Forms of Speeches

Speaking beyond the Speech Classroom

Sample Speeches

Reference and Research Appendices

Quick Access Menu
Using *A Speaker's Guidebook*

The menu to the left briefly displays the book's content. Each menu box corresponds to a tabbed divider in the text. The dividers contain more detailed menus for each section and are followed by "Speaker's Reference" pages that offer executive-like summaries of the subsequent chapters.

At the back of the book, you will find other reference aids:

- The index
- A list of feature boxes and checklists
- A list of sample speeches
- A list of visual guides

Using *A Speaker's Guidebook* Online Tools

 Icons throughout the book refer the reader to the *Speaker's Guidebook* companion Web site, where a wealth of online learning tools are available to support and extend concepts in the book and help with the speech-building process — chapter quizzes, sample speeches, more than 300 video clips including short examples and full speeches, suggested speech topics, outlining and bibliography tools, and much more.

Some online tools require premium access, which is free when packaged with the book or an affordable option available on the book's companion Web site. **bedfordstmartins.com/speakersguide**

To Find Out More

For more on using the book's reference aids and online tools, turn to "How to Use This Book" (p. iii), which includes tutorials that show you how to get quick answers to your questions.

FOURTH EDITION

A Speaker's Guidebook

Text and Reference

Dan O'Hair
University of Oklahoma

Rob Stewart
Texas Tech University

Hannah Rubenstein

Bedford/St. Martin's
Boston ◆ New York

For Bedford/St. Martin's

Executive Editor for Communication: Erika Gutierrez
Developmental Editor: Lai T. Moy
Editorial Assistant: Mae Klinger
Production Editor: Monique Calello
Production Supervisor: Andrew Ensor
Marketing Manager: Adrienne Petsick
Art Director: Lucy Krikorian
Text Design: Claire Seng-Niemoeller
Copy Editor: Denise Quirk
Photo Research: Sue Brekka
Cover Design: Donna L. Dennison
Composition: Pre-Press PMG
Printing and Binding: Quebecor World Taunton

President: Joan E. Feinberg
Editorial Director: Denise B. Wydra
Director of Development: Erica T. Appel
Director of Marketing: Karen R. Soeltz
Director of Editing, Design, and Production: Marcia Cohen
Assistant Director of Editing, Design, and Production: Elise S. Kaiser
Managing Editor: Shuli Traub

Library of Congress Control Number: 2008931066

Manufactured in the United States of America.

4   3   2   1

j   i   h   g

For information, write: Bedford/St. Martin's, 75 Arlington Street, Boston, MA 02116   (617-399-4000)

ISBN-10: 0-312-47282-X
ISBN-13: 978-0-312-47282-5

Acknowledgments
Acknowledgments and copyrights appear at the back of the book on pages 582–583, which constitute an extension of the copyright page.

How to Use This Book

A Speaker's Guidebook: Text and Reference has been carefully designed to help you easily and quickly access the information you need to prepare speeches and presentations. The text may be used not only in a public speaking course but also in other college courses, in your working life after college, and in your civic activities in your community.

The Main Menu and Table of Contents

The twelve tab dividers (discussed in more detail on the next page) allow the book to flip open easily, and the book's binding lets it lie flat. On the inside front cover you will find the **Main Menu** that offers a listing of the thirty chapters in the text and a visual link to help you find each one. For even more information or to find a specific topic, simply turn to the full **table of contents** on page xxv.

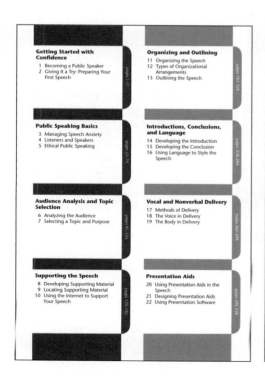

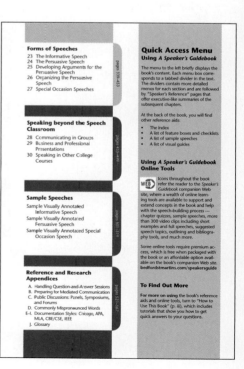

The Tabs

A Speaker's Guidebook is divided into twelve tabbed sections that are arranged into four color banks — red, green, yellow, and blue. Each section opens with a tab divider; the front of the tab divider identifies the tab name and the chapters contained in that section. The back indicates chapter titles and detailed information about major topics covered. To find the specific information you want, look for the appropriate tab and open the book to it.

The back of each tab divider offers a table of contents for the chapters within that tabbed section. The **Speaker's Reference** pages for the chapters within the section follow each tab divider.

PUBLIC SPEAKING BASICS
(33–79)

Speaker's Reference Sections

You may well find one of the most useful features of *A Speaker's Guidebook* to be its **Speaker's Reference** pages that immediately follow each tab divider. These pages provide executive-like summaries of the material covered within the subsequent chapters. A list of key terms in the chapters appears at the end of the Speaker's Reference pages, just before the opening of the first chapter within that tabbed section.

Speaker's Reference pages offer a quick review of the most important information in subsequent chapters through summaries and key terms.

To refer to the full in-text coverage of a topic, simply flip to the page indicated in parentheses.

Speaker's Reference
Public Speaking Basics

Speaker's Reference

3. Managing Speech Anxiety

Recognize What Underlies the Fear of Public Speaking

- A lack of public speaking experience: It can be difficult to put the anxiety that often precedes new experiences into perspective. (p. 42)
- Feeling different: Everyone is different from everyone else and even seasoned speakers experience anxiety. (p. 42)
- Being the center of attention: The audience won't notice things about you that you don't want to reveal. (p. 42)

Pinpoint the Onset of Your Anxiety and Plan to Overcome It

- Some people become anxious upon hearing that they must give a speech (pre-preparation anxiety). (p. 44)
  Don't allow your anxiety to deter you from planning your speech.
- For some, the onset of anxiety occurs as they begin to prepare the speech (preparation anxiety). (p. 44)
  Beware of avoidance and procrastination.
- Some people don't feel anxious until it's time to rehearse the speech (pre-performance anxiety). (p. 44)
  Practice your speech to build confidence.
- Many people don't experience public speaking anxiety until they actually begin to deliver the speech (performance anxiety). (p. 45)
  Practice stress-control breathing and other relaxation techniques.

To Build Confidence, Prepare and Practice

- Manage your time wisely during the preparation phase. (p. 44)
- Rehearse until you know how you want to express yourself. (p. 45)

Try to View Giving a Speech as a Positive Opportunity

- Lessen anxiety by using positive thoughts prior to delivery. (p. 47)
- Picture the speech as an extension of an ordinary conversation. (p. 47)

35

A Speaker's Guidebook New Media

WEB Icons throughout the book refer the reader to the book's companion Web site, where a wealth of online learning tools are available to support and extend concepts in the book and help you with the speech-building process. Some assets require premium access, which is *free* when packaged with the book or an affordable option available directly through the book's companion Web site.

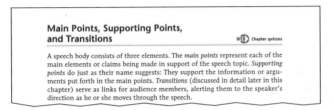

Main Points, Supporting Points, and Transitions   WEB Chapter quizzes

A speech body consists of three elements. The *main points* represent each of the main elements or claims being made in support of the speech topic. *Supporting points* do just as their name suggests: They support the information or arguments put forth in the main points. *Transitions* (discussed in detail later in this chapter) serve as links for audience members, alerting them to the speaker's direction as he or she moves through the speech.

Visual Guides

Visual Guides (ten total) walk you through the most challenging aspects of the speechmaking process—from research and organization through creating presentation aids. A complete list of visual guides is available on the inside back cover.

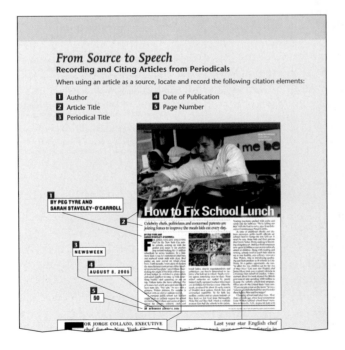

The Checklists

Useful general checklists located throughout the text are another hallmark of *A Speaker's Guidebook*. These checklists offer step-by-step directions, assessment exercises, and content reviews. Consult one of the 104 checklists to review key concepts and to get tips on applying those concepts to your own presentations. For a full list of *Checklists*, see p. 601.

Checklists appear throughout the text, highlighting key concepts and offering useful tips and guidelines.

 CHECKLIST

Minimizing Distractions

✓ If you have trouble seeing or hearing at a distance, arrive early and sit in the front.

✓ If you are going to a group meeting and you have trouble hearing when others are talking at the same time, sit next to the leader so that most of the messages will be communicated toward your side of the room.

✓ Monitor yourself for lapses in attention and consciously redouble your efforts to concentrate on listening.

✓ Monitor yourself for signs of defensive listening.

✓ Don't assume ahead of time that you know what the speaker will say.

The Glossary

When you wish to verify the meaning of a key term, refer to the glossary that begins on p. 548. There you will find explanations of the many terms associated with the fields of rhetoric and communication. These important terms are vital to your understanding of the book's content and are likely to appear on tests.

List of Boxed Features and Full-Text Speeches

Throughout *A Speaker's Guidebook* you will find three types of special boxed features. "Public Speaking in Cultural Perspective" explores the many ways that culture informs public speaking; "ESL Speaker's Notes" offer detailed guidance for non-native speakers; and "Ethically Speaking" boxes offer students ways to ensure an ethical stance when speaking. Throughout, you also will find twelve full-text sample speeches that can serve as models to help you learn the art and craft of creating your own speeches. For a full list of the boxes and sample speeches, refer to p. 600 and the inside back cover.

Preface

A Speaker's Guidebook: Text and Reference is a pioneering public speaking text that offers better solutions to the wide range of challenges that students face. Adopted at more than four hundred schools since the first edition was published in 2001, the book grew out of the realization that public speaking courses are not ends in themselves. The principles and skills taught in this book are meant to be of lasting use to students, to help them beyond merely meeting the requirements of the course — in their other college courses, in their working lives after college, and in whatever roles they play in their communities. The book functions not only as a brief yet comprehensive classroom text but also as a unique and useful post-classroom reference, one that will prove an invaluable resource in any public speaking situation.

The key goal of *A Speaker's Guidebook* has always been to effectively address the fundamental challenges of public speaking, both inside and outside the speech classroom. With the support of hundreds of instructors nationwide, we have developed a book that students use and keep, that reinforces basic skills, and that helps students apply what they've learned to their own speeches.

The Story of the New Edition

In preparing this new edition, we turned to more than fifty instructors and experts from across the United States to learn about new developments in the field and to find out about the course challenges they face today. These instructors told us that students often don't see the relevance of the public speaking class to their lives beyond the classroom. They also told us that students keep bumping up against the same obstacles that have derailed them for years, such as speech anxiety and the inability to apply lessons from the course to their own speeches. In the fourth edition, we aimed directly at these perennial problems. We thus make clear why public speaking matters, and then we give students unique and innovative tools for overcoming the most common obstacles:

- A focus on civic engagement that shows the relevance of public speaking skills
- Tips *from* students *for* students on reducing speech anxiety
- Unique visual tutorials that help students with basic skills such as research, organizing, outlining, and much more
- Visually annotated sample speeches and a wealth of online speech videos that provide models that help students apply what they learn to their own speeches

In developing this edition, we have also harnessed the power of digital media to offer additional tools that will help students overcome fundamental course challenges in ways impossible even a few years ago.

A NEW EMPHASIS ON CIVIC ENGAGEMENT

Students often doubt that public speaking can be a relevant part of their own lives. Nor do they see that it can be a powerful force that informs the cultural and political conversations that surround them every day. To help students make these connections, and to help them see how they can make their own voices heard, throughout this new edition we show how public speaking skills can help students enter the public conversation about key social issues. Further, we show how public address exerts a profound influence on our culture and indeed our democracy. Along with highlighting civic awareness in several chapters, including ethics, topic selection, and persuasive speaking, and in boxed features such as "Ethically Speaking" and "Public Speaking in Cultural Perspective," the fourth edition offers the following:

- **"Become an Engaged Citizen."** This new section in Chapter 1 addresses the fundamental question, "Why Study Public Speaking?" Here we place special emphasis on the idea that public speaking is a powerful tool for inspiring and effecting social change. We also offer useful links that guide students to online sites that focus on major policy debates and that offer an even deeper look at civic engagement.

- **A Focus on Vital Topics of the Day.** Examples throughout the text focus on the most important issues facing our contemporary society, while new sample speeches from student and professional speakers cover a wide range of vital topics, such as the challenges of immigration; the importance of community service; a call to arms to engage with global proverty; and the need for reform in health care.

MORE HELP WITH OVERCOMING SPEECH ANXIETY

Speech anxiety continues to be one of the greatest challenges facing today's students, and in this edition we've paid more attention to addressing this problem than ever before. Our full chapter titled "Managing Speech Anxiety" has been moved up from Chapter 5 to Chapter 3. In speaking with instructors across the United States, as we have found from our own teaching, students who fear public speaking are often comforted by stories from other students who have been in their shoes and shared their same fears. Thus, throughout Chapter 3, we now offer new advice and dozens of tips *from* students *for* students on how they have dealt with their own speech apprehension. For example, student Kristen Obracay notes, "I focus on the information. I try not to think about being graded. I also practice my speech a ton to really make sure I do not speak too quickly. I time myself so that I can develop an average time. This makes me more confident with time requirements. And, because I know that I am well prepared, I really try to just relax." Student Stephanie Meagher adds, "I take a deep breath in and out to calm myself when I feel nervous. I also picture myself in a calm environment like the beach. . . . this helps to calm my nerves."

NEW TOOLS THAT HELP STUDENTS MASTER BASIC SKILLS

Because many students struggle throughout the speech preparation process—from choosing and narrowing a topic and researching the speech to organizing, outlining, and preparing visual aids—this new edition offers more help than ever before on these fundamental skills. In the third edition of *A Speaker's Guidebook*, we offered four "From Source to Speech" visual research guides—unique tutorials that use words and images to give students an overview of a specific skill or process in a single glance. Reaction was so postive to this feature that this edition features six new visual tutorials (making a total of ten) that walk students through the most challenging stages in the speechmaking process. New guides focus on selecting a topic and narrowing it effectively, demonstrating the reliability and credibility of sources, incorporating transitions, and designing and presenting effective PowerPoint slides.

MORE TOOLS THAT HELP STUDENTS APPLY WHAT THEY LEARN TO THEIR OWN SPEECHES

Because we understand that students learn more when they see visual illustrations of specific concepts in action, the fourth edition includes a host of new visual learning tools.

Six new "visually annotated" model speeches (nine total)   Each of these full-text model speeches offers traditional textual annotations (that help students understand the language, organization, and arguments used in a speech) alongside innovative "visual annotations"—photographs that show action shots of speakers delivering their presentations. These visual annotations go beyond the traditional printed page by bringing the elements and analysis of speech delivery into clear focus.

New speeches include student Ashley White giving an engaging introductory speech titled "The Dance of Life," student David Kruckenberg's informative speech on an experimental cure for cancer, and a persuasive speech by Professor Anita Taylor titled "Tales of the Grandmothers" that skillfully incorporates the narrative pattern of arrangement.

***Video Central for Public Speaking* offers over 300 speech videos online**   *A Speaker's Guidebook* now offers more video online than any competing college-level public speaking text. This online speech video library is available as a premium resource that can be packaged *free* with each new copy of *A Speaker's Guidebook*. Not only does *Video Central for Public Speaking* include every student speech included in the main text, it also includes hundreds of additional speech clips that bring virtually every concept in the book to life. These excellent models are searchable by chapter and integrated directly into the premium *A Speaker's Guidebook e-Book*. Students can read about a specific concept in the text and then watch that concept come to life by watching an associated video clip.

Enduring Features

The following features have made *A Speaker's Guidebook: Text and Reference* extremely successful in its first three editions:

A COMPREHENSIVE CLASSROOM TEXT

A Speaker's Guidebok covers all the topics included in the standard public speaking texts — and much more. Although we designed the coverage to be accessible, we didn't lose sight of the need for comprehensiveness. *A Speaker's Guidebook* covers all the traditional topics, including listening, speaking ethically, managing speech anxiety, analyzing the audience, selecting a topic and purpose, locating and using supporting materials, organizing and outlining ideas, using language, creating presentation aids, delivering the speech, and constructing various speech types. But *A Speaker's Guidebook* offers much more than traditional texts, including chapters on using the Internet to support the speech, using presentation software, preparing business and professional presentations, and speaking in other courses.

This text has been built on the assumption that students will incorporate the Internet and other technological tools into every step of the of the speechmaking process; thus we offer a special chapter on using the Internet as well as integrating relevant discussion of technology throughout the text. Widely praised by reviewers and expanded in this new edition, Chapter 10, "Using the Internet to Support Your Speech," teaches students how to research effectively on the Internet. Chapter 22, "Using Presentation Software," shows students how to use the latest hardware and software to produce powerful presentation aids and includes a tutorial on using Microsoft's PowerPoint.

To give students advice that is grounded in the theory of speech communication, we have included references to current communication research and classical rhetorical theory throughout the book, using them as the basis for concrete suggestions in real-world speaking situations. Examples range from coverage of individual contemporary theorists and their work to discussions of rhetorical proofs and the classical canons of rhetoric.

Because persuasive speaking is a major aspect of most speech courses, the text offers three full chapters on persuasion, more than any other text. The unique Chapter 26, "Organizing the Persuasive Speech," demonstrates how to organize persuasive speeches using Monroe's motivated sequence, cause-effect, comparative-advantage, and refutative patterns.

A Speaker's Guidebook also offers students a wealth of resources to help them adapt their speeches to the cultural requirements of the speech situation. Along with extensive coverage within chapters, **Public Speaking in Cultural Perspective** boxes feature such topics as comparing cultural values, vocal delivery and culture, and variations in nonverbal communication.

Special consideration has also been given to the non-native speaker. **ESL Speaker's Notes** boxes focus on critical areas of concern to speakers whose first language is not English and offer practical ways to address those concerns. Sample features include "Avoiding the Pitfalls of Manuscript Delivery" and "Vocal Variety and the Non-Native Speaker." Another characteristic that defines *A Speaker's Guidebook* is its strong focus on ethics. Chapter 5, "Ethical Public Speaking," is devoted to this topic and includes an in-depth consideration of the role that values play in the ethical quality of speeches. **Ethically Speaking** boxes appear throughout the text, continually reminding students that ethical conduct should apply to all aspects of the speechmaking process.

Finally, *A Speaker's Guidebook* recognizes the importance of solid sample speeches, and it provides twelve total. Speeches include two speeches of introduction, one speech of demonstration, three informative speeches, four persuasive speeches, and two special occasion speeches. All of the sample speeches are excellent models for student study and analysis, and nine of them include innovative visual annotations.

AN INVALUABLE REFERENCE BEYOND
THE SPEECH CLASSROOM

A Speaker's Guidebook features a unique, user-friendly design, convenient and accessible reference features throughout, and extensive reference and research appendices.

The information in *A Speaker's Guidebook* is designed for quick and easy retrieval. Twelve tabbed dividers allow the book to flip open easily, and a comb binding lets it lie flat. A **Main Menu** on the inside front cover listing all tabs and chapters, paired with a full table of contents beginning on p. xxv, quickly directs students to the sections they need.

Speaker's Reference pages at the beginning of each tabbed section allow students to quickly access and review the most important information in each chapter; convenient cross-references enable readers to flip quickly to a full discussion of the material, should they so choose.

Every chapter in *A Speaker's Guidebook* contains **checklists**, offering step-by-step directions, self-assessments, and content review checks. Widely praised by reviewers for their precision and conciseness, these checklists help students and professionals both plan their speeches and assess their efforts.

The **Sample Speeches** appendix and a wealth of **Reference** appendices — including "Commonly Mispronounced Words" and a useful glossary of key terms — allows students to easily access practical information.

A SUPERIOR RESOURCE IN ANY PUBLIC SPEAKING SITUATION

Along with providing students with an accessible, up-to-date classroom guide, *A Speaker's Guidebook* contains many features that will make it an invaluable resource in other college courses and *after* the public speaking course.

"Speaking in Other College Courses"   Chapter 30 provides guidance for creating the kinds of oral presentations students are likely to deliver in other college courses, from the social sciences and humanities to science and engineering. Separate sections describe sample presentations in technical, scientific and mathematical, arts and humanities, social science, and education courses, along with a new section on speaking in nursing and allied health courses.

More about public speaking on the job   *A Speaker's Guidebook* gives students more in-depth preparation than any other text for the kinds of speaking situations they are likely to encounter on the job. Chapters 28 and 29 cover business and professional speeches, sales presentations, status reports, and staff reports.

Extensive help with the research process   In addition to three full chapters dedicated to finding and developing supporting material (Chapters 8–10), *A Speaker's Guidebook* includes unique appendices showing students how to use the *Chicago*, APA, MLA, CBE/CSE, and IEEE documentation styles.

Microsoft PowerPoint tutorial   Generating presentation aids in a presentation software program has become one of the key challenges for the contemporary public speaker and presenter. Chapter 22, "Using Presentation Software," includes a tutorial on using Microsoft's PowerPoint that teaches readers how to enter and edit text, insert objects into slides, and use PowerPoint's text animation and transition effects.

Resources for Students and Instructors

ONLINE RESOURCES FOR STUDENTS

Free and open book companion site at bedfordstmartins.com/speakersguide offers access to a host of useful tools and resources including: multiple-choice self-assessment quizzes for each chapter in the book; suggested speech topics plus speech topics research links to help students develop their own ideas; a how-to guide for using Microsoft PowerPoint; tutorials for evaluating online sources and avoiding plagiarism; additional full-text sample speeches; and much more.

A Speaker's Guidebook e-Book, **available free when packaged with a new copy of the main text** or priced affordably as a stand-alone   The e-book includes all the content in the print book and enables students to add notes, highlight, and assess their understanding through quizzing. Instructors can customize the e-book by adding their own content and deleting or reordering chapters. In addition, accessing the e-book allows students seamless access to a host of premium resources integrated with the e-book itself including:

- *Video Central for Public Speaking.* This powerful resource offers access to more video than any competing speech text and includes over 300 speech clips along with every sample student speech in the book. These videos help students learn best public speaking practices as well as master the skills described in the book. Clips are organized alphabetically and by chapter and are integrated directly onto each page of the *A Speaker's Guidebook e-Book.* Viedo clips are also linked with every key concept in the text, allowing students to read about a specific concept onscreen and then immediately see that concept come to life.
- *The Bedford Speech Outliner* walks the student through the outline-building process with targeted feedback.
- *Video Quizzes* help students review fundamental speech concepts in a fun and interactive way.
- *Relaxation Audio Download* aids students in overcoming their own communication apprehension.
- **All materials from the book companion site** are integrated as well, including chapter quizzes, learning tools, and links, enabling students to study and review as they read.

To order the book/e-book package, use ISBN 0-312-56336-1.

Powerful *Video Theater 3.0* interactive CD-ROM, available *free* when packaged with a new copy of the main text   We designed the student CD-ROM to provide examples and tools that a text alone cannot. An innovative *Video Theater 3.0* offers full student speeches — informative, persuasive, special occasion, and demonstration — along with professional speech clips. These video examples work not just as models but as powerful teaching tools. For each full speech we offer a speech outline and text, and much more. We analyze each speech in five areas — audience analysis; content and supporting ideas; introduction, transitions, and conclusion; delivery; and visual aids — and offer "hotlinks" so that while reading about a specific example, students or instructors can click and see the point exemplified. The CD-ROM also offers a tutorial to help students use visual aids effectively. To order the book/CD-ROM package, use ISBN 0-312-56387-6.

PRINT RESOURCES FOR STUDENTS

The Essential Guide to Rhetoric   (0-312-47239-0) by William M. Keith, University of Wisconsin, Milwaukee, and Christian O. Lundberg, University of North Carolina, Chapel Hill. This guide — available as a *free* package with any new copy of *A Speaker's Guidebook* — is a powerful addition to the public speaking class, providing an accessible and balanced overview of key historical and contemporary rhetorical theories. Written by two leaders in the field, this brief guide uses concrete, relevant examples and jargon-free language to bring these concepts to life.

The Essential Guide to Presentation Software (0-312-53819-7) by Allison Ainsworth, Gainesville State College, and Rob Patterson, James Madison University. This completely revised guide shows students how presentation software can be used to support, not overtake, their speeches. Sample screens and practical advice make this an indispensable resource for students preparing electronic visual aids.

The Essential Guide to Interpersonal Communication (0-312-45195-4) **and** *The Essential Guide to Group Communication* (0-312-45194-6) by Dan O'Hair and Mary Wiemann. These brief and readable guides offer succinct yet comprehensive coverage of key aspects of interpersonal and group communication, covering basic concepts and theories backed by current scholarship.

Outlining and Organizing Your Speech (0-312-53817-0) by Merry Buchanan, University of Central Oklahoma. This student workbook provides step-by-step guidance for preparing informative, persuasive, and professional presentations and gives students the opportunity to practice the critical skills of conducting audience analysis, dealing with communication apprehension, selecting a speech topic and purpose, researching support materials, organizing and outlining, developing introductions and conclusions, enhancing language and delivery, and preparing and using presentation aids.

Media Career Guide: Preparing for Jobs in the 21st Century, **Sixth Edition** (0-312-46914-4) by James Seguin, Robert Morris College. Practical and student-friendly, this revised guide includes a comprehensive directory of media jobs, practical tips, and career guidance for students considering a major in communication studies and mass media.

Research and Documentation in the Electronic Age, **Fourth Edition** (0-312-44339-0) by Diana Hacker, Prince George's Community College, and Barbara Fister, Gustavus Adolphus College. This handy booklet covers everything students need for college research assignments at the library and on the Internet, including advice for finding and evaluating Internet sources.

RESOURCES FOR INSTRUCTORS

Instructor's Resource Manual (0-312-53816-2) by LeAnne Lagasse, Texas Tech University; Jennifer Emerling Bone, State University of New York, Oneonta; Elaine Wittenberg-Lyles, University of Texas at San Antonio; and Melinda Villagran, George Mason University. This revised comprehensive manual is a valuable resource for new and experienced instructors alike. It offers extensive advice on topics such as helping students use their public speaking skills to become more engaged citizens; ideas for preparation and practice to reduce speech anxiety; setting and achieving student learning goals; managing the classroom; facilitating group discussion; understanding culture and gender considerations; dealing with ESL students; evaluating speeches (for both instructors and students); and evaluating Internet resources. In addition, each chapter of the main text is broken down into chapter challenges, detailed outlines, suggestions for facilitating class discussion from topics covered in feature boxes, additional activities and exercises, and recommended supplementary resources. The new edition includes more guidelines for first-time instructors, advice for integrating technology into the speech class, and expanded suggestions for videos and other classroom resources.

ESL Students in the Public Speaking Classroom: A Guide for Teachers (0-312-53814-6) by Robbin Crabtree, Fairfield University, and Robert Weissberg, New Mexico State University. As the United States increasingly becomes a nation of non-native speakers, instructors must find new pedagogical tools to aid students for whom English is a second language. This guide specifically addresses the needs of ESL students in the public speaking course and offers instructors valuable advice for helping students deal successfully with the challenges they face.

Print and Electronic *Test Bank* (Print: 0-312-53815-4; Electronic: 0-312-55668-3) by LeAnne Lagasse, Texas Tech University; Jennifer Emerling Bone, State University of New York, Oneonta; and Merry Buchanan, University of Central Oklahoma. *A Speaker's Guidebook* offers a complete testing program, available both in print and for Windows and Macintosh environments. Each chapter includes multiple-choice, true-false, and fill-in-the-blank exercises, as well as essay questions. Sample midterm and final examinations are also included in the testing program.

Instructor's materials at at bedfordstmartins.com/speakersguide   The companion Web site to *A Speaker's Guidebook,* Fourth Edition, offers rich teaching resources for new and experienced instructors, including a downloadable version of the *Instructor's Resource Manual,* completely revised PowerPoint slides for each chapter in the text, speech assignment suggestions, discussion questions for sample speeches, an electronic gradebook for online quizzing, and links to course management software including WebCT, Blackboard, and Angel.

Microsoft PowerPoint slides   These slides, completely revised by Allison Ainsworth, Gainesville State College, for the fourth edition, provide visual support for the key concepts covered in each chapter and are available to be downloaded from the instructor's section of the book's companion Web site at bedfordstmartins.com/speakersguide.

VIDEO RESOURCES ON DVD

Professional Speeches (0-312-19222-3)   Available in DVD and VHS formats, Volume 19 of the esteemed *Great Speeches* series offers dynamic contemporary speeches for today's classroom. The most recent in the series, this video features compelling speeches including President Clinton's 1998 State of the Union Address, Madeleine Albright's first speech as secretary of state, Christopher Reeve's address to the 1996 Democratic National Convention, and a speech on spirituality by the Dalai Lama. Additional videos are available from the Bedford/ St. Martin's Video Library.

Student Speeches (0-312-39300-8)   A 3-video set of student speeches provide students with attainable models for study, analysis, and inspiration. Included are a variety of speeches that fulfill the most common assignments in public speaking — informative and persuasive speeches — by students of varying ability from Texas Tech and the University of Oklahoma.

Acknowledgments

We are especially thankful for the contributions of several experts who helped us develop this edition of *A Speaker's Guidebook*. We would like to thank Carol Koris of Johnson & Wales University–North Miami, and Emily Holler of Kennesaw State University and their students for suggestions to improve the book, tips for fellow students, and new speeches. We are also very grateful to the Phi Rho Pi organization and their students — especially those involved in the 2007 National Tournament — for their extensive contributions to this edition as well as allowing us to use their speeches in the book and in our new *Video Central for Public Speaking*. We would like to thank LeAnne Lagasse of Texas Tech University for her excellent work revising the *Instructor's Resource Manual* (originally created by Elaine Wittenberg-Lyles of the University of Texas at San Antonio and Melinda Villagran of George Mason University, and revised for the third edition by Jennifer Emerling Bone of the State University of New York, Oneonta) and Test Bank (originally created by Tom Howard of the University of Oklahoma and Merry Buchanan of the University of Central Oklahoma, and updated by Jennifer Emerling Bone). We much appreciate the contributions of Allison Ainsworth of Gainesville State College, in particular the PowerPoint slides she created to accompany this edition, her revision of the *Essential Guide to Presentation Software*, and her expert guidance on using presentation software in public speaking. Thank you also to Alexis Sparks of Texas Tech University for her work on Web content to accompany *A Speaker's Guidebook*, Fourth Edition.

We very much appreciate the assistance of the hundreds of reviewers whose feedback and advice allowed us to make *A Speaker's Guidebook: Text and Reference,* Fourth Edition, better. Please see the following pages for a list of each of these reviewers.

It has been a privilege to work with the pioneering editors and publishers of Bedford/St. Martin's, whose innovative ideas led to the format of this text.

President Joan Feinberg, Editorial Director Denise Wydra, Executive Editor Erika Gutierrez, and Director of Development Erica T. Appel understand how to deliver information to readers in ways that are most useful and also most compelling, and we are grateful to them for sharing their expertise with us. A special thanks to Development Editor Lai T. Moy for sharing her insight, creativity, and attention to detail and for shepherding this edition from its earliest stages. Managing Editor Shuli Traub and Project Editor Monique Calello expertly guided the text through a complicated production process, while Production Supervisor Andrew Ensor helped turn the book from a manuscript into a beautiful publication. We thank Editorial Assistant Mae Klinger for her always swift and efficient help, hard work, and good instincts, as well as for her thoughtful and diligent efforts on the *Instructor's Resource Manual* and Test Bank that accompany the fourth edition. Thank you also to Sandy Schechter and Sue Brekka for their tireless pursuit of permissions. Finally, for their work in developing the Web site and other technology products, we are grateful to Jessica Chesnutt, Allison Hart, Harriet Wald, and Nick Carbone.

Reviewers and Survey Respondents, Fourth Edition

Stephanie Ahfeldt, *Concordia College*

Allison Ainsworth, *Gainesville State College*

Timothy Anderson, *Elgin Community College*

Dencil K. Backus, *California University of Pennsylvania*

Robert Betts, *Rock Valley College*

Thomas Bovino, *Suffolk County Community College*

Amanda Brown, *University of Wisconsin, Stout*

Christa Brown, *Minnesota State University*

Edward Clift, *Woodbury University*

Michael D. Crum, *Coastal Carolina Community College*

Kevin Cummings, *Mercer University*

Julie Davis, *College of Charleston*

Gary Deaton, *University of Transylvania*

Cynthia Dewar, *City College of San Francisco*

Thomas F. Downard, *Northeastern University*

Fred Fitch, *Kean University*

James J. Floyd, *University of Central Missouri*

Sonia Margarita Gangotena, *Blinn College*

Ron Gephart, *Southwest Tennessee Community College*

Valerie Manno Giroux, *University of Miami*

Keith H. Griffin, *University of South Carolina*

Diane Gruber, *Arizona State University*

Deborah Hefferin, *Broward Community College*

Emily Holler, *Kennesaw State University*

Brendan B. Kelly, *University of West Florida*

Carol Koris, *Johnson & Wales University, North Miami*

Lynn Kuechle, *Minnesota State University, Mankato*

Victoria Leonard, *College of the Canyons*

Nancy Levin, *Palm Beach Community College*

Natabhona Mabachi, *University of Kansas*

Anne McIntosh, *Central Piedmont Community College*

Marjorie Keeshan Nadler, *Miami University*

Phyllis Ngai, *The University of Montana, Missoula*

Kekeli Nuviadenu, *Bethune-Cookman College*

Keith Perry, *Abraham Baldwin Agricultural College*

Brian Pilling, *Westminster College*

Roger D. Priest, *Ivy Tech Community College*

Paul Raptis, *Gainesville State College*

Kenna J. Reeves, *Emporia State University*

John Reffue, *Hillsborough Community College*

Rebecca Robideaux, *Boise State University*

Karin Russell, *Keiser University*

John Saunders, *Columbus State University*

James M. Schnoebelen, *Washburn University*

Karen Michelle Scott, *Savannah College of Art & Design*

Pam Speights, *Wharton County Junior College*

Erik Stroner, *Iowa Central Community College*

Bonnye Stuart, *Winthrop University*

Sarah Elizabeth Symonds, *Coastal Carolina Community College*

Laura R. Umphrey, *Northern Arizona University*

Steve Vrooman, *Texas Lutheran University*

Marta Walz, *Elgin Community College*

Stephanie Webster, *University of Florida*

Kristopher Robert Weeks, *Montclair State University*

David E. Williams, *Texas Tech University*

Jim Wilson, *Shelton State Community College*

Reviewers and Survey Respondents, Third Edition

Helen Acosta, Bakersfield College; Nedra Adams-Soller, College of Lake County; Sue Aiello, New York Institute of Technology–Main Campus; Robert Alexander, Bucks County Community College; Jason Ames, Chabot College; James Anderson, Johnson & Wales University; Robert Arend, San Diego Miramar College; Mike Armstrong, Tallahassee Community College; Jay Baglia, San Jose State University; Kaylene Barbe, Oklahoma Baptist University; Cameron Basquiat, Community College of Southern Nevada; Kimberly Batty-Herbert, Broward Community College North; Elizabeth Bell, University of South Florida; Ray Bell, John C. Calhoun State Community College; Christina Benac, Ball State University; Mary Jane Berger, College of Saint Benedict; Kathy Berggren, Cornell University; Mark Bergmooser, Monroe County Community College; Sandra Berkowitz, University of Maine; Constance Berman, Berkshire Community College; Bob Betts, Rock Valley College; Pete Bicak, Rockhurst University; Rochelle Bird, Utah Valley State College; T. Black, Shepherd College; Marian Blue, Skagit Valley Community College–Oak Harbor; Jennifer Emerling Bone, University of Colorado–Boulder; Robert Bookwalter, Marshall University; Jennifer Boyenga, Indian Hills Community College; Chris Braden, Alverno College; Linda Brigance, SUNY College at Fredonia; Joel Brouwer, Montcalm Community College; Jin Brown, University of Alaska–Fairbanks; Nate Brown, Santa Monica College; Ferald Bryan, Northern Illinois University; Glenn Byrne, Stonehill College; Lisa Callihan, Florence Darlington Technical College; Diana Cameron, North Iowa Area Community College; Amy Capwell-Burns, University of Toledo; Harry Carrell, Missouri Valley College; Karishma Chatterjee, Ohio State University–Main Campus; Susan Childress, Santa Rosa Junior College; Sally Cissna,

Milwaukee School of Engineering; Carolyn Clark, Salt Lake Community College; Annie Clement, Winona State University; Robert Cohen, Ohio State University–Mansfield; Jennifer Cohen-Rosenberg, Los Angeles Pierce College; Linda Combs, Daytona Beach Community College; Melanie Conrad, Midwestern State University; John Cook, University of Texas at Brownsville; Diana Cooley, North Harris College; Kimberly Corey, McIntosh College; Ed Coursey, Palm Beach Community College Glades Center; Ken Cox, Florence Darlington Technical College; Sandra Coyner, Southern Oregon University; Christine Cranford, East Carolina University; Rita Crockett, Howard College; Billye Currie, Samford University; Daniel Dahlquist, University of Wisconsin at Platteville; Phillip Dalton, Stetson University; William Davidson, University of Wisconsin–Stevens Point; Dale Davis, University of Texas at San Antonio; Thomas DelVecchio, Iona College; Andrew Denhart, Stetson University; Ron Dluger, North Park University; Paul Duax, American River College; Betty Dvorsen, City College of San Francisco; Jarvis Elena, Daytona Beach Community College; Dennis Elkins, Savannah College of Art & Design; Scott Ellis, San Jacinto College–Central Campus; Valerie Endress, Rhode Island College; Carolyn Engdahl, Fitchburg State University; David Engel, Marshalltown Community College; Kathleen M. Farrell, St. Louis University; Judy Ferrand, Wor-Wic Community College; William Ferreira, Houston Community College Southwest; Nilo Figur, Concordia University; Sondra Fishinger, Union County College; Peter Fjeld, Berkeley College; Charles Fleischman, Hofstra University; James J. Floyd, Central Missouri State University; Marjorie Ford, Stanford University; Christine Foster, Ramapo College of New Jersey; James Friauf, Milwaukee School of Engineering; William Furnell, Santa Monica College; James Gallagher, New Mexico State University at Alamogordo; Pat Gehrke, University of South Carolina; John Gillette, Lake City Community College; Susan Gilpin, Marshall University; Valerie Giroux, University of Miami; Curt Gilstrap, Drury University; Louis Giuliana, Holy Family College; Susan Giusto, Francis Marion University; Eric Gnezda, Ohio Wesleyan University; Robert Gobetz, University of Indianapolis; William "Bubba" Godsey, John C. Calhoun State Community College; Janna Goodwin, Regis University; Luke Gordon, Portland State University; Michelle Gorthy, City College of San Francisco; Frank Gray, Ball State University; Neil Gregersen, University of Wisconsin at Waukesha; Laura Gregg, Saginaw Chippewa Tribal College; Jean Groshek, Alverno College; Diane Gruber, Arizona State University–West; Phil Hamilton, San Bernardino Valley College; Greg Hammond, New Mexico Junior College; Reeze Hanson, Haskell Indian Nations University; Eric Harlan, Mississippi University for Women; John Hatch, University of Dubuque; Linda Heil, Harford Community College; Mark Henderson, Jackson State University; Andrew Herman, State University of New York at Genesee; Dan Higgins, Heidelberg College; Rick Hogrefe, Crafton Hills College; Angela Holland, Community College of Southern Nevada; Emily Holler, Kennesaw State University; Victoria Howitt, Grossmont College; Kevin Howley, DePauw University; Karen Huck, Central Oregon Community College; W. A. Kelly Huff, Truett-McConnell–Watkinsville; Lynette Jachowicz, Maple Woods Community College; Dale Jenkins, Virginia Technical College; Ronald C. Jones, Norfolk State University; Linda Karch,

Norwich University; Susan Katz, University of Bridgeport; Bill Keith, University of Wisconsin–Milwaukee; Tim Kelley, Northwest-Shoals Community College; Helen Kingkade, Midlands Technical College–Airport; David Kosloski, Clark College; Jeffrey Kotz, University of Connecticut; Mary Lahman, Manchester College; Jon Larson, Inver Hills Community College; Betty Jane Lawrence, Bradley University; Peter Lee, Golden West College; Diana Leonard, University of Arizona; Victoria Leonard, College of the Canyons; Douglas Lepter, Trevecca Nazarene University; Wendy Leslie, Missouri Valley College; Jason Lind, Skagit Valley College; Linda Linn, Western Wyoming College; Steven Long, Wayland Baptist University; Bob Loss, Barton County Community College; Louis Lucca, La Guardia Community College, CUNY; Thomas Marshall, Robert Morris University; Ben Martin, Santa Monica College; Michael McFarland, Stetson University; Lee McGavin, University of Texas–Permian Basin; Libby McGlone, Columbus State Community College; Annie McKinlay, North Idaho College; Gordon McLean, Arizona Western College; Scott McLean, Arizona Western College; Miriam McMullen-Pastrick, Pennsylvania State University at Erie, Behrend; Rebecca Meisnebach, Concord College; Deborah Meltsner, Old Dominion University; Andrew Merolla, Ohio State University; John Morrison, Rollins College; Alfred Mueller, Pennsylvania State University at Mont Alto; Lisa Mueller, Northeast Iowa Community College; Donna Munde, Mercer County Community College; Diana Karol Nagy, University of Florida; Helen Nelson, Spalding University; Linda Norris, Indiana University of Pennsylvania; Kathleen Norris, Loyola Marymount University; Karen O'Donnell, Finger Lakes Community College; Jennifer O'Dorisio, Pomona High School; Richard Olsen, University of North Carolina at Wilmington; Susan Ondercin, Carroll Community College; Elenie Opffer, Regis University; Donald Painter Jr., University of South Florida; Teresa Palmitessa, Pennsylvania State University at Erie, Behrend; Emily Paramonova, Cogswell Polytechnical College; Daniel Paulnock, Saint Paul College; Holly Payne, Western Kentucky University; Karl Payton, Le Tourneau University; Kimberly Pearce, De Anza College; Sheila Peebles, Baldwin-Wallace College; Ray Penn, Lincoln Memorial University; Pamela Perkins, San Diego City College; Jean Perry, Glendale Community College; William Petkanas, Western Connecticut State University; Chuck Pierce, Central Carolina Technical College; Dann Pierce, University of Portland; Michael Pitts, Los Angeles Southwest College; Dwight Podgurski, Colorado Christian University; Linda Powers, Wofford College; Joyce Puls, Baker College; Kathleen Quimby, Messiah University; Susan Rabideau, University of Wisconsin–Fox Valley; Alan Ragains, Windward Community College; Gail Reid, State University of West Georgia; Pamela Reid, Copiah-Lincoln Community College; Paula Reif, Carl Albert State College; Larry Reynolds, Johnson City Community College; William Richter, Lenoir-Rhyne College; Lisa Riede, Lockhaven University of Pennsylvania; Nita Ritzke, University of Mary; Rick Roberts, University of San Francisco; Patricia Rockwell, University of Louisiana at Lafayette; Rita Rosenthal, Boston College and Stonehill College; Susan Sanders, Northern Essex Community College; Carol Saunders, Chipola Junior College; Kimberly Schwartz, University of Dubuque; Steve Schwarze, University of Montana; Marlene Sebeck, Wheeling

Jesuit University; Lois Self, Northern Illinois University; Susan Selk, El Paso Community College; Colleen Shaughnessy-Zeena, Salem State College; Charla Markham Shaw, University of Texas at Arlington; Alisa Shubb, American River College; Elizabeth Simas, California State University at Northridge; Jacqueline Simon, Palomar College; John Kares Smith, SUNY Oswego State University; Andrew Snyder, Saint Gregory's University; Jay Soldner, Western Wisconsin Technical College; Rick Soller, College of Lake County; Pam Speights, Wharton County Junior College; Ebba Stedillie, Casper College; Susan Stehlik, Rutgers University–Newark Campus; Lesa Stern, Southern Illinois University–Edwardsville; James Stewart, Tennessee Technical University; Pamela Stovall, University of New Mexico–Gallup; Anthony Stubbs, Iowa Lakes Community College South; Pat Sutherland, Tennessee Wesleyan College; Michael Swinford, Shorter College; Sarah Symonds, Coastal Carolina Community College; Kelly Tait, University of Nevada–Reno; Georgia Talsma, Mount Marty College; April Dupree Taylor, University of South Alabama; Katherine Taylor, University of Louisville; Donna Thomsen, Johnson & Wales University; Ray Tipton, Walters State Community College; Hank Tkachuk, Concordia College-Moorehead; Candice Todd, Lynchburg College; Michael Tomaschyk, Cuyahoga Community College–Western; Amy Trombley, Western Michigan University; Anita Turpin, Roanoke College; Clint Uhrich, Luther College; Joseph Valcourt, Central Carolina Technical College; Marilyn Valentino, Lorain County Community College; Jay VerLinden, Humboldt State University; Valerie Vlahakis, John Wood Community College; Steve Vrooman, Texas Lutheran University; Chris Wagner, Cosumnes River College; Anthony Wainwright, Onondaga Community College; Lisa Waite, Kent State University–Stark Campus; Bill Wallace, Northeastern State University; Dennis Waller, Northwest Nazarene University; David Weinandy, Aquinas College; Nancy Wendt, Oregon State University; Estelle Wenson, Stonehill College; Beverly West-Dorny, San Joaquin Delta College; Steven Wiegenstein, Culver-Stockton College; Thomas Wilkinson, Rowan University; David Williams, Texas Technical University; Frances Winsor, Pennsylvania State University at Altoona; Marianne Worthington, Cumberland College; Miriam Zimmerman, Notre Dame de Namur University; Joe Zubrick, University of Maine–Fort Kent.

Reviewers and Survey Respondents, Second Edition

Cameron Basquiat, Community College of Southern Nevada; Carolyn Clark, Salt Lake Community College; Letitia Dace, University of Massachusetts–Dartmouth; Francis Dance, University of Denver; Layne Dearden, Brigham Young University–Idaho; Rebecca Faery, Massachusetts Institute of Technology; Joyce Fernandes, Bristol Community College; John Giertz, Bakersfield College; Heather Grace, University of Pittsburgh–Bradford; Marc Martin, San Francisco State University; Charles McMahan, Vincennes University; Deborah Meltsner, Old Dominion University; Andrea Morgan, Georgia Perimeter College; Dann Pierce, University of Portland; Patricia Rockwell, University of Louisiana-Lafayette; Robert Sadowski, University of Michigan–Flint; Michael Searcy, University of

Iowa, Scott Community College; Lisa Stefani, Grossmont College; Elena Strauman, Auburn University; Jeremy Teitelbaum, California Polytechnic State University; Gregory Thomas, Morgan Community College; and Robert Witkowski, Midlands Technical College.

Reviewers and Survey Respondents, First Edition

Linda Brown, El Paso Community College; Tamara Burk, Columbia College; Lawrence J. Chase, California State University-Sacramento; Helen Chester, Milwaukee Area Technical College; Jeanine Congalton, Fullerton College; Lauren Sewell Coulter, University of Tennessee-Chattanooga; Karen D. Covey, New River Community College; Michal Dale, Southwest Missouri State; William F. Ferreira, Houston Community College, Southwest; Eric Fife, College of Charleston; William Fustield, University of Pittsburgh; Kathleen M. Galvin, Northwestern University; Kelby Halone, Clemson University; William J. Jordan, North Carolina State University; Ruth Ann Kinzey, University of North Carolina-Charlotte; Lt. Col. George Luker, USAF Academy; Joseph Martinez, El Paso Community College; Virgil Moberg, Flagler College; Carlos Perez, Maple Woods Community College; Jean Perry, Glendale Community College; Tina Pieraccini, State University of New York-Oswego; Lora Sager, Greenville Technical College; Dr. Roy Schwartzmann, Northwest Missouri State University; John Kares Smith, State University of New York-Oswego; Kimberly Terrill, Francis Marion University; and Glenda Treadaway, Appalachian State University.

Contents

Public Speaking Basics

Audience Analysis and Topic Selection

Supporting the Speech

Organizing and Outlining

Introductions, Conclusions, and Language

Vocal and Nonverbal Delivery

Presentation Aids

Forms of Speeches

Speaking beyond the Speech Classroom

Sample Speeches

Reference and Research Appendices

Getting Started with Confidence

Getting Started with Confidence

Speaker's Reference
Getting Started with Confidence

1. Becoming a Public Speaker

Recognize the Many Benefits of Public Speaking

- Enhance your professional and personal goals. (p. 6)
- Aid your work as a student. (p. 7)
- Learn to share your values and explore the values of others. (p. 8)
- Hone your critical thinking and listening skills. (p. 8)

Become an Engaged Citizen

- Use public speaking to become more involved in solving social problems. (p. 8)
- Learn the rules of engagement for effective and ethical public discourse. (p. 9)

Recognize the Enduring Nature of the Study of Public Speaking

- The *canons of rhetoric*, a five-part speechmaking process developed in ancient Greece, remains relevant for today's public speaker. (p. 10)

Recognize the Similarities between Public Speaking and Other Forms of Communication

- As in *conversation*, you attempt to make yourself understood, involve and respond to your conversational partner, and take responsibility for what you say. (p. 12)
- As in *small group communication*, you address a group of people who are focused on you and expect you to clearly discuss issues that are relevant to the topic and to the occasion. (p. 12)
- As in *mass communication*, you must understand and appeal to audience members' interests, attitudes, and values. (p. 12)

Recognize the Differences between Public Speaking and Other Forms of Communication

- Opportunities for feedback are fewer than in conversation or in small group communication, and greater than in mass communication. (p. 13)
- The level of preparation required is greater than in other forms of communication. (p. 13)

3

- The degree of formality tends to be greater than in other forms of communication. (p. 13)

As You Prepare Your Speeches, Consider the Rhetorical Situation

- The rhetorical situation is the circumstance that calls for a public response. Successful speeches fulfill the conditions that call for the speech. (p. 16)

Set Clearly Defined Goals for Your Speeches

- Establish a set of goals early in the speechmaking process. (p. 16)
- Keep a clear focus in mind. (p. 16)

Don't View Your Speech as Complete until You've Assessed the Outcome

- Ask yourself whether you accomplished what you set out to do. (p. 16)
- Use constructive feedback for self-evaluation and improvement. (p. 16)

Draw on the Familiar Skills of Conversation and Writing

- Consider that in both conversation and writing, you try to uncover the audience's interests and needs before speaking. (p. 17)
- Consider that in both conversation and writing, you check to make certain that you are understood, and adjust your speech to the listeners and to the occasion. (p. 17)
- Much of what you've learned about organizing written papers can be applied to organizing your speeches. (p. 17)

Foster a Sense of Inclusion in All of Your Speeches

- Try to identify and respectfully address the diversity of values and viewpoints held by audience members. (p. 18)
- Work toward making every member of the audience feel recognized and included in your message. (p. 18)

2. Giving It a Try: Preparing Your First Speech

To Gain Confidence, Deliver a Brief First Speech

Use This Overview to Construct and Deliver the First Speech

- Select a topic. (p. 19)
- Analyze the audience. (p. 20)
- Determine the speech purpose. (p. 20)

- Compose a thesis statement. (p. 20)
- Develop the main points. (p. 21)
- Gather supporting materials. (p. 21)
- Separate the speech into its major parts: introduction, body, and conclusion. (p. 21)
- Outline the speech using coordinate and subordinate points. (p. 22)
- Consider presentation aids. (p. 24)
- Practice delivering the speech. (p. 24)

KEY TERMS

Chapter 1

oratory	style	feedback
rhetoric	memory	audience perspective
agora	delivery	message
forum	dyadic communication	channel
public forum	small group communication	noise
forensic oratory	mass communication	shared meaning
deliberative oratory	public speaking	rhetorical situation
epideictic oratory	source	culture
canons of rhetoric	encoding	ethnocentrism
invention	receiver	cultural intelligence
arrangement	decoding	

Chapter 2

topic	main points	coordinate points
audience analysis	supporting material	subordinate points
general speech purpose	introduction	organizational pattern
specific speech purpose	body	presentation aids
thesis statement	conclusion	

① Becoming a Public Speaker

As a student of public speaking, you are joining a very large and venerable club. People have studied public speaking in one form or another for well over two thousand years. Indeed, public speaking may be the single most studied skill in history. Since before the time of the great Greek thinker Aristotle (384-322 B.C.E.) and the brilliant Roman statesman and orator Cicero (106-43 B.C.E.), practitioners of this ancient art have penned countless volumes bearing advice on how to address an audience. Our own frenzied era of electronic communication has not diminished the need for this singularly effective form of communication, and public speaking remains an indispensable vehicle for the expression of ideas. Whatever people care deeply about, public speaking offers a way to communicate their concerns with others. Indeed, few other activities offer quite the same opportunity to make one's voice heard.

This guidebook contains the tools you need to create and deliver effective speeches, from brief presentations made to fellow students, co-workers, or fellow citizens to major addresses given to large audiences. Here you will discover the basic building blocks of any good speech, as well as the requirements for delivering presentations in a variety of specialized contexts ranging from the college psychology class to the business and professional arena. You'll also find proven techniques to build your confidence by overcoming the anxiety associated with public speaking.

Why Study Public Speaking?

 WEB⟩ Other college courses

The ability to speak confidently and convincingly in public is an asset to anyone who wants to take an active role in the classroom, workplace, and community. As you master the skills of public speaking, you'll find that it is a powerful vehicle for professional and personal growth.

ADVANCE YOUR PROFESSIONAL GOALS

Whatever your career, chances are that public speaking will be a valuable, even crucial, skill to master. As a report entitled "What Students Must Know to Succeed in the Twenty-first Century" states:

> Clear communication is critical to success. In the marketplace of ideas, the person who communicates clearly is also the person who is seen as thinking clearly. Oral and written communication are not only job-securing, but job-holding skills.[1]

Skill in public speaking tops the list of skills that are sought after by many organizations. Dozens of surveys of corporate managers and executives reveal that oral communication is the most important skill they look for in a college graduate. In a recent survey of employers, for example, oral communication skills ranked first in such critical areas as interpersonal, analytical, teamwork, and computer skills (see Table 1.1).

TABLE 1.1 • Top Personal Qualities/Skills Rated by Employers

1. Communication skills (written and verbal)
2. Honesty/integrity
3. Interpersonal skills (relates well to others)
4. Motivation/initiative
5. Strong work ethic
6. Teamwork skills (works well with others)

Source: "Employers Cite Communication Skills, Honesty/Integrity as Key for Job Candidates." *Job Outlook 2007 Survey,* March 15, 2007. National Association of Colleges and Employers. www.naceweb.org/press/display.asp?year=2007&prid=254. Accessed April 25, 2007.

ACCOMPLISH PERSONAL GOALS

Perhaps more than any other course of study, public speaking offers both key theories of communication and a set of extraordinarily useful skills that can lead to greater confidence and satisfaction in life. Whether you want to stand up with poise in front of classmates, feel more comfortable expressing yourself in group situations, or parlay your skills in the public arena, public speaking offers you a way to fulfill your goals.

ENHANCE YOUR CAREER AS A STUDENT

Preparing speeches involves numerous skills that you can use in other courses. Many forms of writing or composition, for example, also require that you research topics, analyze audiences, support and prove claims, and select patterns for organizing ideas. In addition, courses as diverse as engineering and art history include an oral-presentation component. Students in technical disciplines and the sciences are often called upon to explain complex information clearly and accessibly. Charts, graphs, and other presentation aids are often an important part of such presentations (Chapters 20-22), as are effective introductions and conclusions (Chapters 14 and 15). Identifying target audiences (Chapter 6) and selecting appropriate modes of delivery (Chapters 17-19) are critical skills for everyone, and no less so for the business major who must communicate with multiple audiences, including co-workers, managers, clients, and customers. Other applications of public speaking skills across the curriculum are the focus of Chapter 30, "Speaking in Other College Courses."

EXPLORE AND SHARE VALUES

A speech is an occasion for speaker and audience to focus on ideas and events about which they feel strongly, even passionately. Thus public speaking offers a unique opportunity to explore values, deep-seated feelings, and ideas about what is important in life. Public speaking enables you to express your values and explore those of others in civil discourse, regardless of whether the audience shares your viewpoint. Speaking to an audience whose knowledge or opinions differ from your own can be an equally and sometimes even more satisfying experience than addressing a like-minded audience, especially when speaker and listeners end up gaining a fuller appreciation of each other.

HONE CRITICAL THINKING AND LISTENING SKILLS

Public speaking training will sharpen your ability to reason and think critically. As you study public speaking, you will learn to construct claims and then present evidence and reasoning that logically support them. As you practice organizing and outlining speeches, you will become skilled at structuring ideas so that they flow logically from one to another. You will be able to identify the weak links in your thinking and work to strengthen them.

Public speaking training also hones the highly valued skill of listening. "The difference between 'speaking' and 'listening,'" notes communication scholar W. Barnett Pearce, "is not just a matter of using one's ears rather than one's mouth. It is the assumption of different positions, which are defined by clusters of rights, duties, responsibilities, and obligations."[2] As you learn what goes into a good argument, you will become a more critical receiver of information of all kinds. In a world in which misleading information is often disguised as logic for purposes of selling, deception, or exploitation — or when people are merely mistaken — the ability to listen critically enables you to separate fact from falsehood.

Become an Engaged Citizen

While public speaking skills contribute to both career advancement and personal enrichment, they also offer you ways to enter the public conversation and to deliberate on key policy debates — in other words, to become a more engaged citizen.

Climate change, energy, social security, immigration reform — such large public issues require our considered judgment and action. Yet today too many of us leave it up to politicians, journalists, and other "experts" to make decisions about them. This seems to be a growing trend, with negative implications for our democracy.[3] At its base, democracy only works when decisions affecting "the common good" actually reflect the will of the people — of the voting majority. Today, however, only about 35 percent of people in the United States regularly vote. Of these, only 22 percent are 18-29 years old.[4]

When citizens speak up in sufficient numbers, change occurs. Before the Civil Rights movement of the 1950s and 1960s, for example — a movement largely spearheaded by college students and clergy — racial segregation was legal in the South. In the face of sustained and mass protest, however, Congress passed a series of laws culminating in the Voting Rights Act of 1965, which made it easier for African Americans to make their voices count.

Today the health of the environment is at the forefront. Yet as with civil rights, change will not occur without many people coming together to address key issues and work out their differences. Leaving problems such as pollution and global warming to others is an invitation to special interest groups, who may or may not act with our best interests in mind. As Rebecca Rimel, president of the Pew Charitable Trusts, noted in a recent speech:

> Imagine, for a moment, our nation in 20 years time if our citizenry remains as disengaged — and special interests remain as engaged — as they are now. We'd have a democracy that responds to the particular interests of the few over the pressing demands of the many . . . a society increasingly alienated from its government and each other.[5]

As you study public speaking, you will have the opportunity to research topics that are meaningful to you, such as the environment, consider alternate viewpoints, and if appropriate, choose a course of action.[6] You will learn to distinguish between argument that advances constructive goals and uncivil speech that serves merely to inflame and demean others. You will learn, in short, the "rules of engagement" for effective public discourse.[7] As you do, you will gain confidence in your ability to join your voice with others in pursuit of issues you care about.

Table 1.2, "Civic Engagement on the Web," lists Web sites devoted to education about key policy debates and engagement in them through online conversations, petitions to policymakers, and participation in polls.

TABLE 1.2 • Civic Engagement on the Web

Public Agenda www.publicagenda.org	**Public Agenda** aims to provide nonbiased research that explains public attitudes about complex policy issues. The Web site contains Issues Guides on topics ranging from abortion to terrorism.
The Public Forum Institute www.publicforuminstitute.org	**The Public Forum Institute** Similar to Public Agenda, the Public Forum Institute offers unbiased research on a variety of important public issues, such as oceans under stress and homeland security.
Project Vote Smart www.vote-smart.org	**Project Vote Smart** offers a wealth of information about political candidates and elected officials, including their voting records, campaign contributions, public statements, biographical data, and evaluations of them generated by over one hundred competing special interest groups.
e.thePeople www.e-thepeople.org	**e.thePeople** explores political issues and allows you to publish "conversations" for the *e.thePeople* community to read and respond to. You may also express your opinion by taking polls and circulating petitions to policymakers.

The Classical Roots of Public Speaking

 Links

The practice of **oratory**, also called **rhetoric**, emerged full force in Greece in the fifth century B.C.E. and referred to making effective speeches, particularly those of a persuasive nature. The ancient city-state of Athens, the site of the world's first recorded direct democracy, was governed by some forty thousand free, property-holding males (neither women nor slaves had the rights of citizens). The Athenians believed that citizenship demanded active participation in public affairs, a principle that endures to this day, and they demonstrated their involvement through oratory in a public square or marketplace called the **agora**. Later, in the Roman republic (the Western world's first known representative democracy), citizens met in a public space called a **forum**, and today the term **public forum** denotes a variety of media for the voicing of ideas, including traditional physical spaces such as town squares as well as a plethora of print and electronic media.

CLASSICAL TERMS AND THE CANONS OF RHETORIC

For the Greeks, oratory was an essential tool in settling civil disputes, determining public policy, and establishing laws. In cases involving major crimes, for example, juries usually included five hundred members.[8] Since people served as their own advocates, their chances of persuading jurors to vote in their favor depended on their oratorical skills. The Greeks called such legal speech **forensic oratory**; speech given in legislative or political contexts, **deliberative**; and speech delivered in special ceremonies, such as celebrations and funerals, **epideictic**. The great Athenian leader-general Pericles, for example, used his considerable powers of political persuasion, or *deliberative oratory*, to convince Athenians to rebuild the Acropolis and erect other great temples, such as the Parthenon, that would endure and amaze the world for centuries to come.

To learn the art of rhetoric, families with means sent their boys to study with private tutors, including such illustrious classical scholars as Protagoras and Plato. Aristotle (384-322 B.C.E.), one of the greatest classical rhetoricians and teachers, divided the process of preparing a speech into five parts — *invention, arrangement, style, memory,* and *delivery* — called the **canons of rhetoric**. **Invention** refers to adapting speech information to the audience in order to make your case. **Arrangement** is organizing the speech in ways that are best suited to the topic and the audience. **Style** is the way the speaker uses language to express the speech ideas. **Memory** is the practice of the speech until it can be artfully delivered. Finally, **delivery** is the vocal and nonverbal behavior you use when speaking. The Roman orator Cicero (106-43 B.C.E.) renamed these canons *inventio* (discovering the speech material), *dispositio* (arranging the material), *elocutio* (styling the speech), *memoria* (remembering all the various lines of argument to prove a case), and *pronounciatio* (vocal and nonverbal delivery).

Table 1.3, "Classical Rhetoric on the Web," lists several sites on the Web devoted to classical rhetoric.

TABLE 1.3 • Classical Rhetoric on the Web	
Silva Rhetoricae humanities.byu.edu/rhetoric/silva.htm	Sponsored by Brigham Young University, this site offers detailed descriptions of the canons of rhetoric, along with entries of thousands of rhetorical terms.
Virtual Salt: A Handbook of Rhetorical Devices www.virtualsalt.com/rhetoric.htm	Virtual Salt contains definitions and examples of more than sixty traditional rhetorical devices useful for improving your speeches.
A Glossary of Rhetorical Terms with Examples (University of Kentucky, Division of Classics) www.uky.edu/AS/Classics/rhetoric.html	From the University of Kentucky Classics Department, this site offers brief definitions of rhetorical strategies and a number of examples to illustrate the concept.

A RICH AND RELEVANT HERITAGE

Although scholars such as Aristotle and Cicero surely didn't anticipate the omnipresent PowerPoint slide show that accompanies so many contemporary speeches, the speechmaking structure they bequeathed to us as the canons of rhetoric remains remarkably intact. Although these canons are often identified by terms other than the original ones, they continue to be taught in current books on public speaking, including this one. For example, Chapters 6-10 and 24-25 (analyzing the audience; selecting and researching a topic; composing arguments) correspond to *invention*. Chapters 11-13 and 26 (on outlining and organizing the speech) represent *arrangement*. Chapter 16 (on language) focuses on *style*. Finally, Chapters 17-19 describe the process of *practice* (*memory*) and *delivery* (see Table 1.4).

Public Speaking as a Form of Communication

Public speaking is one of four categories of human communication: dyadic, small group, mass, and public speaking. **Dyadic communication** is a form of communication between two people, as in a conversation. **Small group communication** involves a small number of people who can see and speak directly with one another. **Mass communication** occurs between a speaker and a large audience of unknown people. In mass communication the receivers of the message are not present with the speaker, or are part of such an immense crowd that there can be little or no interaction between speaker and listener. Television, radio news broadcasts, and mass rallies are examples of mass communication.

In **public speaking** a speaker delivers a message with a specific purpose to an audience of people who are present during the delivery of the speech. Public speaking always includes a speaker who has a reason for speaking, an audience that gives the speaker its attention, and a message that is meant to accomplish a specific purpose.[9] Public speakers address audiences largely without interruption and take responsibility for the words and ideas being expressed.

TABLE 1.4 • The Classic Canons of Rhetoric and Speechmaking Today

The Canons of Rhetoric	Addressed in *A Speaker's Guidebook*
1. Invention (Selecting and adapting speech material to the audience; constructing arguments)	Chapter 6: Analyzing the Audience
	Chapter 7: Selecting a Topic and Purpose
	Chapter 8: Developing Supporting Material
	Chapter 9: Locating Supporting Material
	Chapter 10: Using the Internet to Support Your Speech
	Chapter 24: The Persuasive Speech
	Chapter 25: Developing Arguments for the Persuasive Speech
2. Arrangement (Ordering the speech)	Chapter 11: Organizing the Speech
	Chapter 12: Types of Organizational Arrangements
	Chapter 13: Outlining the Speech
	Chapter 26: Organizing the Persuasive Speech
3. Style (Use of language, including figures of speech)	Chapter 16: Using Language to Style the Speech
4. Memory (Practice of the speech)	Chapter 17: Methods of Delivery
	Chapter 18: The Voice in Delivery
5. Delivery (Vocal and nonverbal delivery)	Chapter 19: The Body in Delivery

SIMILARITIES BETWEEN PUBLIC SPEAKING AND OTHER FORMS OF COMMUNICATION

Like small group communication, public speaking requires that you address a group of people who are focused on you and expect you to clearly discuss issues that are relevant to the topic and to the occasion. As in mass communication, public speaking requires that you understand and appeal to the audience members' interests, attitudes, and values. And like dyadic communication, or conversation, public speaking requires that you attempt to make yourself understood, involve and respond to your conversational partners, and take responsibility for what you say.

A key feature of any type of communication is sensitivity to the listeners. Whether you are talking to one person in a coffee shop or giving a speech to a hundred people, your listeners want to feel that you care about their interests, desires, and goals. Skilled conversationalists do this, and so do successful public speakers. Similarly, skilled conversationalists are in command of their material and present it in a way that is organized and easy to follow, believable, relevant, and interesting. Public speaking is no different. Moreover, the audience will expect you to be knowledgeable and unbiased about your topic and to express your ideas clearly.

DIFFERENCES BETWEEN PUBLIC SPEAKING
AND OTHER FORMS OF COMMUNICATION

Although public speaking shares many characteristics of other types of communication, several factors distinguish public speaking from these other forms. These include (1) opportunities for feedback, (2) level of preparation, and (3) degree of formality.

Public speaking presents different opportunities for *feedback,* or listener response to a message, than does dyadic, small group, or mass communication. Opportunities for feedback are high both in conversation and in small group interactions. Partners in conversation continually respond to one another in back-and-forth fashion; in small groups, participants expect interruptions for purposes of clarification or redirection. However, because the receiver of the message in mass communication is physically removed from the messenger, feedback is delayed until after the event, as in TV ratings.

Public speaking offers a middle ground between low and high levels of feedback. Public speaking does not permit the constant exchange of information between listener and speaker that happens in conversation, but audiences can and do provide ample verbal and nonverbal cues to what they are thinking and feeling. Facial expressions, vocalizations (including laughter or disapproving noises), gestures, applause, and a range of body movements all signal the audience's response to the speaker. The perceptive speaker reads these cues and tries to adjust his or her remarks accordingly. Because feedback is more restricted in public speaking situations than in dyadic and small group communication, *preparation* must be more careful and extensive. Because you have fewer opportunities to know how your listeners feel about what you are saying, you must anticipate how they will react to your remarks. With each audience member focused on you, it is important to be in command of your material. In dyadic and small group communication, you can always shift the burden to your conversational partner or to other group members. Public speaking offers no such shelter, and lack of preparation stands out starkly.

Public speaking also differs from other forms of communication in terms of its *degree of formality.* In general, speeches tend to occur in more formal settings than do other forms of communication. Formal gatherings such as graduations, weddings, religious services, and the like naturally lend themselves to speeches; they provide a focus and give form — a "voice" — to the event. In contrast, with the exception of formal interviews, dyadic communication (or conversation) is largely informal. Small group communication also tends to be less formal than public speaking, even in business meetings.

Thus public speaking shares many features of everyday conversation, but because the speaker is the focal point of attention in what is usually a formal setting, listeners expect a more systematic presentation than they do in conversation or small group communication. As such, public speaking requires more preparation and practice than the other forms of communication.

Public Speaking and the Communication Process

Communication, whether between two people or between one person and an audience of many listeners, is an interactive process in which people exchange and interpret messages with one another.

ELEMENTS OF COMMUNICATION

In any communication event, including public speaking, several elements are present. These include the source, the receiver, the message, the channel, and shared meaning, as well as context, goals, and outcome (see Figure 1.1).[10]

The Source

The **source**, or sender, is the person who creates a message. The speaker transforms ideas and thoughts into messages and sends them to a receiver, or an audience. The speaker decides what messages are to be sent and how they will be sent. The process of organizing the message, choosing words and sentence structure, and verbalizing the message is called **encoding**. Encoding is this cumulative process of the source transforming thoughts into messages and delivering them to the audience.

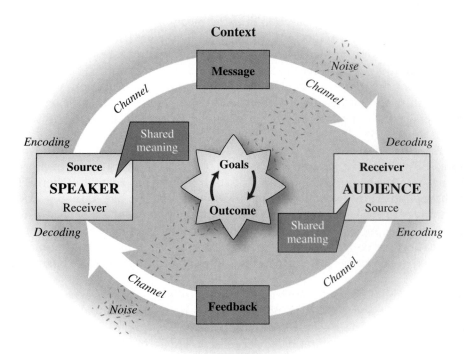

Figure 1.1 The Communication Process

The Receiver

The recipient of the source's message is the **receiver**, or audience. The process of interpreting the message is called **decoding**. Audience members decode the meaning of the message selectively, based on their own experiences and attitudes. **Feedback**, the audience's response to a message, can be conveyed both verbally and nonverbally. For example, an audience member may blurt out, "I don't think so," or may smile and nod. Feedback from the audience often indicates whether a speaker's message has been understood. Note that feedback is a message sent by the receiver to the speaker. In this way, the original receiver is now in the role of source (an audience member is encoding a message) and the original source is in the role of receiver (the speaker is decoding a message). This change in roles between speaker and audience represents the interactive nature of public speaking.

Often, speakers deliver ineffective or inappropriate messages because they do not know or do not understand their audience (the receivers). Whether you are speaking to an audience of one or a hundred, always adopt an **audience perspective** — that is, try to determine the needs, attitudes, and values of your audience before you begin speaking. Let their relevant interests and background guide you in constructing your speech (see Chapter 6).

The Message

The **message** is the content of the communication process: thoughts and ideas put into meaningful expressions. Content can be expressed verbally (through the sentences and points of a speech) and nonverbally (through eye contact and gestures). Miscommunication can happen when audience members misinterpret the speaker's intended message, or when the speaker misreads audience feedback.

The Channel

The medium through which the speaker sends a message is the **channel**. If a speaker is delivering a message in front of a live audience, the channel is the air; sound waves deliver the message by traveling through the air. Other channels include telephones, televisions, and computers. If interference, or noise, occurs, the message may not be understood. **Noise** is any interference with the message. Although noise includes physical sounds such as a slamming door or ringing cell phone, it can also include psychological distractions, such as heated emotions, and environmental interference, such as a frigid room or the presence of unexpected people.

Shared Meaning

Shared meaning is the mutual understanding of a message between speaker and audience. Shared meaning occurs in varying degrees. The lowest level of shared meaning exists when the speaker has merely caught the audience's attention. As the message develops, depending on the method of encoding selected by the source, a higher degree of shared meaning is possible. Thus it is listener and speaker together who truly make a speech a speech — who co-create its meaning.

Context and the Rhetorical Situation

Context includes anything that influences the speaker, the audience, or the occasion — and thus, ultimately, the message itself. In the case of classroom speeches, context would include (among other things) recent events on campus or in the outside world, the physical setting (e.g., a small classroom or large auditorium), the order and timing of speeches, and the cultural orientations of audience members. Considering context reminds us that successful communication can never be divorced from the concerns and expectations of others.

Part of the context of any speech is the situation that created the need for it in the first place. All speeches are delivered in response to a specific **rhetorical situation**, or circumstance, that calls for a public response.[11] A funeral, for example, calls for a eulogy; a graduation calls for a commencement address. Politicians deliver speeches in response to various events, such as major policy shifts or natural disasters. Considering the rhetorical situation helps us remember the reason for the speech itself, and, closely aligned to this, the expectations of our audience.

Goals

Goal setting is one of the primary tenets of most communication models. A clearly defined goal is a prerequisite for an effective speech. What is it that you want the audience to learn or do or believe as a result of your speech? How much ground do you want to cover? What do you personally want to achieve by delivering the speech? Establishing a set of goals early in the speechmaking process and writing them down in the form of concise sentences will help you proceed through speech preparation and delivery with a clear focus in mind. All the steps you take will be in concert with the clearly articulated goals that you have set. (See Chapter 7 for more on formulating the speech goal.)

Outcome

A speech is not truly complete until its effects have been assessed and you decide whether you have accomplished what you set out to do. Usually this assessment is informal, as in listening to audience reactions. Sometimes it is more formal, as in receiving an evaluation from an instructor or from the audience itself. Constructive feedback is an invaluable tool for self-evaluation and improvement. (See Chapter 5 for further discussion and tips on giving and receiving constructive criticism.)

Learning to Speak in Public

None of us is born knowing how to speak in public. Even seemingly effortless communicators such as Los Angeles Mayor Antonio Villaraigosa and Marian Wright Edelman, founder of the Children's Defense Fund, have worked hard — perhaps hardest of all — to achieve good results. Similarly, the student activist who convinces the college administration to divest its shares from companies that support the government of Sudan, the lab worker who clearly describes his or her latest experiment to colleagues, and the PTA parent who builds a groundswell of opposition to lengthening the school year all succeed because they have devoted time and effort to preparing their speeches.

DRAW ON FAMILIAR SKILLS

Learning any new skill involves mastering a set of techniques and then practicing them until you gain proficiency. Usually, the process can be made less daunting by drawing on related skills that you already have.

Conversation and Public Speaking

Planning and executing the delivery of a speech, according to contemporary scholars, is much the same as engaging in a particularly important conversation. Although it requires more thinking and effort than ordinary conversation, delivering a speech rests on the same basic principles. Intuitively, you are already familiar with many of the basic principles of public speaking. For example, when speaking with a friend, you automatically check to make certain that you are understood and then adjust your meaning accordingly. You also tend to discuss issues that are appropriate to the circumstances. If you're speaking to someone you know quite well, you're likely to address any number of topics with ease. When a relative stranger is involved, however, you try to get to know his or her interests and attitudes before revealing any strong opinions.

These instinctive adjustments to your audience, topic, and occasion represent critical steps in putting a speech together. Although the means of discovering what is important to a larger audience are of necessity more involved, both the conversationalist and the public speaker try to uncover the audience's interests and needs before speaking.

Speaking and Writing

Preparing a speech also has much in common with writing. For example, as author Robert Perrin notes, both effective speaking and effective writing depend on having a focused sense of who the audience is.[12] Both speaking and writing often require that you research a topic, offer credible evidence, employ effective transitions to signal the logical flow of ideas, and use persuasive appeals. The principles of organizing a speech parallel those of organizing an essay, including offering a compelling introduction, a clear thesis statement, supporting ideas, and a thoughtful conclusion.

RECOGNIZE PUBLIC SPEAKING'S UNIQUE REQUIREMENTS

Although public speaking has much in common with everyday conversation and with writing, it is, obviously, "its own thing." More so than writers, successful speakers generally use familiar words, easy-to-follow sentences, straightforward syntax (subject-verb-object agreement), and transitional words and phrases. Speakers also routinely repeat key words and phrases to emphasize ideas and help listeners follow along, and even the briefest speeches make frequent use of repetition (see Chapter 16).

Spoken language is often more interactive and inclusive of the audience than written language. The personal pronouns *we, I,* and *you* occur more frequently in spoken than in written text. Audience members want to know what the speaker thinks and feels, and that he or she recognizes them and relates them to the message. Speakers accomplish this by making specific references to themselves and to the audience.

Yet because public speaking usually occurs in more formal settings than does everyday conversation, listeners expect a somewhat more formal style of communication from the speaker. When you give a speech, listeners expect you to speak in a clear, recognizable, and organized fashion. Thus, in contrast to conversation, in order to develop an effective oral style you must practice the words you will say and the way you will say them.

BECOME A CULTURALLY SENSITIVE SPEAKER

Every audience member wants to feel that the speaker has his or her particular needs and interests at heart, and to feel recognized and included in the speaker's message. To create this sense of inclusion, the public speaker must attempt to understand the audience's beliefs and norms and to be *culturally sensitive.* **Culture** — the language, beliefs, values, norms, behaviors, and even material objects that are passed from one generation to the next — touches almost every aspect of who and what we are.[13] Whether addressing classmates in a public speaking class or delivering a business presentation to a group of foreign executives, a speaker who is culturally sensitive will assume differences. He or she will try to determine what those differences are and then address them with interest and respect.

The flip side of cultural sensitivity is **ethnocentrism**, the belief that the ways of our own culture are superior to those of other cultures. Ethnocentric speakers don't bother to consider other perspectives or ways of behaving. No matter how passionately they believe in an issue, our most admired public speakers strive to acknowledge and respectfully consider alternative viewpoints.

More than ever, public speakers must demonstrate not only cultural sensitivity but also **cultural intelligence**.[14] As David C. Thomas and Kerr Inkson explain, cultural intelligence means

> being skilled and flexible about understanding a culture, learning more about it from your ongoing interactions with it, and gradually reshaping your thinking to be more sympathetic to the culture and to be more skilled and appropriate when interacting with others from the culture.[15]

As a public speaker, you will continually confront values that are different from your own. In this guidebook you will find numerous suggestions for increasing your cultural intelligence so that you can become a more culturally sensitive speaker. These discussions range from assessing audience members' cultural values (see Chapter 6), avoiding stereotypes, and refraining from hate speech (see Chapter 5) to the crucial role that language plays in creating a culturally sensitive speech (see Chapter 16).

Giving It a Try: Preparing Your First Speech

Novice speakers in any circumstances — at school, at work, or in the community — will benefit from preparing and delivering a first short speech of between two and five minutes. An audience of as few as two other people will suffice to test the waters and help you gain confidence in your ability to "stand up and deliver." Experts will tell you that the best way to overcome nervousness about speaking in public is to get up and deliver a speech. After all, you can't learn how to swim if you don't get wet.

A Brief Overview of the Speechmaking Process

WEB ▷ Chapter quizzes

As a beginning speaker preparing your first classroom speech, you will not be required to know all the conventions of speechmaking as described in subsequent chapters. However, it is helpful to have a sense of the various steps involved in putting together and delivering a speech or a presentation (see Figure 2.1).

SELECT A TOPIC

The first step in creating a speech involves finding a **topic**, or something to speak about. Unless the topic is assigned, let your interests — your passions — be your guide. What deeply engages you? What recent local, national, or world events have drawn your attention? What are your areas of expertise? Your hobbies? Are there controversies brewing on campus or at your workplace that you might wish to address? Beware, however, that personal interest should not be the only criterion for selection. It's equally important that you feel confident that your topic will be of interest to the audience. Whatever you settle on, make sure to consider your audience members and their interests.

ANALYZE THE AUDIENCE

Audiences have personalities, interests, and ambitions all their own. These factors affect how receptive an audience will be toward a given topic. Thus it is imperative that you learn as much as you can about the similarities and differences among the members of your audience. **Audience analysis** is actually a highly systematic process of getting to know your listeners relative to the topic and the speech occasion. The process involves studying the audience through techniques such as interviews and questionnaires (see Chapter 6). However, for this first speech assignment it should be sufficient to ask three or

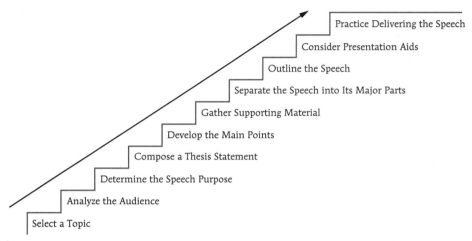

Figure 2.1 Steps in the Speechmaking Process

four people who will be part of your audience a few questions about your topic. For example, What do they already know about it? Does it interest them? Consider also some fairly easily identifiable *demographic characteristics:* ratio of males to females, racial and ethnic differences represented in the group, noticeable age variations, and proportion of the group that is from out of state or out of the country. Next, consider how different people (e.g., older and younger, men and women, international and native-born) might think or feel differently about your topic.

DETERMINE THE SPEECH PURPOSE

Once you settle on a topic, the next step is to decide what you wish to convey about it—and why. As you will learn in Chapter 7, there are three **general speech purposes** toward which you should direct your speeches: *to inform, to persuade,* or *to mark a special occasion.* Thus you need to decide whether your goal is to inform your audience about an issue or event, to persuade them to accept one position to the exclusion of other positions, or to mark a special occasion such as a wedding, a funeral, or a dinner event. Your speech should also have a **specific purpose**. This is a declarative sentence stating what you expect the speech to accomplish. For example, if your general purpose is to inform, your specific purpose might be "to inform my audience about three key reasons why tuition will be raised." Write your specific purpose on a sheet of paper or on a Post-it note placed on the edge of your computer monitor. It will be an important guide in developing the rest of the speech.

COMPOSE A THESIS STATEMENT

Once you've identified the general and specific speech purposes, you need to compose a **thesis statement** that clearly expresses the central idea of your speech. While the specific purpose describes what *you* want to achieve with the speech, the thesis statement concisely identifies for your audience, in a single sentence, what the speech is about:

GENERAL PURPOSE: To inform

SPECIFIC PURPOSE: To inform my audience about the evolution of the MTV network.

THESIS STATEMENT: MTV has evolved from a single music video cable station to a multichannel, multientertainment network.

Wherever you are in the planning stage, always refer to the thesis statement to make sure that you are on track to illustrate or prove your thesis.

DEVELOP THE MAIN POINTS

Organize your speech around two or three **main points**. These are the primary pieces of knowledge (in an informative speech) or the key arguments in favor of your position (in a persuasive speech) (see Chapter 11). If you create a clear, specific purpose statement for your speech, the main points will be easily identifiable (if not explicit).

SPECIFIC PURPOSE: To inform my audience about the evolution of the MTV network.

    I. MTV began strictly as a source of music videos.

    II. After its first few years, MTV programming included other types of music shows.

    III. Now MTV programming consists largely of variety and reality shows.

GATHER SUPPORTING MATERIAL

Supporting material illustrates the main points by clarifying, elaborating, and verifying the speaker's ideas. Supporting material includes the entire world of information available to you — from personal experiences to statistics from outside sources. Unless your speech is about yourself (or focuses on an extraordinarily compelling personal experience), plan to research your topic for supporting material. For short classroom speeches, your research might be as minimal as a few comments that other people have made about the topic, editorials in the campus newspaper, or statistics gathered from a reputable Internet site. As your assignments become more involved, so too will your research. Chapters 8-10 describe developing, locating, and using many kinds of supporting material.

SEPARATE THE SPEECH INTO ITS MAJOR PARTS   Video quizzes

The three major parts to every speech are the introduction, body, and conclusion (see Table 2.1). Develop each part separately, then bring them together using transition statements (see Chapters 11 and 13).

Introduction

The **introduction** serves to introduce the topic and the speaker and to alert audience members to your specific speech purpose. A good introduction should catch the audience's attention and interest. Some of the many ways in which speakers do this include making a startling statement, telling a story, or using humor (see Chapter 14).

Speech Body

Just like the body of a written essay, the speech **body** contains the speech's main points and subpoints, all of which support the speech's thesis. It is here that you should illustrate or argue each of your main ideas, using the supporting material you have gathered to clarify, elaborate, or substantiate your points.

Conclusion

The **conclusion** restates the speech purpose and reiterates how the main points confirm it. Because the conclusion represents your last opportunity to motivate your listeners and to state your theme in a memorable manner, make sure to end on a strong note (see Chapter 15).

OUTLINE THE SPEECH

 WEB Outliner

An outline provides the framework upon which to arrange the elements of your speech in support of your thesis. Outlines are based on the principle of *coordination* and *subordination* — the logical placement of ideas relative to their importance to one another. **Coordinate points**, more often referred to as main points, are of equal importance and are indicated by their parallel alignment. **Subordinate points**, also called sub-points, are given less weight than the main points they support and are identified in outlines by their placement

TABLE 2.1 • Major Speech Parts		
Introduction	**Body**	**Conclusion**
• Welcome your audience. • Introduce yourself, your topic, and your speech purpose. • Catch the audience's attention and interest with the use of a quote, a short story, an example, or another kind of supporting material. • Provide a clear transition statement to the body of the speech.	• Introduce the main ideas of the speech and illustrate them with a variety of supporting material. • Organize your ideas and evidence in a structure that suits your topic, audience, and speech occasion. • Use transition statements and phrases to move between main points and to the conclusion.	• Restate the specific speech purpose and reiterate how the main points confirm it. • Leave your audience with something to think about. • Answer questions.

to the right of the points they support. A smooth flow of thought among and within coordinate points requires using clear transition statements, ideally written into the outline. (For a full discussion of outlining, see Chapter 13.)

As your speeches become more involved, you will need to select an appropriate **organizational pattern** (see Chapters 12 and 26). You will also need to familiarize yourself with developing both *working* and *speaking* outlines (see Chapter 13). To allow for the full development of your ideas, *working outlines* generally contain points stated in complete sentences, including the transition statements. As a rule, *speaking outlines* (also called presentation outlines) are far briefer than working outlines and are usually prepared using either short phrases or key words.

Following is a working full-sentence outline created by a beginning public speaking student for a speech of introduction (see speech below):

TOPIC:	Speech of Introduction for Lisa Tran
SPEECH PURPOSE:	To inform
SPECIFIC SPEECH PURPOSE:	To inform my audience about my odyssey as a refugee from war-torn Vietnam to a person fulfilling her potential and realizing her dreams in America

Introduction

(Captures audience attention — in this case, with a startling statement and select dramatic details of her story.) My story begins in Saigon, where my father was imprisoned. We fled the country without taking any belongings. The boat ride was horrific, and we arrived to harsh media attention. We first settled in Kansas, where we were finally reunited with Dad.

(States thesis statement and previews main points. In a brief speech, the preview can act as a transition.) We set forth on American soil some years ago, but my journey has just begun. Little did I dream then of what was in store for me. Little do I know of what my future will bring.

Body

I. We become American citizens, and I achieve things I never dreamed of.

    A. I become the first Asian pom captain at the University of Oklahoma.

    B. I become a member of Kappa Kappa Gamma and the 1999 Miss Greek OU.

II. My achievements could not have occurred if I did not have some knowledge of the difficulties and hardships of life.

    A. Though I could not afford lessons in Vietnam, as a child I trained myself to dance.

        1. Nine years later, I earned honors as a dancer and today I teach dance.

        2. In 1999, I was crowned the first Asian Miss Greek OU.

B. Thanks to the love and support of my sorority, my friends, and my family, I have come far.

C. The journey is not over.

Conclusion

(Restates the thesis in a memorable way.) As an anonymous poet once wrote, "Dream what you want to dream, go where you want to go, be what you want to be, because you have only one life and one chance to do all the things you want to do." Rather than proving my self-worth, my accomplishments merely symbolize the true passion and drive we have for living and succeeding.

(Leaves the audience with a motivating message.) We are what we learn and take with us during this journey we call life. I am the past because I have appreciation; I am the present because I have learned humbleness; I am the future because I have so much more to learn.

CONSIDER PRESENTATION AIDS

As you prepare your speech, consider whether using visual or audio aids, a combination of the two, or other **presentation aids** will help your audience understand your points. A presentation aid can be as simple as writing the definition of a word on a blackboard or as involved as a multimedia slide show. Presentation aids that summarize and highlight information, such as charts and graphs, can often help the audience to retain ideas and understand difficult concepts (see Chapter 20).

PRACTICE DELIVERING THE SPEECH

The success of even your first speech in class depends on how well prepared and practiced you are. You will want to feel and appear "natural" to your listeners, an effect best achieved by rehearsing both the verbal and nonverbal elements of your speech. So practice your speech — often. It has been suggested that a good speech is practiced at least six times. For a four- to six-minute speech, that's only thirty to forty minutes (figuring in re-starts and pauses) of actual practice time.

As you practice your speech, pay attention to:

1. Adjusting the volume of your speaking voice to cover the room.
2. Modulating the rate at which you speak, aiming to be neither too slow nor too fast.
3. Pronouncing words correctly.
4. Smiling and animating your face in ways that feel natural and appropriate to your topic.
5. Making eye contact with your audience members.
6. Using gestures that feel natural to you without exaggerating your movements.

CHECKLIST

Using the Audio Recorder to Bolster Confidence

Many public speaking experts agree that of the vast array of high-tech audio-visual gizmos available, the tape recorder, or the digital audio recorder, along with the video camera (see Chapter 20), are among some of the few truly indispensable aids to building confidence in public speaking. Listening to your speech helps to make it real and, therefore, less scary.

✓ Record yourself at least one of the six times that you rehearse your speech.

✓ As you play back the recording, listen for clarity. Is your pronunciation clear?

✓ Listen to the tempo of your sentences. Are they too long? Too choppy?

✓ Have you included any tongue twisters that cause you to stumble as you speak?

✓ Time your speech as you record it. This will help you decide how to edit it and where to add or cut.

✓ Use positive self-imagery. Close your eyes and visualize yourself standing in front of the audience and being well received. Let the sound of your voice relax you as you sit back and appreciate all the good work you've done.[1]

1. Ron Hoff, *I Can See You Naked,* rev. ed. (Kansas City, Mo.: Andrews McMeel, 1992), 66.

ESL Speaker's Notes
Identifying Linguistic Issues as You Practice Your Speech

As noted in the preceding checklist, most experts recommend that you prepare for delivering your first speech (as well as for subsequent speeches) by practicing with an audio recorder. Non-native speakers may wish to pay added attention to pronunciation and articulation as they listen. *Pronunciation* is the correct formation of word sounds. *Articulation* is the clarity or forcefulness with which the sounds are made, regardless of whether they are pronounced correctly. It is important to pay attention to and work on both areas. If possible, try to arrange an appointment with an instructor to help you identify key linguistic issues in your speech practice tape. If instructors are unavailable, try asking a fellow student.

 Because languages vary tremendously in the specific sounds they use and the way in which these sounds are produced by the vocal chords, each of us will speak a non-native language a bit differently from native speakers. That is, we will have some sort of accent. This should not concern you in and of itself. What is important is identifying which specific features of your pronunciation, if any, seriously interfere with your ability to make yourself understandable. Listening to your speech with an audio recorder or a videotape, perhaps in the presence of a native speaker, will allow you to identify trouble spots. Once you have identified which words you tend to mispronounce, you can work to correct the problem.

(Continued)

As you listen to your recording, watch as well for your articulation of words. ESL students whose first languages don't differentiate between the /sh/ sound and its close cousin /ch/, for example, may say "share" when they mean "chair" or "shoes" when they mean "choose."[1] It is therefore important that you also check to make sure that you are using the correct meaning of the words you have selected for your speech.

1. Based on Robbin Crabtree and Robert Weissberg, *ESL Students in the Public Speaking Classroom* (Boston: Bedford/St. Martin's, 2000), 23.

Take the Plunge

 **WEB** Sample speeches

As you prepare for your first speech, it is very important that you fulfill each of the steps in the speechmaking process described in the previous section. Keep track of your progress and stay aware of your feelings about the whole process — from the time the assignment is given to the few minutes immediately following the speech. Remember, the first speech is usually simple and fun, so try not to focus all your energies on how nervous or anxious you're feeling — even the most experienced speakers go through some degree of anxiety. But by taking as many opportunities that come their way to speak in public, and by practicing extensively, they learn to control their fear — you can, too.

✓ SELF-ASSESSMENT CHECKLIST

My First Speech

Consider each item in the following checklist in two ways — as something to accomplish during preparation, and as something to consider after you have presented your speech. Use this self-assessment tool to improve future speeches by isolating areas where you need improvement.

Introduction

_____ 1. How will/did I capture attention?

_____ 2. What is/was my thesis statement?

_____ 3. What will/did I say to relate the topic to the audience?

_____ 4. What will/did I say to preview the main points of the speech?

_____ 5. What will/did I say to make the transition from my introduction to my first main point?

Body

_____ 1. Is/was the arrangement of my main points clear and logical?

_____ 2. What transition statements will/did I use between main points?

_____ 3. Do I have/did I use appropriate support material for each point?

(Continued)

Conclusion

_____ 1. How will/did I restate the thesis/purpose of my speech?
_____ 2. What will/did I say to summarize the main points?
_____ 3. What memorable thought will/did I end the speech with?

Delivery

_____ 1. What will/did I do to assure consistent eye contact?
_____ 2. What will/did I do to project appropriate vocal qualities (rate and volume, clear articulation)?
_____ 3. What will/did I do to ensure proper posture, gestures, and general movement?

My overall assessment of this speech is: _____

What I consider strengths in this speech: _____

Elements I need to improve on: _____

Goals for my next speech: _____

Sample Visually Annotated Introductory Speech

 WEB Video

The Dance of Life

ASHLEY WHITE

Warm smile connects with audience

We are on a lifelong journey to find our identity. On this journey, we look for those things that make us unique, that bring us success, and that hold us back, and we discover how they define our personality. We set standards for ourselves and observe our boundaries. We take so many extraordinary measures, but when exactly are we supposed to discover who we are? Is there a specific moment? Is there an initiation age? Is it ever certain? What happens if what defines us must suddenly be let go? How do we find new purpose with what is left? •

I have always identified myself as a dancer. Since age three I have been in dance classes, but since birth I have danced. It is not a path for the faint of heart, and yet seldom are dancers taken very seriously. Few people outside of the discipline understand the

• Even though the speaker's topic is herself, she draws the audience in with the personal pronoun "We." This captures the audience's attention and makes listeners feel included. The speaker's use of a series of rhetorical questions is a dramatic way to introduce her thesis—the search for identity and purpose in life—and to preview the main points.

commitment, the scrutiny, the self-sacrifice, the physical and emotional pain — and the unspeakable joy — that dance affords its chosen ones. Dance truly does offer an inexpressible enjoyment, whether performed in the classroom, in rehearsal, or on stage. It becomes more than a hobby. It is self-defining. •

    My dance teacher was the first to notice the curve, and then I was formally diagnosed with scoliosis at the age of ten. Scoliosis is a lateral curvature of the spine ranging from slight to severe. It often gets worse during adolescent growth and stops worsening when growth stops. It affects girls and boys, but it is not life threatening. •

Quick pause to glance at notecard

    At eleven, I was wearing a back brace at night, and at twelve, both day and night. Adolescence is a difficult time to deal with any anomaly. During a time when everyone was trying to fit the norm, the brace made me feel different. This caused me much anxiety and depression. Dance class was my only time of liberation, which made my desire to dance even stronger.

    I stopped wearing the brace once I got to high school because I had stopped growing; but during my second semester of college I received troubling news. My curve had worsened by fifteen degrees in four years, and it was time to consider surgery. The doctor informed me from the start that, with the surgery, dancing professionally would not be likely, although I would be able to dance recreationally. He also advised that without the surgery, my spine would continue to curve, leaving me with lifelong discomfort and misshapenness. I went through with the surgery in July 2007. The doctors placed two titanium rods on either side of my spine, held in place by hooks. Two months later, I am still recovering and have little pain.

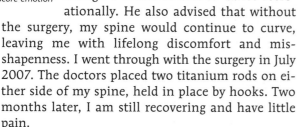

Effective gestures underscore emotion

    I am thankful for my overall health, for the success of the surgery, that one day soon I will dance again, and that amongst all this emotional turmoil, I have found a new passion. This art is expressed in

• The speaker's first main point introduces dance as her passion.

• The speaker introduces her second point, that she developed scoliosis. She adds drama by signaling, in story form, that something has gone wrong with her chosen path.

Ashley turns to address audience members in all corners of the room

the kitchen, not in the dance studio, and my training begins here at Johnson and Wales University. Cooking and dancing require many of the same skills: discipline, artistry, technique. However, knowledge of food can also provide me with endless career opportunities, whereas as a dancer I might never have worked steadily. •

This transition of redefining myself has been a difficult one, and I have learned that it is actually an ongoing one. Being in touch with oneself requires constant learning, redefining, and reapplying, and not just being dedicated to a single interest. This lifelong journey I am on? I know now that this is just the beginning of finding my own identity. •

• In a surprise twist, the speaker tells us that she has found a new passion. This is her third main point.

• The speaker concludes by returning to the theme she introduced in her introduction: the quest for identity.

Sample Introductory Speech

Past, Present, and Future

LISA TRAN

Introduction

• Everybody has a history; some, perhaps, more interesting than others. Mine began nearly twenty-one years ago in Saigon, Vietnam. My father, who was an affluent businessman, was taken captive along with many other men by the Vietnamese communist government and imprisoned because of his Chinese descent. All of our money, property, and rights were stripped away from us. My mother, three sisters, brother, and I escaped with thousands of other Vietnamese and Chinese refugees in search of safety and freedom. For six long months, my family and I survived the most horrific boat ride to the United States. Hundreds

• The speaker captures the audience's attention with a short but dramatically phrased introductory statement.

of people died due to the grotesque conditions and diseases prevalent on the boat. Nevertheless, we landed on the coast of California only to find harsh media attention focused on us upon our arrival. A program was implemented by placing each refugee family with an American caretaker. • For three years, my family and I resided in Caney, Kansas, with Father Mike. In 1981, my family and I were finally reunited with my father, who was released by the strict communist government. Due to the untimely death of Father Mike, we moved south to Tulsa, Oklahoma, where my family and I have lived for almost twenty years. • Although my journey seemed to begin in Vietnam, it has only just begun.

Body

Through the trials and tribulations my family and I have undergone, we are lucky and fortunate to have become American citizens. • I never dreamed that I would be the first Asian pom captain at the University of Oklahoma, a member of Kappa Kappa Gamma, and the 1999 Miss Greek OU. I could not have accomplished these honors without knowing the difficulties and hardships of life. • As a young child, I would mimic the choreography performed by the dancers on the television show *Star Search*. However, because we were poor, I could not afford dance lessons each week. Through hard work and perseverance, I trained myself to dance. Nine years later, I have earned individual honors as a dancer and have been teaching dance for a national company. Because of my ability to dance, my sorority encouraged me to enter a pageant. I had never been in a pageant before, and was apprehensive from the moment my sorority voted me in. The house was confident in me, though, and offered support throughout the weeks I was training. On April 23, 1999, I was crowned Miss Greek OU. This title has allowed me to be a role model for young women in my community. • Most important, I have also been given the opportunity to represent my culture as one of the first Asian women to be voted Miss Greek OU. I could not have achieved this honor without the love and support of my sorority, my

• Even in a short speech like this, the speaker probably should offer a little information about Father Mike.

• This preview—that the speaker's journey "has only just begun"—also acts as a transition statement.

• In just one sentence the speaker sets up three main, coordinate points—becoming pom captain, a sorority member, and a pageant winner.

• A series of subordinate points shows how the speaker overcame several personal trials and attained several noteworthy accomplishments.

• Rather than merely reciting a list of her accomplishments, the speaker frames them within the larger context of support from family, friends, and community.

friends, and my family. These three accomplishments have shown me how far my life has come. My story does not end here, because the journey is not over.

Conclusion

• "Dream what you want to dream, go where you want to go, be what you want to be, because you have only one life and one chance to do all the things you want to do." I do not let the achievements that I have accomplished prove my self-worth. They merely symbolize the true passion and drive we have for living and succeeding. • We are what we learn and take with us during this journey we call life. I am the past because I have appreciation; I am the present because I have learned humbleness; I am the future because I have so much more to learn.

• This quotation reinforces the inspirational nature of the speech. Using her own life as an example, the speaker exhorts others to use their time wisely.

• The speaker's strong conclusion leaves the audience with something to think about as we ponder the precise meaning of her near-poetic statement, "I am the past because. . . ."

Public
Speaking
Basics

IN GOD WE TRUST

Public Speaking Basics

Speaker's Reference
Public Speaking Basics

3. Managing Speech Anxiety

Recognize What Underlies the Fear of Public Speaking

- A lack of public speaking experience: It can be difficult to put the anxiety that often precedes new experiences into perspective. (p. 42)
- Feeling different: Everyone is different from everyone else and even seasoned speakers experience anxiety. (p. 42)
- Being the center of attention: The audience won't notice things about you that you don't want to reveal. (p. 42)

Pinpoint the Onset of Your Anxiety and Plan to Overcome It

- Some people become anxious upon hearing that they must give a speech (pre-preparation anxiety). (p. 44)
  Don't allow your anxiety to deter you from planning your speech.
- For some, the onset of anxiety occurs as they begin to prepare the speech (preparation anxiety). (p. 44)
  Beware of avoidance and procrastination.
- Some people don't feel anxious until it's time to rehearse the speech (pre-performance anxiety). (p. 44)
  Practice your speech to build confidence.
- Many people don't experience public speaking anxiety until they actually begin to deliver the speech (performance anxiety). (p. 45)
  Practice stress-control breathing and other relaxation techniques.

To Build Confidence, Prepare and Practice

- Manage your time wisely during the preparation phase. (p. 44)
- Rehearse until you know how you want to express yourself. (p. 45)

Try to View Giving a Speech as a Positive Opportunity

- Lessen anxiety by using positive thoughts prior to delivery. (p. 47)
- Picture the speech as an extension of an ordinary conversation. (p. 47)

Use Visualization and Relaxation Techniques to Gain a Sense of Control

- Learn about visualization. (p. 47)
- Learn how to use stress-control breathing, natural gestures, and movement as you speak. (p. 50)

Remember: Audience Members Are Evaluating Your Message, Not You

- Try to lessen your fear of being judged: Listeners tend to evaluate the content of a message rather than who the speaker is as a person. (p. 51)

Focus on the Enjoyable and Empowering Aspects of Speaking

- You have the chance to influence others. (p. 52)
- You can express your own views. (p. 52)
- You can inform, persuade, entertain, or even console others. (p. 52)

4. Listeners and Speakers

As You Prepare, Consider Factors That Influence Listening

- People pay attention to what they hold to be important. (p. 54)
- People pay attention to information that touches their experiences and backgrounds. (p. 54)
- People filter new information based on what they already know. (p. 54)

Incorporate the Factors That Influence Listening into Your Speech

- Try to uncover what is important to your listeners. (p. 54)
- When explaining unfamiliar concepts, consider using analogies, metaphors, and other figures of speech. (p. 54)
- When introducing new information, associate it with something with which your listeners are already familiar. (p. 54)
- Appeal to your listeners' experiences and backgrounds. (p. 54)
- Use dialogic communication to balance speaking and listening. (p. 55)

Anticipate and Cope with Common Obstacles to Listening

- Plan ahead in order to minimize the impact of external distractions such as noise, movement, light, darkness, heat or cold, and so forth. (p. 55)

- Channel your energy into truly listening. (p. 55)
- As a speaker be sensitive to any distractions your audience may face. (p. 55)
- Internal distractions such as daydreaming, time pressures, emotional turmoil, or fatigue due to illness or lack of sleep can disrupt concentration. (p. 56)
- Beware of listening defensively: Wait for the speaker to finish before devising your own mental arguments. (p. 56)
- Don't assume that you already know what the speaker will say. (p. 57)
- Don't judge the speaker on the basis of his or her accent, appearance, or demeanor. Focus instead on what is actually being said. (p. 58)
- Reveal your needs to the speaker, try to gain clarification, and ask questions. (p. 58)

Use Strategies to Become a More Active Listener

- Set listening goals that encourage action. (p. 59)
- Listen for main ideas, take notes, and focus on the organizational pattern. (p. 59)
- Watch for nonverbal cues: eye contact, body language, facial expressions, and gestures. (p. 59)

Listen Critically to the Speaker's Evidence and Arguments

- Evaluate the speaker's evidence for accuracy and credibility. (p. 61)
- Analyze the speaker's assumptions and biases. (p. 61)
- Assess the speaker's reasoning: Look for faulty logic or inappropriate causal relationships. (p. 61)
- Resist false assumptions, overgeneralizations, and either-or thinking. (p. 61)
- Consider multiple perspectives. (p. 61)
- Summarize and assess the relevant facts and evidence before deciding how you will act on the speaker's information or argument. (p. 62)

Offer Constructive Feedback When Evaluating Speeches and Presentations

- Be honest and fair in your evaluation. (p. 62)
- Do not judge the message's content on the basis of the speaker's communication style. (p. 63)
- Be compassionate in your criticism: Start with something positive; focus on the speech, not on the speaker; and be selective in your criticism. (p. 63)

Speaker's Reference

5. Ethical Public Speaking

Take Responsibility for Your Power to Influence Others

* Be morally accountable for your message. (p. 65)
* Accept responsibility for the stands you take. (p.65)

Earn the Audience's Trust

* Display good character (ethos). (p. 65)
* Develop a solid grasp of your subject (competence). (p. 66)
* Display sound reasoning skills. (p. 66)
* Present information honestly and without manipulation. (p. 66)
* Be genuinely interested in the welfare of your listeners. (p. 66)

Recognize and Respect Audience Values

* Consider what your audience's core values might be, and address them with sensitivity. (p. 66)
* When your topic is controversial, consider both sides of an issue and look for common ground. (p. 66)
* To get a better sense of your own and others' values, analyze them using the instruments in the text. (p. 67)

Recognize That Legal Speech Is Not Always Ethical Speech

* The First Amendment provides protection both to truthful speakers and to speakers whose words are inflammatory and offensive. (p. 67)
* Codes of ethical speech are built on moral rather than legal principles: Though often legally protected, racist, sexist, homophobic, and pornographic speech are clearly unethical. (p. 69)

Be Aware That Certain Types of Speech Are Illegal

* Speech that provokes people to violence ("fighting words") (p. 69)
* Speech that can be proved to harm an individual's reputation (slander or defamatory statements) (p. 69)
* Words spoken with a reckless disregard for the truth (p. 69)

Contribute to Positive Public Discourse

* Advance constructive goals. (p. 70)
* Avoid introducing conversation stoppers into public discourse. (p. 70)
* Follow the rules of engagement for civil public discourse. (p. 70)

Exhibit Trustworthiness, Respect, Responsibility, and Fairness

- Tell the truth, don't distort information, and acknowledge sources. (p. 71)
- Avoid ethnocentrism, stereotyping, and any hint of hate speech. (p. 72)
- Focus on issues, not on personalities. (p. 72)
- Make sure that your topic is socially constructive. (p. 72)
- Strive hard for accuracy. (p. 74)
- Acknowledge alternative and opposing views so that the audience can make informed decisions. (p. 74)

Avoid Plagiarism

- Orally acknowledge any source that requires credit in written form: other people's ideas, opinions, theories, evidence, and research; direct quotations; paraphrased information; facts and statistics. (p. 75)

Know the Copyright Law

- Copyright law protects *intellectual property* (original authorship or expression). (p. 75)
- Facts and statistics that are common knowledge cannot be copyrighted but must be orally credited in your speech. (p. 76)
- The fair use doctrine permits limited use of copyrighted materials without permission; such material must be orally credited in your speech. (p. 78)

KEY TERMS

Chapter 3

public speaking anxiety (PSA)	preparation anxiety	visualization
pre-preparation anxiety	pre-performance anxiety	
	performance anxiety	

Chapter 4

feedback loop	active listening	defensive listening
listening	listening distraction	critical thinking
selective perception	external listening distraction	valid generalization
dialogue	internal listening distraction	overgeneralization
dialogic communication		

Speaker's Reference

Chapter 5

responsibility
ethics
ethos
speaker credibility
values
First Amendment
free speech
fighting words
slander
reckless disregard
for the truth

invective
conversation stopper
rules of engagement
dignity
integrity
trustworthiness
respect
heckler's veto
ethnocentrism
stereotype
hate speech

fairness
plagiarism
wholesale plagiarism
patchwrite plagiarism
direct quotation
paraphrase
common knowledge
copyright
public domain
intellectual property
fair use

Managing Speech Anxiety

Nothing in life is to be feared. It is only to be understood.
                                                    -Marie Curie

Everyone, even accomplished speakers, can feel jittery before they give a speech. According to one study, at least 75 percent of students in public speaking courses approach the course with anxiety.[1] It turns out that feeling nervous is not only normal but desirable. Channeled properly, nervousness can boost performance.

> I am really susceptible to severe nervousness. . . . I usually take deep breaths and remember that everyone is going through the same thing. I also find that just going first helps to boost my confidence.   — *Shaye Weaver, student*

The difference between seasoned public speakers and the rest of us is not that the seasoned speakers don't feel nervous or anxious. It's just that they're more practiced at making it work *for* rather than *against* them. They've also mastered specific techniques that help them cope with and minimize their tension. You, too, can develop your own techniques for dealing with speech anxiety:

> I focus on the information. I try not to think about being graded. I also practice my speech a ton to really make sure I do not speak too quickly. I time myself so that I can develop an average time. This makes me more confident [in dealing] with time requirements. And, because I know that I am well prepared, I really try to just relax.   — *Kristen Obracay, student*

What Makes Speakers Anxious?

Researchers have identified several factors that underlie the fear of addressing an audience.[2] These include lack of public speaking experience (or having had a negative experience), feeling different from members of the audience, and uneasiness about being the center of attention. Each factor can lead to the onset of **public speaking anxiety (PSA)** — that is, fear or anxiety associated with either actual or anticipated communication to an audience as a speaker.[3]

LACK OF POSITIVE EXPERIENCE

Anxious anticipation is a natural reaction to new experiences. For those who have had no public speaking experience, anxiety about what to expect is only natural, but it's hard to put into perspective. It's a bit of a vicious circle. Some people react by deciding to avoid making speeches altogether. Unfortunately, they also lose out on the considerable rewards speechmaking brings. Lack of experience may be particularly hard on women. One study found that female executives experience markedly higher levels of speech anxiety (42 percent) than their male counterparts (15 percent) when they make only occasional speeches.[4]

Anxious anticipation also results from previous negative experiences with public speaking. For example, some speakers lose track of their thoughts or misjudge audience expectations. Gaining more speaking experience affords opportunities to adapt to different kinds of audiences and unexpected occurrences. Furthermore, it only increases the likelihood of more successful speech experiences and helps build confidence.

FEELING DIFFERENT

Novice speakers often feel alone — as if they were the only person ever to experience the dread of public speaking. Moreover, the prospect of getting up in front of an audience makes them extra-sensitive to their personal idiosyncrasies, such as a less-than-perfect haircut, a slight lisp, or the belief that no one could possibly be interested in anything they have to say.

As novice speakers, we become anxious because we assume that being different somehow means being inferior. Actually, everyone is different from everyone else in many ways. Just as true, nearly everyone experiences nervousness about giving a speech. The following students would agree:

> The way I deal with the stress of public speaking is being well-prepared, staying focused, and understanding that just about everyone gets nervous giving a speech. — *Brian Wardach, student*

> I control my anxiety by mentally viewing myself as being 100 percent equal to my classmates. — *Lee Morris, student*

> It's always scary to speak in front of others, but you just have to remember that everyone is human. They are just as scared as you are when they deliver *their* speeches. Nobody wants you to fail; they're not waiting on you to mess up. If I keep that in mind, I can survive giving a speech. — *Mary Parrish, student*

BEING THE CENTER OF ATTENTION

Certain audience behaviors — such as lack of eye contact with the speaker, pointing, conversing with a neighbor — can be disconcerting. When these behaviors occur, our tendency is to think that we must be doing something inappropriate;

we then wonder whether the entire audience has noticed a flaw in the presentation. Left unchecked, this thinking diverts our attention away from the speech and focuses it on "me." As a result, we develop an oversensitivity to things we think we might be doing wrong. This concern only makes us feel more conspicuous and anxious, when actually (and ironically), an audience notices very little wrong about us that we don't want to reveal. Keeping this in mind should help reduce your anxiety about being the center of attention, especially if the speech is well developed and effectively delivered. Remind yourself that you see yourself more critically than the audience does, so relax and focus on delivering your message.

✓ **CHECKLIST**

Recognizing and Overcoming Your Underlying Fears about Public Speaking

Problem	Solution
✓ Are you intimidated by a lack of experience?	Prepare and practice rehearsing your speech at least several times. Do it in front of at least one other person. This way, you'll feel more confident that you have experience with your present speech.
✓ Are you worried about appearing different from others?	Remember that everyone is different from everyone else in many ways. Dress well, be well groomed, and trust that you will make a good impression.
✓ Are you uncomfortable about being the center of attention?	Remind yourself that the audience won't notice anything about you that you don't want to reveal, especially if your speech is well planned and rehearsed. Put the focus on the speech instead of on yourself.

Pinpointing the Onset of Public Speaking Anxiety

Different people become anxious at different times during the speechmaking process. For some people PSA arises as soon as they learn that they will have to give a speech at some point in the future. For others it arises as they approach the podium. Research suggests that females may experience higher anxiety than males at all stages of the speechmaking process.[5] Thus, it is particularly important that females experiment with the anxiety-reducing techniques described in this section. Figure 3.1 illustrates the different points during the speechmaking process at which PSA can occur.[6]

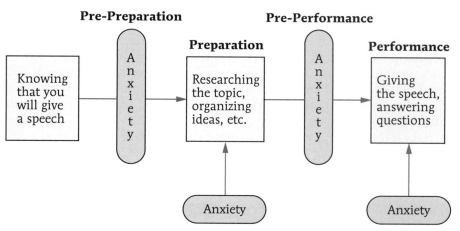

Figure 3.1 Where Anxiety Can Occur in the Speechmaking Process

PRE-PREPARATION ANXIETY

Some people feel anxious the minute they know they will be giving a speech. **Pre-preparation anxiety** can be a problem for two reasons. First, a highly anxious person may be reluctant to begin planning for the speech. Second, anxiety can preoccupy the person to such an extent that he or she misses vital information that is required to fulfill the speech assignment.

PREPARATION ANXIETY

For a few people, anxiety arises only when they actually begin to prepare for the speech. They might feel overwhelmed at the amount of times and planning required, or hit a roadblock that puts them behind schedule, or they might be unable to locate adequate support for a critical point. These kinds of pressures produce more stress, avoidance of the process, and procrastination — all of which contribute to **preparation anxiety**. Research has shown, however, that for the great majority of people, anxiety is lowest during the preparation phase.[7] If you do find yourself feeling anxious during this stage of the speechmaking process, consider doing what student Katelyn Brock does:

> When I start to get really frustrated, I take short breaks. . . . My breaks are usually between 15 and 30 minutes long, and I do something relaxing, like watch television. I just know I have to do something to get my mind off the speech topic. The short breaks help more than anything else.   — *Katelyn Brock, student*

PRE-PERFORMANCE ANXIETY

Some people experience anxiety as they rehearse their speech, when the reality of the situation sets in: Soon they will face an audience that will be watching and listening only to them. Or they may feel that their ideas don't sound as focused or as interesting as they should. Or they sense that time is short. If this **pre-performance anxiety** is strong enough, and is interpreted negatively, they may even decide to stop rehearsing.

> I experience anxiety before, during, and after the speech. My "before speech" anxiety begins the night before my speech, but then I begin to look over my notecards, and I start to realize that I am ready for this speech. I practice one more time and I tell myself I am going to be fine. — *Paige Mease, student*

PERFORMANCE ANXIETY

 WEB Relaxation audio

For most people, anxiety tends to be highest just before speaking begins.[8] **Performance anxiety** is probably most pronounced during the introduction of the speech, when the speaker utters the first words of the speech and is most aware of the audience's attention. In fact, the speaker's perceptions of the audience are important here — an audience perceived to be hostile or negative usually elicits higher anxiety in the speaker than either positive or neutral audiences.[9] However, experienced speakers agree that if they control their nervousness during the introduction, the rest of the speech comes relatively easily.

> Before my speech, I just make sure to focus on getting my work done. I sit down and do the research; I get the information I need and I transfer it to my speech. Before my speech, to calm myself down, I just remind myself that everyone is doing a speech. This isn't something unexpected and I am prepared for it. During the speech, when I struggle more than I normally do with anxiety, I focus on getting through the facts and information I had researched.
> — *Mark Burkhead, student*

Strategies for Getting Started with Confidence

Depending on when it strikes, the consequences of public speaking anxiety can include everything from procrastination to poor speech performance. The important thing to remember is to manage your anxiety and not let it manage you. The first step in effective management of speech anxiety involves planning and practicing your speech. Professional speaker Lenny Laskowski sums it up pithily in the 9Ps: "Prior Proper Preparation Prevents Poor Performance of the Person Putting on the Presentation."[10]

PREPARE AND PRACTICE

There's nothing magical about gaining confidence in public speaking — except, of course, the glow of accomplishment that sets in after the hard work is done and the speech is over. The surest route to confidence is through preparation and practice. Canadian speech coach John Robert Colombo asserts that the best way to work out your fear of speaking is to *overwork* it.[11] That is, take every opportunity you can to confront what scares you — practice as often as you can,

ESL Speaker's Notes
Confidence and Culture: When English Isn't Your First Language

For native English speakers, the fear of being at center stage is normal. If you are a non-native speaker, anxiety about delivering a speech in a non-native language is equally normal. It is important to know that you are not alone.

Try to think about public speaking as an opportunity to learn more about the English language and how to use it. As you listen to your classmates' speeches, for example, you will gain exposure to spoken English. Exercises throughout this text will help you outline, write, and rehearse your speeches, as well as help you gain confidence in your written and spoken language skills. Following are some tips that all novice speakers, regardless of whether English is your first language, will find helpful:

1. Take your time and speak slowly as you introduce the purpose and the main points of your speech. This will give your listeners time to get used to your voice and to focus on your message.
2. Practice saying any English words that may be troublesome for you five times. Then say the words again, five times. Progress slowly until the word becomes clearer and easier to pronounce. This type of practice will give you time to work on any accent features you might want to improve.[1]
3. Avoid using jargon (see Chapter 16 and the Glossary). Learn to use a thesaurus to find *synonyms,* or words that mean the same thing, that are simpler and easier to pronounce.
4. Offer words from your native language as a way of drawing attention to a point you're making. This helps the audience appreciate your native language and your accent. For example, the Spanish word *corazón* has a more lyrical quality than its English counterpart *heart.* Capitalize on the beauty of your native tongue.

Remember, practicing oral English is the surest way to master it.

1. J. E. Flege, J. M. Munro, and I. R. A. MacKay, "Factors Affecting Strength of Perceived Foreign Accent in a Second Language," *Journal of the Acoustical Society of America* 97 (1995): 3125ff.

and, in the future, accept as many speaking engagements as appropriate. If you are confident that you know your material and have adequately rehearsed your delivery, you're far more likely to feel confident at the podium than otherwise. Thus preparation should begin as soon as possible after a speech is assigned. Once you have prepared the speech, you should rehearse it several times. Recent research points to the advantages of practicing your speech in front of a small audience of, say, seven or eight people.[12] Students who practiced this way received significantly higher evaluations of their classroom speeches than students who didn't practice or practiced in different ways. And whereas practicing didn't correlate directly with reduced speech anxiety, the overall greater performance outcomes for those who did practice suggests that even the students who were more anxious were better able to control their anxiety.

Note the following student testimonials about practice:

> Knowing your material is crucial! The worst anxiety comes when you feel un-
> prepared. You just can't help but be nervous, at least a little. If you are confi-
> dent about what you're speaking the anxiety fades and you'll feel more
> comfortable.   — *Shea Michelle Allen, student*

> In order to calm myself, I just try to make sure I know everything I am going to talk
> about pretty well. I also practice my speech a few times in front of my roommates.
>   — *Josh Beck, student*

> For one speech, I only practiced one time before I presented it to the class.
> This made me very nervous because I am the type of person who has to prac-
> tice everything several times before I feel comfortable doing it in front of other
> people. I did have a chance to calm myself before the speech though. I had to
> reassure myself that nothing horrible was going to happen, and that I was
> going to do fine.   — *Lauren Ditthart, student*

MODIFY THOUGHTS AND ATTITUDES

Negative thoughts increase speech anxiety.[13] Maintaining a positive attitude,
however, results in lowered heart rate and reduced anxiety during delivery of
the speech.[14] Thus, from start to finish, it's important to regard your speech as
a valuable, worthwhile, and challenging activity. Remind yourself of all the reasons that public speaking is helpful personally, socially, and professionally. Tell
yourself that it is an opportunity, not a threat. One communication researcher
has shown that altering one's thinking about public speaking from a "performance orientation" to a "communication orientation" can significantly increase
confidence.[15] Rather than thinking of your speech as a formal performance
where you will be judged and critiqued, try thinking of it as a kind of ordinary
conversation. By doing so, you will feel less threatened and more relaxed about
the process. And with each successive speech experience, your attitude about
public speaking will grow more positive. Here's what one student had to say:

> Just before a speech those feelings of anxiety undoubtedly try to sneak in. The
> way I keep them from taking over is to not let my mind become negative!
> As long as I keep positive thoughts of confidence in my head, anxiety doesn't
> stand a chance!   — *Morgan Verdery, student*

VISUALIZE SUCCESS

Visualization — also called guided imagery or mental rehearsal[16] — is a highly
successful way to reduce nervousness and help you prepare effectively for your
speech.[17] The technique is popular among athletes, who use it to "see" the
outcome of their performance in a game or an event. By concentrating on the

---

✓ SELF-ASSESSMENT CHECKLIST

Preparation and Practice Check

Note the date each item is started and completed. Place a check mark in the space at the front of each item to indicate its completion. Start by asking yourself when did I receive the assignment? When will I complete it?

Activity	Date Activity Started	Date Completed
• In advance of preparing my speech, have I planned what I need to do and where I need to get it done?	____	____
• Have I selected an appropriate speech topic and purpose?	____	____
• When will I need to spend time in the library?	____	____
• When will I need to work on a computer?	____	____
• Have I tried to discover as much information as possible about the audience and the speaking environment? (See Chapter 6.)	____	____
• Have I allowed enough time to thoroughly research the material required to support my key points? (See Chapters 8–10.)	____	____
• Have I organized and outlined main and supporting points? (See Chapters 11–13.)	____	____
• Have I rehearsed delivering my speech, beginning two or three days prior to the speech date? (See Chapters 17–19.)	____	____
• Have I planned and constructed any necessary presentation aids? (See Chapters 20–22.)	____	____
• Am I confident that I know how I want to express myself?	____	____
• Have I checked out the site where I will be speaking?	____	____
• Have I made sure that any audiovisual equipment I plan to use is in good working order?	____	____

---

vision of a successful outcome, an athlete is able to summon feelings and actions consistent with effective performance.[18] Speech communication professors at Washington State University have been working for several years to develop visualization techniques for increasing positive expectations associated with speechmaking.[19] Next is their script for visualizing success on a public speaking occasion. The exercise requires you, the speaker, to close your eyes and visualize a series of positive feelings and actions that will occur on the day of your speech.

> Close your eyes and allow your body to get comfortable in the chair in which you are sitting. Move around until you feel that you are in a position that will continue to be relaxing for you for the next ten to fifteen minutes. Take a deep, comfortable breath and hold it . . . now slowly release it through your nose. Now take another deep breath and make certain that you are breathing from the diaphragm . . . hold it . . . now slowly release it and note how you feel while doing this. Now one more deep breath . . . hold it . . . and release it slowly . . . and begin your normal breathing pattern. Shift around if you need to get comfortable again.
>
> Now begin to visualize the beginning of a day in which you are going to give an informative speech. See yourself getting up in the morning, full of energy, full of confidence, looking forward to the day's challenges. You are putting on just the right clothes for the task at hand that day. Dressing well makes you look and feel good about yourself, so you have on just what you want to wear, which clearly expresses your sense of inner well-being. As you are driving, riding, or walking to the speech setting, note how clear and confident you feel, and how others around you, as you arrive, comment positively regarding your fine appearance and general demeanor. You feel thoroughly prepared for the target issue you will be presenting today.
>
> Now you see yourself standing or sitting in the room where you will present your speech, talking very comfortably and confidently with others in the room. The people to whom you will be presenting your speech appear to be quite friendly and are very cordial in their greetings and conversations prior to the presentation. You feel absolutely sure of your material and of your ability to present the information in a forceful, convincing, positive manner.
>
> Now you see yourself approaching the area from which you will present. You are feeling very good about this presentation and see yourself move eagerly forward. All of your audiovisual materials are well organized, well planned, and clearly aid your presentation.[20]

Practicing the mental exercise of seeing yourself give a successful speech will help you prepare with confidence and strengthen your positive attitudes and expectations for speechmaking.

USE RELAXATION TECHNIQUES

Just as you would warm up before taking a lengthy jog, you should practice *relaxation techniques* before — and even during — your speech. The goal is to feel a sense of control over the heightened physiological reactions you're experiencing, keeping in mind that physiological changes are normal when you are under the stress of a speech situation. According to public speaking experts Laurie Schloff and Marcia Yudkin,[21] the following techniques will lessen anxiety before and during a speech.

✓ CHECKLIST

Acquiring and Maintaining Confidence

Upon each successful completion of a speech assignment, your confidence will grow, but you need to work conscientiously at building confidence. As you prepare for each speech assignment, follow these general steps as outlined in more detail in this chapter.

1. *Prepare and practice.* As soon as you have been given an assignment to speak, start planning not only your topic but also when and where you will practice your speech. Also plan to mentally practice your speech as you work on different parts of it and when you bring the parts together.

2. *Modify thoughts and attitudes.* Think of each speech assignment as an opportunity to have an extended conversation with a large group of people about a topic that really interests you and that you believe will interest and have some relevance to your audience. Keep your thoughts positive, concentrating on what works and makes good sense as you develop your topic, and on the positive outcomes that will result from your speech.

3. *Visualize success.* On the day of your speech, and even when rehearsing it the day before, use the visualization exercise to practice seeing yourself in an optimistic frame of mind with well-developed speech points that you deliver enthusiastically and effectively. Envision yourself having confidence and great success.

4. *Utilize relaxation techniques.* Whenever you feel ill-at-ease during preparation and rehearsal of your speech, and particularly as the moment for giving your speech approaches, use the techniques of stress-control breathing, natural gesturing, and general movement while speaking to help yourself relax.

5. *Learn from the task and enjoy it.* Think of your speech assignment as a learning opportunity rather than just another hurdle to jump for your degree. Enjoy the opportunity to share what you learn about your topic with others.

Stress-Control Breathing

When you feel stressed, the center of your breathing tends to move from the abdomen to the upper chest, leaving you with a reduced supply of air. The chest and shoulders rise, and you feel out of breath. With *stress-control breathing*, you will feel more movement in the stomach than in the chest. Try stress-control breathing in two stages.

Stage One. Inhale air and let your abdomen go out. Exhale air and let your abdomen go in. Do this for a while until you get into the rhythm of it.

Stage Two. As you inhale, use a soothing word such as *calm* or *relax,* or a personal mantra, as follows: "Inhale *calm,* abdomen out, exhale *calm,* abdomen in."

Go slowly. Each inhalation and exhalation of stress-control breathing takes about three to five seconds.

Begin practicing stress-control breathing several days before you're scheduled to speak. Then, once the speaking event arrives, begin stress-control breathing while awaiting your turn at the podium. (You can even place your hand on your abdomen unobtrusively to check how you're doing.) After you've been called to the podium, you can focus on breathing once more while you're arranging your notes and getting ready to begin.

> I get very anxious before I'm about to speak, so I have two ways to cope with my nervousness. I take a couple deep breaths through my stomach; I breathe in through my nose and out of my mouth. This allows more oxygen to the brain so you can think clearly. I also calm myself down by saying, "Everything will be okay, and the world is not going to crumble before me if I mess up."
> — *Jenna Sanford, student*

Or, try combining stress-control breathing with calming thoughts:

> I take a deep breath in and out to calm myself when I feel nervous. I also picture myself in a calm environment like the beach . . . this helps to calm my nerves.
> — *Stephanie Meagher, student*

Natural Gestures

Practice some controlled, natural gestures that might be useful in enhancing your speech, such as holding up your index finger when stating your first main point. Think about what you want to say as you do this, instead of thinking about how you look or feel. (See Chapters 2 and 19 for tips on practicing natural gestures.)

Move as You Speak

You don't have to stand perfectly still behind the podium when you deliver a speech. Walk around as you make some of your points. Movement relieves tension and helps hold the audience's attention.

According to experts at the Mayo Clinic, practicing relaxation techniques can improve how you respond to stress by slowing your heart rate, lowering your blood pressure, slowing your breathing rate, increasing blood flow to major muscles, and reducing muscle tension, all of which help you feel better in the stressful situation.[22] Such techniques result in better concentration and sharper performance as a speaker.

LEARN FROM THE SPEECH EVALUATION

Speech evaluations help to identify ways to improve what you do. Evaluation allows you to compare what you were assigned to do and what you planned to do with what you actually do, and thus reveals what works and what doesn't, what can be added and what can be avoided for a more effective speech. You can learn a lot by evaluating your own behavior, but objective evaluations of others often are more helpful because self-evaluations tend to be distorted.[23] Although no one likes to feel evaluated, it is a necessary part of a speech class; inevitably, your speech assignments will be evaluated by your instructors and probably by your classmates as well. Whether the evaluation is formal (i.e., written and graded) or informal, it's easy but not necessary to take it personally.

First, your instructor and your classmates don't know everything about you; they know only how you've presented a speech. Second, if that speech is planned and delivered well, your listeners will be most aware of your message, not of you personally. Audience members will be deciding whether the information is relevant and accurate and interesting. Your concern as a speaker should be with the audience's evaluation of your message, not of you as a person. Your classmates and instructor will provide practical feedback to help you do better in your next speech. Using their evaluations is part of learning to be an effective speaker.

ENJOY THE OCCASION

 WEB Chapter quizzes

Tara's course schedule for the new semester included a speech course. She says that she dreaded it all summer long. On her way to class on the first day she seriously considered bypassing it and going straight to her adviser's office to drop it. But she went to class anyway, perhaps realizing that she would have to take the course or one very much like it before she can graduate. "I was surprised after the first day of class to feel optimistic about it," she says. "The instructor was friendly and seemed to understand the students with concerns like mine." Hearing some of her classmates comment about how they looked forward to the challenge of giving speeches gave Tara a sense that the course could be worthwhile. But the clincher came after the instructor had each student stand and say a few words about themselves and their ambitions. "It was obvious that some of my classmates were nervous about this activity, but it was also easy to see that, really, all of them enjoyed talking to the class." It made her feel that she had something meaningful in common with them. She left the class feeling much better than when she walked in; not fully confident yet, but at least wanting to see what she can do.

Most people ultimately find that giving speeches can indeed be fun. It's satisfying and empowering to influence people, and a good speech is a sure way to accomplish that goal. Preparing and practicing, maintaining a positive attitude, managing the inevitable stress of public speaking by making it work for you, and visualizing success — all of this makes public speaking both challenging and exciting. Think of it in these terms, and chances are it will come out that way.

Listeners and Speakers 4

As a student of public speaking, you wear two hats — those of speaker and listener. Listeners and speakers are interdependent: Listeners need someone to whom they will listen, and speakers need someone to whom they will address their remarks. Thus it is listener and speaker together who truly make a speech a speech — who "co-create" its meaning. Successful speakers adjust their message based on their listeners' reactions, and vice versa. Communication scholars call this continual flow, or *circular response* between speaker and listener, the **feedback loop**.

Listening is a communication activity that you do more than any other. Studies show that you listen 40 percent of the time, but speak only 35 percent. Executives listen even more, spending upwards of 50 percent of their day listening to others.[1] Because listening research reveals that most people retain only half of what they hear immediately and only 35 percent of what they heard after twenty-four hours, it is essential to hone your listening skills.[2] This course is the perfect place to do so.

The more skilled you are at listening to speeches, the more you will learn about what will and won't work for your speech. Focusing on the art of listening will also serve you well in many arenas other than public speaking. Numerous studies show that competent listeners tend to be efficient and successful in both their personal and professional lives and tend to be better problem solvers and more engaged citizens.

The Selective Nature of Listening WEB Chapter quizzes

Most of us understand that giving a speech involves preparation and practice, but fewer recognize the hard work that listening requires. Rather than being a passive activity that simply "happens" to us, listening is a complex behavior. In contrast to hearing, which is the physiological process of perceiving sound, **listening** is the conscious act of recognizing, understanding, and accurately interpreting the messages communicated by others. While *hearing* is largely reflexive or automatic in nature, listening is a proactive and discriminating process.

Can you recall sharing reactions with a friend about a lecture, movie, or other event and noticing that even though you both attended the same affair, you formed quite different impressions? In any given situation, no two listeners will process information in exactly the same way. The reason lies in **selective**

perception — people pay attention selectively to certain messages while ignoring others. Several factors influence what we listen to and what we ignore:

1. *We pay attention to what we hold to be important.* We are most motivated to listen to others if we think that what is being said will be of consequence to us. This is why audience analysis is so crucial to speechmaking (see Chapter 6). People look for information that reflects their interests, needs, values, attitudes, and beliefs.

2. *We pay attention to information that touches our experiences and backgrounds.* If we listen to something that is foreign to us, chances are we'll just zone out. To catch and sustain listeners' attention, a speaker must in some way touch upon audience members' experiences and backgrounds.

3. *We sort and filter new information on the basis of what we already know.* According to learning theory, all new concepts are understood as analogies to previous concepts.[3] As listeners, this means that we try to understand new information by comparing it with what we already know.

As a speaker, in line with these principles, try to uncover what is important to your audience. To capture listeners' attention, appeal to their experiences and backgrounds. When introducing new information, make it relevant by associating it with something with which your listeners are already familiar. Consider clarifying your meaning through analogies, similes, metaphors, and other figures of speech, and help listeners visualize your ideas with presentation aids (see Chapters 16 and 20–22).

ESL Speaker's Notes
Learning by Listening

As every student of a foreign language knows, listening is the key to learning a language. Using textbooks to study usage and grammar is important, but it is through the spoken language — hearing it and speaking it — that we gain fluency.

Listening to the speeches of colleagues or classmates, as well as those broadcast by television channels such as C-Span, can help you hone the skills you need to become a better speaker. Nearly all college libraries own many DVDs, videocassettes, and other recorded materials made specifically for ESL speakers such as yourself, and the reference librarian will be happy to locate them for you. The Internet also offers many helpful listening resources. Among the many sites you will find is the *Merriam-Webster Online Dictionary* (**www.webster.com**), which includes an audio feature that allows you to hear the correct pronunciation of words. You can also download and listen to speeches directly on the Internet.

As you listen to these resources, you can:

- Build your vocabulary.
- Improve pronunciation through guided repetition.
- Learn new idioms, or informal expressions, used by native speakers of English.
- Observe body posture, gestures, intonation, and other nonverbal aspects of delivery.

Listening and Speaking as Dialogic Communication

Dialogue, from the Greek, means "through words" (*dia,* "through" and *logos,* "word").[4] **Dialogic communication** is the sharing of ideas and open discussion through words. In contrast to *monologue,* in which we try merely to impose what we think on another person, true dialogue encourages both speaker and listener to reach conclusions together. For listeners, this means suspending certainty and practicing empathy. For the speaker it means approaching a speech not as an argument that must be "won," but as an opportunity to achieve understanding with audience members. As communication scholar Ronald D. Gordon notes, in dialogue both speaker and listener let one another know that:

> We can relate to and understand what they are saying, that we can suspend our own point of view and put ourselves in their positions and imagine how things might seem and feel from their point of view.[5]

In the public sphere, where so many people of diverse backgrounds and opinions converge in the attempt to solve problems, dialogic communication is especially important. In this spirit, we stand a better chance of avoiding conflict and discord and achieving workable compromises.[6]

Barriers to Active Listening

Active listening is focused, purposeful listening. It is a multistep process of gathering and evaluating information. Before reviewing these steps, however, consider the following stumbling blocks to active listening. The poor listening habits that tend to plague college students include inattentiveness and being prone to distraction, scriptwriting and defensive listening, and laziness and overconfidence.[7] Active listening isn't possible unless we recognize and overcome these habits.

LISTENING DISTRACTIONS

A **listening distraction** is anything that competes for attention that you are trying to give to something else. You may have every intention of listening to someone's presentation but instead find yourself thinking about an upcoming exam. Or perhaps you're hungry, tired, or angry about a recent incident. Distractions can originate outside of us, in the environment (external distractions), or within us, in our thoughts and feelings (internal distractions).

External Distractions

Virtually anything in the environment—noise, movement, light, darkness, heat, or cold —can be considered an **external listening distraction**. The din of jackhammers or competing conversations may make it impossible to listen well.

> ✓ **CHECKLIST**
>
> **Minimizing Distractions**
>
> ✓ Eat or drink something light before arriving at the speech.
>
> ✓ Extend your walk into the speech site to raise your heart rate and level of alertness; for example, use the stairs instead of the elevator.
>
> ✓ Arrive early and consider sitting in the front.
>
> ✓ Sit away from open windows, open doors, heating and cooling vents, bright lights, or other features that cause visual or noise distractions.
>
> ✓ Tell yourself that you will hear something unanticipated in the speech. Don't assume you know what the speaker will say. Check your emotions about the speech topic and the speaker or even other audience members.
>
> ✓ Listen for what is new and what is familiar, thus avoiding lapses in attention.
>
> ✓ Listen for how the facts relate to the purpose and thesis of the speech, avoiding defensive listening and concentrating on critical listening.

The problem may be poor lighting or people walking into or out of a meeting. The room may be excessively warm or cold.

To minimize external distractions, try to anticipate and plan for them — even if you do so just minutes before a presentation begins. If you have trouble seeing or hearing at a distance, arrive early and sit in the front. If you have trouble hearing at group meetings, sit near the leader so that most messages will be communicated to your side of the room.

Paying attention to external distractions is also critical for speakers. As a speaker, try to address promptly any distractions your audience may face. For example, you can close windows and doors against intruding noise or ask audience members to move closer to you.

Internal Distractions

Internal listening distractions are thoughts and feelings, both positive and negative, that intrude on our attention. Internal distractions can take the form of daydreaming, anxiety due to time pressures, distress over an argument, fatigue owing to lack of sleep or illness, or any kind of strong emotion, including negative reactions to a speech that you find disagreeable. Optimally, distracting strong emotions are best dealt with before you enter the listening environment.

SCRIPTWRITING AND DEFENSIVE LISTENING

Instead of focusing on the speaker, people who are "scriptwriters" are thinking about what they, rather than the speaker, will say next.[8] Similarly, people who engage in **defensive listening** decide either that they won't like what the speaker is going to say or that they know better. This usually occurs when listeners sense that their attitudes or opinions are being challenged.

Ethically Speaking
The Responsibilities of Listening in the Public Arena

As a speaker you have the power of the podium, but as a listener you also have considerable power that you can wield constructively or destructively. An example of the latter includes rude listening behaviors such as heckling, name-calling, interrupting out of turn, and other breaches in civility. Beyond short-circuiting communication, these acts can easily lead to explosive results — from menacing clashes among activists on opposite sides of a cause to eruptions at school board meetings and other civic venues.

Perhaps you have witnessed the fallout of such clashes on your college campus in the form of student demonstrations gone awry. In one such instance, at San Francisco State University, a heated exchange arose between pro-Palestinian student demonstrators and a group of Jewish students; the police were ultimately called to maintain order. In another instance, this one at a school board meeting in Connecticut, an audience member who took exception to a board member's proposal threw a pitcher of ice water in his face. Visibly shaken, the board member had to be escorted out of the room by the police. The meeting was adjourned abruptly, some on the board considered resigning, and many parents were fearful of attending other meetings.

The ability to dissent from prevailing opinion is one of the hallmarks of a free society. As listeners, we are ethically bound to refrain from disruptive and intimidating tactics that are meant to silence those with whom we disagree. If we find the arguments of others morally offensive, we are equally bound to speak up in refutation. Only in this manner can we preserve the freedom to express our ideas. Clearly, the power to listen can translate into being socially responsible or socially destructive.

When you find yourself scriptwriting or listening with a defensive posture, hear the speaker out. Try to focus on the speaker's motives for the remarks that offend you. Try to listen with empathy. You may still end up disagreeing with the speaker, but at least you'll do so from a position of actually having heard what he or she has said. Remind yourself that effective listening precedes effective rebuttal.[9]

LAZINESS AND OVERCONFIDENCE

Sometimes we think we already know, or perhaps don't need to know, the speaker's message. Close cousins to defensiveness, laziness and overconfidence can manifest themselves in several ways: We expect too little from speakers, ignore important information, or display an arrogant attitude. Later, we discover that we missed important information. Never assume that you already know what a speaker will say. You'll very seldom be right. And remember the value of modesty. Rarely do we know as much as we think we do.

CULTURAL BARRIERS

Differences in dialects or accents, nonverbal cues, word choice, and even physical appearance can serve as barriers to listening. Nonverbal cues such as gestures can also throw a listener off. Most gestures are culture-specific rather than universal. For example, a thumbs-up gesture in the United States usually means "good job" or "things are going fine." In Australia and Nigeria the same gesture is considered rude and insulting. In the United States, students of public speaking are counseled to maintain eye contact when they speak. In some Eastern cultures, however, direct eye contact is seen as disrespectful or even intolerable. And in Korea lowering the eyes signals rejection.

Active listeners can take action to manage these potential barriers to communication. One strategy is to refrain from judging a speaker on the basis of his or her accent, appearance, or demeanor, and to focus instead on what is actually being said. Put yourself in the speaker's shoes, and imagine what it would be like if you were addressing an audience in a new language. Instead of judging the speaker, reveal your needs to him or her whenever possible. Try to gain clarification by asking questions. Turn confusion into curiosity and an opportunity to learn about other people's experiences.

Overcoming cultural barriers to listening is important in all contexts of communication, including public discourse. When listening to (and delivering) speeches on such culturally laden public policy issues as border security and immigration reform, you must do your part to help diverse members of your audience actively listen to and understand your message. Whether as a speaker or an audience member, grappling with conflicts rooted in cultural differences demands empathetic listening and the suspension of disbelief characteristic of dialogic communication.

Public Speaking in Cultural Perspective
Helping Diverse Audiences Understand You

To help your audience listen effectively and truly get your message, consider reviewing your speech or presentation for the following cultural barriers to understanding:

1. Do you use *idioms,* or colloquial expressions such as "under the weather," "apple of his eye," and "bad-mouth," that non-native speakers aren't likely to know? Watch for such expressions and either eliminate them or pause and define them for your audience. (See Chapter 16 for additional tips on using language in a culturally sensitive manner.)

2. Do you speak at an appropriate rate—one that is neither too fast nor too slow? By paying particular attention to speech rate, pronunciation, and articulation, you can help non-native speakers of English understand what you are saying (see Chapter 18).

3. Are you alert to nonverbal cues that suggest that your listeners may not comprehend you? Be alert to confused expressions, and ask your listeners if you can clarify points for them.

Becoming a More Active Listener **Links**

Active listeners use their eyes as well as their ears to decode a speaker's nonverbal and verbal cues. They listen for the speaker's main points and critically evaluate evidence used to support claims. Active listeners:

- Set listening goals.
- Listen for main ideas.
- Watch for the speaker's nonverbal cues.

SET LISTENING GOALS

Setting listening goals helps you prepare to get the most from a listening situation. What do you need and expect from the listening situation? Keep these goals in mind as you listen. Try to state your listening goals in a way that encourages action. Table 4.1 illustrates the steps in setting listening goals.

TABLE 4.1 • Steps in Setting Listening Goals
Identify Need: "I have to know Suzanne's speech thesis, purpose, main points, and type of organization in order to complete and hand in a written evaluation."
Indicate Performance Standard: "I will get a better grade on the evaluation if I am able to identify and evaluate the major components of Suzanne's speech."
Make Action Statement (Goal): "I will minimize distractions and practice the active listening steps during Suzanne's speech. I will take careful notes during her speech and ask questions about anything I do not understand."
Assess Goal Achievement: "Before I leave the classroom, I will review my notes carefully to make sure that I covered everything."

LISTEN FOR MAIN IDEAS

No one has perfect retention. To ensure that you hear and retain the speaker's most important points, try these strategies:

- *Listen for the speaker's organizational pattern* (see Chapters 12 and 26). Knowing the sequence and structure of a speech makes it easy for you to understand and remember the content.

- *Listen for introductions, transitions, and conclusions to alert you to the main points.* Most speakers will introduce their main points in their introductory remarks. This gives the listener the chance to identify these points and focus on their discussion later: "I have three points I want to make tonight. First, . . ."

   Transitions can also alert the listener to the fact that a main point is about to be discussed: "My next major point is. . . ." Speakers often use many of the following transitions to preview a main idea: "One, two, three, . . . ,"

"First, second, third, . . ."; "Most important, . . ."; "Another point (issue) I would raise. . . ."

Conclusions are a valuable place to recheck your memory of the main points: "Let me recap those three rules for living overseas. One, . . ."

- *Watch for a more direct eye gaze.* Speakers are more likely to look at you when they are trying to make an important point. In addition, they are likely to shift their gaze to a different part of the audience when moving from one main point to another.

- *Take notes on the speaker's main points.* Several different methods of note taking are possible when listening to public speeches. The bullet, column, and outline methods can be helpful (see Table 4.2 on note-taking methods).

TABLE 4.2 • Methods of Note Taking		
Method	**Description**	**Example**
Bullet	Notes list the main points and/or supporting material in bullet form.	• Bipolar disorder is actually a spectrum of disorders. • Adults suffer more classical patterns of mood swings.
Column	Notes are taken in two columns. One column is used for verbatim notes, and the other is used for interpretations or notes to yourself.	"Make sure your hands are dry." Grip the ball with the thumb and first two fingers.
Outline	Notes are taken according to the organizational format or outline that the speaker is using (see Chapters 12 and 26).	

 CHECKLIST

Strategies for Active Listening

1. Set listening goals and state them in a way that encourages action: "In my colleague's presentation, I will learn why it took the team six months to complete the last phase."
2. Listen for the speaker's main ideas.
3. Take notes.
4. Try to detect the speaker's organizational pattern.
5. Seek out main ideas in the speaker's introduction, use of transitions, and conclusion.
6. Watch for the speaker's nonverbal cues.
7. Take note of body language, eye contact, facial expressions, and gestures.

WATCH FOR NONVERBAL CUES

Much of a message's meaning is communicated nonverbally, and you can use this information as you listen to speeches. *Body language* is an excellent source of information. Watch the speaker's stance and posture. Do they seem rigid and wooden? If so, the speaker may be nervous and may not feel comfortable with the material he or she is presenting. *Facial expressions* also provide cues to help you listen better. Speakers who are committed to their material are more likely to display facial expressions that are consistent with their commitment to the message. Smiling, frowning, raising eyebrows, and other expressions of emotion are useful cues in determining the speaker's sincerity and enthusiasm for the message. The same cues can betray the speaker's real feelings. If verbal and nonverbal messages do not correspond, the nonverbal cues are usually the more honest ones.

Active Listening and Critical Thinking

Active listening and critical thinking go hand in hand. The use of one skill builds the other. **Critical thinking** is the ability to evaluate claims on the basis of well-supported reasons. Critical thinkers are able to look for flaws in arguments and resist claims that have no supporting evidence.[10] They don't take things at face value.

As you listen to speeches, use your critical faculties to:

- *Evaluate the evidence.* Is the evidence accurate? What is the source of the evidence? Is the source credible? How does the source compare to a source you would use? Is it a source available to the wider public? Do you sense any emotional reactions or other distractions owing to the evidence and its source?

- *Assess an argument's logic.* Does the speaker's reasoning betray faulty logic? (See Chapter 25.) Is the speaker's reasoning consistent with or different from what a majority of people contend? Is it based on evidence that most people are aware of or can find themselves?

- *Resist false assumptions, overgeneralizations, either-or thinking, and other fallacies in reasoning.* A **valid generalization** is supported by different types of evidence from different sources, but it does not make claims beyond a reasonable point. **Overgeneralizations** are unsupported conclusions (e.g., "All welfare recipients are lazy"). Test the validity of a generalization by determining if the basis of support is biased in any way. *Either-or thinking* is dominated by just two choices and creates false dilemmas that do not in fact exist. (See Chapter 25 for additional fallacies of reasoning.)

- *Consider multiple perspectives.* There is often more than one way to look at things. Similarly, there are often multiple solutions to problems. Consider different perspectives, and realize that both your own perspective

---

CHECKLIST

Using the Thought/Speech Differential to Listen Critically

Did you know that we think at a much faster rate than we speak? We speak at the rate of between ninety and two hundred words a minute; we think at a rate of perhaps as much as five hundred to six hundred words per minute. This differential between "thought speed" and "speech speed" is one reason we are so easily distracted. But rather than using the thought/speech differential as an excuse to let your mind wander, you can turn it into an opportunity to apply your critical thinking skills. The next time you find yourself "thinking ahead" of the speaker — usually by thinking of something that's unrelated to the speech — use the time instead to listen with the following questions in mind:

✓   What's the speaker saying?

✓   What does it really mean?

✓   Is he or she leaving anything out?

✓   Is this an assumption? A generalization? A fact or an opinion?

✓   Are my biases intruding on my listening?

✓   How can I use what the speaker is telling me?[1]

1. Thomas E. Anastasi Jr., *Listen! Techniques for Improving Communication Skills* (Boston: CBI Publishing, 1982), 35.

---

and that of the speaker are subject to error. How does the speaker's perspective and your own compare to perspectives of public figures who speak on the topic?

•   *Summarize and judge.* Summarize the speaker's facts and evidence for yourself. If the speaker asks for an action on the part of listeners (as is often the case in persuasive speeches; see Chapter 24), decide how you will act on the basis of the evidence. Will you be more apt to act on the evidence itself, or in line with what you think most people will do?

Guidelines for Evaluating Speeches and Presentations

As public speakers, we want to know the results of our efforts. While audience members' reactions during the speech provide clues to their feelings about it, more specific feedback is needed if we are to gain insight into our strengths and weaknesses. By critically evaluating the speeches of others, you'll be better able to assess your own strengths and weaknesses as a speaker.

BE HONEST AND FAIR IN YOUR EVALUATION

Keep in mind the need to be honest and fair in your evaluation. Sometimes we have a tendency to focus on certain aspects of a speech and, as a result, minimize some of the most important elements. Focusing on a topic that you really like or dislike, for example, may cause you to place undue importance on that speech element. It is also important to remain open to ideas and beliefs that differ from your own. This openness will help your ideas, as well as your role as a citizen engaged with public issues, prosper. You can always learn something from differing viewpoints, and, likewise, honest and fair listeners will learn from your viewpoints.

ADJUST TO THE SPEAKER'S STYLE

Each of us has a unique communication style, a way of presenting ourselves through a mix of verbal and nonverbal signals. As listeners, we form impressions of speakers based on this communication style. Depending on our own preferences, we may find some speakers dull, others dynamic, still others off-putting, and so on. Adjusting to a speaker means not judging the content of that speaker's message based on his or her communication style. As listeners, it's up to us to identify which impressions create the most difficulty and then develop techniques for overcoming any listening problems. Accents, awkward grammatical phrases, and word choice are not good reasons to "tune out" a speaker. Maintaining respect for all types of speakers is a sign of good listening.

BE COMPASSIONATE IN YOUR CRITICISM

How can you critically evaluate a presentation in a way that's constructive rather than cruel? In keeping with the biblical injunction to "do unto others," consider the following approach:[11]

1. *Start by saying something positive.* No one's speech is all bad, so why not start off by saying something nice? The benefits of this are twofold: You'll boost the speaker's self-confidence, and he or she will probably be more receptive to the criticism you do offer.

2. *Focus on the speech, not on the speaker.* Cne of the most challenging aspects of giving a speech is the feeling of being exposed to others. Don't confirm the speaker's fears of being ripped apart. When a speaker's ideas conflict with your own, concentrate on what you find disagreeable with his or her arguments, rather than judging the speaker as a person. People are more similar than we think, even when our viewpoints differ. Address your remarks to the characteristics of the speech, not to the speaker.

3. *Target your criticism.* Global statements such as "I just couldn't get into your topic" or "That was a great speech" don't give the speaker any information that he or she can use. If something fell short, be as specific as possible in describing it: "I wanted to hear more about the importance of such and such as it related to. . . ."

Peer Evaluation Form

In the space below, offer your evaluation of the speaker. Make your evaluation honest but constructive, providing the sort of feedback that you would find helpful if you were the speaker.

Did the speaker seem confident?   Yes   Somewhat   No
Suggestions: _____
_____

Did the speaker use appropriate volume?   Yes   Somewhat   No
Suggestions: _____
_____

Did the speaker use good eye contact?   Yes   Somewhat   No
Suggestions: _____
_____

Did the speaker use effective vocal expression?   Yes   Somewhat   No
Suggestions: _____
_____

Did the speaker use appropriate gestures
and facial expressions?   Yes   Somewhat   No
Suggestions: _____
_____

Was the speaker's introduction effective?   Yes   Somewhat   No
Suggestions: _____
_____

Was the speaker's conclusion effective?   Yes   Somewhat   No
Suggestions: _____
_____

Could you easily identify and remember
the speaker's main points?   Yes   Somewhat   No
Suggestions: _____
_____

Did the speaker's organizational patterns
make sense to you?   Yes   Somewhat   No
Suggestions: _____
_____

Did the speaker use effective supporting
evidence?   Yes   Somewhat   No
Suggestions: _____
_____

The best thing about the speaker was: _____
_____

The best thing about the speech was: _____
_____

Recommendations for improvement: _____
_____

Ethical Public Speaking ⬤ 5

One of the most consistent expectations that we as listeners bring to any speech situation is that the speaker will be honest and straightforward with us. Why else give our attention to someone unless we believe that he or she is sincere? Yet, while we assume an attitude of trust, we instinctively remain alert to hints that might signal dishonesty. As we listen to the actual words the speaker utters, for example, we are simultaneously evaluating his or her posture, tone of voice, gaze, and other potential markers of sincerity or lack thereof.

How can you ensure that your listeners will find you worthy of their trust? As ethicist Michael Josephson[1] has noted, there are both practical and moral reasons for maintaining an ethical stance in public speaking. At the practical level, you must establish credibility with listeners before they will accept your message. Credibility is based on trust, honesty, and believability. You also have a moral obligation to treat your listeners with respect — to behave ethically toward them. Central to ethical public speaking is responsibility to oneself and others.

Take Responsibility for Your Words WEB Chapter quizzes

Public speakers are in the unusual position of being able to influence or persuade people and, at times, move them to act — for better or for worse. With this power to affect the minds and hearts of others comes **responsibility** — the heart of ethics. One definition of *responsibility* is "a charge, trust, or duty for which one is accountable."[2] **Ethics** is the study of moral conduct — how people should act toward one another. In terms of public speaking, ethics refers to the responsibilities we have toward our audience and ourselves. It also encompasses the responsibilities listeners have toward speakers.

While laws dictate what we *must* do, ethics suggests what we *ought* to do. When network executives fired radio personality Don Imus in 2007 for making racist and sexist remarks about the Rutgers women's basketball team members, it wasn't because he broke the law, but because the executives regarded Imus's speech as beyond the pale of civil discourse.

EARN YOUR LISTENERS' TRUST

Ethics is derived from the Greek word *ethos*, meaning "character." According to the ancient Greek rhetorician Aristotle, audiences listen to and trust speakers who demonstrate positive ethos (positive character). Positive ethos includes *competence* (as demonstrated by the speaker's grasp of the subject matter), *good moral character* (as reflected in the speaker's trustworthiness, straightforward-ness, and honest presentation of the message), and *goodwill* (as demonstrated by the speaker's knowledge and attitude of respect toward the audience and the particular speech occasion).

For Aristotle, speakers were regarded positively only when they were well prepared, honest, and respectful toward their audience. Some 2,500 years after Aristotle, surprisingly little has changed. Modern research on **speaker credibility** reveals that people place their greatest trust in speakers who

- have a solid grasp of the subject,
- display sound reasoning skills,
- are honest and straightforward, and
- are genuinely interested in the welfare of their listeners.[3]

Listeners tend to distrust speakers who deviate even slightly from these qualities. However, merely being an expert is not enough to inspire listeners' trust. Studies reveal that we trust only those speakers who we believe have our best interests in mind.[4]

RESPECT YOUR LISTENERS' VALUES

Our ethical conduct is a reflection of our **values** — our most enduring judg-ments or standards of what's good and bad in life, of what's important to us. Values shape our worldview, drive our behavior, and form the basis on which we judge the actions of others. Our ethical choices — including those we make in our speeches — are our values in action.

Like human behavior itself, values are not a tidy affair but can conflict or clash. The larger and more diverse the society, such as exists in the United States, the greater these clashes will tend to be. One only has to think of the so-called *values divide* in the United States between "red states" (representing conservative values) and "blue states" (representing liberal values).

Conflicting values lie at the heart of many controversies, making it difficult to address certain topics without challenging cherished beliefs. The United States is a country of immigrants, for example, but half of the population with only a high-school education believes that immigrants threaten traditional American values, while only a quarter of Americans who are college-educated agree.[5] We treasure freedom of religion, but some of us want prayer in the schools while others believe in maintaining the separation of church and state. Although we cherish our right to privacy, some of us believe in the value of the Patriot Act, which gives the government sweeping powers to conduct surveillance of U.S. citizens, while others claim that the act violates our civil liberties.

As you prepare your speech, anticipate that audience members will hold a range of values that will differ not only from your own, but from each other's, and proceed with sensitivity. Of course, the more you understand about your listeners beforehand, the more effectively you will be able to prepare a message that will engage them while remaining true to yourself (see Chapter 6 on the differences between attitudes, beliefs, and values and how to identify each in audience members).

BRING YOUR OWN VALUES INTO FOCUS

Analyzing the underlying values that lead you to your position on an issue can help you do the same for audience members. What basic values underlie your support of or opposition to the death penalty? What personal characteristics might lead others to take a different position?

Through extensive research, psychologist Milton Rokeach identified thirty-six values important to a large cross section of people, distinguishing between two kinds of values: instrumental and terminal. *Instrumental values* are socially desirable behavioral characteristics, such as being courageous. *Terminal values* are desirable states of being, such as living a comfortable life.

To bring some of your personal values into focus, complete the self-assessment exercise in the accompanying checklist. To identify which values mean the most to you, rank both terminal and instrumental values from least to most important. Then compare what you care about with what your audience analysis indicates that your listeners might value (see Figure 5.1). Where your values overlap those of your audience, you may be able to identify some common ground from which to present your topic.

Use Your Rights of Free Speech Responsibly

As a public speaker, you must balance the rights of free speech with the responsibilities that accompany it. Perhaps no other nation in the world has as many built-in safeguards for its citizens' right to free expression as the United States. The **First Amendment** of the U.S. Constitution plays a pivotal role in enforcing these safeguards by guaranteeing freedom of speech ("Congress shall make no law . . . abridging the freedom of speech . . ."). However, it is often difficult for our state and federal judges (who are charged with interpreting the

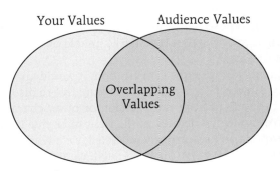

Figure 5.1 Comparing Values

SELF-ASSESSMENT CHECKLIST

Identifying Values

As a way of uncovering where your values lie, rank each item from *1* to *10* (from least to most important). From these, select your top five values and write them down in the circle labeled "Your Values" in Figure 5.1. Repeat the exercise, but this time rank each value in terms of how important you think it is to your audience. Select the top five of these values and place them in the circle labeled "Audience Values." Finally, draw arrows to the overlapping area to indicate where your highest values (of those listed) coincide with those you think are most important to your listeners.

Terminal Values (states of being you consider important)	*Instrumental Values (characteristics you value in yourself and others)*
A comfortable life	Ambitious
An exciting life	Broadminded
A sense of accomplishment	Capable
A world at peace	Cheerful
A world of beauty	Clean
Equality	Courageous
Family security	Forgiving
Freedom	Helpful
Happiness	Honest
Inner harmony	Imaginative
Mature love	Independent
National security	Intellectual
Pleasure	Logical
Salvation	Loving
Self-respect	Obedient
Social recognition	Polite
True friendship	Responsible
Wisdom	Self-controlled

Source: Milton Rokeach, *Value Survey* (Sunnydale, Calif.: Halgren Tests, 1967).

Constitution) to find a satisfactory balance between our right to express ourselves (our *civil liberties*) and our right to be protected from speech that harms us (our *civil rights*). Whose rights, for example, should be protected? Should a "shock jock's" right to spew racist remarks be upheld over the objections of the victims of those remarks?

As today's judges interpret the Constitution, it would appear that radio announcers such as Howard Stern and Don Imus are free to disparage groups and individuals on the basis of their race, gender, or other characteristics. In the United States, **free speech** — defined as the right to be free from unreasonable constraints on expression[6] — is strongly protected, even when the targets of that speech claim that it infringes on their civil rights to be protected from discrimination.

Nevertheless, there remain important limits on our right to speak freely, and as a public speaker it is critical that you are aware of these limitations. For example, certain types of speech are actually illegal, including the following:

- Speech that provokes people to violence (incitement or "**fighting words**") and is, in the words of First Amendment expert David L. Hudson, "of such slight social value as a step to the truth that any benefit that may be derived from [the speech] is clearly outweighed by the social interest in order and morality."[7]
- Speech that can be proved to be defamatory (termed **slander**), or potentially harmful to an individual's reputation at work or in the community.
- Speech that invades a person's privacy, such as disclosing personal information about an individual that is not in the public record.

The law makes a distinction between whether the issues or individuals you are talking about are public or private. If you are talking about a public figure or a matter of public concern, you have much more latitude to say what you think, and you will not be legally liable unless it can be shown that you spoke with a **reckless disregard for the truth**. That is, you can be legally liable if it can be shown that you knew that what you were saying was false but said it anyway. If, on the other hand, in your speech you talk about a private person or private matters involving that person, it will be easier for that person to successfully assert a claim for defamation. You will then have the burden of proving that what you said was true.[8]

While a limited range of speech is not legal, speakers who seek to distort the truth about events often can do so and not suffer any consequences. You may express an opinion questioning the severity of the Holocaust or the suffering of African Americans under slavery. The fact that this sort of offensive speech is *legal*, however, does not necessarily mean that it is ethical. In fact, in most instances the First Amendment ensures protection to both the speaker who treats the truth — and other people — with respect *and* those whose words are inflammatory and offensive. While there are various approaches to evaluating ethical behavior, common to all of them are the fundamental moral precepts of not harming others and telling the truth. Seen from this perspective, many kinds of legally protected speech — whether they are racist, sexist, homophobic, pornographic, antireligious, or just plain mean — are clearly unethical.

CONTRIBUTE TO POSITIVE PUBLIC DISCOURSE

One way to evaluate whether your speech is ethical is to consider whether or not it makes a positive contribution to *public discourse* — exchanges (including speeches) involving issues of importance to the larger community, such as debates on campus about the war in Iraq or on the need to take action to slow climate change.

Public Speaking in Cultural Perspective
Comparing Cultural Values

Do the criteria for an ethical speaker outlined in this chapter— that is, displaying the qualities of trustworthiness, respect, responsibility, and fairness— apply equally in different cultures? For example, does telling the truth always take precedence over other qualities, such as being eloquent or protecting the interests of your clan or group? Are ethical standards for speeches merely a product of a particular culture? What about the concept of plagiarism? In the United States, speakers who fail to acknowledge their sources meet with harsh criticism and often suffer severe consequences, even if, as in the case of a recent college president (see p. 74), the speaker is otherwise highly respected. Is this universally true?[1] Can you think of examples in which ideas of ethical speech expressed in this chapter are not necessarily shared by other cultures? Do you personally hold values for ethical speech that are different from those cited here?

1. For an instructive article about plagiarism in China, in which the author disputes the notion of cultural relativity regarding plagiarism in that country, see Dilin Liu, "Plagiarism in ESOL Students: Is Cultural Conditioning Truly the Major Culprit?" *ELT* 59 (2005): 234–41.

What might constitute a positive contribution to public debates of this nature? Perhaps most important is the *advancement of constructive goals*. Speaking merely to inflame and demean others, on the other hand, degrades the quality of public discourse. Consider the case of the right-wing commentator Ann Coulter. In 2006, Coulter harshly criticized several of the widows of victims of the 9/11 attack who had pushed for and succeeded in establishing the bipartisan 9/11 Commission. Disliking the conclusions of the commission, Coulter charged, "These broads are millionaires, lionized on TV and in articles about them, reveling in their status as celebrities and stalked by grief-arazzies. I have never seen people enjoying their husbands' death so much."[9] Her accusation caused a furor, with most people on both sides of the political fence finding Coulter's statement an unacceptable *ad hominem* attack—an argument that targets a person instead of the issue at hand (see Chapter 25 for a review of this and other fallacies of reasoning).

Coulter's **invective**, or verbal attack, served as a **conversation stopper**— speech designed to discredit, demean, and belittle those with whom one disagrees. Conversation stoppers and other forms of attack breach the acceptable "rules of engagement" for public conversations. As communication scholar W. Barnett Pearce explains, the concept of the **rules of engagement**, originally used as a military term, can also be applied to the ways we relate to one another in the public arena:

> Comparable to the orders about the circumstances in which soldiers may use their weapons are the rights and responsibilities to speak, to speak the truth, to disclose one's purposes, to respond to others, to respond coherently, to listen, and to understand. . . .[10]

To ensure that your speech fulfills these rights and responsibilities, consider the following ground rules for ethical speaking.

Observe the Ground Rules for Ethical Speaking

The qualities of dignity and integrity should infuse every aspect of a speech. **Dignity** refers to ensuring that your listeners feel "worthy, honored, or respected" as individuals.[11] Each of us wants to be accorded dignity. **Integrity** signals the speaker's incorruptibility—that he or she will avoid compromising the truth for the sake of personal expediency.[12] For example, slanting facts in your favor during a speech to persuade others to take your side demonstrates a lack of integrity. Speakers who demonstrate dignity and integrity care about themselves and their listeners. They exhibit a hallmark of ethical speaking: concern for the greater good.

Speaking ethically also requires that we adhere to certain "pillars of character,"[13] including being trustworthy, respectful, responsible, and fair in our presentations.

BE TRUSTWORTHY

We find speakers trustworthy when we sense that they are honest about their intentions and about the information they present. **Trustworthiness** is a combination of honesty and dependability. Trustworthy speakers don't sacrifice the truth to achieve their aims. At the broadest level, being a trustworthy speaker is essential to the democratic process because democracy depends on an informed citizenry.[14]

Manipulating data to achieve a particular purpose is untrustworthy, as are any attempts to deceive an audience by misrepresentation, omission, or making up of information (see Chapter 8 on the ethical use of statistics). Ethically, you are required to support your points truthfully and accurately. Truth telling can be an especially difficult issue in persuasive speeches (see Chapters 24–26). When the goal is to try to persuade others, the temptation is to fashion the information in a way that fits the goal, even if it means omitting a fact here or there that would convince the audience otherwise. But all kinds of speeches, not just persuasive ones, should be built on the truth. This means acknowledging rather than omitting relevant alternative viewpoints (see Chapter 25 for guidelines on addressing competing arguments). Acknowledging sources is also an essential aspect of being a trustworthy speaker. To do otherwise is to commit plagiarism (discussed later in this chapter).

DEMONSTRATE RESPECT

A shorthand definition for **respect** is "treating people right." Speakers demonstrate respect by addressing audience members as unique human beings and refraining from any form of personal attack.

Focus on issues rather than personalities. Civil disagreement is quite appropriate in a speech. Personal attacks on the character of those with whom you disagree are not.

Allow the audience the power of rational choice. Audiences deserve to hear information in a way that permits them to exercise the power of rational choice. Sensationalist or lurid appeals rob people of this power. In most cases, it's not necessary to use graphic pictures or upsetting verbal descriptions just to make a point. Similarly, drowning out a speaker's message with which you disagree—called a **heckler's veto**—robs us of the ability to make up our own minds about an issue and silences the free expression of ideas.

Avoid in-group and out-group distinctions. Each of us wants to feel included. One of the most unethical things a public speaker can do is make some members of the audience feel excluded or, worse, victimized. Promoting such distinctions violates the universal rule of avoiding harm to others.

One simple but very effective thing you can do to make audience members feel included is maintain eye contact. This assures audience members that they aren't seen as passive objects but as unique human beings. (Preferences for eye contact do vary by culture, so be certain to consider your audience.) Also, try to use language that everyone can understand.

A serious ethical breach is the expression of ethnocentrism, stereotypes, or outright prejudice in a speech. Speakers who exhibit **ethnocentrism** act as though everyone shares their point of view and points of reference, whether or not this is the case. They may tell jokes that require a certain context or refer only to their own customs. Ethical speakers, by contrast, assume differences and address them respectfully. Generalizing about an apparent characteristic of a group and applying that generalization to all of its members is another serious affront to people's dignity. When such racial, ethnic, gender, or other **stereotypes** roll off the speaker's tongue, they pack a wallop of indignation and pain for the people to whom they refer.

Hate speech is the ultimate vehicle for promoting in-group and out-group distinctions. **Hate speech** is any offensive communication—verbal or nonverbal—that is directed against people's racial, ethnic, religious, gender, or other characteristics. Racist, sexist, or ageist slurs, gay bashing, and cross burnings are all forms of hate speech. Ethically, you are bound to scrupulously avoid any hint of ethnocentrism, stereotyping, and hate speech.

MAKE RESPONSIBLE CHOICES

Communication is a strong tool for influencing people, and even one message has the potential to change people's lives. When preparing a speech, consider the following:

Topic and purpose. Will learning about your topic in some way benefit listeners? Are your overall speech aims socially constructive? What effect

Ethically Speaking
Speech Codes on Campus: Civility versus Free Speech

U.S. colleges and universities have long been at the center of the debate over what constitutes free speech versus hate speech. On the one side are those who resist censorship of any kind, often in support of the constitutional rights of the First Amendment. On the other side are advocates of speech codes and policies that limit what students and faculty can and cannot say and do; these advocates argue that such codes are necessary to ensure a tolerant and safe environment.

In the 1980s and early 1990s, hundreds of schools, both public and private, instituted hate speech codes prohibiting certain forms of offensive speech and acts that were deemed intimidating or hostile to individuals or groups. Many of these codes were later found to be unconstitutional, but anti-harassment policies designed to do much the same thing remain in place today.[1] These, along with federal laws designed to protect students from a hostile learning environment, allow administrators to punish students and faculty for what they judge to be offensive speech.

Responding to legal challenges, many campuses have replaced hate speech codes with "anti-harassment" policies, with a corresponding shift from a focus on offensive speech per se (such as hurling a racial epithet at someone) to a focus on "harassing speech" and conduct (such as sexually harassing someone by word and/or deed). But as with earlier hate speech codes, anti-harassment policies have also come under fire. The Foundation for Individual Rights in Education (FIRE), for example, a First Amendment watchdog group, maintains that like earlier hate speech codes, the majority of these anti-harassment policies are unconstitutional.[2]

Many colleges and universities limit student protests and demonstrations to designated areas on campus called "free speech zones"; and these too have proved to be controversial. At the University of Massachusetts, Dartmouth, for example, students have staged several protests over the university's policy of restricting all demonstrations and rallies to a specific half-acre "Public Forum Zone" in a corner of the campus. A message on one of the flyers posted around campus read "Do you know what a free speech zone is? According to our Federal Constitution, the United States is a free speech zone, not selective areas."[3]

Free speech zones and speech codes and policies raise important ethical questions. Supporters of such policies claim that they are necessary to protect students from racial or sexual intimidation, to ensure equal opportunity, and to enforce the norms of a civil society.[4] Detractors argue that limits on free speech prevent students with unpopular or politically incorrect views from freely expressing themselves. As Kermit L. Hall, president of Utah State University, has written:

> Free speech at public universities and colleges is at once the most obvious and the most paradoxical of constitutional principles. It is obvious because given the nature of academic inquiry, only an open, robust and critical environment for speech will support the quest for truth. At the same time, universities are at once communities that must balance the requirements of

(Continued)

free speech with issues of civility, respect and human dignity. They are also part and parcel of the larger social order with its own, often competing, set of values.[5]

What do you think?

1. David L. Hudson, "Hate Speech and Campus Speech Codes," First Amendment Center Web site, www.firstamendmentcenter.org (accessed May 17, 2007); Markkula Center for Applied Ethics Web site, "The Price of Free Speech: Campus Hate Speech Codes," from *Issues on Ethics 5*, no. 2 (Summer 1992), www.scu.edu/SCU/Centers/Ethics/ publications/iie/v5n2/codes.html (accessed June 26, 2002).
2. Ibid.
3. Rachel Fish, "Students React to Free-Speech Zone," *The Torch,* March 15, 2007, www.umassd.edu/torch/06-07/i21v53/ (accessed June 20, 2007).
4. Jon B. Gould, "Returning Fire," *Chronicle of Higher Education,* April 20, 2007, chronicle.com/weekly/v53/i33/33b01301.htm (accessed May 16, 2007).
5. Kermit L. Hall, "Free Speech on Public College Campuses," First Amendment Center Web site, www.firstamendmentcenter.org (accessed February 8, 2005).

will your speech have on your listeners? (See Chapter 7 for more on selecting an ethical topic and purpose.)

Evidence and reasoning. Are your arguments sound? Sloppy evidence and reasoning distort the truth.

Accuracy. Is the content of your message accurate? Are the facts correct? Accuracy is a hallmark of ethical speaking.

Honest use of emotional appeals. Using emotional appeals supported by facts is a legitimate way to achieve your goal (see Chapter 24). However, using them as a crutch when your argument is weak on evidence or facts is a breach of ethics.

DEMONSTRATE FAIRNESS

Few subjects are black and white; rarely is there only one right or wrong way to view a topic. **Fairness** is ensured when you make a genuine effort to see all sides of an issue and to be open-minded. Using only information that helps your case is unfair to listeners because it prevents them from making informed decisions.[15] Speakers who do so also betray a lack of sensitivity to other people's values and moral stances.

Avoid Plagiarism

 Tutorial

To their everlasting regret, more than one otherwise honorable speaker has succumbed to the pressure of creating a moving speech by appropriating someone else's ideas or words. For example, Eugene Tobin, a historian and the president of Hamilton College, stepped down in 2002 after admitting that he failed to credit his sources in his speeches. The plagiarism came to light after a faculty member pointed out similarities in Tobin's words and those of a book reviewer at Amazon.com. Tobin issued an apology for "the omissions that resulted from the way I develop and present my speeches."[16]

Crediting sources is a crucial aspect of any speech. **Plagiarism** — the passing off of another person's information as one's own — is unethical. To plagiarize is to use other people's ideas or words without acknowledging the source. **Wholesale plagiarism** occurs when you simply "cut-and-paste" material from sources into your speech and represent it as your own. **Patchwrite plagiarism** is copying material into your speech draft from a source and then changing or rearranging words and sentence structures here and there to make the material appear as if it were your own.[17] For example, one form of plagiarism in a public speaking course is taking a written essay and turning it into a speaking outline.[18] A student might read an article in the *Atlantic Monthly* on problems faced by refugees fleeing from war-torn Darfur. The student bases the entire presentation on this one article, outlining it point-by-point and turning it into a speech. Even if he or she acknowledges the source of the information, this is an act of plagiarism because the student copied *the organization and structure* of another person's work. As much if not more than the facts and ideas contained in the article is the unique manner in which the author expresses them.

Whether it's done intentionally or not, plagiarism in any form is stealing and is a serious breach of ethics. When you present plagiarized material as your own speech material, you abuse the trust that an audience places in you. More than any other single action, acknowledging sources lets listeners know that you are trustworthy and will represent both fact and opinion fairly and responsibly.

RULES FOR AVOIDING PLAGIARISM

The basic rule for avoiding plagiarism as a public speaker is straightforward: *Any sources that require credit in written form should be acknowledged in oral form.* These include direct quotations, paraphrased information, facts, statistics, and most other kinds of information that was gathered and reported by someone other than yourself. For each source, plan on alerting audience members to the following:

1. *Type of source* (e.g., magazine, book, personal interview, or Web site)
2. *Author or origin of the source* (e.g., "In a documentary on New York produced by Ken Burns . . ." or "On the National Science Foundation Web site . . .")
3. *Title or description of the source* (e.g., "In *Endangered Minds,* author Jane Healy . . ." or "In an article on sharks . . .")
4. *Publication date of the source* (e.g., "In an article on sharks published in the October 10, 2005, issue of *Oceanography* . . .")

Oral presentations need not include full bibliographic references (including full names, dates, titles, and volume and page numbers). However, you should include complete references in a bibliography or works cited list or at the end of the speech outline. (For detailed guidelines on creating a bibliography or list of works cited for a speech, see Chapter 13 and Appendices E–I.)

Orally Credit Direct Quotations

Direct quotations are statements quoted verbatim, or word for word, from a source. Direct quotes should always be acknowledged in a speech. Although it is not a requirement, you can call attention to a source's exact wording with phrases such as "And I quote" and "As [the source] put it." For example:

> As my esteemed colleague Dr. Vance Brown told an audience of AIDS researchers at the International AIDS Convention last year, *and I quote,* "The cure may be near or it may be far, but the human suffering is very much in the present."

> *As Shakespeare would say,* "A rose by any other name would smell as sweet."

Orally Credit Paraphrased Information

A **paraphrase** is a restatement of someone else's ideas, opinions, or theories in your own words.[19] Because paraphrases alter the form but not the substance of another person's ideas, you must acknowledge the original source. After all, the ideas are not your ideas.

When you paraphrase in a speech, restate the idea from the original source, making sure to use your own words and sentence structure:

Orginal Version

> It was in the 1980s that food began disappearing from the American super-market, gradually to be replaced by "nutrients," which are not the same thing. Where once the familiar name of recognizable comestibles — things like eggs or breakfast cereal or cookies — claimed pride of place on the brightly colored packages crowding the aisles, now new terms like "fiber" and "cholesterol" and "saturated fat" rose to large-type prominence. More important than mere foods, the presence or absence of these invisible substances was now generally believed to confer health benefits on their eaters.　　　　　*—Nir Rosen*

Oral Paraphrase

> In an essay on "The Age of Nutritionism" published in the January 28, 2007, issue of the *New York Times Magazine,* Nir Rosen says that we have taken our focus off real food and put it on its chemical composition — on the nutrients in it. Thus we no longer eat apples and oranges, but "an important source of soluble and insoluble fiber" and "80 fat-free calories containing a healthy dose of vitamin C." Nir says that rather than the actual food we eat, we now believe it is the unseen substances such as cholesterol, saturated fat, and fiber, that make us healthy or sick.

Orally Credit Facts and Statistics

The source for any data that was not gathered by you should be cited in your speech. You don't have to cite **common knowledge** — information that is likely to be known by many people, but such information must truly be widely disseminated. For example, it is common knowledge that terrorists flew two planes into the World Trade Center towers on September 11, 2001. It is not common knowledge that the towers were respectively, 1,368 and 1,362 feet high. These facts require acknowledgment of a source, in this case the Port Authority of New York and New Jersey, the owners of the World Trade Center.[20] The following three examples illustrate how you can orally acknowledge and cite facts and statistics in a speech.

> *According to the public information office of the Port Authority of New York and New Jersey, which owned the World Trade Center towers,* the towers were, respectively, 1,368 and 1,362 feet high. The center was actually a complex of seven buildings on sixteen acres.

AVOID PLAGIARISM ON THE INTERNET

Just as with print sources, information found on the Internet including direct quotations, paraphrased information, facts, statistics, or other content that was gathered and reported by someone other than yourself must be accurately credited. This includes information obtained from Web sites, blogs, electronic publications, mailing lists, newsgroups, and online databases. (For specific guidelines on acknowledging Internet sources, see Chapter 10 and Appendices E–I. For additional direction on orally crediting sources of various types, see Chapter 8, "Developing Supporting Material.")

 CHECKLIST

Steps to Avoid Plagiarism

1. Keep track of your sources as you collect them.
2. Create a system for tracking sources (using notecards, Microsoft Word, EndNote, or another note-tracking program).
3. Be especially careful to keep track of and cite Internet sources (see Chapter 10).
4. Review your speech to ensure that you've credited any quoted, paraphrased, and summarized information drawn from others' work.

Respect the Laws of Copyright and Fair Use

Copyright is a legal protection afforded original creators of literary and artistic works.[21] When including copyrighted materials in your speeches — such as reproductions of graphs or photographs, a video or sound clip, and so forth — you must determine when and if you need permission to use such work.

When a work is copyrighted, you may not reproduce, distribute, or display it without permission from the copyright holder or you will be liable for copyright infringement. For any work created from 1978 to the present, the copyright is good for the author's lifetime, plus fifty years. After that time, unless extended, the work falls into the **public domain**, which means that anyone may reproduce it. Not subject to copyright are federal (but *not* state or local) government publications, common knowledge, and select other categories.

Copyright laws are designed to protect **intellectual property** — the ownership of an individual's creative expression. As publishing attorney Steve Gillen explains:

> Copyright law concerns authorship or expression, i.e., words and images, not the underlying facts or ideas. . . . Facts, statistics, and concepts can be recited without permission [though failure to cite the source for them constitutes plagiarism unless they are common knowledge]. What you cannot do is copy or plagiarize the original or creative manner in which the original data was expressed.[22]

An exception to the prohibitions of copyright restrictions is the doctrine of **fair use**, which permits the limited use of copyrighted works without permission for the purposes of scholarship, criticism, comment, news reporting, teaching, and research.[23] This means that when preparing speeches for the classroom, you have much more latitude to use other people's creative work (with credit in all cases) without seeking their permission. For example, as long as you acknowledged your source, you could use a song from David Cook's CD as part of an in-class presentation. Different rules apply to the professional speaker, whose use of copyrighted materials is considered part of a for-profit "performance." In this event, you would need to obtain a performance license from a performing rights society such as ASCAP (American Society of Composers, Authors, and Publishers).

The same principles of fair use that apply to music apply to any graphics you might have decided to project during your presentation. Bear in mind, however, that while the *data* within a table or chart may not be copyrighted, its particular visual arrangement usually is.[24] Thus, you must accurately credit both the *source of the data* as well as the *creator of its graphic display*. For example, suppose that for a speech on women in the sciences you locate a graph in *Time* magazine that visually illustrates the percentage of men versus women who receive Ph.D.s in the sciences and engineering. The source of the data is a federal government agency, which falls within the public domain. However, as the creator of the graph, *Time* magazine owns the copyright for this particular display of the data.

The long and short of it? If you are a professional public speaker who makes use of copyrighted materials in your speeches, you must obtain copyright clearance. For speeches created for onetime use in the classroom or for other nonprofit, educational purposes, accurately crediting your sources will often suffice. (For more on copyright, visit the U.S. Copyright Office online at www.copyright.gov.)

SELF-ASSESSMENT CHECKLIST

An Ethical Inventory

_____ 1. Do I distort any information to make my point?

_____ 2. Does my speech focus on issues rather than on personalities?

_____ 3. Do I try to foster a sense of inclusion?

_____ 4. Is my topic socially constructive?

_____ 5. Is the content of my message as accurate as I can make it?

_____ 6. Whenever appropriate, do I acknowledge alternative and opposing views so that my audience can make informed decisions?

_____ 7. Do I acknowledge each of my sources?

_____   Direct quotations

_____   Paraphrased information

_____   Facts and statistics gathered from any source other than your own research

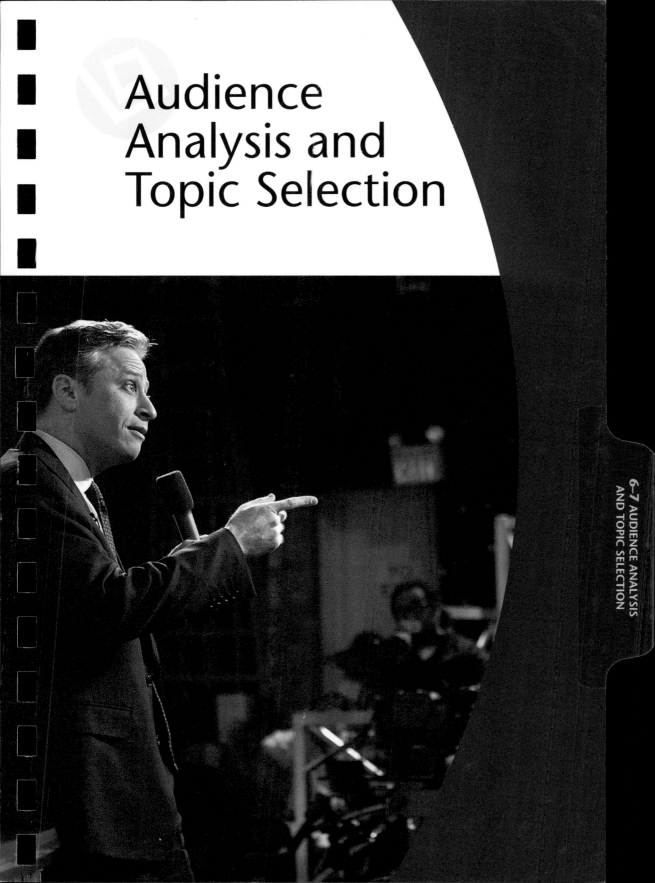

Audience Analysis and Topic Selection

Audience Analysis and Topic Selection

AUDIENCE ANALYSIS AND
TOPIC SELECTION (81–123)

Speaker's Reference
Audience Analysis and Topic Selection

6. Analyzing the Audience

Learn about Your Audience and Adapt Your Message Accordingly

- Identify what your audience needs and wants to know. (p. 89)
- Show audience members why the topic should interest them. (p. 90)

Evaluate Audience Attitudes, Beliefs, and Values toward the Topic

- Directly appeal to listeners' core values in your message. (p. 88)
- Adjust your approach depending on whether they have positive, negative, or neutral values, attitudes, and beliefs. (p. 90)

Establish Common Bonds Between Yourself and the Audience

- Focus on areas of agreement. (p. 90)
- Stress mutual bonds through shared experiences. (p. 90)

Anticipate Audience Expectations of the Speech Occasion

- Adjust your speech to the occasion. (p. 91)
- Adjust your speech when addressing a captive audience. (p. 91)

Address the Age Range of Your Audience

- Offer examples they will recognize and find relevant. (p. 92)

Consider the Socioeconomic Status of Your Audience

- Know that personal attitudes, beliefs, and goals are closely tied to occupational status. (p. 93)
- Use examples that are appropriate to the audience's level of sophistication and education. (p. 93)

Consider Religious and Political Affiliations

- Identify potential religious sensitivities and tread carefully. (p. 93)
- To the extent possible, gauge the audience's degree of political involvement and tread sensitively. (p. 94)

Avoid Judgments Based on Gender Stereotypes and Avoid Sexist Language

- Treat gender-related issues evenly. (p. 94)
- Anticipate listeners' attitudes with respect to gender. (p. 94)

Consider How Disability May Affect Audience Members

- Review both your topic and your delivery in light of the potential disabilities of audience members. (p. 95)
- Use language and examples that are respectful of persons with disabilities. (p. 95)

Adapt to Cultural Differences

- Identify the ethnic and cultural background of audience members. (p. 96)
- Identify listeners' major values and cultural orientation related to your topic and adapt your speech accordingly. (p. 97)
- Consult cross-national polls to further identify audience attitudes. (p. 98)
- Focus on universal values. (p. 98)

Gather Information about Your Audience from a Variety of Sources

- Consider interviewing one or more representatives of the audience. (p. 100)
- For classroom speeches, consider questionnaires or instant polls. (p. 100)
- Look for information about the audience in published sources, such as company Web sites, brochures, articles, and other related materials. (p. 102)

Investigate the Logistics of the Speech Setting

- Find out in advance what the physical setting will be like. (p. 103)
- Plan appropriately for the length of your speech, and be on time. (p. 103)
- Learn about the seating arrangement and where you will be placed. (p. 103)
- Be sensitive to recent events that may affect audience members. (p. 103)
- Consider the meaning of the speech event to audience members and the underlying reason for your speech (the rhetorical situation). (p. 103)

7. Selecting a Topic and Purpose

Be Aware That Speech Topics May or May Not Be Assigned

Select from the Three General Speech Purposes

- Use an informative speech to increase audience understanding and awareness. (p. 106)
- Use a persuasive speech to effect change in audience attitudes, beliefs, values, or behavior. (p. 106)
- Use a special occasion speech when the specific event calls for entertainment, celebration, commemoration inspiration, or setting a social agenda. (p. 108)

Consider Various Approaches to Selecting Your Topic

- Rely on your own interests. (p. 109)
- Survey current events. (p. 110)
- Consider controversial and community issues. (p. 110)
- Avoid overused topics. (p. 111)

Try Brainstorming to Generate Ideas

- Use lists and word association. (p. 111)
- Diagram your ideas on paper using a topic map. (p. 112)
- Use subject indexes at Internet search sites. (p. 112)

Narrow Your Topic and Purpose

- Narrow your topic to align with time constraints, audience expectations, and the occasion. (p. 118)
- Use action terms to develop your specific purpose. (p. 119)

Formulate the Thesis Statement

- State the thesis as a single, declarative sentence that poses the central idea of your speech. (p. 119)
- Use the thesis to help you develop main points. (p. 120)
- Make the thesis statement relevant and motivating by adding key words or phrases and considering audience interests. (p. 123)

Speaker's Reference

KEY TERMS

Chapter 6

audience analysis
audience-centered approach
pandering
attitudes
beliefs
values
perspective taking
identification
captive audience
demographics
target audience
generational identity
socioeconomic status (SES)

gender
sexist language
gender stereotypes
persons with disabilities (PWD)
co-culture
individualistic cultures
collectivist cultures
uncertainty avoidance
high-uncertainty avoidance cultures
low-uncertainty avoidance cultures

power distance
linear-active cultures
multi-active cultures
reactive cultures
interview
questionnaire
closed-ended question
fixed alternative question
scale question
open-ended question

Chapter 7

general speech purpose
informative speech
persuasive speech

special occasion speech
brainstorming
word association

topic map
specific speech purpose
thesis statement

Analyzing the Audience 6

Have you ever seen an advertisement that was so convincing that you made a mental note to purchase the product it described? What was it about the ad that made such an impression? Perhaps it featured a pair of athletic shoes or a particular brand of jeans. Did the ad suggest that it could fulfill a personal need? Did it portray an image that you wanted to project?

Advertisers are shrewd analysts when it comes to reading people's needs and wants. The best of them can closely target both our desires and our fears. In at least one sense, to make a successful speech or presentation you must function like an advertiser. To capture an audience's attention and bring your listeners to your point of view, you too must present a topic in ways that are meaningful to them. **Audience analysis** is the process of gathering and analyzing information about audience members *with the explicit aim of adapting your message to the information you uncover.* What are your listeners' views with respect to your topic? What do they need or want to know? How much do audience members have in common with one another? How familiar are they with the speech topic? What most concerns them about it?

Adapt to Audience Psychology

 WEB Chapter quizzes

One of the most important lessons you can learn as a speaker is that people tend to evaluate messages in terms of their own — rather than the speaker's — attitudes, beliefs, and values. As a result, you are far more likely to engage your listeners' attention if you let their relevant interests and background guide you in constructing your speech.

Maintaining an **audience-centered approach** while preparing a speech — from the beginning steps of selecting the speech topic to making decisions about how you will organize, word, and deliver it — is the only way to ensure that your message will be meaningful to your audience. However, being audience-centered does *not* mean that you must abandon your own convictions or cater to the audience's whims. This practice, called **pandering**, will only undermine your credibility in the eyes of the audience. Think of audience analysis as an opportunity to get to know and establish common ground with audience members, just as you might do with a new acquaintance. The more you find out about someone, the more you can discover what you share in common and how you differ.

IDENTIFY AUDIENCE MEMBERS' ATTITUDES, BELIEFS, AND VALUES

The audience members' attitudes, beliefs, and values provide crucial clues to how receptive they will be toward your topic and your position on it. While we tend to use these three terms interchangeably, each reflects a distinct mental state that reveals a great deal about us.

Attitudes are our general evaluations of people, ideas, objects, or events.[1] To evaluate something is to judge it as relatively good or bad, useful or useless, desirable or undesirable, pretty or ugly, tasteful or tasteless, and so on. People generally act in accordance with their attitudes (although the degree to which they do so depends on many factors).[2] If listeners have a positive attitude toward reading, for example, they're likely to read and to want to listen to a speaker discuss books. If they have a negative attitude toward religion, chances are they'll avoid attending religious services — as well as speeches praising the value of religion.

Attitudes are based on **beliefs** — the ways in which people perceive reality.[3] They are our feelings about what is true. Whereas attitudes deal with how we feel about some activity or entity ("Reading is good" or "God is good"), beliefs refer to our level of confidence about the very existence or validity of something ("I believe God exists" or "I'm not so sure that God exists"). The less faith listeners have that something exists — UFOs, for instance — the less open they are to hearing about it.

Both attitudes and beliefs are shaped by **values** — our most enduring judgments about what's good and bad in life, as shaped by our culture and our unique experiences within it. For some of us, the sanctity of marriage between a man and woman is a core value. For others, the value of social justice supersedes that of material comfort. Whatever the nature of our core values, they are central to our sense of who we are. We have fewer values than either attitudes or beliefs, but they are more deeply felt and resistant to change.

In the United States, researchers have identified a set of core values, including *achievement and success, equal opportunity, material comfort, hard work, practicality and efficiency, change and progress, science, democracy,* and *freedom.*[4] A survey of several Asian societies reveals such core values as the spirit of *harmony, humility toward one's superiors, awe of nature,* and a *desire for prosperity.*[5] People in every culture also possess values related to their personal relationships, religion, occupation, and so forth. Table 6.1 illustrates some of these values in China, India, Mexico, and Iraq.

If you can determine your listeners' relevant core values, you can refer to them in your speech, potentially making your message far more personally relevant and motivating. For example, seeking to uncover core values relating to the environment, the Biodiversity Project asked a representative sample of Americans to choose their most important personal reason for protecting the environment.[6] The three values most widely cited included: (1) wanting one's family to enjoy healthy surroundings; (2) feeling responsible for future generations (stewardship); and (3) believing that nature is God's creation and as such, sacred. Based on this information, the organization counseled its

TABLE 6.1 • Core Values in China, India, Mexico, and Iraq

China	India	Mexico	Iraq
• Modesty	• Family orientation	• Group loyalty	• Devoutness
• Tolerance	• Material success and creativity	• Mañana (cyclical time)	• Hospitality
• Filial piety			• Gender inequality
• Stoicism	• Fatalism	• Machismo	• Values rhetoric
• Respect for hierarchy	• Do-it-yourself mentality	• Family closeness	• Pride in ancient heritage
• Pride (not losing face)	• Honor of family and group	• Saving face at all costs	• Moralistic
• Wisdom	• Problem-solving	• Deference to age	
		• Mysticism, fatalism	

Source: Adapted from material in Richard D. Lewis, *When Cultures Collide: Leading across Cultures,* 3rd ed. (Boston, Mass.: Intercultural Press-Nicholas Brealey International, 2005).

speakers to directly touch upon these values in their presentations, offering the following as an example:

> We care about our family's health, and we feel a responsibility to protect our loved ones' quality of life. The local wetland provides a sanctuary to many plants and animals. It helps to clean our air and water and provides a space of beauty and serenity. All of this is about to be destroyed by irresponsible development.[7]

IDENTIFY LISTENERS' DISPOSITION TO THE TOPIC, SPEAKER, AND OCCASION

With any speech, it's important to try to uncover the audience's feelings and expectations — or *disposition* — toward (1) the topic of your speech, (2) you as the speaker, and (3) the speech occasion. This **perspective taking** will help you see things from your listeners' point of view.

Gauge Listeners' Disposition toward the Topic

As a general rule, people pay more attention to and feel more positively about topics that are in keeping with their values and beliefs. The less we know about something, the more indifferent we tend to be. One way to gauge an audience's attitude toward a topic is by asking: What do my listeners know about the topic? What is their level of interest? How do they feel about it? Then you can adjust the speech accordingly. Table 6.2 on the following page contains some general guidelines for addressing different types of audiences.

Gauge Listeners' Disposition toward the Speaker

How audience members feel about you will have considerable bearing on their attentiveness and responsiveness to your message. A speaker who is well liked can gain at least an initial hearing by an audience even if listeners are unsure

TABLE 6.2 • Guidelines for Appealing to Different Types of Audiences

Type of Audience	Strategy
If the topic is *new to listeners* . . .	Start by showing why the topic is relevant to them. Relate the topic to familiar issues and ideas about which they already hold positive attitudes.
If listeners know *relatively little* about the topic . . .	Stick to the basics, explain the topic's relevance, and include background information. Steer clear of jargon, and define any unclear terms.
If listeners hold *negative attitudes* toward the topic . . .	Focus on establishing rapport and credibility. Don't directly challenge listeners' attitudes; look instead for areas of agreement and move from there. Offer evidence from sources they are likely to accept in order to demonstrate why a negative attitude is unfounded, and then give good reasons for developing a positive attitude toward the topic.[1] (See Chapters 24 and 25 on persuasion.)
If listeners hold *positive attitudes* toward the topic . . .	Tell stories with vivid and colorful language that reinforces listeners' attitudes.[2]
If listeners are a *captive audience* . . .	Pay close attention to the length of your speech, especially if other speakers precede and follow you. Motivate listeners to pay attention by focusing as much as possible on what is most relevant to them.

1. James C. McCroskey, Virginia P. Richmond, and Robert A. Stewart, *One-on-One: The Foundations of Interpersonal Communication* (Englewood Cliffs, N.J.: Prentice-Hall, 1986), 76.

2. Herbert Simon, *Persuasion in Society* (Thousand Oaks, Calif.: Sage, 2001), 385–87.

of what to expect from the message itself. Conversely, an audience that feels negatively toward the speaker will disregard even the most important or interesting message. We tend to put up barriers against people whom we hold in low regard.

Listeners have a natural need to identify with the speaker and to feel that he or she shares their perceptions,[8] so look for ways to establish a common bond, or **identification**, between you and the audience. Many speakers do this by emphasizing those aspects of the topic about which the audience members are likely to agree. When speaking to an audience of abortion rights activists, for example, Senator Hillary Clinton called on opposing sides in the debate to find "common ground" by focusing on education and abstinence:

> We should all be able to agree that we want every child born in this country and around the world to be wanted, cherished, and loved. The best way to get there is to do more to educate the public about reproductive health, about how to prevent unsafe and unwanted pregnancies.[9]

Clinton clearly was attempting to reach out beyond her core constituency and achieve some measure of identification with those who oppose abortion.

Sharing a personal story, emphasizing a shared role, and otherwise stressing mutual bonds all help to create identification. So too does the strategic use of inclusive language such as *we, you, I,* and *me.* Notice, for example, how Clinton uses the personal pronoun *we* to encourage identification with the speech goal (see Chapter 16 for more on inclusive language) and to build a sense of community within the audience. Even your physical presentation can foster identification. We're more apt to identify with the speaker who dresses like us (or in a manner we aspire to) than with someone whose style and grooming seems strange or displeasing.

 CHECKLIST

Respond to the Audience as You Speak

As you deliver your speech, monitor the audience for signs of how they are receiving your message. Look for bodily clues as signs of interest or disengagement:

✓ Large smiles and eye contact suggest a liking for and agreement with the speaker.

✓ Arms closed across the chest may signal disagreement.

✓ Averted glances, slumped posture, and squirming usually indicate disengagement.

Be prepared to adjust your speech to audience reactions. If audience interest seems to be flagging, consider a change of pace by:

✓ Asking the audience a few questions related to their experiences on the topic.[1]

✓ Sharing a story linked to your topic that might encourage identification.

1. Nick Morgan, *Working the Room: How to Move People to Action through Audience-Centered Speaking* (Cambridge, Mass.: Harvard Business School Press, 2003), 181–97; 2.

Gauge Listeners' Disposition toward the Occasion

Part of any audience analysis is anticipating audience reactions to the rhetorical situation. Depending on the occasion, people bring different sets of expectations and emotions to a speech event. Imagine attending your college graduation ceremonies. Your general feelings of joy and goodwill are likely to spill over to the commencement speaker, and unless he or she does quite poorly, you will probably enjoy the speech. In contrast, imagine being a businessperson attending a conference — it's your third night away from home, you're tired from daylong meetings, and now you're expected to listen to company executives explain routine production charges for the coming fiscal year. Unlike the graduation ceremony, your presence at the business meeting is a requirement, so you may not feel as enthused about this speech occasion. Obviously, a **captive audience** will tend to present greater challenges than one that is voluntary (see Table 6.2 for tips on appealing to a captive audience).

Adapt to Audience Demographics

 Links

Another way to discover valuable insights about audience members is to learn demographic information about them. **Demographics** are the statistical characteristics of a given population. Six characteristics typically considered when analyzing speech audiences are *age, socioeconomic status* (including *income, occupation,* and *education*), *religious and political affiliations, gender, disability,* and *ethnic and cultural background*. Bear in mind that any number of other traits—for example, place of residence and group membership—may be important to investigate. This also holds true with regard to persons of different cultural backgrounds. Kenyan students, for instance, report that birthplace, specifically whether they are of rural or urban origin, and literacy level are key demographic characteristics to consider when addressing them as an audience.[10]

Knowing audience demographics will help you identify your **target audience**—those individuals whom you are most likely to influence in your direction. Think about a student preparing his or her first speech for a public speaking class at a community college. According to the American Association of Community Colleges, the average age of community college students is twenty-nine years. Students as young as 16 attend classes alongside 40-year-olds. Thirty-nine percent are the first generation to attend college, and twenty-seven percent of full-time students work full time.[11] Community college students also bring a mix of racial and ethnic backgrounds to the classroom. How does your own classroom compare? Are you just as likely to engage a 40-year-old single mother of two school-aged children about the need for an all-volunteer military as the 19-year-old single male classmate sitting nearby? While it is always preferable to reach as many people as possible, if your audience is diverse and you know you cannot reach everyone equally, plan your remarks with specific attention to your target audience.

AGE

Age can be a very important factor in determining how listeners will react to a topic. Each age group brings with it its own concerns and, broadly speaking, psychological drives and motivations. The quest for identity in adolescence (around the ages of 12–20), for example, differs markedly from the need to establish stable careers and relationships in early adulthood (ages 20–40). Similarly, adults in their middle years (40–65) tend to grapple with a full plate of issues related to career, children, aging parents, and an increased awareness of mortality. And as we age (65 and older), physical changes and changes in lifestyle (from work to retirement) assume greater prominence.

In addition to sharing the concerns associated with a given life stage, people of the same generation often share a familiarity with significant personages, local and world events, noteworthy popular culture, and so forth. Thus, bearing in mind the **generational identity** of your audience can help you evaluate your topic from an audience-centered perspective. Americans born in the United States in the 1950s, for example, are likely to retain vivid memories of

John F. Kennedy's assassination as well as television shows such as *The Mickey Mouse Club* and *Gunsmoke.* If you mention these TV programs to younger people, however, chances are you'll draw blank stares. By the same token, most older people take little notice of today's popular youth figures or the current stars of hip-hop and Top 40 music.

SOCIOECONOMIC STATUS

Socioeconomic status (SES) includes income, occupation, and education. Knowing roughly where an audience falls in terms of these key variables can be critical in effectively targeting your message.

Income

Income determines people's experiences on many levels. It directly affects how they are housed, clothed, and fed, and determines what they can afford. Beyond this, income has a ripple effect, influencing many other aspects of life. For example, depending on income, health insurance is either a taken-for-granted budget item or an out-of-reach dream. The same is true for travel and leisure activities. Given how pervasively income affects people's life experiences, insight into this aspect of an audience's makeup can be quite important.

Occupation

In most speech situations, the occupation of audience members is an important and easily identifiable demographic characteristic that the speaker should try to determine in advance. The nature of people's work has a lot to do with what interests them. Occupational interests are tied to several other areas of social concern, such as politics, the economy, education, and social reform. Personal attitudes, beliefs, and goals are also closely tied to occupational standing.

Education

Level of education strongly influences people's ideas, perspectives, and range of abilities. For example, studies show that people who have a college education work in higher-status occupations and generally earn higher pay than do non-college graduates. A higher level of education, moreover, appears to be associated with greater fluctuation in personal values, beliefs, and goals. In other words, people with higher levels of education may be more open to changing their minds.

If the audience is generally well educated, your speech may need to be quite sophisticated. When speaking to a less-educated audience, you may choose to clarify your points with more examples and illustrations.

RELIGION

The *Encyclopedia of American Religions* identifies more than 2,300 different religious groups in the United States,[12] from Seventh-day Adventists to Zen Buddhists, so don't assume that everyone in your audience shares a common religion. Furthermore, don't assume that all members of the same spiritual tradition agree on all issues. For example, people who identify themselves as Catholic disagree on birth control and divorce, Jews disagree on whether to recognize same-sex unions, and so forth. Awareness of an audience's general religious orientation can be especially helpful when your speech addresses a topic as potentially controversial as religion. Stem-cell research, capital punishment, same-sex marriage, and teaching about the origins of humankind — all are rife with religious overtones and implications.

POLITICAL AFFILIATION

As with religion, beware of making unwarranted assumptions about an audience's political values and beliefs. Some people like nothing better than a lively debate about public-policy issues. Others avoid anything that smacks of politics. And many people are very touchy about their views on political issues. Unless you have prior information about the audience's political values and beliefs, you won't know where your listeners stand.

GENDER

Gender is another important factor in audience analysis, if only as a reminder to avoid the minefield of gender stereotyping. Distinct from the fixed physical characteristics of biological sex, **gender** is our social and psychological sense of ourselves as males or females.[13] Making assumptions about the preferences, abilities, and behaviors of your audience members based on their presumed gender can seriously undermine their receptivity to your message. Using **sexist language**, language that casts males or females into roles on the basis of sex alone, will also swiftly alienate many listeners. Equally damaging to credibility is the inclusion of overt **gender stereotypes** — oversimplified and often severely distorted ideas about the innate nature of what it means to be male or female.

Beyond ensuring that you treat issues of gender evenly, try to anticipate the audience members' attitudes with respect to gender and plan accordingly. Consider the case of the speaker, Brianna, whose speech focused on the role of women in the U.S. military:

> Brianna's audience consisted of Korean-, Vietnam-, and Gulf-war-era veterans. Brianna's thesis was that although females cannot fight in combat units, a result of the military's combat exclusion rule, women in fact serve in many frontline capacities: as combat medics, as members of support deployment battalions, and as pilots of attack helicopters and fighter jets.
>
> As Brianna described the harrowing conditions facing some of these soldiers, she noticed several of the older veterans frowning and fidgeting. Then, one veteran in the back of the auditorium shouted out that women didn't belong in the military. "They're not built for combat," he said. "They're only built for performing with the USO."

Feeling flustered but quickly regaining her footing, Brianna paused for a moment, then said, "Women in the military have a long and honorable history, especially as nurses, and they've made heroic contributions. So I think your comment is sexist. However, things *are* very different today, and it is probably shocking to hear about some of the issues they now face."

Brianna then threw out a question. "How likely was it," she asked the audience, "for a woman to fly an attack helicopter during the Korean or Vietnam wars?"

"None of the girls flew planes in those days," said one veteran.

"All the girls were nurses then," commented another.

Although Brianna had anticipated that a number of audience members might find her topic controversial, she was surprised both by the strength of the audience's reactions and the blatant sexism that was expressed. Wisely, she responded to the sexist remark evenly and without anger and facilitated a limited discussion before continuing with her prepared remarks.

The demographic of age played a large role in audience members' attitudes toward Brianna's topic. Depending on audience composition, ethnic and cultural background could have also come into play. In certain cultures, for example, it is unthinkable that women would take any role in the military.

DISABILITY

According to the U.S. Census Bureau, more than 18 percent of the population five years and older (excluding persons who are institutionalized) has some sort of mental, physical, emotional, or employment disability; 12 percent have a severe disability. Over 14 percent of those enrolled in college and graduate school are counted as disabled.[14] Problems range from sight and hearing impairments to constraints on physical mobility and employment. Thus disability is another demographic variable to consider when analyzing an audience. Keep **persons with disabilities (PWD)** in mind when you speak and use language and examples that afford them respect and dignity.

ETHNIC OR CULTURAL BACKGROUND

An understanding of and sensitivity to the ethnic and cultural composition of your audience are also key factors in delivering a successful — and ethical — speech. As a speaker in a multicultural and multiethnic society, you are all but certain to encounter audience members of different national origins (or first-generation Americans). Some may have a great deal in common with you. Others may be fluent in a language other than yours and must struggle to understand you. Still other members of the audience may belong to a distinct **co-culture**, a social community whose values and style of communicating may or may not mesh with your own.

In the United States, at least 30 percent of the population belongs to a racial or ethnic minority group, and 34 million people, or 11 percent, are

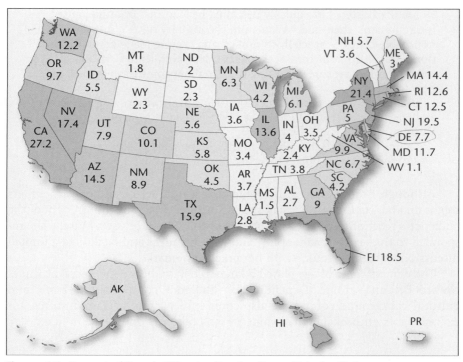

Figure 6.1 Percent of People Who Are Foreign Born, State by State
Note: Data are limited to the household population and exclude the population living in institutions, college dormitories, and other group quarters.
Source: U.S. Census Bureau, 2005 American Community Survey.

foreign-born (see Figure 6.1).[15] Worldwide, there are more than two hundred recognized countries, and many more distinct cultures within these countries.[16] How might you prepare to speak in front of an ethnically and culturally diverse audience, including that of your classroom? In any speaking situation, your foremost concern should be to treat your listeners with dignity and to act with integrity. You do this by infusing your speech with the pillars of character described in Chapter 5: trustworthiness, respect, responsibility, and fairness. Since values form the basis of people's attitudes and actions, identifying those of your listeners can help you to communicate with sensitivity and appeal to their interests and needs in an appropriate manner.

Adapt to Cultural Differences

Cross-cultural scholars offer numerous models that compare and contrast differing values and associated behavioral patterns among various cultures. Two that may be particularly helpful to you as a public speaker include Geert Hofstede's *value dimensions* and Richard D. Lewis's *cultural types*.

HOFSTEDE'S VALUE-DIMENSIONS MODEL

Geert Hofstede has identified the following five major "value dimensions" as being significant across all cultures, but in widely varying degrees;[17] he then ranks forty countries in terms of how they compare on these dimensions.

Individualism versus Collectivism.   **Individualistic cultures** tend to emphasize the needs of the individual rather than those of the group, upholding such values as individual achievement and decision making. In **collectivist cultures**, by contrast, personal identity, needs, and desires are viewed as secondary to those of the larger group. For example, audience members who share collectivist values may believe that the wishes of parents and the family group must come before their own. In Hofstede's analysis, the United States, Australia, Great Britain, and Canada rank highest on individualism. Venezuela, Peru, Taiwan, and Pakistan rank highest in collectivist characteristics.

High Uncertainty versus Low Uncertainty.   **Uncertainty avoidance** refers to the extent to which people feel threatened by ambiguity. **High-uncertainty avoidance cultures** tend to structure life more rigidly and formally for their members, while **low-uncertainty avoidance cultures** are more accepting of uncertainty in life and therefore allow more variation in individual behavior. Among the nations Hofstede investigated, Portugal, Greece, Peru, Belgium, and Japan rank highest in uncertainty avoidance; the United States, Sweden, Denmark, Ireland, and Norway rank lowest.

High Power Distance versus Low Power Distance.   **Power distance** is the extent to which a culture values social equality versus tradition and authority. Cultures with *high levels of power distance* tend to be organized along more rigidly hierarchical lines, with greater emphasis placed on honoring authority. Those with *low levels of power distance* place a higher value on social equality. High power distance countries include India, Brazil, Singapore, Greece, Venezuela, and Mexico. Austria, Finland, Denmark, Norway, New Zealand, and Israel rank lowest on this dimension. The United States ranks somewhat above the midpoint range among the nations in Hofstede's survey.

Masculine versus Feminine.   The *masculinity and femininity dimension* refers to the degree to which a culture values traits that it associates with masculinity and with femininity. Traditional masculine traits include ambition, assertiveness, performance, and overt displays of manliness. Feminine traits stress nurturance and cooperation. In Hofstede's analysis, Ireland, the Philippines, Greece, and South Africa ranked highest in masculinity, while Sweden, Norway, Finland, and Denmark ranked highest in femininity. The dominant values in the United States were weighted toward masculinity.

Long- versus Short-term Time Orientation.   Hofstede's *time orientation* dimension refers to the degree to which a culture values behavior that is directed to future rewards, such as perseverance and thrift, versus behavior that is directed toward the present, such as expecting quick results. In Hofstede's analysis, China, Hong Kong, Taiwan, and South Korea ranked highest in long-term orientation, while Great Britain, Canada, the Philippines, Germany, and Australia ranked highest in short-term orientation.

LEWIS'S CULTURAL TYPES MODEL

In place of value dimensions, Richard D. Lewis offers a model that classifies cultures according to whether they are linear-active, multi-active, or reactive.[18]

Linear-active Cultures.   People in **linear-active cultures** approach tasks system-atically, preferring to do one thing at a time and in organized fashion. They tend to be cool, factual, decisive planners. In Lewis's model, Germany, Switzerland, the United States, and Great Britain rank highest in linear-active traits; Argentina, Brazil, Mexico, Sub-Saharan Africa, and the Arab Middle East rank lowest.

Multi-active Cultures.   Persons in **multi-active cultures** tend to do many things at once, are people-oriented, and extroverted. They tend to be warm, emotional, talkative, and impulsive. Argentina, Mexico, Brazil, Chile, and the Arab Middle East rank highest in multi-active traits.

Reactive Cultures.   In **reactive cultures**, people rarely initiate discussions or actions, preferring to listen to what others have to say first. They tend to be courteous, accommodating, and good listeners. Japan, China, Vietnam, Korea, and Thailand rank highest in reactive traits.

Bear in mind that the value dimensions and cultural patterns identified by Hofstede and Lewis reflect those of the *dominant culture;* they do not necessarily reflect the behaviors of all the groups living within a society. Although individu-alism characterizes the dominant culture of the United States, for example, vari-ous co-cultures, such as Hispanic Americans, Native Americans, and, to varying degrees, African Americans, have been described as collectivist in nature.[19]

CONSULT CROSS-CULTURAL POLLS

To hone in on how persons from other cultures might view specific issues, you can consult cross-cultural polls, such as those conducted by the World Values Survey (www.worldvaluessurvey.org). The accompanying Public Speaking in Cultural Perspective box, "Cross-National Comparisons of Attitudes, Values, and Beliefs," offers suggestions on investigating attitudes, beliefs, and values across cultures; see also "Published Sources" on p. 102.

FOCUS ON UNIVERSAL VALUES

As much as possible, it is important to try to determine the attitudes, beliefs, and values of audience members. At the same time, you can focus on certain values that, if not universally shared, are probably universally aspired to in the

Public Speaking in Cultural Perspective
Cross-National Comparisons of Attitudes, Values, and Beliefs

Cross-national surveys can be extremely useful for learning about how values vary across cultures. Globally, the largest-scale cross-national surveys are the World Values Survey (www.worldvaluessurvey.org) and those conducted by the International Social Survey Program (ISSP) (www.issp.org/data.shtml). Using representative national samples of at least one thousand individuals, the World Values Survey offers a fascinating look at the values and beliefs of people in sixty-six countries. Through this resource you can discover how people of other nations feel about work, family, religion, and even who should do the housework.

The International Social Survey Program surveys forty-three nations on the following broad topics: environment, family and changing gender roles, national identity, religion, role of government, social inequality, social networks, and work orientations. Researchers pose the same series of questions to a representative sample in each of the forty-three member nations. For example: "What percentage of people believe that the Bible is the actual word of God?" In Great Britain, only 5 percent believe that it is, whereas in the United States, 30 percent hold this belief. To investigate attitudes, values, and beliefs related to your topic, go to the ISSP archive Web site (www.gesis.org/en/data_service/issp/search/index.htm) and click on "Search in Codebooks and Question." Then insert a phrase or a key term (e.g., "belief in God"). A list of surveys that focus on your terms may appear; you can then examine the individual surveys.

ESL Speaker's Notes
Comparing Cultural Values

As you consider your own values, think about the influence of culture. Can you identify values that you hold but that your listeners probably will not share? What role does culture play in these values? Are there certain values your listeners are likely to hold that you do not share? What are these? Have you experienced clashes of values between yourself and others regarding what you believe to be good and bad, important and unimportant? As you think about your own values, the role culture plays in them, and the values of those around you, consider how you can use this information to develop a speech that will best express what you want to say.

human heart. These include love, truthfulness, fairness, freedom, unity, tolerance, responsibility, and respect for life.[20]

Techniques for Learning about Your Audience

Now that you know the kind of information to look for when analyzing an audience, how do you actually uncover it? Unlike a professional pollster, you cannot survey thousands of people and apply sophisticated statistical techniques to analyze your results. On a smaller scale, however, you can use the same techniques. These include the interview, the survey, and published sources.

INTERVIEWS

An **interview** is a face-to-face communication for the purpose of gathering information. Interviews, even brief ones, can reveal a lot about the audience's interests and needs. You can conduct interviews one-on-one or in a group, in person, or by telephone or e-mail, depending on the time and the feasibility of making such arrangements. Rather than interviewing everyone in an audience, which often would be impractical, consider interviewing a smaller sampling or even just *one* knowledgeable representative of the group that you will address. As in questionnaires (see next page), interviews usually consist of a mix of open and closed-ended questions. (See Chapter 9 for more on conducting interviews.)

SURVEYS

Written surveys, or **questionnaires**, are designed to gather information from a pool of respondents. Because you can distribute them simultaneously to large groups, questionnaires offer a more efficient means of gathering information from a pool of people than do interviews.

A questionnaire consists of a series of questions containing a mix of open- and closed-ended questions. **Closed-ended questions** are designed to elicit a small range of specific answers supplied by the interviewer:

> "Do you or did you ever smoke cigarettes?"
> Yes _____   No _____   Sometimes _____

Answers will be "Yes," "No," or "I smoked for *x* number of years." Closed-ended questions are especially helpful in uncovering shared attitudes, experiences, and knowledge of audience members.

Closed-ended questions may be either fixed alternative or scale questions. **Fixed alternative questions** contain a limited choice of answers, such as "Yes," "No," or "Sometimes" (as in the preceding example). **Scale questions** — also called *attitude scales* — measure the respondent's level of agreement or disagreement with specific issues:

> "Flag burning should be outlawed":
> Strongly agree _____   Agree _____   Undecided _____   Disagree _____
> Strongly disagree _____

In addition to agreement, scale questions can be used to measure how important listeners judge something to be and how frequently they engage in a particular behavior:

> "How important is religion in your life?"
> Very important _____   Important _____   Moderately important _____
> Of minor importance _____   Unimportant _____
> "How frequently do you attend religious services?"
> Very frequently _____   Frequently _____   Occasionally _____   Never _____

Open-ended questions are designed to allow respondents to elaborate as much as they wish:

"How do you feel about using the results of DNA testing to prove innocence or guilt in criminal proceedings?"

Open-ended questions are particularly useful for probing beliefs and opinions. They elicit more individual or personal information about the audience members' thoughts and feelings. They are also more time-intensive than closed-ended questions.

Often, it takes just a few questions to get some idea of where audience members stand on each of the demographic factors. By using a mix of open- and closed-ended questions, you can draw a fairly clear picture of the backgrounds and attitudes of the members of your audience.

Sample Audience Analysis Questionnaire

Part I: Demographic Analysis

1. What is your age?   _____ years
2. What is your sex?   _____ Male   _____ Female
3. Please indicate your primary heritage:
   _____ American Indian   _____ African American
   _____ Asian American   _____ European
   _____ Latino   _____ Middle Eastern   _____ Other
4. Please indicate your level of formal education:
   _____ High school   _____ Some college
   _____ College degree   _____ Other (please specify)
5. What is your approximate annual income range?
   _____ less than $10,000   _____ $10,000–$25,000
   _____ $25,000–$50,000   _____ $50,000–$75,000
   _____ $75,000–$100,000   _____ over $100,000
6. With which political party are your views most closely aligned?
   _____ Democratic   _____ Republican   _____ Neither (Independent)
7. Please check the box below that most closely matches your religious affiliation:
   _____ Buddhist   _____ Christian
   _____ Hindu   _____ Jewish
   _____ Muslim   _____ Not religious   _____ Other (please specify)
8. How would you characterize your religious involvement?
   _____ Very religious _____ Somewhat religious _____ Not very religious
9. How would you characterize your political position?
   _____ Liberal   _____ Conservative   _____ Moderate

(Continued)

Part II: Analysis of Attitudes, Values, and Beliefs on a Specific Topic

Indicate your answers to the following questions about stem cell research by checking the appropriate blank.

10. It is unethical and immoral to permit any use of stem cells for medical research.

_____ Strongly agree _____ Agree   _____ Undecided

_____ Disagree   _____ Strongly disagree

11. Do you think the government should or should not fund stem cell research?

_____ Should   _____ Should not   _____ Neutral

12. Rather than destroy stem cells left over from *in vitro* fertilization, medical researchers should be allowed to use them to develop treatments for diseases.

_____ Strongly agree _____ Agree   _____ Undecided

_____ Disagree   _____ Strongly disagree

13. What kind of cells come to mind when you think of stem cell therapy?

_____

14. Which of the following has had the biggest influence on your thinking about stem cell research?

_____ Media reports   _____ Opinions of friends and family

_____ Your religious beliefs   _____ Personal experience

PUBLISHED SOURCES

Another avenue to explore when analyzing your audience is published sources. Organizations of all kinds publish information describing their missions, goals, operations, and achievements. Sources include Web sites and related online articles, print brochures, newspaper and magazine articles, annual reports, and industry guides. These materials often contain a wealth of information that you can use to identify salient information about your listeners.

You might also consider consulting published opinion polls, such as the following:

- Pew Research Center: pewresearch.org/
- National Opinion Research Center (NORC): www.norc.uchicago.edu
- Roper Center for Public Opinion Research: ropercenter.uconn.edu
- The Gallup Organization: www.gallup.com

Polls offer excellent insight into the range of attitudes that exist about a given issue as well as how representative state, national, or international samples responded to questions about your issue. You may also wish to use the published data as supporting material for your speeches (see Chapter 8).

Analyze the Speech Setting

As important as analyzing the audience is assessing (and then preparing for) the setting in which you will give your speech — size of audience; location, time, and length of speech; and rhetorical situation.

SIZE OF AUDIENCE AND PHYSICAL SETTING

The size of the audience and the physical setting in which a speech occurs can have a significant impact on the outcome of the speech. The atmosphere of a classroom is different from that of a banquet room, an outdoor amphitheater, or a large auditorium. The larger the group, the less you are likely to interact with the audience; you will also need to plan how to position yourself and adjust your voice, sometimes with the aid of acoustical equipment.

TIME AND LENGTH OF SPEECH

Both the time at which your speech is scheduled and its length will affect listeners' receptivity to it. People gathered at breakfast, lunch, or dinner meetings, for example, come to the speech occasion with more than one agenda. They may wish to hear you, but they will also want time to eat and converse with other people. Your boss or fellow employees may expect to receive information quickly so that they can proceed to other business.

In any speaking situation, always find out how long you are expected to speak. Bear in mind that few matters of speech etiquette are as annoying to an audience as a speaker's apparent disregard for time. Start on time and end well within the time allotted to you. Table 6.3 includes typical lengths for various presentations.

TABLE 6.3 • Typical Length of Presentations	
Kind of Presentation	**Length**
In-depth speech	15–20 minutes
Presentation to boss	1–10 minutes
Toast	1–2 minutes
Award acceptance speech	3–5 minutes

THE SPEECH CONTEXT (RHETORICAL SITUATION)

Any speech or presentation you deliver will always occur in a particular context. You may be the third of six speakers on a panel, for instance. You might precede or follow a speaker who is more dynamic or well known than you are. Your listeners may be preoccupied with unusual circumstances — a local sports team just won a championship, extreme weather conditions have disrupted everyday life, the president of the company just resigned, and so forth. By being alert to any of these contingencies, you can address them in your speech.

✔ **CHECKLIST**

Analyzing the Speech Situation

_____ 1. Where will the speech take place?

_____ 2. How long am I expected to speak?

_____ 3. How many people will attend?

_____ 4. Will I need a microphone?

_____ 5. How will any projecting equipment I plan to use in my speech, such as an LCD projector, function in the space?

_____ 6. Where will I stand or sit in relation to the audience?

_____ 7. Will I be able to interact with listeners?

_____ 8. Who else will be speaking?

_____ 9. What special events or circumstances of concern to my audience should I acknowledge?

✔ **CHECKLIST**

Reviewing Your Speech in Light of Audience Demographics

1. Have you reviewed your topic in light of the age range and generational identity of your listeners? Do you use examples they will recognize and find relevant?

2. Have you avoided making judgments based on stereotypes?

3. Is your speech free of biased, insensitive language?

4. Does your speech acknowledge potential differences in values and beliefs and address them sensitively?

5. Have you evaluated your vocabulary for potentially confusing meanings?

6. Have you considered the appropriateness of your topic in relation to the demographic factors you have uncovered about your audience?

7. Are your explanations and examples at a level that is appropriate to the audience's sophistication and education?

8. Do you make any unwarranted assumptions about the audience's political or religious values and beliefs?

9. Does your topic carry religious or political overtones that are likely to stir your listeners' emotions in a negative way?

10. Do you address the concerns of both male and female listeners?

Selecting a Topic and Purpose 7

The first task in preparing any speech is to select a topic and purpose that are appropriate to the audience, the occasion, and the overall speech situation (i.e., the *rhetorical situation*). Choosing the topic and identifying the purpose of your speech answers three key questions: "What precisely is my speech about?" "What is my goal in speaking to the audience?" and "What specifically do I want my listeners to know or do?" Considering these questions as you prepare your speech can help you stay focused and convey a coherent message using directly relevant material that is immediately useful to your audience.

Assigned versus Self-Selected Topics

In your speech course you will probably be assigned a variety of speeches, some of which might have a specified topic. In work, civic, and other speech contexts, you may or may not select your own speech topic. Your boss might ask you to prepare a talk explaining how your group developed its latest product. The local Chamber of Commerce might request that you address "businesses that grow a town's tax base." Often speakers are invited because of their expertise in a subject area, so they cover the same general topic in every speech.

Even speakers who give frequent speeches on the same general topic never give the same speech twice. Similarly, even though you might be assigned a topic, or speak on the same topic over and over, you still must refine and adapt to each speech situation. You must decide on a specific purpose or goal for each talk. Even when the choice of topic is your decision, you are usually given some direction as to how your talk should be presented. For example:

- You may be given a *purpose*. The adviser for the youth group you volunteer for asks you to speak at the next meeting to "boost morale." The topic you select for this is yours to decide.

- You are given *time constraints*. Your boss informs you that you are on the agenda to talk to a group of grade-school visitors for three to five minutes next Monday. How you fill this time is up to you.

- You are given a *challenge*. The master of ceremonies for a roast to honor a retiring local newspaper writer asks you to "make the audience laugh."

Seldom does anyone mean it when he or she tells you, "Whatever you talk about is fine." Yes, the topic may be fine, but in most cases the person who invited you to speak has an outcome or end result in mind. In other words, when you select a topic for a speech, you are also held accountable for accomplishing a certain purpose.

Identifying the General Speech Purpose   Chapter quizzes

Public speeches can be classified as addressing one of three general speech purposes: to *inform,* to *persuade,* or to *mark a special occasion.* The **general speech purpose** for any speech answers the question "Why am I speaking on this topic for this particular audience and occasion?"

The general speech purpose is sometimes indicated by the occasion. Often, however, rather than specifically dictating a speech purpose, the occasion only suggests parameters of appropriateness. For example, one commencement speaker may decide to prepare a persuasive speech that exhorts the graduates to contribute time after graduation to public service, whereas another speaker might decide to entertain the audience with a lighthearted look at what the students' degrees will, or perhaps will not, do for them in the future. Although the two speakers select different general speech purposes (one to persuade and the other to entertain), both select and adapt their topics to ensure appropriateness to the occasion.

WHEN THE GENERAL SPEECH PURPOSE IS TO INFORM

Your purpose in an informative speech is to share your knowledge or point of view about a subject with others. To do so, you define, describe, explain, or demonstrate this knowledge. Thus the general purpose of an **informative speech** is to increase the audience's understanding and awareness of a topic. You want the audience to learn something.

When selecting a topic for an informative speech, try to gauge how much the audience already knows about it. There's no surer way to lose audience members' attention than to speak over — or under — their heads. If the speech topic assumes a lot of background knowledge, make certain that the audience has it. Likewise, if the audience is familiar with the topic, it's important to present it in a way that is fresh and interesting. Everyone knows about taxes, for instance, but we're always eager to hear about new ways to avoid paying them. Just about any topic is appropriate for an informative speech (see Tables 7.1 and 7.2), as long as you present it with the goal of giving the audience something new to expand their understanding and awareness.

WHEN THE GENERAL SPEECH PURPOSE IS TO PERSUADE

Persuasive speeches also increase listeners' knowledge of a topic. But the general purpose of a **persuasive speech** goes further — it is to effect some degree of change in the audience's attitudes, beliefs, or even basic values (the latter being the hardest to change). Or the purpose may be to change specific behaviors (e.g., "Don't practice unsafe sex") or reinforce existing behaviors (e.g., "Keep practicing safe sex").

TABLE 7.1 • Some General Categories of Informative Topics					
Objects	**People**	**Events**	**Concepts**	**Processes**	**Issues**
Their construction, function, symbolic or concrete meaning. For example, how wind energy generators work; what's behind Native American cliff dwellings.	Their biographies, noteworthy achievements, anecdotes about them. For example, the early life of Barack Obama; the identity of Osama bin Laden.	Noteworthy or unusual occurrences, both past and present. For example, rebuilding of New Orleans; criminality in professional sports.	Abstract and difficult ideas or theories. For example, the nature of love; the definition of peace; the theory of intelligent design.	A series of steps leading to an end result. For example, how one becomes an astronaut; how to succeed in a college internship.	Problems or matters of dispute. For example, U.S. border security; whether reality television is really real.

TABLE 7.2 • Sample Informative Speech Topics

- The Importance of Sleep to General Well-Being
- Getting the Most from the Campus Recreation Center
- Trends in Religion in the Workplace
- Low-Carb Cooking
- Careers in Forensic Science
- Mentoring Teens
- Switching from a PC to a Mac
- Advances in Breast Cancer Treatment

Topics or issues on which there are competing perspectives are particularly suitable for persuasive speeches. Controversial issues such as immigration reform, stem cell research, and binge drinking naturally lend themselves to a persuasive purpose because people hold strongly contrasting opinions about them. But other topics can be suitable as well. The only requirement is that the topic allow the speaker to fashion a message that is intended to effect some degree of change in the audience (see Table 7.3).

Consider the topic of binge drinking. A persuasive purpose (e.g., "To persuade my audience to avoid binge drinking") would be appropriate if:

- The audience feels considerably different about the topic than you do (e.g., members of the audience engage in binge drinking).

- The audience holds similar attitudes and beliefs about the topic as you do but needs direction in taking action (e.g., the audience consists of people who want to help friends avoid binge drinking and are seeking strategies to do so).

- The audience agrees with your position but is likely to encounter opposing information or circumstances in the near future (e.g., beer will be readily available at an upcoming annual celebration of college students).

TABLE 7.3 • Sample Persuasive Speech Topics

- Take College Courses Online
- Study Abroad for a Semester
- Avoid Cosmetic Surgery
- Take Nutritional Supplements for Better Health
- Plagiarism Will Ruin Your Career
- Switch to Hands-Free Cell Phones in Cars
- Let's Restructure the College Football Championships
- Adopt a Senior Citizen
- Learn Another Language

WHEN THE GENERAL SPEECH PURPOSE IS TO MARK A SPECIAL OCCASION

Some speeches are prepared for a purpose dictated by a special occasion. **Special occasion speeches** include speeches of introduction, speeches of acceptance, speeches of presentation, roasts and toasts, eulogies, and after-dinner speeches, among others. Depending on the specific event, the general purpose of a special occasion speech will be variously to entertain, celebrate, commemorate, inspire, or set a social agenda (see Chapter 27). Special occasion speeches sometimes have secondary specific purposes to inform or to persuade. For example, a speech to mark the occasion of Veterans Day might include a message to devote more time to volunteering with the local Veterans Hospital.

 CHECKLIST

Identifying Your General Speech Purpose

✓ Is your goal in speaking primarily to increase the audience's knowledge of a topic or to share your point of view? (Your general purpose is to inform.)

✓ Is it primarily to effect some degree of change in the way your listeners view things? (Your general purpose is to persuade.)

✓ Is it primarily to mark a special occasion? (Your general purpose will be variously to entertain, celebrate, commemorate, inspire, or set a social agenda.)

Choosing a Topic for the Classroom Speech Topics

Selecting a topic for a classroom speech can be approached from a variety of angles. You can begin "at the top," so to speak, by focusing on broad social issues of national or even global consequence; or you can start closer to the ground, by considering your own interests and life experiences. Once you settle on a topic, the real challenge becomes taming your enthusiasm to fit the available time and the audience's interests.

PERSONAL INTERESTS: LOOKING WITHIN

Selecting a topic you are familiar with—and, most important, enthusiastic about—offers many advantages. Because you are interested in the topic, researching it will be enjoyable. You'll look forward to learning more about it and will probably pay more attention to what you discover. You'll bring a sense of genuine enthusiasm to your presentation. Depending on the depth of your background knowledge, you may convey great competence and thereby encourage the audience to see you as a highly credible speaker. In the classroom, your instructor, as well as your classmates, may be much more interested in learning about topics based on your own experiences and expertise.

As seen in Table 7.4, personal interests run the gamut from favorite activities and hobbies to deeply held goals and values. Personal experiences provide powerful topics, especially if, by your sharing them, the audience in some way benefits from your experience. "What it's like" stories also yield interesting topics.

TABLE 7.4 • Identifying Topics

Favorite Hobbies	Personal Experiences	Values	Goals
• Sports • Volunteering* • Cars • Fashion • Reading • Video games • Music • Travel • Outdoor life	• Exotic travel destinations • Service in the armed forces • Volunteer work in a foreign country* • Immigration • Life-threatening disease • Service vacations*	• Building a greater sense of community* • Spirituality • Philanthropy* • Political activism*	• Being a high-tech entrepreneur • Attending graduate or professional school • Starting a family • Being fit* • Learning more about my religion
Specific Subject Interests	**Social Problems**	**Health and Nutrition**	**Current Events**
• Local history* • Ancient history • Politics* • Art* • Religion • Science	• Road rage* • Violence in the schools • Lack of affordable child care • Environmental issues*	• Diets • Herbal and vitamin supplements • Exercise regimens • HMOs • Health insurance* • Assisted living	• Pending legislation—crime bills, property taxes, land use* • Political races • Race relations • National security
Grassroots Issues	**New or Unusual Angles**	**Issues of Controversy**	
• Land development versus conservation* • Local organizations* • School issues	• Unsolved crimes* • Unexplained disappearances • Scandals	• Creationism versus evolution • Airport security • Stem cell research	

*Note: Topics marked with an asterisk are good possibilities for speeches on civic responsibility.

For example, what is it like to go hang gliding in the Rocky Mountains or to be part of a medical mission's team working in Uganda?

Some personal interest topics are particularly amenable for speeches addressing civic responsibility. For example, the purpose of a speech based on your experience in taking a service vacation (e.g., building homes in a Mexican village) could be to generate interest in establishing a local organization for promoting and structuring service vacations, or for encouraging the development of a local chapter of Habit for Humanity, an organization that builds homes for low-income families. Or you could use your interest in video games to develop a speech about how occupational therapists use video game technology to provide elderly persons with activities that engage physical and mental fitness, and argue that this technology can be placed in senior citizen centers for recreational purposes.

CURRENT EVENTS AND CONTROVERSIAL ISSUES

People are constantly barraged with newsworthy topics, but few of us have the time to delve into them. What is actually behind the oil-for-food scandal involving the United Nations and Iraq? What can and cannot be done to better secure our nation's borders? Similarly, controversial issues of the day—patenting human genes, Bible study in the schools, and so on—usually earn their place in the limelight because they reflect our deepest concerns and profoundly affect us as individuals and as members of society. Many of us appreciate and even hunger for information that broadens our understanding of these topics. As an interested and responsible citizen of your community, you are surrounded by issues that beg for attention and action. Select the ones that are most important to you and your audience, and see if you can make a difference.

GRASSROOTS ISSUES: OPPORTUNITIES FOR CIVIC ENGAGEMENT

Most people respond with interest to issues that affect them directly, and, barring war and federal tax hikes, these tend to be of a local nature. Parents want to know about quality day care in the area; town residents need information about upcoming referendums. People are also interested in what other people in their communities are doing. Are you involved in a club on campus, or do you volunteer for a local charity? Consider giving a speech about the organization's mission, membership, or upcoming event. Review your community's newspapers for the local headlines; conduct a Google or Yahoo! search on local community news. Research of this kind can produce numerous topics of current interest. Here are a few examples:

- A Google News search of "Cincinnati, Ohio, local issues" turns up "Poverty in City Ranks Third in U.S."

- A Google News search of "Beckley, West Virginia, local issues" reveals "Storm Water Utility Faces Big Challenge."

- A search of Yahoo! News for "Santa Fe, New Mexico, local issues" shows "N.M. Resumes Planning for Medical Marijuana Program."

- A Windows Live News Search for "Bellevue, Washington, local issues" presents "Local Hospital Promoting Sober Driving."
- A Windows Live News Search for "Columbia, Missouri, local issues" reveals "Bar Patio Sparks Downtown Debate."

Similar issues face the town or city in which your college or university is located.

Moving from community-related topics to a purpose for your speech will not be as difficult as it may seem, especially if you are focusing on issues that are relevant and meaningful to your audience. And, because such topics are in the news, you should be able to find ample materials to develop your speech.

AVOID TOPICS THAT ARE OVERDONE: YOU BE THE EXPERT

Even though there an almost limitless number of speech topics, the same ones seem to appear repeatedly in student classroom speeches across the country. Imagine how many students give speeches on the following topics each year: abortion, gun control, steps for getting a job, how to change a flat tire, Oprah Winfrey, *Star Wars,* and spring break vacations.

Students so often select topics like these because they are popular, they touch upon some deep-seated beliefs and values, and they are relatively easy to research. But because it's very hard to come up with any new claims or arguments, you are unlikely to change anyone's mind on the topic and may cause an in-class controversy. Equally important, you are likely to bore your instructor, who has probably heard dozens, if not hundreds, of speeches on this same topic.

You stand a better chance of engaging the interests of your classmates and your instructor if you avoid very common topics and develop ones that are novel or unique. One way to do this is to consider your own expertise, ranging from an unusual hobby (collecting rare books on eBay; hiking city neighborhoods) or uncommon job for people your age (opening your own tea room; piloting a shrimp boat) to a particular skill you possess (constructing Web sites; managing small investments; refereeing youth sports). Fresh ideas based on firsthand knowledge and experiences are more intriguing and provide an opportunity for others to get to know you better.

Using Brainstorming to Generate Ideas

Brainstorming is a problem-solving technique that involves the spontaneous generation of ideas through word association, topic mapping, or even Internet browsing of subject indexes.

WORD ASSOCIATION

To brainstorm by **word association**, write down *one* topic in which you are interested and that you think will appeal to your audience. If you have trouble getting started, simply write down a word related to anything — music, relationships, food — that currently interests you. Then jot down the first thing that comes to mind when you read the word or words you have just written. It doesn't have to be related to the first topic. As soon as your words remind you of something, write it down. Now read the second item on the list, and write down your next thought. If a word or words remind you of more than one thing, write down all of them. Try writing your thoughts as quickly as you can, without analyzing them as topics. Repeat the process until you have a list of fifteen to twenty items.

Once you have generated a list, review each item as a potential topic. Narrow the list to two or three, and then select a final topic. The following list is an example of the word-association brainstorming technique:

- health ⇒ alternative medicine ⇒ naturopathy ⇒ fraud
- children ⇒ parenting ⇒ working ⇒ day care ⇒ living expenses
- diving ⇒ snorkeling ⇒ Bahamas ⇒ conch shells ⇒ deep-sea fishing
- Internet ⇒ Web sites ⇒ blogging ⇒ MySpace
- exercise ⇒ StairMaster ⇒ weight lifting ⇒ swimming

TOPIC MAPPING

If you find it helpful to visualize ideas, try drawing a **topic map** (see Figure 7.1). Put a potential topic in the middle of a piece of paper and draw a circle around it. As related ideas come to you, write them down as shown in Figure 7.1. Keep going until you hit upon an idea that appeals most to you.

INTERNET SEARCH INDEXES

Popular Internet portals offer alphabetized directories covering a wide range of topics; examples include Yahoo! Web Directory, Lycos Topics, and MSN Directory. To access these directories, consult the portal's home page for a link to an

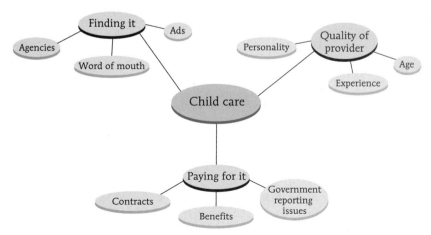

Figure 7.1 A Topic Map

A–Z list of topics. Then click on any one of the categories (e.g., "Arts") to access a page full of links to subtopics within that category, some of which lead to pages with even more subtopics. Essentially what you get is an electronic version of word-association brainstorming, except that Web servers provide the keywords; all you need to do is isolate the topic that interests you. (See Chapter 10 for more on using subject directories.)

Some Internet search portals, such as Ask.com, present search results in the form of the familiar list of related words. In a space right at the top of the page is an encyclopedia-type entry that gives a definition and description of, say, "black bears" with a link to more information. In the right-hand margin of the page is a section that gives links to blogs that contain references to the search subject "black bear." Just below the blog listing is a list of results from a diction-ary search for the term, showing a couple of definitions for "black bear." In the left-hand margin of the page is a list of alternative searches you could choose to pursue, labeled "Expand Your Search, including Grizzly Bears, Brown Bears, and Polar Bears." Even more useful, perhaps, is another list in the left-hand margin, labeled "Narrow Your Search," listing, in this case, options to search:

American **Black** Bear

What Do **Black Bears** Eat

Where Do **Black Bears** Live

Facts about **Black Bears**

Black Bear Information

How Long Do **Black Bears** Live

Black Bears Habitat

North American **Black Bear**

How Fast Can a **Black Bear** Run

Are **Black Bears** Endangered

Our point in describing this kind of search page is to show you how the Internet can be a helpful tool for identifying and narrowing a speech topic, a part of the process we take up next.

✓ **CHECKLIST**

Criteria for Selecting a Topic

_____ 1. Is the topic appropriate to the occasion?

_____ 2. Will the topic appeal to my listeners' interests and needs?

_____ 3. Is the topic something I can speak about with enthusiasm and insight?

_____ 4. Can I research and report on the topic in the time allotted?

_____ 5. Will I be able to offer a fresh perspective on the topic?

From Source to Speech
Brainstorming on the Web

Why Brainstorming?

The ability to move instantaneously from one link to another makes the Web an excellent brainstorming tool. With just a few clicks of a mouse, you can move quickly among informative text, images, video, and audio, resulting in surprising connections among ideas. This ease of navigation makes the Web an excellent tool for narrowing a topic if you search it efficiently.

Methods for Brainstorming Online

To brainstorm effectively on the Web, consider what stage you are at in the speechmaking process.

IF YOU DON'T YET HAVE A TOPIC . . .

. . . conduct a general search in the Yahoo! Directory, which will provide you with a wealth of information in various formats, including articles, books, and images.

IF YOU HAVE AN IDEA BUT ARE UNSURE WHAT TO SAY ABOUT IT . . .

. . . read what peers and subject experts have to say about such topics as business and finance, health and fitness, and music and entertainment on About.com, or other specialized search engines.

IF YOU'RE LOOKING FOR CROSS-DISCIPLINARY SCHOLARSHIP . . .

. . . link to Google Scholar for a trove of credible sources, including peer-reviewed papers, theses, books, abstracts, and articles.

IF YOU ARE ACTUALLY READY TO RESEARCH MATERIALS . . .

. . . go straight to your town or university library portal for sources that have been vetted by experts for reliability and credibility.

114

Sample Results from Brainstorming on the Web

A visual learner, Andrea chose to start brainstorming on Google Images. In the general search bar, she typed in the name of her favorite actress, "Audrey Hepburn." This search resulted in several intriguing images of the Hollywood icon.

A close look at her favorite photo of the elegant star left Andrea wondering if perhaps Audrey's long cigarette holder was part of her glamour.

Do stars portrayed as smokers in contemporary films influence audience perception of those stars? Of smoking? Curious, Andrea searched Google Scholar for *impact of smoking in movies*. Her search displayed all abstracts and articles containing each word in the search field.

Had Andrea used quotation marks around her terms, i.e., "impact of smoking in movies," only articles containing this exact phrase would have appeared in the results.

Andrea located several abstracts by reputable sources stressing the negative impact of smoking in the movies, especially on young audiences. She settled on this as a topic, then moved to a library portal to locate the full articles, as well as to conduct further research—the next step in developing her thesis.

From Source to Speech
Narrowing Your Topic Using a Library Portal

One of several ways to research your topic is to use a library's online portal. Wanting to narrow down the topic of smoking in the movies, Andrea searched the Brooklyn Public Library portal. There, she located relevant and available books and gained immediate access to online periodical databases. These databases allowed her access to full-text articles from sources that have been evaluated for reliability by librarians, and they helped her avoid the paid links and unreliable sources that general search sites such as Google typically include in their listings.

Navigating the Library Portal

Andrea selected from the menu of links on the portal home page to find different sources: "Library Catalog" to find books, the "Articles and Databases" to find full-text articles and materials from the "invisible" Web.

A basic search within "Articles and Databases" resulted in multiple hits, all with numerous articles from various databases.

This recent psychology journal article reveals a level of results that general search engines do not find—an article that has undergone peer review and can be viewed in full-text, PDF form.

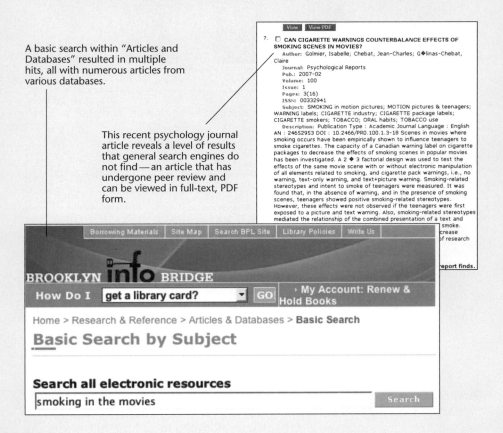

7. ☐ **CAN CIGARETTE WARNINGS COUNTERBALANCE EFFECTS OF SMOKING SCENES IN MOVIES?**
Author: Golmier, Isabelle; Chebat, Jean-Charles; G◆linas-Chebat, Claire
Journal: Psychological Reports
Pub.: 2007-02
Volume: 100
Issue: 1
Pages: 3(16)
ISSN: 00332941
Subject: SMOKING in motion pictures; MOTION pictures & teenagers; WARNING labels; CIGARETTE industry; CIGARETTE package labels; CIGARETTE smokers; TOBACCO; ORAL habits; TOBACCO use
Description: Publication Type : Academic Journal Language : English AN : 24652953 DOI : 10.2466/PRO.100.1.3-18 Scenes in movies where smoking occurs have been empirically shown to influence teenagers to smoke cigarettes. The capacity of a Canadian warning label on cigarette packages to decrease the effects of smoking scenes in popular movies has been investigated. A 2 ◆ 3 factorial design was used to test the effects of the same movie scene with or without electronic manipulation of all elements related to smoking, i.e., no warning, text-only warning, and text+picture warning. Smoking-related stereotypes and intent to smoke of teenagers were measured. It was found that, in the absence of warning, and in the presence of smoking scenes, teenagers showed positive smoking-related stereotypes. However, these effects were not observed if the teenagers were first exposed to a picture and text warning. Also, smoking-related stereotypes mediated the relationship of the combined presentation of a text and ... smoke. ... crease ... f research

... eport finds.

Borrowing Materials | Site Map | Search BPL Site | Library Policies | Write Us

BROOKLYN info BRIDGE

How Do I [get a library card? ▼] [GO] › My Account: Renew & Hold Books

Home > Research & Reference > Articles & Databases > **Basic Search**

Basic Search by Subject

Search all electronic resources

[smoking in the movies] [Search]

Sample Results from an Advanced Library Portal Search

To focus her research and to steer clear of unwanted sources, Andrea conducted an advanced search. This function allowed her to better distill the specific purpose of her speech and to develop her thesis statement.

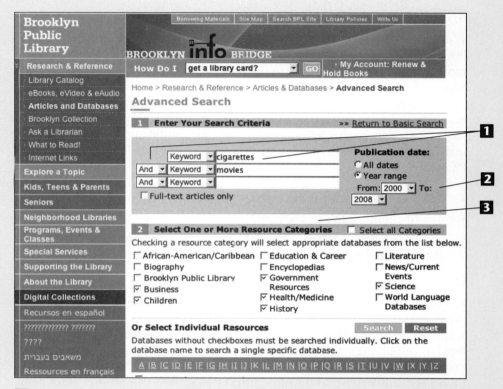

1 Linking search terms *cigarettes* and *movies* by Boolean operator "AND" resulted in hits containing both these terms.

2 Limiting search from 2000 to 2008 ensured that only articles in this period appeared.

3 Limiting the resource categories yielded results that covered only the areas on which she wanted to focus her thesis.

Refining the Topic and Purpose

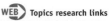 **WEB** Topics research links

Once you have an idea of what you'd like to speak about and have established the general speech purpose, you need to narrow your focus so that it's in line with time constraints, audience expectations, and the nature of the occasion.

NARROWING THE TOPIC

When you narrow a topic, you focus on specific aspects of it to the exclusion of others. Naturally, you focus on those aspects of the topic that interest you the most. You also carefully evaluate them in light of audience interests, knowledge, and needs.

What is the purpose of your speech? How long is the speech to be? How much time do you have to do research? How much information can you responsibly review so that you avoid distorting or falsifying the material? Imagine, for example, how your approach to the topic "Americans' Love of Cell Phones" may change as you consider the following factors:

- The speech is for an informative speaking assignment.
- The time limit is five to seven minutes.
- The library does not have a copy of a recent telecommunications industry report on cell phone use, and your computer is down.

Just as brainstorming can be used to discover a general topic, it can also be helpful in narrowing one. One way of doing this is to brainstorm by category. What sorts of categories can you break your general topic into? Do an Internet search as described on page 113 to generate some categories. For the general topic of cell phones, some related categories are models, manufacturers, and calling plans. As you brainstorm by category, ask yourself, "What questions do I have about the topic? Am I more interested in how cell phones work or in how much they cost? What aspect of cell phones is my audience most likely to

 CHECKLIST

Narrowing Your Topic

✓ What is my audience most likely to know about the subject?
✓ What are my listeners most likely to want to learn?
✓ What aspects of the topic are most relevant to the occasion?
✓ Can I develop the topic using just two or three main points?
✓ How much can I competently research and report on in the time I am given to speak?

want to hear about?" You can also use topic mapping or browsing an Internet directory to narrow your topic. Here's how it's done:

*   Write your topic in the middle of a blank piece of paper and circle it.
*   Using the topic circle as the spoke of a wheel, surround it with as many categories as you can associate it with.
*   Keep breaking down the categories until you settle on an aspect of the topic that will interest your audience and that you can research and report on in the time allotted.

FORMING A SPECIFIC SPEECH PURPOSE

The **specific speech purpose** zeroes in on the goal of the speech. It expresses both the topic and the general speech purpose in action form and in terms of the specific objectives you hope to achieve with your speech. The specific purpose statement answers the question, "Precisely what is it about my topic that I want the audience to learn/do/reconsider/agree with?"

Consider the topic of cooking. Say you've narrowed the topic to "Alternative Cooking Methods" and further to "Solar Cooking," and selected an informative speech purpose. Now you would need to decide what you want to accomplish in your speech. Given that your speech goal is to inform, perhaps you want audience members to understand the process and benefits of solar cooking. Or perhaps you want to provide your listeners with resources for obtaining equipment and recipes for solar cooking. Your primary objective becomes your specific speech purpose:

GENERAL TOPIC:	Alternative Cooking Methods
NARROWED TOPIC:	The Process and Benefits of Solar Cooking
GENERAL PURPOSE:	To inform
SPECIFIC PURPOSE:	To inform my audience about the benefits associated with the process of solar cooking

From Topic and Purpose to Thesis Statement

Now that you know your topic and have devised your general and specific purposes, your next step is to formulate a thesis statement. The **thesis statement** is the theme or central idea of the speech stated in the form of a single, declarative sentence. The thesis statement concisely expresses what the speech will attempt to support from the speaker's point of view. It is a single line that serves to connect all the parts of the speech, much like a backbone. The main points, the supporting material, and the conclusion all emanate from and relate to the thesis.

Ethically Speaking
Ethical Considerations in Selecting a Topic and Purpose

Respect for your audience members and adaptation to their needs and interests should always guide your topic choices. What makes a speech ethical or unethical depends on how it empowers the audience to think or act. In other words, ethical considerations begin with your goal or purpose. Speakers who select persuasive purposes should be particularly careful; under pressure to sway an audience, some speakers may be tempted to tamper with the truth. As you review your speech goal, consider the following:

• Have you deliberately distorted information to achieve a desired result?
• Is it your intent to deceive?
• Do you try to coerce the audience into thinking or acting in a certain way?
• Have you knowingly tried to appeal to harmful biases?

   Although few hard-and-fast rules exist when it comes to ethical guidelines for selecting topics, some areas are clearly off-limits — at least in U.S. culture:

• The topic shows an audience how to perform actions prohibited by law.
• The topic provides audience members with information that may result in their physical or psychological harm.
• The topic humiliates or degrades the fundamental values of an audience's culture, religion, or political system.

The thesis statement and the specific purpose are closely linked. Both state the speech topic, but in different forms. The thesis statement concisely identifies, in a single idea, what the speech is about; *the specific purpose describes in action form what you want to achieve with the speech.* Note also that even though the specific speech purpose is seldom spoken by the speaker (whereas the thesis must be clearly stated because the entire speech rests on it), it is important to formulate the specific purpose for yourself (and to state it in writing for your instructor). By clearly stating the goal for your speech, you set in your mind exactly what you want it to accomplish.

USE THE THESIS STATEMENT TO CONVEY THE CENTRAL IDEA

The thesis statement conveys the central idea or core assumption about the topic (see Figure 7.2). Whether the speech is informative or persuasive, the thesis offers your comment on the topic. For instance, the thesis statement "Three major events caused the United States to go to war in 1941" expresses your view that three factors played a part in the U.S. entry into World War II. The speech is then developed from this thesis, presenting facts and evidence to support it.

   The thesis statement aids you in developing a coherent, understandable speech. Without the thesis statement, the audience cannot easily follow the

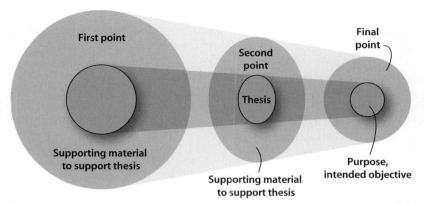

Figure 7.2 Supporting points maintain the thesis on idea through to the speech's specific purpose or intended objective.

ideas that make up the body of the speech. Thus you should postpone the development of main points and supporting material until you have correctly formulated the speech purpose and thesis statement (see Chapter 11).

The nature of the thesis statement varies according to the speech purpose. In a persuasive speech, your comment on the speech as stated in the thesis represents what you are going to prove in the address. All the main points in the speech are arguments that develop this position. Consider the following examples (all with the general purpose of persuading the audience):

Example 1

GENERAL PURPOSE: To persuade

SPECIFIC PURPOSE: To persuade the audience to raise money on behalf of the Sierra Club

THESIS: A donation to the Sierra Club is an investment in nature.

Example 2

SPECIFIC PURPOSE: To persuade the audience to vote for a political candidate

THESIS: A vote for Senator Juarez is a vote for progress.

Example 3

SPECIFIC PURPOSE: To persuade the audience that abstinence is the way to avoid the harm alcohol can cause

THESIS: Abstinence is the best way to avoid the harm alcohol can cause.

Notice that in each case, after you read the thesis you find yourself asking "Why?" or thinking "Prove it!" This will be accomplished by the evidence you give in the main points (see Chapter 11).

The thesis statement in an informative speech conveys the scope of the topic, the steps associated with the topic, or the underlying elements of the topic. It describes what the audience will learn. Consider the following examples:

Example 1

GENERAL PURPOSE:	To inform
SPECIFIC PURPOSE:	To educate the audience about how the U.S. government is structured
THESIS:	The three branches of the U.S. government form our unique representative democracy.

Example 2

SPECIFIC PURPOSE:	To enable audience members to invest their money properly
THESIS:	There are six steps to investing in the stock market.

Example 3

SPECIFIC PURPOSE:	To establish the chronology of the U.S. entry into World War II
THESIS:	Three major events caused the United States to go to war in 1941.

USE THE THESIS STATEMENT TO GUIDE YOUR SPEECH PREPARATION

The point of creating a thesis statement is to help you identify precisely what your speech is about. As you develop the speech, use the thesis to keep yourself on track. Depicted as the inner core of a cylinder, as in Figure 7.2, the thesis is a straight and narrow path from when it is first stated to when it reaches your last point and fulfills the speech purpose. As you research materials, review them in the light of whether they contribute to the thesis or stray from it. When you actually draft your speech, work your thesis statement into it and restate it where appropriate. Doing so will encourage your audience to understand and accept your message.

Following are some examples of student speech topics and the corresponding general and specific speech purposes and thesis statements:

Example 1

SPEECH TOPIC:	Blogs
GENERAL SPEECH PURPOSE:	To inform
SPECIFIC SPEECH PURPOSE:	To inform my audience of three benefits of keeping a Web log

THESIS STATEMENT:	Maintaining a Web log provides the opportunity to practice writing, a means of networking with others who share similar interests, and the chance to develop basic Web site management skills.

Example 2

SPEECH TOPIC:	Student Internships
GENERAL SPEECH PURPOSE:	To persuade
SPECIFIC SPEECH PURPOSE:	To persuade my audience that internships are beneficial
THESIS STATEMENT:	To prepare for a difficult job market and enhance your résumé, you should get a student internship to help link your academic studies.

✓ **CHECKLIST**

Formulating the Thesis Statement

_____ 1. Does my thesis statement sum up in a single sentence what my speech is about?

_____ 2. Is it restricted to a single idea?

_____ 3. Is it in the form of a complete declarative sentence?

_____ 4. Is it stated in a way that is relevant to the audience?

Making the Thesis Statement Relevant and Motivating

As you refine the draft of your speech, try to express the thesis statement in a way that will motivate the audience to listen. In many cases, creating a relevant thesis can be accomplished quite easily by adding a few key words or phrases. You can preface an informative thesis statement with a phrase such as "Few of us know" or "Contrary to popular belief" or "Have you ever." A persuasive thesis statement can also be adapted to establish relevance for the audience. Phrases such as "As most of you know" or "As informed members of the community" or "As concerned adults" can attract listeners' attention and interest and help them see the topic's relevance.

The exact phrasing or rewording of your thesis statement depends on the type of audience to which you are speaking. Once you gain some information about your audience members, you won't have trouble making the topic relevant for them.

Supporting
the Speech

Supporting the Speech

Speaker's Reference
Supporting the Speech

8. Developing Supporting Material

Alternate among Different Types of Supporting Materials

- Provide more than your own personal opinions or experiences. (p. 133)
- Illustrate each main point with several different types of supporting material. (p. 133)

Orally Cite Your Sources

- Reveal the source of your ideas in your speech. (p. 133)
- Provide enough context to establish the source's credibility. (p. 133)

Choose Accurate, Relevant, and Compelling Supporting Material

- Seek out compelling *examples* to illustrate or describe your ideas. (p. 134)
- Share *stories,* either real or hypothetical, to drive your point home. (p. 135)
- Use firsthand findings in the form of *testimony.* (p. 137)
- Hunt for relevant *facts,* or documented occurrences. (p. 139)
- Consider whether you need *statistics,* or quantified evidence, including frequencies, percentages, and averages. (p. 140)
  Draw your statistics from reliable sources and present them in context. Beware of cherry-picking and other unethical ways of presenting data.

Convince Listeners to Accept Your Supporting Material as Reliable and Credible

- To establish credibility, briefly mention the source's relevant credentials and past performance. (p. 146)
- To establish reliability, emphasize the source's trustworthiness. (p. 146)
- Use multiple credible and reliable sources, especially when making controversial claims. (p. 147)

9. Locating Supporting Material

Consider Using Both Primary and Secondary Sources

- *Primary research* includes interviews and surveys you conduct yourself. (p. 148)

129

Speaker's Reference

- Sources for *secondary research* include all credible information gathered by others, such as a library's holdings. (p. 148)

Plan a Research Strategy

- Avoid wasting time in the wrong places. (p. 148)
- Keep in mind your goal of substantiating your thesis. (p. 148)
- Consult reference librarians. (p. 149)
- When searching databases, consult the Search Tips section. (p. 150)

Consider Various Secondary Sources

- Books (p. 150)
- Newspapers and periodicals (p. 150)
- Government publications (p. 151)
- Reference works (e.g., encyclopedias, almanacs, books of quotations, poetry collections, and atlases) (p. 151)

Consider Conducting Interviews to Uncover Information

- Plan your questions well in advance; beware of vague, leading, and loaded questions. (p. 155)
- Strive to make a positive first impression. (p. 156)
- Use active listening strategies such as paraphrasing. (p. 157)
- Close the interview effectively. (p. 157)

Consider Conducting Surveys to Learn about Audience Attitudes

Develop an Effective System for Documenting Your Sources

- Accurately record each of your references. (p. 158)
- Record appropriate bibliographic information for each piece of evidence. (p. 158)
- Select a method to organize your sources, and follow it systematically. (p. 159)

As You Gather Your Research, Evaluate Its Credibility

- How was the data gathered? (p. 161)
- What is the author's background in the field of study? (p. 166)
- How credible is the publication? Who is the publisher? What are the contributors' qualifications? (p. 166)
- How reliable is the data? (p. 166)
- How recent is the reference? (p. 166)

10. Using the Internet to Support Your Speech

Strive for a Mix of Print and Internet Sources

- Recognize that much information is available only in print. (p. 167)
- Some materials are more readily accessible online, including those collected by the U.S. government. (p. 167)

Start Your Search at Your Library's Home Page

- Library portals provide an entry point for sources drawn from library holdings, including electronic holdings, that have been vetted for quality. (p. 167)
- Library holdings are organized systematically by professionals. (p. 168)
- Portals and virtual libraries can help you access the invisible Web. (p. 169)

Critically Evaluate All Information Found Online

- Check the most authoritative Web sites first. (p. 170)
- Evaluate authorship and sponsorship. (p. 170)
- Check for currency. (p. 170)
- Check that the site credits its sources and that sources are credible. (p. 170)
- Distinguish information from misinformation, propaganda, and disinformation. (p. 172)

Make the Most of Internet Search Tools

- *Search engines* automatically index the contents of the Web. (p. 173)
- *Meta-search engines* search several search engines simultaneously. (p. 174)
- *Specialized search engines* focus on specific topics. (p. 174)
- *Subject (Web) directories* contain searchable databases of sites organized by subject and reviewed by human editors. (p. 174)

Know When to Use a Search Engine or Subject Directory

- To find very defined information, use a *search engine* first. (p. 175)
- To find sites on a given subject, use a *subject (Web) directory*. (p. 176)
- To narrow a topic, use a *subject (Web) directory* first. (p. 176)

Know That Commercial Influences Can Taint Search Results

- For a fee, some search tools guarantee a higher ranking ("paid placement"). (p. 176)
- For a fee, some search tools guarantee inclusion, without guaranteeing higher ranking ("paid inclusion"). (p. 176)

Use Search Commands to Enhance Results

- Use the basic search commands correctly. (p. 177)
- Refine your search with field searching. (p. 178)

Record Your Sources Systematically

- Orally reveal the source of your ideas located online. (p. 179)
- Do not use Internet sources that you have not verified as to authorship, currency, reliability, and credibility. (p. 179)

KEY TERMS

Chapter 8

supporting material	anecdote	percentage
example	testimony	average
brief example	expert testimony	mean
extended example	lay testimony	median
hypothetical example	facts	mode
story	statistics	cherry-picking
narrative	frequency	

Chapter 9

invention	Dewey decimal number	almanac
primary research	periodical	fact book
secondary research	U.S. Government Printing Office (GPO)	atlas
database		interview
full-text database	encyclopedia	working bibliography
reference librarian	general encyclopedia	fabrication
Library of Congress call number	specialized encyclopedia	

Chapter 10

library portal	information	meta-search engine
virtual library	propaganda	specialized search engine
World Wide Web	misinformation	subject (Web) directory
invisible Web	disinformation	paid placement
domain	search engine	paid inclusion
tilde (~)	individual search engine	field searching

Developing Supporting Material

Often, the most important element in a good speech is not the topic itself but how it is developed and supported. You can easily see this in speeches on the same topic prepared by different speakers. Good speeches contain accurate, relevant, and interesting **supporting material** in the form of memorable examples, narratives, testimony, facts, and statistics. These "flesh out" the speech—they give substance to the speech's thesis or central idea.

Broadly speaking, supporting material performs three functions: (1) It creates interest and engages attention; (2) it illustrates, clarifies, and elaborates on the meaning of your ideas; and (3) it substantiates or proves that a statement is correct. As you gather supporting material, consider how you can use it to generate interest and to add solid evidence to your assertions.

Use a Variety of Supporting Materials   Research room

Virtually any speech you deliver will require a variety of supporting material other than your own personal opinion or experience. This holds true whether or not you possess expert knowledge on a topic. People want to know the truth about a given matter, and they will not merely accept your word for it. In general, listeners respond most favorably to a variety of supporting materials derived from multiple sources to illustrate each main point.[1] Alternating among different types of supporting material—moving from a story to a statistic, for example—will make the presentation more interesting and credible while simultaneously appealing to your audience members' different learning styles.

Refer Orally to Your Sources    Chapter quizzes

Equally important as the types of supporting material you select is mentioning the sources for them in your speech. Listeners place more value on conclusions drawn by multiple sources that they find credible.[2] Unlike a written bibliography, there is no set format for orally citing sources. As long as you clearly identify where your information came from and provide your listeners with enough context to accurately interpret it, you can vary your wording to suit your needs (see "From Source to Speech: Demonstrate Your Sources' Reliability and Credibility," pp. 144–145).

Offer Examples

"We learn by example" became a popular saying because it is indeed true. **Examples** illustrate, describe, or represent things. Their purpose is to aid understanding by making ideas, items, or events more concrete.

Study the text of any engaging speech and you will see that it is liberally sprinkled with good examples that clarify and enliven the speaker's message. Examples are particularly helpful when they are used to describe or explain things with which the audience may not be familiar. Examples can be brief or extended and may be either factual or hypothetical.

BRIEF EXAMPLES

Brief examples offer a single illustration of a point. Barrington D. Parker, in a speech about visa problems among foreign-born graduate students, uses the following brief example to illustrate that unlike students in many other countries, relatively few U.S. students pursue degrees in science and engineering:

> Your children and mine gravitate towards humanities and social science majors as opposed to the quantitative ones such as mathematics, natural science, or engineering. . . . This aspect of our culture is radically different from many other places in the world. For example, a member of the Yale Corporation originally from Bombay told us that if you were at a social gathering of professionals there, and a son or daughter was going to college, you would be positively embarrassed to admit that he or she was studying humanities or liberal arts. This meant you had somehow failed. The ablest, hardest-working students there are expected to become scientists, physicians, or engineers.[3]

EXTENDED EXAMPLES

Sometimes it takes more than a brief example to effectively illustrate a point. **Extended examples** offer multifaceted illustrations of the idea, item, or event being described, thereby getting the point across and reiterating it effectively. Risa Lavizzo-Mourey, M.D., uses an extended example to illustrate how the physicians in her audience could use their knowledge to shift the course of childhood obesity:

> In the questions you ask about childhood obesity, and in the answers you find, you will hold the power to alter the course of America's health history as it occurs. . . . For example, I can think of at least three moments in the past half century that dramatically shifted the course of America's medical and scientific history. The first time came exactly 51 years ago today—March 26, 1953—when Jonas Salk called a press conference to announce the discovery of a polio vaccine. The second time, amazingly, came just four weeks later, when Watson and Crick published their discovery of the double helix structure of DNA. The third time was in 1964, when U.S. surgeon general Luther Terry courageously

reported that cigarette smoking does cause cancer and other deadly diseases. For many of you, that was the first day of what turned into a 40-year movement to alter a culture of harm that was anchored in centuries of acceptable behavior. Your science and determination helped America turn the tide against tobacco and smoking — saving the lives of millions.[4]

CHECKLIST

Possible Forms for Citing Examples

✓ "Let me give you two examples of outsourcing . . ."
✓ "Lance Armstrong's Livestrong Foundation is an example of a fiscally effective charity . . ."
✓ "For example, what if, in five years, the average temperature of the Pacific Ocean rises one half of one degree Fahrenheit?"

HYPOTHETICAL EXAMPLES

In some speeches you may need to make a point about something that could happen in the future if certain things occurred. For example, if you argue the thesis "We should eliminate summer vacations for all school-age children," you automatically raise the question of what will happen if this comes to pass. Since it hasn't happened yet, you'll need a **hypothetical example** of what you believe the outcome will be. Republican Representative Vernon Ehlers of Michigan offered the following hypothetical example when he spoke at a congressional hearing in support of a bill to ban human cloning:

> What if in the cloning process you produce someone with two heads and three arms? Are you simply going to euthanize and dispose of that person? The answer is no. We're talking about human life.[5]

Share Stories

Often, one of the most powerful means of conveying a message is through a **story,** or **narrative**. Narratives tell tales, both real and imaginary, about practically anything under the sun. Scholars of narratives have commented that all human history consists of stories. "Most of our experience, our knowledge, and our thinking is organized as stories," notes language scholar Mark Turner. "One story helps us make sense of another."[6] A growing body of neuroscientific evidence also suggests that it is through stories that we organize our thinking.[7]

Stories come in many guises, from simple recitations of an event to fairy tales, legends, parables (short moral lessons), biblical narratives, and myths. They can be Horatio Alger–type success stories or Charles Dickens–type hard-luck tales. Many stories are passed down orally from one generation to the next. Common to all narratives are the essential storytelling elements of plot,

CHECKLIST

Selecting the Right Example or Story

_____ 1. Does the example or story truly illustrate or prove the point I need to make?

_____ 2. Is it credible?

_____ 3. Is it compelling enough?

_____ 4. Is it suitable for my audience's background and experiences, or would another illustration be more appropriate?

character, setting, and some sort of time line. Stories can be brief and simple descriptions of short incidents worked into the body of the speech, or relatively drawn-out accounts that constitute most of the presentation. In either event, the key to a successful story is choosing one that will strike a responsive chord with the audience.

Personal experiences can be the basis for powerful stories. In a keynote address delivered to the annual convention of the Asian American Journalists Association (AAJA), Helen Zia, a Chinese American writer and activist, revealed a personal experience that shed light on growing up as an Asian American in the 1950s and 1960s:

> I, like most of you, remember what it was like never to see people who looked like me in the world beyond my immediate circle. When I was growing up in the 1950s, Asians were nowhere to be found in the media, except occasionally in the movies. There at the Saturday matinee, my brothers and I would sit with all the other kids in town watching old World War II movies — you know, where the evil Zero pilots would be heading for their unsuspecting prey, only to be thwarted by the all-American heroes, who were, of course, always white. These movies would have their defining moment, that crescendo of emotion when the entire theater would rise up, screaming "Kill them!" "Kill them!" "Kill them!" ("Them" being the Japanese.) When the movie was over and the lights came on, I wanted to be invisible so that my neighbors wouldn't direct their red-_white_-and-blue fervor toward me.[8]

CHECKLIST

Possible Forms for Citing Narratives

✓ "In J. R. R. Tolkien's classic trilogy *The Lord of the Rings*, a young Hobbit boy named Frodo . . ."

✓ "Some of you will recall when, in the animated movie *The Incredibles*, a family of superheroes — including Mr. Incredible, his wife Elastigirl, and their three kids — try to blend into the suburbs . . ."

✓ "I can never forget the day . . ."

✓ "At 9 A.M. on December 3, 2008, Shawn Bailey left her home for work . . ."

ESL Speaker's Notes
Broadening Your Listeners' Perspectives

As a non-native speaker of English, consider sharing a personal experience with the audience. Stories from other lands and other ways of life often fascinate listeners. Unique cultural traditions, eyewitness accounts of newsworthy events, or tales passed down orally from one generation to the next are just some of the possibilities. Depending on the goal of your speech, you can use your experiences as supporting material for a related topic or as the topic itself.

One adult public speaking student from Poland related what life for her was like after the fall of communism in 1989. She described how goods she had never seen before suddenly flooded the country. A wondrous array of fruit and meat left the most vivid impression on the then 11-year-old, as both had been nearly impossible to find under the old regime. The speaker's audience was fascinated with her firsthand account of historical events, and she found that sharing her unique experiences boosted her confidence in her speaking ability.

Many speakers, whether they're ministers at the Sunday morning pulpit or high-tech entrepreneurs rallying the troops, liberally sprinkle their speeches with **anecdotes** — brief stories of interesting and often humorous incidents based on real life. Obviously, the most effective anecdotes are those that the audience hasn't heard before and that link back to the speaker's theme. In a speech about the need to preserve our national parks, Brock Evans, the director of the Endangered Species Coalition, does this artfully:

> One of the leaders of the fight was a fifth-generation rancher, Carroll Noble. . . . [H]e had a spread over near Pinedale. I'll never forget how he loved this Wyoming land, and how he expressed his feelings about it. One day, we were having dinner at his place. He had a big picture window there, framing that whole magnificent vista of the Wind River Range, its snow-capped jagged peaks, and the great tumbling mass of green forest spilling down its flank to the lake. At one point, he gestured out there, and turned to me with the greatest sadness: "You see that?" he said. "If they start cutting that, I'll never look out that window again."[9]

Draw on Testimony

When looking for supporting material, consider quoting or paraphrasing people who have an intimate knowledge of your topic. **Testimony** (from the Latin word for "witness") includes firsthand findings, eyewitness accounts, and opinions by people, both lay (nonexpert) and expert. **Expert testimony** includes any findings, eyewitness accounts, or opinions by professionals who are trained to evaluate or report on a given topic. A medical doctor may

CHECKLIST

Possible Forms for Citing Testimony

✓ "According to John Miller, one of the three founders of the community's rapid-transit committee . . ."

✓ "Teresa Allen, fund-raising chairperson from the Chicago Society of the Performing Arts, gave some insight into the proper way to obtain donations when she said . . ."

✓ "Dr. Mary Klein, a stem cell researcher from the Brown University School of Medicine, echoed this sentiment when she spoke Monday at the Public Health Committee meeting . . ."

provide cutting-edge information on the threat of cholesterol. A representative of an organization can appear before a government committee to testify for or against a proposed bill. **Lay testimony**, or testimony by nonexperts, can also serve as powerful supporting material. For example, eyewitnesses, such as residents of New Orleans who survived Hurricane Katrina, can reveal compelling firsthand information that may be unavailable to others, often in a powerful way.

Credibility plays a key role in the effectiveness of testimony. It's up to you to establish the source's reputation, and to do so in as compelling and accurate a manner as possible. When citing testimony, supply the name and qualifications of the person whose testimony you use and inform your listeners when and where the testimony was offered. It isn't always necessary to cite the exact

CHECKLIST

Evaluating the Credibility of Testimony

✓ Are the experts I've cited proven in their fields?
✓ Is the lay testimony reliable?
✓ Do the sources have any obvious biases?
✓ Is their testimony timely? Is it relevant?
✓ Do their views effectively support my thesis?
✓ Do their views add power to my assertions or arguments?
✓ Are there reasons that the audience may not react favorably to the testimony?[1]

Testimony that does not meet these standards is likely to do more harm to your speech than good.

1. The idea for these questions was prompted by O. M. Walter and R. L. Scott, *Thinking and Speaking: A Guide to Intelligent Oral Communication,* 3rd ed. (New York: Macmillan, 1973), 52.

date (though do keep a written record of this); in the oral presentation, terms such as "recently" and "last year" are fine:

> In testimony before the U.S. House Subcommittee on Human Rights and Wellness last week, Derek Ellerman, co-executive director of the Polaris Project said, "Many people have little understanding of the enormity and the brutality of the sex trafficking industry in the United States. When they think of sex slavery, they think of Thailand or Nepal — not a suburban house in the DC area, with $400,000 homes and manicured lawns. . . ."[10]

Provide Facts and Statistics

 WEB Links

Most people require some type of evidence, usually in the form of facts and statistics, before they will accept someone else's claims or position.[11] **Facts** represent documented occurrences, including actual events, dates, times, people involved, and places. Facts are truly facts only when they have been independently verified by people other than the source. For example, we accept as true that Abraham Lincoln was the sixteenth president of the United States because this fact has been independently verified by eyewitnesses, journalists, historians, and so forth. Listeners are not likely to accept your statements as factual unless you back them up with credible evidence.

Statistics are quantified evidence that summarize, compare, and predict things, from batting averages to birthrates. Statistics can clarify complex information and help make abstract concepts or ideas concrete for listeners. For

TABLE 8.1 • Types and Functions of Supporting Material

Type of Supporting Material	Definition	Purpose
Example	Illustrates, describes, or represents things; it can be brief or extended, and real or hypothetical.	Aids understanding by making ideas, items, or events more concrete; creates interest.
Narrative	A story, either real or imaginary, short or drawn-out in length. Can constitute a small part of the presentation or serve as a basis for the speech itself.	Generates interest and identification.
Testimony	Firsthand findings, eyewitness accounts, and opinions by people, both lay (nonexpert) and expert.	Provides evidence and aids credibility.
Facts	Actual events, dates, times, and places that can be independently verified.	Provides evidence (including people involved) and demonstrates points.
Statistics	Data that demonstrate relationships.	Summarizes information, demonstrates proof, makes points memorable.

example, rather than simply stating, "We are selling millions of songs on iTunes," Steve Jobs, CEO of Apple Computer, Inc., described iTune's success this way: "We're selling over five million songs a day now. Isn't that unbelievable? That's 58 songs every second of every minute of every hour of every day."[12]

USE STATISTICS ACCURATELY

Audience members often accept a speaker's statistics without question, believing that "numbers never lie" and that the speaker will be ethical in his or her use of them. Unfortunately, this may not always be the case. So that your statistics have value as supporting evidence, you should understand what the statistics actually mean and use terms that describe them correctly.

Use Frequencies to Indicate Counts

A common type of statistic used in speeches, a **frequency** is simply a count of the number of times something occurs:

"On the midterm exam there were 8 As, 15 Bs, 7 Cs, 2 Ds, and 1 F."

Frequencies can help listeners understand comparisons between two or more categories, indicate size, or describe trends:

- According to *Census 2000,* the total population of the State of Colorado comprised 2,165,983 males and 2,135,278 females.[13] *(compares two categories)*
- Inside the cabin, the Airbus A380 has room for at least 550 passengers — and as many as 1,000.[14] *(shows size)*
- According to the CDC, the birth rate among young adolescents aged 10 to 14 has declined steadily from a peak of 12,901 in 1994, to the current low of 7,315.[15] *(describes a trend)*

Use Percentages to Express Proportion

As informative as frequencies can be, the similarity or difference in magnitude between things may be more meaningfully indicated in percentages. A **percentage** is the quantified portion of a whole. Describing the frequencies of males and females in the 2000 Colorado population (2,165,983 and 2,135,278, respectively) in percentages shows even more clearly how similar the two amounts are: 50.36 percent male and 49.64 percent female. (Common practice in speeches permits us to round off the figures, using such terms as "roughly.")

Percentages are especially useful when comparing categories or classes of something, as, for example, in the reasons for delays of domestic flights:

Nearly 8 percent of April 2007 flights were delayed by aviation system delays, over 7 percent by late-arriving aircraft; over 6 percent by factors within the airline's control, such as maintenance or crew problems; 0.70 percent by extreme weather; and 0.06 percent for security reasons.[16]

Because audience members cannot take the time to pause and reflect on the figures as they would with written text, speakers must help listeners interpret the numbers, as in this example:

> As you can see, late-arriving flights caused far more delays than did security measures, which accounted for just about one half of a percentage point.

(See Chapter 16 for more on the differences between oral and written language.)

Use Averages to Describe Typical Characteristics

An **average** describes information according to its typical characteristics. Usually we think of the average as the sum of the scores divided by the number of scores. This is the *mean,* the arithmetic (or computed) average. But there are two other kinds of averages — the *median* and the *mode*. As a matter of accuracy, in your speeches you should distinguish among these three kinds of averages.

Consider a teacher whose nine students scored 5, 19, 22, 23, 24, 26, 28, 28, and 30, with 30 points being the highest possible grade. The following illustrates how she would calculate the three types of averages:

- The **mean** score is 22.8, the *arithmetic average,* the sum of the scores divided by nine.
- The **median** score is 24, the *center-most score in a distribution* or the point above and below which 50 percent of the nine scores fall.
- The **mode** score is 28, the *most frequently occurring score* in the distribution.

The following speaker, claiming that a rival organization misrepresented the "average" tax rate, illustrates how the inaccurate use of the different types of averages can distort reality:

> The Tax Foundation determines an *average* [*mean*] tax rate for American families simply by dividing all taxes paid by the total of everyone's income. . . . For example, if four middle-income families pay $3,000, $4,000, $5,000, and $6,000, respectively, in taxes, and one very wealthy family pays $82,000 in taxes, the *average* [*mean*] tax paid by these five families is $20,000 ($100,000 in total taxes divided by five families). But four of the five families have a tax bill equaling $6,000 or less. . . . [Many] analysts would define a *median* income family — a family for whom half of all families have higher income and half have lower income — to be the "typical family" and describe the taxes paid by a such a median-income family as the taxes that typical middle-class families owe.[17]

PRESENT YOUR STATISTICS ETHICALLY

Whether done inadvertently or intentionally, offering listeners inaccurate statistics is unethical. Following are some steps you can take to reduce the likelihood of using false or misleading statistics in your speeches:

Ethically Speaking
Assessing Statistics for Reliability and Validity

Researchers use many different statistical tools to analyze their data. Unfortunately, it's extremely easy to misuse any of these methods. If misuse does occur, whether intentionally to advance an agenda or accidentally, through error, the conclusion may misrepresent an important relationship or effect.[1] The flawed data that results from such misinterpretations often evolves into widespread misconceptions. One classic example is the oft-quoted statement that 95 percent of all dieters never lose weight, and 95 percent of those who do lose weight will not keep it off. In fact, this figure is based on a study done in the 1950s of one hundred patients in an obesity clinic.[2] Clearly, the study's results cannot be extrapolated with any degree of accuracy to today's general population.

Before using statistics in your speeches, be sure to take the time to assess their reliability and validity. Consider whether the data were collected scientifically and interpreted objectively. Ask yourself "What is the sample size? Are the results statistically relevant? Was the experiment well designed?"

If you are reporting on a poll, ask yourself "Who took the poll, and when was it conducted? Who paid for the poll, and why was it taken? How many people were interviewed for the survey, and how were they chosen? What area (nation, state, or region) or group (teachers, lawyers, Democratic voters, etc.) were these people chosen from? Are the results based on the answers of all the people interviewed? Who should have been interviewed and was not? What is the sampling error for the poll results? What other kinds of factors could have skewed the poll results?"[3]

1. John S. Gardenier and David B. Resnik, "The Misuse of Statistics: Concepts, Tools, and a Research Agenda" (proceedings of 2001 conference, "Investigating Research Integrity," U.S. Department of Health and Human Services, Office of Research Integrity), ori.dhhs.gov/multimedia/acrobat/papers/gardenier.pdf (accessed July 2, 2002).

2. Gary Taubes, *Bad Science: The Short Life and Weird Times of Cold Fusion* (New York: Random House, 1993).

3. Excerpted from Sheldon R. Gawiser and G. Evans Witt, "Twenty Questions a Journalist Should Ask about Poll Results." Earl Babbie, *The Practice of Social Research* (Belmont, CA: Wadsworth, 1998). National Council on Public Opinion Polls Web site www.ncpp.org/qajsa.htm (accessed July 2, 2002).

Choose Your Sources Carefully.   Be discerning about the sources for your statistics. This is particularly important given our tendency to place our faith in numbers. Are they taken from trustworthy and reputable sources? Are they drawn from a secondary or tertiary source such as a media outlet or personal Web site, or from a primary source such as a polling organization or a government statistical repository (e.g., FirstGov.gov)? Bear in mind that the more information that is available about the methods used to generate the data, including how and why it was collected and what researchers hoped to learn from it, the more authoritative the source of the information is likely to be.

Present Statistics in Context.   Statistics are meaningful only within a proper context. To help audience members accurately interpret statistical information, indicate why the statistics were collected, who or what they are intended to represent, what methods were used to collect them, and what period of time they refer to. The best and maybe only sure way to answer these questions is to know the sources of your statistical information.

Note how this speaker describes when the data were collected (2003), the method used to collect the data (survey), and the scope of the research (national):

> According to a report posted on the Centers for Disease Control and Prevention Web site, 70 percent of all deaths among youth and young adults aged 10–24 years result from only four causes: motor-vehicle crashes (32 percent), other unintentional injuries (12 percent), homicide (15 percent), and suicide (12 percent). These figures represent data collected during 2003, the latest year such data were collected, from questionnaires distributed to all public and private schools in the U.S. with students in at least one of grades 9–12 in the 50 states and the District of Columbia.[18]

Avoid Confusing Statistics with "Absolute Truth."   Rather than the absolute or only truth, statistics represent a quantification of something at a given point in time. Thus, statistics are rarely definitive. Even the most recent data available

---

SELF-ASSESSMENT CHECKLIST

Using Statistics in Your Speech: An Ethical Inventory

✓   Do I include statistics from the most authoritative sources I can locate?
✓   Do I briefly tell listeners about the method(s) used to collect the statistics (such as a survey), the scope of the research (e.g., sample size), and where the data is drawn from?
✓   Do I alert listeners to when the statistics were collected?
✓   Do I offer the data as they appropriately represent my point or claim, but refrain from declaring that these data are absolute?
✓   Do I refrain from using or ignoring statistics selectively to make my point (cherry-picking)?

CHECKLIST

Possible Forms for Citing Facts and Statistics

✓   "As published in the October 2008 edition of *Nature* . . ."
✓   "According to the U.S. Department of Health and Human Services Web site, accessed on May 18, 2008 . . ."
✓   "According to a January 2008 report posted on the Centers for Disease Control and Prevention Web site, 70.8 percent of all deaths . . ."
✓   "In a May 2008 study published in *Morbidity and Mortality Weekly Report,* available online at the Centers for Disease Control and Prevention Web site . . ."

From Source to Speech
Demonstrating Your Sources' Reliability and Credibility

How Can I Lead the Audience to Accept My Sources as Reliable and Credible?

- If the source is affiliated with a respected institution, identify that affiliation for your audience.
- If citing a study linked to a reputable institution, identify the institution.
- If a source has relevant credentials, note the credentials.
- If the source has relevant real-life experience, mention that experience.

In the following excerpt from a speech about emergency room care in the United States, the speaker omits information about her key sources that would help to convince the audience that her evidence and sources are trustworthy:

> According to a series of three reports by the Institute of Medicine on the breakdown of our emergency room system, the need for emergency rooms has increased by 26% since 1993. Today, we'll uncover the catastrophic conditions existing in America's emergency rooms, discover what is causing these conditions, and look at how to restore faith in a system that has — to quote from a New York editorial — "reached a breaking point."

Below we see a much more convincing use of the same sources.

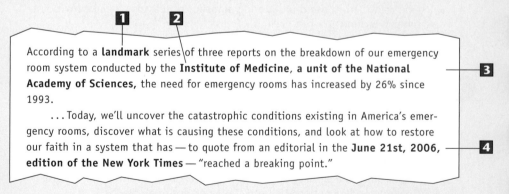

> According to a **landmark** series of three reports on the breakdown of our emergency room system conducted by the **Institute of Medicine, a unit of the National Academy of Sciences,** the need for emergency rooms has increased by 26% since 1993.
>
> ... Today, we'll uncover the catastrophic conditions existing in America's emergency rooms, discover what is causing these conditions, and look at how to restore our faith in a system that has — to quote from an editorial in the **June 21st, 2006, edition of the New York Times** — "reached a breaking point."

1 The speaker wisely includes the adjective "landmark" to signal credibility for her evidence.

2 The speaker communicates relevant affiliations, connecting the source to an entity that raises audience's confidence level.

CONTACT

Institute of Medicine
500 Fifth Street NW
Washington DC 20001

iomwww@nas.edu

tel: 202.334.2352
fax: 202.334.1412

Staff Directory

>> LATEST WEBCASTS & PRESENTATIONS

> Agenda. 2006 IOM Annual Meeting: Ste
> Agenda. 2007 IOM Annual Meeting: Evi
> Agenda. 2005 IOM Annual Meeting: Pha

■ more webcasts & presentations

> RSS

Home | About | Topics | Projects| Memberships| Boards | Events | Reports | Sitemap
Copyright © 2008 National Academy of Sciences. All rights reserved.

3 The speaker identifies the source as a respected government agency. Listeners are more likely to trust the source if it is connected to a trusted entity.

4 The speaker supports her thesis that a crisis exists with a quotation from a notable source: *The New York Times,* a well-known, well-respected national paper.

The New York Times

Opinion

| WORLD | U.S. | N.Y. / REGION | BUSINESS | TECHNOLOGY | SCIENCE | HEALTH | SP |

EDITORIALS   COLUMNISTS   CONTRIBUTORS   LETTERS   N.Y./RE(

EDITORIAL
Emergency in the Emergency Rooms

Published: June 21, 2006

The nation's emergency rooms have been stretched thin for at least a decade or more, but a new analysis suggests that they have reached a breaking point. Their plight underscores how dreadfully unprepared on a subject will change the next time the data are collected. Nor are statistics necessarily any more perfect than the people who collect them.

One way to avoid presenting statistics as definitive is to present them as tentative information. Offer the data as they appropriately represent your point or claim, but refrain from declaring that these data are absolute.

Avoid Cherry-Picking.   To **cherry-pick** is to selectively present only those statistics that buttress your point of view while ignoring competing data.[19] Cherry-picking is a popular tool of politicians and policymakers, who are often accused of selectively referring to only those statistics that boost their arguments and policies.

When you find yourself searching for statistics to confirm an opinion or belief you already hold, you are probably engaging in cherry-picking.[20] Choosing from among the mean, median, and mode of a distribution the one average that makes the best case for your point, when in fact one of the other averages is the better indicator of what your data represent, is an instance of cherry-picking. Researching statistical support material is not a trip through a buffet line to select what looks good and discard what doesn't. You must locate as much information as possible that is pertinent to your particular point, and then present it in context or not at all.

USE VISUAL AIDS WHENEVER POSSIBLE

When your speech relies heavily on statistical information, use appropriate tables, graphs, and charts to display the statistics (see Chapters 20–22).

Win Acceptance of Your Supporting Materials

Too often, inexperienced speakers orally credit the sources of their supporting material in bare-bones fashion — for example, mechanically citing the publication name and date but leaving out key information that could convince the audience to accept the source as reliable and its conclusions as true. But discerning listeners will accept your examples, narratives, testimony, facts, and statistics as legitimate only if they believe that they are derived from sources that are reliable and credible. *Reliability,* in this context, refers to our level of trust in the source's credentials and past performance. If you support a scientific claim by crediting it to an unknown 14-year-old's personal blog, for example, most listeners won't find it as reliable as if you credited it to a scientist affiliated with a reputable institution.

Credibility is our judgment about the probable truth of a source's statement. While a source that is reliable is usually credible, this is not always so.[21] Sometimes we have information that contradicts what we are told by a reliable source. For example, a soldier based in Iraq might read a news article in the *Wall Street Journal* that describes a battle in which he or she participated. The soldier knows that certain facts in the story are false, because the soldier was there. In general, however, the soldier finds the *Wall Street Journal* a reliable source. Because even the most reliable source can sometimes be wrong, it is better to offer a variety of supporting materials rather than a single source. This is especially the case when your claims are controversial.

Convincing audience members to accept your evidence is not the same as convincing them of your *personal credibility* as a speaker, although the two are certainly related. If audience members do not trust you, they will be reluctant to believe much of what you say, regardless of the quality of your sources. (For a discussion of personal credibility, or ethos, see Chapter 5.)

Further, different audiences do require varying amounts and types of evidence, especially in persuasive speeches, as discussed in Chapter 25. The attitudes of your audience toward your topic, for example — whether they are hostile, critical and conflicted, sympathetic, or uninformed or apathetic toward it — can play an important role in whether they require more evidence (hostile audiences) or less evidence (sympathetic audiences). (See "Target Audience" in Chapter 26; see also "Using Evidence to Support Your Claims" in Chapter 25.)

"From Source to Speech" on pp. 144–145 illustrates how you can orally cite your sources in a way that listeners will accept them as reliable and credible, even when they do not agree with your position (see also a "Using Evidence to Support Your Claims" in Chapter 25).

9 Locating Supporting Material

The search for supporting material can be one of the most enjoyable parts of putting together a speech. It is at this stage that you can delve into your subject, sift through sources, and select material that best conveys and supports your message. Classical rhetoricians termed the process of selecting information to illustrate or prove your points **invention**. According to Aristotle, one of the speaker's most important tasks is to select from among the many different types of evidence available those materials that are most likely to lead listeners to accept the speaker's point of view.[1]

To find the right mix of examples, facts and statistics, opinions, stories, and testimony for your speech, you will want to conduct primary research, secondary research, or a combination of the two. **Primary research** is original or first-hand research, such as interviews and surveys conducted by you, the speaker. **Secondary research** is the vast world of information gathered by others.

The main sources for primary research are interviews and surveys; secondary research resides in a nearly infinite number of library and Internet resources. As you gather these materials, consider how you can use them to generate interest, illustrate and clarify your meaning, and add solid evidence to your assertions.

Before You Begin: Plan a Research Strategy

 WEB Research room

A common pitfall of research is getting sidetracked. In reviewing secondary research particularly, the biggest pitfall is wasting time in the wrong places. By keeping the reason for your search — to substantiate your thesis with material that is most likely to be accepted by your audience — clearly in mind, you stand a better chance of avoiding this trap.

Before beginning your search, take a few moments to review your thesis statement. Consider what you need to support it. What do you need to elaborate upon, explain, demonstrate, or prove? What kinds of evidence will your audience most likely accept? (See Chapter 25.) Different topics suggest different research methods, so reflect on what might work best for your particular topic, purpose, and occasion. A topic such as drinking habits on campus clearly begs for primary research in the form of interviews, surveys, or personal observations. Other topics can be supported only through secondary research. Nearly all topics benefit from a mix of both.

Making an Inventory of Your Research Needs

_____ 1. What do I personally know about my topic?

_____ 2. What does my thesis statement require me to explain, demonstrate, or prove?

_____ 3. What type of supporting material does my topic call for?

     _____ Primary research such as interviews or surveys?

     _____ Facts and statistics?

     _____ Examples that will clarify material?

     _____ Stories that will capture attention and make a point?

     _____ Testimony that will bolster my argument?

_____ 4. What type of supporting material will most influence my audience?

     _____ Primary research such as interviews or surveys?

     _____ Facts and statistics?

     _____ Examples that will clarify material?

     _____ Stories that will capture attention and make a point?

     _____ Testimony that will bolster my argument?

Secondary Resources: Print and Electronically Stored Sources

WEB Bibliographer

Secondary research includes all information recorded by individuals other than actual participants in an event or study. The most likely sources of secondary research include books, newspapers, periodicals, government publications, and reference works such as encyclopedias, almanacs, books of quotations, and atlases. In the past, these sources appeared only in print. Increasingly, the information they contain is being stored in online databases. A **database** is a searchable place, or "base," in which information is stored and from which it can be retrieved. A **full-text database** is one in which at least some of the records in the database contain the full text of articles.

LIBRARY RESOURCES TO FACILITATE YOUR SEARCH

If you conduct your search in a library, you may wish to begin by consulting two essential resources: the reference librarian and the library catalog. (See Chapter 10 for information on resources to facilitate your searches on the Internet.)

The Reference Desk

Every library contains a unique mix of print works and database subscription services. At the reference desk you can find out what this mix is and, with the help of a reference librarian, learn how to use these resources to research your topic. **Reference librarians** are information specialists who are trained to help you in your search.

The Library Catalog

You can find out what the library owns by consulting the library catalog, which is searchable by author, title, and subject. Libraries organize books and other holdings according to the **Library of Congress call number** or the **Dewey decimal number**. Once you've located an entry in the catalog, jot down or print out this call number so that you can locate it on the shelves.

The Search Tips Section

Whatever it is you want to locate on a database—book, newspaper, magazine, journal article, or other media—smart search techniques will make your job less stressful and more productive. Every database has its own way of conducting searches, so it is vital that you consult the "Search Tips" section (see also Chapter 10, "Using the Internet to Support Your Speech").

BOOKS

Books explore topics in depth. A well-written book provides detail and perspective and can serve as an excellent source of supporting examples, stories, facts, and statistics. To locate a book in your library's holdings, refer to the library's catalog. To search the titles of all books currently in print in the United States, refer to *Books in Print* (in print form) or *Books in Print* Online (www.booksinprint.com/bip/). Alternatively, log on to an online bookseller such as Amazon.com and key in your topic; because *Books in Print* is a subscription-based service (i.e., it charges a fee), many librarians search for books in this manner.[2]

NEWSPAPERS AND PERIODICALS

Newspapers are a rich source of support material. In addition to reports on the major issues and events of the day, many newspaper stories—especially feature articles—also include detailed background or historical information. Three comprehensive online sources for searching newspaper articles include *Lexis-Nexis Academic Universe News Service, InfoTrac Newspaper Collection, ProQuest National Newspapers,* and *Newsbank.* Several Web sites are also devoted to newspapers, in such categories as newspaper archives (e.g., www.newspaperarchive .com), U.S. newspapers (www.newsvoyager.com), and online world newspapers (world-newspapers.com). Indexes to individual newspapers such as the *New York Times* and *Wall Street Journal* are also available on microfiche. News reported on television and radio may be accessed on sites such as NPR.org, CNN.com, and BBC.co.uk.

A **periodical** is a regularly published magazine or journal. Periodicals can be an excellent source for speeches because they usually include the various types of supporting material discussed in Chapter 8 (examples, narratives, testimony, facts, and statistics). Periodicals include general-interest magazines such as *Time* and *Newsweek,* as well as the thousands of specialized academic, business, and technical magazines, newsletters, and refereed journals in circulation. Articles in *refereed journals* are evaluated by experts before being published and supply sources for the information they contain. Articles in *general-interest magazines,* by contrast, rarely contain citations and may or may not be written by experts on the topic. Most general-interest magazines are available in *Infotrac Online.* Many libraries offer access to *Academic Search Premier* and *EBSCO Academic Search Elite,* both of which cover both general periodicals and more specialized scholarly journals.

In addition, an ever-increasing number of periodical databases are devoted to special topics. For business-related topics, consider using *ABI/Inform, Lexis-Nexis Academic,* and *EBSCO Business Source Complete.* If you plan to talk about a health or medical topic, examine Health and Wellness Resource Center (www .galegroup.com/HealthRC) or PubMed (www.ncbi.nlm.nih.gov/entrez/query.fcgi). See Table 9.1 for a list of specialized databases available in many college libraries.

GOVERNMENT PUBLICATIONS

Part of every tax dollar supports the constant production of publications by the **U.S. Government Printing Office (GPO)**, and the result is a resource that every citizen should enjoy. The GPO is responsible for publishing and distributing all information collected and produced by federal agencies, from the U.S. Census Bureau to the Department of Education and the Environmental Protection Agency. GPO publications also include all congressional reports and hearings. Most federal, state, and local government agencies provide statistics and other information freely and in a timely manner.

Finding and using government documents can be a daunting task, but, given that nearly all the information comes from primary sources, it's usually well worth the effort. Get started by logging on to www.access.gpo.gov, where you will find an "A to Z Resource List." Alternatively, go directly to FirstGov.gov, the official portal to all government information and services. FirstGov.gov contains links to millions of Web pages from federal, local, and tribal governments to foreign nations around the world. The site includes links to statistics of every kind. You may also wish to access FirstGov en Español, which offers resources in Spanish. Translations in twenty-eight other languages are also available.

Online, the University of Michigan's Document Center (www.lib.umich.edu/ govdocs) is another excellent starting point for government documents, whether local, state, federal, foreign, or international.

REFERENCE WORKS

Reference works include, but are not limited to, encyclopedias, almanacs, biographical reference works, books of quotations, poetry collections, and atlases.

Encyclopedias

Encyclopedias summarize knowledge that is found in original form elsewhere. Their usefulness lies in providing a broad overview of subjects and in helping you to generate a list of key terms for your search. **General encyclopedias**

TABLE 9.1 • Specialized Databases Found in Many Libraries

Database	Description
WorldCat *(Accessed through Firstsearch)*	WorldCat lets you search collections of more than 10,000 libraries worldwide, making it the world's largest network of library content.
ABI/INFORM	Covers business, management, economics, and a wide range of related fields. Contains abstracts and full text.
ALT-HEALTH WATCH	Focuses on the many perspectives of complementary, holistic, and integrated approaches to health care and wellness; offers full-text articles from more than 170 international journals, periodicals, booklets, and book excerpts.
ERIC (Education Resources Information Center)	The world's largest digital library of educational information, with more than 1.1 million citations of education-related documents and journal articles; 1966–present. Also offers free access to more than 107,000 full-text nonjournal documents published between 1993 and 2004 (www.eric.ed.gov).
Ethnic NewsWatch	ENW presents a comprehensive, full-text collection of more than 250 publications (dating from 1990) offering both national and regional coverage from a multiethnic perspective.
American Rhetoric	Database of and index to 5000+ full-text, audio and video versions of public speeches, sermons, legal proceedings, lectures, debates, interviews, and other recorded media events (www.americanrhetoric.com).
Scirus	Searches millions of science-specific Web pages, allowing you to find the latest scientific, scholarly, technical, and medical data on the Web (douglassarchives.org/).
PsycINFO	Includes indexes and summaries of journal articles, book chapters, books, and reports—all in the field of psychology, psychiatry, and related disciplines. Journal coverage, spanning 1887–present, includes international material selected from more than 1,700 publications.
PubMed	The National Library of Medicine's database of citations to more than 15 million articles in the biomedical fields; includes a growing list of full-text entries (www.ncbi.nlm.nih.gov/entrez/query/fcgi).
FedStats	U.S. government database of statistics from 100 federal agencies such as the Bureau of Prisons and the National Cancer Institute (www.fedstats.gov).

attempt to cover all important subject areas of knowledge; **specialized encyclopedias** delve deeply into one subject area. The most comprehensive of the general encyclopedias is the *Encyclopedia Britannica*, which is available in print and online. Because almost one-third of the encyclopedia is devoted to biographies, it is an ideal reference for topics involving people.

For a more in-depth look at a topic, there are specialized encyclopedias of all types, ranging from the *McGraw-Hill Encyclopedia of Science and Technology* to the *Encyclopedia of Religion* and the *Oxford Encyclopedia of Latinos and Latinas in the United States*. Your reference librarian will help you identify those in your school's library collection.

Public Speaking in Cultural Perspective
Multicultural Reference Works—Filling the Gap

Until fairly recently, standard reference works such as encyclopedias and almanacs claimed to be comprehensive but, in fact, generally paid little attention to the culture and accomplishments of the many groups that make up the United States. Today many publishers are addressing the long-standing need for detailed information on these groups' experiences. The *Gale Encyclopedia of Multicultural America,* for example, contains 152 original essays on specific minority and ethnic groups in the United States, from Arab Americans to the Yupiat.[1] Macmillan publishes the *Encyclopedia of African-American Culture and History,* while Grolier publishes *Encyclopedia Latina.* Routledge publishes the *Encyclopedia of Modern Jewish Culture.*

Among biographical resources, Gale Research publishes *African American Biography, Contemporary Black Biography, Hispanic American Biography, Asian American Biography, Arab American Biography,* and *Native American Biography.* All are multivolume sets that contain portraits, quotes, interviews, and articles about prominent men and women.

Among specialized almanacs, available now are the *Asian American Almanac, Muslim Almanac, St. James Press Gay and Lesbian Almanac, Native North American Almanac, African American Almanac,* and *Hispanic American Almanac* (all published by Gale Research), along with a host of similar publications. Each reference work contains essays that focus on all major aspects of group life and culture. One way to see what's available is to search a database such as WorldCat.

1. Robert Von Dassanowski, ed., *Gale Encyclopedia of Multicultural America,* 2nd ed. (Detroit, Mich.: Gale Publications, 2000).

Almanacs

To find facts and statistics that support your topic, **almanacs** and **fact books** are a good choice. (See also the U.S. government publications listed previously.) As with encyclopedias, there are both general and specialized almanacs. In the general category, one of the most comprehensive sources is the *World Almanac and Book of Facts.* This reference work's well-organized alphabetical index gives readers easy access to subjects. It contains facts and statistics in many categories, including those related to historical, social, political, and religious subjects, plus the top ten news stories of the year, notable Supreme Court decisions, notable quotes of the year, and a complete listing of vital statistics for all nations of the world. Other helpful almanacs include the *Information Please Almanac; Famous First Facts: A Record of First Happenings, Discoveries, and Inventions in American History; People's Almanac;* and *Guinness Book of Records* (see also the Guinness World Records Web site at www.guinnessworldrecords.com, which provides facts on world records of all kinds). Information from almanacs can supplement other research for your speech. As with encyclopedias, however, don't rely on almanacs as your only means of support.

Biographical Resources

For information about famous or noteworthy people, the *Biography and Genealogy Master Index* is an excellent starting point. This comprehensive resource indexes biographical material from a rich range of sources. For analyses and criticism of the published works of individuals you may be speaking about, consider such biographical resources as *Current Biography, Dictionary of American Biography, Famous Hispanics in the World and in History* (access is free at coloquio.com/famosos/alpha.htm), and *The African American Biographical Database (AABD)*.

Books of Quotations

For public speakers, books of quotations are an indispensable tool. Quotations are often used in the introductions and conclusions of speeches; they are also liberally sprinkled throughout examples, narratives, and, of course, testimony. First published in 1855, *Bartlett's Familiar Quotations* contains a collection of passages, phrases, and proverbs traced to their sources in ancient and modern literature. Many collections are targeted specifically at public speakers, including *Quotations for Public Speakers: A Historical, Literary, and Political Anthology,* by Robert G. Torricelli,[3] and *Nelson's Complete Book of Stories, Illustrations, and Quotes: The Ultimate Contemporary Resource for Speakers,* by Robert J. Morgan.[4]

Poetry Collections

Lines of poetry, if not entire poems, are often used by speakers both to introduce and conclude speeches and to illustrate points in the speech body. Every library has a collection of poetry anthologies as well as the collected works of individual poets. Updated yearly, the *Columbia Granger's Index to Poetry* indexes poems by author, title, and first line. Online, you can search for contemporary poetry at the *Electronic Poetry Center* (epc.buffalo.edu/e-poetry). To search for classic works, see Bartleby.com (www.bartleby.com/index.html), the *American Verse Project* (quod.lib.umich.edu/a/amverse), and *Poetry Archive.com* (www.poetryarchive.org/poetryarchive/home.do).

Atlases

An **atlas** is a collection of maps, text, and accompanying charts and tables. As well as serving to locate a particular locale (and to learn about its terrain, demographic information, and proximity to other places), many atlases use the medium of maps to explore art history, human anatomy, and even dog breeds. For straightforward geographic atlases, consult *National Geographic Atlas of the World* and *Rand McNally Commercial Atlas and Guide.* Both are in print form; online you can access maps at the National Geographic Web site (www.nationalgeographic.com/maps/index.html).

To learn about what atlases can offer beyond geographical information, consider conducting a search of atlases related to your topic. A subject search involving the keywords *art* AND *atlas,* for example, would likely lead to the highly regarded *Atlas of World Art,* published by Oxford University Press (2004).

Primary Resources: Interviews and Surveys

Supporting material drawn from primary research can include any source developed directly by the participants involved. The Declaration of Independence is a primary document created by the founding fathers of the United States. Firsthand oral or written histories, diaries, letters, and recordings of meetings and other events are also primary sources. Two additional types of primary research commonly used to support speeches are interviews and surveys that you conduct yourself. Both methods can provide valuable kinds of information to support and enliven a speech.

INTERVIEWS

Even with all the print and online information available today, oftentimes you can gain considerably more insight into a topic by speaking personally to someone who has expertise on the subject. An **interview** is a face-to-face communication for the purpose of gathering information. Productive interviews require advance planning.

Preparing for the Interview

Many people make the mistake of treating an interview as they would a conversation, assuming that things will "just flow." In fact, getting the information you need from a subject requires advance planning. Questions should be carefully prepared and written down; take care to avoid posing poorly phrased questions[6] that are vague, leading, or loaded.

- *Vague questions* don't give the person being interviewed enough to go on. He or she must either guess at what you mean or spend time asking you for clarification. Vague questions waste the interviewee's time and reflect the interviewer's lack of preparation.
- *Leading questions* encourage, if not force, a certain response and reflect the interviewer's bias: "Like most intelligent people, are you going to support candidate X?"
- *Loaded questions* are likewise phrased to reinforce the interviewer's agenda. They may also have a hostile intent: "Isn't it true that you've never supported school programs?"

As you draft your questions, aim to create *neutral questions,* or those that don't lead the interviewee to a desired response. Usually, neutral questions consist of a mix of open, closed, primary, and secondary questions (see Table 9.2).

TABLE 9.2 • Forms of Interview Questions	
Question Form	Description/Purpose in the Interview
Open/closed	• **Open questions:** Allow the interviewee to elaborate as he or she desires.
	• **Closed questions:** Permit only "Yes," "No," or other limited responses (see Chapter 6; section on questionnaires).
Primary/secondary	• **Primary questions:** Introduce new topics or areas of questioning (e.g., "What made you want to become a veterinarian?").
	• **Secondary questions:** Expand upon topics introduced in primary questions (e.g., "Did you go to veterinary school right after college?" and "Was it difficult to get student loans?").
Types of Secondary Questions: Questions seeking clarification Questions seeking elaboration "Clearinghouse" questions	• **Questions seeking clarification:** Designed to clarify the interviewee's statements (e.g., "By 'older mothers,' do you mean over 30, over 40, or over 50?").
	• **Questions seeking elaboration:** Designed to elicit additional information (e.g., "Were there other reasons that you chose your profession?").
	• **"Clearinghouse" questions:** Designed to check that all important information has been discussed (e.g., "Have we covered all the important points?").

H. Dan O'Hair, Gustave W. Friedrich, and Linda D. Dixon, *Strategic Communication in Business and the Professions,* 4th ed. (Boston: Houghton Mifflin, 2002), 216.

Structuring the Interview

Think about an interview as having the same broad structure as a speech, with an introduction (the opening), a body, and a conclusion (the closing).

The Opening: Getting off to a Good Start. A spirit of collaboration is crucial in the interview setting, so focus on creating a positive first impression. It is at this stage that your interviewee will decide whether you are credible and trustworthy:

- Acknowledge the interviewee and express respect for his or her expertise.
- Briefly summarize your topic and informational needs.
- State a (reasonable) goal — what you would like to accomplish in the interview — and reach agreement on it.
- Establish a time limit for the interview and stick to it.

The Body: Posing the Questions. It is in the body of the interview that you will pose your substantive questions. Using your prepared questions as a guide, permit the interviewee to introduce new topics and elaborate as he or she sees fit. Don't be afraid to ask for clarification or to repeat your questions if they remain unanswered.

It is vital to listen well as your subject answers your questions. As journalist Jim Short counsels, "Listen to what the subject is saying, not just to what you

---

✓ **CHECKLIST**

Preparing for the Interview

_____ 1. Do I have a written set of questions?

_____ 2. Can each of the questions be answered within a reasonable time frame, or within the time agreed upon with the interviewee?

_____ 3. Are each of my questions relevant to the central idea and purpose of my speech?

_____ 4. Are my questions posed in a well-thought-out sequence in relation to my topic?

_____ 5. Are my questions free of bias or hostile intent?

_____ 6. Are controversial questions reserved until the end of the interview?

_____ 7. Have I obtained advance permission to record the interview?

_____ 8. Do I have a working writing implement and ample notepaper (or a working laptop)?

_____ 9. Am I thoroughly comfortable about operating any recording equipment I plan to use during the interview?

---

want to hear." In addition, strive to use the active listening strategies described in Chapter 4 (e.g., set goals, listen for main ideas, and watch for nonverbal cues). Don't break in when the subject is speaking or interject with leading comments. *Paraphrase* the interviewee's answers where appropriate in order to establish understanding. Ask for *clarification* and *elaboration* when necessary.

The Closing: Recheck and Confirm.   Too often, people who conduct interviews end them in haste. Before ending the interview, recheck your notes and, if necessary, confirm them:

- Check to see that your notes have been properly recorded and are legible.
- Briefly offer a positive summary of important things you learned in the interview.
- Offer to send the interviewee the results of the interview, as in a printed speech.
- Send a written note of thanks.

Recording the Interview

More than one interview has gone splendidly — and entirely — unrecorded. As a result, the interviewer had to reconstruct from memory what was said, with the result usually being a slew of inaccuracies. You can avoid this pitfall by taking detailed notes, tape-recording the interview, or using a combination of note taking, recording, and videotaping. To establish an air of authenticity, you might even decide to replay short excerpts during your speech.

SURVEYS

Like interviews, a *survey* is useful both as a tool to investigate audience attitudes (see Chapter 6) and as supporting material. Surveys are an especially effective source of support for topics related to the attitudes, values, and beliefs of people in your immediate environment. Perhaps, for example, your central idea is, "School-age children who regularly attend religious services have a greater sense of well-being than those who don't." Although secondary research would be necessary to prove your claim, a survey of students at a local school could serve as an excellent source of additional support with direct relevance to your audience. (For information on creating surveys, refer to Chapter 6.)

Remember, however, that any informal survey you conduct is unlikely to be statistically sound enough to be taken as actual proof of your claims. Present your findings to the audience in a manner that acknowledges this, and be certain to shore up any informal survey research you conduct with other, more credible forms of support. (See Chapter 8 for a discussion of using statistics in speeches.)

Documenting Your Resources

Doing research can be fascinating, but organizing it can be frustrating. Fortunately, a few simple steps can help you keep track of your sources and their origins. (For visual guidelines on citing print sources and incorporating source material into your speech, see "From Source to Speech" on citing books, pp. 162–163, and on citing periodical articles, pp. 164–165.)

RECORD REFERENCES AS YOU GO

One of the biggest problems any researcher encounters is keeping track of bibliographic information. The easiest way to avoid this problem is to maintain a **working bibliography** as you review potential sources. Whether you are photocopying an article, downloading it from the Internet, or copying a passage by hand, make sure to record the information outlined in the accompanying checklist for each source. (See Chapter 10 for more on how to organize Internet sources.)

Of course, you won't cite all of this information in the speech itself. (See Chapter 8 for examples of how to acknowledge other people's ideas in your speeches.) You *will* need a complete record of your references, however, for an end-of-speech bibliography. For your written bibliography, the most commonly used documentation systems are the *Chicago Manual of Style,* the APA (American Psychological Association) method, the MLA (Modern Language Association) method, the CSE (Council of Science Editors, formerly Council of Biology Editors) method, and the IEEE (Institute of Electrical and Electronic Engineers) method. (See Appendices E through I for a description of each of these documentation styles.)

✓ CHECKLIST

Creating a Bibliography

For each relevant source, be sure to record the following elements:

_____ 1. Names of author(s) or editor(s) as cited

_____ 2. Title of publication

_____ 3. Volume or edition number, if applicable

_____ 4. Name of publisher

_____ 5. Place of publication (city and state); if published only online, give Internet address

_____ 6. Date and year of publication

_____ 7. Page number on which the material appears

_____ 8. All relevant information for any direct quotations, paraphrases, or specific ideas or theories put forth by others

_____ 9. The source of the facts and statistics used in the speech

_____ 10. All relevant bibliographic information for any examples and stories supplied by someone else

_____ 11. The source of any testimony presented in the speech, including the name of the person who offered the testimony and the date and context of the testimony

_____ 12. Any relevant information related to any presentation aids you plan to use, including charts and figures based on other people's data; photographs or videos produced by other people; music composed and performed by others; objects or models created by another

---

CHOOSE HELPFUL TOOLS

Rather than jotting down your notes helter-skelter, develop a system for organizing your research. Use notecards, spiral notebooks, and computer bookmarks and file folders to store your research. Insert the reference for each source directly onto the applicable note. Use Microsoft Word's footnote function, or consider software programs such as EndNote to organize your bibliography.

IDENTIFY QUOTED, PARAPHRASED, AND SUMMARIZED MATERIAL

To avoid plagiarism (see Chapter 5), insert quotation marks around directly quoted material. When paraphrasing someone else's words or summarizing passages in articles, books, or other sources, record the page number on which the original quotation or passage appears (see Figures 9.1, 9.2, and 9.3).

CRITICALLY EVALUATE YOUR SOURCES

Respect for the written word is deeply ingrained in many of us, and for good reason. Yet not all words are created equal. Some are written by people who

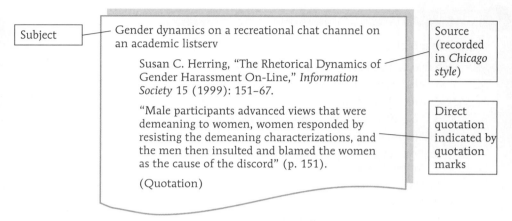

Figure 9.1 Sample Note for a Direct Quotation

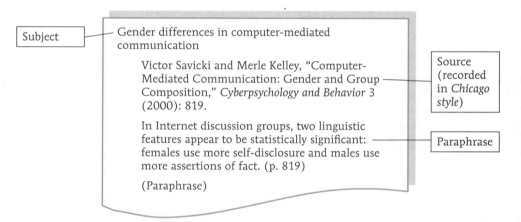

Figure 9.2 Sample Note for a Paraphrase

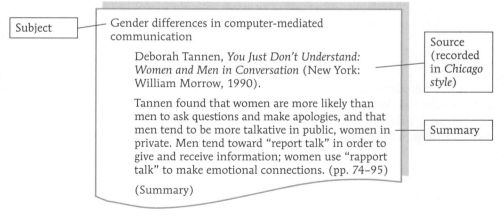

Figure 9.3 Sample Note for a Summary

Ethically Speaking
Researching Your Speech in an Ethical Manner

As you research your speech topic, it's helpful to remind yourself of your ethical responsibilities. As discussed in Chapter 5, central to conducting ethical research is avoiding plagiarism by using your own organization and ideas and properly citing sources when using the work of others. In addition to plagiarism, fabricating information, deceiving research subjects about your real purposes, and breaching confidentiality are equally unethical. **Fabrication** is the making up of information, such as falsifying data or experiments or claiming a source when none exists. Perhaps the most widely publicized case of fabrication in recent times was that of former *New York Times* reporter Jayson Blair. According to an investigation by the *New York Times,* Blair

> filed dispatches that purported to be from Maryland, Texas and other states, when often he was in New York; fabricated comments; concocted scenes and lifted material from other newspapers and wire services; also he selected details from photographs to create the impression he had been somewhere or seen someone, when he had not.[1]

Fabrication can also include altering quotes to "fit" a point; claiming credentials or expertise for yourself that you don't possess, in an effort to boost your credibility; inflating figures to promote your point; and so forth. Each of these examples represents an act of deception.

Conducting research ethically extends to any interviews or surveys that you undertake. In some cases, for example, people will not talk with you or provide information unless you agree to maintain their anonymity. Ethically, it is the speaker's responsibility to protect his or her source's confidentiality when requested. This is true whether the source is a respondent to a questionnaire to whom you have promised anonymity or an expert in a field who gives you an inside tip.

Ethical conduct in public speaking goes beyond doing no harm. The goal of any speech should be to in some way serve the audience well. For example, by investigating whether a certain food ingredient can harm the body, a speaker may help audience members live healthier and longer lives. By conducting research into the pros and cons of different savings options, a speaker may assist audience members in better preparing for retirement. Use your research to advance the knowledge of others or to show them a new way of viewing a problem or an issue.

1. Dan Barry, David Barstow, Jonathan D. Glater, Adam Liptak, and Jacques Steinberg, "Correcting the Record: *Times* Reporter Who Resigned Leaves Long Trail of Deception," *New York Times,* May 11, 2003.

distort the facts, either knowingly or unknowingly. In an age of exploding information, it is now easier than ever for both the honest and the dishonest to get into print — or its electronic equivalent online. (See Chapter 10 for more on evaluating Internet sources.) Thus it is vital to critically evaluate sources before using them. Whether you are reviewing a book, a newspaper article, or any other source, consider the following:

From Source to Speech
Recording and Citing Books

When using a book as a source, locate and record the following citation elements:

1 Book Title

2 Author

3 Publisher

4 City and State of Publication

5 Year of Publication

6 Page Number

1

THE BIG PICTURE

☆ The New Logic of Money and Power in Hollywood ☆

2

Edward Jay Epstein

RANDOM HOUSE ☆ NEW YORK
© 2005

3
RANDOM HOUSE

4
NEW YORK

5
© 2005

6
18

18 ☆ THE BIG PICTURE

title. But while the studios spent an average of $59 million per film just to get audiences and prints into American theaters, they recovered from the box office only $20.6 million on average per film. So in 2005 they wound up paying more to alert potential moviegoers and supply theaters with prints for an opening than they were getting back from those who bought tickets. (The story was similar with overseas theaters, for which, in addition to prints and advertising, the studios had to pay the cost of dubbing and additional editing to tailor the films to foreign audiences.) These new marketing costs had grown so large by 2005 that even if the studios had somehow managed to obtain all their movies for free, they would still have lost money on their American releases.

But studios, of course, did *not* make these movies for free. And, to make matters far worse, the costs of producing a film have also risen astronomically. At the end of the studio-system era, in 1947, the cost of producing an average studio film, or negative cost, was $732,000. In 2005 it was $63.8 million. To be sure, the dollar had decreased in value sevenfold between 1947 and 2005, but even after correcting for inflation, the cost of producing films had increased more than sixteen times since the collapse of the studio system.

Part of the studios' cost problem is the result of stars being freed from their control. Instead of being tethered to studios by seven-year contracts, stars are now auctioned off—with the help of savvy agents—to the highest bidder for each film. Since there are fewer desirable stars than film projects, they can command eight-digit fees. By 20 getting not only between $20 and $50 million a fi tion and perks but a percentage of the film's total cash outlays.

For example, Arnold Schwarzenegger received tract, a $29.25 million fixed fee for his role in the 2 *Rise of the Machines*, as well as a $1.5 million perk private jets, a fully equipped gym trailer, three-be locations, round-the-clock limousines, and persona tion, once the film reached its cash break-even po anteed him 20 percent of the gross receipts from (including video, DVD, theatrical box office, tele Under any scenario—whether the film failed, b profit—the star was assured of making more mo

At the end of the studio-system era, in 1947, the cost of producing an average studio film, or negative cost, was $732,000. In 2003 it was $63.8 million. To be sure, the dollar had decreased in value sevenfold between 1947 and 2003, but even after correcting for inflation, the cost of producing films had increased more than sixteen times since the collapse of the studio system.

Part of the studios' cost problem is the result of stars being freed from their control. Instead of being tethered to studios by seven-year contracts, stars are now auctioned off—with the help of savvy agents—to the highest bidder for each film.

Record Notes

When taking notes, create a separate heading for each idea and record each of the citation elements (author, title, and so forth). Indicate whether the material is a direct quotation, a paraphrase, or a summary of the information. Following are sample notes for a paraphrase and a summary.

NOTE FOR A PARAPHRASE:

Subject

Source

Paraphrase

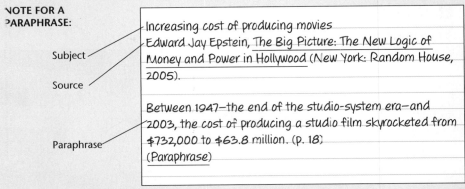

Increasing cost of producing movies
Edward Jay Epstein, The Big Picture: The New Logic of Money and Power in Hollywood (New York: Random House, 2005).

Between 1947—the end of the studio-system era—and 2003, the cost of producing a studio film skyrocketed from $732,000 to $63.8 million. (p. 18)
(Paraphrase)

NOTE FOR A SUMMARY:

Subject

Source

Summary

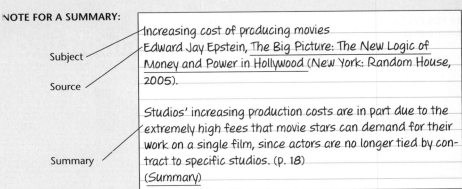

Increasing cost of producing movies
Edward Jay Epstein, The Big Picture: The New Logic of Money and Power in Hollywood (New York: Random House, 2005).

Studios' increasing production costs are in part due to the extremely high fees that movie stars can demand for their work on a single film, since actors are no longer tied by contract to specific studios. (p. 18)
(Summary)

Orally Cite Sources in Your Speech

In your speech, alert the audience to the source of any ideas not your own:

SPEECH EXCERPT INDICATING A PARAPHRASE

> Hollywood studios now need deeper pockets than ever before. In addition to rising promotion, advertising, and distribution costs, studios face rapidly increasing production costs. In his book ***The Big Picture: The New Logic of Money and Power in Hollywood,*** **Edward Jay Epstein notes that** between 1947—the end of the studio-system era—and 2003, the cost of producing a studio film skyrocketed from $732,000 to $63.8 million.

SPEECH EXCERPT INDICATING A SUMMARY

> **According to Edward Jay Epstein in *The Big Picture: The New Logic of Money and Power in Hollywood,*** studios' increasing production costs are in part due to the extremely high fees that today's stars can demand. No longer tied by contracts to studios, stars' salaries are now settled by bidding wars.

163

From Source to Speech
Recording and Citing Articles from Periodicals

When using an article as a source, locate and record the following citation elements:

1 Author

2 Article Title

3 Periodical Title

4 Date of Publication

5 Page Number

1 BY PEG TYRE AND SARAH STAVELEY-O'CARROLL

2

3 NEWSWEEK

4 AUGUST 8, 2005

5 50

How to Fix School Lunch

Celebrity chefs, politicians and concerned parents are joining forces to improve the meals kids eat every day.

BY PEG TYRE AND SARAH STAVELEY-O'CARROLL

FOR JORGE COLLAZO, EXECUTIVE chef for the New York City public schools, coming up with the perfect jerk sauce is yet another step toward making the 1.1 million schoolkids he serves healthier. In a little more than a year, he's introduced salad bars and replaced whole milk with skim. Beef patties are now served on whole-wheat buns. Until recently, "every piece of chicken the manufacturers sent us was either breaded or covered in a glaze," says Collazo.

Last year star English chef Jamie Oliver took over a school cafeteria in a working-class suburb of London. A documentary about his work shamed the British government into spending $500 million to revamp the nation's school-food program. Oliver says it's the United States' turn now. "If you can put a man on the moon," he says, "you can give kids the food they need to make them lighter, fitter and live longer."

For guidelines on various citation styles including *Chicago*, APA, MLA, CBE/CSE, and IEEE see Appendices E–I.

Record Notes

When taking notes, create a separate heading for each idea and record each of the citation elements (author, title, and so forth). Indicate whether the material is a direct quotation, a paraphrase, or a summary of the information.
  Following are sample notes for a direct quotation and a paraphrase.

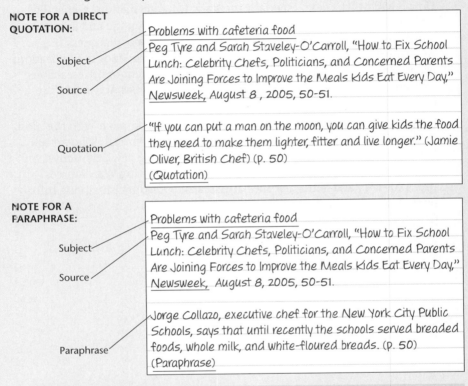

NOTE FOR A DIRECT QUOTATION:

Subject

Source

Quotation

Problems with cafeteria food
Peg Tyre and Sarah Staveley-O'Carroll, "How to Fix School Lunch: Celebrity Chefs, Politicians, and Concerned Parents Are Joining Forces to Improve the Meals Kids Eat Every Day," Newsweek, August 8 , 2005, 50-51.

"If you can put a man on the moon, you can give kids the food they need to make them lighter, fitter and live longer." (Jamie Oliver, British Chef) (p. 50)
(Quotation)

NOTE FOR A PARAPHRASE:

Subject

Source

Paraphrase

Problems with cafeteria food
Peg Tyre and Sarah Staveley-O'Carroll, "How to Fix School Lunch: Celebrity Chefs, Politicians, and Concerned Parents Are Joining Forces to Improve the Meals Kids Eat Every Day," Newsweek, August 8, 2005, 50-51.

Jorge Collazo, executive chef for the New York City Public Schools, says that until recently the schools served breaded foods, whole milk, and white-floured breads. (p. 50)
(Paraphrase)

Orally Cite Sources in Your Speech

In your speech, alert the audience to the source of any ideas not your own:

SPEECH EXCERPT INDICATING A DIRECT QUOTATION

The drive to improve nutrition in schools is not restricted to the United States. **According to an article on fixing school lunches published in the August 8, 2005, edition of** *Newsweek*, star chef Jamie Oliver's success in transforming cafeteria food in England has led him to claim that the U.S. should do the same. *Newsweek* **quoted Oliver as saying,** "If you can put a man on the moon, you can give kids the food they need to make them lighter, fitter and live longer."

SPEECH EXCERPT INDICATING A PARAPHRASE

As reported in the August 8, 2005, edition of *Newsweek*, Executive chef Jorge Collazo of the New York City public schools claimed that until recently, virtually every piece of chicken that was served was breaded or glazed; students drank whole rather than skim milk, and ate white rather than whole-wheat bread.

- What is the author's background — for example, his or her experience, training, and reputation — in the field of study?

- How credible is the publication? Who is the publisher? Is the person or organization reputable? What other publications has the author or the organization published?

- How reliable is the data, especially the statistical information? Generally, statistics drawn from government documents and scientific and academic journals are more reliable than those reported in the popular press (e.g., general-interest magazines). This is because the former kinds of publications print primary data officially collected by the government or by researchers who are subject to peer review. (See also "Using Statistics Accurately" in Chapter 8.)

- How recent is the reference? As a rule, it is best to be familiar with the most recent source you can find, even when the topic is historical. Scholars are continually uncovering new information and offering new perspectives on past events. (See also "From Source to Speech: Evaluating Web Sources" [pp. 170–171] and "Ethically Speaking: Learn to Distinguish among Information, Propaganda, Misinformation, and Disinformation" [p. 172] in Chapter 10.)

Using the Internet to Support Your Speech 10

The Internet represents a vast world of possibilities for discovering material for your speech. In this often unruly and unregulated electronic universe, you can consult daily newspapers from Asia to Africa — and translate them into any one of a dozen languages. You can study Supreme Court decisions, access government documents, browse museum holdings, and drill for information lying deep within the recesses of little-known databases. As with conducting research in a library, the key to a productive search in cyberspace lies in a well-thought-out research strategy, an understanding of the kinds of information that are available on the Internet, and a grasp of how to use Internet search tools effectively.

Begin Your Search at a Library Portal   Research links

Easy access to the Internet may lead you to rely heavily or even exclusively on popular search engines such as Google or Yahoo! to locate speech materials. Doing so, however, presents a host of potential problems, from finding false and/or biased information, to overlooking key sources not found on these sites, to sheer information overload. For these reasons, when researching online it is a good idea to begin your search at your school's **library portal**, or electronic entry point into its holdings (e.g., the library's home page).

✓ CHECKLIST

Evaluating the Credibility of a Web Site

✓ Have I sought out the most authoritative sources for my topic? For example, have I searched for the official Web site(s) of the sponsoring organization related to my topic? Have I consulted government Web sites?

✓ Does the home page of each Web site offer information about its author or organization?

✓ Can I locate additional information about the credibility of the site's author or organization in other sources, such as newspaper articles?

✓ Is the "date last modified/updated" indicated at the top or bottom of each Web site or page? Does it seem that the author or organization routinely updates the site to ensure the information is accurate and current?

Libraries classify and order their resources, both print and electronic, according to well-defined standards. No such standards exist for popular Web search engines.

In considering what library holdings offer that popular Web search engines such as Google and Yahoo! do not, reference librarian Susan Gilroy[1] notes that library holdings are built through careful and deliberate selection processes by trained professionals. When you select a speech source from a library's resources, be it a quotation from an e-journal article, a statistic from a government publication, or an example from a nonfiction book, you can be assured that an information specialist has vetted that source for reliability and credibility.

The databases and other resources you will find on a library's portal are as much a part of its holdings as are its shelved materials. Table 10.1 lists the types of online resources available at most college libraries.

VIRTUAL LIBRARIES

In addition to the home pages of actual libraries, a host of **virtual libraries** can be found on the Internet. The oldest of these is the WWW Virtual Library (www.vlib.org) founded by Tim Berners-Lee, who also founded the **World Wide Web**. Both this and the Internet Public Library (www.ipl.org) offer links to a rich array of resources. A list of virtual libraries appears in Table 10.2.

TABLE 10.1 • Typical Resources Found on Library Portals

- Full-text databases (newspapers, periodicals, journals)
- Reference works (dictionaries, encyclopedias, quotation resources, fact books, directories)
- Books and monographs
- Statistical resources (e.g., FedStats.gov and *Statistical Abstract*)
- Journals
- Digitized texts (primary documents; digitized books)
- Digitized image collections (e.g., ARTstor Digital Library and Internet Archive)
- Video collections

TABLE 10.2 • Selected Virtual Libraries

- **WWW Virtual Library:** vlib.org
- **Librarians' Index to the Internet:** lii.org/search
- **Internet Public Library (IPL):** www.ipl.org
- **Academic Info:** www.academicinfo.net
- **Digital Librarian:** www.digital-librarian.com
- **The Library of Congress:** www.loc.gov/rr/index.html
- **Infomine:** infomine.ucr.edu

Figure 10.1 Virtual Research Library from the Library of Congress

Because library portals and virtual libraries often take you to links that do not readily appear in general search engines and subject directories, they are sometimes considered part of the **invisible Web** — the large portion of the Web that general search engines fail to find. Countless documents and Web sites form part of the invisible Web; this is yet another reason why you should not rely solely on popular search engines for your speech sources.

Be a Critical Consumer of Information

Apart from a library's electronic resources section, how can you distinguish between information on the Internet that is reputable and credible and information that is untrustworthy? As discussed in the Ethically Speaking box on p. 172, search engines cannot discern the quality of information; only a human editor can do this. Each time you examine a document, especially one that has not been evaluated and rated by credible editors, ask yourself, "When was the information posted, and is it timely? Will these sources be accepted by my audience as credible?" (See "From Source to Speech: Demonstrating Your Sources' Reliability and Credibility," pp. 144–145.) "Who put this information here? Why did they do so? Where is similar information found?"[2]

From Source to Speech
Evaluating Web Sources

Check the Most Authoritative Web Sites First

Seek out the most authoritative Web sites on your topic. If your speech explores the NBA draft, investigate the NBA's official Web site first. Check government-sponsored sites such as *www.usgov.gov*. Government-sponsored sites are free of commercial taint and contain highly credible primary materials.

Evaluate Authorship and Sponsorship

1 *Examine the **domain** in the Web address*—the suffix at the end of the address that tells you the nature of the site: educational (.edu), government (.gov), military (.mil), nonprofit organization (.org), business/commercial (.com), and network (.net). A **tilde (~)** in the address usually indicates that it is a personal page rather than part of an institutional Web site. Make sure to assess the credibility of each site, whether it is operated by an individual, a company, a government agency, or a nonprofit group.

2 *Look for an "About" link that describes the organization or a link to a page that gives more information.* These sections can tell a great deal about the nature of the site's content. Be wary of sites that do not include such a link.

3 *Identify the creator of the information.* If an individual operates the site, does the document provide relevant biographical information, such as links to a résumé or a listing of the author's credentials? Look for contact information. A source that doesn't want to be found, at least by e-mail, is not a good source to cite.

Check for Currency

4 *Check for a date that indicates when the page was placed on the Web and when it was last updated.* Is the date current? Web sites that do not have this information may contain outdated or inaccurate material.

Check That the Site Credits Its Sources and That Sources Are Trustworthy

5 *Check that the Web site documents its sources.* Reputable Web sites document the sources they use. Follow any links to these sources, and apply the same criteria to them that you did to the original source document. A good rule of thumb is to verify information you find with at least two other reputable and independent sources.

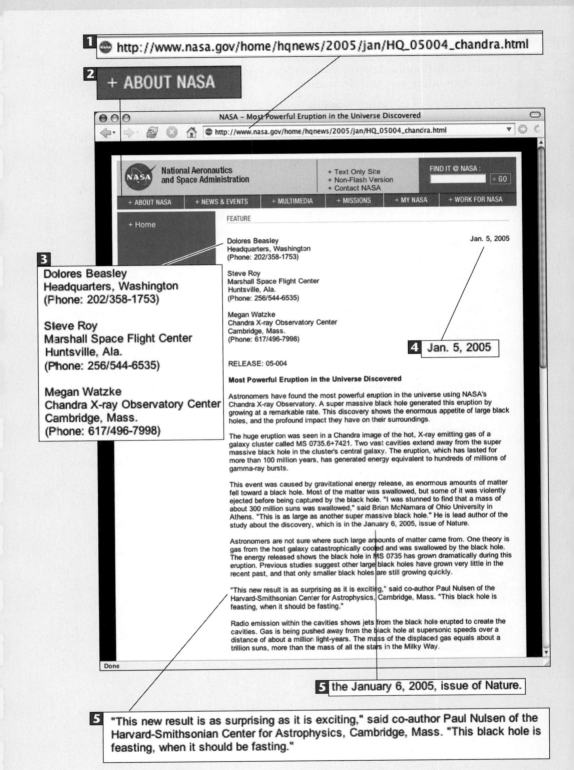

1 http://www.nasa.gov/home/hqnews/2005/jan/HQ_05004_chandra.html

2 + ABOUT NASA

3
Dolores Beasley
Headquarters, Washington
(Phone: 202/358-1753)

Steve Roy
Marshall Space Flight Center
Huntsville, Ala.
(Phone: 256/544-6535)

Megan Watzke
Chandra X-ray Observatory Center
Cambridge, Mass.
(Phone: 617/496-7998)

4 Jan. 5, 2005

NASA – Most Powerful Eruption in the Universe Discovered

http://www.nasa.gov/home/hqnews/2005/jan/HQ_05004_chandra.html

National Aeronautics
and Space Administration

+ Text Only Site
+ Non-Flash Version
+ Contact NASA

FIND IT @ NASA :

+ GO

+ ABOUT NASA   + NEWS & EVENTS   + MULTIMEDIA   + MISSIONS   + MY NASA   + WORK FOR NASA

+ Home

FEATURE

Dolores Beasley
Headquarters, Washington
(Phone: 202/358-1753)

Steve Roy
Marshall Space Flight Center
Huntsville, Ala.
(Phone: 256/544-6535)

Megan Watzke
Chandra X-ray Observatory Center
Cambridge, Mass.
(Phone: 617/496-7998)

Jan. 5, 2005

RELEASE: 05-004

Most Powerful Eruption in the Universe Discovered

Astronomers have found the most powerful eruption in the universe using NASA's Chandra X-ray Observatory. A super massive black hole generated this eruption by growing at a remarkable rate. This discovery shows the enormous appetite of large black holes, and the profound impact they have on their surroundings.

The huge eruption was seen in a Chandra image of the hot, X-ray emitting gas of a galaxy cluster called MS 0735.6+7421. Two vast cavities extend away from the super massive black hole in the cluster's central galaxy. The eruption, which has lasted for more than 100 million years, has generated energy equivalent to hundreds of millions of gamma-ray bursts.

This event was caused by gravitational energy release, as enormous amounts of matter fell toward a black hole. Most of the matter was swallowed, but some of it was violently ejected before being captured by the black hole. "I was stunned to find that a mass of about 300 million suns was swallowed," said Brian McNamara of Ohio University in Athens. "This is as large as another super massive black hole." He is lead author of the study about the discovery, which is in the January 6, 2005, issue of Nature.

Astronomers are not sure where such large amounts of matter came from. One theory is gas from the host galaxy catastrophically cooled and was swallowed by the black hole. The energy released shows the black hole in MS 0735 has grown dramatically during this eruption. Previous studies suggest other large black holes have grown very little in the recent past, and that only smaller black holes are still growing quickly.

"This new result is as surprising as it is exciting," said co-author Paul Nulsen of the Harvard-Smithsonian Center for Astrophysics, Cambridge, Mass. "This black hole is feasting, when it should be fasting."

Radio emission within the cavities shows jets from the black hole erupted to create the cavities. Gas is being pushed away from the black hole at supersonic speeds over a distance of about a million light-years. The mass of the displaced gas equals about a trillion suns, more than the mass of all the stars in the Milky Way.

Done

5 the January 6, 2005, issue of Nature.

5 "This new result is as surprising as it is exciting," said co-author Paul Nulsen of the Harvard-Smithsonian Center for Astrophysics, Cambridge, Mass. "This black hole is feasting, when it should be fasting."

Ethically Speaking
Learn to Distinguish among Information, Propaganda, Misinformation, and Disinformation

Elizabeth Kirk of the Johns Hopkins University's Sheridan Libraries offers important distinctions among information, propaganda, misinformation, and disinformation (see Figure 10.2). Bearing in mind these distinctions when evaluating both print and Internet sources can help you to critically assess their credibility.

- **Information** is data set in a context for relevance. We obtain information by observing and investigating. Information tells us something that is understandable and has the potential to become knowledge when we view it critically and add it to what we already know. To illustrate the difference between data and information, Kirk offers this example:

  "Eight million" and "nine percent" are . . . bits of data. However, "The population of New York City in 2000 was reported to top 8,000,000 persons, a growth of 9% since 1990" is . . . information.

- **Propaganda.** Many people believe that propaganda is based on false information, but this is not necessarily so. Instead, propaganda may well be based in fact, but the facts are presented in a way intended to provoke a certain response. The purpose of propaganda is to instill a particular attitude in order to gain public support for a cause or issue. Usually presented as advertising or publicity, propaganda encourages you to think in a particular way. Military posters that encourage you to enlist are an example of propaganda.

- **Misinformation.** While propaganda may include information that is in fact true, misinformation always refers to something that is not true. One common form of misinformation on the Internet is the *urban legend*—a fabricated story passed along by unsuspecting people.

- **Disinformation.** Propaganda emphasizes one point of view, and misinformation mistakenly represents something as true when it is in fact false. Disinformation is the deliberate falsification of information. For example, doctored photographs and falsified profit-and-loss statements are examples of disinformation in action. Unfortunately, the Internet is widely used for disinformation.

Meaningful speeches are based on sound information rather than on misinformation, propaganda, or disinformation. Being alert to such distinctions is important both as a consumer of speeches and as an ethical speaker and citizen.

Source: Elizabeth E. Kirk, "Information and Its Counterfeits," Sheridan Libraries of Johns Hopkins University, 2001, www.library.jhu.edu/researchhelp/general/evaluating/counterfeit.html (accessed May 4, 2005).

Information ➔	**Propaganda** ➔	**Misinformation** ➔	**Disinformation**
Data set in a context for relevance. *Example:* A fact	Information represented in such a way as to provoke a desired response. *Example:* An advertisement to conserve energy	Something that is not true. *Example:* An urban legend	Deliberate falsification of information. *Example:* A falsified profit-and-loss statement

Figure 10.2 Information, Propaganda, Misinformation, and Disinformation

Make the Most of Internet Search Tools

Just as you wouldn't look for a book in a library without first locating its placement in a card catalog (computerized or otherwise), neither should you simply log on to the Internet and expect to stumble upon the information you need. To locate information on the Internet efficiently, you must be familiar with the function of search engines and subject (Web) directories.

DISTINGUISHING AMONG TYPES OF SEARCH ENGINES

Search engines index the contents of the Web. These engines use powerful software programs (called spiders, crawlers, or bots) that "crawl" the Web, automatically scanning millions and, in the case of the largest engines, billions of documents that contain the keywords and phrases you command them to search. Results are generally ranked from most to least relevant, though search engines use markedly different criteria to determine relevance. Some search engines search only the Web. Others also scan the files of publicly accessible personal journals (called "blogs"), worldwide public discussion groups or newsgroups ("Usenet"), and discussion groups that occur via mass e-mail distribution such as Windows Live Groups at groups.live.com ("mailing lists"). Some engines index more Web pages than others or index pages more often than others.

Individual versus Meta-Search Engines

Search engines are distinguished by whether or not they compile their own databases. **Individual search engines** compile their own databases of Web pages. Three of the largest individual search engines are:

- Google (google.com)
- Yahoo! (search.yahoo.com)
- Windows Live (live.com)

Of these, Google indexes the most Web pages and offers searches that focus on images, maps, news, and blogs, among other options.

Rather than compiling their own databases, **meta-search engines** scan a variety of individual search engines simultaneously. Since meta-search engines scan multiple search engines, why use an individual search engine? Meta-search engines run wide but not necessarily deep. Existing meta-search engines can produce disappointing results that include only the top listings from each search engine and far too many paid listings.[3] As a result, some librarians no longer recommend using them.[4] With that disclaimer, here are several of the most comprehensive meta-search engines:

- Dogpile (www.dogpile.com)
- Ixquick (ixquick.com)
- Metacrawler (www.metacrawler.com)

Specialized Search Engines

A **specialized search engine** lets you conduct narrower but deeper searches into a particular field. Specialized search engines are databases created by researchers, government agencies, businesses, or other parties with a deep interest in a topic. Examples include Scirus, a scientific-only search engine, and Bioethics.gov, a specialized search engine sponsored by the President's Council on Bioethics.

To find a search engine geared specifically to your topic, begin your search at your school's library home page by typing in the topic term with the keywords *search engine*. For example, a search for *global warming* AND *search engine* will lead you to many dedicated sites.

New specialized search engines emerge all the time; here are three well-known (and comparatively broad) ones geared to college students and researchers:

- GoogleScholar.com (lets you search specifically for scholarly literature, including peer-reviewed papers, theses, books, preprints, abstracts, and technical reports from all broad areas of research)
- FindArticles.com (culls articles from leading academic, industry, and general-interest publications)
- Answers.com (a reference search service that provides concise answers drawn from over a hundred authoritative encyclopedias, dictionaries, glossaries, and atlases)

UNDERSTANDING HOW SUBJECT (WEB) DIRECTORIES WORK

A **subject (Web) directory** is a searchable database of Web sites organized by categories (see Figure 10.3). Three of the most comprehensive subject directories on the Web are:

- Open Directory Project or DMOZ (www.dmoz.org)
- Yahoo! Directory (dir.yahoo.com)
- Academic Info (www.academicinfo.net)

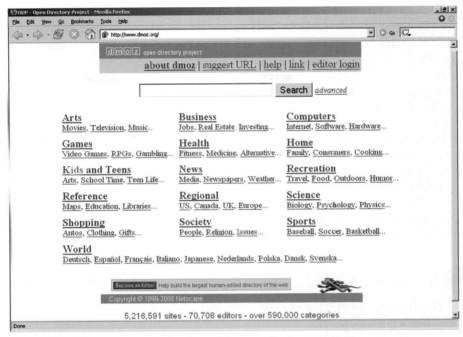

Figure 10.3 Home Page for the Open Directory Project (DMOZ)

Subject directories allow you to progressively narrow your search, or "drill down" your topic, until you find what you are looking for. If your speech is on some aspect of baseball teams, for example, you would follow these links, continuing until you find what you want:

sports ⇒ baseball ⇒ amateur ⇒ leagues ⇒ teams

If you attempt to search in a manner other than by subject (e.g., by proper name), the directory will not return results.

Unlike search engines, which rely on automated crawlers to retrieve documents matching your keywords, people create and manage subject directories. (Note that directories do vary in how and to what extent submissions are assessed.) To find a subject directory for a specific topic or field, try using one of the general directories or search engines listed earlier. If your topic is Afghanistan, for example, key in *Afghanistan* AND *directory* or *Web directories*. Among other hits, this search yields the excellent specialized directory Afghana! at www.afghana.com.

KNOWING WHEN TO USE SEARCH ENGINES AND SUBJECT DIRECTORIES

Both search engines and subject directories offer valuable help in locating supporting material for your speech, but each is best used for a somewhat different purpose. Because search engines index so many documents, they often find information that isn't listed in subject directories, making them extremely useful when you want to locate a wide variety of materials. In addition, because they scan the full text of a document rather than just its title, first few pages, or URL address, search engines are the tool of choice when you need to find very defined information (such as specific terms, facts, figures, or quotations) that may be buried within documents.

In contrast, subject directories are more useful in both finding and narrowing a topic (see Chapter 7). When you are looking for information on a general topic such as automobiles, for instance, subject directories offer a far easier and less time-consuming way of surveying information. In this case, you might find links to fifty sites that have been selected by the editors or maintainers of the directory; these selected sites may have a higher probability of being relevant to your search. With a search engine, you would be faced with the task of sifting through countless documents containing the word *automobile,* many of which would not be relevant.

 CHECKLIST

Choosing between a Subject Directory and a Search Engine

✓   If you are looking for a list of reputable sites on the same subject, use a subject directory.

✓   If you are looking for a specific page within a site, use a search engine.

✓   If you need to find specific terms, facts, figures, or quotations that may be buried within documents, use a search engine.

✓   If you want to locate a wide variety of materials related to your search, use a subject directory first and then use a search engine.

BEING ALERT TO COMMERCIAL FACTORS AFFECTING SEARCH RESULTS

When researching your topic outside of a library portal, you will want to consider any commercial influence on your search results — specifically, whether a particular listing appears in your search results merely because an advertiser has paid to put it there. Advertising on the Internet is now a billion-dollar industry, and much of the revenue search engines garner from it come from (1) fees that companies pay them for a guaranteed higher ranking within search results (called **paid placement**) and (2) fees that companies pay to be included in a search engine or subject directory's full index of possible results, without a guarantee of ranking (called **paid inclusion**).[5] When you are looking to purchase something, finding links that advertisers have paid to include is not necessarily a bad thing. But when you need unbiased information of a factual nature, it clearly is a problem.

Identifying paid-placement listings is relatively easy: Look for a heading labeled "Sponsored Links" or "Sponsored Results" at the top, side, or bottom of the main page. Be aware that these headings are in an inconspicuous color or small typeface and may be hard to read. Identifying paid-inclusion listings is much more difficult because they are mixed in with the main results. Sometimes they may be grouped under headings such as "Web Results" or "Web Pages," but most often there is no way to identify whether or not someone paid to include the listing in the search engine's index (recall that paid inclusion does not guarantee any particular ranking in the listings). Google and AOL have never sponsored paid-inclusion programs. However, many other search engines continue to offer paid-inclusion programs, prompting the *Consumer Reports WebWatch*[6] to offer tips on ways to minimize the potential influence of commercial interests on your search (see the accompanying checklist).

 CHECKLIST

Identifying Paid Listings in Search Results

✓ Look for a heading labeled "Sponsored Links" or "Sponsored Results" at the top, side, or bottom of the main page. This indicates a paid-placement listing.

✓ Use multiple search engines and compare the results.

✓ Beware of meta-search engines, which often include many paid-inclusion listings.

✓ Click beyond the first page of your search results to find relevant sites.

✓ Read the fine print on a search engine's disclosure pages to find its policy on paid inclusion.

Conduct Smart Searches

 WEB Chapter quizzes

To maximize the odds of finding the materials you need, take some time to familiarize yourself with the search commands of the search tools you select. Go to the Help command located near the search window. Here you will find tips for entering your search commands most efficiently. Most search tools provide guidance for conducting both simple and more advanced searches. Advanced search functions allow you to further refine your search criteria — by looking for sites in a particular language, limiting the search by date, or searching for specific kinds of files (such as sound or picture files).

USE BASIC SEARCH COMMANDS

Most search tools are programmed to respond to the following basic commands:

- Quotation marks (" ") to find exact phrases (e.g., *"white wine"*). Without the quote marks, search tools will list all relevant sites with the word *white* as well as those with the word *wine*.

- *Boolean operators,* words placed between the keywords in a search that specify how the keywords are related, include AND, OR, and NOT. They act as filters to help you eliminate potential items that are unrelated to your search.

  - AND *narrows* your search to the words you include. For example, *Bill Gates* AND *speeches* AND *Bill and Melinda Gates Foundation* eliminates speeches given by Bill Gates about other topics, such as those about Microsoft.

  - OR *expands* your search by permitting results that contain alternative terms. For example, (*preschool* OR *nursery school*). Note: Include OR searches within parentheses. This search will find documents that contain *preschool, nursery school,* or both.

  - NOT *restricts* your search by excluding specific terms from the results. For example, *"bed and breakfasts"* NOT *motels* will find all documents that contain the exact phrase *bed and breakfasts* but that aren't motels.

- Plus (+) and minus (–) signs placed directly in front of keywords indicate whether you want the term included or excluded from the search (e.g., *+publishing –printing*).

USE FIELD SEARCHING TO FURTHER NARROW RESULTS

Field searching goes beyond the basic search commands to narrow results even further. Using this function (also called an advanced search) will take you slightly longer at the start, but it can save considerable time overall by returning closer matches.

Search engines sort results according to several attributes or "fields" common to all pages on the World Wide Web. Most search tools provide advanced search options that enable you to target these more specific search parameters to further narrow search results. To locate the field search option, look for a link on the front page of any given search engine.

A field search option generally includes the following fields:

- *Keywords:* "All," "exact phrase," "at least one," and "without" filter results for keywords in much the same way as the basic search commands. Keyword field searches allow you the option of limiting your search to a Web site's title or URL.

- *Language* includes search results with pages written in the specified language. A search for the exact phrase *"gas prices"* and the language specified as Polish produces results listing sites originating in English and sites originating in Polish.

- *Country* searches result in documents originating in the specified country.

- *File format* returns results with links to particular document formats, such as Microsoft Word (.doc), Adobe Acrobat (.pdf), PowerPoint (.ppt), and Excel (.xls).

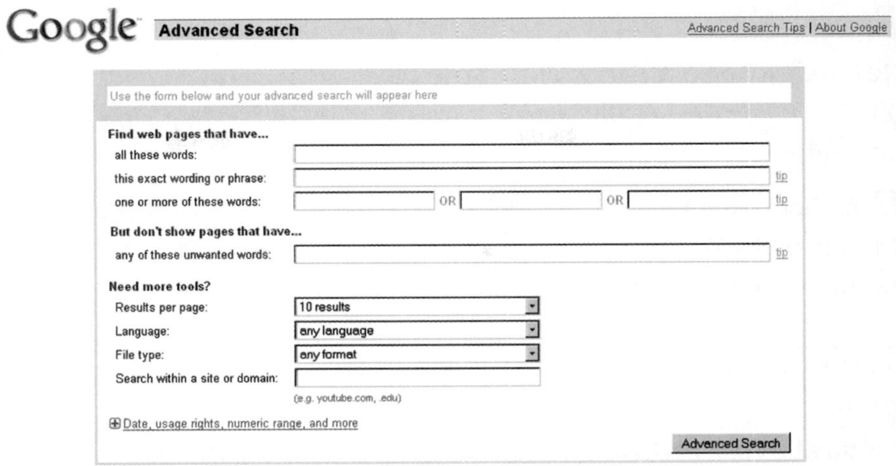

Figure 10.4 Google's Advanced Search Page for Conducting Field Searches

- *Domain* searches limit results to sites residing in the specified Internet domain (e.g., .com, .edu, .gov, .org). Both Yahoo! and Google enable more restricted domain searching to specific sites (e.g., harvard.edu; fcc.gov). (See Figure 10.4.)

- *Date* searches focus on a specified range of time. For example, if you search early in the semester on your topic and later want to know if new information has appeared, you could limit your search to the last three months or even the last week.

- *Safe-search,* usually the default setting in the major search engines, filters out most obscene and adult-oriented material and in some instances information that is potentially violent or hate-oriented. Safe-search is an especially important feature when doing image searches or searches on sensitive topics, although it is by no means fail-safe.

- *Page-specific* searches attempt to obtain a very limited set of results by seeking pages that contain the same basic information as a known page does or that link to the known page.

Record and Cite Internet Sources

Because Internet sites often change, it is especially important to keep track of your speech sources. Remember that when you give a speech, you are in the spotlight. Your information may be challenged by an audience member, and you will need to prove that you have based your speech on credible information from reliable sources. If there is any chance that your speech may be published, the publisher will want to include a list of references. Refer to Chapter 9, p. 158, for instructions on maintaining a working bibliography.

From Source to Speech
Recording and Citing Web Sources

When using a Web document as a source, locate and record the following citation elements:

1 Author of the Work
2 Title of the Work
3 Title of the Web Site
4 Date of Publication/Last Update
5 Site Address (URL) and Date Accessed

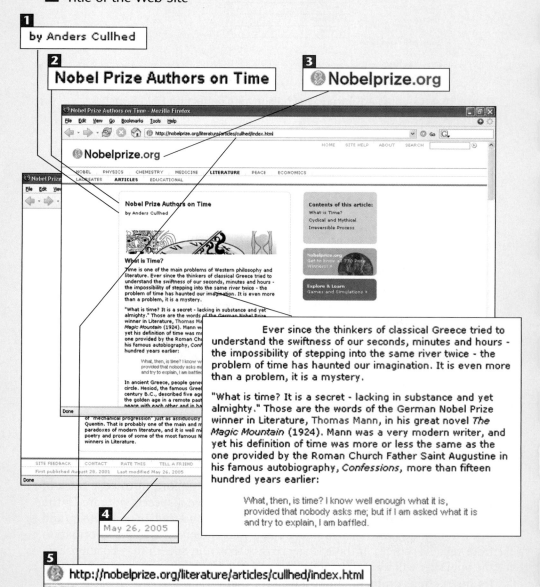

1
by Anders Cullhed

2
Nobel Prize Authors on Time

3
Nobelprize.org

Ever since the thinkers of classical Greece tried to understand the swiftness of our seconds, minutes and hours - the impossibility of stepping into the same river twice - the problem of time has haunted our imagination. It is even more than a problem, it is a mystery.

"What is time? It is a secret - lacking in substance and yet almighty." Those are the words of the German Nobel Prize winner in Literature, Thomas Mann, in his great novel *The Magic Mountain* (1924). Mann was a very modern writer, and yet his definition of time was more or less the same as the one provided by the Roman Church Father Saint Augustine in his famous autobiography, *Confessions*, more than fifteen hundred years earlier:

What, then, is time? I know well enough what it is, provided that nobody asks me; but if I am asked what it is and try to explain, I am baffled.

4
May 26, 2005

5
http://nobelprize.org/literature/articles/cullhed/index.html

For guidelines on various citation styles including *Chicago*, APA, MLA, CBE/CSE, and IEEE see Appendices E–I.

Record Notes

When taking notes, create a separate heading for each idea and record the citation elements from your source. Indicate whether the material is a direct quotation, a paraphrase, or a summary of the information. Following are sample notes for a quotation and a paraphrase.

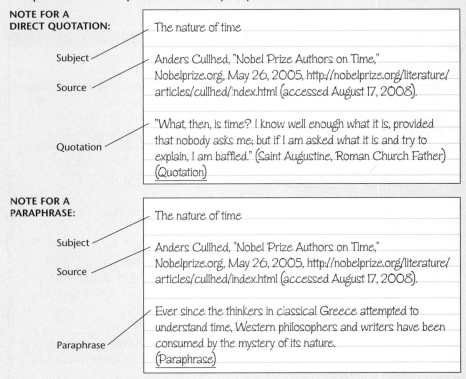

NOTE FOR A DIRECT QUOTATION:

Subject

Source

Quotation

The nature of time

Anders Cullhed, "Nobel Prize Authors on Time," Nobelprize.org, May 26, 2005, http://nobelprize.org/literature/articles/cullhed/index.html (accessed August 17, 2008).

"What, then, is time? I know well enough what it is, provided that nobody asks me; but if I am asked what it is and try to explain, I am baffled." (Saint Augustine, Roman Church Father) (Quotation)

NOTE FOR A PARAPHRASE:

Subject

Source

Paraphrase

The nature of time

Anders Cullhed, "Nobel Prize Authors on Time," Nobelprize.org, May 26, 2005, http://nobelprize.org/literature/articles/cullhed/index.html (accessed August 17, 2008).

Ever since the thinkers in classical Greece attempted to understand time, Western philosophers and writers have been consumed by the mystery of its nature. (Paraphrase)

Orally Cite Sources in Your Speech

In your speech, alert the audience to the source of any ideas not your own:

SPEECH EXCERPT INDICATING A DIRECT QUOTATION

Many famous thinkers have grappled with the concept of time. For example, Saint Augustine wrote in his biography, *Confessions*, "What, then, is time? I know well enough what it is, provided that nobody asks me; but if I am asked what it is and try to explain, I am baffled."

SPEECH EXCERPT INDICATING A PARAPHRASE

In an article on the nature of time posted on the Web site Nobleprize.org, professor of comparative literature Anders Cullhed notes that beginning with thinkers in ancient Greece, Western philosophers and writers have tried to understand the nature of time.

During delivery of your speech, always reveal to your audience the source of any direct quotations, paraphrased information, facts, opinions, statistics, or other types of information that are not your own and are outside the pool of common knowledge (see Chapter 5). For visual guidelines on recording and citing Web sources, see "From Source to Speech" on this topic on pp. 180–181.

 CHECKLIST

Documenting Internet Sources

As in documentation of print sources, styles of documenting Internet sources for a written bibliography vary according to discipline. Three of the most widely used formats are the American Psychological Association (APA) style, the Modern Language Association (MLA) style, and the *Chicago* style. (See Appendices E through I for specific documentation guidelines.) Each referencing style varies in the precise ordering and formatting of information, but all generally require that you provide as much of the following information as possible:

✓ Name of the author, editor, or site maintainer (if applicable). (Some sources may be identified only by a log-in name.)

✓ Publication information of any print version

✓ Date of electronic publication or last revision (if known)

✓ Title of document, whether it's a scholarly project, database, periodical, or, for a professional or personal site with no title, a description such as a home page

✓ Title of complete work of which it is a part (if relevant)

✓ Other relevant information (volume number, page numbers, etc.)

✓ Retrieval date statement (e.g., "Retrieved March 16, 2008" or "Accessed March 16, 2008")

✓ URL

Source: Andrew Harnack and Eugene Kleppinger, *Online! A Reference Guide to Using Internet Sources* (Boston: Bedford/St. Martin's, 2002).

Organizing and Outlining

Organizing and Outlining

Speaker's Reference
Organizing and Outlining

11. Organizing the Speech

Create Main Points That Express Your Key Ideas and Major Claims

- Use the specific purpose and thesis statements as guides. (p. 191)
- Check that each main point flows directly from these statements. (p. 191)

Restrict the Number of Main Points, and Focus on One Idea per Point

- Strive to cover between two and five main points. (p. 191)
- Focus each main point on a single idea. (p. 193)
- Present each main point as a full-sentence statement. (p. 194)
- Reflect the main points back to the purpose statement. (p. 194)

Use Supporting Points to Substantiate or Prove Your Main Points

- Create supporting points with your research materials. (p. 194)
- Ensure that supporting points follow logically from main points. (p. 194)
- Check that supporting points are in fact subordinate in weight to main points. (p. 195)

Create Speech Points That Are Unified, Coherent, and Balanced

- State the points of your speech in parallel form. (p. 193)
- Focus each point, whether main or subordinate, on a single idea. (p. 196)
- Review the logical connections between points. (p. 196)
- Dedicate roughly the same amount of time to each main point. (p. 197)
- Ensure that the introduction and the conclusion are approximately of the same length and that the body is the longest part of the speech. (p. 198)
- Substantiate each main point with at least two supporting points. (p. 198)

Use Transitions to Signal Movement from One Point to Another

- Use clear transitions to move from point to point. (p. 198)
- Use full-sentence transitions to move from one main point to another. (p. 198)

- Use internal previews to help listeners anticipate what's ahead. (p. 202)
- Use internal summaries to help listeners review what's been said. (p. 202)

12. Types of Organizational Arrangements

Be Audience-Centered When Arranging Main Points

- Select a pattern that listeners can easily follow. (p. 204)
- Select a pattern that helps you achieve your speech goals. (p. 204)
- Subpoints need not always follow the pattern selected for main points. (p. 204)

Choose from a Variety of Organizational Patterns

- To stress natural divisions or categories in a topic, consider a *topical pattern*. (p. 204)
- To motivate listeners to adopt a course of action, consider *Monroe's motivated sequence*. (p. 204 and Chapter 26)
- To demonstrate the superiority of one viewpoint or proposal over another, consider the *comparative advantage pattern*. (p. 204 and Chapter 26)
- To disprove an opposing claim to your position, consider the *refutation pattern*. (p. 204 and Chapter 26)
- To describe a series of developments in time or a set of actions occurring sequentially, consider a *chronological pattern*. (p. 206)
- To emphasize physical arrangement, consider a *spatial pattern*. (p. 206)
- To demonstrate a topic in terms of its underlying causes (or its effects), consider a *causal (cause-effect) pattern*. (p. 207)
- To demonstrate a problem and then provide justification for a solution, consider a *problem-solution pattern*. (p. 208)
- To convey speech ideas through a story, consider a *narrative pattern*. (p. 209)
- To demonstrate how each speech idea builds on the previous idea and in turn supports the thesis, consider a *circular pattern*. (p. 210)

13. Outlining the Speech

Plan on Developing Two Outlines before Delivering Your Speech

- Begin by creating a working outline in sentence format. (p. 212)
- Transfer your ideas to a speaking outline in phrase or key-word format. (p. 212)

Become Familiar with Sentence, Phrase, and Key-Word Outlines

• Sentence outlines express speech points in full sentences. (p. 212)
• Phrase outlines use shortened versions of the sentence form. (p. 214)
• Key-word outlines use just a few words associated with the specific point. (p. 214)

Know the Benefits and Drawbacks of the Three Outline Formats

• Sentence outlines offer the most protection against memory lapses but sacrifice eye contact. (p. 214)
• The less you rely on your outline notes, the more eye contact you can have with the audience. (p. 214)
• Key-word outlines promote eye contact and natural delivery, *if* you are well rehearsed. (p. 214)

Plan Your Speech with a Working Outline

• Check for correct coordination and subordination of speech points. (p. 213)
• Treat the working outline as a document to be revised and rearranged. (p. 215)
• Include everything you want to say in your working outline. (p. 215)
• Separate the introduction and conclusion from the body of the speech. (p. 215)
• Create a bibliography. (p. 215)
• Assign the speech a title. (p. 216)

Create a Speaking Outline to Deliver the Speech

• Condense the working outline into a phrase or key-word outline. (p. 220)
• Clearly indicate delivery cues. (p. 220)
• Print large enough for your words to be seen at a glance. (p. 221)

KEY TERMS

Chapter 11

arrangement	indentation	full-sentence transitions
outlining	roman numeral outline	signposts
introduction	unity	restate-forecast form
body	coherence	rhetorical questions
conclusion	coordination and subordination	preview statement
main points		internal preview
parallel form	balance	internal summary
supporting points	transitions	

Chapter 12

topical pattern of arrangement

chronological pattern of arrangement

spatial pattern of arrangement

causal (cause-effect) pattern of arrangement

problem-solution pattern of arrangement

narrative pattern of arrangement

circular pattern of arrangement

Chapter 13

working outline

speaking outline

sentence outline

phrase outline

key-word outline

delivery cues

Organizing the Speech

Audience members quickly note the difference between a well-organized speech and one that has been put together haphazardly, with decidedly negative results when the speech is disorganized. Listeners' understanding of a speech, for example, is directly linked to how well it is organized.[1] Apparently, a little bit of disorganization won't ruin a speech if the speaker is otherwise engaging. Audience attitudes plummet when the speech is very disorganized.[2] Listeners also find speakers whose speeches are well organized more credible than those who present poorly organized ones.[3] Given all this, you won't want to skip the crucial steps of arranging and outlining speech points.

Organizing the speech (also called **arrangement** by classical scholars) is the strategic process of deciding how to order speech points into a coherent and convincing pattern for your topic and audience. **Outlining** is the physical process of plotting those speech points on the page in hierarchical order of importance. An *outline* is an essential tool that lets you check for logical inconsistencies in the placement of speech points and pinpoint weaknesses in the amount and kind of support for them. Rather than making the job of drafting a speech harder, outlining your speech provides a vivid snapshot of its strengths and weaknesses and clearly points to how you can fix the flaws. Although a few famous speakers have managed to deliver successful speeches without first arranging and outlining them, for the vast majority of us, the success or failure of a speech will depend on doing so.

Beyond the Speech: Organizing as a Life Skill

As well as being of immense practical value in fashioning better speeches, skill in arranging and outlining information can have far-reaching positive effects on many aspects of your academic and professional life. As noted in Chapter 1, written and verbal skill in communication rank first in employers' "wish list" for employees.[4] Employers seek workers who can communicate ideas logically and convincingly. Nearly all professional-level jobs, for example, require you to prepare well-organized written and oral reports, PowerPoint presentations, and so forth. Similarly, written assignments in the classroom depend upon how convincingly and logically you present your viewpoint. Learning how to arrange ideas into a coherent pattern and gaining proficiency with outlining — a skill that depends on the logical coordination and subordination of ideas (see p. 196) — will serve you well as a public speaker and in these other arenas (see Tables 11.1 and 11.2).

A speech structure is quite simple, composed of just three general parts: an introduction, a body, and a conclusion. The **introduction** establishes the

TABLE 11.1 • Sample Outline Format

Extended Outline Format:

I. Main point
    A. Subordinate to main point I
    B. Coordinate with subpoint A
        1. Subordinate to subpoint B
        2. Coordinate with sub-subpoint 1
            a. Subordinate to sub-subpoint 2
            b. Coordinate with sub-subpoint 2
                (1) Subordinate to sub-sub-subpoint b
                (2) Coordinate with sub-sub-sub-subpoint (1)
II. Main point: Coordinate with main point I

purpose of the speech and shows its relevance to the audience. It lets listeners know where the speaker is taking them. The **body** of the speech presents main points that are intended to fulfill the speech purpose. Main points are developed with various kinds of supporting material to fulfill this purpose. The **conclusion** ties the purpose and the main points together. It brings closure to the speech by restating the purpose and reiterating why it is relevant to the audience, and by leaving audience members with something to think about. In essence, the introduction tells listeners where they are going, the body takes them there, and the conclusion lets them know that they have arrived.

Chapters 12 and 13 describe the various patterns you can use to order speech points and illustrate the three types of outline formats — sentence, phrase, and key word. Chapters 14 and 15 focus on how to create effective introductions and conclusions. In this chapter, we explore the body of the speech.

Main Points, Supporting Points, and Transitions

 WEB Chapter quizzes

A speech body consists of three elements. The *main points* represent each of the main elements or claims being made in support of the speech topic. *Supporting points* do just as their name suggests: They support the information or arguments put forth in the main points. *Transitions* (discussed in detail later in this chapter) serve as links for audience members, alerting them to the speaker's direction as he or she moves through the speech.

Main Points: Making the Claim

Main points express the key ideas and major themes of the speech. Their function is to represent each of the main elements or claims being made in support of the speech topic. The first step in creating main points is to identify the central ideas and themes of the speech. What are the most important ideas you seek to convey? As you review your research, what important ideas emerge? What ideas can you substantiate with supporting material? Each of these ideas or claims should be expressed as a main point.

USING THE PURPOSE AND THESIS STATEMENTS AS GUIDES

You can use the specific purpose and thesis statements as reference points to help generate main points. As discussed in Chapter 7, the *specific purpose statement* expresses the goal of the speech. Formulating it in your mind allows you to articulate precisely what you want the speech to accomplish (without stating it directly in the speech itself). The *thesis statement* (which *is* stated in the speech) expresses the speech's theme or central idea. It concisely lays out what the speech is about. The main points should flow directly from these two statements expressing the speech goal and the central idea, as seen in the following examples:

SPECIFIC PURPOSE: (what you want your audience to get from the speech; not stated in speech itself): To show my audience, through a series of easy steps, how to perform meditation.

THESIS: (the central idea of the speech; thesis is expressed in speech): When performed correctly, meditation is an effective and easy way to reduce stress.

Main Points:

I.   The first step of meditation is "positioning."

II.   The second step of meditation is "breathing."

III.   The third step of meditation is "relaxation."

THESIS STATEMENT: To ensure financial security in retirement, young adults need to set investment goals, invest early, and commit to the long haul.

Main Points:

I.   Setting investment goals is the first step that young adults need to take to ensure financial security in retirement.

II.   Young adults should begin investing as early as they can and put away as much as possible.

III.   It is important that young adults invest for the long haul.

NUMBER OF MAIN POINTS

Most speakers find that audiences can comfortably take in only between two and five main points. (Although most classroom speeches fit this category, research has shown that in longer speeches listeners can follow up to seven main points.[5]) As a rule, the fewer main points in a speech, the greater are the odds

✓ **SELF-ASSESSMENT CHECKLIST**

Do the Speech Points Illustrate or Prove the Thesis?

_____ 1. Are the most important ideas in your speech expressed in the main points?

_____ 2. Are any key ideas implied by your thesis not addressed by main points?

_____ 3. Does each supporting point offer sufficient evidence for the corresponding main point?

_____ 4. Do your supporting points reflect a variety of appropriate supporting material, such as examples, narratives, testimony, and facts and statistics?

that you will keep your listeners' attention. Listeners have a better recall of the main points made at the beginning and at the end of a speech than of those made in between (unless the ideas made in between are far more striking than the others). Thus, if it is especially important that listeners remember certain ideas, introduce those ideas near the beginning of the speech and reiterate them at the conclusion.

STRATEGIES FOR LIMITING MAIN POINTS

Audiences become overwhelmed when presented with too much information, tending to tune out in response. Therefore, if you find you have too many main points while organizing your speech, consider whether your topic is sufficiently narrow (see Chapter 7). At the same time, check whether you amply support each main point with a variety of sources. This "narrow but deep" approach helps prevent loss of attention and encourages audience members to follow your message.

If the problem does not lie in an overly broad topic, review your main and supporting points for proper subordination. Do any points more properly belong as subpoints to other main points? In a speech draft about interviewing and etiquette training, University of Oklahoma student Amber Pointer found this to be the case when she saw that she had created six main points:

I. Interviewing is competitive and requires preparation.

II. As in sports, interviewing requires training to compete well against others.

III. When you sell yourself in an interview, you want to make your best impression.

IV. When you take a course on interviewing, you become more competitive.

V. Dressing appropriately is critical to making a good impression.

VI. Proper table manners are key to making a positive impression during a luncheon interview.

Upon examination, Amber realized that main points II and IV are actually sub-points of point I:

I.   Interviewing is competitive and requires preparation.
~~II.~~ a.   As in sports, interviewing requires training to compete well against others.
~~IV.~~ b.   When you take a course on interviewing, you become more competitive.

Similarly, points V and VI are subpoints of point III (which now becomes main point II):

II.   When you sell yourself in an interview, you want to make your best impression.
~~V.~~ a.   Dressing appropriately is critical to making a good impression.
~~VI.~~ b.   Proper table manners are key to making a positive impression during a luncheon interview.

As she examined her outline, Amber realized that she had introduced ideas toward the end of her speech that properly supported the first main point and presented material early on that was actually subordinate to her second main point. Rather than six main points, Amber's speech in fact consists of just two.

FORM OF MAIN POINTS

A main point should not introduce more than one idea. If it does, it should be split into two (or more) main points:

Incorrect:
I.   West Texas has its own Grand Canyon, and South Texas has its own desert.

Correct:
I.   West Texas boasts its own Grand Canyon.
II.   South Texas boasts its own desert.

Whenever possible, main points should also be stated in **parallel form** — that is, in similar grammatical form and style. (See Chapter 16 for a discussion of parallelism.) This helps listeners understand and retain the points and lends power and elegance to your words:

THESIS STATEMENT: The Group of Eight (G8) of the world's leading industrial nations should take stronger steps at its next summit to reduce carbon dioxide emissions linked to global warming.

Incorrect:

I.   The U.S. must adopt new stricter policies to reduce carbon dioxide emissions.

II.   Canada failed to adopt a sound global-warming policy.

III. Switzerland didn't do anything either.

Correct:

I.   The U.S. must adopt stricter policies to reduce carbon dioxide emissions.

II.   Canada must readdress the question of carbon dioxide emissions in its next session of parliament.

III. Switzerland must reevaluate its position on carbon dioxide emissions in its next plenary session.

Always create your main points as full sentences, and strive to express them as declarative sentences or sentences that state a fact or an argument. Presenting each main point as a declarative statement emphasizes the point and alerts audience members to the main thrusts of your speech. For instance, if one of your main points is that poor children are suffering because of changes in welfare laws, you should clearly state, "Today, poor children are suffering because of changes in the welfare laws." Main points reflect back to the purpose statement, and this connection between purpose statement and main points keeps the audience on track.

Supporting Points: Substantiating the Claim

Supporting points represent the supporting material you have gathered to fill out or justify the main points and lead the audience to accept the purpose of the speech (see Chapter 8). It is here that you substantiate or prove your thesis with examples, narratives, testimony, and facts and statistics.

Listeners respond most favorably to a variety of supporting materials derived from multiple sources to illustrate each main point.[6] Alternating among different types of supporting material — such as beginning with a short story, followed by examples, statistics, and perhaps credible testimony — sparks interest and builds credibility while simultaneously appealing to listeners' different learning styles. For example, to support the claim that Michael Jordan was the most dominant player in the history of basketball, you could relate a story about how he won the final game of the 1998 NBA championship against the Utah Jazz team, quote from journalist David Halberstam's biography of Jordan, and then provide some of Jordan's lifetime stats.

To determine whether they have the right amount and kind of supporting points, some speakers check them against a series of questions used by journalists: *who* (did it), *what* (did they do), *when* (did they do it), *where* (did it occur), *why* (did it happen), and *how* (did it happen)? This formula dictates that every news story should answer these questions, usually in descending order of importance in case the story has to be shortened. While these particular questions may not reflect the most relevant criteria for your selection of supporting materials, the idea is to carefully evaluate whether your subpoints satisfactorily flesh out your main claims and that they do so with a mix that is likely to appeal to listeners.

POSITION OF SUPPORTING POINTS

In an outline, supporting points appear in a subordinate position to main points. This is indicated by **indentation**. As with main points, supporting points should be ordered in a logical fashion — that is, arranged in order of their importance or relevance to the main point. The most common format is the **roman numeral outline** (used thus far in this chapter). Main points are enumerated with uppercase roman numerals (I, II, III . . .), supporting points are enumerated with capital letters (A, B, C . . .), third-level points are enumerated with arabic numerals (1, 2, 3 . . .), and fourth-level points are enumerated with lowercase letters (a, b, c . . .), as seen in the following format (see also Table 11.2):

I.   Main point
    A.   Supporting point
       1.   Sub-supporting point
          a.   Sub-sub-supporting point
          b.   Sub-sub-supporting point
       2.   Sub-supporting point
          a.   Sub-sub-supporting point
          b.   Sub-sub-supporting point
    B.   Supporting point
II.   Main point

Here is an example from a speech about children's negative attitudes toward school:

I.   The increase in study drill sessions in preparation for standardized tests, from one hour to three hours daily, is causing school-age students to experience anxiety about attending school.

    A.   Teachers report that students' reactions to the lengthened study drills have been negative.

       1.   Teachers report a noticeable rise in acting-out behaviors.

       2.   Teachers report a tenfold increase in class-time requests to visit the nurse.

    B.   During the past two months, two hundred parents have lodged complaints with the principal about the extended study drill sessions.

       1.   The majority (85%) said that their children complained about the lengthy study sessions.

       2.   A minority (15%) reported that their children resisted going to school.

II. The elimination of the art and science classes in favor of longer drill sessions has only increased students' negative feelings toward school.

 A. Art classes have long been a favorite of school-age children.

 B. Student reaction to the elimination of science classes has been strongly negative.

  1. Students staged a sit-down strike in the cafeteria to protest the elimination of science classes.

  2. Several students transferred to other schools in order to take science classes.

Note that different levels of points are also distinguished by different levels of indentation. These differences clearly indicate the direction of your speech. They also enhance your recollection of points and make it easy for you to follow the outline as you speak.

Principles of Organizing Main and Supporting Points

 WEB Outliner

Whether you are creating a painting, an essay, a musical composition, or a speech, certain principles of good form apply. A well-organized speech is characterized by unity, coherence, and balance. Try to adhere to these principles as you arrange your speech points.

UNITY

There is a type of skilled speaker — often a preacher — who routinely seems to meander off point, only to surprise the audience at the end by artfully tying each idea to the speech theme. Such speeches retain the quality of unity, if only at the last minute. A speech exhibits **unity** when it contains only those points that are implied by the purpose and thesis statements. Nothing is extraneous or tangential. Each main point supports the thesis, and each supporting point provides evidence for the main points. Each subpoint supports each supporting point. Each point focuses on a single idea.

COHERENCE

Coherence refers to clarity and logical consistency. A coherent speech is one that is organized logically. The speech body should follow logically from the introduction, and the conclusion should follow logically from the body. Within the body of the speech itself, the main points should follow logically from the thesis statement, and the supporting points should follow logically from the main points. Transitions (discussed in the next section) serve as logical bridges that help establish coherence.[7] You can ensure coherence by adhering to the principle of **coordination and subordination** — the logical placement of ideas relative to their importance to one another. Ideas that are *coordinate* are given equal weight. An idea that is *subordinate* to another is given relatively less weight. Outlines are based on the principle of coordination and subordination. Coordinate points are indicated by their parallel alignment, and subordinate points are indicated by their indentation below the more important points:

I.   The electronic media have profoundly altered the form and substance of political campaigns.
   A.   Today's campaigns rely largely on television's fast-paced visual images and sound bites.
      1.   Politicians must manage themselves "telegenically."
      2.   Politicians must compress issues into phrases that can fit into two-minute reports on the evening news and into thirty-second commercials.
   B.   Politicians and their pollsters now use the Internet to reach voters.
II. The altered form of political campaigns threatens the health of our democracy.
   A.   Politicians use the new technology to constantly take the public's "temperature."
   B.   Politicians now spend more time reacting to minute shifts in public opinion polls than they do in governing.

As you can see, coordinate points are aligned with one another, while subordinate points are indented below the points that they substantiate. Thus main point II is coordinate with main point I, subpoint A is subordinate to main point I, subpoint B is coordinate with subpoint A, and so forth.

TABLE 11.2 • Principles of Coordination and Subordination

- Assign ideas that are coordinate equal weight.
- Assign ideas that are subordinate relatively less weight.
- Indicate coordinate points by their parallel alignment.
- Indicate subordinate points by their indentation below the more important points.
- Every point must be supported by two points or none at all (consider how to address one "dangling" point in the point above it).

BALANCE

One common mistake on the part of many inexperienced public speakers is to give overly lengthy coverage to one point and insufficient attention to others. Another mistake is to give scanty evidence in the body of the speech after presenting an impressive introduction. Yet another error is jumping right into the speech without properly introducing the topic. The principle of **balance** suggests that appropriate emphasis or weight be given to each part of the speech relative to the other parts and to the theme.

The body of a speech should always be the longest part, and the introduction and the conclusion should be roughly the same length. Stating the main points in parallel form is one aspect of balance. *Assigning each main point at least two supporting points is another.* Students often forget this and assign a main point only one subpoint. If you have only one subpoint, consider how you might incorporate it into the superior point. Think of a main point as a tabletop and supporting points as table legs; without at least two legs, the table cannot stand.

✓ CHECKLIST

Do the Speech Points Reflect Unity, Coherence, and Balance?

_____ 1. Does each main point refer directly to your specific purpose or thesis statement?

_____ 2. Does each point focus on a single idea?

_____ 3. Do your main points follow logically from your thesis statement?

_____ 4. Do your supporting points follow logically from the main points?

_____ 5. Do you spend roughly the same amount of time on each main point?

_____ 6. Is each main point substantiated by at least two supporting points?

_____ 7. Are the speech points stated in parallel form?

Transitions: Giving Direction to the Speech Links

Transitions are words, phrases, or sentences that tie the speech ideas together and enable the speaker to move smoothly from one point to the next. Transitions (also called *connectives*) can be considered the "neurosystem" of speeches: They provide consistency of movement from one point to the next and cue the audience that a new point will be made. (See Table 11.3 for a list of common transitions.) As you develop your speech, think about using transitions to move listeners from one main point to the next, from main points to supporting points, and from one supporting point to another supporting point. Transitions are also used to move from the introduction to the body of the speech, and from the body to the conclusion. Transitions can take the form of full sentences, phrases, or single words.

TRANSITIONS AMONG MAIN POINTS

When moving from one main point to another, **full-sentence transitions** are especially effective. For example, to move from main point I in a speech about sales contests ("Top management should sponsor sales contests to halt the decline in sales over the past two years") to main point II ("Sales contests

TABLE 11.3 • Transitional Words and Phrases	
Function	**Example**
To show comparisons	similarly, in the same way, likewise, in comparison, just as
To contrast ideas	on the other hand, and yet, at the same time, in spite of, however, in contrast
To illustrate cause and effect	as a result, therefore, hence, because, thus, consequently, so the evidence shows, for this reason
To illustrate sequence of time or events	first, second, third, following this, before, after, later, earlier, at present, in the past, until now, tomorrow, next week, eventually
To indicate explanation	for example, to illustrate, in other words, to simplify, to clarify
To indicate additional examples	not only, in addition to, let's look at
To emphasize significance	most importantly, above all, remember, keep in mind
To summarize	as we have seen, altogether, in summary, finally, in conclusion, let me conclude by saying

will lead to better sales presentations"), the speaker might use the following transition:

> Next, let's look at exactly what sales contests can do for us.

In a speech on spyware (see Chapter 13), student John Coulter effectively transitions between his first and second main points:

> But leaving aside the finer distinctions between spyware and other types of computer menaces, what is crystal clear is that spyware represents a growing threat. Consider some of the symptoms and problems associated with spyware.

TRANSITIONS AMONG SUPPORTING POINTS

Transitions among supporting points can be handled with full sentences. For example, the transition from supporting point A ("Sales personnel will be motivated by competition") to supporting point B ("Contests are relatively inexpensive") could be made by the following transition:

> Another way that sales competitions will benefit us is by their relative cost effectiveness.

Likewise, the transition from supporting point B1 ("Contests cost less than losses in sales revenues") to supporting point B2 ("Contests cost less than training new sales staff") could be stated as follows:

> In addition to costing less than a loss in revenues, sales competitions are less expensive than training new people.

From Point to Point
Using Transitions to Guide Your Listeners

Transitions direct your listeners from one point to another in your speech, leading them forward along a logical path while reinforcing key ideas along the way. At a bare minimum, plan on using transitions to move between:

- The introduction and the body of the speech
- The main points
- The subpoints, whenever appropriate
- The body of the speech and the conclusion

Introduction

I.   Today I'll explore the steps you can take to create a greener campus...
(Transition: Let's begin by considering what "going green" actually means.)
Body

I.   "Going green" means taking action to promote and maintain a healthy environment.
(Transition: So how do you go green?)
A.   Get informed—understand what is physically happening to your planet
(Transition: Understanding the issues is only part of going green, however. Perhaps most importantly....)
B.   Recognize that change starts here, on campus, with you....

While transitions help guide your listeners from point to point, they can also do a lot more, including:

- Signal explanations and examples
- Emphasize, repeat, compare, or contrast ideas
- Introduce propositions (major speech points)
- Illustrate cause and effect
- Summarize and preview information
- Suggest conclusions from evidence

Following is an excerpt from a working outline on a speech about campuses going green. Note how the student edits himself to ensure that he (1) uses transitions to help listeners follow along and retain his speech points and (2) uses transitions strategically to achieve his goal of persuading the audience.

Student inserts a transition (**rhetorical question**) to introduce a new proposition (e.g., main point).	(Transition: Why are environmentalists targeting college campuses?)
	I. College campuses generate the waste equivalent of many large towns...
Student realizes he needs to insert this transitional phrase to signal a **cause-effect relationship**.	(Transition: As a result...)
	A. Colleges face disposal issues, especially of electronics...
	B. Administrators face decisions about mounting energy costs...
Student uses a transition to **move to the next proposition**.	(**Transition:** Following are some ideas to create a greener campus. First...)
	II. Promote a campus-wide recycling program
This transitional phrase **introduces additional examples**.	(**Transition:** For example...)
	A. Decrease the availability of bottled water and disposable...
	B. Insist on recycling bins at all residence hall...
	C. Encourage computer centers to recycle...
Student inserts an **internal summary** to help listeners retain information and transition to the next main point.	(Transition: Recycling is a critical part of going green. Decreasing the consumption of plastic and paper, installing recycling bins, and responsibly disposing of print cartridges will make a huge difference. Another aspect of going green is using sustainable energy...)
	III. Lobby administrators to investigate solar, wind, and geothermal...
	A. Make an argument for "eco-dorms..."
	B. Explore alternative heating....
Student inserts an **internal summary** to move to the next main point.	(Transition: So far, we've talked about practical actions we can take to encourage a greener lifestyle on campus, but what about beyond the campus?)
	IV. Get involved at the town government level
	A. Town-grown committees...
	B. Speak up and voice your concerns...
Student inserts a transition to signal a **shift to his concluding point**.	(Transition: As you can see, we have work to do...)
	Conclusion
	I. If we want our children and our children's children to live to see a healthy earth, we must take action now...

Conjunctions or phrases (sometimes called **signposts**) such as the following can be just as effective:

Next, . . .
First, . . . (second, third, and so forth)
We now turn . . .
Finally, let's consider . . .
If you think that's shocking, . . .
Similarly, . . .

SAMPLE TECHNIQUES FOR POSING TRANSITIONS

Transitions are often posed in **restate-forecast form**. That is, the transition restates the point just covered and previews the point to be covered next:

Now that we've established a need for sales contests (*restatement*), let's look at what sales contests can do for us (*forecast*).

Transitions can also be stated as **rhetorical questions**, or questions that do not invite actual responses. Instead, they make the audience think (see Chapter 14):

Will contests be too expensive? Well, actually . . .
How do the costs of contests stack up against the expense of training new people?

USING INTERNAL PREVIEWS AND SUMMARIES AS TRANSITIONS

Previews are transitions that tell the audience what to expect next. In a speech introduction, the **preview statement** describes what will be covered in the body of the speech (see Chapter 14). In the body itself, **internal previews** can be used to alert audience members to ensuing main points:

Victoria Woodhull was a pioneer in many respects. Not only was she the first woman to run her own brokerage firm, but she was also the first to run for the presidency of the United States, though few people know this. Let's see how she accomplished these feats. . . .

Similar to the internal preview, the **internal summary** draws together ideas before proceeding to another speech point. Internal summaries help listeners review and evaluate the thread of the theme thus far:

It should be clear that the kind of violence we've witnessed in the schools and in our communities has a deeper root cause than the availability of handguns. Our young children are crying out for a sense of community, of relatedness and meaning, that they just aren't finding in the institutions that are meant to serve them.

(See Chapter 13 for more on how to include transitions in the speech outline.)

✔ **SELF-ASSESSMENT CHECKLIST**

Using Transitions

_____ 1. Do you include enough transitions to adequately guide your listeners through your speech?

_____ 2. Do you use appropriate transitions when making comparisons, showing cause and effect, illustrating a sequence in time, contrasting ideas, summarizing information, and so forth?

_____ 3. Do you include full-sentence transitions that alert listeners to shifts from one main point to the next?

_____ 4. Do you make appropriate use of internal previews and summaries? The restate-forecast technique? Rhetorical questions?

_____ 5. Do you use a transition to alert listeners to the conclusion of the speech?

12 Types of Organizational Arrangements

Once you select the main points for your speech, you must decide on a type of organizational arrangement or combination of arrangements for them. Public speeches make use of at least a dozen different organizational arrangements. Here we look at seven commonly used patterns for all forms of speeches: topical, chronological, spatial, causal (cause-effect), problem-solution, narrative, and circular. In Chapter 26 you will find three additional patterns of organization, two designed specifically for persuasive speeches: *Monroe's motivated sequence* and *refutation,* which are designed specifically for persuasive speeches, as well as *comparative advantage.* (See Table 12.1 and Chapter 26.)

As you review these organizational designs, bear in mind that there are multiple ways to organize a speech. Each method communicates something different, even if the topic is the same. Your goal should be to choose one that your audience can easily follow and that will best achieve your speech purpose.

Once you select an organizational arrangement, you can proceed to flesh out the main points with subordinate ideas. *Your subpoints need not always follow the pattern you select for your main points.* For instance, for a speech about the recent history of tattooing in the United States, you might choose a chronological pattern to organize the main points but switch to a cause-effect arrangement for some of your subpoints about why tattooing is on the rise today. (See Table 12.1 for descriptions of patterns.) Organization, whether of main points or subpoints, should be driven by what's most effective for the particular rhetorical situation.

Arranging Speech Points Topically

 Chapter quizzes

When each of the main points is a subtopic or category of the speech topic, the **topical pattern of arrangement** (also called the *categorical pattern*) may be most appropriate. Consider preparing an informative speech about choosing Chicago as a place to establish a career. You plan to emphasize three reasons for choosing Chicago: the strong economic climate of the city, its cultural variety, and its accessible public transportation. Of relatively equal importance, these three points can be arranged in any order without affecting each other or the speech purpose negatively. For example:

THESIS: Chicago is an excellent place to establish a career.

    I. Accessible transportation

    II. Cultural variety

    III. Economic stability

TABLE 12.1 • Types and Functions of Organizational Arrangements

Function	Pattern of Organization
Topical	To stress natural divisions in a topic; allows points to be moved around to emphasize listeners' needs and interests
Chronological	To describe a series of developments in time or a set of actions occurring sequentially
Spatial	To describe or explain the physical arrangement of a place, scene, event, or object
Causal (Cause-Effect)	To explain or demonstrate a topic in terms of its underlying causes or effects
Problem-Solution	To demonstrate the nature and significance of a problem and provide justification for a proposed solution
Narrative	To convey ideas through the medium of a story with characters, settings, and a plot
Circular	To demonstrate how one idea leads to another and then another, all of which leads back to the speech thesis
Monroe's Motivated Sequence	To motivate listeners to adopt a course of action (see Chapter 26)
Refutation	To disprove an opposing claim to your position (see Chapter 26)
Comparative Advantage	To demonstrate the superiority of one viewpoint or proposal over another (see Chapter 26)

This is not to say that when using a topical arrangement you should arrange the main points without careful consideration. If your main points permit it, you may want to arrange them in ascending or descending order according to their relative importance, complexity, or timeliness. Perhaps you have determined that listeners' main concern is the city's economic stability, followed by an interest in its cultural variety and accessible transportation. You may then decide to arrange the points in the order of the audience's most immediate needs and interests:

I.   Economic stability

II. Cultural variety

III. Accessible transportation

Topical arrangements give you the greatest freedom to structure main points according how you wish to present your topic. You can approach a topic by dividing it into two or more categories, for example, or you can lead with your strongest evidence or leave your most compelling points until you near the conclusion. If your topic does not call out for one of the other patterns described in this chapter, be sure to experiment with the topical pattern.

Arranging Speech Points Chronologically

Some speech topics lend themselves well to the arrangement of main points according to their occurrence in time relative to each other. The **chronological pattern of arrangement** (also called the *temporal pattern*) follows the natural sequential order of the main points. To switch points around would make the arrangement appear unnatural and might confuse the audience. Topics that describe a series of events in time (such as events leading to the adoption of a peace treaty) or develop in line with a set pattern of actions or tasks (such as plans for building a model car, procedures for admitting patients to a hospital) call out to be organized according to a chronological pattern of arrangement. A speech describing the development of the World Wide Web, for example, calls for a chronological, or time-ordered, sequence of main points:

THESIS STATEMENT: The Internet evolved from a small network designed for academic scientists into a vast system of networks used by billions of people around the globe.

I. The Internet was first conceived in 1962 as the ARPANET to promote the sharing of research among scientists in the U.S.

II. In the 1980s a team created TCP/IP, a language that could link networks, and the Internet as we know it was born.

III. At the end of the cold war, the ARPANET was decommissioned and the World Wide Web made up the bulk of Internet traffic.

IV. The Internet celebrates its twenty-fifth anniversary, with 10 million people connected.[1]

In addition to topics that involve time lines, the chronological arrangement is appropriate for any topic that involves a series of sequential steps. A scientist might describe the steps in a research project on fruit flies, for example, or a cook might explain the steps in a recipe.

Arranging Speech Points Using a Spatial Pattern

When the purpose of your speech is to describe or explain the physical arrangement of a place, a scene, or an object, logic suggests that the main points be arranged in order of their physical proximity or direction relative to each other. This calls for the **spatial pattern of arrangement**. For example, you can select a spatial arrangement when your speech provides the audience with a "tour" of a particular place:

THESIS STATEMENT: El Morro National Monument in New Mexico is captivating for its variety of natural and historical landmarks.

   I.   Visitors first encounter an abundant variety of plant life native to the high-country desert.

   II.   Soon visitors come upon an age-old watering hole that has receded beneath the 200-foot cliffs.

   III.   Beyond are the famous cliff carvings made by hundreds of travelers over several centuries of exploration in the Southwest.

   IV.   At the farthest reaches of the magnificent park are the ancient ruins of a pueblo dwelling secured high atop "the Rock."

In a speech describing a computer company's market growth across various regions of the country, a student speaker uses the following spatial arrangement:

THESIS STATEMENT: Sales of Digi-Tel Computers have grown in every region of the country.

   I.   Sales are strongest in the Eastern Zone.

   II.   Sales are growing at a rate of 10 percent quarterly in the Central Zone.

   III.   Sales are up slightly in the Mountain Zone.

   IV.   Sales in the Western Zone are lagging behind the other regions.

Arranging Speech Points Using a Causal (Cause-Effect) Pattern

Some speech topics represent cause-effect relationships. Examples might include (1) events leading to higher interest rates, (2) reasons students drop out of college, and (3) causes of spousal abuse. In speeches on topics such as these, the speaker relates something known to be a "cause" to its "effects." The main points in a **causal (cause-effect) pattern of arrangement** usually take the following form:

I.   Cause

II.   Effect

Sometimes a topic can be discussed in terms of multiple causes for a single effect, or a single cause for multiple effects:

Multiple Causes for a Single Effect (Reasons Students Drop Out of College)	**Single Cause for Multiple Effects (Reasons Students Drop Out of College)**
I. Cause 1 (lack of funds)	I. Cause (lack of funds)
II. Cause 2 (unsatisfactory social life)	II. Effect 1 (lowered earnings over lifetime)
III. Cause 3 (unsatisfactory academic performance)	III. Effect 2 (decreased job satisfaction over lifetime)
IV. Effect (drop out of college)	IV. Effect 3 (increased stress level over lifetime)

Some topics are best understood by presenting listeners with the effect(s) first and the cause(s) subsequently. In an informative speech on the 1988 explosion of Pan Am flight 103 over Lockerbie, Scotland, for instance, a student speaker arranges his main points as follows:

THESIS STATEMENT: The explosion of Pan Am flight 103 over Lockerbie, Scotland, killed 270 people and resulted in the longest-running aviation investigation in history.

    I. (Effect) Two hundred and fifty-nine passengers and crew members died; an additional eleven people on the ground perished.

    II. (Effect) To date, it is the longest-running aviation investigation in history.

    III. (Cause) The court found that the cause was a terrorist act; specifically, a bomb planted by Libyan citizen Al Megrahi.

    IV. (Cause) Many people believe that Megrahi did not act alone, if he acted at all.

In this case, the speaker presents the effects of the airplane explosion as the first two main points. He subsequently addresses the causes of the explosion in the ensuing main points.

Arranging Speech Points Using a Problem-Solution Pattern

The **problem-solution pattern of arrangement** organizes main points both to demonstrate the nature and significance of a problem and to provide justification for a proposed solution. This type of arrangement can be as general as two main points:

I. Problem (define what it is)

II. Solution (offer a way to overcome the problem)

However, many problem-solution speeches require more than two points to adequately explain the problem and to substantiate the recommended solution:

I.   The nature of the problem (identify its causes, incidence, etc.)
II. Effects of the problem (explain why it's a problem, for whom, etc.)
III. Unsatisfactory solutions (discuss those that have not worked)
IV. Proposed solution (explain why it's expected to work)

Following is a partial outline of a persuasive speech about teen pregnancy arranged in a problem-solution format (see also Chapter 26):

THESIS STATEMENT: Once you realize the nature and probable causes of the problem of teen pregnancy, it should be clear that current solutions remain unsuccessful and an alternative solution — peer counseling — should be considered.

    I.   Early unwed pregnancies
        A.   Average age of teen mothers
        B.   National and local incidence
    II. Probable causes of teen pregnancy
        A.   Lack of knowledge about contraception
        B.   Lack of motivation to use contraception
        C.   Dysfunctional social relationships
    III. Unsuccessful solutions
        A.   School-based sex education
        B.   Mass-media campaigns encouraging abstinence
    IV. Peer counseling as a possible solution
        A.   How peer counseling works
        B.   Peer counseling coupled with school-based sexuality curriculum

Arranging Speech Points Using a Narrative Pattern

Storytelling is often a natural and effective way to get your message across. In the **narrative pattern of arrangement**, the speech consists of a story or a series of short stories, replete with characters, settings, plot, and vivid imagery. However, most speeches built largely upon a story (or a series of stories) are likely to incorporate elements of other organizational arrangements described in the chapter. For example, you might present the story in a time sequence, thus using a chronological design. Or the story could be organized in an effect-cause design, in which you first reveal why something happened (such as a drunken driving accident) and then describe the events that led up to the accident (the causes).

Whatever the structure, simply telling a story is no guarantee of giving a good speech. Any speech should include a clear thesis, a preview, well-organized main points, and effective transitions. In a speech entitled "Tales of the Grandmothers,"[2] professor of communication Anita Taylor illustrates her thesis—that the U.S economy would not be what it is today without the range of "home work" that women have traditionally performed—by relating an extended story about her female ancestors, beginning in 1826. Although the story dominates the speech, Taylor frequently leaves off and picks up its thread in order to orient her listeners and drive home her theme. In addition to explicitly stating her thesis, Taylor pauses to preview main points:

My grandmothers illustrate the points I want to make. . . .

Taylor also makes frequent use of transitions, including internal previews, summaries, and simple signposts, to help her listeners stay on track:

But, let's go on with Luna Puffer Squire Nairn's story.

And here, Taylor signals the conclusion:

So here we are today. . . . And finally. . . .

For a full text of "Tales of the Grandmothers," see p. 507.

Arranging Speech Points Using a Circular Pattern

In the **circular pattern of arrangement**, the speaker develops one idea, which leads to another, which leads to a third, and so forth, until he or she arrives back at the speech thesis.[3] This type of organization can be useful when you want listeners to follow a particular line of reasoning, especially when your main goal is persuasion. In a speech on the role that friendship plays in physical and mental well-being, a student speaker showed how acts of consideration

---

✓ **CHECKLIST**

Matching the Organizational Pattern to the Audience

_____ 1. Does the arrangement move the speech along in a logical and convincing fashion?

_____ 2. Do my ideas flow naturally from one point to another, leading to a satisfying conclusion?

_____ 3. Does the organizational pattern lend my speech momentum?

_____ 4. Does the organizational plan convey the information listeners expect or need in a way that they will be able to grasp?

and kindness lead to more friendships, which in turn lead to more social support, which then results in improved mental and physical health. Each main point leads directly into another main point, with the final main point leading back to the thesis.

Public Speaking in Cultural Perspective
Arrangement Formats and Audience Diversity

Studies confirm that the way you organize your ideas affects your audience's understanding of them.[1] Another factor that may affect how we organize relationships among ideas is culture.[2] Are certain organizational formats better suited to certain cultures? Consider the chronological arrangement format. It assumes a largely North American and Western European orientation to time because these cultures generally view time as a linear (or chronological) progression in which one event follows another along a continuum, with events strictly segmented. In contrast, some Asian, African, and Latin American cultures view time more fluidly, with events occurring simultaneously or cyclically.[3] Thus, when a speaker follows a chronological arrangement of the typical linear fashion, audience members from cultures with different time orientations may have difficulty making the connections among the main points. For these audiences, an alternative arrangement, such as the narrative or circular pattern, may be a more appropriate form in which to express speech ideas.

1. R. G. Smith, "Effects of Speech Organization upon Attitudes of College Students," *Speech Monographs* 18 (1951): 547–49; E. Thompson, "An Experimental Investigation of the Relative Effectiveness of Organizational Structure in Oral Communication," *Southern Speech Journal* 26 (1960): 59–69.
2. Devorah A. Lieberman, *Public Speaking in the Multicultural Environment,* 2nd ed. (Englewood Cliffs, N.J.: Prentice Hall, 1997).
3. Edward T. Hall, *The Dance of Life: Other Dimensions of Time* (New York: Doubleday, 1983); J. K. Burgoon, D. B. Buller, and W. G. Woodall, *Nonverbal Communication: The Unspoken Dialogue* (New York: Harper & Row, 1989).

⑬ Outlining the Speech

Producing an outline lies at the very heart of creating a speech, being at once a tool for brainstorming and a blueprint for the presentation. By plotting ideas in hierarchical fashion (such that coordinate ideas receive relatively equal weight and subordinate ideas relatively less so), and by using indentation to visually represent this hierarchy, you can't help but examine the underlying logic of the speech and the relationship of ideas to one another.[1] (For a review of the principles of coordination and subordination and the mechanics of outlining, see Chapter 11.)

Plan on Creating Two Outlines

As you develop a speech, you will actually create two outlines: a working outline and a speaking, or delivery, outline. A **working outline** (also called a *preparation outline*) is an essential tool in composing a speech. Here you refine and finalize the specific purpose and thesis statements, firm up and organize main points, and develop supporting points to substantiate them. It is at this point that you decide what supporting material you want to keep or need to add, and how it can best be incorporated into a coherent train of thought.

Once you complete the working outline, you must transfer its ideas to a **speaking outline** (also called a *delivery outline*) — the one you will use when you are practicing and actually presenting the speech. (See Table 13.1.) Speaking outlines, which contain your ideas in condensed form, are much briefer than working outlines.

Some instructors may require three distinct outlines — working, formal, and speaking — with a *formal outline* containing the entire speech, worded much as the speaker plans to present it and including a title and bibliography. Alternatively, as shown in this chapter, you can simply refine the working outline until it in essence becomes a formal outline.

Before we look at the working outline, let's consider the three different types of formats speakers use to outline speeches.

TYPES OF OUTLINE FORMATS

Speeches can be outlined in complete sentences, phrases, or key words.

The Sentence Outline Format

Sentence outlines represent the full "script," or text, of the speech. In a **sentence outline** each main and supporting point is stated in sentence form as a declarative

TABLE 13.1 • Steps in Organizing and Outlining the Speech
1. Create the Main Speech Points
2. Note Any Obvious Subpoints
3. Select an Organizational Pattern
4. Create a Working Outline
• Organize Main Points and Subpoints
• Check Main Points and Subpoints for Coordination and Subordination
• Revise Thesis Statement in Light of Final Organization
5. Transfer the Working Outline to a Speaking Outline Using Phrases or Key Words

sentence (one that makes a statement or an assertion about a subject). So, too, are the introduction, the conclusion, and the transition statements. Often, these sentences are stated in the way the speaker wants to express the idea during delivery.

Generally, sentence outlines are used for working outlines but not for speaking outlines, although they may be recommended for use in delivery under the following conditions:

1. When the issue is highly controversial or emotion-laden for listeners and precise wording is needed to make the point as clear as possible
2. When the material is highly technical and exact sentence structure is critical to an accurate representation of the material
3. When a good deal of material relies on quotations and facts from another source that must be conveyed precisely as worded

While one or more of these conditions may suggest the use of a sentence outline, most speaking professionals recommend the actual speaking outline be prepared using phrases or key words. If there are points in your speech where you want to note exact quotations or precisely state complicated facts or figures, you can write those out in full sentences within your key-word or phrase speaking outlines.

The following is an excerpt in sentence format from a speech by Mark B. McClellan on keeping prescription drugs safe:[2]

I. The prescription drug supply is under unprecedented attack from a variety of increasingly sophisticated threats.
   A. Technologies for counterfeiting — ranging from pill molding to dyes — have improved across the board.
   B. Inadequately regulated Internet sites have become major portals for unsafe and illegal drugs.

The Phrase Outline Format

A **phrase outline** uses a partial construction of the sentence form of each point, instead of using complete sentences that present precise wording for each point. The idea is that the speaker is so familiar with the speech that a glance at a few words associated with each point will serve as a reminder of exactly what to say. A section of McClellan's sentence outline would appear as follows in phrase outline form:

I. Drug supply under attack
    A. Counterfeiting technologies more sophisticated
    B. Unregulated Internet sites

The Key-Word Outline Format

The briefest of the three forms of outlines, the **key-word outline**, uses the smallest possible units of understanding to outline the main and supporting points. A section of McClellan's outline would appear as follows in key-word outline form:

I. Threats
    A. Counterfeiting
    B. Internet

EFFECTS OF OUTLINE FORMAT ON DELIVERY

The type of outline you select will affect how well you deliver the speech. Of the three types of outline formats (sentence, phrase, and key word), sentence outlines permit the least amount of eye contact with listeners, which is why they are not recommended for use during delivery. Eye contact is essential to the successful delivery of a speech. While sentence outlines offer the most protection against memory lapses, they may prompt you to look at the outline rather than at the audience. The less you rely on your outline notes, the more eye contact you can have with audience members. For this reason, phrase outlines or key-word outlines are recommended over sentence outlines in delivering most speeches, with the key-word outline often being the preferred format.

Key-word outlines permit more eye contact, greater freedom of movement, and better control of your thoughts and actions than any of the other outline formats. They are also less conspicuous to the audience. However, if at any time during the speech you experience stage fright or a lapse in memory, a key-word outline may not be of much help. This is why preparation is essential when using one. You must be confident in knowing the topic and the speech arrangement well enough to deliver the speech extemporaneously. *Extemporaneous speeches* are carefully planned and practiced in advance and are then delivered from a key-word or phrase outline. (See Chapter 17 for a discussion of extemporaneous and other types of speech delivery.)

Begin with a Working Outline

As the name implies, working outlines are works in progress. They are meant to be changed as you work through the mass of information you've collected. At several points in this process, you will probably find it necessary to rearrange the main points or to omit and add different kinds of supporting materials before deciding on the precise arrangement you want to use.

The outline should give you confidence that you've satisfactorily fleshed out your ideas. Instead of worrying about whether you will have enough to say, or whether your speech will be well organized, you'll have a realistic picture of what you'll be able to communicate. Rather than writing out the speech word for word, however, focus on charting a coherent and well-supported course. This will give you the freedom to "think on your feet" during delivery.

SEPARATE THE INTRODUCTION AND CONCLUSION FROM THE BODY

Whether in a working or speaking outline, the introduction and the conclusion are separate from the main points. The introduction is the preface; the conclusion is the epilogue. The actual main points — or body — of the speech come between the preface and the epilogue, or the head and the feet.

In outlines, treatments of the introduction can vary. You can use such labels as *Attention Getter, Thesis,* and *Preview* to indicate how you will gain the audience's attention, introduce the thesis, and preview the speech topic and main points (see Chapter 14 for more on developing the introduction). Alternatively, your instructor may prefer that you assign the introduction its own numbering system or simply write it out in paragraph format.

Similarly, in the conclusion you can indicate where you signal the close of the speech, summarize main points, reiterate the thesis and purpose, and leave the audience with something to think about (or otherwise offer a memorable close) — or, again, assign it its own numbering system or write it out. (See Chapter 15 for more on developing the conclusion.)

LIST YOUR SOURCES

As you work on the outline, clearly mark where speech points require source credit. Directly after the point, either insert a footnote *or* enclose in parentheses enough of the reference to be able to retrieve it in full. Once you complete the outline, order the references alphabetically and place them on a sheet titled "Works Cited" and/or "Works Consulted." (Some instructors may prefer that you order the sources consecutively, as they appear in the speech, and label them "Sources" or "References.") For guidelines on what to include in a source note, see Chapters 9 and 10 (especially the From Source to Speech sections); see Appendices E–I for particular citation styles.

CREATE A TITLE

As the last step, assign the speech a title. Neatly crafted titles communicate the essence of a speech. At times, you might even refer to the title in the introduction, as a means of previewing the topic. Whether mentioned or not, a title should inform any readers of the speech of its subject, and in a way that invites them to read it.

✔ **CHECKLIST**

Steps in Creating a Working Outline

_____ 1. Write out your topic, general purpose, specific speech purpose, and thesis—to keep them in focus.

_____ 2. Establish your main points (optimally two to five).

_____ 3. Flesh out supporting points.

_____ 4. Check for correct subordination and coordination; follow the numbering system shown in Table 11.2 (p. 197).

_____ 5. Label each speech part (e.g., introduction, body, and conclusion).

_____ 6. Write out each speech point in sentence form (unless directed otherwise).

_____ 7. Label and write out transitions.

_____ 8. Note sources in parentheses.

_____ 9. Prepare a list of sources, and append it to the outline.

____ 10. Assign the speech a title.

SAMPLE WORKING OUTLINE

The following outline is from a speech delivered by John Coulter at Salt Lake Community College. It uses the sentence format and includes labeled transitions.

Staying Ahead of Spyware

JOHN COULTER
Salt Lake Community College

TOPIC:	Problems and solutions associated with spyware
SPECIFIC PURPOSE:	To inform my audience members of the dangers of spyware so that they may take appropriate steps to prevent infection
THESIS STATEMENT:	Computer users must understand the nature of spyware and how it works in order to take the necessary steps to protect themselves.

Introduction

I. Imagine how you would feel if someone was tracking everything you did on the Internet, including recording your passwords and credit card numbers. *(Attention getter)*

II. A type of software known as spyware can install itself on your computer without your knowledge and harvest this sensitive information.

III. To protect yourself, you need to understand how spyware works. *(Thesis)*

IV. Today, I'll talk about what spyware is, the harm it causes, who it affects, and how to keep your computer from becoming infected. *(Preview)*

TRANSITION: So, what exactly is spyware?

Body

I. Spyware is relatively new and appears in many guises.

    A. Until the year 2000, *spyware* referred to monitoring devices on cameras. (FTC, March 2004 report)

        1. Its first link to a software context apparently was in connection with the introduction of a security program called ZoneAlarm.

        2. Today, the Federal Trade Commission defines spyware as any computer code that installs itself on your computer, gathers data from it, and sends it back to a remote computer without your consent. (FTC, *Consumer Alert*)

            a. Spyware includes software that will advertise on your computer.

            b. It also includes software that collects personal information.

TRANSITION: You may be wondering how spyware gets into your computer and what it does once it gets there.

    B. Spyware installs itself silently, often "piggybacking" onto other downloaded programs such as file-sharing applications and games.

        1. Links in pop-up ads and the "unsubscribe" button in spam are known sources.

        2. Some types of spyware track your Web-browsing habits and sell this information to marketers.

        3. A type of spyware called adware loads ads onto the computer but doesn't monitor browsing habits.

        4. The most dangerous (and rarest) type of spyware, keystroke logging, records and transmits keystrokes to steal such personal information as tax returns, Social Security numbers, and passwords.

C. Distinctions remain fuzzy between spyware and other kinds of programs that install themselves on computers. (FTC, March 2004)

1. Industry people disagree over whether software that the manufacturer discloses in the licensing, but in print so fine that it isn't
likely to be read or understood, should be considered spyware or
adware.

2. Disagreement exists over whether software that the manufacturer
"piggybacks" onto free downloads in order to advertise itself, but
that doesn't install monitoring code, should be called spyware or
adware.

3. People agree that to qualify as spyware, it must serve the interests
of someone other than the user: "Spyware alters the PC's behavior
to suit the interests of outside parties rather than the owner or
user." (Mossberg, *WSJ*, July 14, 2005)

TRANSITION: There's a lot of confusion regarding the differences
between spyware and computer viruses — and even whether
there are any.

D. Spyware is different from a virus in a variety of ways.

1. Viruses are generally written by individuals in order to brag about
causing damage. (CNET.com video)

2. Spyware is written by teams employed by companies, not all of
them shady, to make money.

3. Viruses have been around for more than two decades; everyone
agrees on how to define them; and they are illegal.

4. Few laws exist governing spyware, though legislation is pending in
many states and on the federal level.

TRANSITION: Leaving aside the finer distinctions between spyware and
other types of computer menaces, what is crystal clear is
that spyware represents a growing threat.

II. Users can learn to recognize the symptoms and problems associated with
spyware.

A. One sign of infiltration is a constant stream of pop-up ads. (Vara,
WSJ, July 18, 2005)

B. Strange toolbars may appear on the desktop.

C. Browser settings may be hijacked, forcing users to strange Web pages.

D. The computer may behave sluggishly or become unstable.

1. Files may become displaced or disappear.

2. The computer may crash.

III. Spyware is the leading cause of computer-related problems today.

   A. Tanner Nielson of Totally Awesome Computers in Salt Lake City, Utah, reports that the majority of problems brought into the store are spyware related. (Nielson interview)

   B. A 2005 *Consumer Reports* national survey finds that spyware is a leading cause of computer malfunction. (*Consumer Reports*, 2005)

      1. Within the past two years, one-third of users with home Internet access experienced severe computer problems and/or financial losses.

      2. Eighteen percent said that their hard drives were so seriously infected that the contents had to be erased.

TRANSITION: Spyware can do some nasty things to your computer as well as to your wallet.

IV. Prevention is the best way to avoid spyware's harmful and potentially dangerous effects.

   A. Keep your browser up-to-date to take advantage of security updates.

   B. Invest in one of the three top antispyware programs recommended by *Consumer Reports:* Webroot's Spy Sweeper, Computer Associates' Pest-Patrol, and Spybot's Search & Destroy. (*Consumer Reports*, 2005)

   C. Don't install any software without reading the fine print.

   D. Download free software only from sites you know and trust.

   E. Don't click on links in pop-up windows.

   F. Don't reply to or even open spam or any email that isn't from someone you know.

   G. Don't hit the "unsubscribe" button in spam because spyware is known to lurk here.

   H. Exercise caution when surfing online: Spyware tends to be loaded onto disreputable sites containing pornography and even on sites advertising spyware solutions.

Conclusion

I. The makers of spyware are in it for the money, so the problem is likely to be long lasting. (*Signals close of speech*)

II. Spyware can do serious damage to your computer and your finances, but by taking the right steps you can avoid major problems. (*Summarizes main points*)

   A. An increasing number of solutions to spyware exist, including more secure browsers and good antispyware programs.

   B. The steps I've laid out should help you protect your computer from becoming infected.

C. One final piece of advice is to keep abreast of developments related to spyware by reading reputable computer publications such as *PC Magazine* and visiting reputable Web sites such as CNET.com. *(Leaves audience with something to think about)*

III. Forewarned is forearmed. Good luck! *(Memorable close)*

Works Cited

Federal Trade Commission. Monitoring Spyware on Your PC: Spyware, Adware, and Other Software. Mar. 2005. 8 Aug. 2005 www.ftc .gov/os/2005/03/050307spywarerpt.pdf.

Federal Trade Commission. Web Site for the Consumer. "Consumer Alert on Spyware." 8 Aug. 2005 www.ftc.gov/bcp/conline/pubs/alerts/ spywarealrt.htm.

Mossberg, Walter J. "Despite Others' Claims, Tracking Cookies Fit My Spyware Definition." Wall Street Journal 14 July 2005. 19 July 2005 http://ptech.wsj.com/archive/ptech-20050714.html.

"Net Threat Rising." Consumer Reports Sept. 2005: 12–15.

Nielson, Tanner. Personal interview. 12 May 2005.

Vara, Vauhini. "Lurking in the Shadows." Wall Street Journal 18 July 2005. 19 July 2005 http://online.wsj.com/article/0,,SB112128460774484814, 00-search.html.

"Virus vs. Spyware." CNET.com. Videos section. 9 Aug. 2005 http://reviews .cnet.com/Virus_vs_spyware/4660-10620_7-6273711.html.

Preparing the Speaking Outline Video quizzes

Once you complete a full-sentence working outline, it is time to transfer your ideas to a speaking outline, using a key-word or phrase format. While the speaking outline uses the same numbering system (see Table 11.2 on p. 197) and parallel form as the working version, it contains just enough words to jog your memory. Exceptions are made for any quotations, statistics, or other information that you will deliver word for word; these should be written out in full.

CLEARLY INDICATE DELIVERY CUES

Include in the speaking outline any brief reminder notes, or **delivery cues**, that will be part of the speech. As seen in Table 13.2, common delivery cues include transitions, timing, speaking rate and volume, presentation aids, quotations, statistics, and difficult-to-pronounce names or words. So that they are easily visible at a glance, you might capitalize the cues, place them in parentheses, and/or highlight them.

Place the outline on 4 × 6-inch notecards or 8.5 × 11-inch sheets of paper. Some speakers dislike notecards, finding them too small to contain enough material and too easily dropped. Others find notecards small enough to be handled

TABLE 13.2 • Common Delivery Cues in a Speaking Outline

Delivery Cue	Notes to Self in Outline
Transitions	(TRANSITION)
Timing	(PAUSE)
	(SLOW DOWN)
	(REPEAT)
Speaking rate and volume	(SLOWLY)
	(LOUDER)
	(SOFTLY)
Presentation aids	(SHOW MODEL)
	(SHOW MAP)
	(SLIDE 3)
Sources	(*Atlanta Constitution,* August 2, 2005)
Statistics	(2002, boys to girls = 94,232; U.S. Health Human Services)
Quotations	Eubie Blake, 100: "If I'd known I was gonna live this long, I'd have taken better care of myself."
Difficult-to-pronounce names or words	Eowyn (A-OH-win)

✓ **CHECKLIST**

Tips on Using Notecards or Sheets of Paper

_____ 1. Leave some blank space at the margins to find your place as you glance at the cards.

_____ 2. Number the notecards or sheets so that you can follow them with ease.

_____ 3. Instead of turning the cards or sheets, slide them under one another.

_____ 4. Do not staple notes or sheets together.

_____ 5. If you use a lectern, place the notes or sheets near eye level.

_____ 6. Do not use the cards or sheets in hand gestures, as they become distracting pointers or flags.

---

unobtrusively but large enough to accommodate key words (assuming about one main point and supporting points per card). Whichever you use, be sure to print large and bold enough so that your words will be easily seen at a glance.

PRACTICE THE SPEECH

The key to the successful delivery of any speech, and particularly one delivered with an outline in a phrase- or key-word format, is practice. The more you rehearse your speech, the more comfortable you will become when you speak

✓ **CHECKLIST**

Steps in Creating a Speaking Outline

_____ 1. Select large notecards or sheets of paper that you can easily handle without distraction.

_____ 2. If the outline is prepared on a computer, use a large-size print (at least 14 points) that can be comfortably read at a glance. If it's handwritten, use easy-to-read ink and large letters.

_____ 3. Identify each main and subpoint with a key word or phrase that is likely to jog your memory accurately.

_____ 4. Include delivery cues.

_____ 5. Write out quotations word for word as well as other information that you need to cite verbatim.

_____ 6. Using the speaking outline, practice the speech at least five times.

from the key-word outline. For additional information on rehearsing the speech, see Chapter 19, "The Body in Delivery."

SAMPLE SPEAKING OUTLINE

Staying Ahead of Spyware

JOHN COULTER
Salt Lake Community College

TOPIC:	Problems and solutions associated with spyware
SPECIFIC PURPOSE:	To inform my audience members of the dangers of spyware so that they may take appropriate steps to prevent infection
THESIS STATEMENT:	Computer users must understand the nature of spyware and how it works in order to take the necessary steps to protect themselves.

Introduction

I.   Imagine, feel? (_Attention Getter_)

II. Can happen; spyware installs, harvests

III. To protect, understand how (_Thesis_)

IV. What, harm, who affects, avoid (_Preview_)

(TRANSITION: So, what exactly . . . ?)

   [PAUSE]

Body

I.   Relatively new, many guises

    A.   Until 2000, monitoring devices on cameras (FTC, March 2004 report)

        1.   First link to software content, ZoneAlarm

        2.   FTC defined: installs, gathers data, sends to remote computer, no consent

            a.   Install advertising

            b.   Collect personal data

(TRANSITION: May be wondering . . .)

    B.   Installs silently, "piggybacks"

        1.   Known sources — pop-up ads, "unsubscribe" button in spam

        2.   Some track browsing habits, sell info

        3.   Adware loads ads; no monitoring

        4.   Keyloggers steal info [SHOW SLIDE]

    C.   Fuzzy distinctions (FTC, March 2004)

        1.   Disclosed in licensing agreement, fine print?

        2.   Free downloads; no code?

        3.   All agree serves others: "Spyware alters the PC's behavior to suit the interests of outside parties rather than the owner or user." (Mossberg, *WSJ*, July 14, 2005)

(TRANSITION: There's a lot of confusion . . .)

    D.   Different from virus

        1.   Individuals; to brag, damage (CNET.com video)

        2.   Spyware — teams, companies, money

        3.   Viruses two decades; all defined; illegal

        4.   Few laws

(TRANSITION: Leaving aside distinctions, growing threat . . .)

II.   Recognize symptoms, problems

    A.   Stream pop-ups (Vara, *WSJ*, July 18, 2005)

    B.   Toolbars on desktop [SHOW SLIDE]

    C.   Browser settings hijacked

    D.   Computer sluggish, unstable

        1.   Files displaced, disappear

        2.   Crash

III. Leading cause computer problems
   A. Nielson; majority of problems (Nielson interview)
   B. *Consumer Reports,* 2005 survey
      1. Past two years; one-third severe problems computer and/or financial
      2. 18% hard drives seriously infected; erase

(TRANSITION: Nasty things to computer, wallet)

IV. Prevention key
   A. Update browser; security updates
   B. Antispyware: Webroot's Spy Sweeper, Computer Associates' PestPatrol, Spybot's Search & Destroy (*Consumer Reports,* 2005) [SHOW BOX]
   C. Don't install w/o fine print
   D. Beware free downloads
   E. Don't click pop-up links
   F. Links in spam
   G. "Unsubscribe" button
   H. Caution! Disreputable sites, even spyware solutions!

[PAUSE]

Conclusion

I. Money, problem long lasting
II. Damage computer, finances, right steps
   A. Solutions, browsers, antispyware
   B. Steps laid out
   C. *PC Magazine,* CNET.com
III. Forewarned is forearmed. Good luck!

FULL-TEXT SPEECH

Following is the full text of the speech outlined in this chapter. John's assignment was to deliver a four- to five-minute informative speech citing at least three authoritative sources, incorporating at least one presentation aid, and including a list of references in either APA or MLA style.[3]

Staying Ahead of Spyware

JOHN COULTER

Salt Lake Community College

How would you feel if someone was watching and recording everything you typed on the Internet — your passwords, personal letters, and perhaps even your credit card numbers? Well, it just might be. There are plenty of software programs out there that can install themselves on your computer without your knowledge. Once they're installed, they're able to harvest sensitive information such as this. •

In order to protect yourself, it is necessary to understand how these types of programs, known as spyware, work. •

Today, I'll talk about the danger of spyware and how to avoid it. I'll discuss four main points relating to spyware: what it is, the harm it causes, who it affects, and how to keep your computer from becoming infected by it. •

So, what exactly is spyware? •

To begin, spyware is relatively new. According to a March 2004 report by the Federal Trade Commission (FTC), until the year 2000 the term *spyware* referred to monitoring devices on cameras. Its first link to a software context apparently was in connection with the introduction of a security program called ZoneAlarm. Today, the FTC defines spyware as any computer code that installs itself on your computer, gathers data from it, and sends it back to a remote computer without your consent. • This includes software that will advertise on your computer, collect personal information, and change your computer's configuration.

You may be wondering how spyware gets into your computer and what it does once it gets there. •

Spyware installs itself silently, often "piggybacking" onto other downloaded software programs such as file sharing applications and games. Links in pop-up ads and the "unsubscribe" button in spam are other known sources. Some types of spyware track your Web-browsing habits and sell this information to marketers; other kinds, sometimes called adware, merely load ads on your computer but don't monitor your browsing habits. The most dangerous (and rarest) type of

* John gains listeners' attention by relating the topic to their concerns.

* He introduces the speech thesis.

* He previews the main points.

* John uses a transition to signal the move into the body of the speech.

* John alternates among a mix of credible sources throughout the speech, beginning here with a government report.

* This transition shifts the focus from definitions of spyware to examples of it.

spyware, keystroke logging, or simply keyloggers, records and transmits keystrokes. Keyloggers can steal information as personal as your tax returns, Social Security number, and passwords, sending it along to identity thieves.

Each of these examples represents an instance of spyware. Yet, as noted in the report by the FTC, distinctions remain fuzzy between spyware and other kinds of software programs that install themselves on computers.

Is it spyware, for example, if the manufacturer discloses what the software does in the licensing agreement, but in print so fine that it isn't likely to be read or understood? Some people in the industry say yes; others, no. Is it spyware if the manufacturer "piggybacks" it onto a free download in order to advertise itself on your computer, but otherwise doesn't install monitoring code? • Here again, opinion is divided. People do agree that to qualify as spyware, it must serve the interests of someone other than the user. As computer guru Walter Mossberg of the *Wall Street Journal* put it in his July 14, 2005, column, "Spyware alters the PC's behavior to suit the interests of outside parties rather than the owner or user."

• Repetition of a rhetorical question— "Is it spyware . . . ?" lends rhythm to this section.

You may be wondering about the differences between spyware and computer viruses—or whether there are any. •

• Internal preview alerts the audience to what's ahead.

Spyware is different from a virus in a variety of ways. According to a video tutorial on the Web site CNET.com, viruses are generally written by individuals in order to brag or cause damage. Spyware is written by teams employed by companies, many but not all of them shady, in order to make money. Viruses have been around for more than two decades; everyone agrees on how to define them; and they are illegal. Currently, few laws exist governing spyware, though legislation is pending in many states and on the federal level.

But leaving aside the finer distinctions between spyware and other types of computer menaces, what is crystal clear is that spyware represents a growing threat. Consider some of the symptoms and problems associated with spyware. •

• Restate-forecast transition: Restates the point just covered and previews the upcoming one.

As described by Vauhini Vara in the July 18, 2005, edition of the *Wall Street Journal,* one sign that your computer's been infiltrated with spyware is a constant stream of pop-up ads. Another is the appearance of strange toolbars on your desktop or even a different homepage. The settings on your browser may be changed or "hijacked," forcing you to strange Web pages and ignoring the addresses you type in. Your computer may behave sluggishly or become unstable. The monitor may start to do weird things; files may become displaced or disappear altogether. The worst case scenario? Your computer crashes.

How many people are plagued by problems such as these? •

• Transition stated as a rhetorical question.

In a conversation with Tanner Nielson of Totally Awesome Computers right here in Salt Lake City, Utah, the majority of issues on computers brought into their store are spyware related. Nielsen's observation is borne out by a nationally representative survey conducted in 2005 by *Consumer Reports.* It found that within the past two years one-third of users with home Internet access experienced severe problems with their computer systems and/or financial losses. Eighteen percent said that their hard drives were so seriously infected that the contents had to be erased.

So spyware can do some nasty things to your computer as well as to your wallet. Prevention is the best way to avoid these harmful and potentially dangerous effects. • A recent Federal Trade Commission *Consumer Alert* advises keeping your browser up-to-date so that it can take advantage of security updates. Second, invest in an antispyware program. The three top antispyware programs cited by *Consumer Reports* are Webroot's Spy Sweeper, Computer Associates' PestPatrol, and Spybot's Search & Destroy. Third, don't install any software without reading the fine print, and download free software only from sites you know and trust. Fourth, do *not* click on links in pop-up windows. Don't reply to or even open any e-mail that isn't from someone you know. Never reply to spam, and don't hit the "unsubscribe" button. Spyware is known to lurk here.

• Another restate-forecast transition.

Finally, be careful about the Web sites you visit. Spyware tends to be loaded onto disreputable sites containing pornography and even Web sites advertising solutions to spyware. Know the nature of the sites you visit whenever possible. •

Unlike individuals who create computer viruses, the makers of spyware are in it for the money. Thus, the problem is likely to be a long-lasting one. At the same time, much is being done to counteract spyware, including making browsers more secure and developing effective antispyware programs.

Spyware can do serious damage to your computer and to your finances. The steps I've laid out should help you protect your computer from becoming infected. The antispyware programs I've mentioned are easy to install and very helpful. One final piece of advice is to keep abreast of developments related to spyware by reading reputable computer publications such as *PC Magazine* and visiting reputable Web sites such as CNET.com.

Forewarned is forearmed. Good luck! •

• Signal words—"first," "second," "finally"— move listeners from one point to another.

• Concluding paragraphs signal the close of the speech, reiterate the theme, offer a summary, and end with a memorable phrase.

Introductions, Conclusions, and Language

keep a child

Introductions, Conclusions, and Language

Speaker's Reference
Introductions, Conclusions, and Language

14. Developing the Introduction

Use the Introduction to Capture the Audience's Attention

- Lead with a quotation. (p. 235)
- Tell a story. (p. 236)
- Pose questions. (p. 237)
- Say something startling. (p. 238)
- Bring in humor. (p. 238)
- Refer to the occasion. (p. 239)
- Establish common ground. (p. 239)

Alert the Audience to Your Speech Topic and Purpose

- Declare what your speech is about and what you hope to accomplish. (p. 239)

Preview the Main Points

- Help listeners mentally organize the speech by introducing the main points and stating the order in which you will address them. (p. 240)

Demonstrate Why the Audience Should Care about Your Topic

- Consider emphasizing the topic's practical implications. (p. 241)
- Consider specifying what the audience stands to gain by listening. (p. 242)

Establish Your Credibility

- Briefly state your qualifications for speaking on the topic. (p. 242)
- Emphasize some experience, knowledge, or perspective you have that is different from or more extensive than that of your audience. (p. 242)

Prepare the Introduction

- Prepare the introduction after you've completed the speech body. (p. 242)
- Keep the introduction brief: It should occupy no more than 10 to 15 percent of the overall speech. (p. 242)

15. Developing the Conclusion

Alert the Audience to the Conclusion of Your Speech

- Use transitional words or phrases. (p. 243)
- Indicate in the manner of your delivery that the speech is coming to an end. (p. 243)
- Once you've signaled the conclusion, finish the speech promptly. (p. 243)

Summarize the Key Speech Points

- Reiterate the main points of your speech, but don't do it in a rote way. (p. 244)
- Remind listeners of the topic and purpose of your speech. (p. 244)

Challenge the Audience to Respond to Your Ideas or Appeals

- If the goal is informative, challenge listeners to respond to the appeal of your message. (p. 245)
- If the goal is persuasive, challenge listeners to act in line with your message. (p. 245)

Employ Vivid Language and Attention-Getting Devices

- Use quotations. (p. 246)
- Tell a story. (p. 246)
- Pose rhetorical questions. (p. 247)

Prepare the Conclusion

- Keep the conclusion brief: It should be only one-sixth the length of the overall speech. (p. 247)
- Carefully consider your use of language. (p. 247)

16. Using Language to Style the Speech

Strive for Simplicity

- Try to say what you mean in short, clear sentences. (p. 250)
- Steer clear of unnecessary jargon. (p. 250)
- Avoid words unlikely to be understood by your audience. (p. 250)

Aim for Conciseness

- Use fewer rather than more words to express your thoughts. (p. 250)
- Use contractions (*it's* instead of *it is*). (p. 251)
- Experiment with phrases and sentence fragments. (p. 252)

Use Repetition and Transitions

- Repeat key words and phrases to emphasize important ideas and to help listeners follow your logic. (p. 252)
- Make liberal use of transitional words and phrases, internal previews, and internal summaries. (p. 253)

Use Personal Pronouns

- Make specific references to yourself and to the audience. (p. 253)
- Foster a sense of inclusion by using the personal pronouns *I, you,* and *we.* (p. 253)

Use Culturally Sensitive and Unbiased Language

- Avoid language that relies on unfounded assumptions, negative descriptions, or stereotypes of a group's characteristics. (p. 254)
- Avoid colloquial expressions the audience may not understand. (p. 254)
- Work toward developing *cultural intelligence.* (p. 256)

Choose Concrete Words

- Use concrete nouns and verbs. (p. 256)
- Avoid abstract language that is open to interpretation — unless that is your intent. (p. 257)

Use Vivid Imagery

- Use colorful language. (p. 257)
- Appeal to listeners' senses: smell, taste, sight, hearing, and touch. (p. 257)
- Use *similes, metaphors, analogies,* and other figures of speech. (p. 258)

Choose Language That Builds Your Credibility

- Use language that is appropriate to the audience, occasion, and subject. (p. 259)
- Use language accurately. (p. 260)
- Choose words that are both denotatively (literally) and connotatively (subjectively) appropriate for the audience. (p. 260)

Choose Words That Express Confidence and Conviction

- Use the active voice. (p. 260)
- Use "I" language. (p. 261)
- Avoid powerless speech, such as hedges and tag questions. (p. 261)

Choose Language That Creates a Lasting Impression

- Repeat key words, phrases, or sentences at various intervals (anaphora). (p. 262)
- Choose words that repeat the same sounds in two or more neighboring words or syllables (alliteration). (p. 263)
- Arrange words, phrases, or sentences in similar form (parallelism). (p. 263)
- Use *antithesis* (juxtaposing two ideas in balanced opposition to each another) or *triads* (grouping concepts into threes). (p. 264)

KEY TERMS

Chapter 14

anecdote
rhetorical question

ethical appeal

Chapter 15

call to action

Chapter 16

style
rhetorical device
jargon
contractions
biased language
colloquial expression
sexist pronoun
persons with
disabilities (PWD)
cultural intelligence
concrete language
abstract language
figures of speech

simile
metaphor
cliché
mixed metaphor
analogy
personification
understatement
irony
allusion
hyperbole
onomatopoeia
malapropism

denotative meaning
connotative meaning
active voice
hedges
tag questions
anaphora
alliteration
hackneyed
parallelism
antithesis
triad

Developing the Introduction 14

Many inexperienced speakers think that if the body of their speech is well developed they can "wing" the introduction and conclusion. Leaving these elements to chance, however, is a formula for failure. Although the introduction and conclusion are not more important than the body of the speech, they are essential to its overall success. Introductions set the tone and prepare the audience to hear the speech. A good opening previews what's to come in a way that invites listeners to stay the course. An effective conclusion ensures that the audience remembers the speech and reacts in a way that the speaker intends.

This chapter describes the techniques speakers use to lead into their speeches. Chapter 15 addresses the conclusion.

Functions of the Introduction WEB Chapter quizzes

The choices you make about the introduction can affect the outcome of the entire speech. In the first several minutes (one speaker pegs it at ninety seconds[1]), audience members will decide whether they are interested in the topic of your speech, whether they will believe what you say, and whether they will give you their full attention. A good introduction serves to:

- Arouse your audience's attention and willingness to listen.
- Introduce your topic and purpose.
- Preview the main points.
- Motivate the audience to accept your goals.
- Make the topic relevant.

GAIN ATTENTION: THE FIRST STEP

The first challenge faced by any speaker is that of winning the audience's attention. Some of the more time-honored techniques for doing this include using quotations, telling a story, posing questions, saying something startling, using humor, referring to the occasion, and establishing a feeling of common ground with the audience.

Use a Quotation

A good quotation, one that elegantly and succinctly expresses an idea, is a very effective way to draw the audience's attention. Quotations can be culled from literature, poetry, film, or directly from individuals.

Audiences instinctively confer credibility on speakers who adroitly weave statements by people of renown into their remarks. In a sense, the speaker "borrows" the source's status. In the following example from a speech on the importance of history, historian David McCullough uses quotes from Harry Truman, eighteenth-century author Lord Bolingbroke, and historian Daniel Boorstein to capture his audience's attention and introduce a central point of his speech:

> Harry Truman once said the only new thing in the world is the history you don't know. Lord Bolingbroke, who was an 18th century political philosopher, said that history is philosophy taught with example. An old friend, the late Daniel Boorstein, who was a very good historian and Librarian of Congress, said that trying to plan for the future without a sense of the past is like trying to plant cut flowers. We're raising a lot of cut flowers and trying to plant them, and that's much of what I want to talk about tonight.[2]

Quotations need not be restricted to the famous. Clever sayings of any kind, whether spoken by a 3-year-old child or by a wise friend, may express precisely the idea you are looking for.

Tell a Story

Noted speechwriter and language expert William Safire once remarked that stories are "surefire attention getters."[3] Speakers like to use stories (also known as *narratives*) to illustrate points, and audiences like to hear them, because they make ideas concrete and colorful.[4] Stories personalize issues, encouraging identification and making things relevant. Most important, they entertain.

Recall from Chapter 8 that an **anecdote** is a brief story of interesting, humorous, or real-life incidents. As rhetorical scholar Edward Corbett notes, anecdotes are "one of the oldest and most effective gambits for seizing attention."[5] Corbett's assessment is supported by a 1998 study conducted by Dutch researchers, who found that speeches with anecdotal openers both motivate the audience to listen and promote greater understanding and retention of the speaker's message.[6] The key to successfully introducing a speech with an anecdote is choosing one that strikes a chord with the audience. Here, for example, Antoinette Bailey uses a humorous anecdote to begin her speech on diversity:

> I'd like to begin by retelling a story. . . . Three businessmen — a Frenchman, a Japanese man, and an American — are lined up before a firing squad. According to ancient custom, each is granted a final wish. The Frenchman says he would die happy if he could sing "La Marseillaise" one more time. He does . . . and he sings this old revolutionary song so well that it brings tears to the eyes of the riflemen. Even so, they take steady aim and shoot the Frenchman dead.
>
> The Japanese businessman is inspired by the patriotic example of the Frenchman. He expresses his desire to give one last speech on *Kaizen,* the Japanese method for encouraging incremental improvements in the production

system. However, before he can get started, the American rises and insists that he be the next to go. "I will die happy," says the American, "if I don't have to listen to one more lecture on Japanese management."[7]

Bailey uses the anecdote to make the point that her topic, diversity, has become "one of the buzzwords in American businesses and society" and that "anything that buzzes is likely to be a source of annoyance." Having acknowledged the often hackneyed treatment of her topic, Bailey proceeds to treat it with insight and originality.

Like a joke, stories should be able to stand on their own. People want to be entertained. They don't want to listen to the speaker's explanation of what the story means. Of course, not all stories have to be real. Hypothetical stories can serve the same purpose as real ones. Just remember that the hypothetical story must be plausible and will seem more effective if you connect it to yourself.

Pose Questions

Can you recall a speech that began with a question? Posing questions is an effective opening technique. Doing so draws the audience's attention to what you are about to say. Questions can be real or rhetorical. **Rhetorical questions** (like the one that opens this paragraph) do not invite actual responses. Instead, they make the audience think, as with, "What is my real purpose in life?"

Whenever you use a rhetorical question in an introduction, always let the audience know that your speech will attempt to answer it:

> Are you tired of paying more and more taxes every year? Are you fed up with having no control over how your money is spent? If so, we are in this together. Today I'm going to talk with you about some concrete steps you can take to lessen your tax burden.

Posing questions that seek an actual response, either in a show of hands or by verbal reply, also sparks interest. Here is an example of how a speech about dieting might be introduced by using real, or "polling," questions:

> How many of you have tried to diet? (*Speaker waits for a show of hands.*) How many of you kept the weight off when you stopped dieting? (*Speaker waits for a show of hands.*) How many of you would like to try a diet that doesn't make you feel starved all the time? (*Speaker waits for a show of hands.*) As you can see by looking around this room, you are not alone. Today I'm going to discuss a way of eating that is both satisfying and healthful.

Polling audience members is an effective way to gain their attention, but there are several potential drawbacks to this approach. It is possible that no one will respond, that the responses will be unexpected, or that you will be called on to answer in unanticipated ways. If you incorporate questions, make sure that you feel comfortable improvising or adapting if things don't go according to plan.

Say Something Startling

 Links

"Did you know that virtually no one is having babies anymore in parts of Western Europe?" Surprising audience members with startling or unusual information is one of the surest ways to get their attention. Such statements stimulate your listeners' curiosity and make them want to hear more about your topic.

Speakers frequently base their startling statements on statistics, a powerful means of illustrating consequences and relationships—how one thing affects another. As you learned in Chapter 8, statistics can quickly bring things into focus. In the following example, a student addressing the issue of minimum wages uses statistics to drive home the main point:

> Imagine going to work for nine hours a day, five days a week, fifty-two weeks a year, and having only about $8,600 to show for it (before taxes). Now imagine having to support not only yourself but your spouse and kids as well. The next step to imagine is you standing in welfare lines.

Use Humor

Few things build rapport and put people at ease as effectively as humor. Introducing a speech with a short joke or a funny story can set a positive tone for what's to follow. Handled well, humor is also an excellent way to make key points and introduce the theme of a speech. The drier and more difficult or complex the topic, the greater are the odds that a speech will be enlivened by humor.

Yet you should use humor with caution. Simply telling a series of unrelated jokes might initially attract the audience's attention, but unless the jokes make a relevant point they will probably detract from your purpose. Moreover, few things turn an audience off more quickly than tasteless or inappropriate humor. Speech humor should always match the audience, topic, purpose, and occasion. It should also match your personal style. Humor or sarcasm that belittles others—whether on the basis of race, sex, ability, or otherwise—should be strictly avoided in any speech.

✓ SELF-ASSESSMENT CHECKLIST

Using Humor Appropriately

_____ 1. Is your humor appropriate to the occasion?

_____ 2. Does your humor help you make a point about your speech topic or the speech occasion?

_____ 3. Have you avoided any potentially offensive targets, such as race or religion?

_____ 4. Is your humor likely to insult or demean anyone?

_____ 5. Will the audience understand your humor?

_____ 6. Have you given your humor a trial run?

_____ 7. Is your humor funny?

Self-deprecating humor often gets a chuckle, and it's usually safe. In the following example, Charlton Heston made light of his age with a quip:

> My daughter called me with some words of advice for today's talk. She said, "Don't tell them any funny stories about me when I was a child, or how tough you had it during the Great Depression."[8]

Refer to the Occasion

Introductions that include references to the speech occasion and to any relevant facts about the audience also tend to capture attention and, crucially, establish goodwill. People appreciate a direct reference to the event, and they are interested in the meaning the speaker assigns to it. In a speech on management, Vance Coffman began in this fashion:

> Let me say, right here at the beginning, that it is an honor — and a great personal pleasure — to be invited to participate in this Executive Forum of Mercer University. I understand that this is the 20th anniversary season of these innovative forums, so let me congratulate you and wish you every good fortune in continuing its success for at least another 20 years.[9]

Establish Common Ground

Just as friendships are formed by showing interest in others, audiences are won over when speakers express interest in them and show that they share similar interests and goals. Establishing a feeling of common ground demonstrates interest and respect, and thereby builds speaker credibility.

When Nelson Mandela, an anti-apartheid leader in South Africa who later became the country's president, was first released from prison after twenty-seven years of incarceration, he addressed a huge crowd of supporters. He began this way:

> Friends, comrades, and fellow South Africans. I greet you all in the name of peace, democracy, and freedom for all. I stand here before you not as a prophet but as a humble servant of you, the people. Your tireless and heroic sacrifices have made it possible for me to be here today. I therefore place the remaining years of my life in your hands.[10]

Although Mandela had just tasted his first hours of freedom after more than two decades in prison, he chose to focus on the members of the audience rather than on himself, expressing respect and establishing common ground. In response, Mandela's listeners could not help but hold him in even higher esteem.

INTRODUCE THE PURPOSE AND TOPIC

The introduction should alert the audience to the speech topic and purpose. In the attention-getting phase of the introduction, you may already have alluded to your topic, sometimes very clearly. If not, however, you now need to declare

Public Speaking in Cultural Perspective
Humor and Culture: When the Jokes Fall Flat

While humor can be a highly effective tool for introducing speeches, it can also be the cause of communication breakdowns. As one scholar notes, "Humor goes beyond language; it takes us into the heart of cultural understanding."[1] Humor assumes shared understanding. When that understanding is absent, the jokes fall flat. Humor breakdowns can occur any time audience members do not share the same cultural assumptions as the speaker. These assumptions may be based on gender, social class, educational background, ethnicity, or nationality.[2] A new employee may not get a joke told by a presenter with a long history in the corporate culture. A non-native speaker may not be familiar with an idiom used to express humor or may not share the underlying belief on which the humor is based. An English-speaking American may find the humor in other English-speaking countries baffling.

How can you avoid using humor that your audience won't understand? The obvious answer is to carefully consider your audience. Be as confident as possible that your material will make sense and be humorous to your listeners. Be particularly alert to nonverbal feedback. If you receive puzzled stares, consider clarifying your meaning. You might even acknowledge the cultural assumptions that your humor tacitly expresses.

1. William Lee, "Communication about Humor as Procedural Competence in Intercultural Encounters," in *Intercultural Communication: A Reader,* 7th ed., Larry A. Samovar and Richard E. Porter (Belmont, Calif.: Wadsworth, 1994), 373.
2. Ibid., 381.

what your speech is about and what you hope to accomplish by incorporating your thesis statement (see Chapter 7). Note an exception to this rule: When your goal is to persuade, and the audience is not yet aware that this is your intention, such "forewarning" may predispose listeners in the opposite direction. However, when the audience knows of your persuasive intent, previewing the topic and purpose can enhance understanding.[11]

Topic and purpose are clearly explained in this introduction to a speech by Marvin Runyon, postmaster general of the United States:

> This afternoon, I want to examine the truth of that statement — "Nothing moves people like the mail, and no one moves the mail like the U.S. Postal Service." I want to look at where we are today as a communications industry, and where we intend to be in the days and years ahead.[12]

PREVIEW THE MAIN POINTS

After indicating the topic and purpose, your introduction should preview the main points of the speech. Previewing the main points helps audience members mentally organize the speech and helps you, the speaker, keep their attention. Introductory previews are straightforward. You simply tell the audience what the main points will be and in what order you will address them.

For example, you might state, "First, I will address the issue of . . ." followed by "Second, I will provide information on. . . ."

In a speech titled "U.S. Roads and Bridges: Highway Funding at a Crossroads," the president of the American Automobile Association, Robert L. Darbelnet, effectively introduces his topic, purpose, and main points:

> Good morning. When I received this invitation, I didn't hesitate to accept. I realized that in this room I would find a powerful coalition: the American Automobile Association; the National Asphalt Pavement Association. Where our two groups come together, no pun intended, is where the rubber meets the road.
>
> Unfortunately, the road needs repair.
>
> My remarks today are intended to give you a sense of AAA's ongoing efforts to improve America's roads. Our hope is that you will join your voices to ours as we call on the federal government to do three things:
>
> Number one: Perhaps the most important, provide adequate funding for highway maintenance and improvements.
>
> Number two: Play a strong, responsible yet flexible role in transportation programs.
>
> And Number three: Invest in highway safety.
>
> Let's see what our strengths are, what the issues are, and what we can do about them.[13]

When previewing your main points, simply mention those points, saving your in-depth discussion of each one for the body of your speech.

MOTIVATE THE AUDIENCE TO ACCEPT YOUR GOALS

A final function of the introduction is to motivate the audience to care about your topic and believe what you have to say about it. In order for this to occur, audience members must believe that (1) the topic is relevant and (2) you are qualified to address it.

✔ **SELF-ASSESSMENT CHECKLIST**

How Effective Is Your Introduction?

_____ 1. Does the introduction capture the audience's attention?
_____ 2. Does the introduction establish a positive bond with listeners?
_____ 3. Does the introduction alert listeners to the speech purpose and topic?
_____ 4. Does the introduction motivate listeners to accept your speech goals?

MAKE THE TOPIC RELEVANT

A good introduction demonstrates why your listeners should care about your topic. One way to do this is to describe the practical implications the topic has for them. Another is to convince audience members that your speech purpose is consistent with their motives and values. Yet another strategy is to specify what the audience stands to gain by listening to you. A student speech about groundwater shows how this can be accomplished:

> Anytime we are thirsty, water is available through a tap or drinking fountain. None of us ever stops to think about where water comes from or how it's processed. It may surprise you to learn that frequently in the United States simple tap water has been found to contain dozens of pollutants and impurities. Fertilizers from irrigation fields, petroleum products from leaking underground storage facilities, and even the motor oil your neighbor dumped in the alley may end up in your drinking water.

ESTABLISH CREDIBILITY AS A SPEAKER

During the introduction, audience members make a decision about whether they are interested not just in your topic but also in you. They want to know why they should believe you, and they will look to you for reasons to do so. Thus **ethical appeals** are particularly important when the audience does not know you well and when it is important to establish your professionalism.[14] To build your credibility, make a simple statement of your qualifications for speaking on the topic at the particular occasion and to the specific audience. Briefly emphasize some experience, knowledge, or perspective you have that is different from or more extensive than that of your audience. If your goal, for example, was to persuade your audience to be more conscientious about protecting city parks, you might state, "I have felt passionate about conservation issues ever since I started volunteering with the city's local chapter of the Nature Conservancy four summers ago."

Guidelines for Preparing the Introduction   Chapter quizzes

Although the introduction comes first in a speech, it should be prepared after you've completed the speech body. When you then turn to the introduction, you will know exactly what your speech message is and what you need to preview.

Keep the introduction brief—as a rule, it should occupy no more than 10 to 15 percent of the overall speech. Nothing will turn an audience off more quickly than waiting interminably for you to get to the point. Finally, practice delivering your introduction until you feel confident that you've got it right. Use a tape recorder and seek out friends or colleagues who will give you constructive feedback.

 CHECKLIST

Guidelines for Preparing the Introduction

✓ First complete the body of the speech.
✓ Review your research for material that you can use in the introduction.
✓ Keep the introduction brief. As a general rule, it should make up no more than 10 to 15 percent of the entire speech.
✓ Time your introduction before delivery.
✓ Revise the introduction freely until you're completely satisfied.

Developing the Conclusion

Just as a well-crafted introduction gets your speech effectively out of the starting gate, a well-constructed conclusion ensures that you go out with a bang and not a whimper. Conclusions give you the opportunity to drive home your purpose, and they offer you a final chance to make the kind of impression that will accomplish the goals of your speech. Conclusions also provide the audience with a sense of logical and emotional closure, as well as further opportunity for you to build a relationship with your audience.

Functions of Conclusions

Like introductions, conclusions consist of several elements that work together to make the end of a speech as memorable as the beginning. Conclusions serve to:

- Signal to the audience that the speech is coming to an end and provide closure.
- Summarize the main points and goals.
- Reiterate the thesis or central idea of the speech.
- Challenge the audience to respond.

SIGNAL THE CLOSE OF A SPEECH AND PROVIDE CLOSURE

People who listen to speeches are taking a journey of sorts, and they want and need the speaker to acknowledge the journey's end. The more emotional the journey, as in speeches designed to touch hearts and minds, the greater is the need for logical and emotional closure.

One way to alert the audience that a speech is about to end is by using a transitional word or phrase to signal closure: *finally, looking back, in conclusion, in summary, as I bring this to a close,* or *let me close by saying* (see Chapter 11). You can also signal closure more subtly by adjusting your manner of delivery; for example, you can vary your tone, pitch, rhythm, and rate of speech to indicate that the speech is winding down (see Chapter 18).

Few things annoy listeners more than hearing a speaker say "in conclusion," and then having to sit through another twenty minutes of the speech. Once you've signaled the end of your speech, conclude in short order (though not abruptly). Although there are no hard-and-fast rules about length, as a general rule about one-sixth of the speech can be spent on the introduction, one-sixth on the conclusion, and the remaining four-sixths on the body of the speech.[1]

SUMMARIZE THE MAIN POINTS AND GOALS

One bit of age-old advice for giving a speech is: "Tell them what you are going to tell them (in the introduction), tell them (in the body), and tell them what you told them (in the conclusion)." The idea is that emphasizing the main points three times will help the audience to remember them.

Summarizing the main points in the conclusion accomplishes the last step of "telling them what you've told them." However, the summary or review should be more than a rote recounting. Consider how Holger Kluge, in a speech titled "Reflections on Diversity," summarizes his main points:

> I have covered a lot of ground here today. But as I draw to a close, I'd like to stress four things.
> First, diversity is more than equity. . . .
> Second, weaving diversity into the very fabric of your organization takes time. . . .
> Third, diversity will deliver bottom line results to your businesses and those results will be substantial, if you make the commitment. . . .
> Fourth, and above all, remember this. Diversity means recognizing the uniqueness of another person whether they are a customer, an employee, or ourselves. It means acknowledging their right to be who they are.[2]

As the speaker reiterates each point, audience members are able to mentally check off what they've heard during the speech. Did they get all the main points? A restatement of points like the one above brings the speech full circle and helps give the audience a sense of completion.

REITERATE THE TOPIC AND SPEECH PURPOSE

Another function of the conclusion is to reiterate the topic and speech purpose — to imprint it in the audience's memory. In the conclusion to a speech about preventing school violence, William Kirwan reminds his audience of his central idea:

> What I've tried to convey this afternoon are the kinds of efforts it will take for us to save the next Nick Johnson and all the other tragedies like his that are lurking out there. We can build a network of metal detectors and surveillance cameras and hope that we catch a future Nick before he fires. Or, we can build a community that could save him long before he turns down the road toward destruction. Do we want to catch him, or do we want to save him?[3]

Reminding listeners of your speech purpose links their frame of reference to yours, thus allowing your audience to determine how well they've comprehended your central idea.

CHALLENGE THE AUDIENCE TO RESPOND

A strong conclusion challenges audience members to put to use what the speaker has taught them. This applies to both informative and persuasive speeches. In an *informative speech,* the speaker challenges audience members to use what they've learned in a way that benefits them. In a *persuasive speech,* the challenge usually comes in the form of a **call to action.** Here the speaker challenges listeners to act in response to the speech, see the problem in a new way, change their beliefs about the problem, or change both their actions and their beliefs about the problem.

A concluding challenge is important because it shows audience members that the problem or issue being addressed is real and personally relevant to them. In the introduction, part of the goal is to show audience members how the topic is relevant to them; the call to action is a necessary part of completing that goal in the conclusion.

Note how Hillary Rodham Clinton makes a specific call to action in her conclusion to an address presented to the United Nations Fourth World Conference on Women:

> Now it is time to act on behalf of women everywhere. If we take bold steps to better the lives of women, we will be taking bold steps to better the lives of children and families too. . . . As long as discrimination and inequities remain so commonplace around the world — as long as girls and women are valued less, fed less, fed last, overworked, underpaid, not schooled and subjected to violence in and out of their homes — the potential of the human family to create a peaceful, prosperous world will not be realized. Let this conference be our — and the world's — call to action.[4]

In this direct call to action, Rodham Clinton appeals to her audience to act to better the lives of women around the world. Moreover, she specifically calls the conference a "call to action" to highlight the fact that she wants audience members to personally take steps to fulfill this goal.

Make the Conclusion Memorable

Beyond summarizing and providing closure, a key function of the conclusion is to make the speech memorable. A good conclusion increases the odds that the speaker's message will linger after the speech is over. A speech that makes a lasting impression is one that listeners are most likely to remember and act on.

Effective conclusions are crafted with vivid language that captures the audience's attention (see Chapter 16). Conclusions rely on (but are not limited to) the same devices for capturing attention as introductions — quotations, stories, questions, startling statements, humor, and references to the audience and the occasion. Here we offer examples of speech conclusions that make use of quotations, stories, and rhetorical questions.

Making the Conclusion Memorable

✓ Use quotations—including poetry, lyrics, and pertinent statements from others.

✓ Pose rhetorical questions to make your audience think about the speech topic and your speech goals.

✓ Tell a story that illustrates or sums up a key speech idea.

✓ Use appropriate humor.

✓ Issue a challenge.

✓ Make a startling statement.

✓ Link back to the introduction to give the audience a sense of having come full circle.

USE QUOTATIONS

As with introductions, using a quotation that captures the essence of the speech can be a very effective way to close a speech. Note how Sue Suter quotes a character in *Star Trek* to conclude her speech on discrimination and the disabled:

> That brings us to the final lesson from *Star Trek*. I'd like to leave you with two quotations from Captain Picard that define what it means to be human. In *The Next Generation,* Picard confronts discrimination by agreeing that, yes, we may be different in appearance. Then he adds, "But we are both living beings. We are born, we grow, we live, and we die. In all the ways that matter, we are alike."[5]

Quoting from poetry is also a highly effective way to conclude a speech, as seen in this commencement address given by Oprah Winfrey to graduates of Wellesley College:

> I want to leave you with a poem that I say to myself sometimes. . . . Maya Angelou wrote a poem and I don't know a poem more fitting than "Phenomenal Woman" for this crowd, because you are and these words are for you.
>   She says, "Pretty women, honey, they wonder just where my secret lies 'cause I'm not cuter, built to suit a fashion model size, but when I start to tell them, they say, Girl, you're telling lies and I said, no, honey, it's in the reach of my arms, it's in the span of my hips, it's in the stride of my stepping, it's in the curl of my lips, 'cause I'm a woman, honey, phenomenally, phenomenal, phenomenal woman."[6]

TELL A STORY

A short concluding story, or *anecdote,* can bring the entire speech into focus very effectively. It helps the audience to visualize the speech:

> I would conclude with a story that applies to all of us in this industry. In ancient times there was a philosopher who had many disciples. . . .

How Effective Is Your Conclusion?

Does your conclusion . . .

_____ 1. Alert the audience that the speech is ending?

_____ 2. Actually come to an end soon after you say you will finish?

_____ 3. Last no more than about one-sixth of the time spent on the body of the speech?

_____ 4. Reiterate the main points?

_____ 5. Remind listeners of the speech topic and purpose?

_____ 6. Challenge the audience to respond to your ideas or appeals?

_____ 7. Provide a sense of closure and make a lasting impression?

Another technique is to pick up on a story or an idea that you mentioned in the introduction, bringing the speech full circle:

> Remember the story of Timmy that I told in the beginning, the young hero who gave up everything he ever wanted to help his family? Well, I am happy to tell you that Timmy, or I should say Tim, is today one of the most successful entrepreneurs in the state of Florida.

POSE A RHETORICAL QUESTION

Yet another effective way to make a speech linger is to leave the audience with a *rhetorical question*. Just as such questions focus attention in the introduction, they can drive home the speech theme in the conclusion. A speech on groundwater contamination, for example, might end with a rhetorical question:

> Water has been cheap and plentiful, for most of us, for our entire lives. Easy access to our most necessary resource is now greatly threatened. Given this danger, we need to ask ourselves, "How long can we ignore the dangers of groundwater contamination?"

Guidelines for Preparing the Conclusion WEB Video quizzes

As with the introduction, prepare the conclusion after you've completed the speech body. Keep it brief—as a rule, no more than about one-sixth of the overall speech. And, just as you should outline the introduction in full-sentence and then key-word form, do so for the conclusion (see Chapter 13). Carefully consider your use of language in the conclusion. More than other parts of the speech, the conclusion can contain words that inspire and motivate (see Chapter 16).

Finally, practice delivering the conclusion until you feel confident that you've got it right. Use a tape recorder or video camera, and seek out friends or colleagues for constructive feedback. While practicing, work on ensuring that audience members will understand the speech is ending through your word choice and vocal intonation (see Chapter 18), and be sure to rehearse how you will leave the podium or speech area (see Chapter 19).

✔ **CHECKLIST**

Guidelines for Preparing the Conclusion

✓ During the research phase, be on the lookout for material that you can use in the conclusion.

✓ Do not leave the conclusion to chance. Prepare both a full-sentence outline and a key-word outline.

✓ Keep the length of the conclusion to about one-sixth of the overall speech.

✓ Practice delivering the conclusion often, using your peers as sounding boards.

Using Language to Style the Speech 16

Words are the public speaker's tools of the trade, and the words you choose to style your speech will play a large role in how well it is received. **Style** involves both the specific word choices and **rhetorical devices** (techniques of language) that speakers use to express their ideas and achieve their speech purpose.

Used in all its richness, language allows us to visualize an image and even get a sense of sound or smell. Poets and novelists use descriptive language to breathe life into that someone or something and to make their words leap off the page into the reader's mind. In public speaking, you too can use the evocative power of language to captivate your audience. Carefully choosing the right words and images is crucial to connecting with your audience. Doing so will increase the odds that your listeners will understand, believe in, and retain your message.[1]

Prepare Your Speeches for the Ear Chapter quizzes

> In the book *Reagan: In His Own Hand,* former Secretary of State George P. Shultz recalls how President Ronald Reagan once approved a foreign policy speech that Shultz was about to deliver but then added, "Of course, if I were giving that speech, it would be different." The text, he opined to an abashed Shultz, had been written to be read in the *New York Times,* not to be spoken aloud. Flipping through the manuscript, Reagan penciled in a few changes and marked out the section that contained, or should contain, the "story." Nothing of substance was altered, but, writes Shultz, "I saw that he had changed the tone of my speech completely."[2]

A masterful public speaker, President Reagan was keenly aware that written language and oral language differ in several respects. Whereas readers who fail to understand something can go back and reread a passage until they are satisfied that they understand what the writer means, listeners have only one chance to get the message. If the language in your speech is unclear, listeners will have a tough time getting the meaning you intend to convey.

The next time you listen to a speech or even a classroom lecture, consider how the presenter's language differs from that of this textbook. Here are some things you are likely to note:

- More so than written texts, effective speeches use familiar words, easy-to-follow sentences, and straightforward syntax (subject-verb-object agreement).

- Speeches make much more frequent use of repetition and transitions than do most forms of written communication.

- Because you cannot "rewind" a speaker's words, speeches must be more clearly organized than written language. A clear organizational pattern provides listeners with the necessary framework to follow spoken messages.

- Spoken communication is more interactive than written language. When you deliver a speech, you can adjust the content based on audience feedback. If listeners appear not to understand you, for example, you can supply additional examples or otherwise attempt to increase shared meaning.

Keeping these differences between oral and written language in mind, consider how you can use the following tips to write your speeches to be heard rather than read.

STRIVE FOR SIMPLICITY

To make certain that your audience understands you, strive for simplicity of expression in your speeches. When selecting between two synonyms, choose the simpler term. Avoid pretentious and/or empty terms such as *extrapolate* for "guess" and *utilize* for "use." And unless the audience consists of specialized professionals, translate **jargon** — the specialized, "insider" language of a given profession — into commonly understood terms. As former presidential speechwriter Peggy Noonan notes in her book *Simply Speaking:*

> Good hard simple words with good hard clear meanings are good things to use when you speak. They are like pickets in a fence, slim and unimpressive on their own but sturdy and effective when strung together.[3]

William Safire, another master speechwriter, puts it this way:

> Great speeches steer clear of forty-dollar words. Big words, or terms chosen for their strangeness — I almost said "unfamiliarity" — are a sign of pretension. What do you do when you have a delicious word, one with a little poetry in it, that is just the right word for the meaning — but you know it will sail over the head of your audience? You can use it, just as FDR used "infamy," and thereby stretch the vocabulary of your listeners. But it is best if you subtly define it in passing, as if you were adding emphasis.[4]

AIM FOR CONCISENESS

Concise wording is another feature of an effective speech. As a rule, use fewer rather than more words to express your thoughts. As you work on your speech drafts, edit any unnecessary words and phrases, bearing in mind that, in general, easy-to-pronounce words and shorter sentences are more readily understood. Because they reflect how the English language is actually spoken, use

contractions — shortened forms of the verb *to be* and other auxiliary verbs in conjunction with pronouns (*I, he, she, you, we*) and proper nouns (*John, Juanita*). Thus, rather than

> I am so happy to be here today. I will first turn . . .

say,

> I'm happy to be here. I'll first turn . . .

Refer to the accompanying ESL Speaker's Notes for a list of common English contractions.

ESL Speaker's Notes
Using Contractions

Learning to use contractions is an excellent way for non-native speakers to sound like experienced speakers of English. Using contractions will make your language sound more natural, thereby helping your audience to feel more at ease with your speech patterns. As you work on your speeches, practice using the contraction forms in this chart.

Auxiliary Verb Form	Contractions with Pronouns	Contractions with Nouns	Contractions with Question Words
am	*I'm* swimming this morning.		*What'm* I supposed to do? (Common only in spoken English.)
is	*She's* going to come. *She's* a teacher. *It's* easy!	*Ahmed's* at home. *Joan's* playing the piano at the moment.	*Who's* on the telephone? *What's* he doing?
are	*You're* a great cook! *They're* playing tennis this afternoon.	The *books're* on their way. (Common only in spoken English.)	*What're* you going to do? (Common only in spoken English.)
has	*He's* been to Cairo twice. *It's* been such a long time! *She's* been painting all day.	*Mary's* gone to the store.	*What's* she been doing? *Who's* been invited?

(Continued)

have	*I've* eaten for the day. *They've* got six dogs.	The *students've* finished their homework. (Common only in spoken English.)	*Where've* you been all day? (Common only in spoken English.)
had	*He'd* been outside all day. *We'd* better be going.		*What'd* you done before that? (Common only in spoken English.)
will	*I'll* find your book tomorrow. *We'll* be there soon.	*Peter'll* catch the train to New York. (Common only in spoken English.)	*What'll* we do? *Where'll* you take us? (Common only in spoken English.)
would	*I'd* like some food. *They'd* like to ask her some questions.	*Jane'd* love to come. (Common only in spoken English.)	*Where'd* you like to go? (Common only in spoken English.)

Source: Adapted from "Using Contractions," About.com section on English as a second language, with Kenneth Beare, http://esl.about.com/library/grammar/blgr_contractions.htm (accessed May 12, 2002).

CONSIDER PHRASES AND SENTENCE FRAGMENTS

Although they are often avoided in written language, phrases and sentence fragments can sometimes help to communicate an oral message concisely. The following example, by a speaker trained as a physician, demonstrates how they can add punch to a speech:

> I'm just a simple bone-and-joint guy. I can set your broken bones. Take away your bunions. Even give you a new hip. But I don't mess around with the stuff between the ears. . . . That's another specialty.[5]

Beware of shortening merely for shortening's sake, however. Your first goal should always be to help the audience see the connection between ideas.[6] Repetition and transitions can often help you to accomplish this.

MAKE FREQUENT USE OF REPETITION AND TRANSITIONS

Good speeches often repeat key words and phrases. Indeed, even very brief speeches make use of this extremely important linguistic device. Repetition adds emphasis to important ideas, helps listeners follow the speaker's logic, and

---

✓ SELF-ASSESSMENT CHECKLIST

Does Your Speech Incorporate Effective Oral Style?

_____ 1. Can you use fewer rather than more words to clearly express your thoughts?

_____ 2. Is your speech free of unnecessary jargon?

_____ 3. Do you steer clear of terms that are difficult to pronounce (and therefore difficult to decipher)?

_____ 4. Do you avoid any unnecessary "forty-dollar words"?

_____ 5. Do you use frequent transitions, internal previews, and summaries (see Chapter 11)?

_____ 6. Do you judiciously use the personal pronouns *I* and *you* to personalize the occasion and foster a sense of inclusion?

_____ 7. Would interjecting some phrases and sentence fragments in place of full sentences add punch to your speech?

_____ 8. Do you make sufficient use of repetition and transitions?

---

imbues language with rhythm and drama. Similarly, threaded through a typical speech are numerous transitional words, phrases, and sentences, such as *next, first, second, third,* and so forth; and *we now turn to.* Along with more lengthy internal previews and internal summaries, these transitions guide the listener from one main point to the next, from main points to supporting points, and from one supporting point to another (see Chapter 11).

USE PERSONAL PRONOUNS

Oral language is often more interactive and inclusive of the audience than is written language. The personal pronouns *we, us, I,* and *you* occur more frequently in spoken than in written text. Audience members want to know what the speaker thinks and feels, and to be assured that he or she recognizes them and relates them to the message. Speakers accomplish this by making specific references to themselves and to the audience, as in this excerpt from a speech to a group of people working in public relations:

> My talk today is about you. Each one of you personally. I know you hear many presentations. For the most part, they tend to be directed mostly to others with very little for you. My presentation today is different; the topic and the information will be important to every one of you, especially if you're at all interested in having a happy, successful, and important life. I'm going to show and tell each of you how to become a verbal visionary.[7]

Consult the accompanying checklist for additional tips on personalizing your speech with personal pronouns.

✓ **CHECKLIST**

Personalizing Your Speech with Personal Pronouns

✓ "*I* am indebted to the ideas of . . ."

✓ "Those of *us* who have lived during a world war . . ."

✓ "*We* cannot opt out of this problem . . ."

✓ "To *me,* the truly great lessons . . ."

✓ "Some of *you* will recall . . ."

Choose Language That Encourages Shared Meaning

Words have a power that goes beyond mere description. They can encourage shared meaning or serve as obstacles to understanding. They can build trust or engender hostility. Language that encourages shared meaning is dialogic in nature. Recall from the listening chapter (Chapter 4) that *dialogic communication* seeks to find common ground through the sharing of ideas and open discussion. Such language is culturally sensitive and unbiased, concrete, and vivid.

USE CULTURALLY SENSITIVE AND UNBIASED LANGUAGE

Perhaps more than any other aspect of human society, language defines and creates culture. Through language people are able to communicate with one another — to share meaning. *Language* is the distinctive words, phrases, and colloquial expressions that pass from one generation to the next and that define and perpetuate a unique culture.

As a public speaker, it is critical to be sensitive to cultural variations in language, whether you are addressing people of another nationality or audiences for whom local variations in language are significant. Demonstrating sensitivity to your audience begins with using language that is free of bias. **Biased language** relies on unfounded assumptions, negative descriptions, or stereotypes of a given group's age, class, gender, disability, geographic, ethnic, racial, or religious characteristics. In addition to being unethical, biased language reflects poorly on a speaker's credibility and may lead to the audience's rejecting both the speaker and the message of the speech. (See the Public Speaking in Cultural Perspective box on p. 255.)

As you review your speech draft, consider whether you use sayings specific to a certain region or group of people (termed **colloquial expressions** or idioms) that may confuse listeners. Expressions such as "back the wrong horse," "hit the nail on the head," and "wet behind the ears" can add color and richness to your speech, but only if your listeners understand them, so be sure to include simple definitions for any idiomatic expressions that you include in your speech.

Public Speaking in Cultural Perspective
Adapting Your Language to Diverse Audiences

Using language that is appropriate to each of your listeners is one of the most important challenges facing you as a public speaker. Consider, for example, that many students at your school may be Arab, Jewish, Asian, African, or Hispanic American. Others may have families that come from Europe, Canada, Mexico, and elsewhere.

How do members of the co-cultures in your audience want you to refer to them? Are there important regional differences in languages you should address? Rather than being a monolithic group, Asian Americans and Pacific Islanders in the United States include those of Chinese, Samoan, Pakistani, Bangladeshi, Native Hawaiian, Vietnamese, Korean, Thai, and Japanese descent, and this is merely a partial listing of countries of origin. Some Asian Americans have limited English proficiency (LEP) and live in linguistically isolated households in which all members fourteen years and older speak limited English,[1] while others excel at elite universities and in high-powered careers. Rather than treating any individual merely as a member of a broad category, audience members want to be addressed as individuals and to be recognized for their unique characteristics and life circumstances.

Similarly, a common misconception of Arab Americans is that they are a homogeneous group. For example, many people believe that all Arab Americans are practicing Muslims. In fact, the largest portion are Catholics (42 percent); most of the six million Muslims in this country are not Arab Americans. Rather than sharing a religion, Arab Americans belong to many religions, including Islam, Christianity, Druze, Judaism, and others.[2] Using biased language based on these and other misconceptions can only alienate your listeners.

All people look to speakers to use language that is respectful and inclusive of them. As you prepare your speeches, consider whether you include terms that might leave your listeners feeling less than respected. For the long term, make learning about other cultures an ongoing endeavor. In this way, you will truly be able to address the sensitivities of diverse audiences.

1. "The Diverse Face of Asians and Pacific Islanders in California," National Asian Pacific American Legal Consortium (San Francisco: 2005), www.napalc.org/?id=61&cid=4&pid=3&oid=1 (accessed April 28, 2005).
2. Arab American Institute, "About Arab Americans," www.aaiusa.org/definition.htm (accessed April 28, 2005).

(See Chapter 4 for more on cultural barriers to understanding, and Chapter 6 for more on adapting to differing ethnic and cultural backgrounds.)

One common mistake that persists despite ongoing attempts to remedy it is the use of **sexist pronouns**, which unnecessarily restrict the gender of the person or persons in question. Steer clear of the generic pronoun *he* to refer to both women and men, using *she or he* instead. Also avoid stereotyping jobs or social roles by gender. For example, a speaker who continually refers to engineers as "he" and to nurse practitioners as "she" is guilty of using sexist language. Try to use gender-neutral terms when possible, such as *chairperson* instead of *chairman.*

Another mistake many speakers make is failing to recognize the range of physical and mental disabilities that their listeners may experience. Yet about one out of every five people in the United States has some sort of physical or mental disability.[8] Thus another way that you can demonstrate cultural sensitivity is to familiarize yourself with issues that are important to **persons with disabilities (PWD)**, and then ensure that your language accords them dignity, respect, and fairness.

As described in Chapter 1, **cultural intelligence**[9] is the willingness to learn about other cultures and gradually reshape your thinking and behavior in response to what you've learned.[10] As you craft the language in your speech, consider your own cultural intelligence quotient (see the accompanying checklist).

CHECKLIST

Considering Your Cultural Intelligence Quotient

✓ Have you learned about the background of your audience members?

✓ Can you identify cultural values and attitudes that may affect how audience members will receive your speech?

✓ Have you considered your use of colloquial expressions?

✓ Does your language include any unintentional assumptions about a given group, such as assigning all members a general characteristic?

✓ Does your language reflect any disparagement toward a person's or a group's nationality, geographic origin, or religion?

CHOOSE CONCRETE WORDS

Another way to build common ground is by using **concrete language** — language that is specific, tangible, and definite. The flip side of concrete language is **abstract language** — language that is general or nonspecific. Studies show that listeners retain concrete nouns and verbs more easily than they retain abstractions. In fact, each time listeners hear an abstract word they try to find a concrete reference for it, and if you haven't given it they will search their own experience for it. The meaning they ultimately attach to the word may not match yours and, furthermore, if they are sufficiently puzzled they will be distracted from focusing on the remainder of your message.

Note the following ten words, all of which are among the most overused abstractions in student speeches:[11]

old	bad	a lot	short	good
thing	big	long	new	late

The following examples illustrate abstract versus concrete language:

ABSTRACT:	The road was rough.
CONCRETE:	The road was pitted with muddy craters and nearly swallowed up by huge outcroppings of dark gray granite.
ABSTRACT:	That iPhone has a lot of accessories.
CONCRETE:	Along with the iPhone itself, she purchased a Bluetooth headset and dual dock.

 CHECKLIST

Is Your Speech Language Concrete?

As you construct your speech, consider which words and phrases may be abstract. Consult a dictionary or thesaurus to find more concrete words that would strengthen your message. For example, consider the following levels of concreteness:

Abstract	*Less Abstract*	*Concrete*
summer ⟶	hot weather ⟶	sweltering heat
congestion ⟶	traffic jam ⟶	gridlock

OFFER VIVID IMAGERY

Vivid images paint a mental picture for listeners, inviting them to use their imaginations and thereby become involved in your message. Paint vivid images with colorful and concrete words that appeal to the senses and with figures of speech, such as similes, metaphors, and analogies.

Select Words That Are Colorful and Concrete

Merely by modifying nouns and verbs with descriptive adjectives and adverbs, you can create many colorful and concrete images. For example, rather than characterizing the sky merely as "blue," you can specify it as "faint blue," "sea blue," "blue with feathers of white," or "blue with pillows of dark gray."

Appeal to the Senses

Use language that appeals to listeners' sense of smell, taste, sight, hearing, or touch. Consult the checklist on concrete language above, as well as the following discussion of similes and metaphors, for more on translating abstractions into vivid images that appeal to the senses.

Use Figures of Speech

Figures of speech, including similes, metaphors, and analogies, make striking comparisons that help listeners visualize, identify with, and understand the speaker's ideas. A **simile** explicitly compares one thing to another, using *like* or *as* to do so: "He works *like* a dog" and "The old woman's hands were *as* soft as a baby's." A **metaphor** also compares two things, but does so by describing one thing as actually *being* the other. Metaphors do not use *like* or *as:* "Time is a thief," "All the world's a stage," and "Love is a rose." Used properly, metaphors express ideas compactly and cleverly. However, try not to use overused metaphors that are **clichéd**, or predictable and stale (as in the above examples). Similarly, beware of using clichéd similes. In addition, beware of using **mixed metaphors**, or those that juxtapose or compare unlike images or expressions: "Burning the midnight oil at both ends" incorrectly joins the expressions "burning the midnight oil" and "burning a candle at both ends."

An **analogy** is simply an extended metaphor or simile that compares an unfamiliar concept or process to a more familiar one to help listeners understand the unfamiliar one.[12] When Martin Luther King Jr. delivered his now-famous "I Have a Dream" speech on the steps of the Lincoln Memorial in 1963, he began with a financial metaphor of a bad check. As he spoke, he extended the metaphor to include the "bank of justice" and the "vaults of opportunity":

> In a sense we have come to our nation's capital to write a check. When the architects of our republic wrote the magnificent words of the Constitution and the Declaration of Independence, they were signing a promissory note to which every American has fallen heir. This note was a promise that all men would be guaranteed the unalienable rights of life, liberty, and the pursuit of happiness.
>
> It is obvious today that America has defaulted on this promissory note insofar as her citizens of color are concerned. Instead of honoring this sacred obligation, America has given the Negro a bad check; a check which has come back marked "insufficient funds." But we refuse to believe that the bank of justice is bankrupt. So we refuse to believe that there are insufficient funds in the great vaults of opportunity of this nation.[13]

More recently, African American minister Phil Wilson used metaphoric language in his 2001 sermon to a Los Angeles congregation about the dangers of AIDS:

> Our house is on fire! The fire truck arrives, but we won't come out, because we're afraid the folks from next door will see that we're in that burning house. AIDS is a fire raging in our community and it's out of control![14]

See Table 16.1 for other figures of speech that contribute to vivid imagery, including **personification**, **understatement**, **irony**, **allusion**, **hyperbole**, and **onomatopoeia**.

TABLE 16.1 • Figures of Speech		
Figure of Speech	**Description**	**Example**
Personification	Endowing abstract ideas or inanimate objects with human qualities.	"Computers have become important members of our family."
Understatement	Drawing attention to an idea by minimizing or lowering its importance.	"Flunking out of college might be a problem."
Irony	Using humor, satire, or sarcasm to suggest a meaning other than the one that is actually being expressed.	"Our football players are great. They may not be big, but they sure are slow."
Allusion	Making vague or indirect reference to people, historical events, or concepts to give deeper meaning to the message.	"His meteoric rise to the top is an example for all of us."
Hyperbole	Using obvious exaggeration to drive home a point.	"Have you seen those students carrying backpacks the size of minivans filled with five-course dinners, cell phones, and an occasional textbook or two?"
Onomatopoeia	The imitation of natural sounds in word form; it adds vividness to the speech.	"The rain dripped a steady *plop plop plop* on the metal roof; the bees *buzzed* through the wood."

Source: Some examples taken from Andrea A. Lunsford, *The St. Martin's Handbook,* 6th ed. (Boston: Bedford/St. Martin's, 2008).

Choose Language That Builds Credibility Links

As you draft your speeches, consider whether your language builds trust and credibility. When you wield words correctly—that is, by being appropriate, being accurate, and showing confidence in your topic—you demonstrate the competence and trustworthiness that audiences look for in a speaker.

USE APPROPRIATE LANGUAGE

The language you use in a speech should be appropriate to the audience, the occasion, and the subject matter. As a rule, strive to uphold the conventional principles of grammar and usage associated with standard written English, but as prepared for the ear. The more diverse the audience and the more formal the occasion, the closer you will want to remain within these bounds. Sometimes, however, especially when the audience is more homogeneous, it may be appropriate to mix casual language, regional dialects, or even slang in your speech, especially if most members of the audience also use the expressions. As long as the meaning is clear, interposing such terms into a speech can simultaneously reveal who you are and add vivid imagery to your speech. Consider the following excerpt:

> On the gulf where I was raised, *el valle del Rio Grande* in South Texas — that triangular piece of land wedged between the river *y el golfo* which serves as the Texas–U.S./Mexican border — is a Mexican *pueblito* called Hargill.[15]

USE LANGUAGE ACCURATELY

Words can evoke powerful responses in listeners. To build trust and credibility, language must be accurate — that is, it must be both correct in usage and truthful in expression. (See also the discussion of slander in Chapter 5 and of fallacies of reasoning in Chapter 25.) One error that speakers sometimes commit is the **malapropism** — the inadvertent use of a word or a phrase in place of one that sounds like it.[16] Malapropisms — "It's a strange *receptacle*" for "It's a strange *spectacle*" — do nothing to enhance the speaker's credibility.

More broadly, speakers sometimes fail to choose words that are both denotatively and connotatively appropriate for the audience. The **denotative meaning** of a word is its literal, or dictionary, definition. Although some concrete words have mainly denotative meanings — *surgery* and *saline,* for example — through long use most words have acquired special associations that go beyond their dictionary definitions. The **connotative meaning** of a word is the special association that different people bring to bear on it. For instance, you may like to be called slender but not skinny, or thrifty but not cheap.

Ask yourself whether the words you have chosen carry connotative meanings to which the audience might react negatively. For example, members of a mainstream church or synagogue may associate the word *cult* with an off-center or even bizarre religious group. But to people who belong to an emerging religious group (which, according to sociologists of religion, is the denotative meaning of *cult*) being described as a cult may be offensive.

CHOOSE WORDS THAT CONVEY CONFIDENCE AND CONVICTION

To inspire trust in your listeners, you must express yourself with confidence and conviction. Three ways to convey these qualities are by using the *active voice,* using *personal pronouns* or "I" language, and *avoiding hedges and tag questions.*

Use the Active Voice

Voice is the feature of verbs that indicates the subject's relationship to the action. A verb is in the **active voice** when the subject performs the action. A verb is in the *passive voice* when the subject is acted upon or is the receiver of the action.[17] As in writing, speaking in the active rather than the passive voice will make your statements clear and assertive instead of indirect and weak:

PASSIVE: A test was announced by Ms. Carlos for Tuesday.
                         A president was elected by the voters every four years.

ACTIVE: Ms. Carlos announced a test for Tuesday.
                               The voters elect a president every four years.

Use "I" Language

As well as fostering a sense of inclusion, "I" language (as expressed through the personal pronouns *I, me,* and *my*) creates an impression of conviction. Instead of saying "This is a good idea for our university," it would be more convincing for you to say "I personally support this idea." If audience members are expected to accept your ideas and arguments, you must indicate convincingly that you accept them as well. Unless audience members believe you to be an expert on your topic, however, in most cases they will want you to back up your assertions with credible supporting material drawn from other sources (see Chapter 8 for more on supporting your speech).

Avoid Powerless Speech

Despite the great strides made toward gender equality in the United States, research shows that many women, and to a lesser extent men, tend to use weak language that undermines their message. In addition to the passive voice, linguists Robin Lakoff and Deborah Tannen, among others, note that women are particularly prone to using weak language forms such as hedges and tag questions.[18] **Hedges** are unnecessary words and phrases that qualify or introduce doubt into statements that should be straightforward. Hedges make you sound as if you doubt your own words, thereby undermining your authority in the eyes of the audience. Examples of hedges include:

I guess my question is . . .

In my opinion . . .

I may not be right, but . . .

✓ SELF-ASSESSMENT CHECKLIST

Does Your Language Build Trust and Credibility?

_____ 1. Is your language appropriate to the audience, occasion, and subject matter?

_____ 2. Is your speech free of slander?

_____ 3. Are your word choices accurate?

_____ 4. Do any of the words you have chosen carry connotative meanings to which the audience might react negatively?

_____ 5. Do you construct your sentences using the active voice?

_____ 6. When appropriate, do you use the personal pronoun *I* to express conviction and ownership of your ideas?

_____ 7. When appropriate, do you use the personal pronoun *you* to foster a sense of recognition and a feeling of inclusion in your listeners?

_____ 8. Is your language free of hedges and tag questions?

Tag questions are unnecessary questions that are appended to statements or commands. Like hedges, tag questions undermine the speaker's authority by turning straightforward statements into questions that are left to the audience to resolve. Examples include:

> The project was poorly managed, *or at least I thought so.*
>
> The proposal was too expensive, *wasn't it?*
>
> I will next address the issue of economics, *okay?*

Choose Language That Creates a Lasting Impression

Just as certain lyrics and bits of music replay themselves in our minds, oral language that is artfully arranged and infused with rhythm leaves a lasting impression on listeners. You can create the cadenced arrangement of language through rhetorical devices such as repetition, alliteration, and parallelism.

USE REPETITION FOR RHYTHM AND REINFORCEMENT

One of the most effective strategies for creating a lasting impression in a speech is *repetition*. Repeating key words, phrases, or even sentences at various intervals throughout a speech creates a distinctive rhythm and thereby implants important ideas in listeners' minds. This technique captures the audience's attention and brings the speaker closer to his or her listeners. Repetition works extremely well when it is delivered with the appropriate inflections and pauses. Note, for example, then Presidential candidate Barack Obama's use of repetition in a speech to supporters in New Hampshire:

> Yes we can to justice and equality. Yes we can to opportunity and prosperity. Yes we can heal this nation . . .[19]

In a form of repetition called **anaphora**, the speaker repeats a word or phrase at the beginning of successive phrases, clauses, or sentences. Obama uses anaphora in the preceding example ("Yes we can . . ."), as does Martin Luther King Jr. in his famous "I Have a Dream" speech, repeating the phrase "I have a dream" numerous times, each with an upward inflection followed by a pause.

Speakers have made use of anaphora since the earliest times: For example, Jesus preached: "*Blessed are* the poor in spirit. . . . *Blessed are* the meek. . . . *Blessed are* the peacemakers. . . ."[20]

In a speech about becoming an organ donor, Manchester Community and Technical College student Ed Partlow uses anaphora this way:

> Today *I'm going to talk about* a subject that can be both personal and emotional.
>
> *I'm going to talk about* becoming an organ donor.

In addition to reinforcing key ideas, repetition can help you create a thematic focus for your speech. Speakers often do this by using both anaphora and epiphora in the same speech. In anaphora you repeat words or phrases at the beginning of successive statements; in *epiphora* you repeat a word or phrase at the end of successive statements. In the same speech to his New Hampshire supporters, note how Barack Obama used epiphora to establish a theme of empowerment:

> Some of them are illiterate and can't read the want-ad sections. And when they can, they can't find a job that matches their address. *They work hard every day*. I know. I'm one of them.[21]

> I know they work. I'm a witness. They catch the early bus. *They work every day* . . . They raise other people's children. They work every day . . .

In addition to capturing the audience's attention and reinforcing key ideas, anaphora and other kinds of repetition can be used to create a thematic focus for your speech. Speakers do this by repeating key phrases that emphasize a central or recurring idea. The theme words generally appear first in the introduction, then the idea is repeated in the body, and the words or phrases are repeated in the conclusion. In the following example from a speech delivered to a conference of teenagers in Atlanta, the Reverend Jesse Jackson repeats the theme that teenagers "are somebody":

> This morning I want to speak on the subject "It's Up to You," for it is important for you to get involved and be part of what's happening. You must feel that you count in order to appreciate yourself and develop yourself in relation to other people.
> People to my right, I am. [Audience answers] "I am." Now don't sound all scared and timid. I know better. I am. [Audience answers] "I am." Somebody. [Audience answers] "Somebody."[22]

Jackson continues in this vein, repeating the phrase "I am somebody" at various points throughout the speech. He concludes by saying:

> My mind is a pearl. I can learn anything in the world. I am somebody. Nobody will save us but us. Right on![23]

USE ALLITERATION FOR A POETIC QUALITY

Alliteration is the repetition of the same sounds, usually initial consonants, in two or more neighboring words or syllables. Political campaign slogans often use alliteration to catch the attention of voters. Phrases such as Jesse Jackson's "Down with dope, up with hope" and former U.S. vice president Spiro Agnew's disdainful reference to the U.S. press as "nattering nabobs of negativism" are *classic* examples of alliteration in speeches.

Alliteration lends speech a poetic, musical rhythm. When used well, it drives home themes and leaves listeners with a lasting impression. When alliteration is poorly crafted or **hackneyed**, it can distract from a message. Use only those alliterative phrases that convey your point more concisely and colorfully than it can otherwise be conveyed.

USE PARALLELISM TO DRIVE YOUR POINTS HOME

Another rhetorical device that is characteristic of memorable speeches is **parallelism** — the arrangement of words, phrases, or sentences in a similar form. Parallel structure can help the speaker emphasize important ideas in the speech. Like repetition, parallelism creates a sense of steady or building rhythm.[24] Orally numbering your points — for example, "first, second, and third" — is one use of parallel language. Another method, which works well when your speech contains chronological material, is to state the relevant years, months, or days when introducing an idea or presenting evidence. A speaker recapping the major events of World War II might begin each main point with a phrase such as "December 1942" or "March 1943," followed by a pause.

Parallelism in speeches often makes use of **antithesis** — setting off two ideas in balanced (parallel) opposition to each other to create a powerful effect:

> One small step for a man, one giant leap for mankind. — Neil Armstrong on the moon, 1969

> To err is human, to forgive divine. — Alexander Pope, 1711

> For many are called, but few are chosen. — Matthew 22:14

Speakers often make use of three parallel elements or **triads**. This combination of three elements may be natural to a speech (such as in one describing the three branches of the U.S. government). In other cases, a speech may be manipulated to accommodate the use of triads. In fact, many speeches are carefully confined to three main points in order to take advantage of triads. There is something powerful about grouping concepts or ideas into threes. Consider the following examples:

> . . . of the people, by the people, and for the people. — Abraham Lincoln

> If 60 million Anglo-Saxons can have a place in the sun,
> If 60 million Japanese can have a place in the sun,
> If 7 million Belgians can have a place in the sun,
> I cannot see why 400 million black people cannot. — Marcus Garvey

As these examples indicate, when parallelism is used appropriately, it creates a powerful, poetic effect for the audience.

Vocal and Nonverbal Delivery

Vocal and Nonverbal Delivery

Speaker's Reference
Vocal and Nonverbal Delivery

17. Methods of Delivery

Strive for Naturalness in Your Delivery

- Think of your speech as a particularly important conversation. (p. 271)
- Rather than behaving theatrically, strive for naturalness. (p. 271)

Show Enthusiasm

- Show enthusiasm for your topic and for the occasion. (p. 272)
- Speak about what excites you. (p. 272)

Project a Sense of Confidence and Composure

- Focus on the ideas you want to convey rather than on yourself. (p. 272)
- Inspire audience members' confidence in you by appearing confident. (p. 272)

Engage Your Audience by Being Direct

- Establish eye contact with your listeners. (p. 272)
- Use a friendly tone of voice. (p. 272)
- Smile whenever it is appropriate. (p. 272)
- Consider positioning yourself close to the audience. (p. 272)

If You Must Read from a Prepared Text, Do So Naturally

- Vary the rhythm of your words. (p. 273)
- Become familiar with the speech so you can establish some eye contact with the audience. (p. 274)
- Consider using compelling presentation aids. (p. 274)

In General, Don't Try to Memorize Entire Speeches

- Consider memorizing parts of your speech, such as quotations. (p. 275)
- Brief remarks, like toasts, can be well served by memorization. (p. 275)
- When delivering material from memory, know it well enough to do so with enthusiasm and directness. (p. 275)

When Speaking Impromptu, Maximize Any Preparation Time

- Anticipate situations that may require impromptu speaking. (p. 275)
- Consider what would best serve the audience. (p. 276)
- As you wait your turn to speak, take notes on what others are saying. (p. 276)
- Jot down a few key ideas in key-word form. (p. 276)
- Stay on topic. (p. 276)

In Most Situations, Select the Extemporaneous Method of Delivery

- Prepare and practice your speech in advance of delivery. (p. 276)
- Speak from an outline of key words and phrases. (p. 276)
- Use eye contact and body orientation and movement to maximize delivery. (p. 277)

18. The Voice in Delivery

Adjust Your Speaking Volume

- The bigger the room and the larger the audience, the louder you need to speak. Yet the volume must not be too loud for those in front. (p. 279)
- Be alert to signals from the audience indicating problems in volume. (p. 279)

Beware of Speaking in a Monotone

- Vary your intonation to reflect meaning. (p. 280)
- Use pitch to animate your voice. (p. 280)

Adjust Your Speaking Rate for Comprehension and Expressiveness

- To ensure that your speaking rate is comfortable for your listeners (neither too fast nor too slow), be alert to their reactions. (p. 281)
- Vary your speaking rate to indicate different meanings. (p. 281)

Use Strategic Pauses and Avoid Meaningless Vocal Fillers

- Use pauses to emphasize points, to draw attention to key thoughts, or to allow listeners a moment to contemplate what you've said. (p. 281)
- Eliminate distracting vocal fillers, such as "uh," "hmm," "you know," "I mean," and "it's like." (p. 281)

Vocal Variety

- Use the various vocal elements—volume, pitch, rate, and pauses—to create an effective delivery. (p. 282)
- Use a mix of these elements throughout your speech. (p. 283)

Be Conscious of How You Pronounce and Articulate Words

- Learn to pronounce words correctly. (p. 283)
- If you use a dialect, make sure that your audience understands it. (p. 284)
- Don't mumble or slur your words. (p. 284)

19. The Body in Delivery

Remember the Importance of Your Nonverbal Behavior

- Audiences are attuned to a speaker's vocal delivery (how you say something) and physical actions (facial expressions, gestures, body movement, and physical appearance). (p. 286)
- Audiences notice discrepancies between what you say and how you say it. (p. 287)
- Audiences do not so much listen to a speaker's words as they "read" the speaker who delivers them. (p. 288)

Animate Your Facial Expressions in Appropriate Ways

- Avoid a deadpan expression. (p. 288)
- Establish rapport with your audience with a smile. (p. 288)
- Avoid expressions that are out of character for you. (p. 288)

Maintain Eye Contact with Your Audience

- Establish eye contact to indicate that you recognize and respect listeners. (p. 288)
- Scan the room with your eyes, pausing to gaze at selected listeners. (p. 289)

Use Gestures That Feel Natural to Fill in Gaps in Meaning

- Use gestures to clarify your message. (p. 289)
- Avoid exaggerated gestures, but make them broad enough to be visible. (p. 289)
- Use appropriate gestures that arise from your feelings. (p. 289)

Avoid Standing Stiffly behind the Podium

- As space and time allow, try to get out from behind the podium. (p. 289)
- Move around at a comfortable, natural pace. (p. 290)
- Be aware of your posture. Stand erect, but not ramrod straight. (p. 290)

Pay Attention to Your Clothes and Grooming

- Choices of clothing and grooming will probably be the first thing your listeners notice about you. (p. 290)
- Dress appropriately for the occasion: dark-colored suits convey a sense of authority, while medium-blue or navy suits enhance credibility. (p. 290)
- Keep your hands free of distracting objects, such as pens and notecards. (p. 292)

Practice Your Speech Using a Speaking Outline

- Focus on your speech ideas rather than on yourself. (p. 292)
- After you've practiced several times, record or videotape your delivery. Incorporate changes and record it again. (p. 292)
- Rework unsatisfactory parts of your speech as you practice. (p. 293)
- Practice under realistic conditions. (p. 293)
- Visualize the audience as you speak. (p. 293)
- Practice using your speaking notes unobtrusively. (p. 293)
- Ask at least one other person to serve as a constructive critic. (p. 293)
- Time each portion of your speech (introduction, body, conclusion). (p. 293)
- Evaluate and adjust your rate of speech. (p. 293)
- Don't wait until the last minute to begin practicing. (p. 293)
- For an extemporaneous speech, plan to practice five times. (p. 293)

KEY TERMS

Chapter 17

effective delivery	TelePrompTer	speaking impromptu
elocutionary movement	speaking from memory	speaking
speaking from manuscript	oratory	extemporaneously

Chapter 18

volume	intonation	pronunciation
lavalier microphone	speaking rate	articulation
handheld or fixed microphone	vocal fillers	dialects
pitch	pauses	mumbling
	vocal variety	lazy speech

Chapter 19

aural channel	visual channel	talking head
paralanguage	scanning	

Methods of Delivery 17

I wish you to see that public speaking is a perfectly normal act, which calls for no strange, artificial methods, but only for an extension and development of that most familiar act, conversation.　　　—James Albert Winans, *Public Speaking*[1]

The process of putting together a speech may be challenging, but what often creates the bigger challenge for most of us is contemplating or actually getting up in front of an audience and speaking. Added to this uneasiness is the unfounded idea that speech delivery should be formulaic, mechanical, and highly exaggerated—that it is, in a way, unnatural or artificial. But as the early public-speaking scholar James Albert Winans noted, a speech is really just an enlarged conversation, "quite the natural thing."

Just as in a conversation, each component of your speech "performance," from the quality of your voice to your facial expressions, gestures, and manner of dress, affects how your listeners respond to you. As audience members listen to your words, they are simultaneously reacting to you on a nonverbal level— how you look, how you sound, and how you respond to them. This means that you must be attentive to your behavior while speaking, and thus while practicing. What you want to achieve through nonverbal behavior in your speeches is an appearance of naturalness rather than theatricality. As communications scholar James C. McCroskey has noted, effective delivery rests on the same natural foundation as everyday conversation. It doesn't call attention to itself.[2]

Qualities of Effective Delivery

 WEB Video quizzes

Speakers who deliver well-received speeches or presentations share several characteristics at the podium: They are natural, enthusiastic, confident, and direct. **Effective delivery** is the skillful application of natural conversational behavior in a way that is relaxed, enthusiastic, and direct. As Winans has noted, effective delivery is characterized by "a style at once simple and effective."[3]

STRIVE FOR NATURALNESS

Had you been a student in the early 1900s, during the heyday of the **elocutionary movement**, feeling uneasy about delivery would have been justified. The elocutionists regarded speechmaking as a type of performance, much like acting.[4] Students were given a rigid set of rules on how to use their eyes, faces, gestures, and voices to drive home certain points in the speech and to manipulate audience members' moods. Delivery was emphasized to such an extent that it often assumed more importance than the content of the speech.

Today, the content or message itself, rather than the delivery, is seen as being most important. Nevertheless, delivery remains a critical part of successful speechmaking. Instead of stressing theatrical elements, contemporary delivery emphasizes naturalness. To appear natural is to appear smooth, polished, and unrehearsed, even though you have rehearsed, and because you have rehearsed you have learned the message so well that you can present it with enthusiasm, confidence, and directness.

SHOW ENTHUSIASM

Enthusiasm is contagious. When you talk about something that excites you, you talk more rapidly, use more gestures, look at your listeners more frequently, use more pronounced facial expressions, and probably stand closer to your listeners and perhaps even touch them more. Your enthusiasm spills over to your listeners, drawing them into your message. As their own enthusiasm grows, they listen more attentively because they want to know more about the thing that excites you. In turn, you sense their interest and responsiveness and realize that you are truly connecting with them. The value of enthusiastic delivery is thus accomplished: It focuses your audience's attention on the message.

PROJECT A SENSE OF CONFIDENCE

Speeches delivered with confidence and composure inspire the audience's confidence in you and in your message. Your focus is on the ideas that you want to convey, not on memorized words and sentences and not on yourself. Instead of thinking about how you look and sound, you're thinking about the idea you're trying to convey and how well your listeners are grasping it. Confident delivery directs the audience's attention to the message and away from the speaker's behavior.

BE DIRECT

To truly communicate with an audience, you must build rapport with your listeners. You need to show that you care about them and their reasons for listening to you. This is generally done in two ways: by making your message relevant to the interests and attitudes of audience members, and by demonstrating your interest and concern for them in your delivery. The best way to do the latter is by being direct: Maintain eye contact; use a friendly tone of voice; animate your facial expressions, especially positive ones such as smiling; and position yourself so that you are physically close to the audience. Of course, you don't want to go overboard by becoming annoying or overly familiar with the audience. But neither do you want to appear distant, aloof, or uncaring. Both extremes draw audience attention away from the message. (Chapters 18 and 19 focus on techniques for using your voice and body, respectively, to achieve a natural, enthusiastic, confident, and direct delivery. In the following section, we consider the major methods of delivery.)

Select a Method of Delivery

As a speaker, you can choose from four basic methods of delivery: speaking from manuscript, speaking from memory, impromptu speaking, and extemporaneous speaking. Each method is distinguished by the expressive voice and body behaviors it uses or restricts, and by the qualities of delivery it promotes or impedes (see Table 17.1).

SPEAKING FROM MANUSCRIPT

When **speaking from manuscript**, you read a speech verbatim — that is, from prepared written text (either on paper or on a **TelePrompTer**) that contains the entire speech, word for word.

As a rule, speaking from manuscript restricts eye contact and body movement, and may also limit expressiveness in vocal variety and quality. Watching a speaker read a speech can be monotonous and boring for the audience. Quite obviously, the natural, relaxed, enthusiastic, and direct qualities of delivery are all limited by this method. Commenting on the dangers of reading from a

TABLE 17.1 • Methods of Delivery and Their Probable Uses

Method of Delivery	Description	Probable Uses
Manuscript	Speech is read from fully prepared text.	When precise wording is called for; for instance, when a speaker wants to avoid being misquoted or misconstrued, or when he or she is communicating exact descriptions and directions.
Memory	Speech is delivered entirely from memory.	When a speaker is called on in special occasion circumstances, such as short toasts and introductions; when quotations are used (partial memorization).
Impromptu	Speech is delivered without preparation or practice.	When a speaker is called on or elects to speak without prior planning or preparation; this occurs in many speaking situations.
Extemporaneous	Speech is well practiced and delivered from a key-word or phrase outline.	When the goal is to deliver a speech exhibiting a natural conversational quality of delivery that is nonetheless well prepared and practiced; this is the most widely used form of delivery.

TelePrompTer, for instance, columnist and former speechwriter William Safire notes that it can make the speaker appear "shifty and untrustworthy."[5]

At certain times, however, it is advisable or necessary to read a speech, such as when you must convey a very precise message. As with politicians and business leaders, you may know that you will be quoted and must avoid misinterpretation. Or perhaps it is your responsibility to explain an emergency so you will need to convey exact descriptions and directions (see Chapter 28 on crisis communication). In some speech circumstances, such as when an award is being presented, tradition may dictate that your remarks be read from a manuscript.

When you must give a speech from manuscript, practice reading it often until you are satisfied that your delivery is expressive. Use a large font and double- or triple-space the manuscript so that you can read without straining. Vary the rhythm of your words (see Chapter 18), and become familiar enough with the speech text so that you can look at the audience occasionally. Consider using some compelling presentation aids to add interest and movement to your delivery (see Chapter 20).

SPEAKING FROM MEMORY

The formal name for **speaking from memory** is *oratory*. The term is reminiscent of ancient public speakers whose speeches (some of which were extremely long) were fully committed to memory. If you were to use the oratorical style, you would put the entire speech, word for word, into writing and then commit

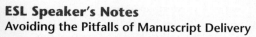

ESL Speaker's Notes
Avoiding the Pitfalls of Manuscript Delivery

Speaking from manuscript may be difficult and perhaps even ill-advised for some ESL speakers. Reading a speech aloud, word for word, is likely to exaggerate existing problems with pronunciation and word stress, or the emphasis given to words in a sentence. These emphasized words or syllables are pronounced more loudly and with a higher pitch. Robbin Crabtree and Robert Weissberg note:

> One of the most characteristic features of spoken English is the tendency of native speakers to take one word in every sentence and give it a stronger push than the others. This feature is called *primary stress*. If you try out a couple of sample sentences, you'll note that the primary stress normally falls at the end, or very close to the end, of the sentence:
> "That was one of the best speeches I've ever heard."
> "Let me know if you have trouble; and I'll be glad to help."[1]

If you have difficulty with word and sentence stress and you find that you need to deliver a speech from manuscript, follow the advice described in these pages. In addition, spend extra practice time reading your speech with the aim of ensuring that your word and sentence stress align with the meaning you intend.

1. Robbin Crabtree and Robert Weissberg, *ESL Students in the Public Speaking Classroom: A Guide for Teachers* (Boston: Bedford/St. Martin's, 2000), 24.

it to memory. In the United States, instances of speaking from memory rarely occur, though this form of delivery is common in other parts of the world.[6] Memorization is not a natural way to present a message. It stifles authentic and sincere enthusiasm, and it poses a considerable threat to maintaining a relaxed delivery. Since you are required to recall exact words from memory, true eye contact with the audience is unlikely (try maintaining eye contact with someone while you recall something from memory; you'll notice a loss of directness if you can manage to maintain eye contact at all). Moreover, memorization invites potential disaster during a speech, because there is always the possibility of a mental lapse or block. When a mental block occurs, you are left with no or few options because you have focused practice on nothing else but the exact wording of the speech—when recall of words is lost, strained silence often results.

Some kinds of brief speeches, however, such as toasts and introductions, can be well served by memorization. Sometimes it's helpful to memorize a part of the speech, especially when you must present the same information many times in the same words, or when you use direct quotations as a form of support. By and large, though, there will seldom be a need for you to memorize an entire speech of any kind. If you do find an occasion to use the memorization strategy, be sure to learn your speech so completely that in actual delivery you can focus on conveying enthusiasm and directness.

SPEAKING IMPROMPTU

The word *impromptu* means "unpracticed, spontaneous, or improvised." **Speaking impromptu** involves speaking on relatively short notice with little time to prepare. It's not advisable to speak impromptu when you've been given adequate time to prepare and practice a speech (that's called procrastination). However, there are many occasions that require you to make some remarks on

---

✓ **CHECKLIST**

Speaking Off-the-Cuff: Preparing for the Impromptu Speech

To succeed at giving impromptu speeches, follow these steps:

_____ 1. Find a pen and a piece of paper as quickly as possible.

_____ 2. Take a minute to reflect on how you can best address the audience's interests and needs. Take a deep breath, and focus on your expertise on the topic or on what you really want to say.

_____ 3. Jot down in key words or short phrases the ideas you may want to cover.

_____ 4. Stay on the topic. Don't wander off track.

_____ 5. If your speech follows someone else's, acknowledge that person's statements.

_____ 6. State your ideas, and then summarize them.

_____ 7. Use transitions such as *first, second,* and *third,* both to organize your points and to help listeners follow them.

the spur of the moment. For example, an instructor may invite you to summarize key points from the weekend reading assignment; a fellow employee who was scheduled to speak on the new marketing plan may be sick, and your boss asks you to take his or her place; or during a meeting you might feel compelled to state your opposition to a proposal.

To succeed in delivering impromptu remarks:

- *Follow the lead of Academy Award nominees: Be prepared.* Try to anticipate situations that may require you to speak impromptu. If there is any chance that this might occur, prepare some remarks beforehand.

- *Think on your feet — and think first about your listeners.* Consider their likely needs and interests, and try to shape your remarks accordingly. For example, who are the people present, and what are their views on the issue?

- *As you wait your turn to speak, listen to what others around you are saying.* Take notes in a key-word or phrase format and arrange them into ideas or main points from which you can speak. The proverbial speech on a napkin has some real practicality for impromptu speaking. Organizing a few thoughts beforehand will help you make your point and prevent you from talking aimlessly. Refrain from spending what little time you do have on trying to devise a joke or funny story. Just work with whatever appropriate thoughts come to mind at the moment.

- *When you do speak, give a brief statement, if appropriate, summarizing what you've heard from others.* Then state your own position, make your points, and restate your position, referring as needed to your notes.

Taking steps like these will enhance your effectiveness because you will maintain the qualities of natural, enthusiastic, and direct delivery. And having even a hastily prepared plan can give you greater confidence than having no plan at all.

SPEAKING EXTEMPORANEOUSLY

Speaking extemporaneously falls somewhere between impromptu and written or memorized deliveries. In an extemporaneous speech, you prepare well and practice in advance, giving full attention to all facets of the speech — content, arrangement, and delivery alike. Instead of memorizing or writing the speech word for word, you speak from an outline of key words and phrases (see Chapter 13), having concentrated throughout your preparation and practice on the ideas you want to communicate.

Probably more public speeches — from business presentations and special occasion speeches to formal public addresses — are delivered by extemporaneous delivery than by any other method. Because extemporaneous speaking is the technique that is most conducive to achieving a natural, conversational quality of delivery, many speakers consider it to be the preferred method of the four types of delivery. In fact, since special occasion speeches — such as toasts, introductions, tributes, and eulogies — are among the most common types of speeches made beyond the classroom, mastering the extemporaneous method of delivery can be especially beneficial. Knowing your idea well enough to present it without memorization or manuscript gives you greater flexibility in adapting to the specific speaking situation. You can modify wording, rearrange your points, change examples, and omit information in keeping with the audience and the setting. You can have more eye contact, more direct body orientation, greater freedom of movement, and generally better control of your thoughts and actions than with any of the other delivery methods.

However, keep in mind several possible drawbacks to extemporaneous delivery. For one, it is relatively easy to get off track when using this method. Because you aren't speaking from specifically written or memorized text, you may become repetitive and wordy. Fresh examples or points may come to mind that you want to share, so the speech may take longer than you anticipated. Occasionally, even a glance at your speaking notes will fail to jog your memory on a point that you wanted to cover, and you may momentarily find yourself searching for what to say next. The remedy for these potential pitfalls is, of course,

Ethically Speaking
A Tool for Good and Evil

The philosopher Plato believed that the art of public speaking — or rhetoric, as the ancients referred to it — was too often corrupt.[1] Plato's cynicism toward public speaking was the result of unethical practices that he witnessed among his peers and other leaders in ancient Greece. From his perspective, rhetoric (at least as practiced) too often distorted the truth. Today, few people condemn public speaking per se as a dishonest form of communication. But many are aware of the power of delivery to corrupt. If history is any guide, these fears are well founded: one has only to think of such modern-day dictators as Mao Tse-tung, Joseph Stalin, Adolf Hitler, and Saddam Hussein, all of whom deliberately used delivery as a means of manipulation. Hitler's forceful delivery — a scorching stare, gestures, and a staccato voice — so mesmerized his listeners that millions accepted the horrific idea that an entire people should be annihilated. Historians note how Hitler spent countless hours practicing his vocal delivery and body language to achieve maximum hypnotic effect. As he did this, he would have himself photographed so that he could hone individual gestures to perfection.[2]

Like any tool, delivery can be used for both ethical and unethical purposes. Countless speakers, from Abraham Lincoln to Martin Luther King Jr., have used their flair for delivery to uplift and inspire people. Yet there will always be those who try to camouflage weak or false arguments with an overpowering delivery. You can ensure that your own delivery is ethical by reminding yourself of the ground rules for ethical speaking described in Chapter 5: trustworthiness, respect, responsibility, and fairness. Always reveal your true purpose to the audience, review your evidence and reasoning for soundness, and grant your audience the power of rational choice.

1. Thomas M. Conley, *Rhetoric in the European Tradition* (New York: Longman, 1990).
2. Ian Kershaw, "The Hitler Myth," *History Today* 35, no. 11 (1985): 23.

practice. If you practice delivering your speech using a speaking outline often enough, you will probably have no difficulty staying on target. In fact, you will be more likely to deliver a speech that is effectively natural, enthusiastic, confident, and direct.

✓ **CHECKLIST**

Ready for the Call: Preparing for the Extemporaneous Speech

Follow these general steps below to prepare effective extemporaneous speeches:

_____ 1. Focus your topic as assigned or as appropriate to the audience and occasion.

_____ 2. Prepare a thesis statement that will serve as the central point or idea of your speech.

_____ 3. Research your topic in a variety of sources to gather support for your thesis and add credibility to your points.

_____ 4. Outline main and subordinate points.

_____ 5. Practice the speech at least six times.

(See Chapter 2 for more on speech preparation.)

The Voice in Delivery 18

Used properly in the speaking situation, your voice is a powerful instrument of expression that should express who you are and convey your message in a way that engages listeners. Your voice also indicates your confidence and affects whether the audience perceives you to be in control of the situation.[1] Regardless of the quality and importance of your message, if you have inadequate mastery of your voice, you may lose your audience's attention and fail to deliver a successful speech. Fortunately, you can learn to control each of the elements of vocal delivery as you practice your speech. These include volume, pitch, rate, pauses, vocal variety, and pronunciation and articulation.

Volume

 Chapter quizzes

Volume, the relative loudness of a speaker's voice while giving a speech, is usually the most obvious and frequently cited vocal element in speechmaking. If you do not speak loud enough for the entire audience to hear you, your speech is essentially a failure. *The proper volume for delivering a speech is somewhat louder than that of normal conversation.* Just how much louder depends on three factors: (1) the size of the room and the number of people in the audience, (2) whether or not you use a microphone, and (3) the level of background noise.

Speaking at the appropriate volume is critical to how credible your listeners will perceive you to be. Speakers whose volume is too low are viewed less positively than those who project their voices at a pleasing volume. One expert suggests that if your tendency is to speak softly as a rule, you will initially have to project more than you think is necessary:

> As you breathe from your diaphragm, you will gain the force for vocal projection from your diaphragm — not your vocal cords. So don't strain your vocal cords; instead, start the breath with your diaphragm and let it propel your voice beyond the last row of the audience.[2]

The easiest way to judge whether you are speaking too loudly or too softly is to be alert to audience feedback. You need to increase volume if audience members appear to be straining to hear you. Some might even be so helpful as to hold a cupped hand up to an ear to show that it is difficult to hear what you are saying.

✓ **CHECKLIST**

Tips on Using a Microphone

_____ 1. Perform a sound check with the microphone at least several hours before delivering your speech.

_____ 2. When you first speak into the microphone, ask your listeners if they can hear you clearly.

_____ 3. Speak directly into the microphone; if you turn your head or body, you won't be heard.

_____ 4. To avoid broadcasting private statements, beware of "open" mikes.

_____ 5. When wearing a **lavalier microphone** attached to your lapel or collar, speak as if you were addressing a small group. The amplifier will do the rest.

_____ 6. When using a **handheld** or **fixed microphone**, beware of _popping_, which occurs when you use sharp consonants, such as _p, t,_ and _d,_ and the air hits the mike. To prevent popping, move the microphone slightly below your mouth and about six inches away.

Source: Susan Berkley, "Microphone Tips," _Great Speaking_ 4, no. 7 (2002), www.antion.com/ezine/v4n7.txt (accessed July 16, 2005).

Pitch

Imagine the variation in sound between the left-most and the right-most keys of a piano. This variation represents the instrument's **pitch**, or range of sounds from high to low (or vice versa). Pitch is determined by the number of vibrations per unit of time; the more vibrations per unit (also called _frequency_), the higher the pitch, and vice versa.[3] The classic warm-up singing exercise _"Do re mi fa so la ti do"_ is an exercise in pitch. Vocal pitch is important in speechmaking — indeed, in talk of any kind — because it powerfully affects the meaning associated with spoken words. For example, say "Stop." Now, say _"Stop!"_ Hear the difference? The rising and falling of vocal pitch across phrases and sentences, termed **intonation**,[4] conveys two very distinct meanings. Intonation, or pitch, is what distinguishes a question from a statement:

> It's time to study already.

> It's time to study al_ready?_

Additionally, as you speak, pitch conveys your mood, reveals your level of enthusiasm, expresses your concern for the audience, and signals your overall commitment to the occasion. When there is no variety in pitch, speaking becomes monotonous. A monotone voice is the death knell to any speech. Speakers who are vocally monotone rapidly lose the audience's attention and goodwill. To avoid speaking in monotone, practice and listen to your speeches with a tape recorder. You will readily identify instances that require better inflection.

Rate

The most effective way to hold an audience's attention, as well as to accurately convey the meaning of your speech, is to vary your **speaking rate**, the pace at which you convey speech. A slow rate at the right time indicates thoughtfulness, seriousness, solemnity, reverance, concern, and the like. A lively pace indicates excitement, adventure, happiness, enthusiasm, and so on.

The normal rate of speech for adults is estimated to be between 120 and 150 words per minute. The typical public speech occurs at a rate slightly below 120 words per minute, but there is no standard, "ideal," or most effective rate. Being alert to the audience's reactions is the best way to know whether your rate of speech is too fast or too slow. An audience will get fidgety, bored, listless, perhaps even sleepy if you speak too slowly. If you speak too rapidly, listeners will appear irritated and confused, as though they can't catch what you're saying. One recent study suggests that speaking too fast will cause listeners to perceive you as tentative about your control of the situation.[5] Learn to control your rate this way: select a section of ten words from your speech; write out a sentence or two if you don't already have a manuscript of your speech. Read the selection aloud over and over for thirty seconds. You should be able to repeat the selection seven or eight times in thirty seconds, or about fifteen times in one minute. If you are stating the words more than eight times in thirty seconds, you need to slow your rate. If you are repeating the set of words fewer than seven times in thirty seconds, you need to increase your rate.

Pauses

Many novice speakers are uncomfortable with pauses. It's as if some social stigma is attached to any silence in a speech. This tendency is probably a carryover from everyday conversation, where we cover pauses with unnecessary and undesirable **vocal fillers**, such as "uh," "hmm," "you know," "I mean," "it's like," and "anyways." Like pitch, however, pauses are important strategic elements of a speech. **Pauses** enhance meaning by providing a type of punctuation, emphasizing a point, drawing attention to a key thought, or just allowing listeners a moment to contemplate what is being said. In short, they make a speech far more effective than it might otherwise be. Both the speaker and the audience need pauses.

In his well-known "I Have a Dream" speech, Martin Luther King Jr. exhibits masterful use of strategic pauses. In what is now the most memorable segment of the speech, King pauses, just momentarily, to secure the audience's attention to the next words that are about to be spoken:

> I have a dream [*pause*] that one day on the red hills of Georgia. . . .
>
> I have a dream [*pause*] that one day even the great state of Mississippi. . . .[6]

Imagine how diminished the impact of this speech would have been if King had uttered "uh" or "you know" at each of these pauses!

Vocal Variety

 WEB Chapter quizzes

Rather than operating separately, all the vocal elements described so far — volume, pitch, rate, and pauses — work together to create an effective delivery. Indeed, the real key to effective vocal delivery is to vary all these elements, thereby demonstrating **vocal variety**. For example, as King speaks the words "I have a dream," the pauses are immediately preceded by a combination of reduced speech rate and increased volume and pitch — a crescendo, you might say. The impact of this variety leaves an indelible impression on anyone who has heard his speech.

✓ **SELF-ASSESSMENT CHECKLIST**

Practice Check for Vocal Effectiveness

_____ 1. As you practice, does your voice project authority?

_____ 2. Is your voice too loud? Too soft?

_____ 3. Do you avoid speaking in a monotone? Do you vary the stress or emphasis you place on words to clearly express your meaning?

_____ 4. Is your rate of speech comfortable for listeners?

_____ 5. Do you avoid unnecessary vocal fillers, such as "uh," "hmm," "you know," and "I mean"?

_____ 6. Do you use silent pauses for strategic effect?

_____ 7. Does your voice reflect a variety of emotional expressions? Do you convey enthusiasm?

ESL Speaker's Notes
Vocal Variety and the Non-Native Speaker

Learning to deliver a speech with the vocal variety that English-speaking people in the United States expect can be particularly challenging for non-native speakers. In addition to having concerns about pronunciation and articulation, the non-native speaker may also be accustomed to patterns of vocal variety — volume, pitch, rate, and pauses — that are different from those discussed in this chapter.

The pronunciation of English depends on learning how to combine a series of about forty basic sounds (fifteen vowels and twenty-five consonants) that together serve to distinguish English words from one another. Correct pronunciation also requires that the speaker learn proper word stress, rhythm, and intonation or pitch.[1] As you practice your speeches, pay particular attention to these facets of delivery. Seek feedback from others to ensure that your goal of shared meaning will be met whenever you deliver speeches.

1. Maryann Cunningham Florez, "Improving Adult ESL Learners' Pronunciation Skills," National Clearinghouse for ESL Literacy Education, 1998, www.cal.org/caela/digests/Pronun.htm (accessed July 16, 2005).

One key to achieving effective vocal variety is enthusiasm. Vocal variety comes quite naturally when you are excited about what you are saying to an audience, when you feel it is important and want to share it with your listeners. If you strive for these kinds of feelings when planning and practicing your speeches, vocal variety should follow naturally. However, be careful not to let your enthusiasm overwhelm your ability to control your vocal behavior. Talking too rapidly can lead to more filled pauses because you forget what you want to say. Overexcitement can also result in a consistently high pitch that becomes monotonous. Hence, it is essential to practice your vocal delivery even when you are already enthusiastic about a speech.

Pronunciation and Articulation

Another important element of vocal delivery involves correctly saying the words you speak. Few things distract an audience more than improper pronunciation or unclear articulation of words. **Pronunciation** is the correct formation of word sounds. **Articulation** is the clarity or forcefulness with which the sounds are made, regardless of whether they are pronounced correctly. In other words, you can be articulating clearly but pronouncing incorrectly. In this way, good articulation may betray poor pronunciation. It is important to pay attention to and work on both areas.

Consider these words that are routinely mispronounced:

- effect *(ee-fect)* is stated as *uh-fect.*
- anyway *(any-way)* is said as *any-ways.*
- mobile *(mo-bile)* is said as *mo-bull* or *mo-bill.*
- leaves *(leevz)* is stated as *leephs.*

Public Speaking in Cultural Perspective
Vocal Delivery and Culture

Every culture has subcultural variations on the preferred pronunciation and articulation of its languages. These variations represent **dialects** of the language. In the United States, for example, there is so-called Standard English, Black English (or, more recently, Ebonics), Tex-Mex (a combination of Spanish and English spoken with a distinct Texas drawl or accent), and such regional variations as those found in the South, New England, and along the border with Canada. In parts of Texas, for example, a common usage is to say "fixin' to" instead of "about to," as in "We're fixin' to go to a movie."

Your own dialect may be a factor in the effectiveness of your delivery when speaking to an audience of people whose dialect is different. At the least, your dialect might call attention to itself and be a distraction to the audience. One strategy that you can use is to determine which words in your usual vocabulary are spoken dialectically and then practice articulating them in Standard English pronunciation.

> ✓ **CHECKLIST**
>
> **Overcoming Articulation Problems**
>
> _____ 1. If you mumble, practice speaking more loudly and with emphatic pronunciation.
>
> _____ 2. If you tend toward lazy speech, put more effort into your articulation.
>
> _____ 3. Consciously try to say each word clearly and correctly.
>
> _____ 4. Practice clear and precise enunciation of proper word sounds. Say _articulation_ several times until it seems to roll off your tongue naturally.
>
> _____ 5. Do the same for these words: _want to, going to, Atlanta, chocolate, sophomore, California._
>
> _____ 6. As you practice giving a speech, consider words that might pose articulation and pronunciation problems for you. Practice saying them over and over until doing so feels as natural as saying your name.

Incorrect pronunciations are a matter of habit. Normally you may not know that you are mispronouncing a word because most people you talk with probably say the word much the same way you do. This habit may be associated with a regional accent or dialect. In that case, speaking to an audience of local origin may pose few problems if you pronounce words in regionally customary ways.

But if you are speaking to members of an audience for whom your accent and pronunciation patterns are not the norm, it becomes especially important to have practiced and to use correct pronunciations to the fullest extent possible. In fact, the better your pronunciation all around, the more enhanced will be the audience's perceptions of your competence, and the greater will be the potential impact of your speech. (See Table 18.1 and Appendix D for lists of commonly mispronounced words.)

Articulation problems are also a matter of habit. (Exceptions are problems associated with oral, periodontal, or other conditions that impede articulate speech, such as wearing orthodontics, having a cleft palate or a tongue thrust, or having injuries to the teeth or gums.) A very common pattern of poor articulation is **mumbling** — slurring words together at a very low level of volume and pitch so that they are barely audible. Sometimes the problem is **lazy speech**. Common examples include saying "fer" instead of "far," "wanna" instead of "want to," "gonna" instead of "going to," and "theez' er" instead of "these are." Like any habit, poor articulation can be overcome by practicing and by unlearning the problem behavior (see the accompanying checklist on overcoming articulation problems).

TABLE 18.1 • Thirteen Commonly Mispronounced Words

Correct Spelling	Wrong Pronunciation	Right Pronunciation
acts	aks	akts
asked	aks	askt
et cetera	ek set er uh	et set er uh
facts	faks	fakts
fifth	fith or fif	fifth
genuine	jen yu wine	jen yu in
hundred	hun dert	hun dred
international	innernashunal	in ter na shuh nal
introduce	innerdoos	in tro dyoos
nuclear	nookyouluhr	nook klee uhr
picture	pi chur	pik chur
products	prah duks	prah dukts
recognized	rekunized	re kug nized

Source: Lilyan Wilder, *Seven Steps to Fearless Speaking* (New York: Wiley, 1999), 210–11. Reprinted with permission.

19 The Body in Delivery

Beyond the actual words that are spoken, audiences receive information from a speech through two nonverbal channels of communication: the aural and the visual. The **aural channel** is made up of the vocalizations that form and accompany spoken words. These vocalizations, or paralanguage, include the qualities of volume, pitch, rate, variety, and pronunciation and articulation described in Chapter 18. **Paralanguage** refers to *how* something is said, not to *what* is said.

The **visual channel** includes the speaker's physical actions and appearance—facial expressions, gestures, general body movement, physical appearance, dress, and objects held. These nonverbal elements have been called the *silent language*. Paralanguage and the visual elements of a speech are critical to an audience's full understanding of the message you wish to convey. According to one study, listeners derive only 7 percent of the meaning of any message about feelings and attitudes from the speaker's words, the verbal component, while 38 percent comes from the speaker's voice and 55 percent comes from the speaker's facial expressions and body movements, the nonverbal component.[1]

Functions of Nonverbal Communication in Delivery

Researchers have identified several ways in which nonverbal communication works together with the verbal component of a speech:[2]

- Nonverbal communication clarifies the meaning of verbal messages.
- Nonverbal communication facilitates feedback, creating a loop of communication between speaker and audience.
- Nonverbal communication helps establish a relationship between speaker and audience.
- Nonverbal communication helps establish speaker credibility.

CLARIFY VERBAL MESSAGES

The impact of the verbal component of your speech—what you say—depends largely on your vocal and bodily actions while saying it. The same words spoken with different body movements or different vocal emphasis convey different meanings. For instance, consider how saying "I hate you" jokingly to a friend who just got a new car that you want differs in tone and emphasis from screaming "I *hate* you!" to someone who has done you a grave injustice. Similar shifts in meaning occur with gestures. If you said "I hate you" while screwing your face up into a nasty grimace and shaking your fist, you would convey a greater sense of vehemence than would be the case if you said it in a flat tone without this gesture.

FACILITATE FEEDBACK

Listeners use a host of body cues — head shaking (either in agreement or in disagreement), smiles or frowns, arms rigidly folded across the chest, and friendly gazes or facing-away postures — to communicate their pleasure or displeasure with a speech. Being alert to such feedback and responding to it can mean the difference between an alienated audience and one that feels recognized and respected. Coughing and excessive shifting around, for example, may indicate difficulty in hearing and flagging interest. In response, you might try to increase your speaking volume and look in the direction of the affected listeners more frequently and for longer periods. If you receive negative cues such as frowns and head shaking, you might try presenting some additional evidence or interjecting some relevant humor.

ESTABLISH RELATIONSHIPS BETWEEN SPEAKER AND AUDIENCE

Nonverbal behavior, such as how you position yourself vis-à-vis your listeners, allows you to adjust your relationship with them, establishing a level of familiarity and closeness that is suitable to the topic, purpose, and occasion. To stimulate a sense of informality and closeness, for example, you can move out from behind the podium and walk or stand among audience members. Talk-show host and comedian Jay Leno opens each of his nightly shows by walking to the front edge of the stage to greet and shake hands with members of the audience. His friendly, open behavior establishes a casual communicative atmosphere and a direct relationship with his audience. Conversely, remaining at a distance from the audience, such as behind the speaker's stand, using a more reserved vocal quality, and speaking at a somewhat slower and consistent rate establish a more formal relationship with listeners.

ESTABLISH SPEAKER CREDIBILITY

Nonverbal communication plays a key part in the audience's perception of your competence, trustworthiness, and character.[3] For example, audiences are more readily persuaded by speakers who emphasize vocal variety, eye contact, nodding at listeners, and standing with an open body position than by those who minimize these nonverbal cues.[4] Audience members also respond more positively to speakers whom they perceive to be well dressed and attractive. They are apt to take them more seriously and are more objective in their responses than they are to speakers whom they do not find attractive.

Pay Attention to Body Movement

 WEB Chapter quizzes

Audience members are quick to detect discrepancies between what you say and how you say it. As they listen to you, they are simultaneously evaluating the cues sent by your facial expressions, eye behavior, gestures, and general body movements. Audiences do not so much listen to a speaker's words as they "read" the speaker who delivers them.[5]

ANIMATE YOUR FACIAL EXPRESSIONS

From our facial expressions, audiences can gauge whether we are excited about, disenchanted by, or indifferent to our speech — and the people to whom we are presenting it. Facial expressions are an asset to public speakers, but only if they make use of them.

Few behaviors are more effective for building rapport with an audience than *smiling*. A smile is a sign of mutual welcome at the start of a speech, of mutual comfort and interest during the speech, and of mutual goodwill at the close of a speech. Smiling when you feel nervous or otherwise uncomfortable can help you relax and gain more composure. Of course, facial expressions need to correspond to the tenor of the speech. Doing what is natural and normal for the occasion should be the rule.

✔ **SELF-ASSESSMENT CHECKLIST**

Tips for Using Effective Facial Expressions

_____ 1. Avoid a deadpan expression.

_____ 2. Use animated expressions that feel natural and express your meaning.

_____ 3. Never use expressions that are out of character for you or inappropriate for the speech occasion.

_____ 4. In practice sessions, loosen your facial features with exercises such as widening the eyes and moving the mouth.

_____ 5. Align your facial expressions with your feelings.

_____ 6. Establish rapport with the audience by smiling naturally when appropriate.

MAINTAIN EYE CONTACT

If smiling is an effective way to build rapport, maintaining eye contact is mandatory in establishing a positive relationship with your listeners. Eye contact with the audience is one of the most, if not *the* most, important physical actions in public speaking. Eye contact maintains the quality of directness in speech delivery. It lets people know they are recognized, indicates acknowledgment and respect, and signals to audience members that the speaker sees them as unique human beings.

With an audience of a hundred to more than a thousand members, it's impossible to look at every listener. But in most speaking situations you are likely to experience, you should be able to look at most people in the audience by using a technique called **scanning**. When you scan an audience, you move your gaze from one listener to another and from one section to another, pausing as you do so to gaze briefly at each individual. One speaking professional suggests following the "rule of three": Pick three audience members to focus on — one in the middle, one on the right, and one on the left of the room; these audience members will be your anchors as you scan the room.[6] Initially, this may be difficult. But with just a little experience you will find yourself doing it naturally.

USE GESTURES THAT FEEL NATURAL

> Friend 1 to Friend 2: "How was the fishing trip?"
>
> Friend 2: "Great! The best I've had in years."
>
> Friend 1: "Caught a monster, eh? How big was it?"
>
> Friend 2 [*extending two hands, palms facing each other*]: "About this big!"

Words alone seldom convey what we want to express. Head, arm, hand, and even leg gestures are often critical in helping to clarify the meanings we try to convey in words. Physical gestures fill in the gaps, as in illustrating the size or shape of an object (e.g., showing the size of a fish by extending two hands, palms facing each other), expressing the depth of an emotion (pounding a fist on a podium), or emphasizing a certain word (using one's index finger to "write" the word in the air while saying it).

To achieve a natural, relaxed quality in delivery, use gestures to fill in gaps in meaning, as you would in everyday conversation. Gestures should arise from genuine emotions and should conform to your personality.[7]

BE AWARE OF GENERAL BODY MOVEMENT

General body movement is also important in maintaining audience attention and processing of your message. Audience members soon tire of listening to a **talking head** who remains steadily positioned in one place behind a microphone

---

✔ CHECKLIST

Tips for Effective Gesturing

_____ 1. Use natural, spontaneous gestures.

_____ 2. Use gestures to generate interest and clarify your message.

_____ 3. Use gestures that are appropriate to the topic and to the occasion.

_____ 4. Avoid exaggerated gestures, but use gestures that are broad enough to be seen by each member of the audience.

_____ 5. In practice sessions, analyze your gestures for effectiveness.

_____ 6. Practice movements that feel natural to you.

or a podium. When this position is unavoidable, either because there is a fixed microphone at the podium or because there is too little space to allow unrestricted movement, gestures and facial expressiveness become all the more important. But as space and time allow, try to get out from behind the podium and stand with the audience. As you do, move around at a comfortable, natural pace.

A speaker's posture sends a definite message to the audience. Listeners perceive speakers who slouch as being sloppy, unfocused, and even weak. Strive to stand erect, but not ramrod straight. The goal is to appear authoritative, not rigid.

DRESS APPROPRIATELY

As superficial as it may sound, the first thing an audience is likely to notice as you approach the speaker's position is your clothing. How you dress for delivering a speech is important. The critical criteria in determining appropriate dress for a speech are audience expectations and the nature of the speech occasion. If you are speaking as a representative of your business, for example, you will want to complement your company's image.[8] Many jobs and many speaking occasions permit casual dress; but take care not to confuse casual with sloppy or unkempt.[9] Even casual business attire should be professional in the sense that it conveys a responsible, credible, and confident image. Consider Bono, the celebrity activist and front man of the rock group U2, who regularly delivers speeches to international organizations, political gatherings, and universities about the critical economic and health conditions in Africa and developing nations.[10] When speaking Bono tends to choose an outfit that is sensibly casual but appropriate — a dress jacket over dress shirt, with no necktie and with an open collar — attire that reflects his rock star image while respecting the official nature of each occasion.

Your attire reveals an attitude about what you are doing and the amount of effort you seem willing to put into it. The more professional you look, the more professional you will feel, and the more positive the attitude you will convey to

---

✓ **CHECKLIST**

Broad Dress Code Guidelines

_____ 1. Dress well and appropriately for each speech occasion.

_____ 2. For a "power" look, wear a dark-colored suit.

_____ 3. Medium-blue or navy suits, slacks, or skirts paired with white shirts or blouses will enhance your credibility.

_____ 4. When selecting accessories (ties, scarves, kerchiefs, and the like), consider that the color yellow conveys friendliness and the color red focuses attention on you.

_____ 5. Flashy jewelry distracts listeners.

audience members. As noted by fashion expert David Wolfe in the context of job security:

> Dressing down could imply that you don't need to be taken seriously, or don't need the job. People are starting to realize that offices aren't the beach, and work is not a casual occasion.[11]

This advice is no less important for your classroom speeches than it is for speeches given elsewhere. You should dress for your speeches in class just as you would if you were delivering them to a business or professional group that you want to impress. At the very least, it's good practice, and it's likely to benefit your speech by showing your respect for both the occasion and the audience.

Public Speaking in Cultural Perspective
Nonverbal Communication Patterns in Different Cultures

As a speaker, it's important to remember that, like verbal communication, non-verbal communication is also profoundly influenced by culture. Gestures, for example, have entirely different meanings in different cultures, and many an unsuspecting speaker has inadvertently made a rude gesture in his or her host's culture. In the late 1950s, for instance, then-Vice President Richard Nixon made a goodwill tour of Latin America, where there were feelings of hostility toward the United States. On one of his stops, Nixon stepped off his plane and, smiling, gestured with the A-OK sign to the waiting crowd. The crowd booed. In that culture, Nixon's gesture meant "Screw you." Days of delicate diplomacy were undone by two seconds of nonverbal behavior.[1] This same gesture, incidentally, means "zero" in French and "money" in Japan. Roger Axtell catalogs a variety of gestures in his book *Gestures: The Do's and Taboos of Body Language around the World.* This eye-opening account demonstrates how something in one culture can mean literally the opposite in another (e.g., nodding means "yes" in the United States but can mean "no" in the former Yugoslavia and Iran).

The display of emotions is also guided by the social rules of the culture. The Japanese are conditioned to mask emotion, whereas Americans express emotion more freely. Speakers in different cultures thus use different facial expressions to convey emotions. Eye behavior also takes quite different forms; people in the United States and Canada use eye contact as a form of acknowledgment or politeness in greeting, but in other cultures, such as those of Nigeria and Puerto Rico, this is often considered disrespectful. Finally, appearance preferences also change from one culture to another.

No speaker should feel obliged to adopt nonverbal behaviors that are not his or her own. At the same time, a successful speech depends on shared meaning. As such, a thorough audience analysis is needed to anticipate potential misunderstandings that might occur nonverbally.

1. Roger Axtell, *Gestures: The Do's and Taboos of Body Language around the World* (New York: Wiley, 1991).

Source: Adapted from Dan O'Hair et al., *Competent Communication,* 2nd ed. (Boston: Bedford/ St. Martin's, 1997), 146–47.

An extension of dress is having various objects on or around your person while giving a speech — pencil and pen, a briefcase, a glass of water, or papers with notes on them. Always ask yourself if these objects are really necessary. A sure way to distract an audience from what you're saying is to drag a briefcase or backpack to the speaker's stand and open it while speaking, or to hold a pen or other object. Similarly, fumbling around with a pointer can be distracting unless it's being used to refer to certain visual displays.

Practice the Delivery

 Video quizzes

Practice is essential to effective delivery. The more you practice, the greater your comfort level will be when you actually deliver the speech. More than anything, it is uncertainty that breeds anxiety. By practicing your speech using a fully developed speaking outline (see Chapter 13), you will know what to expect when you actually stand in front of the audience.

Indeed, public speaking involves a set of motor skills much like playing a sport does. Consider the amount of time an individual golfer spends on the driving range and putting greens to improve skills and raise scores. When preparing to deliver a speech, mentally going through the motions while seated at your desk will provide some benefit, but practicing by actually standing up and talking out loud is necessary to perform successfully. You will be more comfortable with the sound of your own voice and with your gestures and will be confident that you can pronounce difficult words correctly. You will have a good sense of how your vocal quality will vary from one section of the speech to another. In other words, you will know what you are getting into.

FOCUS ON THE MESSAGE

The purpose of your speech is to get a message across, not to display extraordinary delivery skills. Focusing on your message is likely to make your delivery more natural and more confident.

RECORD THE SPEECH

Once you've practiced your speech several times, talk it out into an audio recorder. At a later stage in the practice process, you can place the recorder across the room from you and practice projecting your voice to the back row of the audience. To accurately gauge how you sound, use a good-quality recording device.

Videotaping two practice sessions can provide valuable feedback. As you watch your initial recording, make notes of the things you'd like to change. Before rerecording, practice several more times until you are comfortable with the changes you've incorporated. Note that no one is ever entirely thrilled with his or her videotaped image, so try to avoid unnecessary self-criticism. Videotape your speech a second time, paying close attention to the areas of speech delivery that you want to improve.

BE PREPARED TO REVISE YOUR SPEAKING NOTES

As you practice, be prepared to revise your speech as needed. If your introduction or conclusion isn't as effective as you would like, rework it. Make other adjustments as necessary to improve your speech and make the outline easier to follow.

PRACTICE UNDER REALISTIC CONDITIONS

Try to simulate the actual speech setting as you practice. Keep the seating arrangement in mind as you speak, picturing the audience as you go along. Turn various objects in the room into imaginary audience members, and project your voice in their direction. Practice scanning for eye contact. Practice with a podium of some kind (unless you know that you won't be using one). Stack some boxes to form a makeshift podium if you have to. Practice working with your speaking notes until you are confident that you can refer to them without overly relying on them. Practice placing your notes on a podium and moving around the podium for effective delivery.

At some point, practice your speech in front of at least one other person. Ask your volunteer(s) to identify the purpose and key points of your speech. Question them about what they did or did not understand. Seek detailed feedback about the quality of your delivery.

TIME YOUR SPEECH

As you practice, time each part of the speech (introduction, body, and conclusion) so that if you exceed your time limit you can adjust these sections accordingly. Recall that, as a general rule, the introduction and the conclusion should make up no more than 10 or 15 percent of your entire speech (see Chapters 14 and 15). If the speech is too long, look for extraneous material that can be cut. Consider your rate of speech. If it is too slow, practice speaking more concisely. If the speech is too short, review your evidence and make certain that you adequately support your main points. If your rate of speech is too fast, practice slowing your tempo.

PLAN AHEAD AND PRACTICE OFTEN

If possible, begin practicing your speech a couple of days before you are scheduled to deliver it. Many expert speakers recommend practicing your speech about five times in its final form. Since few speeches are longer than twenty minutes, and most are shorter, this represents a maximum of two hours of practice time—two hours well spent.

✓ **CHECKLIST**

Practicing Your Speech

_____ 1. Practice with your speaking notes.

_____ 2. Revise those parts of your speech that aren't satisfactory, altering your speaking notes as you go.

_____ 3. Focus on your speech ideas rather than on yourself.

_____ 4. Visualize the setting in which you will speak as you practice, projecting your words to different parts of the space to reach audience members.

_____ 5. Practice your speech several times, and then record it with an audio recorder.

_____ 6. Time each part of your speech—introduction, body, and conclusion.

_____ 7. If possible, videotape yourself twice—once after several practice sessions and again after you've incorporated changes into your speech.

_____ 8. Practice the speech under realistic conditions, paying attention to projecting your voice and working with your speaking notes unobtrusively.

_____ 9. Practice in front of at least one volunteer, and seek constructive criticism.

_____ 10. Schedule your practice sessions early in the process so that you have adequate time to prepare.

_____ 11. Practice your speech at least five times.

Presentation Aids

Presentation Aids

Speaker's Reference
Presentation Aids

20. Using Presentation Aids in the Speech

Using Presentation Aids to Increase Understanding and Retention

- Presentation aids can concisely express complex ideas. (p. 301)
- Statistical relationships can be made clear through graphs and charts. (p. 302)
- Well-prepared presentation aids can boost your credibility. (p. 302)
- Beware of losing credibility with sloppily conceived aids. (p. 302)

Consider Using Props and Models

- Inanimate or live *props* can solidify your descriptions. (p. 302)
- In many areas of study, *models* are a central component of presentations. (p. 302)

Consider Illustrating Key Points with Pictures

- Look for visually arresting *photographs.* (p. 303)
- Create a *diagram* to demonstrate how something is constructed or used. (p. 303)
- Use a *map* to pinpoint an area or illustrate proportions. (p. 303)
- Use a *poster* to convey a brief message forcefully. (p. 304)

Use Graphs and Charts to Show Trends and Demonstrate Relationships

- Select a *line graph* to represent trends and other information that changes over time. (p. 304)
- Choose a *bar graph* to compare quantities or magnitudes. (p. 305)
- Use a *pie graph* to show proportions. (p. 305)
- Use a *pictogram* to characterize comparisons in picture form. (p. 305)
- Use a *flowchart* to diagram a procedure or process. (p. 306)
- Use an *organizational chart* to illustrate hierarchical relationships. (p. 306)
- Use a *table* to summarize large amounts of information. (p. 307)

Think About the Possible Use of Audio and Video to Add Interest

- Choose clips that illustrate ideas or bring humor to the mix. (p. 309)
- Consider incorporating clips into PowerPoint presentations. (p. 309)

Consider Using Multimedia to Enhance Key Speech Points

- Be familiar with presentation software programs that effectively incorporate multimedia. (p. 309)

Consider the Options for Displaying Presentation Aids

- Ensure the smooth display of overhead transparencies. (p. 310)
- Choose the most appropriate graphics and displays for the occasion. (p. 310)
- Write neatly when using a flip chart or chalkboard. (p. 312)
- Time the distribution of handouts. (p. 312)

21. Designing Presentation Aids

Present One Major Idea per Aid

- Limit the amount of information in any single visual. (p. 317)
- Use phrases or short sentences rather than complicated full sentences. (p. 317)
- Limit words to no more than eight per line. (p. 317)
- Limit lines to no more than eight per aid. (p. 317)
- Use parallel sentence structure. (p. 317)

Apply the Same Design Decisions to Each Aid

- Apply consistent colors, fonts, capitalization, and styling. (p. 318)

Use Type Large Enough to Be Read Comfortably

- For slides, use a sans serif typeface for titles and major headings. (p. 319)
- Experiment with a serif typeface for the body of the text. (p. 319)
- Experiment with 36-point type for major headings, 24-point type for subheadings, and 18-point type for the body of the text. (p. 320)
- Use upper- and lowercase type rather than all capitals. (p. 321)

Use Color Wisely

- Use bold, bright colors (yellow, orange, red) to highlight text or objects. (p. 321)
- Use neutral colors such as blue, green, tan, and white for backgrounds. (p. 322)
- For typeface and graphics, use colors that contrast with the background color. (p. 322)
- Restrict the number of colors to two, three, or four, and use the same colors consistently. (p. 322)

22. Using Presentation Software

Remember That You're Giving a Speech, Not a Slide Show

- Don't overuse aids. (p. 323)
- Don't let technical wizardry distract from the focus on message and audience. (p. 323)
- Avoid hiding behind your electronic presentation. (p. 323)

Refer to Chapter Text for Tips on Using Microsoft PowerPoint

- Become familiar with tool and features on the various PowerPoint screens. (p. 324)
- Use the AutoContent Wizard or Slice Layout features for the best assistance in developing your aid. (p. 325)

Practice Using Presentation Aids until They Flow Smoothly with the Speech

KEY TERMS

Chapter 20

presentation aids	bar graph	audio clip
prop	pie graph	video
model	pictogram	multimedia
pictures	chart	overhead transparency
diagram	flowchart	LCD display technology
graph	organizational chart	flip chart
line graph	table	handout

Speaker's Reference

Chapter 21

eight-by-eight rule	font	sans serif typefaces
typeface	serif typefaces	

Using Presentation Aids in the Speech 20

An old cliché states, "A picture is worth a thousand words." To modernize the cliché we should say, "A picture plus sound plus motion and other special effects are worth a thousand words" — that is, of course, when they are used in a context that is appropriate to the topic, the audience, and the occasion (i.e., the rhetorical situation).

Presentation aids include objects, models, pictures, graphs, charts, video, audio, and multimedia. Each of these elements, used alone and in combination, helps listeners to see relationships among concepts and elements. Aids are also helpful to store and remember material and to critically examine key ideas. The strength of a presentation aid lies in the context in which it is used. No matter how powerful a photograph or chart or video may be, the audience will be less interested in merely gazing at it than in discovering how you will relate it to a specific point. If even superior-quality aids are poorly related to a speech, listeners will be turned off. Thus presentation aids should be used to complement rather than to serve as the main source of your ideas.

Functions of Presentation Aids

 WEB Chapter quizzes

Used judiciously, presentation aids can help listeners process and retain information, spark interest, convey information in a time-saving fashion, and enhance an image of professionalism.

HELP LISTENERS PROCESS AND RETAIN INFORMATION

Most people process and retain information best when they receive it in more than one format. Research findings indicate that we remember only about 20 percent of what we hear, but more than 50 percent of what we see *and* hear.[1] Further, we remember about 70 percent of what we see, hear, and actually do. Messages that are reinforced visually and otherwise are often more believable than those that are simply verbalized. As the saying goes, "Seeing is believing."

PROMOTE INTEREST AND MOTIVATION

Effective presentation aids draw audience members into a speech and stimulate their interest. They allow listeners to engage the right side of their brains — the hemisphere that plays an important role in such nonverbal tasks as visualization, music, and drawing. Literally seeing the facts of an argument laid out in front of them can make a significant difference in how listeners respond to an

301

appeal. In an appeal for donations for the homeless, for instance, a photograph that graphically portrays homeless conditions or a chart that starkly illustrates high rates of homelessness often speaks more directly to listeners than any verbal appeals a speaker can summon.

CONVEY INFORMATION CONCISELY

Visual aids are ideal for capturing detail in a quick, at-a-glance fashion. By expressing difficult thoughts and ideas without lengthy explanations, presentation aids facilitate concise communication and save time. For example, a fifteen- to thirty-second video clip can convey the equivalent of as much as ten minutes of verbal explanation.[2] Pictures can vividly represent an object, a scene, or an event instantaneously. Statistical relationships can be communicated more efficiently and effectively through graphs and charts than through verbal description. Audience members can quickly see and understand the difference between two elements of a bar graph or the dips and rises on a line graph.

LEND A PROFESSIONAL IMAGE

Quality visual aids demonstrate that work has gone into the presentation. By giving your listeners the impression that you are approaching the presentation professionally, you motivate them to approach it in the same way. This increases your credibility (ethos), which in turn helps get your message across. Of course, a bad presentation aid will have just the opposite effect, compromising an image of professionalism. A presentation that is too "slick" can also backfire, undermining credibility.

Types of Presentation Aids

 WEB Video quizzes

A variety of presentation aids are at your disposal. Base the ones you choose on the speech content, the audience, and the occasion. Here we move from least to most high-tech. (See Chapter 22 for a discussion of presentations that make use of presentation software.)

PROPS AND MODELS

A **prop** can be any live or inanimate object—a snake or a stone, for instance—that captures the audience's attention and illustrates or emphasizes key points. Sometimes, as in the case of a student bringing a corn snake to class, the prop *is* the subject of the speech. Late-night personalities Jay Leno and David Letterman are famous for using animals on their shows, for instance. (See the accompanying checklist on using props effectively.)

In addition to props, models can be an important, and sometimes necessary, aid to a presentation. A **model** is a three-dimensional, scale-size representation of an object. Presentations in engineering, architecture, medicine, and many other disciplines often make use of models.

> ✓ **CHECKLIST**
>
> **Tips for Using Props Effectively**
>
> _____ 1. Choose props that illustrate and reinforce key points.
>
> _____ 2. Beware of using humorous props, such as wigs or costumes. Unless they match the levity of the topic, such props can easily undermine your credibility.
>
> _____ 3. Make sure the prop is big enough for everyone to see (and read, if applicable).
>
> _____ 4. Show the prop slowly and make sure that every member of the audience can see it.
>
> _____ 5. In most cases, keep the prop hidden until you are ready to use it.
>
> _____ 6. Don't let the prop distract you or the audience. Put it away when you are finished with it.
>
> _____ 7. Practice your speech with the prop.
>
> _Source:_ Selected ideas based on Andrea Nierenberg, "Props Help Bring Content into the Visual Realm," _Presentations_ 16 (April 2002): 4, 54.

PICTURES (PHOTOGRAPHS, DRAWINGS, DIAGRAMS, MAPS, AND POSTERS)

Few verbal descriptions can match the powerful impact that a strong visual image creates. Photographs, drawings, paintings, and other illustrations are all forms of **pictures** — two-dimensional representations of people, places, ideas, or objects produced on an opaque backing. Among the types of pictures commonly used by speakers are photographs, line drawings, diagrams, maps, and posters.

A **diagram** (also called a _schematic drawing_) explains how something works or how it is constructed or operated. Diagrams are best suited to simplifying and clarifying complicated procedures, explanations, and operations. They are the aid of choice when you need to explain how to construct or use something. Figure 20.1 is a diagram that shows how to assemble monitor stand cables for a computer.

A _map_ is a representation of a whole or a part of an area on a flat surface.[3] Maps help audience members to visualize geographic areas and to understand various relationships among them. At the simplest level, maps illustrate the layout of a geographic region. Thus if your speech is about becoming familiar with a company's various offices worldwide, you could incorporate a map depicting the location of the offices into your talk. Maps are also an excellent way to illustrate the proportion of one thing to something else in different areas of a region. You could create a map to illustrate the proportion of manufacturing plants to distribution centers, for example, or of distribution centers to retailers, and so forth. For a speech on making one's way around New York City via public transportation, you could create a slide in which you could embed a map of the New York City subway system.

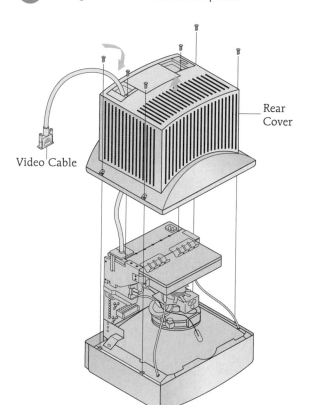

Rear
Cover

Video Cable

Figure 20.1 Diagram of Schematic Drawing of Monitor Stand Cables

A *poster* is a large, bold, two-dimensional design incorporating words, shapes, and, if desired, color, placed on an opaque backing. Posters are used to convey a brief message or point forcefully and attractively. They make a good choice for introducing topics or concepts early in the introductory part of a presentation, as well as later, when simple concepts need to be introduced. Posters are economical and easy to use; they are a good choice for speakers who give the same presentation many times. Easels are useful if you have several posters to show successively, and chalkboard railings can hold posters as well. As described in Chapter 30, posters are featured in one form of presentation called the *poster session*.

GRAPHS AND CHARTS

A **graph** represents numerical data in visual form. Graphs neatly illustrate relationships among components or units and demonstrate trends. Four major types of graphs are line graphs, bar graphs, pie graphs, and pictograms.

A **line graph** displays one measurement, usually plotted on the horizontal axis, and units of measurement or values, which are plotted on the vertical axis.

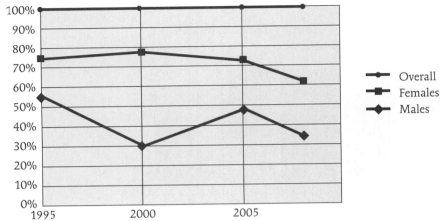

Figure 20.2 Percentage of College Students Who Consider Using a Bicycle for Transportation to Campus

Each value or point is connected with a line. Line graphs are especially useful in representing information that changes over time, such as trends. For example, Figure 20.2 represents fluctuations in the way college students transport to campus over a fifteen-year period. Line graphs remain a favorite among most presenters and listeners because they simplify complex information and are easier to read than more complicated tables and charts of data.

A **bar graph** uses bars of varying lengths to compare quantities or magnitudes. As seen in Figure 20.3, bars may be arranged either vertically or horizontally. Speakers sometimes use multidimensional bar graphs, or bar graphs distinguished by different colors or markings, when they need to compare two or more different kinds of information or quantities in one chart. A **pie graph** depicts the division of a whole. In this type of graph, the pie, which represents 100 percent, is divided into portions or segments called slices. Each slice constitutes a percentage of the whole. A **pictogram** shows comparisons in picture form. The pictures represent numerical units and are drawn to relate to the

---

✓ **CHECKLIST**

Tips for Creating Effective Pictograms

_____ 1. When creating pictograms, choose pictures that symbolize the subject being represented to a broad spectrum of viewers.

_____ 2. To avoid confusing the eye, make all pictograms the same size.

_____ 3. Clearly label what the pictogram symbolizes.

_____ 4. Clearly label the axes of the pictogram graph.

Vertical Bar Graph

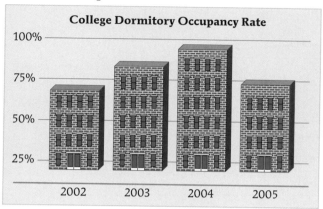

Horizontal Bar Graph

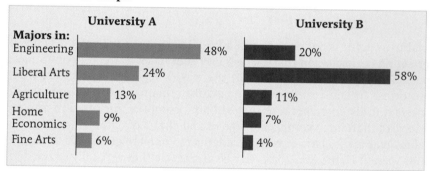

Figure 20.3 Bar Graphs of Quantities and Magnitudes

items being compared. Figure 20.4 is a pictogram that demonstrates an increase in the number of college students.

A **chart** visually organizes complex information into compact form. Several different types of charts are helpful for speakers: flowcharts; organizational charts; and tabular charts or tables. A **flowchart** is a diagram that shows step-by-step progression through a procedure, a relationship, or a process. Usually the flow of a procedure or a process is drawn horizontally or vertically and describes how key components fit into a whole. To show the sequence of activities or the directional flow in a process, the flowchart is the visual aid of choice (see Figure 20.5).

An **organizational chart** illustrates the organizational structure or chain of command in an organization. It shows the interrelationship of the different positions, divisions, departments, and personnel. Figure 20.6 shows an organizational chart for a hypothetical organization.

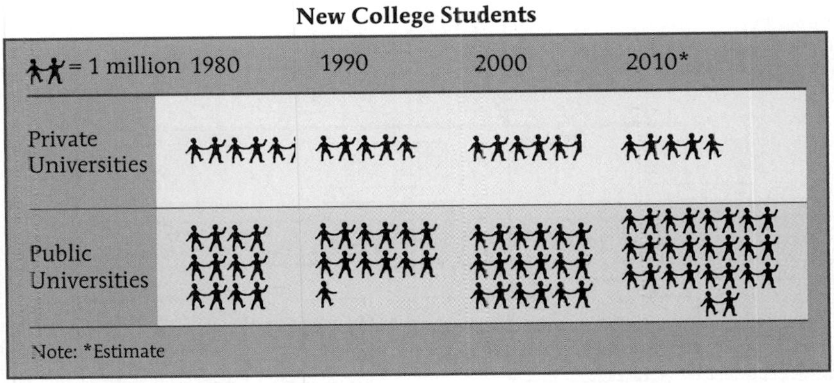

New College Students
= 1 million
1980
1990
2000
2010*
Private Universities
Public Universities
Note: *Estimate

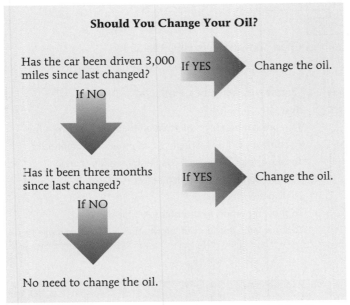

Figure 20.4 Pictogram Showing Increase in College Students

Should You Change Your Oil?
Has the car been driven 3,000 miles since last changed?
If YES
Change the oil.
If NO
Has it been three months since last changed?
If YES
Change the oil.
If NO
No need to change the oil.

Figure 20.5 Flowchart Showing Oil-Changing Decision Process

A tabular chart, or **table**, is a systematic grouping of data or numerical information in column form. Tables are not truly graphics, because they are not really pictures. However, even if they lack visual appeal they often present valuable data that the viewer can examine quickly and make comparisons about easily. Table 20.1, for example, summarizes the best uses of different types of graphs and charts.

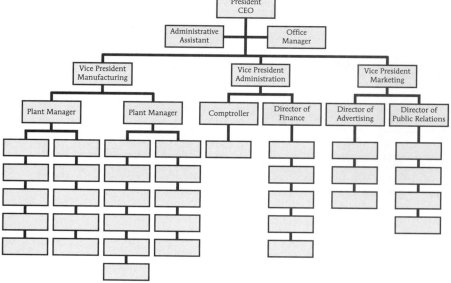

Figure 20.6 Organizational Chart Showing Personnel Hierarchy

TABLE 20.1 • Best Use of Different Types of Graphs and Charts

Type of Graph or Chart	Best Use
Line graph	To represent trends or information that changes over time
Bar and column graph	To compare individual points of information, magnitudes
Pie graph	To show proportions such as sales by region, shares
Pictogram	To show comparisons in picture form
Flowchart	To diagram processes
Organizational chart	To show reporting relationships in a hierarchy
Table	To show large amounts of information in easily viewable form

✓ **CHECKLIST**

Tips for Creating Effective Line, Bar, and Pie Graphs

_____ 1. Make sure that you label both axes of the line or bar graph appropriately.

_____ 2. Start the numerical axis of the line or bar graph at zero.

_____ 3. Compare only like variables.

_____ 4. Put no more than two lines of data on one graph.

_____ 5. Assign a clear title to the graph.

_____ 6. Clearly label all relevant points of information in the graph.

_____ 7. When creating multidimensional bar graphs, do not compare more than three kinds of information.

(Continued)

_____ 8. When creating a pie graph, restrict the number of pie slices to seven.

_____ 9. When creating a pie graph, make sure that you identify the value or percentage of each pie slice, and make sure that each slice of the pie accurately represents the value or percentage (e.g., use half of the pie to show 50 percent).

_____ 10. When creating a pie graph, consider using color or background markings to distinguish the different slices of the pie.

AUDIO AND VIDEO

An **audio clip** is a short recording of sounds, music, or speech. Introducing sound into a speech can add interest, illustrate ideas, and even bring humor to the mix. **Video** — including movie, television, and other recording segments — can also be a powerful presentation aid that combines sight, sound, and movement to illustrate key speech concepts. Because audio and video clips can be linked to PowerPoint slides or other digital devices, both are generally a safe choice as presentation aids.

✓ CHECKLIST

Tips on Incorporating Audio and Video into Your Presentation

_____ 1. If you are using traditional audio or video playback equipment, be sure to cue the audio- or videotape to the appropriate segment before the presentation. Fumbling for the right spot during your speech is a sure way to lose credibility and attention.

_____ 2. Alert audience members to what they will be viewing before you show the video.

_____ 3. Reiterate the main points of the audio or video clip once it is over.

_____ 4. Always check to see whether the audio or video material you are using is copyrighted, and that you are using it in a manner consistent with copyright laws.

MULTIMEDIA

Multimedia combines several media (stills, sound, video, text, and data) into a single production. The idea behind multimedia is that the more senses you evoke, the more memorable the event will be. Studies confirm that the visual and auditory reinforcement of multimedia helps people learn and master information more quickly than they would by conventional means. But even though it's an increasingly popular option, multimedia does require more planning than other forms of presentation aids. It is also more time-consuming.

To produce multimedia, you need to become familiar with presentation software programs such as Microsoft PowerPoint, Adobe Persuasion, and Corel-Draw, to name just a few (see Chapter 22).

Options for Displaying the Presentation Aid

Once you've selected the types of aids that are best suited for communicating your ideas (e.g., chart or graph and so forth), you can select from a variety of options for displaying them during your speech. On the more traditional side, popular devices include overhead transparencies, slide transparencies, flip charts, chalkboards, and handouts. Many presenters create computer-generated graphics, which they then display with computer projection or LCD display technologies (see Chapter 22).

OVERHEAD TRANSPARENCIES

An **overhead transparency** (also called an *overhead acetate*) is an image on a transparent background that can be viewed by transmitted light, either directly or through projection onto a screen or a wall. The images may be written or printed directly onto the transparency. If the transparency is handwritten during the presentation, it can be used much like a chalkboard (see p. 315). Parts of the transparency may be covered with opaque paper and revealed progressively during the presentation. Alternatively, transparencies may be overlaid on each other so that successive details can be added. Objects may also be placed on the stage of the projector to project silhouettes.

Because transparencies have several distinct advantages, they are among the most common presentation media, especially in settings such as schools.

✓ **CHECKLIST**

Tips for Successfully Incorporating Presentation Aids into Your Speech

_____ 1. Talk to your audience rather than to the screen — insofar as possible, don't turn your back to the audience.

_____ 2. Concentrate on maintaining eye contact with the audience.

_____ 3. Avoid putting the aid directly behind you. Place it to one side so that the entire audience can see it and you can move away from it and still face the audience.

_____ 4. Display the aid only when you are ready to discuss it.

_____ 5. Incorporate any aids you plan to use into your practice sessions. Continue to practice with the aids until you are confident that you can handle them without causing undue distractions.

_____ 6. If you decide to use a pointer, don't brandish it about. Once you've indicated the point you wish to make with the pointing instrument, put it down.

First, most facilities that host presentations have overhead projectors. Second, transparencies are inexpensive and overhead projectors are portable and simple to operate. Third, overhead projection is flexible. Material may be added to or taken away from the projector during the presentation, making the overhead a good choice for presentations that require multiple visual aids. Fourth, projection allows you to interact with the audience easily. Unlike writing on a chalkboard or handing out other visual aids, overhead projection allows you to face the audience while using it. In addition, users can keep lights on while using overhead transparencies. The checklist below offers some pointers on using overhead transparencies.

COMPUTER-GENERATED GRAPHICS AND DISPLAYS

With presentation software programs such as Microsoft PowerPoint, many speakers create slides, transparencies, and other presentation aids on a computer. You can project these *computer-generated graphics* directly from a computer

---

✓ **CHECKLIST**

Tips on Using Overhead Transparencies

_____ 1. Practice using your transparencies before your presentation.

_____ 2. Store your transparencies in a sturdy folder or box. Have blank transparencies available so that you can add information during the presentation.

_____ 3. Ensure that the projector is in good order: Make sure it does not block the audience's view; have a spare projector bulb available; tape the power cord to the floor.

_____ 4. Stand to the side of the projector—to the right if you are right-handed or to the left if you are left-handed.

_____ 5. Face the audience, not the projected image.

_____ 6. When adding transparencies, check that they remain clear and properly placed.

_____ 7. Use a pointer to indicate specific sections of a transparency—point to the transparency, not to the screen. Use objects such as a coin, pen, or arrow to mark the slide.

_____ 8. If creating transparencies by writing or drawing during the presentation, use a water-soluble transparency pen and make sure you write clearly.

_____ 9. Use overlays to show successive layers of detail.

_____ 10. Cover transparencies when you are done using them to avoid distracting your audience. Use heavy paper or cardboard so it will not be moved by the projector's fan.

Source: Adapted from Lenny Laskowski, "Using Overhead Transparencies," www.ljlseminars .com/ransp.htm (accessed September 1, 2005); and Media Services, Robert A. L. Mortvedt Library, Pacific Lutheran University, "Using Overhead Projectors," www.plu.edu/~libr/workshops/ multimedia/overhead.html (accessed September 1, 2005).

From Idea to Image
Using Presentation Aids

As you select each aid for your presentation, ask yourself:

- Is the *type* of aid the *best choice* to convey the information?
- Is my *timing* of the aid optimal?
- Will the aid help me achieve my *desired effect*?

Following are examples of one student's effective use of presentation aids in her speech about plastic bags and the environment.

The Plastic Bag Plague

Introduction

I.   Picture a swirling, plastic-laden gyre of ocean waters, twice the size of Texas . . . (*Attention getter*)

The notion of a plastic-laden gyre twice as large as Texas is difficult to fathom without a visual, so to build credibility, the student decides to show a photograph.

Body

I.   Plastic bags choke the land and water . . .

    A.   Americans throw out 30 million tons of plastic annually, or nearly 12 percent of all solid waste, and recycle only 6 percent of it.

Comparing recycling rates of solid wastes, the student uses a bar graph to show how plastic is the least biodegradable.

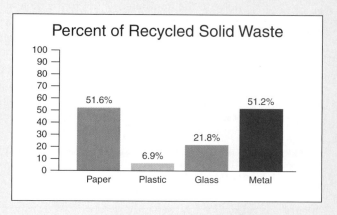

Percent of Recycled Solid Waste

Paper 51.6% Plastic 6.9% Glass 21.8% Metal 51.2%

B. 100,000 marine animals are killed annually . . .

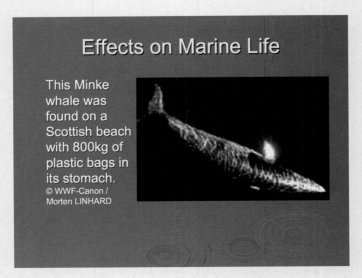

To appeal to the audience's emotions, or pathos, the student shows a video of
marine life suffering the consequences of plastic bag pollution. She hyperlinks
the image to the video URL. On the day of her presentation, she makes sure
the presentation room has an Internet connection and that her hyperlinked
video works.

C. 200,000 plastic bags get deposited in landfills every hour and take
1000 years to decompose . . .

The student illustrates this dramatic statistic with a photograph of a landfill
teeming with plastic.

Conclusion

I.   Prevent major impact on our world . . .

Stop Plastic Bag Waste

➤ Take plastic bags to recycle bin at local grocery store.

➤ Use reusable bags when shopping.

➤ Encourage stores to offer paper bags instead of plastic bags.

➤ Email your senator or representative in support of government regulation on plastics.

Stressing the need to act, the student concludes with a text slide listing actions students can take. Note that she keeps the background color consistent throughout the presentation and selects a font color that contrasts well with it.

II.   Use environmentally friendly bags . . .

The student shows this reusable bag from Whole Foods as a prop to demonstrate her point.

III.   Hold up your reusable bag and say, "No thank you, I brought my own . . ."
Once again, the student holds up a reusable shopping bag to reiterate one of her speech's primary points: Decrease plastic bag consumption.

(using computerized projection and display devices such as LCD projectors; see below), or you can transfer the images to overhead transparencies. (See Chapter 22 for a discussion of how to use presentation software.)

LCD stands for *liquid crystal diode*. **LCD display technology** is now widespread and can be found in laptop computer screens, digital watches, and countless other digitized products. Remember, if you take your presentation on the road, you can never be sure of the quality of the overhead projector that will be provided for you. LCD displays require overhead projectors with a very bright projection light; if the meeting room in which you will be presenting has a poor-quality projector, the projected image may be compromised. LCD projectors, which come with an illumination or light source and thus eliminate the need for an overhead projector, are favored when the speaker wants a freestanding device.

FLIP CHARTS

A **flip chart** is simply a large (27–34 inches) pad of paper on which a speaker can illustrate speech points. Many such aids are prepared in advance, although you can also write and draw on the paper as you speak. As you progress through the speech, you simply flip through the pad to the next exhibit. The flip chart is one of the most inexpensive ways of displaying aids. In terms of equipment, a ruler and colored markers are all that are required. To compete with other kinds of aids, however, you do need some artistic skill so that your images aren't sloppy and awkward.

CHALKBOARDS

On the lowest-tech end of the spectrum lies the *chalkboard* — a black (or white) board on which you can write with chalk (or a marker if the board is the chalkless type). Chalkboards are useful for impromptu explanations, as when someone asks a question for which you do not have an aid but feel you can clarify with words or drawings. In general, try to reserve the chalkboard for quick explanations, such as presenting simple processes that are done in steps. Chalkboards are also useful for engaging the audience in short brainstorming sessions. If you have the time to prepare a speech properly, however, don't rely on a chalkboard. Chalkboards force the speaker to turn his or her back to the audience; they make listeners wait while you write on the board; and they require legible handwriting that will be clear to all viewers.

HANDOUTS

No consideration of presentation aids would be complete without a discussion of the **handout** — page-size items that convey information that is either impractical to give to the audience in another manner or intended to be kept by audience members after the presentation. Handouts can convey large amounts of information to an audience effectively and cost-efficiently because elements may be included that are not covered in depth, or at all, during the actual presentation. Handouts can also be used when it is best to have audience members follow along with you while you go over information.

To avoid distracting your listeners, unless you specifically want them to read the information as you speak, *wait until you are done before you distribute the handout.* If you do want the audience to view a handout during the speech, pass it out only when you are ready to talk about it. Finally, remember that having too many handouts may undercut their effectiveness. Sifting through pages and pages of information may become tiresome for audience members, who may decide that it isn't worth the trouble and lose interest.

Designing Presentation Aids 21

Once you select the types of presentation aids you will use in your speech and decide on the method of displaying them (see Chapter 20), you can begin design and construction. Whether you fashion the aids with pen and paper or generate them on a computer, certain general principles of design apply.

Simplicity

Presentation aids that try to communicate too many messages will quickly overwhelm the audience. To communicate your points effectively in the brief period of time the audience has to view the aid (for slides, this amounts to an average of about thirty seconds[1]), strive for simplicity. Concentrate on presenting one major idea per aid. If you want to cover and discuss a series of points, use a sequential layout of separate aids.

The purpose of a presentation aid is to reinforce, support, or summarize what you say, not to repeat verbatim what you've already verbalized in your speech. Thus, rather than using full sentences that mirror your speech statements, where possible present your points in short phrases. Also, minimize the number of words you use in each presentation aid. Keep them to a maximum of eight words per line and eight lines per aid. Limiting the number of words in an aid lessens the likelihood that the audience will spend too much time reading the aid rather than listening to you.

Another way to keep your aids simple and uncluttered is to construct your text in active verb form and parallel grammatical structure (see Chapter 16 on language). For example, community college student Courtney Phelps delivered an informative speech on the process of looking for a new car. She prepared a PowerPoint slide labeled "Buying a Used Car." Note in Figure 21.1 the differences between her first draft and her final slide.

In reviewing Courtney's first-draft slide, note the lack of parallel structure (each item is constructed differently); her use of wordy full sentences throughout; and the passive construction in point 3 ("It is recommended that . . .").

In her final slide, Courtney switched from passive to active construction (deleting "It is recommended that," leaving only "Shop around . . ."). All of her points became short, crisp sentences. Since the final sentences conformed to the **eight-by-eight rule** — using no more than eight words in a line and eight lines on one slide — her audience members were not likely to be confused by them. Each of these changes increased the clarity of her presentation.

317

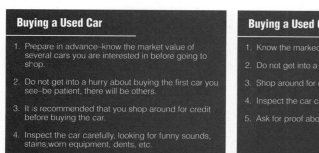

Figure 21.1 Cluttered versus Easy-to-Read Presentation Aid

Continuity

The principle of continuity dictates that you apply the same design decisions you make for one aid to all of the aids you display in a speech. Doing so will ensure that viewers don't become distracted (and irritated) by a jumble of unrelated visual elements.

To help maintain continuity, your choice of any key design elements — colors, fonts, upper- and lowercase letters, styling (boldface, underlining, italics) — should be carried through to each aid. If you select a certain color background for one aid, for instance, repeat the same background for each subsequent aid. Follow the same general page layout throughout, placing repeating elements,

---

✓ **CHECKLIST**

Applying the Principles of Simplicity and Continuity

✓ Restrict your coverage to one idea per aid.
✓ Use as few words as possible to get your ideas across clearly.
✓ Where possible, use key phrases rather than full sentences.
✓ Keep text to no more than eight words per line and eight lines per aid.
✓ Create concise titles that tell viewers what to look for in the aid and that reinforce your message.
✓ Maintain design consistency across all aids. Use the same combinations of fonts, upper- and lowercase lettering, styling (use of boldface, underlining, and italics), and spacing.
✓ Use colors consistently across all aids. If an object is red in one slide and you repeat the same object in another slide, render it in the same color.
✓ Apply the same style and typeface to titles throughout all aids.
✓ Carry through any repeating symbols, such as logos or pictograms, across all aids.

such as titles, in the same place and in the same style and typeface. Use the same symbols in every aid, whether they are colors, pictograms, or logos of one sort or another. For example, if in an aid comparing the computer-buying habits of men and women you illustrated the buying habits of men in red and those of women in green, you would continue using these colors in subsequent aids.

Typeface Style and Font Size

A **typeface** is a specific style of lettering, such as Arial, Times Roman, or Courier. Typefaces come in a variety of **fonts**, or sets of sizes (called the point size) and upper- and lowercases.

Designers divide the thousands of typefaces available today into two categories: serif and sans serif. (There are additional categories, such as script typefaces and those that mimic cursive writing, but these aren't recommended for presentation aids because they are difficult to read from a distance.) **Serif typefaces** include small flourishes, or strokes, at the tops and bottoms of each letter. **Sans serif typefaces** are more blocklike and linear; they are designed without these tiny strokes. Studies have shown that when a body of text is being read, serif typefaces are easier on the eye (see Figure 21.2). Small amounts

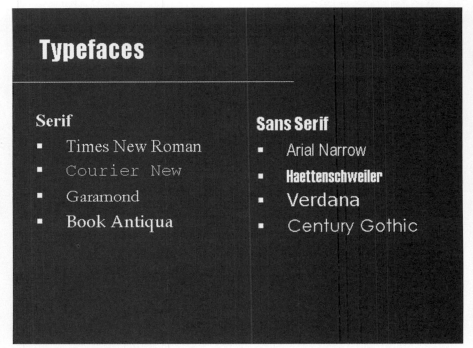

Figure 21.2 Serif and Sans Serif Typefaces

of text, however, such as headings, are best viewed in sans serif type. Depending on how much text you insert into a slide, consider a sans serif typeface for the heading and a serif typeface for the body of the text. If you include only a few lines of text, however, consider using sans serif type throughout.

There are thousands of typefaces beyond those found in word processing programs, many of which can be purchased in separate software packages or downloaded from the Internet. Following are a few key points to observe when selecting type styles for presentations:

1. Whether you are using a hand-drawn poster board or a computer-generated graphic, check your lettering for legibility, taking into consideration the audience's distance from the presentation. Most text for on-screen projection should be a minimum of 18 points or larger. Titles or major headings should be 36 points. One guideline is that major headings within the presentation should be displayed in 36-point type, subheadings should use 24-point type, and regular text should be 18-point type (see Figure 21.3).

2. Check that your lettering stands apart from your background. For example, don't put black type on a dark blue background.

3. Use a typeface that is simple and easy to read, not distracting. It should be consistent with the image you are trying to present and match your meaning.

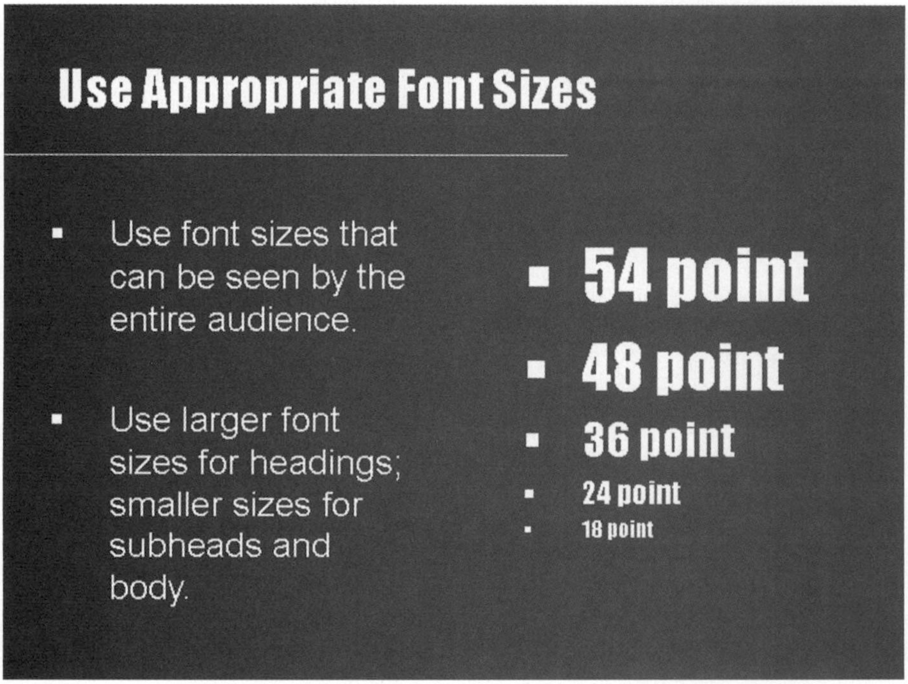

Figure 21.3 Use Appropriate Font Sizes

Tips for Using Typefaces, Fonts, and Sizes Effectively

✓ For on-screen projection, don't use anything smaller than 18-point text. For larger rooms, consider 24-point text or larger.

✓ Avoid ornate typefaces—they are difficult to read.

✓ Use a sans serif typeface for titles and major headings.

✓ Experiment with a serif typeface for the body of the text.

✓ Select a style of type that suits your message.

✓ Experiment with 36-point type for major headings, 24-point type for subheads, and 18-point type for text.

✓ As a rule, use no more than two different typefaces in a single visual aid.

✓ Avoid using all capitals. Use upper- and lowercase type.

✓ Don't overuse boldface, underlining, or italics.

---

4. Don't overuse **boldface**, <u>underlining</u>, or *italics*. Instead, use them sparingly to call attention to or emphasize the most important points.

5. Use upper- and lowercase type. This combination is easier to read than all capitals.

Color

As any artist will attest, color has an amazing ability to stimulate the senses. By doing so, it helps listeners to see comparisons, contrasts, and emphases. The skillful use of color can draw attention to key points, set the mood of a presentation, and make things easier to see. However, color that isn't used wisely can easily backfire. Poor color combinations will set the wrong mood, render an image unattractive, or make it just plain unreadable. Table 21.1 describes the effects of several color combinations.

In addition, because colors evoke distinct associations in people, care must be taken as you design the aid not to summon an unintended meaning or mood. Unless you specifically wish to remind viewers of the holidays of Halloween and Christmas, for example, when addressing audiences in the United States steer clear of combining orange with black and red with green.[2] Table 21.2 describes some of the subjective interpretations different audiences attach to four colors.

TABLE 21.1 • Effect of Color Combinations

Color	Effect in Combination
Yellow	Warm on white, harsh on black, fiery on red, soothing on light blue
Blue	Warm on white, hard to see on black
Red	Bright on white, warm or difficult to see on black

Source: Cheryl Currid, *Make Your Point: The Complete Guide to Successful Business Presentations Using Today's Technology* (Rocklin, Calif.: Prima Publishing, 1995), 75.

TABLE 21.2 • Subjective Interpretations of Color by Different Audiences

Color Hue	Financial Managers	Health Care Professionals	Control Engineers
Blue	Corporate, reliable	Dead	Cold, water
Green	Cool, subdued	Infected, bilious	Safe
Yellow	Important	Jaundiced	Caution
Red	Unprofitable	Healthy	Danger

Source: Adapted from Cheryl Currid, *Make Your Point: The Complete Guide to Successful Business Presentations Using Today's Technology* (Rocklin, Calif.: Prima Publishing, 1995), 74.

Following are some tips for using color effectively in your presentation aids:

- Use *bold, bright colors* to emphasize important points. For instance, speakers often use bright yellow to draw attention to important points. Warm colors such as yellow, red, and orange move to the foreground of a field. For this reason, they are good colors to use when you want to highlight something. But be careful: These colors can be difficult to see from a distance.

- Use *softer, lighter* colors to de-emphasize less important areas of a presentation.

- Keep the *background color* of your presentation constant, and avoid dark backgrounds. As a general rule, the best background colors are the lighter, more neutral colors of tan, blue, green, or white.

- For typeface and graphics, use colors that contrast rather than clash with or blend into the background color.

- Limit the number of colors you use in a graphic to two or three (or four at the most). More color choices can be used in complex and detailed aids.

- Be aware that many presentation software packages provide templates with preselected colors.

 CHECKLIST

Optimizing Your Use of Color

✓ Yellow, orange, and red rank highest in visibility, so use these colors to highlight text or objects within a frame.
✓ To de-emphasize less important areas of a presentation, use softer, lighter colors.
✓ For typeface and graphics, use colors that contrast rather than clash with or blend into the background color.
✓ Use blues, greens, and neutral colors such as tan and white for backgrounds.
✓ Use no more than four colors in a graphic; two or three are even better.
✓ Stay within the same family of hues.

Using Presentation Software

Various presentation software packages offer public speakers powerful tools for creating and displaying professionally polished visual aids. The best known and most available of these programs is Microsoft *PowerPoint*, the one we refer to throughout this chapter. Available since 2006 are Web-based presentation development tools that provide some of the same basic features as PowerPoint but far fewer specialized elements. Examples include Google Docs (docs.google.com) and Zoho Show (show.zoho.com). All of these presentation programs can display visuals directly from a computer via an LCD panel or a projector, or they can be converted into handouts or overhead transparencies for display on a carousel or an overhead projector. Preloaded *templates* provide expert guidelines for font, color, and background combinations, but users can also design their own visual aids. In addition, these presentation software programs allow you to produce multimedia displays by making it possible to import video and sound into your visuals.

It's a Speech, Not a Slide Show

For all its promise, however, the use of PowerPoint or other slides can be fraught with peril. Anyone not having used the program before will need to spend a good deal of time learning it. In addition, with use of any electronic device during a speech, technical errors are always a hazard. In the case of Power-Point slides, common risks include incompatibility of a PowerPoint file with an operating system, projector bulb burnout, or a computer drive freezing when a media file is clicked to play. (The accompanying checklist on preventive maintenance describes steps you can take to avoid these problems.) But perhaps worse than any of these kinds of potential mishaps is the mistaken notion of many speakers that the PowerPoint display itself is the presentation, or that it will somehow save an otherwise poorly planned speech.

No longer is it surprising to hear someone say, "I'm giving a PowerPoint today," instead of "I'm giving a speech today." Some speakers become so enamored of generating graphics or creating glitzy multimedia presentations that they forget their primary mission: to communicate through the spoken word and through their physical presence. Other speakers are tempted to hide behind their visual displays, focusing their attention on the slide show rather than on the audience. As public speaking author Ron Hoff so importantly notes: "It's okay to be partially electronic — everybody can use a bit of glitz — but when all votes are counted and all scores are in, the presenter who is most alive will carry the day."[1] As with any visual support device, careful consideration and a

---

✓ **CHECKLIST**

Preventive Maintenance: Avoiding PowerPoint Technical Glitches

✓ Check to make sure that the operating system of the computer you will use during your speech (e.g., Windows XP, Mac OS X) is compatible with the operating system used to create the aids.

✓ Make sure that the version of the presentation software used to create the aids matches the one that is loaded onto the computer you will use in the presentation. Incompatibilities between versions can cause distortions in your graphics, sound, and video; in some cases one version may not recognize another.

✓ Properly save all the files associated with your presentation (i.e., images, sound files, videos) into the same folder and onto the disk you will use in your presentation.

✓ Verify that the format you've saved the files to, whether it's a floppy disk, zip drive, flash drive, or CD-ROM disk, is compatible with (i.e., will be accepted by) the presentation computer.

✓ Before the speech — if only minutes before — familiarize yourself with the layout and functioning of the presentation computer. This will facilitate smooth operation during the presentation.

✓ If you are concerned about losing your computer-generated presentation — due to a system failure, power outage, or connection error — prepare a hard-copy backup of your presentation. In PowerPoint, for example, you would use the Handout Master and handout printing option to print out your slides for use as handouts.

---

good rationale are needed when you decide to use PowerPoint slides to complement your speeches.

A Brief Guide to Using PowerPoint Web links

Many students today have had exposure to PowerPoint, so you probably already know that it can be used to generate slides containing text, artwork, photos, charts, graphs, tables, clip art, video, and sound. You can upload PowerPoint presentations onto the Web for viewing elsewhere, and with additional software you can broadcast your PowerPoint presentation online in real time. This section offers a brief overview of PowerPoint's primary features. (For more detailed guidance on using PowerPoint, consult *PowerPoint* by Microsoft Press or other similar manuals.) To begin, after opening PowerPoint, familiarize yourself with the toolbars and icons at the top and bottom of the main screen (See Figure 22.1).

Figure 22.1 PowerPoint Toolbars

BECOME FAMILIAR WITH THE PRESENTATION OPTIONS

PowerPoint provides you three options for composing a set of presentation slides.

1. The *AutoContent Wizard* (or *Slide Layout* in PowerPoint 2007) lets you choose the type of presentation you want from about two dozen alternatives, such as Marketing Plan, Introducing a Speaker, Product/Services Overview, and Presenting a Technical Report. AutoContent Wizard then applies an outline for your presentation (see Figure 22.2). You select the presentation medium (on-screen, Web, overheads) in which to enter the information to be presented. The AutoContent Wizard sets up an index of, generally, from six to twelve slides with preloaded slide titles, points, subpoints, colors, and designs.

2. The *Design Template* option includes approximately forty-eight pre-designed templates (see Figure 22.3). You decide how to organize your points and subpoints; the template you select then applies a consistent layout and color scheme to each slide in the presentation. Each template is designed to convey a certain, consistent look or feel.

✓ **CHECKLIST**

Using PowerPoint's AutoContent Wizard or Slide Layout

_____ 1. Choose File New or press CTRL + N. PowerPoint displays the New Presentation dialog box.

_____ 2. Select the AutoContent Wizard option from the right-hand navigation bar (or from the dialog box), and then choose OK. The AutoContent Wizard dialog box appears.

_____ 3. Read the information in the Step 1 dialog box, and then choose the Next button.

_____ 4. Select the type of presentation you want to give, and then choose the Next button.

_____ 5. Select the type of output you want to use, and then choose the Next button.

_____ 6. Enter the information for creating a title slide, and then choose the Next button.

_____ 7. Choose the Finish button to exit the Wizard and create your presentation.

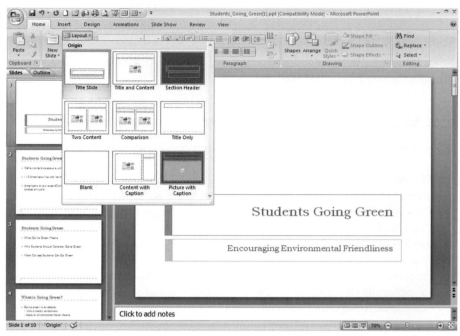

Figure 22.2 PowerPoint's AutoContent Wizard or Slide Layout

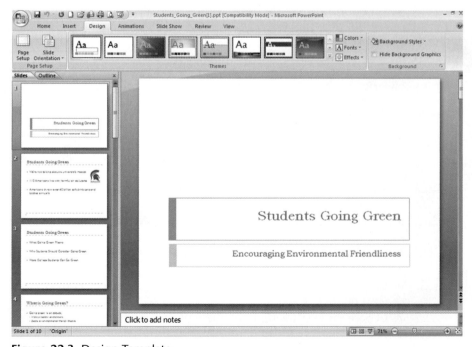

Figure 22.3 Design Template

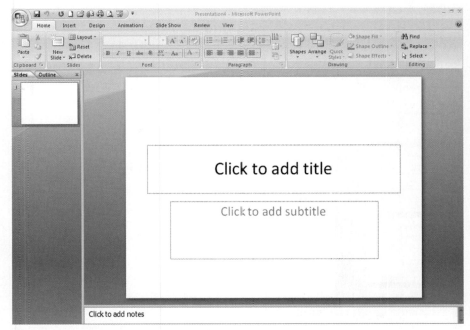

Figure 22.4 Blank Presentation Mode

3. With *Blank Presentation mode*, you customize every aspect of the presentation: layout, color, font, type and size, organization of content, and graphics (see Figure 22.4). This option allows the greatest degree of flexibility. The downside is that each slide's design essentially starts from scratch, but once you have designed a slide with the feature you want, you can select and copy to have each subsequent slide share the same features.

BECOME FAMILIAR WITH VIEW OPTIONS AND SLIDE MASTERS

Current versions of PowerPoint offer three different ways to view slides as you create them: normal view, slide-sorter view, and slide-show view.

1. *Normal view,* the view in which you will do most of your slide preparation work (see Figure 22.5), allows you to view (and edit) one entire slide on the screen. Along the left side of the normal view screen is an outline of the entire presentation (based on the textual content of each slide) or, alternatively, a thumbnail view of each slide as it is created. Below the slide is a space to add notes.

2. *Slide-sorter view* provides a graphical representation of all the slides in the presentation, in the order they were created. In this view you can click and drag slides to reorganize the presentation sequence or to delete slides (see Figure 22.6).

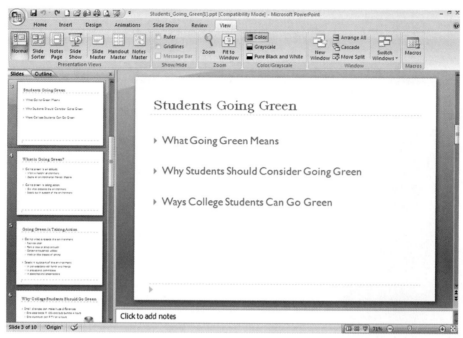

Figure 22.5 Normal View

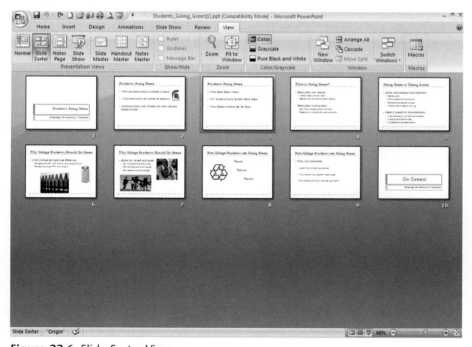

Figure 22.6 Slide-Sorter View

3. *Slide-show view* is the actual view to use for projecting the presentation to an audience. Each slide appears in its proper sequence and fills the entire screen.

For each presentation you create using a Design Template, PowerPoint creates a *Slide Master*. Slide Masters contain the elements (font styles and sizes, background designs, colors, and so forth) that you want to appear on every slide. For example, if you want a logo, image, or line of text to appear on each slide, add that item to the Slide Master, and it will automatically appear on all the slides in your presentation. The *Handout Master* shows a page-size view depicting a number of slides per page (six by default) and lets you alter the orientation of slides on the page. When printed, this view serves as a handout of the slides, useful for audience members to have as a record of the presentation. To display a Master, go to the View menu and scroll down to Master.

During your actual presentation, you can control your slides using the commands listed in Table 22.1.

TABLE 22.1 • Commands to Run a PowerPoint Slide Show

Function	Method
Show the next slide	Click the left mouse button or press the space bar, N, right arrow, down arrow, or Page Down
Show the preceding slide	Click the right mouse button or press Backspace, P, left arrow, up arrow, or Page Up
Show a specific slide	Type the number and press Enter
Access Meeting Minder or pointers	Click the right mouse button and select the appropriate option
Toggle the mouse pointer on or off (show or hide)	Type A or the equal sign
Toggle between a black screen and a current screen	Type B or a period
Toggle between a white screen and a current screen	Type W or a comma
End the show	Press ESC, hyphen, or CTRL-Break
Pause and resume an automatic slide show	Type an S or the plus sign

EDITING TEXT

Whenever you choose a slide layout (other than a blank layout), you replace the sample text in a placeholder or textbox with your own text. PowerPoint text can be edited much like text in a word processor—you can apply bold, italics, and other text modifications. When you finish entering text, deselect the placeholder by clicking a blank area of the slide. After entering text in a text box, you will probably want to change the content or correct errors. Making changes is as easy as clicking and retyping.

USING SLIDE INSERTS

You can easily import photos and images, clip art, and other objects into Power-Point as *slide inserts* to supplement or illustrate your speech points. You use the same procedure as you would when inserting graphical elements into Microsoft Word documents and e-mail messages. With a slide open in normal view, select the Insert menu in the main toolbar at the top of your screen, and click on the type of object you want to insert: Picture, Clip Art, Shapes, Chart, WordArt, or even Movie or Sound.

- *Pictures.* Photos can be inserted from your own picture files, from a disk or portable drive, or from photo Web sites.

- *Clip Art.* You can select clip art from the PowerPoint Clip Art gallery. You can also import clip art from other programs or Web sites such as Microsoft's online Clip Art page (office.microsoft.com/clipart).

- *Charts.* When you select Chart from your Insert menu, you will see a sample chart with data sets (see Figure 22.7). You can select the type of chart you want to create (column, bar, line, pie, and so on) and input the appropriate data. The chart will automatically be inserted into the slide. Inserting a table or worksheet into your slide can serve as helpful

Figure 22.7 Using Charts in PowerPoint Slides

supporting material for a speech — as long as it is simple and large enough to read.

- *Tables.* To insert a table in PowerPoint, select Table from the Insert menu, or import a table from Microsoft Word or Excel.

- *Movie or Sound.* In PowerPoint you can also insert a playable music track from a compact disc or a file from your computer. To do so, select Sound from the Insert menu and then select whether you want to play from a file or from a CD audio track.

✓ CHECKLIST

Inserting Tables and Worksheets into PowerPoint

_____ 1. To create a table or a worksheet using an older version of Power-Point, choose Insert Microsoft Word Table or Insert Microsoft Excel Worksheet in the standard toolbar. A drop-down grid of cells appears.

_____ 2. Click and drag the mouse pointer across the cells in the grid to indicate how many rows or columns you want in your table or worksheet. When you release the mouse button, PowerPoint inserts a special object into your slide. Toolbars for either Word or Excel will replace the PowerPoint toolbars when the special object is selected. In effect, with the special object you are using either Word or Excel inside a PowerPoint window.

_____ 3. To create the content of the table or worksheet, use the mouse, the tab key, or the arrow keys to move from cell to cell and type in the text. When you have entered all of the desired content, select Exit to insert the object into the slide. Deselect the object by clicking in a blank area of the slide.

PowerPoint presentations can include video clips and even portions of movies and television as supporting material for speeches. The growing availability of amateur video on Web sites such as YouTube (www.youtube.com) and Google Video (video.google.com) and the increasing ease of transferring video to computers from portable devices such as iPods, pocket-size hard drives, and cell phones makes the embedding of video even simpler. Rather than having to move from your computer's PowerPoint slides to a separate video player and monitor to show a video clip, you can perform all these functions from one place. However, when attempting to insert video clips into your slides, bear in mind a critical technical difference. Unlike clip art, photos, and charts that can truly be embedded into the PowerPoint presentation, video clips are *merely linked* to your PowerPoint file rather than actually embedded in it. This means that if you move your PowerPoint presentation from one computer to another (by saving it to a CD or to a USB flash drive or by e-mailing it), you will break the link to your video file unless you saved your video file in the same folder as your PowerPoint presentation. It is not difficult to use a video file in a Power-Point presentation, but you may need to practice in order to get it right. To add video to a slide, follow these steps:

1. In normal view, click the slide to which you want to add a movie or an animated file.
2. On the Insert tab, in the Media Clips group (or Movie tab), click the arrow under Movie.
3. Do one of the following:
   - Click Movie from File, locate the folder that contains the file, and then double-click the file that you want to add.
   - Click Movie from Clip Organizer, scroll to find the clip that you want in the Clip Art task pane, and then click it to add it to the slide.

You can also go to Microsoft's PowerPoint Web site (http://office .microsoft.com/en-us/powerpoint/default.aspx) and follow the instructions for adding and playing a movie in a presentation.

Note that you cannot insert portions of a digital movie from a DVD to a PowerPoint slide, but you can use some third-party software to synchronize DVD video during a PowerPoint presentation. Be certain to abide by copyright restrictions when copying or downloading video and audio files. (See Chapter 5 on ethics.)

USING TRANSITIONS AND ANIMATION EFFECTS

As you move from one slide to the next in your presentation or as you move from one point to another within the same slide, you may wish to add transition effects and text animations. *Transition effects* add special motion and sound effects as you click from one slide to another. For example, you can play a "swoosh" sound when the slide appears, or you can make the slides dissolve into black or red as you shift from one to another.

But, a word of warning about transitions and animations: When used sparingly, transition and animation effects can enhance your presentation. When overused, however, they can distract. Too often, these effects appear unprofessional. *Text animations* should also be kept consistent from one slide to the next. If you plan to use the "fly in from left" effect, for example, apply it on all slides that you build as opposed to using it on just one and a different effect for another. The same guidelines apply to slide transitions. A different transition between every slide set tends to distract the audience. Keep the transitions consistent either throughout the entire slide show or within different sections of your presentation. As a rule of thumb, your PowerPoint presentation will not be the poorer if you choose not to use transition and animation effects, but unnecessary use of effects can harm the presentation.

Finding Media for PowerPoint Slides

With PowerPoint, you can import still images, clip art, video, or sound directly into your slides, either by downloading the files from the Internet or accessing them from a computer disk. Depending on your speech topic, you may be able to find clip art video, picture, or sound files on the Internet that meet your needs.

For downloadable digital images, try the following Web sites:

- Corbis.com (pro.corbis.com): Contains more than 2 million photographs, prints, and paintings, 35,000 of which you can download for your personal use (for a fee of about $6 per image).
- Google (www.google.com) and Yahoo! (www.yahoo.com): Popular search engines that have evolved to include image searches.

The following sites contain free photographs and other still images:

- www.mcad.edu
- www.PictureQuest.com
- www.freefoto.com

The following sites offer downloadable music files:

- www.mp3now.com
- www.RioPort.com
- www.mp3.com

Try these sites if you're looking for audio clips:

- www.dailywav.com
- www.4wavfiles.4anything.com
- www.freeaudioclips.com
- www.soundamerica.com
- www.wavcentral.com
- www.wavsounds.com

The following sites contain useful video clips:

- CNN Video Select (www.cnn.com/video) and ABCNews.com Newsclips (abcnews.go.com/sections/us/video_index/video_index.html): Especially useful for speech topics on current events or timely social issues.
- Yahoo! Video Search (video.search.yahoo.com): Offers an advanced search for Creative Commons content to help determine whether a video clip is copyrighted or in the public domain.

From PowerPoint to Presentation
Developing Effective Slides

PowerPoint slides can help listeners visually process information (especially complex statistical data; see From Idea to Image: Using Presentation Aids, p. 312). However, beware of letting your speech turn into a slide show. For each slide of your presentation, carefully consider whether it truly illuminates information for your audience. In addition:

- Use as few slides as possible.
- Simplify text to a minimum.
- Use only those design elements that truly enhance meaning.
- Be prepared to give the same speech without slides.

The following excerpt from a student speech on cycling programs for kids demonstrates the effective use of PowerPoint slides.

Cycling for Kids

Body

I. Cycling is a popular activity for fun, fitness, and volunteering opportunities.

> *To emphasize the popularity of biking for charity, as well as to build credibility, the student inserts a slide listing the top five biking charities.*
>
> *(**Delivery note:** The student stands beside the slide, calling out each of the charities by pointing to them with a laser pointer as she discusses them.)*

Since her focus is on getting involved in local community programs, the speaker lists Trips for Kids as the last bullet of her slide for easy transition to her next main point and to her next slide.

A.   Statistics show that 100 million people in the United States own bikes.
B.   Many cycling organizations provide opportunities for cyclists to get involved in their local communities.
II.   Trips For Kids operates out of the United States and Canada and helps disadvantaged kids discover the joy of mountain biking.

Trips for Kids

- Collects bicycles and safety gear for kids.
- Organizes bike rides for kids.
- Recruits college students to serve as cycling mentors.

TRIPS FOR KIDS NATIONAL

The student lists the organization's primary goals on the slide with the hopes of encouraging other students to get involved in the organization's efforts; for visual effect as well as to build credibility, she also includes the organization's logo on the slide.

A.   Collects bicycles and safety gear for children ages . . .
B.   Organizes bike rides for kids . . .
C.   Recruits college students to serve as cycling mentors

Embedding a single photo of a college student mentoring a child emphasizes the speaker's point, driving home the fact that there are college students who care and want to get involved.

*(**Delivery note:** The student removes the photo before moving to her next main point.)*

III. As a member of the Southeast Off-Road Bicycle Association (SORBA) chapter on campus, I participated in the Trips for Kids program last year.

A. "A typical ride starts Saturday morning with volunteers helping children find just the right size bike and secure their helmets" (SORBA Web site).

The student includes a slide that embeds a link to the Web site for which she volunteers.

*(**Preparation note:** Before showing this slide, the student practices linking to the URL to avoid technical mishaps during her actual presentation.)*

B. We took the kids on rides on various trails in our community.

Transition: Now that you have seen how helping kids ride bicycles is something you can do, you're ready to discover ways to volunteer in the community to encourage cycling.

IV. Become involved with cycling by volunteering at bike trail cleanups

Bike Trail Cleanup

- Energetic volunteers from the Big South Fork Bicycle Club cutting new trail.
- Volunteer at your local trail.

The student shows a slide that includes a photo of an actual bike trail cleanup, again to build credibility and make a strong impact.

*(**Delivery Note:** She leaves it up as background while discussing the various subpoints about bike trail cleanup.)*

A. Look up bike trail information in your community; here's an example of the Chattanooga trails (SORBA Chattanooga Organization).
B. Get together with other cyclists and clean bike trails.

Developing PowerPoint Slides for a Speech

The fundamental principle to using PowerPoint slides for a speech is the same as for any visual support device: make sure that the visuals will add value to your speech and will not distract from or become your speech. Like any visual support, PowerPoint slides are meant to supplement and not to supplant your speech. Often the best place to begin planning your slides is with your speaking outline.

Your speaking outline provides the content elements for your slides, and by thinking through which points in your speech might be better explained to your audience with some kind of visual, you can decide what the content of your slides will be, how many slides you'll need, and how to arrange your slides. A speaking outline may contain between three and five main points. Each main point has at least two subpoints. Are some points more suited for visual display than others? What features should be used for each slide? There is no fixed formula for answering these questions, so you must rely on your own creativity and critical thinking. For an example of how one student thought carefully about which points in his speech could be enhanced by a slide, see the visual guide titled "From PowerPoint to Presentation: Developing Effective Slides" on the previous pages.

CHECKLIST

Tips for Successfully Using PowerPoint Presentations in Your Speech

✓ Don't let the technology get in the way of relating to your audience.

✓ As with nonelectronic presentations, talk to your audience rather than to the screen. Maintain eye contact as much as possible.

✓ Have a backup plan in case of technical errors.

✓ If you use a pointer (laser or otherwise), turn it off and put it down as soon as you have made your point.

✓ Never shine a laser pointer into anyone's eyes. It will burn them!

✓ Incorporate the aids into your practice sessions until you are confident that they strengthen, rather than detract from, your core message.

Forms of Speeches

Forms of Speeches

Speaker's Reference
Forms of Speeches

23. The Informative Speech

Build Awareness and Understanding in Your Informative Speech

- Strive to enlighten (informative intent) rather than to advocate (persuasive intent). (p. 352)
- Use clear transitions, introductions, and conclusions. (p. 352)
- Control your vocal delivery. (p. 352)
- Use presentation aids where appropriate. (p. 352)
- Choose compelling supporting material. (p. 353)

Analyze the Audience's Informational Needs

Consider the Types of Informative Speeches

- Speeches about objects or phenomena. (p. 354)
- Speeches about people. (p. 354)
- Speeches about events. (p. 354)
- Speeches about processes. (p. 354)
- Speeches about issues. (p. 355)
- Speeches about concepts. (p. 355)

Choose Strategies for Conveying Information

- Use *definition* to clarify. (p. 357)
- Provide *descriptions* to paint a picture. (p. 358)
- Provide a *demonstration*. (p. 358)
- Offer an in-depth *explanation*. (p. 358)

Clarify Complex Information

- Build on prior knowledge. (p. 359)
- Use analogies that link concepts to something familiar. (p. 360)
- Demonstrate underlying causes. (p. 360)
- Check for understanding. (p. 360)
- Use visual aids, including models and drawings. (p. 361)

Appeal to Different Learning Styles

- Consider listeners' learning styles as part of your audience analysis. (p. 361)
- Plan on conveying and reinforcing information in a variety of modes — visually, aurally, with text, and with demonstrations. (p. 362)

Arrange Speech Points in an Organizational Pattern

24. The Persuasive Speech

Select a Persuasive Purpose If Your Goal Is To:

- Influence an audience's attitudes, beliefs, or understanding of an issue. (p. 375)
- Influence an audience's behavior. (p. 375)
- Reinforce existing attitudes, beliefs, or behavior. (p. 375)

Increase the Odds of Achieving Your Persuasive Speech Goal By:

- Conducting a thorough audience analysis. (p. 376)
- Making your message relevant to the audience. (p. 376)
- Showing your listeners how the change you seek benefits them. (p. 376)
- Addressing topics that the audience feels strongly about. (p. 376)
- Seeking minor rather than major changes. (p. 377)
- Establishing credibility with your audience. (p. 377)

When Appealing to Emotion, Use Sound Reasoning

- Avoid deliberately arousing fear or otherwise manipulating listeners' emotions. (p. 381)

To Increase the Odds That Listeners Will Act on Your Message:

- Appeal to their needs. (p. 384)
- Appeal to the reasons they act as they do. (p. 385)
- Stress the message's relevance to listeners. (p. 386)
- Present the information at an appropriate level of understanding. (p. 387)
- Establish your credibility: Emphasize your expertise for speeches that stress facts and analysis; emphasize commonality with the audience for personal speeches. (p. 388)

25. Developing Arguments for the Persuasive Speech

Structure the Claims According to the Issue You Are Addressing

- When addressing whether something is or is not true, or whether something will or will not happen, make a *claim of fact.* (p. 394)
- When addressing an issue that relies on individual judgment of right and wrong for its resolution, make a *claim of value.* (p. 395)
- When proposing a specific outcome or solution to an issue, make a *claim of policy.* (p. 395)

Consider the Kinds of Evidence That Best Support Your Claim

- When audience members are aware of the issue in question, consider using evidence with which they are already familiar, based on adequate audience analysis focusing on their opinions of your topic. (p. 398)
- If your knowledge and credentials are such that the audience will find your opinions credible and convincing, consider using your own expertise as evidence. (p. 399)
- If the audience lacks knowledge of the topic and you are not a known expert on the subject, consider using examples, stories, testimony, facts, and statistics from external sources. (p. 400)

Test Your Evidence

- Is it directly relevant to your claim? (p. 400)
- Is it timely? (p. 400)
- Will the audience find the evidence and its source credible? (p. 400)

Employ Appropriate Lines of Reasoning to Validate Claims

- You can use the needs, desires, emotions, and values of audience members as the basis of their accepting some evidence (*motivational warrants*). (p. 401)
- You can rely on audience members' beliefs about the credibility of a source as the basis of their accepting some evidence (*authoritative warrants*). (p. 401)
- You can use audience members' beliefs about the reliability of factual evidence as the basis of their accepting some evidence (*substantive warrants*). (p. 402)
- Use *warrants by cause* when offering a cause-effect relationship as proof of the claim. (p. 402)
- Use *warrants by sign* when the topic allows you to infer that such a close relationship exists between two variables that the presence or absence of

one may be taken as an indication of the presence or absence of the other. (p. 403)

- Use *warrants by analogy* when the topic allows you to compare two similar cases and infer that what is true in one case is true in the other. (p. 404)

Anticipate and Plan on Addressing Counterarguments to Your Position

- If you ignore obvious counterclaims to your position, you may lose credibility. (p. 404)

Beware of Logical Fallacies That Will Weaken Your Arguments

- Avoid *begging the question,* or using circular reasoning to state an argument in such a way that it cannot help but be true. (p. 405)
- Do not rely on popular opinion as evidence that your claim is true (*bandwagoning*). (p. 405)
- Avoid framing your argument as an either-or proposition (*either-or fallacy*). (p. 406)
- Avoid *ad hominem arguments* that attack an opponent instead of attacking the opponent's arguments. (p. 406)
- Avoid relying on irrelevant information to argue your point (*red herring fallacy*). (p. 406)
- Avoid using an isolated instance to make an unwarranted general conclusion (*hasty generalization*). (p. 406)
- Avoid offering conclusions that do not connect to your reasoning (*non sequitur*). (p. 406)
- Avoid claiming that something is true by stating that one example or case will inevitably lead to a series of events or actions (*slippery slope*). (p. 407)
- Avoid *appeals to tradition.* (p. 407)

26. Organizing the Persuasive Speech

Select an Organizational Pattern Based on Your Argument, Audience, and Speech Goal

- Choose a pattern that works with your particular argument and evidence. (p. 408)
- Choose a pattern that will help you appeal to the target audience. (p. 409)
- Consider the refutation or problem-solution pattern for a hostile or a critical and conflicted audience. (p. 409)
- Consider the narrative pattern for sympathetic listeners. (p. 410)

- For an uninformed, less educated, or apathetic audience, focus on gaining listeners' attention and establishing credibility. Consider arranging points logically in a topical pattern. (p. 410)
- Choose a pattern that will help you elicit the reaction you seek from your audience (your *specific speech purpose*). (p. 410)

Use the Problem-Solution Pattern to Demonstrate the Nature of a Problem and Provide Justification for a Solution

- Define the problem and offer a solution (*problem-solution*). (p. 411)
- Define the problem, cite reasons for the problem, and offer a solution (*problem-cause-solution*). (p. 411)

Consider the Motivated Sequence Pattern When Urging Action

- Step 1: *Attention* — address listeners' core concerns. (p. 412)
- Step 2: *Need* — show listeners they have a need or problem that must be satisfied or solved. (p. 413)
- Step 3: *Satisfaction* — introduce the solution to the problem. (p. 413)
- Step 4: *Visualization* — provide a vision of outcomes associated with the solution. (p. 414)
- Step 5: *Action* — make a direct request of listeners. (p. 415)

If the Audience Is Already Aware of an Issue and Agrees That It Should Be Addressed, Consider the Comparative Advantage Pattern

- Determine alternatives to the problem — both pro and con to your position — that the audience will be aware of. (p. 415)
- Organize points to favorably compare your position to alternatives. (p. 416)
- The summary should include brief but compelling evidence demonstrating the superiority or comparative advantage of your option over competing ones. (p. 416)

If Listeners Disagree with You or Are Conflicted, Consider the Refutation Pattern

- State the opposing claim. (p. 417)
- Explain the ramifications of the opposing claim. (p. 417)
- Present your argument and the evidence. (p. 417)
- Show the superiority of your claim through contrast. (p. 417)

27. Special Occasion Speeches

Identify the Primary Purpose of Your Special Occasion Speech

- Is it to *entertain* the audience? (p. 437)
- Is it to *celebrate* or recognize a person, a place, or an event? (p. 437)

- Is it to *commemorate* a person, a place, or an event? (p. 438)
- Is it to *inspire* your listeners? (p. 438)
- Is it to establish or reinforce the goals and values of the group sponsoring the event (*setting a social agenda*)? (p. 438)

Focus Your Speech of Introduction on Motivating the Audience to Listen to the Speaker

- Establish the speaker's credibility by describing relevant facts about his or her background and qualifications for speaking. (p. 439)
- Briefly describe the speaker's topic and establish its relevance to the audience. (p. 439)
- Keep your remarks brief. (p. 439)

Focus Your Speech of Acceptance on Expressing Gratitude for the Honor Bestowed on You

- If you know that you are to receive an award or suspect that you may be honored, prepare the speech in advance. (p. 441)
- Let the audience know what the award means to you. (p. 441)
- Express yourself genuinely and with humility. (p. 441)
- Thank each of the individuals or organizations involved in giving you the award. (p. 442)
- Acknowledge others who helped you attain the achievement. (p. 442)

Focus Your Speech of Presentation on Explaining the Award and the Reason It Is Being Bestowed on the Recipient

- Explain what the award represents. (p. 442)
- Explain why the recipient is receiving the award. (p. 443)

Focus Remarks Made at Roasts and Toasts on the Person Being Honored

- For a roast, prepare a humorous tribute to the person. (p. 443)
- For a toast, pay brief tribute to the person or event. (p. 444)
- Prepare your remarks in advance. (p. 444)
- Rehearse any jokes in advance. (p. 444)
- Keep within your time limits. (p. 444)

When Delivering a Eulogy, Pay Tribute to the Life of the Deceased

- Stay in control of your emotions. (p. 444)
- Refer to each family member of the deceased by name. (p. 445)
- Focus on the person's life rather than on the circumstances of death. (p. 445)
- Emphasize the person's positive qualities. (p. 445)

When Delivering an After-Dinner Speech, Balance Insight and Entertainment

- Begin by recognizing the occasion and linking it to your theme. (p. 446)
- Avoid stand-up comedy. Use humor that is consistent with your personality. (p. 446)
- When addressing serious issues and causes, keep an eye on the audience's comfort level. (p. 447)

Focus Your Speech of Inspiration on Uplifting the Audience

- Seek to arouse the audience's better instincts. (p. 447)
- Focus on creating positive speaker ethos (see Chapter 5). (p. 447)
- Appeal to the audience's emotions through vivid descriptions and emotionally charged words. Consider the use of repetition, alliteration, and parallelism (see Chapter 16). (p. 447)
- Consider using real-life stories and examples. (p. 447)
- Strive for a dynamic delivery style. (p. 448)
- Clearly establish your speech goal. (p. 448)
- Consider using an acronym to organize your message. (p. 448)
- Make your conclusion strong. (p. 449)

KEY TERMS

Chapter 23

informative speaking	definition by example	analogies
preview statement	definition by synonym	learning styles
operational definition	definition by etymology	
definition by negation	(word origin)	

Chapter 24

persuasion	minor premise	ethos
persuasive speaking	deductive reasoning	Maslow's hierarchy of needs
rhetorical proofs	inductive reasoning	expectancy-outcome values theory
logos	hasty overgeneralization	
reasoning	enthymeme	elaboration likelihood model of persuasion (ELM)
syllogism	pathos	
general case	demagogue	central processing
major premise	fear appeal	peripheral processing
specific case	propaganda	speaker credibility

Speaker's Reference

Chapter 25

argument	cultural premises	begging the question
claim	motivational warrants	bandwagoning
evidence	authoritative warrants	either-or fallacy
warrants	substantive warrants	ad hominem argument
claims of fact	warrants by cause	red herring fallacy
speculative claims	warrants by sign	hasty generalization
claims of value	warrants by analogy	non sequitur
claims of policy	inoculation effect	slippery slope
cultural norms	logical fallacy	appeal to tradition

Chapter 26

claim of policy	sympathetic audience	motivated sequence pattern of arrangement
claim of value	uninformed, less educated, or apathetic audience	comparative advantage pattern of arrangement
claim of fact	specific speech purpose	refutation pattern of arrangement
target audience	problem-solution pattern of arrangement	
hostile audience or one that strongly disagrees	problem-cause-solution pattern of arrangement	
critical and conflicted audience		

Chapter 27

special occasion speech	roast	canned speeches
speech of introduction	toast	social agenda–setting
speech of acceptance	eulogy	sermons
speech of presentation	after-dinner speech	speech of inspiration

The Informative Speech 23

Ever wondered how to prune a tree so that it will flower profusely the following year? Or which careers will be most financially rewarding in the next decade? What are the facts about outsourcing? Exactly where are the jobs going, and which jobs are likely to remain in the United States? What about the difference between a stock and a bond? What is a nebula, and how is one formed?

Informative speaking about these and countless other topics is one of the primary ways in which we share knowledge and keep abreast of ideas and events. In the guise of the classroom lecture, you've been exposed to informative speaking since grade school. Beyond the classroom, managers gather employees to explain new procedures and generate enthusiasm for new projects. Researchers report and explain their findings to their colleagues and to the press, while authorities on everything from team sports to terrorism share their expertise from the podium.

Goals and Strategies of Informative Speaking

 WEB Chapter quizzes

To *inform* is to communicate knowledge. The goal of **informative speaking** is to increase the audience's awareness and understanding by imparting knowledge. Informative speeches provide an audience with new information, new insights, or new ways of thinking about a topic. As an informative speaker, you might introduce listeners to new ideas, events, people, places, or processes. You might explain information with which listeners have some familiarity but little real understanding, thereby shaping their perceptions. Your speech might be an in-depth analysis of a complex subject, a simple description of an event, or a physical demonstration of how something works. As long as your audience learns something, the options are nearly limitless.

LOOK FOR WAYS TO INCREASE UNDERSTANDING

People are not simply empty vessels into which you can pour facts and figures and expect them to recognize and remember all that information. Before we can retain information, we must be motivated to listen to it and be able to recognize and comprehend it.[1] Many of the public speaking principles described in previous chapters directly apply to presenting information in a speech. For example, Chapter 8 discusses how to flesh out speech points with compelling supporting materials, such as examples, stories, opinions, and facts. Chapter 16 demonstrates ways you can use language to connect to your audience and help listeners to visualize ideas; it also demonstrates how rhetorical devices such as repetition and parallelism can reinforce information and drive home key themes. Other aspects of speechmaking covered in previous chapters that are necessary ingredients for an effective informative speech include:

- *A well-organized introduction that previews the main points* (see Chapter 14) and a conclusion that concisely summarizes them (see Chapter 15).
- *Clear transitions.* Signal words, phrases, and sentences that tie speech ideas together to help listeners follow the speaker's points (see Chapter 11).
- *An appropriate organizational pattern.* Audience members' understanding of a speech is directly linked to how well it is organized (see Chapters 11–13 and 26).[2]
- *Controlled vocal delivery.* Crucial to communicating any oral message is speaking slowly and clearly enough to permit listeners to process the words (see Chapter 18).
- *Presentation aids.* People process and retain information best when it is reinforced visually and otherwise (see Chapters 20–22).[3]

 CHECKLIST

Help Listeners Process and Retain Information

✓ Make ample use of transitions to help guide listeners.
✓ Concisely preview main points in the introduction and summarize them in the conclusion.
✓ Control your vocal delivery.
✓ Reinforce your message visually and otherwise where appropriate.

DIFFERENTIATE BETWEEN INFORMING AND PERSUADING

The goal of an informative speech stands in contrast to that of the persuasive speech, which explicitly attempts to influence people's attitudes, values, beliefs, or behavior about an issue. Whereas a persuasive speech would seek to modify attitudes or ask the audience to adopt a specific position, an informative speech stops short of this. Yet scholars of public speaking point out that there is no such thing as a purely informative or persuasive speech; that is, there are always elements of persuasion in an informative speech, and vice versa. Rarely are we entirely dispassionate about a subject, especially one that tends to elicit strong reactions. Nevertheless, if you keep in mind the general informative speaking goal, you will be able to deliver an informative speech whose primary function is to enlighten rather than to advocate.

GAUGE THE AUDIENCE'S INFORMATIONAL NEEDS

An understanding of audience members and the factors that affect them is critical to delivering an effective informative speech. Listeners must be able to identify with the topic, see its relevance to their lives, and follow it to its logical conclusion. They must see how they can use and benefit from the information you give them. To ensure that this occurs, you will need to gauge what your listeners already know about a topic as well as what they want and need to know about it (see Chapter 6).

DEMONSTRATE THE TOPIC'S RELEVANCE EARLY ON

Whenever possible, early on in your speech (in your **preview statement**, for example) tell audience members why they should listen to you. Do this by pointing out how what they will learn from your presentation will benefit them. Giving listeners a reason to care can motivate them to pay attention to your message.

PREVIEW MAIN POINTS

Give listeners a sense of the whole before plunging into particulars, and offer them specific signposts they can follow (see Chapter 11). In the introduction, preview your main points and summarize what you want them to gain from the speech:

> I'll begin by defining what the music industry means by "pirating." Next I will discuss the Supreme Court's ruling in *MGM v. Grokster*. . . . By the end of this presentation, I hope that you will. . . .

PRESENT NEW AND INTERESTING INFORMATION

Audiences seek knowledge, which means learning something new. To satisfy this drive, try to uncover information that is fresh and compelling. Seek out unusual sources (but make certain they are credible), novel (but sound) interpretations, startling facts, compelling examples, and moving stories. As professional speaker Vickie K. Sullivan notes:

> The first point that transforms an ordinary speaker into an industry beacon is a new perspective on a major problem. . . . If the speech does not convey provocative information, audience members feel their time has been wasted (and rightfully will feel offended). They expect their thinking to be challenged.[4]

Types of Informative Speeches

Informative speeches are sometimes categorized according to the subject matter they address. Thus an informative speech may be about objects or phenomena, people, events, processes, issues, or concepts. These are not hard-and-fast divisions — a speech can be about both the process of dance and the people who perform it, for example — but they show the range of informative subjects and may point you in the direction of a suitable organizational pattern (see the section on organizing the informative speech on pages 362–363).

SPEECHES ABOUT OBJECTS OR PHENOMENA

Speeches about objects or phenomena explore anything that isn't human; it can be animate, as in the animal kingdom, or inanimate, as in skis or skates. Topics for such speeches run the gamut from ribbons used to raise awareness about diseases such as breast cancer and AIDS to therapy dogs and the musical score for *Spamalot*. Phenomena such as the history of lacrosse as a sport and the evolution of "Texas English" also belong to this broad category.

SPEECHES ABOUT PEOPLE

Speeches about people inform audiences about historically significant individuals and groups, those who have made contributions to society (both positive and negative) or those who for one reason or another we simply find compelling. Who are the Lost Boys of Sudan, and why are they noteworthy? What led Mother Teresa to devote her life to the poor?

Rather than focusing on someone's fame, the key to giving an effective speech about a person is sharing stories that resonate with the audience. People are naturally curious about others, but they also need a reason to care. Often this need can be met by recounting anecdotes or extended stories that stress the person's achievements and human qualities (see Chapter 8).

SPEECHES ABOUT EVENTS

Speeches about events focus on noteworthy occurrences, past and present. What led up to the 1952 proclamation of Puerto Rico as a commonwealth? What occurred at the battle of Puebla in 1862 that led to victory of the Mexican army over the French and is celebrated today as Cinco de Mayo? Speeches about events can have any number of specific purposes. One speaker may wish to paint a vivid picture or description of what it was like to narrowly escape an avalanche while on a snowmobile. Another speech on the same topic might focus more on the incidences of avalanches in the United States, their major causes, and ways to safeguard against them.

SPEECHES ABOUT PROCESSES

Speeches about processes refer to a series of steps that lead to a finished product or end result. In this type of speech you can talk about how something is done, how it is made, or how it works. Sample speech topics might include how a hybrid car works or finishing furniture.

When discussing a process, you will probably have one of two purposes. One is to explain how something works or develops. How will the male birth-control pill work? How do baby penguins develop? The other is to actually teach audience members to perform the process. Such topics might include how to share an electronic photo album online, make salsa at home, or interview for a job.

When describing how to do something, speakers often perform the actual task during the speech, demonstrating each step as they describe it. When it is not possible to perform the task, visual or audio aids may be used to illustrate the steps involved. Visual aids are also essential in explaining processes. To illustrate how to make a Shaker-style table, for example, you might use drawings or photographs showing the table at various stages of construction.

To see the nearly infinite number of processes that can be used as the basis of a speech of demonstration, visit Wikipedia's "how-to" Web site and Google's eHow.com. Both may be found at www.ehow.com. For ideas about visually showing how things work, see HowStuffWorks at www.howstuffworks.com.

SPEECHES ABOUT ISSUES

An *issue* is a problem or a matter in dispute, one that people seek to bring to a conclusion. Informative *speeches about issues* provide an overview or a report of problems in order to increase understanding and awareness. Pornography on the Internet and teaching alternative theories to evolution are examples of issues that might be addressed in an informative speech.

Of the various types of informative speeches, speeches about issues have the greatest potential of "crossing the line" into the persuasive realm. Yet as long as your goal is to inform rather than to advocate, you can legitimately address issues in an informative speech. Thus, in a speech on teenage pregnancy, you might define the nature of the problem and describe the various positions people take with respect to it. Such a speech might also offer explanations of why teenage pregnancy occurs. On the other hand, you would refrain from attributing teenage pregnancy to one cause (such as premarital sex) and advocating one solution to it (such as abstinence).

SPEECHES ABOUT CONCEPTS

Speeches about concepts focus on abstract or complex ideas or theories and attempt to make them concrete and understandable to an audience. What is chaos theory? What is art? Is it a child's drawing, a master's painting, or both? We've heard the term *hate speech*, but we're confused because it seems to encompass everything from racist expressions to racist actions.

Listeners may not be able to see a concept, but a good speaker can deftly evoke its meaning by associating it with certain actions or behaviors. In describing anxiety, for example, the speaker might describe the increased heart rate and distressed facial expressions that accompany the condition. Because they address abstract or complex ideas, speeches about concepts have the potential to confuse audience members. To ensure that this does not occur, follow the guidelines in "Strategies for Reducing Confusion" later in this chapter (p. 359).

Approaches to Conveying Information WEB Video quizzes

Typically, speakers communicate information by defining, describing, demonstrating, and/or explaining. Some informative speeches rely almost exclusively on a single approach (e.g., their main purpose is to demonstrate how something works or to describe what something is). Many speeches, however, employ a combination of strategies in a single presentation. Table 23.1 contains sample

TABLE 23.1 • Types of Informative Speeches, Sample Topics, and Selected Informational Strategies		
Subject Matter	**Sample Topics**	**Informational Strategy** (*definition, description, demonstration, explanation*)
Speeches about objects or phenomena	• Digital cameras • Texas English • Comparison of weight-loss diets • El Niño wind patterns in the western U.S.	*Define* and *describe* the object or phenomenon in question. Depending on your specific speech purpose, either conclude at that point or continue with an in-depth *explanation* or a *demonstration* of the object or phenomenon.
Speeches about people	• Athletes • Authors • Inventors • Political leaders • Soldiers • War or hurricane refugees	Paint a vivid picture of your subject using *description*. Use *explanation* to address the person's (or group's) significance.
Speeches about events	• The New York and Berlin, Germany runners' marathons • Democratic or Republican national conventions • Battle of Gettysburg • National College Cheerleading Finals	Use *description* to paint a vivid picture. Use *explanation* to analyze the meaning of the event.
Speeches about processes	• Isolating DNA in cells • How lightning forms • How the thyroid regulates metabolism • How to practice Power Yoga • Using visualization in sports	If physically showing a process, rely on *demonstration*. If explaining a process, vary strategies as needed.
Speeches about issues	• Racial profiling • Alternative theories to evolution • Politics in the Middle East • Outsourcing • Climate change • No Child Left Behind legislation	Focus on *description* and *explanation*.
Speeches about concepts	• Einstein's theory of relativity • Artificial intelligence • Fractals • Nanotechnology • Free speech	Focus on clear *definitions* and *explanations;* the more difficult a concept is, the more ways you will want to define and explain it. Vivid *description* can also be useful.

topics and strategies for different types of informative speeches. As you prepare your speech, ask yourself, "By which of these means can I best convey my ideas?"

DEFINITION

Informative speaking often involves defining information. When you define information, you identify the essential qualities and meaning of something. What is a fractal? What is cholesterol? What does "equilibrium price" mean in business studies? Many informative speeches focus on questions such as these, addressing the meaning of a new or complex concept. A speaker might choose to define a new software program to a group of colleagues; a corporate spokesperson might define the Americans with Disabilities Act to the heads of various divisions within a company.

You might also select definition when clarifying a complex or controversial idea or issue. For example, many of us are aware that prayer in the public schools has been ruled unconstitutional, but precisely how does the Constitution or its amendments define prayer?

Defining information may sound straightforward, but there are in fact a number of ways to define something, including the following:

- **Operational definition:** Defines something by explaining what it does. For example: "A computer is something that processes information."
- **Definition by negation:** Defines something by describing what it is not. For example: "Courage is not the absence of fear."
- **Definition by example:** Defines something by providing several concrete examples of it. For example: "Health professionals include doctors, nurses, EMTs, and ambulance drivers."
- **Definition by synonym:** Defines something by comparing it to something with which it is synonymous. For example: "A friend is a comrade or a buddy."
- **Definition by etymology (word origin):** Defines something by illustrating the root meaning of the word in question. For example, "Our word *rival*

 CHECKLIST

Define Your Terms

Clear definitions are especially important in informative speeches. If you are unsure whether audience members will know the meaning of a term, plan to define it in one or more of the following ways:

✓ Define your term by explaining what it does.

✓ Define your term by describing what it is not.

✓ Define your term by providing several concrete examples of it.

✓ Define your term by comparing it with something with which it is synonymous.

✓ Define your term by illustrating the root meaning of the term.

derives from the French word, which in turn derives from the Latin word *rivalis*. The original meaning of *rivalis* is 'one living near or using the same stream.' "[5]

DESCRIPTION

When you describe information, you provide an array of details that paint a mental picture of your topic. You may be recounting a bullfight in Pamplona, Spain, or describing the physical ravages wrought by drug abuse. Regardless of the specific subject, the point of speeches relying on description is to offer a vivid portrayal of the topic.

While all types of speeches involve description, some speeches focus on this task more centrally than others. For example, the goal of your speech of description might be to offer your audience a "virtual tour" of the top of Mount Everest, the 1937 World's Fair in Paris, or a painting by Pablo Picasso.

DEMONSTRATION

Yet another approach to presenting information is to explain how something works or to actually demonstrate it. The many "how to" shows on television, ranging from cooking to carpentry, rely on demonstration. Speech topics such as "childproofing your home" or "bidding on eBay" may not include an actual physical demonstration, but the speaker will nevertheless verbally demonstrate the steps involved. Speeches that rely on demonstration often work with the actual object, representations or models of it, or visual aids that diagram it. Table 23.2 contains sample topics for a speech of demonstration.

EXPLANATION

Explanation goes beyond simple clarification of terms or concepts or a description of them. When you explain something, you provide reasons or causes, demonstrate relationships, and offer interpretation and analysis. The classic example of explaining information is the classroom lecture (see Chapter 30). But many kinds of speeches rely on explanation, from those that address

---

TABLE 23.2 • Sample Topics for a Speech of Demonstration

• Mastering the position of attention for a military drill	• Performing the Heimlich maneuver on infants
• Treating a burn	• Pulling a shot of espresso
• Posting videos on YouTube	• Drawing blood from an animal
• Stippling a wall	• Performing an emergency tracheotomy
• Marbleizing furniture	• Making stained glass
• Raising ducks	• Using Adobe Photoshop Elements
• Giving an insulin shot	• Doing genealogy on the Web
• Programming an iPhone	

difficult or confusing theories and processes to ideas that challenge conventional thinking. What is the relationship between the glycemic index, which measures how quickly a carbohydrate raises blood sugar, and glycemic load? Why do researchers say that sometimes emotion makes us more rather than less logical?

See the checklist on p. 361 for strategies for explaining complex processes.

✓ **CHECKLIST**

Use the Power of Language to Connect with the Audience

_____ 1. Use concrete and colorful nouns and verbs that convey your meaning in a specific and tangible way.

_____ 2. Use repetition to help listeners retain information.

_____ 3. Appeal to listeners' sense of smell, taste, sight, hearing, and touch.

_____ 4. Use _similes_ — figures of speech that compare one thing to another (see Chapter 16).

_____ 5. Use _metaphors_ — figures of speech that compare two things by describing one thing as being the other (see Chapter 16).

Strategies for Reducing Confusion

New information can be hard to grasp, so if your topic has the potential for confusion, consider why this might be so. Generally, audience members tend to find information daunting for one or more of the following reasons:[6]

1. The information entails _difficult concepts or terms;_ for example, concepts such as _equilibrium_ in engineering, _liability_ in business, or _tectonics_ in geology.

2. The information involves a _difficult-to-envision process or structure;_ for example, the _process of cloning_ in science, _cash flow management_ in business, or _structure of DNA._

3. The information involves a _counterintuitive idea,_ one that challenges accepted ways of thinking about things. Many scientific concepts challenge common-sense thinking and are hard to grasp; for example, that seemingly solid materials are made of tiny atoms and mostly empty space or that medical studies indicate that drinking one glass of red wine a day is healthy.

Useful for any informative speech, the following strategies are especially helpful when attempting to clarify complex ideas.

USE ANALOGIES TO BUILD ON PRIOR KNOWLEDGE

It is easier to understand a new concept if we can relate it to something that we already know. Indeed, the process of learning itself is sometimes defined as constructing new knowledge from prior knowledge.[7] Explanations that link the unfamiliar with the familiar often take the form of **analogies** (see Chapter 16). For example, to explain the unpredictable paths that satellites often take when they fall to Earth, one speaker likened the phenomenon to dropping a penny into water: "Sometimes it goes straight down, and sometimes it turns end over end and changes direction. The same thing happens when an object hits the atmosphere."[8]

Speakers will sometimes organize part or even all of a speech around an analogy. When explaining how the thyroid functions, for instance, you could liken it to a conductor directing a symphony (the body).[9] Bear in mind, however, that no analogy can exactly represent another concept; at a certain point, the similarities will end.[10] Therefore, you may need to alert listeners to the limits of the comparison. The statement "The heart is like a pump, *except that the heart actually changes size as it pushes blood out*" demonstrates that, though similar, a heart and a pump are not the same.[11]

Analogies, as well as metaphors and similes (see Chapter 16), can help establish a common ground of understanding. Once this occurs, your listeners will have an easier time venturing into new territory, especially if the information you present is counterintuitive.

In the following excerpt from a speech about nanotechnology, Wolfgang Porod explains the size of a nanometer by comparing it to the diameter of the moon. Note how he attempts to reduce confusion by first defining the root *nano* and then comparing it to the size of the moon:

> What is a nano and what is special about a nano? *Nano* is a prefix derived from the Greek word for dwarf and it means one billionth of something. So a nanosecond is a billionth of a second. A nanometer is a billionth of a meter. Now, just saying that doesn't really tell you that much. So what does it mean to have the length scale of a billionth of a meter? Well, imagine the diameter of the moon. It just happens to be, roughly . . . a billion meters. So take that and shrink it down to the length scale of a meter, which is what it means to go a billion size scales. So a nanometer is a billionth of a meter.[12]

DEMONSTRATE UNDERLYING CAUSES

Oftentimes listeners will fail to understand a process because they lack an understanding of its underlying causes. They may believe that something "obviously" works a certain way when in fact it does not. To counter faulty assumptions, first acknowledge common misperceptions and then offer an accurate explanation or causal model.[13]

CHECK FOR UNDERSTANDING

When the speech goal is explanation, audience feedback, always important, becomes even more so. Be alert to nonverbal signals, such as blank stares, that indicate a lack of focus. Don't be afraid to solicit feedback with queries such as "Are you with me?" or "How am I doing?" Direct the question to

---

CHECKLIST

Strategies for Explaining Complex Information

To explain a concept or term:

✓   Build on prior knowledge.
✓   Use analogies that link concepts to something familiar.
✓   Define terms in several ways (e.g., by example, by what it is not).
✓   Simplify terminology wherever possible.
✓   Check for understanding.

To explain a complex process or structure:

✓   All of the above, and:
✓   Make ample use of visual aids, including models and drawings.

To explain a counterintuitive idea:

✓   All of the above, and:
✓   Address the commonly held assumption first, acknowledge its plausibility, and then demonstrate its limitations using familiar examples.

---

the group rather than to one individual; this will ensure that no one feels singled out.

APPEAL TO DIFFERENT LEARNING STYLES

Audience members are more likely to follow your points if you reinforce them visually and, when appropriate, with sound and actual demonstrations. The reason for this is that people have different **learning styles**, or preferred ways of processing information. One learning theory model suggests four such preferences: visual, aural, read/write, and kinesthetic.[14] *Visual learners* will most quickly grasp ideas by viewing visual explanations of them, either through pictures, diagrams, slides, or videos. Understanding for *aural learners* comes most easily through the spoken word, by hearing and speaking. *Read/write learners* are most comfortable processing information that is text-based. *Kinesthetic learners* learn best by experiencing information directly, through real-life demonstrations, simulations, and hands-on experience. Some of us are *multimodal learners*, in that we combine two or more preferences.

Audience analysis can sometimes give you a sense of the types of learners in an audience. For example, it has been shown that mechanics of all types have strong spatial visualization abilities and thus would be classified as visual learners; they may also be kinesthetic learners who want to "test" things for themselves. Often, however, you may not have enough information to

TABLE 23.3 • Different Learning Styles			
Visual	**Aural**	**Read/Write**	**Kinesthetic**
Most easily grasps ideas communicated through pictures, diagrams, charts, graphs, flowcharts, maps.	Most easily grasps ideas communicated through the spoken word, either in live lectures, tapes, group discussions, Webcasts.	Most easily grasps ideas communicated through text-based delivery, handouts, PowerPoint with text-based slides.	Most easily grasps ideas communicated through real-life demonstrations, simulations, and movies, and through hands-on applications.

determine your listeners' learning styles. For this reason, plan on conveying and reinforcing information in a variety of modes. Use charts, diagrams, and other visual representations of ideas to appeal to visual learners. Use colorful and concrete language and strong examples and stories that will engage aural listeners. Prepare text-based slides containing main ideas (but beware of crowding; see p. 318), and, if appropriate, consider distributing handouts at the end of your speech. Use demonstration to appeal to kinesthetic learners. Table 23.3 offers guidelines for presenting information to different types of learners.

Organizing the Informative Speech

Informative speeches can be organized using any of the patterns described in Chapters 12 and 26, including the topical, chronological, spatial, cause-effect, comparative advantage, circular, and narrative patterns. (Note that although the problem-solution pattern may be used in informative speeches, it often is a more logical candidate for persuasive speeches.)

There are any number of ways to organize the various types of informative speeches. A speech about the Impressionist movement in painting, for example, could be organized *chronologically,* in which main points are arranged in sequence from the movement's early period to its later falling out of favor. It could be organized *causally* (cause-effect), by demonstrating that it came about as a reaction to the art movement that preceded it. It could also be organized *topically* (by categories), by focusing on the major figures associated with the movement, famous paintings linked to it, and notable contemporary artists who painted in the style.

Following are some possible pairings of speech types and organizational patterns:

Objects — spatial, topical

People — topical, narrative, chronological

Events — topical, chronological, causal, narrative

Processes — chronological, spatial, causal

Concepts — topical, causal, circular

Issues — topical, chronological, causal, circular

In a speech describing how to buy a guitar, Richard Garza organizes his main points chronologically:

THESIS STATEMENT: Buying and caring for a guitar involves knowing what to look for when purchasing it and understanding how to maintain it once you own it.

MAIN POINTS: I.   Decide what kind of guitar you need.
                           II. Inspect the guitar for potential flaws.
                           III. Maintain the guitar.

In a student speech on using radiofrequency waves to cure cancer, David Kruckenberg organizes his main points topically, dividing his points by categories:

THESIS STATEMENT: An engineer outside of the medical establishment discovers how to refine a medical procedure called radiofrequency ablation, potentially making it a critical tool in the fight against certain kinds of cancer.

MAIN POINTS: I.   Radiofrequency ablation, as currently practiced to treat cancer, poses risks to patients.
                           II. John Kanzius' invention uses nanoparticles to improve upon radiofrequency ablation.
                           III. Kanzius' discovery is currently being tested in several large medical research centers.

 CHECKLIST

Guidelines for Clearly Communicating Your Informative Message

✓ In your introduction, tell audience members what you hope they will learn by listening to you.
✓ Stress the topic's relevance to your listeners.
✓ Use definition, description, explanation, and demonstration to convey your ideas.
✓ Use analogies to make your examples familiar to the audience.
✓ Choose an organizational pattern based on your communication goals, the nature of your topic, and the needs of your audience.
✓ Use presentation aids to reinforce your points.

Sample Speech of Demonstration

An Ounce of Prevention Keeps the Germs Away

CHRISTIE COLLINS

University of Oklahoma

In this speech of demonstration, student Christie Collins uses the chronological pattern of organization to take listeners step by step through the process of proper handwashing.

[*PUT ON RUBBER GLOVES*] Do you ever feel like you need to wear these when you go into the bathroom? I know I do! • According to a 2007 study commissioned by the American Society of Microbiology, researchers lurking in public restrooms discovered a nasty truth: Americans do not always wash up after using the toilet.

> • By putting on rubber gloves, the speaker effectively captures the audience's attention in the introduction.

The society's national survey found that 92 percent of a representative sample of 1,000 men and women surveyed by telephone claim to wash their hands after using the restroom. However, direct observation of more than 6,067 people (half males and half females) in four major U.S. cities revealed that only 77 percent really do so. Men are the worst culprits. Researchers said that only one-third of the males they observed washed their hands in public restrooms. Women fared better, with 88 percent hitting the sinks. •

Hand washing is a critical factor in the spread of food-borne illnesses, colds, flu, and other diseases. • After extensive research and because I am somewhat of a cleaning freak, I have become a master at the art of hand washing. Today, I will be discussing the importance of hand washing, as well as the proper hand-washing technique. •

> • The topic may be time-worn, but the speaker presents new and interesting information about it.
>
> • The speaker demonstrates the topic's relevance and previews the main points of the speech.
>
> • The speaker provides a transition into the body of the speech.

If you really think about it, we live in a very dirty world. Homes, offices, restaurants, classrooms, or just about anywhere you can think of, are all breeding grounds for those pesky little germs. Handle raw, uncooked food, shake someone's hand, take change from a clerk, or turn a doorknob and suddenly you have picked up a host of germs that can make you or others around you sick. For example, almost everyone has experienced a food-borne illness at some point in time. According to the Centers for Disease Control and Prevention (CDC), each year food-borne illnesses kill up to 5,000 people. •

Annually, a whopping 76 million of us get some sort of food-borne sickness. Along with incomplete cooking and washing of foods, dirty hands are an important factor in spreading the bacteria that lead to food-borne illnesses.

Washing your hands is also an important step in preventing colds, flu, infectious diarrhea, and some pretty serious diseases like hepatitis A and meningitis. One of the most common ways people catch colds, for instance, is by rubbing their nose or eyes after their hands have been contaminated with a cold virus. You can lessen the odds of infection by avoiding touching your eyes, nose, and mouth with dirty fingers.

Failure to wash hands after handling money or using a pen or pencil picked up in a public place is common. According to the study sponsored by the American Society of Microbiologists, only 25 percent of us report washing our hands after touching money; fewer still even think about washing their hands after using someone else's writing implement. •

The most important thing that you can do to keep from getting a cold, as well as to keep from contracting more serious illnesses, is to wash your hands. • By frequently washing your hands, you wash away germs that you have picked up from other people, from contaminated surfaces, or from animals.

How do I wash my hands properly, you ask? The procedure, according to the Center for Disease Control and Prevention, is as follows: •

[*PICK UP SOAP AND MOVE NEAR BASIN*] First, you wet your hands with warm running water.

Apply soap. Liquid or bar soap is OK, but liquid soap is easier, and the new antibacterial soaps may provide added protection in food preparation and

• The speaker supports her points with a fact from the CDC.

• Again the speaker offers new information.

• The speaker shows how the information can benefit the audience (e.g., by allowing listeners to stay healthier).

• The speaker physically demonstrates proper procedures.

during illness. If you do use a liquid soap, you'll need to disinfect the container each time before you refill it. If you are using a bar soap, it should be kept in a self-draining holder that is cleaned thoroughly to get rid of bacteria before new bars are put out.

Using gentle friction, vigorously rub hands together, making a soapy lather. Do this away from the water for about twenty seconds, being careful not to wash the lather away. One common bit of advice is to lather as long as it takes to sing "Happy Birthday" to yourself twice. • Make sure you wash the front and back of your hands, as well as between your fingers, your knuckles, and under your fingernails.

• The speaker offers memorable advice by suggesting listeners sing while handwashing.

Rinse your hands well under warm running water. Let the water run back into the sink, not down into your elbows.

Turn off the faucet with a paper towel and dispose of it in a proper receptacle. Remember that you turned the water on with dirty hands, so a barrier such as a paper towel between your clean hands and the faucet prevents resoiling your hands. This is very important in public restrooms!

Dry hands thoroughly with a clean paper towel. To prevent chapping, pat rather than rub hands dry and apply lotion liberally and frequently.

[*WALK TO DOOR AND HOLD DOORKNOB*] • When exiting the restroom, use a paper towel to open the door. Remember the figures I cited earlier? If only one-third of men and women wash their hands in public restrooms, a lot of dirty hands are touching those knobs! Putting a barrier between your hands and the doorknob will prevent the recontamination of your hands.

• The speaker again physically demonstrates her point.

If there is no soap or water available, there are other alternatives. For example, you can use an antibacterial, waterless hand sanitizer, such as Purel brand Instant Hand Sanitizer. You can use the larger bottle at home or maybe on your desk at work. The small bottles fit very nicely in a purse, pocket, tackle box, or glove compartment.

You can also use moist towelettes that contain an antibacterial agent, such as the Wet Ones brand. These can be conveniently kept in a purse or pocket.

You can find these moderately priced hand sanitizers or towelettes in most supermarkets, drugstores, or department stores.

Washing your hands regularly can certainly save a lot of medical bills. • Because it costs less than a penny, you could say that this penny's worth of prevention could save you a 150 dollar visit to the doctor.

• The speaker points to another benefit to the audience, offering yet another new insight on a familiar process.

Now that you understand the importance of hand washing and how to properly wash your hands, practice and teach the proper hand-washing techniques to others, especially children, so that they too can form a good habit of hand washing. •

It's a simple fact. When hand washing is done correctly, it is the number-one means of preventing the spread of infection. • You don't have to take these rubber gloves into the public restroom with you. You just have to follow these simple steps. Doing so will make the world a healthier place for everyone.

• The speaker signals the close of the speech.

• The speaker concludes by reiterating the importance of hand washing.

Works Cited

"Clean Hands Saves Lives!" Centers for Disease Control and Prevention. www.cdc.gov/cleanhands (accessed November 6, 2007).

"Foodborne Illnesses Factsheet." Division of Bacterial and Mycotic Diseases. Centers for Disease Control and Prevention. www.cdc.gov/ncidod/dbmd/diseaseinfo/foodborneinfections_g.htm#howmanycases (accessed November 6, 2007).

"Harris Interactive 2007 Handwashing Survey Fact Sheet." American Society for Microbiology. www.asm.org (accessed November 8, 2007).

Lawhorn, Chad. "KU Prof Touts Hand Washing to Prevent Infectious Diseases." *Lawrence Journal-World*. September 25, 2007. www2.ljworld.com/news/2007/sep/25/ku_prof_touts_hand_washing_prevent_infectious_dise/ (accessed November 6, 2007).

Sample Visually Annotated Informative Speech

WEB ▶ Video

John Kanzius and the Quest to Cure Cancer

DAVID KRUCKENBERG
Santiago Canyon College

In this speech, student David Kruckenberg presents interesting information about a promising new way to treat cancer. The speech is organized chronologically, as the speaker traces the invention from inception to ongoing trials. Note how the speaker helps listeners understand complex processes with the use of frequent transitions, clear definitions, and analogies.

One night Marianne Kanzius awoke to a horrendous clamor coming from downstairs. Investigating, she found her husband John sitting on the kitchen floor, cutting up her good aluminum pie pans with a pair of shears. When Marianne asked him why he was wiring the pans to his ham radio, John told her to go back to bed. So off she went, knowing that her engineer husband wasn't the kind of person to quit until he was satisfied. •

• In the introduction, David draws listeners in with an unusual story.

Making eye contact with every corner engages the whole room. Professional attire supports credibility.

Marianne soon learned that John's late-night experimentation with her pie pans was an attempt to use radio waves to kill the cancer with which he'd recently been diagnosed. In the months and years to come, John Kanzius would go on to refine a cancer treatment technique called radiofrequency ablation, making it a far safer and more effective treatment option. One day soon, John's work might give real hope to the 1.4 million Americans diagnosed with cancer every year, according to the 2006 American Cancer Society Facts and Figures section of its Web site. •

• David introduces the thesis here.

To understand John's discovery, we will explore first the radiofrequency ablation procedure as it is currently practiced, second, John's new approach, and finally the implications of this new hope for treating cancer. •

• Here he previews the three main speech points.

Gestures effectively demonstrate the properties of waves.

Before we can understand radiofrequency ablation, or RFA, we need a crash course in wave physics. • Energy moves in a wave. It is measured in frequency, how quickly it moves up and down. *High frequency waves*, like Superman's x-ray vision, move very quickly, and they are able to penetrate most matter. • However, due to this high frequency, they're likely to cause damage as they collide with molecules and disrupt the atomic balance. *Low frequency waves*, such as radio waves, move very slowly and do not disturb the atomic balance of matter they pass through. • On its Web site, last updated September 10, 2006, the Society of Interventional Radiology explains that radio waves are harmless to healthy cells, as compared to x-rays, which can alter the chemical and genetic state of a cell. This is why radio waves are the perfect choice for cancer ablation. As defined by the National Cancer Institute on January 10, 2007, *ablation* is the medical term for any procedure used to destroy diseased or damaged tissue in the body, either by ingesting hormones, by conventional surgery, or, in this case, by radiofrequency waves. •

The current RFA technique is outlined by the Radiological Society of North America on its Web site, last updated November 8, 2006. Here's how they explain it. •

• First, a local anesthetic is given to numb the skin and the underlying tissue.

Next, a quarter-inch incision is made in the skin so the doctor can insert into it a thin tube called a catheter.

The doctor guides the catheter to the treatment site using an imaging technique such as ultrasound.

The catheter in turn is connected to an electric generator, and once in place, metal prongs extend out of it and into the cancerous tumor.

Next, contact pads, also wired to the generator, are placed on the patient's skin; this completes an electric circuit so that

Reveals photograph of RFA technique.

Combining hand gesture with visual aid helps David explain medical procedure.

• David explains the process underlying RFA.

• David uses an analogy to reduce confusion.

• David clearly defines high and low frequency waves and offers recognizable examples of each.

• David clearly defines a key term of the speech.

• This transition helps listeners focus on the ensuing explanation.

• To help listeners follow the steps in the process, David makes frequent use of transitions, using words such as *first* and *next*. Note that the steps are organized chronologically.

Covers the visual aid at end of discussion to minimize audience distraction.

when the generator is turned on, electric energy in the form of radio waves passes harmlessly through the body, going back and forth between the catheter and the contact pads.

Here's the critical part: ● Every time that the radio waves meet the resistance of the metal prongs at the treatment site, they create heat. It's kind of like an atomic mosh pit, with a crowd of atoms suddenly agitated by radio waves; the electrons begin to bounce around and collide, creating friction and thus heat. ● This heat gets up to 212 degrees Fahrenheit, the temperature at which water boils. As explained on the National Institutes of Health Web site, updated March 21, 2006, the heat destroys the cancerous tumor, essentially cooking it but leaving the surrounding healthy tissue whole.

However, because RFA relies on the use of a catheter, which is invasive and can cause tissue damage, there are limitations to this technique. Enter John Kanzius. ●

John was diagnosed with leukemia in 2002, and his months of being bedridden by chemotherapy sparked a desire in him to find a better way to treat cancer. Now, John had no medical training, but he had worked in the radio industry for forty years. He remembered a time when a colleague who was wearing wire-rimmed glasses got burned because he was standing too close to a radio transmitter. This memory sparked John's late-night kitchen experiment. ●

Two things were amazing about this late-night experiment. First, John was able to replicate RFA in his kitchen. Second, John made a huge improvement upon the technique. Instead of using a catheter to insert the metal prongs into the tumor, he injected tiny metal minerals into a hotdog; he then placed the hotdog between the radio transmitter and receiver so that the radio waves would pass through the meat. When he cut the hotdog open, the area around the minerals was cooked, but the rest remained raw. Kanzius later repeated the experiment with liver, then steak, obtaining the same results.

● David helps reduce confusion by explicitly alerting listeners to key parts of the explanation.

● To help listeners understand a difficult concept, David uses the analogy of a mosh pit.

● David uses an internal preview to alert listeners to what's ahead.

● Notice how David uses the active verb *sparked*, which also relates to the process of heating and burning. Creative use of language engages listeners.

After talking to several doctors, John became aware that he had improved RFA, and he filed for a patent. Word got around, and several prominent cancer centers expressed interest in testing John's theory. He readily agreed, and in August 2005, according to the University of Pittsburgh Medical Center Newsletter of March 22, 2006, researchers tested John's theory. Instead of using a hotdog, they placed a thin test tube between the radio transmitter and the receiver. Inside this tube was a solution of carbon nanoparticles. These particles are actually pieces of metal about 1/75,000 times smaller than the width of a human hair. • A speck of dandruff is like a mountain to a nanoparticle. When they turned on the electricity, the carbon nanoparticles successfully heated to 130 degrees Fahrenheit — the perfect temperature at which to kill cancer cells, according to Dr. Steven Curley in the May 2006 edition of *Reader's Digest*. Dr. Curley further explains that they can use magnets to pull the nanoparticles through the body to the tumor. Dr. Curley, who is a surgical oncologist and cancer researcher at the MD Anderson Cancer Center in Houston, is continuing to test this technique on live animals.

• To help listeners understand the size of a nanometer, David compares it to something with which listeners are familiar — a strand of hair and dandruff.

Now that we understand how RFA works, and I've explained John's major improvement over the previous way of doing RFA, we can examine the implications of his discovery. •

First, because RFA uses electromagnetic energy in the form of radio waves, it's much safer than traditional cancer radiation treatment. As noted, radio waves are harmless to healthy cells as compared to x-rays.

• David uses an internal summary and a preview to transition to his next speech point.

Second, John's new method may solve some of the problems with the current RFA. On its Web site, last updated January 11, 2007, the Mayo Clinic explains that catheters may damage tissues and organs near the treatment site, requiring surgical repair. There's also a risk of hemorrhaging, and in some cases, of infection. John's method prevents these pitfalls with a simple injection of nanoparticles, thus making the procedure safer and less invasive.

Third, on its Web site, last updated January 20, 2007, the University of Southern California Department of Surgery explains that doctors currently use RFA to treat several forms of cancer, such as liver, breast, and prostate, but John's new method can be used to target additional types such as pancreatic and colon cancers. Additionally, as currently practiced, the RFA procedure must be performed several times to target multiple tumors, but John's method makes it possible to target multiple tumors in just a single treatment.

Unfortunately, there are some concerns as to whether the nanoparticles used in this method will leave the body after treatment. If they remain around the treatment site or reenter the bloodstream, it's possible that future exposure to radio waves may cause heat damage to healthy tissues. However, research with nanoparticles detailed in the June 15, 2005, University of Michigan Health System Report indicates that the kidneys can easily filter nanoparticles from the bloodstream and emit them in urine. Of course, we're going to have to wait until this practice becomes common, but considering that the October 14, 2006, *Erie Times-News* says that John recently secured 10 million dollars in investment toward development, we may not have to wait very long. Ironically, John's own method cannot be used to treat his form of leukemia, but fortunately, his chemo regimen has so far been effective.

Today we learned how a man with vision discovered how to cook a hotdog with a ham radio. We explored first the current procedure, then John's new approach, and, finally, the implications of this new hope for treating cancer. Truly it may soon revolutionize the way we fight cancer, saving more lives and doing it more efficiently. ●

Marianne Kanzius was upset when she saw her husband destroying her good pie pans, but now it's clear that the loss of a few pie pans and a hotdog may save millions of lives. ●

● Here David signals the conclusion and summarizes the main points.

● David concludes his speech by returning to his opening story, making the speech come full circle.

Works Cited

"Cancer Facts and Figures, 2006." American Cancer Society. www.cancer.org/docroot/STT/content/STT_1x_Cancer_Facts_Figures_2006.asp (accessed November 8, 2006).

"Dictionary of Cancer Terms." National Cancer Institute. www.cancer.gov/templates/db_alpha. aspx?expand=A (accessed January 11, 2007).

"Nanoparticles Transport Cancer-Killing Drug into Tumor Cells to Increase Efficacy, Lower Drug Toxicity in Mice." University of Michigan Health System. June 15, 2005. www.med.umich.edu/opm/newspage/2005/nanoparticles.htm (accessed January 21, 2007).

"Radiofrequency Ablation . . . Cooking Tumors with Needles" FAQ Sheet. National Institutes of Health. clinicalcenter.nih.gov/drd/rfa/frame=faq.html (accessed January 11, 2007).

"Radiofrequency Ablation for Cancer." Mayo Clinic. www.mayoclinic.org/radiofrequency-ablation/ (accessed January 22, 2007).

"Radiofrequency Ablation of Liver Tumors." Radiological Society of North America. www.radiologyinfo.org/en/info.cfm?PG=rfa (accessed January 15, 2007).

"Radiofrequency Ablation (RFA) of Liver Tumors." Department of Surgery, University of Southern California. www.surgery.usc.edu/divisions/tumor/pancreasdiseases/web%20pages/laparoscopic%20liver%20surgery/radiofrequency%20ablation.html (accessed January 21, 2007).

"Radiofrequency Catheter Ablation." Society of Interventional Radiology. www.sirweb.org/patPub/radiofrequencyAblation.shtml#3 (accessed January 15, 2007).

"Sparks of Genius: Efforts Done by John Kanzius, a Cancer Patient, to Find a Better Cure for Cancer." *Reader's Digest* (May 2006): 132–36.

University of Pittsburgh Medical Center Web Site, *Match* (a publication of the Thomas E. Starzl Transplantation Institute), March 22, 2006.

24 The Persuasive Speech

Persuasive speaking is a type of public speaking you will practice frequently throughout your professional and personal life. To persuade is to influence, advocate, or ask others to accept your views. Whether you are bargaining for a raise, convincing a fellow classmate of the need to join a student protest, or giving a formal speech advocating for a green policy, success or failure rests on how well or how poorly you understand the principles and practices of the art of persuasion.

Persuasive speaking skills are indispensable, especially if you want to make your voice count during public conversations about issues that are important to you, from tuition hikes to terrorism to the future of Social Security. Knowledge of persuasive speaking not only helps you critically assess the persuasive messages of others, but also contributes to the betterment of society and the world. As we saw in Chapter 1, the ability to speak persuasively ensures a healthy democracy. "In a Republican nation," Thomas Jefferson said during his term as the third president of the United States, "whose citizens are to be led by reason and persuasion and not by force, the art of reasoning becomes of first importance."

What Is a Persuasive Speech?

 Chapter quizzes

Persuasive speeches are meant to appeal to the audience's attitudes, beliefs, and values about the issue in question and to sway listeners to the speaker's point of view. Derived from the Greek verb meaning "to believe,"[1] **persuasion** is the process of influencing attitudes, beliefs, values, and behavior. **Persuasive speaking** is a form of speech that is intended to influence the attitudes, beliefs, values, and actions of others.

✓ **CHECKLIST**

Conditions for Choosing a Persuasive Purpose

You should select a persuasive purpose if:

_____ 1. Your goal is to influence an audience's beliefs or understanding about something.

_____ 2. Your goal is to influence an audience's behavior.

_____ 3. Your goal is to reinforce audience members' existing attitudes, beliefs, or behavior so they will continue to possess or practice them.

PERSUASIVE SPEECHES ATTEMPT TO INFLUENCE AUDIENCE CHOICES

Chapter 23 describes the general goal of informative speeches as that of increasing understanding and awareness. Persuasive speeches also serve to increase understanding and awareness. They present an audience with new information, new insights, and new ways of thinking about an issue. In fact, persuasive speeches do all the things informative speeches do. But rather than only seeking to increase understanding and awareness, the explicit goal of the persuasive speech is to influence audience choices.[2] The persuasive speaker tries to somehow influence the opinions or actions of his or her audience. These choices may range from slight shifts in opinion to wholesale changes in behavior.

PERSUASIVE SPEECHES LIMIT ALTERNATIVES

Any issue that would constitute the topic of a persuasive speech represents at least two viewpoints. For example, there are "pro-choice" advocates and "right-to-life" advocates; supporters of candidate Brezinski and supporters of candidate Morales; those who oppose a new holiday bonus plan and those who advocate it; and those who prefer brand X MP3 player over brand Y. With any such issue, it is the objective of a persuasive speaker to limit the audience's alternatives to the side the speaker represents. This is done not by ignoring the unfavorable alternatives altogether but by contrasting them with the favorable alternative and showing it to be of greater value or usefulness to the audience than the other alternatives.

PERSUASIVE SPEECHES SEEK A RESPONSE

By showing an audience the best of several alternatives, the persuasive speaker asks listeners — sometimes explicitly and sometimes implicitly — to make a choice. If the speech is effective, the audience's choice will be limited; that is,

Ethically Speaking
Persuasive Speeches Respect Audience Choices

Even though persuasive speeches present audiences with a choice, the ethical persuasive speaker recognizes that the choice is ultimately the audience members' to make — and he or she respects their right to do so. People take time to consider what they've heard and how it affects them. They make their own choices in light of or despite the best evidence. Your role as a persuasive speaker is not to coerce or force your listeners to accept your viewpoint but to present as convincing a case as possible so that they might do so willingly. For instance, you might want to persuade members of your audience to become vegetarians, but you must also respect their choice not to adopt this path.

listeners will understand that the alternative presented by the speaker is the "right" choice. (See Table 24.1.)

TABLE 24.1 • Characteristics of Persuasive Speeches

- Persuasive speeches attempt to influence the attitudes, beliefs, values, and acts of others.
- Persuasive speeches limit alternatives.
- Persuasive speeches seek a response.
- Persuasive speeches respect audience choices.

The Process of Persuasion

 Video quizzes

Persuasion is a complex psychological process of reasoning and emotion. When you speak persuasively, you try to guide the audience to adopt a particular attitude, belief, or behavior that you favor. But getting people to change their minds, even a little, is challenging and requires considerable skill. Just because you think something is reasonable or right does not guarantee that someone else will think so, too. Each of us has a unique way of looking at the world based on our own particular blend of experiences.

As one expert on persuasion has observed, "Persuasion requires curiosity. It demands a willingness to explore the mind-set of others . . . a Sherlock Holmes mentality."[3] Discovering your listeners' attitudes, beliefs, and values will provide crucial clues to their receptiveness toward your topic and your position on it. (See Chapter 6 for a review of the definitions of these terms.) As in informative speeches, therefore, *audience analysis* is extremely important in persuasive speeches. The more "intelligence" you can gather about audience members, the better you can solve the puzzle of how best to reach them. Be aware, however, that regardless of how thoroughly you have conducted audience analysis or how skillfully you present your point of view, audiences may not respond immediately or completely to a persuasive appeal. Persuasion does not always occur with a single dose. An audience can be immediately "stirred," as the Roman orator Cicero put it, with relative ease. However, producing a lasting impact on listeners' attitudes, beliefs, and behavior is a more difficult matter. Changes tend to be small, even imperceptible, especially at first.

Several key factors increase the odds that your efforts at persuasion will succeed:

- To be most persuasive, your message should be personally relevant to the audience.[4]

- Barring coercion, people are unlikely to change unless they can see how doing so will benefit them.[5]

- People are more likely to act on strong attitudes than on weak ones.[6]

- People who feel highly involved in your message will react differently from those who feel less involved.[7]

✓ **CHECKLIST**

Increasing the Odds of Achieving Your Persuasive Speech Goal

_____ 1. Clearly demonstrate your topic's relevance to the audience.

_____ 2. Clearly demonstrate how any changes you propose will benefit the audience.

_____ 3. Target issues that audience members are likely to feel strongly about. If they don't much care about an issue, it is unlikely that they will pay much attention to it.

_____ 4. Set modest goals. Expect minor rather than major changes in your listeners' attitudes and behaviors.

_____ 5. Establish your credibility with your listeners.

_____ 6. Expect to be more successful when addressing an audience whose position differs only moderately from yours.

_____ 7. Try to convince your listeners that by taking the action you propose they will be rewarded in some way.

- The persuader who seeks only minor changes is usually more successful than the speaker who seeks major ones.

- Audience members' feelings toward you strongly influence how receptive they will be to your message. Attitude change is related to the extent to which the speaker is perceived to be credible.[8]

- People want to feel satisfied and competent. If you can show that an attitude or a behavior might keep them from or help them enter this state, they are more likely to be receptive to change.

- You are more likely to persuade audience members if their position differs only moderately from yours. For example, if you are trying to persuade an audience to support a bill that protects the environment, you are more likely to convince those who in general are favorably disposed toward environmentalism than those who have a consistently strong track record of opposing such legislation.

- In order for change to endure, listeners must be convinced that they will be rewarded in some way. For example, to persuade people to lose weight and keep it off, you must make them believe that they will be healthier and seem more attractive if they do so. Persuaders who achieve this are skilled at motivating their listeners to help themselves.[9]

Following is a brief overview of how the ancient scholars of rhetoric, and Aristotle in particular, viewed the process of persuasion. Much of classical theory on persuasion remains relevant today. Following that discussion is a review of how contemporary social scientists approach persuasion. Both classical and contemporary perspectives provide useful tools for creating successful persuasive speeches. Both approaches recognize that successful persuasion requires a balance of reason and emotion, and that audience members must be well-disposed toward the speaker.

Classical Persuasive Appeals: Using Proofs

 WEB Chapter quizzes

In his treatise on rhetoric, Aristotle explained that persuasion could be brought about by the speaker's use of three types of persuasive appeals, or forms of **rhetorical proofs**. The first concerns the nature of the message in a speech; the second, the nature of the audience's feelings; the third, the qualifications and personality of the speaker. According to Aristotle, and generations of scholars and practitioners who followed him, you can build an effective persuasive speech with any one or a combination of these proofs, termed *logos*, *pathos*, and *ethos*. The best speeches generally make use of all three proofs.

LOGOS: PROOF BY REASON

Many persuasive speeches focus on issues that require considerable thought. Should universities abolish tenure? Should pregnant teenagers be required to seek their parents' permission in order to have an abortion? Are certain television programs too violent for children? When an audience needs to make an important decision or reach a conclusion regarding a complicated issue, appeals to reason and logic are necessary. Aristotle used the term **logos** to refer to persuasive appeals directed at the audience's reasoning on a topic. To **reason** is to draw conclusions based on evidence.

The Syllogism

Aristotle differentiated between two forms of reasoning in speeches. The first is the **syllogism**, a three-part argument consisting of a **general case** (also called a "**major premise**"), a **specific case** ("**minor premise**"), and a conclusion logically following from the first two steps. The classic example is this:

GENERAL CASE:	All men are mortal.
SPECIFIC CASE:	Socrates is a man.
CONCLUSION:	Therefore Socrates is mortal.

Syllogisms are a form of **deductive reasoning**, or reasoning from a general condition to a specific instance.[10] (Reversing direction, **inductive reasoning** moves from specific instances to a general condition.) A well-developed syllogism will lead listeners to a clearer understanding of an issue; one that is poorly thought through will lead them to unfounded conclusions. Here is an example of a contemporary syllogism that is effectively developed:

GENERAL CASE:	Regular exercise enhances your ability to study productively.
SPECIFIC CASE:	Swimming is good exercise.
CONCLUSION:	Swimming regularly will enhance your ability to study productively.

And here is one that is poorly developed:

GENERAL CASE: Rosslyn gets all A's even though she never attends class.

SPECIFIC CASE: Rosslyn is on the college softball team.

CONCLUSION: All college athletes get all A's even though they never attend class.

The preceding example shows how erroneous conclusions can be reached if you begin with a general case that is unfounded. Here, the general case is a **hasty overgeneralization**, or an attempt to support a claim by asserting that a particular piece of evidence (an isolated case) is true for all individuals or conditions concerned. (See the section on fallacies in reasoning in Chapter 25.) Although the specific instance may be true, the conclusion is based on an overgeneralization. In contrast, the first example is an effective syllogism. It reaches a sound conclusion from an accurate general case applied to a specific instance.

As you can see, appeals to reason using syllogism in a persuasive speech require accurate knowledge of the information that forms your general and specific cases. This is a key consideration as you build your arguments.

The Enthymeme

A second form of classical rational appeal, or use of logos, in a persuasive speech is the enthymeme. An **enthymeme** is a syllogism presented as a probability rather than as an absolute, and it states either a general case or a specific case but not both. The case not stated is implied and serves as a mental tool for connecting the speaker and audience.[11] For example, the syllogism about Socrates leads to the absolute conclusion that Socrates is mortal if both of the stated cases are accurate and true. The syllogism about swimming can be restated as an enthymeme so that the conclusion is probably true but not necessarily always true:

GENERAL CASE TO   Regular exercise enhances your ability to study productively,
CONCLUSION: so swimming regularly should enhance your studying.

Implied in this example is that swimming is a good form of exercise. Implied in the next example is that exercise will enhance your ability to study well:

SPECIFIC EXAMPLE   Swimming is good exercise and should enhance
TO CONCLUSION: your studying.

The use of "should" in each case makes the conclusion tentative instead of absolute. Why would you want to offer probable conclusions in a persuasive speech instead of certain conclusions? *Because most arguments are not based on certainty.* It is not absolutely certain, for example, that swimming regularly will enhance your studying because many other factors are involved in studying.

The point is, if your argument is to hold sway, the conclusion has to be certain enough for the audience to accept the premise. The key for both syllogisms and enthymemes is that your premises — your general case and specific instance — be acceptable according to sound reasoning or logic. (See Chapter 25 for detailed advice on building arguments for the persuasive speech.)

PATHOS: PROOF BY EMOTION

Another means of persuasion first described by classical theorists is appealing to listeners' emotions. The term Aristotle used for this is **pathos**. It requires "creating a certain disposition in the audience."[12] Aristotle taught that successful public speakers identify and appeal to four sets of emotions in their listeners.[13] He presented these sets in opposing pairs: anger and meekness, love and hatred, fear and boldness, shame and shamelessness. You can evoke these emotions in a speech by using *vivid descriptions* and *emotionally charged words*. Consider the following example from attorney Elpidio Villarreal, who in 2007 spoke about the value of immigrants to the United States. In this excerpt, he refutes those who claim that this group does not want to assimilate into U.S. culture. Villarreal uses his uncle who died in combat during World War II as an example of the loyalty and sacrifice of Mexican Americans:

> On June 6, 1944, [my Uncle Lupe] landed at a place called Omaha Beach in Normandy, France. He was killed while leading an attack on an enemy bunker that was pinning down his platoon. He was nominated, but did not receive, the Congressional Medal of Honor. My grandparents received a photograph of a road my uncle's unit built in France. The road had been named Villarreal Road. Years ago, I was privileged to walk the battlefields of Normandy, including Omaha Beach, and I visited the great American Cemetery there where lie 17,000 Americans who gave the "last full measure of devotion," as Lincoln so beautifully put it. Simple white marble crosses, interspersed with occasional Stars of David, stretch out for 70 acres. It remains one of the most moving things I have ever seen. I thought about all the brave Americans buried there and of the meaning of their deaths, but I thought especially about my Uncle Lupe, the one who went to war knowing he would die for no other reason than that his country, the one that treated him as a second-class citizen, asked him to.[14] (For a full transcript of Villarreal's speech, see p. 423.)

Although emotion is a powerful means of moving an audience, relying solely on naked emotion to persuade will fail most of the time. As Aristotle stressed, *pathos functions as a means to persuasion not by any persuasive power inherent in emotions per se but by the interplay of emotions — or desire — and sound reasoning.* Emotion gets the audience's attention and stimulates a desire to act on the emotion; reason is then presented as justification for the action. Recent persuasion research confirms this effect.[15] For example, a popular television advertisement depicts a grandfatherly man in a series of activities with family members.

Ethically Speaking
Using Emotions Ethically

The most successful persuaders are those who are able to understand the mind-set of others. With such insight comes the responsibility to use emotional appeals in speeches for ethical purposes only. As history attests only too amply, not all speakers follow an ethical path in this regard. Demagogues, for example, clutter the historical landscape. A **demagogue** relies heavily on irrelevant emotional appeals to short-circuit the listeners' rational decision-making process.[1] Senator Joseph McCarthy, who conducted "witch hunts" against alleged Communists in the 1950s, was one such speaker. Many cult leaders, such as David Karesh, leader of the now-disbanded Branch Davidians, are also masters of manipulating their followers' emotions toward unscrupulous ends. Adolf Hitler played on the fears and dreams of German citizens to urge them toward despicable ends.

Persuasive speakers can manipulate their listeners' emotions by arousing fear and anxiety and by using propaganda.

- *Fear and anxiety.* Some speakers deliberately arouse fear and anxiety in an audience so that listeners will follow their recommendations.[2] Sometimes this is done by offering a graphic description of what will happen if the audience doesn't comply (e.g., people will get hurt, children will starve). If used fairly and carefully, however, the **fear appeal** does have a legitimate place in public speaking. For example, it can be used to demonstrate to children the harm caused by smoking, or to show a group of drunken drivers graphic pictures of the results of their actions. It can also be used to encourage civic involvement to solve pressing social problems,[3] as Al Gore did for climate change with the film *An Inconvenient Truth*. This constructive use of the fear appeal is similar to Aristotle's concept of arousing "civic fear" by appealing to the emotions (pathos) to address a destructive social evil.[4] (Note that for a fear appeal to succeed, it must be delivered by a speaker whom the audience perceives to be highly credible.)[5]

- *Propaganda.* Speakers who employ **propaganda** aim to manipulate an audience's emotions for the purpose of promoting a belief system or dogma. Propagandists tell audiences only what they want their listeners to know, deliberately hiding or distorting opposing viewpoints. For example, news commentator Bill O'Reilly has been accused of using propaganda techniques in his "Talking Points Memo" through his strategic language use.[6] Propagandists engage in name-calling and stereotyping to arouse their listeners' emotions. (See also the Ethically Speaking box in Chapter 10, "Learn to Distinguish among Information, Propaganda, Misinformation, and Disinformation.")

Unlike the ethical persuader, the propagandist does not respect the audience's right to choose; nor does the speaker who irresponsibly uses fear appeals. Ethically, appeals to emotion in a persuasive speech should always be supported by sound reasoning.

1. Charles U. Larson, *Persuasion: Reception and Responsibility,* 6th ed. (Belmont, Calif.: Wadsworth, 1992), 37.

2. James Price Dillard and Michael Pfau, *The Persuasion Handbook: Developments in Theory and Practice* (Thousand Oaks, Calif.: Sage Publications, 2002); Paul A. Mongeau, "Another Look at

(Continued)

Fear-Arousing Persuasive Appeals," in *Persuasion: Advances through Meta-Analysis,* ed. Mike Allen and Raymond W. Preiss (Cresskill, N.J.: Hampton Press, 1998), 53–68; Kim Witte and Mike Allen, "A Meta-Analysis of Fear Appeals: Implications for Effective Public Health Campaigns," *Health Education and Behavior* 27, no. 5 (2000): 591–615.

3. Michael William Pfau, "Who's Afraid of Fear Appeals? Contingency, Courage, and Deliberation in Rhetorical Theory and Practice," *Philosophy and Rhetoric* 40 (2007): 216–37.

4. Ibid.

5. Joseph C. Gardiner, "An Experimental Study of the Effects of Evidence and Fear Appeals on Attitude Change and Source Credibility," research monograph, Department of Communication, Michigan State University, 1969; G. M. Miller and M. A. Hewgill, "Some Recent Research on Fear-Arousing Message Appeals," *Speech Monographs* 33 (1966), 377–91, cited in James C. McCroskey, *An Introduction to Rhetorical Communication,* 8th ed. (Boston: Allyn and Bacon, 2001).

6. Grabe M. Conway, M. E. Grieves, and K. Grieves, "Villains, Victims and the Virtuous in Bill O'Reilly's 'No-Spin Zone,'" *Journalism Studies* 8 (2007): 197–223.

An announcer makes the logical appeal that people with high blood pressure should maintain their prescribed regimen of medication; this is followed by the emotional appeal "If not for yourself, do it for them." The message invokes the desire to stay healthy as long as possible for the benefit of loved ones. The reasoning is sound enough: Blood pressure is controllable with medication, but one must take the medicine in order for it to work. In this case, as in many, emotion helps communicate the idea.

Appealing to an audience's emotions on the basis of sound reasoning ensures that your speech is ethical. However, as seen in the Ethically Speaking box (p. 381), there are a host of ways in which emotions can be used unethically.

ETHOS: PROOF THROUGH SPEAKER CHARACTER

No matter how well reasoned a message is or which strong emotions its words target, if audience members have little or no regard for the speaker they will not respond positively to his or her persuasive appeals. Aristotle believed that speechmaking should emphasize the quality and impact of ideas, but he recognized that the nature of the speaker's character and personality also plays an important role in how well the audience listens to and accepts the message. He referred to this effect of the speaker as **ethos**, or moral character.

Exactly which elements of a persuasive appeal are based on ethos? Let's briefly consider each element in turn, and how you as the speaker can demonstrate them. The first element is *good sense.* Another term for this element of ethos is *competence,* or the speaker's knowledge of and experience with the subject matter. Ethos-based appeals emphasize the speaker's grasp of the subject matter. Skillfully preparing the speech at all stages, from research to delivery, as well as emphasizing your own expertise, evokes this quality.

> ✓ **CHECKLIST**
>
> **Displaying Ethos in the Persuasive Speech**
>
> - Demonstrate your competence as a speaker by knowing your subject well and by emphasizing your expertise.
> - Be straightforward and honest in presenting the facts of your argument as you see them.
> - Reveal your personal moral standards vis-à-vis your topic early in the speech.
> - Demonstrate a genuine interest in and concern for the welfare of your listeners.

The second element of an ethos-based appeal is the speaker's *moral character.* This is reflected in the speaker's straightforward and honest presentation of the message. The speaker's own ethical standards are central to this element. Current research suggests, for example, that a brief disclosure of personal moral standards relevant to the speech or the occasion made in the introduction of a speech will boost audience regard for the speaker.[16] Indeed, you should prepare and present every aspect of your speeches with the utmost integrity so that your audiences will regard you as trustworthy. The fact that you are an honest person will not be the most memorable aspect of your speeches, but the very fact that dishonesty is not expected of you makes it easy to identify in the content or delivery of your message.

The third element of an ethos-based appeal is *goodwill* toward the audience. A strong ethos-based appeal demonstrates an interest in and a concern for the welfare of your audience. Speakers who understand the concerns of their listeners and who address their needs and expectations relative to the speech exhibit this aspect of the ethos-based appeal.

Contemporary Persuasive Appeals: Needs and Motivations

 WEB Links

Classical theories of persuasion describe how appeals to reasoning, emotion, and speaker credibility can bring the audience to the speaker's point of view. Scientific research affirms the centrality of these elements in persuasive appeals,[17] while also investigating other factors that cause us to change or maintain our attitudes. These theories suggest that for persuasion to succeed, the message must effectively target (1) audience members' needs, (2) their underlying motivations for feeling and acting as they do, and (3) their likely approach to mentally processing the persuasive message.

PERSUADING LISTENERS BY APPEALING TO THEIR NEEDS

Have you ever wondered why there are so many fast-food commercials during and after the evening news? Advertisers know that by this time of night many viewers are experiencing a strong need—to eat! Appealing to audience needs is one of the strategies most commonly used to motivate people, whether in advertising or in public speaking.

Perhaps the best-known model of human needs is that formulated by Abraham Maslow in the 1950s.[18] Maslow maintained that each person has a set of basic needs ranging from the essential, life-sustaining ones to the less critical, self-improvement ones. This set includes five categories arranged hierarchically (see Figure 24.1). According to Maslow, an individual's needs at the lower, essential levels must be fulfilled before the higher levels become important and motivating. **Maslow's hierarchy of needs** has long been a basis for motivation-oriented persuasive speeches. The principle behind the model is that people are motivated to act on the basis of their needs; thus to persuade listeners to adopt suggested changes in attitudes, beliefs, or behavior, point to some need they want fulfilled and then give them a way to fulfill it. Critics of this approach suggest that needs may not be organized in a hierarchy and that, in fact, we may be driven as much by wants as by needs.[19] Nevertheless, the theory points to the fact that successful appeals depend on trying to understand what motivates the audience. Table 24.2 describes the five basic needs that Maslow identifies and suggests actions that you as a speaker can take to appeal to them.

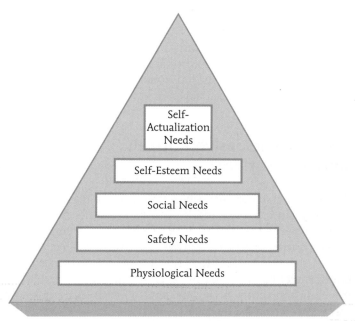

Figure 24.1 Maslow's Hierarchy of Needs

TABLE 24.2 • Using Needs to Motivate Listeners

Need	Speech Action
Physiological needs (the need for basic sustenance, including food, water, and air)	• To ensure that your listeners can give their full attention to your persuasive message, plan for and accommodate the audience's physiological needs in the speech situation (e.g., are they likely to be hot, cold, hungry, thirsty, or bored?).
Safety needs (the need to feel protected and secure)	• Appeal to the safety benefits your listeners will reap by adopting your message (e.g., if you want them to wear seat belts, vote for a bill to stop pollution, or buy a home security system, stress how taking certain steps will protect them from harm).
Social needs (the need to establish and maintain lasting, meaningful relationships with others)	• Appeal to the social benefits your listeners will reap by adopting your message (e.g., if you want an audience of teenagers to quit smoking, stress that if they quit they will appear more physically fit and attractive to their peers; if you want your listeners to oppose a piece of legislation, tell them about other supporters with whom they are likely to positively identify).
Self-esteem needs (the need to feel good about ourselves — that we matter and that we are worthwhile)	• Appeal to the emotional benefits your audience will reap by adopting your position (e.g., when proposing a change in attitudes or behavior, stress that the proposed change will make listeners feel better about themselves).
Self-actualization needs (the need to reach our highest potential; to achieve what we wish to accomplish; to reach the goals that we have set for ourselves)	• Appeal to your listeners' need to fulfill their potential (e.g., stress how adopting your position will help them "be all that they can be").

PERSUADING LISTENERS BY APPEALING TO THE REASONS FOR THEIR BEHAVIOR

The audience is not merely a collection of empty vessels waiting to be filled with whatever wisdom and knowledge you have to offer. Members of an audience are rational, thinking, choice-making individuals. Their day-to-day behavior is directed mainly by their own volition, or will. According to **expectancy-outcome values theory**, which was developed by Icek Ajzen and Martin Fishbein, each of us consciously evaluates the potential costs and benefits (or "value") associated with taking a particular action. As we weigh these costs and benefits, we consider our attitudes about the behavior in question (e.g., "Is this a good or a bad behavior?") as well as what other people who are important to us might think about the behavior (e.g., "My friend would approve of my taking this action"). On the basis of these assessments, we develop expectations about what will happen if we do or do not take a certain action (e.g., "My friend will think more highly of me if I do this"). These expected "outcomes" become our rationale for acting in a certain way. *Thus when you want to persuade listeners to change their behavior, you should try to identify these expected outcomes and use them to appeal to your audience.*[20]

The principles of expectancy-outcome values theory can help you plan a persuasive speech in which the specific purpose is to target behavior. A thorough audience analysis (in the form of a questionnaire) is critical to this approach, however (see the section on surveys in Chapter 6). Putting the theory into practice, as you conduct your audience analysis, you will need to seek out (1) your listeners' attitudes about the behavior you are proposing that they change, as well as (2) their feelings about the consequences associated with that behavior. Consider the case of unsafe sex. If your goal is to persuade audience members to practice safe sex, using a questionnaire you could identify (1) listeners' feelings about the practice and (2) their feelings about the consequences of not practicing safe sex. Assume you find that most audience members consider safe sex to be a good practice and most agree that not practicing safe sex has potentially serious negative risks. Knowing these attitudes, you have a good foundation for presenting your listeners with evidence that will support their attitudes and strengthen your argument that they should practice safe sex.

Third (3), try to determine what audience members believe other significant people in their lives think about the behavior in question, and the audience members' willingness to comply with those beliefs. Continuing with the example of practicing safe sex, you could question audience members about the extent to which they think their partners and close friends care about practicing safe sex and whether the audience members would be more or less willing to comply with these other people's presumed preferences. Assume you find that most audience members believe their partners support practicing safe sex and that most would go along with their partners' preferences. You now have a basis for appealing to your audience's concern for their partners' preferences regarding the practice of safe sex. Figure 24.2 illustrates the steps to take when seeking to persuade an audience to adopt a course of action, based on the principles of expectancy-outcome values theory.

PERSUADING LISTENERS BY FOCUSING ON WHAT'S MOST RELEVANT TO THEM

According to Richard Petty and John Cacioppo's **elaboration likelihood model of persuasion (ELM)**, each of us mentally processes persuasive messages by one of two routes, depending on the degree of our involvement in the message.[21] When we are motivated and able to think critically about the content of a message, we engage in **central processing** of the message. That is, we seriously consider what the speaker's message means to us and who are the ones most likely to act on it. We are the listeners who are most likely to experience a relatively enduring change in thinking that is favorable to the speaker's position.

Not everyone listens critically, however. When we lack the motivation (or the ability) to pay close attention to the issues, we engage in **peripheral processing** of information. In this form of mental processing of the speaker's

1. Investigate listeners' attitudes toward the specific behavior you are targeting in your speech (e.g., practicing safe sex, taking vitamin supplements, adopting a vegetarian diet, etc.).

↓

2. Identify listeners' beliefs about the consequences of their behavior (e.g., "I believe I will contract a sexually transmitted disease if I don't practice safe sex" or "I believe I will remain disease-free even if I don't practice safe sex").

↓

3. Investigate what the audience members believe *significant others in their lives* think about the behavior in question (e.g., my girlfriend is very concerned about health).

↓

4. Demonstrate the positive outcomes of adopting a course of action *favored by audience members' significant others* (e.g., "Practicing safe sex will lead to a great level of trust and intimacy between you and your partner").

Figure 24.2 Steps in Persuading Listeners to Change Their Behavior

persuasive message, we respond to it as being irrelevant, too complex to follow, or just plain unimportant.

Listeners who process messages peripherally are far more likely to be influenced by such non-content issues as the speaker's appearance or reputation, certain slogans or one-liners, and obvious attempts to manipulate emotions. Even though such listeners may "buy into" the speaker's message, they do so not on the strength of the arguments but on the basis of such factors as the speaker's reputation or personal style. In this case, the listener "goes with whatever the speaker says" because of who the speaker is, not because of the quality or substance of the message. Although this may seem like a positive speech outcome, the problem is that such shallow acceptance of a speaker's message has very limited impact on the listener's enduring thoughts and feelings about the matter. Listeners who use peripheral processing are unlikely to experience any meaningful changes in attitudes or behavior. Central processing produces the more long-lasting changes in audience perspective.

To put the principles of the ELM model of persuasion into practice when planning a persuasive speech, (1) make certain that your message is relevant to your listeners, (2) make certain that you present it at an appropriate level of understanding, and (3) establish your credibility with the audience (Figure 24.3). Establish a common bond with your listeners, and ensure that they see you as trustworthy. These steps will increase the odds that your persuasive appeal will produce lasting, rather than fleeting, changes in their attitudes and behavior.

Make your message relevant to your specific audience.

("How many times have you wanted to express your opinion about an important issue such as tuition and fees or stem cell research but haven't been able to find the right forum?")

↓

Present your message at an appropriate level of understanding.

("An intriguing option for expressing your opinions is to post them on blogs. A blog is an online journal offering a writer's thoughts in chronological order and sometimes including space for replies. Let me give you an example . . .")

↓

Establish your credibility with the audience.

("In this screen capture from my own blog, you will see an entry I posted and the almost forty responses that I received.")

Figure 24.3 Steps in Increasing Acceptance of Your Persuasive Message

PERSUADING LISTENERS THROUGH SPEAKER CREDIBILITY

Beyond the qualities of speaker knowledge, moral character, and goodwill toward the audience that ancient scholars such as Aristotle described in terms of ethos, modern behavioral science has identified four other speaker-based factors that affect the outcomes of persuasive messages: expertise, trustworthiness, speaker similarity, and physical attractiveness. Taken as a set, these factors are referred to as **speaker credibility**.

The audience's perceptions of a speaker's expertise and trustworthiness are critical contributors to persuasiveness.[22] Speaker *expertise* contributes to the persuasive outcomes of a speech under two conditions. First, when audience members are relatively unmotivated or unable to fully grasp a message, their responses to the speech will probably be in the speaker's favor if the speaker is perceived as an expert on the subject. Second, when audience members themselves are well informed about the message and perceive the speaker as someone who has expertise, he or she will be more apt to persuade them. Note that "expert" doesn't mean you're a world authority on the topic or issue of your speech. What it does mean is that you have enough knowledge and experience on the subject to be able to help the audience to better understand and accept it.

If there is one speaker attribute that is more important than others, it is probably *trustworthiness*.[23] It's a matter of the "goodwill" that Aristotle taught — audiences want more than information and arguments; they want what's relevant to them from someone who cares. Indeed, audience members who perceive the speaker to be high in credibility will regard the communication as more truthful than a message delivered by someone who is seen to have low credibility.[24]

Speaker Similarity

Two additional critical elements in the speaker-audience relationship that influence the outcome of a persuasive message are speaker similarity and physical attractiveness. *Speaker similarity* involves listeners' perceptions of how similar the speaker is to themselves, especially in terms of attitudes and moral character. Generally, audience members are more likely to respond favorably to the persuasive appeals of a speaker whom they perceive to be a lot like them. This is not always the case, however. In certain situations we attach more credibility to people who are actually dissimilar to us. For example, we are more likely to be persuaded by a dissimilar speaker, especially one viewed as an "expert," when the topic or issue emphasizes facts and analysis. This is why lawyers seek the expert testimony of psychiatrists or other specialists to provide insight into the personality of a suspect, the features of a crime scene, and the like. On the other hand, an audience is more likely to be persuaded by a similar speaker when the subject is personal or relational. For example, we prefer to watch *The Oprah Winfrey Show* instead of *60 Minutes* when the subject is fathers and daughters, or bosses and secretaries. We tend to perceive Oprah Winfrey as being more similar to us in relational concerns than we do Leslie Stahl. But if the issue involves new details in a political scandal or a foreign agreement, we would probably turn to Anderson Cooper as our preferred source. These facts point to an important lesson for the persuasive speaker: *For speeches that involve a lot of facts and analysis, play on whatever amount of expertise you can summon. For speeches that concern matters of a more personal nature, however, it's best to emphasize your commonality with the audience.*

✓ SELF-ASSESSMENT CHECKLIST

Tips for Increasing Speaker Credibility

_____ 1. Prepare well and demonstrate a thorough grasp of your topic.

_____ 2. Enlighten your audience with new and relevant information.

_____ 3. Demonstrate your trustworthiness by presenting your topic honestly and in a way that shows concern for your listeners.

_____ 4. For speeches that involve a lot of facts and analysis, emphasize your expertise on the topic.

_____ 5. For speeches of a more personal nature, emphasize your commonality with the audience.

_____ 6. Be well groomed.

Speaker Attractiveness

Finally, the *physical attractiveness* of the speaker affects persuasive outcomes. A quick look at the physical features of any of a dozen television news anchors and talk-show hosts suggests that physical attractiveness is a significant benefit to speakers. By and large, looking good does pay off for a speaker in terms of persuasive outcomes. In our culture, attractive people are perceived to be competent, in control of themselves, well organized, and confident. We tend to generalize these perceptions to public speakers as well. But there are limitations, even drawbacks, to physical attractiveness as a factor in persuasive speaking. First, highly attractive speakers can be a distraction to an audience, drawing their attention away from the message. Second, physical attractiveness can interfere with persuasive appeals when the speaker's appearance violates expectations for the occasion or the topic. Third, any positive outcomes of a persuasive speech that can be attributed to the speaker's attractiveness will probably be short-term gains at best. Our tendency is to respond positively to attractive speakers because we want to be like them or be associated with them. But responding primarily on that basis leads only to a superficial understanding of the message and fleeting attention to it.

Developing Arguments for the Persuasive Speech 25

The process of reasoning can be defined in different ways depending on the context in which it is applied. One definition of *reasoning* is "the power of comprehending, inferring, or thinking, especially in orderly, rational ways."[1] Reasoning in this sense is the process of critical thinking that we try to engage in throughout our everyday lives and in our roles as public speakers and active listeners. Another definition of *reasoning,* one we introduced in the previous chapter and that applies directly to creating a persuasive speech, is "the process of proving inferences or conclusions from evidence."[2] Reasoning in this sense is synonymous with argument, the topic of this chapter. Reasoning through a persuasive speech is a process of building one or more arguments created to change people's opinions, influence behavior, or justify the arguer's beliefs or actions.[3]

Sound reasoning is based on solid evidence backed by credible sources, and avoids logical fallacies (discussed at the conclusion of this chapter). Sound reasoning is necessary for effective persuasive speaking; it is also the cornerstone of constructive public discourse. When you argue about public issues in a public forum, such as at a student gathering or town meeting, the quality of your reasoning will take center stage. The nearby "Ethically Speaking" box offers guidelines for conducting ethical argument.

This chapter describes how to use argument as a framework for making appeals in persuasive speeches. Most persuasive speeches consist of several arguments.

Ethically Speaking
Engaging in Arguments in the Public Arena

Because the potential to do harm is greater when more people are involved, public discourse carries a greater scope of responsibility and accountability than does private discourse. Consider the following guidelines when engaged in arguments in the public arena:

- Arguing is not "fighting."
- Arguing is reasoning about issues, not attacking personalities.
- Arguing is socially constructive and culturally sensitive.
- Arguing strives for accuracy.
- Arguing acknowledges value in alternative or opposing views.
- Arguing is ethical; the alternative is not.

What Is an Argument?

 WEB Chapter quizzes

An **argument** is a stated position, with support for or against an idea or issue. Persuasive speeches use arguments to present one alternative as superior to other alternatives. Speakers who present arguments ask listeners to accept a conclusion about some state of affairs by providing evidence and reasons that the evidence logically supports the claim. The core elements of an argument consist of a claim, evidence, and warrants:[4]

1. The *claim* states the speaker's conclusion about some state of affairs.
2. The *evidence* substantiates the claim.
3. The *warrants* provide reasons that the evidence is valid or supports the claim.

STATING A CLAIM

To state a **claim** (also called a *proposition*) is to declare a state of affairs. Claims are often (but not always) presented as thesis statements. Claims answer the question "What are you trying to prove?"[5] If you want to convince audience members that they need to be more careful consumers of herbal supplements, you might make this claim: "Many herbal supplements contain powerful substances that may interact in harmful ways with over-the-counter (OTC) or prescription drugs." This claim asserts that taking herbal supplements together with certain OTC or prescription drugs potentially poses a health risk. But unless your listeners already agree with the claim, it's unlikely that they'll accept it at face value. To make the claim believable, the speaker must provide proof, or evidence in support of the claim.

PROVIDING EVIDENCE

Every key claim you make in a speech must be supported with **evidence**, or supporting material that provides grounds for belief (see Chapter 8, "Developing Supporting Material"). In a speech about herbal supplements, for example, to support the claim that they can cause harm by interacting with OTC or prescription drugs, you might provide *statistics* showing the number of persons in a given year who were hospitalized as a result of such interactions. You might then couple these data with *testimony* from individuals who experienced health problems because of such drug interactions or from physicians who treated such patients.

The goal in using evidence is to make a claim more acceptable, or believable, to the audience. If the evidence itself is believable, then the claim is more likely to be found acceptable by the audience.

WARRANTS: JUSTIFYING THE LINK BETWEEN THE CLAIM AND EVIDENCE

Warrants, the third component of arguments, help both to support a claim and to substantiate in the audience's mind the link between the claim and the evidence. They show why the link between the claim and evidence is valid, or *warranted.* Other terms for warrants are *reasoning* and *justification.*

Although a piece of evidence may provide strong support for a claim, in order for listeners to accept the argument, the connection between the claim and the evidence must be made clear and justified in their minds. A warrant serves as a bridge between a claim and evidence. For example, the claim that some herbal supplements, in conjunction with other drugs, can cause health problems may not be clear to listeners. Some good warrants can make the link between claim and evidence clearer. The argument can be supported by showing that:

> According to the American Council on Science and Health, serious side effects have occurred in cases where people consumed prescription blood thinners such as warfarin (Coumadin®) with herbal supplements such as St. John's Wort, Kava, and Valerian. Further, drugs that suppress the immune system, such as cortico-steroids or cyclosporine, have been shown to have harmful effects when interacting with supplements such as Echinacea, St. John's Wort, and Zinc.[6] [EVIDENCE]

The link between the claim and the evidence can be justified by the following:

> Several leading medical journals and organizations, including the American Council on Science and Health, have reported cases documenting harmful interactions between a variety of supplements and medications. [WARRANT]

This provides a justification for accepting the link between the evidence and the claim. The claim is supported.

Diagramming the argument allows you to visualize how the evidence and warrants can be presented in support of your claim. Figure 25.1 illustrates the three components of the preceding argument about the dangers of drug–supplement interactions. As you consider formulating an argument, try to diagram it in a similar fashion:

1. Write down the claim.
2. List each possible piece of evidence you have in support of the claim.
3. Write down the corresponding warrants, or justifications, that link the evidence to the claim.

In the following excerpt from a 2002 address to the United Nations, President George W. Bush speaks about the threat to peace posed by Iraq under the regime of Saddam Hussein. Bush claims that Iraq's decade-long defiance of U.N. demands to comply with its Security Council resolutions can no longer be tolerated. In the speech, Bush makes several claims and offers evidence and support for each of them. Excerpted here are several claims from the speech:

> In 1991 the U.N. Security Council . . . demanded that Iraq denounce all involvement in terrorism and permit no terrorist organizations to operate in Iraq. Iraq's regime agreed. It broke this promise. [CLAIM]

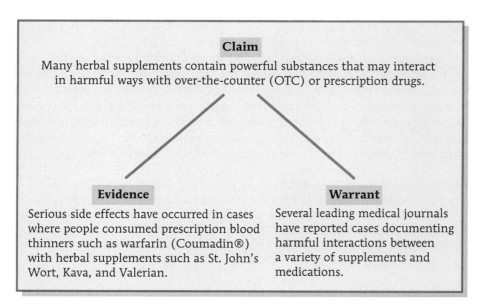

Claim

Many herbal supplements contain powerful substances that may interact in harmful ways with over-the-counter (OTC) or prescription drugs.

Evidence

Serious side effects have occurred in cases where people consumed prescription blood thinners such as warfarin (Coumadin®) with herbal supplements such as St. John's Wort, Kava, and Valerian.

Warrant

Several leading medical journals have reported cases documenting harmful interactions between a variety of supplements and medications.

Figure 25.1 Core Components of Argument

In violation of Security Council Resolution . . . Iraq continues to shelter and support terrorist organizations that direct violence against Iran, Israel, and Western governments. Iraqi dissidents abroad are targeted for murder. . . . In 1993 Iraq attempted to assassinate the emir of Kuwait and a former American president. [EVIDENCE]

The history, the logic and the facts lead to one conclusion: Saddam Hussein's regime is a grave and gathering danger. [WARRANT][7]

Types of Claims, Evidence, and Warrants    Sample speeches

A variety of claims, evidence, and warrants are at your disposal for making an argument. The ones you select will depend on the nature of your topic and the specific purpose of your persuasive speech.

CLAIMS USED IN PERSUASIVE SPEECHES: FACT, VALUE, AND POLICY

Depending on the nature of the issue being addressed, a persuasive speech can consist of three different kinds of claims: of fact, of value, and of policy. Different types of claims require different kinds of supporting evidence.

Persuasive Speeches Making Claims of Fact

Persuasive speeches based on **claims of fact** focus on whether something is or is not true or whether something will or will not happen. Claims of fact usually address one of two kinds of questions: those for which two or more controversial, competing answers exist; or those for which an answer does not yet exist. In the former case, the answer already exists. The question is, Which is the best or right answer? In the latter case, the answer does not yet exist. Questions for which two competing answers exist might include:

- Is *The Office* or *Seinfeld* the funniest sitcom in television history?
- Does affirmative action discriminate against nonminority job applicants?
- Is homosexuality a genetically determined orientation, an outcome of environmental influences, or the result of a combination of factors?

An argument based on any of these questions will need to give evidence in support of one answer as superior to an alternative answer.

The other kind of speech making claims of fact addresses questions for which answers are not yet available. Probable answers to such questions are called **speculative claims**. Such questions might include:

- Will a woman president be elected in the United States within the next ten years?
- Does nanotechnology carry hidden dangers undetected by science?
- Will currency be completely replaced by credit cards within the next ten years?

Persuasive Speeches Making Claims of Value

When relatives or physicians assist a terminally ill patient in planning a suicide, questions arise about the morality of assisted suicide, suicide in general, and the role of medical practitioners in aiding death as they aid life. Situations such as these lie in the realm of claims of value. Persuasive speeches based on **claims of value** address issues of judgment. Is assisted suicide ethical? Should doctors be in the business of helping patients to die as well as to live? When, if ever, is suicide justified? Rather than attempting to prove the truth of something, as in claims of fact, a speaker arguing a claim of value tries to show that something is right or wrong, good or bad, worthy or unworthy.

Like claims of fact, claims of value require evidence. However, the evidence in support of a value claim tends to be more subjective than factual. In defending assisted suicide, for example, a speaker might be able to show that in certain situations compassion requires us to help terminally ill people take their own lives. Likewise, public opinion polls can be used to sway attitudes about a value ("after all, 83 percent of Americans support the death penalty").

Persuasive Speeches Making Claims of Policy

Speakers use **claims of policy** when recommending that a specific course of action be taken, or approved of, by an audience. Legislators regularly construct arguments based on claims of policy: Should we pass a law restricting

Public Speaking In Cultural Perspective
Addressing Culture in the Persuasive Speech

Cultural orientation has a significant effect on responses to persuasion.[1] Although most classroom audiences (and most general audiences) in the United States consist of persons familiar with the values of U.S. culture, individual audience members may hold distinct cultural values related to their country or culture of origin. These range from broad core values to more specific norms related to behavior and beliefs.

Audience members of the same culture share core values, such as *self-reliance* and *individual achievement* (in individualist cultures) and *interdependence* and *group harmony* (in collectivist cultures) (see Chapter 6 on cultural differences). Usually, appeals that clash with core values are unsuccessful, although globalization may be leading to some cross-pollination of values.[2]

Cultural norms are a group's rules for behavior. Attempts to persuade listeners to think or do things contrary to important norms will usually fail.[3] The argument that intermarriage leads to happier couples, for example, will find greater acceptance among Reform rather than Orthodox Jews, since the latter group has strong prohibitions against the practice.

Listeners sharing a common culture usually hold culturally specific values about identity and relationships, called **cultural premises**. Prevalent among the Danes and Israelis, for example, is the premise of egalitarianism, the belief that everyone should be equal. An opposite premise exists in Korea, Japan, and other Asian societies, where status most often is aligned strictly with one's place in the social hierarchy. Bear in mind that it is difficult to challenge deeply held cultural premises.[4]

Culture also influences our responses to emotional appeals. Appeals that touch on *ego-focused* emotions such as pride, anger, happiness, and frustration, for example, tend to find more acceptance among members of individualist cultures;[5] those that use *other-focused* emotions such as empathy, indebtedness, and shame are more apt to encourage identification in collectivist cultures.[6] Usually, it is best to appeal to emotions that lie within the audience's "comfort zone."[7]

Persuasion depends on appeals to values; culture shapes these values. Eliciting a range of emotions may therefore help you appeal to diverse audience members.

1. Jennifer Aaker and Durairaj Maheswaran, "The Impact of Cultural Orientation on Persuasion," *Journal of Consumer Research* 24 (December 1997): 315–28.

2. Jennifer L. Aaker, "Accessibility or Diagnosticity? Disentangling the Influence of Culture on Persuasion Processes and Attitudes," *Journal of Consumer Research* 26 (March 2000): 340–57.

3. Kristine L. Fitch, "Cultural Persuadables," *Communication Theory* 13 (February 2003): 100–123.

4. Ibid.

5. Jennifer L. Aaker and Patti Williams, "Empathy versus Pride: The Influence of Emotional Appeals across Cultures," *Journal of Consumer Research* 25 (1998): 241–61.

6. Ibid.

7. Ibid.

the use of handguns/abortion/firecrackers? Anyone can argue for a claim of policy as long as he or she advocates for or against a given plan. Such claims might include:

- Full-time students who commute to campus should be granted reduced parking fees.
- Students who earn an A average on all speech assignments should be exempt from the final exam.
- Property taxes should be increased to fund classroom expansions at the city's elementary schools.

Notice that in each claim the word *should* appears. A claim of policy speaks to an "ought" condition, proposing that certain better outcomes would be realized if the proposed condition was met.

To build a strong case for a claim of policy, you must provide the audience with a three-part justification consisting of (1) a need or a problem, (2) a solution, and (3) evidence of the solution's feasibility. (See Chapter 26 for more on the problem-solution pattern of arrangement.)

By nature, claims of policy involve claims of fact and often claims of value as well. Consider the following example:

POLICY CLAIM:	The city should provide walking paths in all municipal parks.
FACT:	Almost every park in the city is busy several times each day with recreational walkers. This activity is noticeably greater on weekends.
VALUE:	Walking on properly maintained paths is healthier both for walkers and for the park landscape.

The fact and value claims become, essentially, pieces of evidence in support of the policy claim. The fact statement provides objective evidence, and the value statement offers a more subjective justification of the policy. This suggests that successful speakers need to be quite familiar with all three kinds of argument (see Table 25.1).

So far, we have seen that persuasive speeches can consist of three different kinds of claims: of fact, of value, and of policy. Regardless of the type of claim you make, if you fail to provide convincing evidence in support of it, the audience will not accept it. The following section reviews the different types of evidence used to support these claims.

USING EVIDENCE TO SUPPORT YOUR CLAIMS

In addition to the kinds of evidence described in Chapter 8 (examples, narratives, testimony, facts, and statistics), all of which can be considered as external

TABLE 25.1 • Sample Claims for Arguments of Fact, Value, and Policy

Type of Argument	Claim of fact *(focuses on whether something is or is not true or whether something will or will not happen)*	Claim of value *(addresses issues of judgment)*	Claim of policy *(recommends that a specific course of action be taken, or approved of, by an audience)*
Sample Claim	• Demand for online college courses will be strong in the next decade. • Interactions between herbal supplements and OTC drugs can be harmful. • Breastfeeding is healthier than bottle feeding in the first year.	• The three strikes law is unfair. • The "ideal weight" chart is not ideal. • Title IX hurts male athletes.	• Cigarette prices should be lowered. • Airport security measures should be revamped. • The NBA draft should be changed.

evidence (see p. 400), several other kinds of evidence exist that you can use to persuade audiences to believe your claims.[8] You might, for example, rely on audience members' existing knowledge and opinions — on what listeners already think and believe — as evidence for your claims. Or you might use your own knowledge and expertise as evidence. Finally, you might use the kind of external evidence with which you are already familiar — that of narratives, testimony, facts, and statistics.

Audience Knowledge and Opinions

Research suggests that what your listeners already know or think about your topic ultimately determines their acceptance or rejection of claims you make about it.[9] Nothing is more persuasive to listeners than a reaffirmation of their own attitudes, beliefs, and values, especially when making claims of value and policy. For this reason, the *audience's knowledge and opinions* on the topic can often be the most persuasive evidence. Using the audience's existing knowledge and beliefs as evidence for a claim works something like this:

CLAIM: Natural life support for human activity on the moon may come sooner than we think.

AUDIENCE KNOWLEDGE AS EVIDENCE: You've no doubt read in the papers and seen on the news that scientists recently discovered sources of water on the moon.

WARRANT: Water found on the moon can be used to produce oxygen for human life support.

Here the speaker uses the audience's knowledge of the discovery of water on the moon to support the claim that natural life support will eventually be possible there. The warrant that water on the moon could be converted into oxygen creates a bridge between the evidence and the claim.

The key to using an audience's knowledge and opinions to support your claim is audience analysis. For example, if your topic is privacy on the Internet, you could conduct interviews or distribute surveys that elicit audience members' opinions and gauge what they know about privacy laws or other pertinent information. On the basis of their responses, you could select the evidence with which they are most likely to have some familiarity. Of course, if an audience lacks knowledge on the subject of your claims, you cannot use this kind of evidence. Another kind of evidence is required.

Speaker Knowledge and Opinions

Arguments can sometimes be built on the basis of the *speaker's knowledge and opinions,* or expertise. Doing so, however, will work only if the audience believes the speaker has the authority or credibility to speak on the matter. This credibility may derive from the speaker's personal experience or from his or her original contribution to the topic. As support for a claim, speaker expertise might work like this:

CLAIM:	Natural life support for human activity on the moon may come sooner than we think.
SPEAKER KNOWLEDGE AS EVIDENCE:	My colleagues and I recently found signs of the existence of water on the moon.
WARRANT:	Water found on the moon can be used to produce oxygen for human life support.

In this case, the speaker is one of a group of scientists who discovered that reserves of water exist on the moon. The audience accepts the speaker's professional assertion as evidence.

No matter how credible, the speaker's knowledge and opinion are still "once removed" from the audience. And, as noted, nothing is more persuasive to listeners than a reaffirmation of their own attitudes, beliefs, and values. Nevertheless, if audience members find a speaker credible, they will generally accept his or her knowledge and opinions. To gain acceptance, the speaker will have to establish the appropriate credentials (degrees, past experiences, awards, etc.). Be aware, however, that unless you are truly an expert on a topic, very few speeches can be convincingly built on speaker experience and knowledge alone. Some points in a speech might be substantiated by your own credentials, but not most. For that reason, it is important that you do your research.

If the audience lacks sufficient knowledge to use as evidence and you are not a known expert on the subject, you will need to use yet another type of evidence to support your claims. This is the kind of evidence with which you are already familiar (see Chapter 8).

External Evidence

External evidence is any information in support of a claim that originates with sources other than the audience or the speaker. External evidence consists of the kind of supporting material discussed in Chapter 8 — examples, narratives, testimony, facts, and statistics drawn from outside sources. Importantly, unlike evidence based on audience knowledge and beliefs, external evidence is most powerful when you cite information that the audience has not previously used in forming an opinion.[10] Thus, when using external evidence to prove your claims, seek out information your audience is not likely to know but will find persuasive.

 CHECKLIST

Testing the Strength of Your Evidence

As you identify and apply evidence to a claim, keep in mind the three tests of evidence:

_____ 1. Is the evidence directly relevant to the claim?
_____ 2. Is it timely, or recent and up-to-date?
_____ 3. Will audience members find it credible, or from a source they can trust?

In order for you to successfully support a claim with external evidence, your audience must believe that your information is credible. Consider a speech based on a speculative claim of future fact. In it, you argue that in five years half of all textbooks will be published only in "e-book" format. That is, they will be available to students in electronic form only.

CLAIM:	In five years, half of all the textbooks in the U.S. will be available only in electronic form.
EXTERNAL EVIDENCE:	As chair of the committee on the future of the textbook, I have reports from all major publishers on their plans for electronic publication.
WARRANT:	Apparently, publishers believe that enough students are online and dislike the price of paper textbooks to commit to this course of action.

In this case, the speaker gets evidence for the claim from her own knowledge and opinions. The strength of the evidence for the audience's acceptance of the claim depends on the level of credibility the audience assigns to the outside source — in this case, her position as chair of the committee on the future of the textbook.

TYPES OF WARRANTS USED TO LINK CLAIMS WITH EVIDENCE

As with claims and evidence, depending on the nature and goal of your persuasive speech, you will want to select different kinds of warrants for your arguments. *Motivational warrants* appeal to the audience's needs and emotions. In Aristotle's terms, the motivational warrant makes use of *pathos*. *Authoritative warrants* appeal to the credibility the audience assigns to the source of the evidence; again, in classical terms this appeal is based on *ethos*. *Substantive warrants*, based on *logos*, appeal to the audience's beliefs about the reliability of any factual evidence you offer. (See Chapter 24 for a review of these classical terms.)

Motivational Warrants: Appeals to Emotion

No doubt most readers have seen television and magazine advertisements asking viewers to give just pennies a day to sponsor a starving child in a distant land. The claim may say, "You can easily afford to join this organization dedicated to ending the hunger of thousands of children." The evidence may be stated as "For the price of one soft drink you can feed a child for a week." What's the warrant? "You don't want any child to starve or go without proper medical care." The speaker intends the warrant to motivate listeners by arousing their sympathy for those who lack basic human necessities. **Motivational warrants** use the needs, desires, emotions, and values of audience members as the basis for accepting some evidence as support for a claim, and thus accepting the claim itself. More often than not, motivational warrants are implied rather than stated outright. In terms of the ad to support a starving child, we don't have to be told that we don't want children to starve; if the value or desire is meaningful to us, we realize it while attending to other parts of the message. Here are some other needs and values that can operate as motivational warrants in arguments:

career success	meaningful	health and wellness
quality leisure time	friendships	quality education
financial security	good taste	fine material
physical attractiveness	wealth	possessions
strong marriages	happy families	clean environment

Authoritative Warrants: Appeals to Credibility

Just as one form of evidence relies on the speaker's knowledge and opinions, some warrants rely on an audience's beliefs about the credibility or acceptability of a source of evidence. Such is the case with **authoritative warrants**. For example, in terms of sponsoring a hungry child, the speaker might make the claim that we should contribute financially to an agency that feeds hungry children. The speaker's evidence is that any amount we give, however small, will go far in meeting the agency's objectives. As a warrant, the speaker notes that a certain celebrity or popular politician works with the agency and its recipients; perhaps that individual is even delivering the message.

The success or failure of authoritative warrants rests on how highly the audience regards the authority figure. If listeners hold the person in high esteem, they are more likely to find the evidence and the claim acceptable. Thus authoritative warrants make the credibility of sources of evidence all the more important. In other words, it's possible that naming the source of evidence can also provide the authoritative warrant. For example, in support of the claim that "McDonald's Big Mac sandwiches are among the most popular fast-food sandwiches enjoyed by famous people," you could offer the evidence that "Celebrity X has said that Big Macs are his favorite fast food"; this gives both the evidence (a famous person who eats Big Macs) and the warrant (the specific famous person is Celebrity X) in the same sentence.

If you happen to be highly knowledgeable on a subject, an authoritative warrant can be made by reference to yourself. In this case, the warrant provides the speaker's knowledge and opinions as evidence. For example, in a speech on diet plans that work, you might claim that "Diet Plan B is more effective than Plan A or Plan C for many people" and use yourself both as a source of evidence and as a basis for the warrant: "I have used all three plans and have had the most success with Plan B." Your experience offers evidence for the claim, and you, having had the experience, give warrant to the evidence.

Substantive Warrants: Appeals to Reasoning

Substantive warrants operate on the basis of the audience's beliefs about the reliability of factual evidence. If you claim that your fellow college students should concern themselves more with learning from courses than with the grades they receive, you might offer as evidence the point that what is learned in a course is more applicable to future job responsibilities than the grade received in the course, and you might provide as the warrant a statement that "whereas better grades may lead to more job opportunities, better learning leads to better grades." The relationship between the claim and the evidence is that students will increase their chances for job opportunities if they concentrate on learning instead of on grades; for example, better grades follow from better learning.

There are several types of substantive warrants, or ways of factually linking evidence with a claim. Three that occur most commonly in speeches are *causation*, *sign*, and *analogy*.

Warrants by cause (also called *reasoning by cause*) offer a cause-and-effect relationship as proof of the claim. For example, welfare critics often reason by cause when they suggest that providing funds to people without making them work causes them to be lazy. Their opponents also reason by cause when they rebut this argument. Rather than suggesting a cause-to-effect relationship, however, they might suggest an effect-to-cause relationship, as in: "Welfare mothers don't work outside the home [effect] because the welfare system does not help them with day care [cause]." Similarly, a speaker might argue the following:

CLAIM:	Candidate X lost his 2009 bid for the Senate largely because of his age.
EVIDENCE:	Many available media reports refer to the age issue with which Candidate X had to contend.
WARRANT:	Our society attributes less competence to people who are older versus those who are younger.

Older age is assumed to be a cause of Candidate X's loss in the senatorial campaign. The warrant substantiates the relationship of cause (age) to effect (loss of race) on the basis of society's negative stereotypes of older people.

As pointed out in the accompanying checklist, when using warrants by cause, it is essential to make relevant and accurate assertions about cause and effect.

✓ CHECKLIST

Making Effective Use of Reasoning by Cause

_____ 1. Avoid making hasty assertions of cause or effect on the basis of stereotypes.

_____ 2. Avoid making hasty assertions of cause or effect based on hearsay or tradition.

_____ 3. Be certain that you don't offer a single cause or effect as the only possibility when others are known to exist.

_____ 4. When multiple causes or effects can be given, be sure to note their importance relative to one another.

Warrants by sign (also called _reasoning by sign_) imply that such a close relationship exists between two variables that the presence or absence of one may be taken as an indication of the presence or absence of the other.[11] For example, smoke is a sign of fire. Coughing and sneezing are signs of a cold. A claim and evidence are often associated by sign:

CLAIM:	Summer job opportunities for college students will probably decline at resort locations in the southern Rocky Mountains.
EVIDENCE:	Throughout the southern Rockies in the late winter and early spring, there was a record number of forest fires that destroyed many resorts.
WARRANT:	Widespread natural disasters curtail employment in the affected areas.

In this example, negative effects on employment are an economic sign of natural disasters. The claim is supported by the evidence if the audience accepts the warrant that employment becomes unstable in the wake of natural disasters.

Finally, **warrants by analogy** (also called *reasoning by analogy*) compare two similar cases and imply that what is true in one case is true in the other. The assumption is that the characteristics of Case A and Case B are similar, if not the same, and that what is true for B must also be true for A. Warrant by analogy or comparison occurs frequently in speeches. Consider this example:

CLAIM:	Students will have a better feeling about Mr. Honnacker's speech class if he drops the absence policy.
EVIDENCE:	Student satisfaction increased substantially in Ms. Orlander's math class when she dropped the absence policy.
WARRANT:	Mr. Honnacker's speech class and Ms. Orlander's math class are equivalent with respect to other factors that satisfy students.

Here the speaker compares the speech class with the math class, assuming that both have in common students who are equally satisfied or dissatisfied depending on the nature of the absence policy. The analogy links the evidence from the math class example to the claim about the speech class.

ADDRESSING THE OTHER SIDE OF THE ARGUMENT

There are at least two sides to every argument. Thus all attempts at persuasion are subject to counterpersuasion. Your listeners may be persuaded to accept your claims, but once they are exposed to counterclaims they may change their minds. According to a theory called the **inoculation effect**, by anticipating counterarguments and then addressing or rebutting them, you can "inoculate" your listeners against the "virus" of these other viewpoints. The theory rests on the biological principle of inducing resistance through exposure to small quantities of a harmful substance. Just as you can induce resistance to disease in this manner, the inoculation theory posits that you can induce resistance to counterclaims by acknowledging them.

As noted, if your listeners are unaware of any counterclaims, they may be persuaded by your arguments for a time. However, once they hear other viewpoints, they may change their minds. If listeners are aware of counterclaims and you ignore them, you risk a loss of credibility. As described in the accompanying checklist on addressing competing arguments, however, this does not mean that you need to painstakingly acknowledge and refute all opposing claims.

✓ **CHECKLIST**

Techniques for Addressing Competing Arguments

_____ 1. If the audience knows of claims and evidence that oppose yours, and those claims and evidence can be refuted, raise them in your speech and refute them.

_____ 2. If you don't have time to refute counterclaims that are known to your audience, mention the counterclaims and concede them if your evidence can withstand it. In other words, simply note that there are claims to the contrary, specify the claims, reiterate your own claim, and then move on.

_____ 3. If there are counterclaims that your audience may be unaware of, ignore them if there is no time to refute them. Otherwise, if time permits, state the counterclaims and refute them.

_____ 4. From an ethical perspective, you may ignore competing claims only when they do not severely weaken your own claims and when you have no time to address them adequately.

Source: Adapted from James C. McCroskey, _An Introduction to Rhetorical Communication,_ 6th ed. (Englewood Cliffs, N.J.: Prentice-Hall, 1993).

Fallacies in Reasoning

 Web links

A **logical fallacy** is either a false or erroneous statement or an invalid or deceptive line of reasoning.[12] In either case, you need to be aware of fallacies in order to avoid making them in your own speeches and to be able to identify them in the speeches of others. Many fallacies of reasoning exist; the following are merely a few.

BEGGING THE QUESTION

Begging the question is a fallacy in which an argument is stated in such a way that it cannot help but be true, even though no evidence has been presented. "Intelligent Design is the correct explanation for biological change over time because we can see godly evidence in our complex natural world" is an example of an argument that relies on the kind of circular thinking characteristic of the begging-the-question fallacy. "War kills" is another. In neither statement has the speaker offered any evidence for the conclusion.

BANDWAGONING

Speakers who rely on **bandwagoning** pose arguments that use (unsubstantiated) general opinions as their (false) bases. "Nikes are superior to other brands of shoes because everyone wears Nikes" and "Everyone on campus is voting for her so you should, too" are examples of bandwagoning. The critical listener will ask, "Just who is 'everyone'?"

EITHER-OR FALLACY

The **either-or fallacy** poses an argument stated in terms of two alternatives only, even though there may be many additional alternatives. "If you don't send little Susie to private school this year, she will not gain admission to college" is an example of an argument posed as an either-or fallacy, as is "Either you're with us or against us."

AD HOMINEM ARGUMENT

The **ad hominem argument** targets a person instead of the issue at hand in an attempt to incite an audience's dislike for that person. Examples include: "I'm a better candidate than X because, unlike X, I work for a living" and "How can you accept my opponent's position on education when he has been divorced?"

RED HERRING

In the **red herring fallacy**, the speaker's argument relies on irrelevant premises for its conclusion. For example, "The previous speaker suggests that Medicare is in shambles. I disagree and recommend that we study why the young don't respect their elders." This argument makes no connection between the state of Medicare and the lack of respect for society's elders among the youth. Another example of a red herring fallacy is to say, "I fail to see why hunting should be considered cruel when it gives pleasure to so many people and employment to even more."[13] The speaker offers no statistics to support the truth of this statement.

HASTY GENERALIZATION

When a speaker uses a **hasty generalization**, the argument uses an isolated instance to make an unwarranted general conclusion, as in the following examples: "As shown by the example of a Labrador retriever biting my sister, this type of dog is dangerous and its breeding should be outlawed" and "My neighbor who works for K-Mart is untrustworthy; therefore, K-Mart is not a trustworthy company."

NON SEQUITUR

Non sequiturs "do not follow"; that is, the argument's conclusion does not connect to the reasoning. For example, "Because she lives in the richest country in the world" does not mean that "she must be extremely wealthy." Neither is it accurate to say, "If we can send a man to the moon, we should be able to cure cancer in five years."

SLIPPERY SLOPE

When a speaker uses a **slippery slope** in his argument, he or she is making a faulty assumption that one case will lead to a series of events or actions. For example, "Helping refugees in the Sudan today will force us to help refugees across Africa and around the world" or "If we outsource jobs from the United States, then other companies will outsource jobs, and the U.S. economy will collapse."

APPEAL TO TRADITION

Speakers who use the **appeal to tradition** phrase arguments to suggest that the audience should agree with the claim because that is the way it has always been done. "A marriage should be between a man and a woman because that is how it has always been" is an example of an appeal to tradition, as is "The president of the United States must be a man because a woman has never been president."

26 Organizing the Persuasive Speech

Once you've developed your speech claims, the next step in drafting a persuasive speech is to structure your speech points using one (or more) of the organizational patterns described in Chapter 12 — topical, chronological, spatial, causal (cause-effect), problem-solution, narrative, and circular — and in this chapter. There is no one "best way" to organize a persuasive speech — or any kind of speech. Instead, individual speeches must be put together strategically in ways that will best achieve the goals you have set for them.

Factors to Consider When Choosing an Organizational Pattern

 WEB Outliner

Three factors are critical to consider when selecting an organizational pattern: (1) the nature of your arguments and evidence, (2) the nature of your target audience, and (3) the nature of your specific speech purpose. These considerations apply equally to your selection of types of evidence and persuasive appeals (see Chapter 25). An additional consideration is that of culture (see Chapter 6, p. 96, and the section, "Adapt to Cultural Differences" and the "Public Speaking in Cultural Perspective" box in Chapter 12, p. 211).

ARGUMENTS AND EVIDENCE

As described in Chapter 12, some speech topics or claims clearly suggest a specific design. A speech that argues for a reduction in the price of cigarettes, for example, implies that high cigarette prices represent a *problem* and that lower prices represent a *solution*. Thus one obvious way to arrange speech points is with the *problem-solution pattern* (see Chapter 12 and p. 411). Many such **claims of policy** (e.g., claims that address an "ought condition" and use the word "should") fit naturally into the problem-solution pattern.

Similarly, consider a speech in which it is argued that newborn children do best when their mothers stay home with them full-time for at least the first six months. This **claim of value** (e.g., claims that address issues of judgment) implies that for at least a limited period, staying home is superior to working. One potentially effective way of ordering this claim is with the *comparative advantage pattern of arrangement* (see p. 415). Here, the speaker arranges main points to demonstrate a series of advantages associated with his or her claim versus an alternative position or positions — in this case, mothers who don't stay home.

Finally, consider the **claim of fact** (i.e., claims addressing whether something is or is not true or will or will not happen) that SUVs hurt the environment by releasing up to 30 percent more carbon monoxide and hydrocarbons and 75 percent more nitrogen oxide than passenger cars.[1] The claim implies that greater emissions of noxious gases (cause) lead to degradation of the environment (effect). Hence one way to arrange speech points for this claim is by using the *cause-effect pattern of organization* (see Chapter 12 for a description and sample outlines of this pattern). Alternatively, you could argue this claim in a *problem-solution* or *problem-cause-solution pattern,* so that the first point establishes the problem (SUVs hurt the environment) and subsequent points explain reasons for the problem (SUVs use too much fuel) and provide a solution (enact tougher fuel economy standards).

TARGET AUDIENCE

Another factor to consider when deciding how to arrange your persuasive speech is what your **target audience** knows about the topic and how audience members stand in relation to it (see Chapter 6).

Persuasion scholar Herbert Simon describes four types of potential audiences and suggests a different organizational pattern for each[2] (see Table 26.1). For example, the *refutation pattern of organization,* in which points are arranged as a series of rebuttals of opposing claims, has been shown to soften the reservations

1. Review topic/argument/evidence for likely pattern.

    ↓

2. Determine where the audience stands in relation to the message. Are listeners hostile to it? Sympathetic? Critical? Informed or uninformed? Involved or apathetic?

    ↓

3. Identify the type and degree of change you seek from the audience. Modify attitudes and values? Change behavior? To what degree?

    ↓

4. Consider the cultural composition of the audience (see Chapter 12, p. 211).

    ↓

5. Select an organizational pattern.

Figure 26.1 Factors to Consider When Organizing Your Persuasive Speech

TABLE 26.1 • Persuasive Strategies and Audience Type

Audience	Strategies
Hostile Audience or One That Strongly Disagrees	• Stress areas of agreement. • Address opposing views. • Don't expect major change in attitudes. • Consider the refutation pattern. • Wait until the end before asking the audience to act, if at all.
Critical and Conflicted Audience	• Present strong arguments and evidence. • Address opposing views, perhaps by using the refutation pattern.
Sympathetic Audience	• Use motivational stories (the narrative pattern; emotional appeals) to reinforce positive attitudes. • Stress your commonality with listeners. • Clearly tell your listeners what you want them to think or do.
Uninformed, Less Educated, or Apathetic Audience	• Focus on capturing listeners' attention. • Stress personal credibility and "likability." • Arrange points logically, perhaps using a topical pattern.

of the **hostile audience** or **one that strongly disagrees**, as well as the **critical and conflicted audience**. The *narrative organizational pattern*, in which you frame your speech as a story with characters, plot, and setting, is particularly effective in addressing a **sympathetic audience** that is already on your side (see Chapter 8). For the **uninformed**, **less educated**, or **apathetic audience**, getting your listeners' attention and establishing speaker credibility are critical to their acceptance of your message; of secondary importance is how the speech is organized. One strategy that may work well is arranging points logically, using a *topical pattern of arrangement* (see Chapter 12). Table 26.1 offers strategies for various audiences. Table 26.2 (p. 417) summarizes the patterns discussed in this chapter.

SPECIFIC SPEECH PURPOSE

A third consideration in choosing how you will order speech points is your **specific speech purpose** — how you want your audience to react to your message. Persuasive speeches attempt to influence audience attitudes or behavior. Some speeches attempt to modify audience attitudes and values so that they move in the direction of the speaker's stance, while others aim for an explicit response, as when a speaker urges listeners to donate money for a cause or to vote for a candidate. Sometimes a speech will attempt to modify both attitudes and actions. Thus a final consideration in choosing a pattern for speech points is the type and degree of change you seek in your audience. Do you want to modify attitudes and values? (If so, to what degree?) Do you want to get the audience to act? To do both? Keep in mind that it is far easier to modify attitudes or behavior slightly than it is to do so to a great extent.

Problem-Solution Pattern of Arrangement   Chapter quizzes

One commonly used design for persuasive speeches, especially those based on claims of policy and claims of fact, is the **problem-solution pattern of arrangement** (see Chapter 12). Here you organize speech points to demonstrate the nature and significance of a problem and then to provide justification for a proposed solution:

I. Problem (define what it is)

II. Solution (offer a way to overcome the problem)

But many problem-solution speeches require more than two points to adequately explain the problem and to substantiate the recommended solution. Thus a **problem-cause-solution pattern of arrangement** may be in order:

I. The nature of the problem (identify its causes, incidence, etc.)

II. Reasons for the problem (explain why it's a problem, for whom, etc.)

III. Unsatisfactory solutions (discuss those that have not worked) *(optional step)*

IV. Proposed solution (explain why it's expected to work)

A claim of policy can be organized effectively using the problem-solution or the problem-cause-solution pattern. One way to build a strong claim of policy, for example, is to provide the audience with a four-point justification consisting of: (1) a need or a problem, (2) reasons for the problem, (3) a solution to the need or problem, and (4) evidence of the solution's feasibility.

 CHECKLIST

Organizing a Claim of Policy

✓   Describe the need or problem.

✓   Discuss reasons for the problem.

✓   Offer a solution to the need or problem.

✓   Offer evidence of the solution's feasibility.

First comes a *need* or a *problem.* The policy must speak to a real issue that the audience would like to have resolved. This assumes that the audience will benefit if the proposal is adopted. If your claim is that "the NBA draft should be changed so that young athletes aren't tempted to throw away an opportunity to get an education," the need is for a revamping of the NBA draft policy to encourage athletes to complete their college education. Second, the justification for a policy must provide *reasons for the problem.* Some reasons that the NBA draft needs to be fixed might include the statement that its present policies lure young athletes to pursue unrealistic goals of superstardom and that immature players weaken the quality of the game. Next, you must provide a *solution to the problem,* a specific way to address the need. The policy claim that the NBA draft should be changed must then offer an alternative policy, such as "the NBA draft needs to adopt a minimum age of twenty." Fourth, the justification for the policy claim should offer *evidence of the solution's feasibility.* In this case, the speaker could provide evidence showing that sports organizations in other countries have successfully adopted a minimum age:

GENERAL PURPOSE:	To persuade
SPECIFIC PURPOSE:	To persuade my audience that the NBA draft should be changed so that young athletes are no longer tempted to throw away their chance to get an education.
THESIS STATED AS NEED OR PROBLEM:	The NBA draft should be changed so that athletes like you aren't tempted to throw away an opportunity to get an education.
MAIN POINTS:	I. The NBA draft should be revamped so that college-age athletes are not tempted to drop out of school. *(Need/problem)*
	II. Its present policies lure young athletes to pursue unrealistic goals of superstardom while weakening the quality of the game with immature players. *(Reasons for the problem)*
	III. The NBA draft needs to adopt a minimum age of 20. *(Solution to the problem)*
	IV. National leagues in countries X and Y have done this successfully. *(Evidence of the solution's feasibility)*

Monroe's Motivated Sequence

 Web links

The **motivated sequence pattern of arrangement**, developed in the mid-1930s by Alan Monroe,[3] is a five-step process that begins with arousing listeners' attention and ends with calling for action. This time-tested variant of the problem-solution pattern of arrangement is particularly effective when you want the audience to do something — buy a product, donate time or money to a cause, and so forth. Yet it is equally useful when you want listeners to reconsider their present way of thinking about something or continue to believe as they do but with greater commitment.

STEP 1: ATTENTION

The *attention step* addresses listeners' core concerns, making the speech highly relevant to them. Here is an excerpt from a student speech by Ed Partlow on becoming an organ donor:

> Today I'm going to talk about a subject that can be both personal and emotional. I am going to talk about becoming an organ donor. Donating an

organ is a simple step you can take that will literally give life to others — to your husband or wife, mother or father, son or daughter — or to a beautiful child whom you've never met.

There is one thing I want to acknowledge from the start. Many of you may be uncomfortable with the idea of becoming an organ donor. I want to establish right off that it's OK if you don't want to become a donor.

Many of us are willing to donate our organs, but because we haven't taken the action to properly become a donor, our organs go unused. As a result, an average of fifteen people die every day because of lack of available organs.

In this first step, the speaker makes the topic relevant to listeners by showing how their actions could help those closest to them. He further involves the audience by acknowledging the sensitive nature of his topic and assuring them that he respects their right to make up their own minds. The statistics he cites underscore the seriousness of his purpose.

STEP 2: NEED

Sometimes called the problem step, the *need step* isolates and describes the issue to be addressed. Referring to it as a "need" reminds us that if you can show the members of an audience that they have an important need that must be satisfied or a problem that must be solved, they will have a reason to listen to your propositions (see Chapter 24). Continuing with the organ donor speech, here the speaker establishes the need for organ donors:

According to the U.S. Department of Health and Human Services, there are approximately 80,000 people on the waiting list for an organ transplant. Over 50,000 are waiting for kidney transplants alone, and the stakes are high: 90 percent of patients who receive a kidney from a living donor live at least ten years after the transplant. One of the people on the waiting list is Aidan Malony, who graduated from this college two years ago. Without a transplant, he will die. It is agonizing for his family and friends to see him in this condition. And it is deeply frustrating to them that more people don't sign and carry organ donor cards. I have always carried my organ donor card with me, but I didn't realize the extreme importance of doing so before talking to Aidan.

Every sixteen minutes another name joins that of Aidan Malony and is added to the National Transplant Waiting List.

STEP 3: SATISFACTION

Once you have gotten your listeners' attention and have established a need or a problem that is personally important to them, you are ready to introduce your proposed solution to the problem. The *satisfaction step* identifies the solution. This step begins the crux of the speech, offering audience members a proposal to reinforce or change their attitudes, beliefs, and values regarding the need at hand. Here is an example from the speech on organ donation:

> It takes only two steps to become an organ donor.
> First, fill out an organ donor card and carry it with you. You may also choose to have a note added to your driver's license the next time you renew it.
> Second and most important, tell your family that you want to become an organ donor and ask them to honor your wishes when the time arrives. Otherwise, they may discourage the use of your organs should something happen to you. Check with your local hospital to find out about signing a family pledge—a contract where family members share their wishes about organ and tissue donation. This is an absolutely essential step in making sure the necessary individuals will honor your wish to become an organ donor. Despite what you see on *ER* (the television program), often medical personnel do not get access to your license or your card. I've been a firefighter for over twenty years and can verify this.

The satisfaction step continues by providing more detail about the solution. In this case, the speaker goes on to provide support for why organ donation leads to so many lives being saved. In general, support in the satisfaction step includes evidence that illustrates or demonstrates the feasibility of the proposed solution and its superiority to other alternatives and to the status quo.

STEP 4: VISUALIZATION

In the *visualization step*, you provide the audience with a vision of anticipated outcomes associated with the solution. The purpose of the step is to carry audience members beyond accepting the feasibility of your proposal to seeing how it will actually benefit them:

> There are so many organs and such a variety of tissue that may be transplanted. One organ donor can help up to fifty people. Who can forget the story of 7-year-old

---

 CHECKLIST

Steps in the Motivated Sequence

✓ **Step 1: Attention**   Address listeners' core concerns, making the speech highly relevant to them.

✓ **Step 2: Need**   Show listeners that they have an important need that must be satisfied or a problem that must be solved.

✓ **Step 3: Satisfaction**   Introduce your proposed solution to the problem.

✓ **Step 4: Visualization**   Provide listeners with a vision of anticipated outcomes associated with the solution.

✓ **Step 5: Action**   Make a direct request of listeners that involves reconsidering their present way of thinking about something, continuing to believe as they do but with renewed vigor, or implementing a new set of behaviors or plan of action.

American Nicholas Green, the innocent victim of a highway robbery in Italy that cost him his life? Stricken with unfathomable grief, Nicholas's parents, Reg and Maggie Green, nevertheless immediately decided to donate Nicholas's organs. As a direct result of the donation, seven Italians thrive today, grateful recipients of Nicholas's heart, corneas, liver, pancreas cells, and kidneys. Today, organ donations in Italy are twice as high as they were in 1993, the year preceding Nicholas's death. The Italians called this phenomenon "The Nicholas Effect."

STEP 5: ACTION

The *action step,* the final element in the motivated sequence, involves making a direct request of the audience. Here the speaker asks audience members to act according to their acceptance of the message. This may involve reconsidering their present way of thinking about something, continuing to believe as they do but with greater commitment, or implementing a new set of behaviors or plan of action. The speaker seeks an implicit or explicit response of "I agree with you all the way. I am going to do it." Here, the speaker makes an explicit call to action:

> It takes courage to become an organ donor.
> You have the courage to become an organ donor.
> All you need to do is say yes to organ and tissue donation on your donor card and/or driver's license and discuss your decision with your family.
> Be part of "The Nicholas effect."

The nature of the issue you are addressing will dictate how you implement the motivated sequence. If you're presenting a highly complex problem, you may need to spend much of the speech detailing the characteristics and effects of the problem. If you're talking to an audience that is familiar with the problem, you'll need only to highlight the problem and spend most of the speech on satisfaction and visualization. The extent of the material required for the attention step and the nature of the specific statement of action will depend on your own relationship with your listeners — how well they know you, your experience with the problem, and so on.

Comparative Advantage
Pattern of Arrangement

 Chapter quizzes

Another way to organize speech points is to show how your viewpoint or proposal is superior to one or more alternative viewpoints or proposals. This design, called the **comparative advantage pattern of arrangement**, is most effective when your audience is already aware of the issue or problem and agrees that a need for a solution (or an alternative view) exists. Because listeners are alert to the issue, you don't have to spend time establishing its existence. Instead, you can proceed directly to favorably comparing your position with the alternatives. With this strategy, you are assuming that your audience is open to various alternative solutions.

In order to maintain your credibility, it is important that you identify alternatives that your audience is familiar with as well as those that are supported by opposing interests. If you omit familiar alternatives, your listeners will wonder if you are fully informed on the topic and become skeptical of your comparative alternative as well as your credibility. The final step in a comparative advantage speech is to drive home the unique advantages of your option relative to competing options with brief but compelling evidence.

Using the comparative advantage pattern, the main points in a speech addressing the best way to control the deer population might look like this:

THESIS:	Rather than hunting, fencing, or contraception alone, the best way to reduce the deer population is by a dual strategy of hunting and contraception.
SPECIFIC SPEECH PURPOSE:	To convince my audience that controlling the deer population through a combination of hunting and contraception is superior to a strategy of fencing, hunting, or contraception alone.
MAIN POINT I:	A combination strategy is superior to hunting alone because many areas are too densely populated by humans to permit hunting; in such cases contraceptive darts and vaccines can address the problem. (*Advantage over alternative No. 1*)
MAIN POINT II:	A combination strategy is superior to relying solely on fencing because fencing is far too expensive for widespread use. (*Advantage over alternative No. 2*)
MAIN POINT III:	A dual strategy is superior to relying only on contraception because only a limited number of deer are candidates for contraceptive darts and vaccines. (*Advantage over alternative No. 3*)

Refutation Pattern of Arrangement

 Chapter quizzes

Similar to debate, the **refutation pattern of arrangement** addresses each main point and then refutes (disproves) an opposing claim to your position. The aim here is to bolster your own position by disproving the opposing claim. Note that it is important to refute strong rather than weak objections to the claim, since refuting weak objections won't sway the audience.[4] Further, it is probably best to use this pattern when you are confident that the opposing argument is weak and vulnerable to attack. If done well, refutation may influence audience members who either disagree with you or are conflicted about where they stand.

Main points arranged in a refutation pattern follow a format similar to this:

MAIN POINT I: State the opposing position.

MAIN POINT II: Describe the implications or ramifications of the opposing claim.

MAIN POINT III: Offer arguments and evidence for your position.

MAIN POINT IV: Contrast your position with the opposing claim to drive home the superiority of your position.

Consider the speaker who argues for increased energy conservation versus a policy of drilling for oil in protected land in Alaska:

THESIS: Rather than drilling for oil in Alaska's Arctic National Wildlife Refuge (ANWR), as politicians propose, we should focus on energy conservation measures as a way of lessening our dependence on foreign oil.

SPECIFIC PURPOSE: To convince my audience that rather than drilling for oil in the ANWR, we should maintain the refuge's protected status and focus instead on conserving energy.

MAIN POINT I: Politicians claim that drilling in the Arctic refuge is the only way to increase our energy independence; that it will have little negative impact on the environment; and that if we don't take this step our reliance on foreign energy will only increase. *(Describes opposing claims)*

TABLE 26.2 • Organizational Formats

Organizational Format	Description
Problem-Solution	Speech points arranged to demonstrate a problem and then to offer solution.
Problem-Cause-Solution	Speech points arranged in order to demonstrate problem, reasons for problem, and solution to problem.
Monroe's Motivated Sequence	Speech points arranged to motivate listeners to act on something or to shift their attitudes in direction of speaker's.
Cause-Effect	Speech points arranged to demonstrate that a particular set of circumstances leads to a specific result (either desirable or undesirable) or, conversely, that various results (effects) follow from a particular set of circumstances. See Chapter 12 for the description of this pattern.
Comparative Advantage	Speech points arranged to demonstrate that your viewpoint or proposal contrasts favorably with (is superior to) one or more alternative positions.
Refutation	Speech points arranged to disprove opposing claims.

MAIN POINT II:
By claiming that drilling in the refuge is the only solution to our reliance on foreign energy, politicians sidestep the need for stricter energy conservation policies, as well as the need to protect one of the last great pristine lands. *(Describes implications and ramifications of opposing claims)*

MAIN POINT III:
The massive construction needed to access the tundra will disturb the habitat of thousands of species and shift the focus from energy conservation to increased energy consumption, when the focus should be the reverse. *(Offers arguments and evidence for the speaker's position, as developed in subpoints)*

MAIN POINT IV:
The politicians' plan would encourage consumption while also endangering the environment; my plan would encourage stricter energy conservation while protecting one of the world's few remaining wildernesses. *(Contrasts the speaker's position with the opposition's to drive home the former's superiority)*

Sample Visually Annotated Persuasive Speech

 WEB Video

Emergency in the Emergency Room

LISA ROTH

Illinois Central College

The following speech by college student Lisa Roth investigates the crisis in emergency room care and advocates a claim of policy—that our emergency room system should be overhauled. Note that the organizational format of the speech is problem-cause-solution, and to help build her argument, Lisa offers a variety of types of claims, evidence, and reasoning (in classical terms, "proofs") to back up her assertions.

Last year, 49-year-old Beatrice Vance began experiencing some alarming symptoms—nausea, shortness of breath, and chest pain. She called her daughter, Monique, and asked to be driven to the emergency room at Vista Medical Center in Lake County, Illinois. Upon arrival, a nurse briefly met with her. She asked Ms. Vance to wait until she could be seen by a doctor, as patients are treated in order of severity. •

Fully two hours later, when her name was finally called, Beatrice didn't respond. In fact, hospital officials found her slumped over in her chair, ten feet or so from the admitting station, unconscious and without a pulse. According to an *ABC*

• This dramatic incident serves as an effective attention getter.

Nightly News report on September 18, 2006, Beatrice had already died from a massive heart attack while waiting to be seen by a doctor. •

Sadly, Beatrice is not the only one who suffers at the hands of an overwhelmed, sometimes inconsistent, and sometimes incompetent emergency room staff. Hospitals across the country are plagued by problems. According to experts on the frontline, such as Dr. Brent Eastman, Chief Medical Advisor at Scripps Health Hospital in San Diego, America's emergency rooms are in a crisis that could jeopardize everyone in this room and all their loved ones. •

Effective hand gesture emphasizes gravity of crisis

Today, we'll uncover the catastrophic conditions existing in America's emergency rooms, discover what is causing these conditions, and look at how to restore our faith in a system that has — to quote from an editorial in the June 21, 2006, edition of the *New York Times* — "reached a breaking point." •

Uses body language and facial expression to add emphasis

To begin, emergency rooms are desperately overcrowded. • According to a landmark series of three reports on the breakdown of our emergency room system conducted by the Institute of Medicine, • the need for emergency rooms has increased by 26 percent since 1993; during the same period, 425 emergency departments closed their doors. The average emergency room wait is now almost four hours, according to a report broadcast on *Good Morning America* on September, 18, 2006, and patients could be asked to wait up to forty-eight hours before they are allowed into an inpatient bed.

The United States emergency care system is also seriously understaffed, especially with regard to specialists. • As reported in the *New York Times* editorial, emergency rooms find it very difficult to get specialists to take emergency room and trauma center calls. Furthermore, specialists such as neurosurgeons shy away from emergency room procedures. They don't like the lack of compensation associated with treating so many uninsured patients. They also worry about seeing their malpractice premiums rise.

Not only are emergency rooms understaffed; existing staff often are unprepared for disasters. An

• This vivid description of Beatrice Vance's unnecessary death is Lisa's first bid to prove that a problem exists. This appeal targets listeners' emotion (pathos).

• Here Lisa states her thesis, using expert authority to back it up. She wisely notes the speaker's job title and institutional affiliation.

• Lisa's speech preview indicates that it will be organized using a problem-cause-solution pattern, with three main points focusing in turn on the problems, causes, and solutions of the ER crisis, beginning with overcrowding.

• Lisa introduces the problems plaguing the ER system.

• Lisa wisely includes the adjective *landmark* to signal credibility for her evidence.

• Lisa introduces the second problem — understaffing.

investigation in the July 6, 2006, edition of the *Columbus Dispatch* found that EMTs received only one hour of training for major disaster preparation. What's even scarier, say a team of reporters at the *Fort Worth Star Telegram* on June 15, 2006, is that with one major disaster our emergency care service could fall apart completely.

The third problem with our current system is not surprising. There simply isn't enough money to adequately fund our emergency rooms.

The *New York Times* reports that emergency rooms are "notorious money losers." While most emergency rooms have operating budgets well in the millions, they receive only a fraction of what they need even while being asked to operate securely and safely. Additionally, as reported in the June 16, 2006, edition of the *Pittsburgh Tribune Review*, because of the lack of money, there are now 200,000 fewer hospital beds in the United States than there were in 1993, even as the need for them has increased tremendously.

So, our emergency rooms are broke, overcrowded, and understaffed. Don't you feel secure? •

We can pinpoint three specific causes for the emergency room crisis. These include the highly fragmented emergency medical care system, the uninsured patients, and the lack of money. •

Fragmentation occurs on all levels because there are no standardized procedures and no clear chain of command. On the regional level, emergency vehicles fail to communicate effectively with ER and trauma care centers, causing poorly managed patient flow. On the national level, there are no standardized procedures for the training and certification of emergency room personnel.

To complicate matters even more, there is no lead agency to control emergency room and trauma care centers.

So, as you can see, this lack of organization, from poorly managed patient flow to the absences of standardized training and certifying of personnel, causes chaos and confusion in what should be a streamlined and secure service industry.

Consider the second cause of the crisis. •

• Throughout the speech, Lisa makes effective use of transitions, offering many internal previews and internal summaries to move the listener from one idea to the next. Here she briefly summaries the nature of the problem. She follows this with an internal preview of the causes of the crisis.

• Lisa now turns to the causes of the crisis, beginning with fragmentation.

• Lisa uses a transition to lead into the second cause.

Uninsured patients cause about as much chaos in the emergency room as does fragmentation. According to the July 6, 2006, *Columbus Dispatch*, through no fault of their own, there are now 46 million uninsured in the United States. This of course leads to more unpaid ER bills, which leads to more financial problems for the emergency rooms.

But please understand, I am not blaming the patients who simply cannot afford or are not offered health insurance. They are merely the effect of a larger cause: a society that doesn't place a premium on affordable health care. A lack of affordable health care only perpetuates the cycle in which no affordable health care means no insurance, which in turn leads to unpaid ER bills.

The vast numbers of uninsured leads us to the third and final cause of the emergency room breakdown. Emergency rooms are plagued by insufficient reimbursements from insurers and insufficient funding by the government. •

● Lisa transitions from the second to the third cause of the crisis.

Lack of money is a major cause of the shortage of capacity and staffing stability in emergency rooms. The June 15, 2006, *Fort Worth Star Telegram* tells us that emergency rooms received only 4 percent of the $3.38 billion that was allotted to them by the Homeland Security Department in 2002 and 2003 for emergency medical preparation. As government budgets continue to be slashed, the quality of our health care will continue to deteriorate.

Lisa uses the entire presentation space and connects with audience in all corners of the room

So, how can we renovate a cycle that seems beyond control? Well, we can look to solutions on a national level and then on a personal level. •

● Lisa turns to solutions to the problem.

The first step to defeating the chaos in the emergency rooms is to create a coordinated, regionalized system with national standards and a lead agency. Everyone — from 911, to ambulances, to emergency care services — needs to coordinate their operations effectively and efficiently in order to ensure each patient a safe and secure emergency room visit. Additionally, the Institute of Medicine suggests that a lead agency be started in the Department of Health and Human Services in order to control emergency room and trauma care centers.

On a personal level, the National Association of Emergency Physicians asks us to be responsible before going to the emergency room. Before going to the emergency room, ask yourself, do I really need to go to the emergency room, or can my primary care physician take care of my needs? Take steps to lessen the impact of the uninsured on emergency rooms by following the lead of the people of Columbus, Ohio, who, according to the July 6, 2006, edition of the *Columbus Dispatch*, are building affordable primary care clinics in some of the poor neighborhoods. •

• Lisa gives listeners something concrete they can do toward solving the problem. This is in a sense a call to action, albeit a rather weak one. Perhaps she could have offered additional concrete suggestions.

Lisa's professional dress fits her serious topic

Today we have uncovered some of the catastrophic conditions existing in America's emergency rooms. Armed with a greater understanding of what is causing these issues — overcrowding, lack of specialization and training, and poor funding — we can now look to the future and focus our energy on solving this national crisis. •

• Lisa signals the close of her speech and summarizes the main points.

Unfortunately, while it is too late for Beatrice Vance, because she was not given an EKG within ten minutes of admission to the emergency room, authorities recently ruled that her death was a homicide. This paves the way for criminal prosecution of the Vista Medical Center. It also puts emergency rooms across the country on notice that they too could be found liable should they be found similarly negligent.

Perhaps this terrible tragedy will turn out to be the wake-up call that the United States has needed in order to restore safety and stability to our emergency care system.

Works Cited

Rob Amen. "Emergency Rooms Turn Away More Patients." *Pittsburgh Tribune Review,* June 16, 2006.

Arian Campo-Flores. "How to Stop the Bleeding." *Newsweek,* May 8, 2007. www.newsweek.com/id/34803 (accessed September 26, 2007).

"Code Blue." *Columbus Dispatch,* July 6, 2006, 18A. Editorial. www.dispatch.com (accessed September 29, 2007).

Committee on the Future of Emergency Care in the United States Health System. *Emergency Medical Services: At the Crossroads*. Bethesda, Md.: National Academies Press, 2007.

"Emergency in the Emergency Rooms." *New York Times*, June 21, 2006, Opinion. www.nytimes.com/2006/06/21/opinion/21Wed4.html?ex=1189137600&en=fdd466fef8f1534c&ei=5070 (accessed September 29, 2007).

"Illinois Woman's ER Wait Death Ruled a Homicide." *Good Morning America.* September 17, 2006. http://abcnews.go.com/GMA/Health/story?id=2454685&page=1 (accessed September 26, 2007).

"Inexcusable Death." *ABC Nightly News.* September 18, 2006. http://abcnews.go.com/Video/playerIndex?id=2457808 (accessed September 26, 2007).

Maria M. Perotin, "Serious Condition," *Fort Worth Star Telegram*, June 15, 2006, C1.

National Association of EMS Physicians. Summary of "Future of Emergency Care: Hospital-Based Emergency Care at the Breaking Point" Recommendations. www.naemsp.org (accessed September 26, 2007).

Sample Visually Annotated Persuasive Speech

Choosing the Right Path

ELPIDIO VILLARREAL

This special occasion speech delivered by Elpidio Villarreal, a laywer from Connecticut, is persuasive in nature. Delivered to the Puerto Rican Legal Defense and Education Fund Gala in New York City on October 26, 2006, the speech deals with the large public issue of immigration. It addresses a claim of value (see p. 395) that Mexican American immigrants benefit rather than harm the United States. The occasion of Mr. Villarreal's speech was an award ceremony in his honor; thus we can assume that he is addressing a largely sympathetic audience. Mr. Villarreal links his claims with evidence through various types of appeals. He appeals to the audience's emotions (pathos), citing the sacrifices and achievements of Mexican Americans. He also appeals to his own credibility (ethos), citing his personal experiences as a Mexican American. He also appeals to reason (logos), citing facts and statistics demonstrating the contribution of Mexican Americans to the United States. The speech is broadly organized along the lines of the refutation pattern, in which the speaker states and then refutes opposing arguments.

The tuxedo is appropriate attire for a gala

Thank you, Linda Willett, for that kind introduction. My sincere gratitude to the PRLDEF for this great honor. . . .

I want to spend just a few minutes sharing my personal opinions on an issue dividing the nation in this election year — immigration. In particular, I want to talk about how my own history and that of my family colors my view of this issue. I will not suggest that this nation does not have a right to control and police its own borders. This right is, in fact, an essential attribute of nationhood. Nor do I mean to suggest that immigration is not a legitimate subject of national debate; it surely is. But I think it is important that the debate be framed by facts, not fictions. •

Underlying the ongoing debate over immigration is one central idea — that somehow the current wave of Mexican immigrants coming to this country is fundamentally different from prior waves of immigrants. Mexicans, so the argument goes, are "different" for two main reasons:

(1) They are disloyal. They allegedly remain loyal to Mexico and harbor a desire to return the Southwestern United States to Mexico — either politically or, at the very least, culturally and linguistically — the so-called La Reconquista. (2) They refuse to assimilate. In particular, we are told that they are not learning English and will never learn it, and they will never succeed in America. It is my purpose here tonight to take issue with and to challenge both of these "fictions." •

There are three particularly prominent advocates of the view that Mexican Americans are "different" — (1) Harvard Professor Samuel P. Huntington; (2) political pundit and ex-presidential candidate Pat Buchanan; and (3) Representative Tom Tancredo of Colorado. Here is what they have to say. •

Samuel Huntington — "The assimilation successes of past [immigrants] are unlikely to be duplicated with the contemporary flood of immigrants from Latin America." "Mexicans and other Latinos have not assimilated into mainstream U.S. culture, forming instead their own political and linguistic enclaves — from Los Angeles to Miami — and rejecting

● As Mr. Villarreal previews his topic, he immediately anticipates potential objections to his claims and attempts to "inoculate" himself against them (see pp. 404–405); he also reveals that he will base parts of his arguments on his own authority.

● Here the speaker states his thesis, which is that he will refute two major claims that purport to explain why Mexican immigrants pose a threat to the well-being of the United States. He also establishes how the speech will be organized, which is along the lines of the refutation pattern (see pp. 416–418).

● Mr. Villarreal lays out the competing arguments he will refute by quoting from three advocates of the opposite position.

the Anglo-Protestant values that built the American dream." "There is no Americano dream. There is only the American dream created by an Anglo-Protestant society. Mexican Americans will share in that dream and in that society only if they dream in English."

Pat Buchanan — "A spirit of separatism, nationalism, and irredentism is alive in the barrios." "We are inviting La Reconquista, the reconquest of the Southwest by Mexico, even as Ferdinand and Isabella effected

La Reconquista of Spain in 1492 from the Moors who had invaded eight hundred years before." "What Mexico's elites are systematically pursuing is a sharing of sovereignty in these lost lands and their ultimate recapture, culturally and linguistically, by Mexico."

Pauses to ensure accuracy of quote

Tom Tancredo — "For years I have witnessed a difference in the kinds of people coming into the United States." "Too many immigrants continue to be loyal to their native countries. They desire to maintain their own language, customs and culture. Yet, they seek to exploit the success of America while giving back as little in return as possible."

I have to tell you that when I listen to these guys (let's call them Los Tres Amigos) — when I listen to Los Tres Amigos describe Mexican Americans it's like an out-of-body experience. I am 46 years old and I've been a Mexican American all my life. The people Los Tres Amigos describe in such derogatory and paranoid terms are nothing like the Mexican Americans I know. Nothing at all. •

Let us deal first with this Reconquista idea. I realize that there are a very few Mexican Americans who do talk about La Reconquista, but they are hardly typical or representative of Mexican Americans as a whole. Indeed, I suspect there are more White Southerners who openly call for a return of the Confederacy than there are Mexican Americans who call for the "reconquest" of California and Texas. Lincoln thought the Mexican War of 1848 was immoral because it was fought to advance the interests of the slaveholding class, but I know no Mexican Amercans who care to refight that war. History has no rewind button. Indeed, the notion that Mexican Americans are disloyal is not only wrong, but offensive. • Mexican Americans have won

• Starting off on a humorous note, Villarreal uses his own authority/credibility to begin refuting the claims (e.g., "They are nothing like the Mexican Americans I know").

• Here Villarreal makes a claim of value ("wrong [and] offensive").

proportionately more Congressional Medals of Honor than any other ethnic group in the nation's history. Next time you catch the Honor Roll of the Dead on the PBS *Nightly News Hour* notice how many of the names and faces are Mexican, or other Hispanic. These Mexican Americans sure have a peculiar way of demonstrating their disloyalty. •

• The speaker refutes the claim of disloyalty among Mexican Americans by citing the high proportion who have received military medals for valor; this works both as factual evidence and as an appeal to emotion.

Pat Buchanan complains bitterly about the fact that some of the people protesting the immigration "reform" proposals pending before Congress this spring were waving Mexican flags. He cites this as proof that their political allegiance remains with Mexico. But ethnic flag waving is hardly unusual in this country. Ever been to a St. Patrick's Day parade? Or to a March in support of Israel? • My late grandmother, Elena Villarreal, who came to this country as a refugee from political violence during the Mexican Civil War, had 11 children—nine sons— one of whom died in childhood. Six of her sons served in this country's armed forces. My uncles have fistfuls of medals to prove their bravery, but I want to talk about the bravest one of all—the one who didn't want to go.

• Here Villarreal rebuts the claim of disloyalty by pointing to other older ethnic groups who are now well established in the mainstream. This is a *warrant by analogy*— comparing two similar cases and inferring that what is true in one case is true in the other.

My Uncle Guadalupe was drafted during the Second World War. But he didn't want to go. He became, in fact, a draft dodger. One day, the MPs came to the family house to get him. My uncle hid in a shed in the back of the yard. The MPs knew he was home and they told my grandfather that if he persuaded his son to come with them peacefully, they would not hurt him. My grandfather went to my Uncle Lupe and told him that he had to go. My uncle said he didn't want to go because he knew, he knew in his heart, that he would die. He had foreseen his own death. My Grandfather told him that it didn't matter. Even if it were true, and even if he was destined to die, he still had to go because this was our country now.

My Uncle Lupe surrendered peacefully to the MPs. On June 6, 1944, he landed at a place called Omaha Beach in Normandy, France. He was killed while leading an attack on an enemy bunker that was pinning down his platoon. He was nominated, but did not receive, the Congressional Medal of Honor. My grandparents received a photograph of a road my uncle's unit built in France. The road had been named Villarreal Road. Years ago, I was privileged to walk the battlefields of Normandy, including Omaha Beach, and I visited the great American Cemetery there where lie 17,000 Americans who gave the "last full measure of devotion," as Lincoln so beautifully put it. Simple white marble crosses, interspersed with occasional Stars of David, stretch out for 70 acres. It remains one of the most moving things I have ever seen. I thought about all the brave Americans buried there and of the meaning of their deaths, but I thought especially about my Uncle Lupe, the one who went to war knowing he would die for no other reason than that his country, the one that treated him as a second-class citizen, asked him to. •

Like I said, these Mexican Americans have a peculiar way of demonstrating their disloyalty. The fact is that, in all my life, I have never heard any member of my large family voice even one unpatriotic word. It sickens me to hear Los Tres Amigos question their loyalty. "Never mind about all that," say Los Tres Amigos. The real problem is that "you people" are not assimilating, not becoming "real" Americans, not learning the beautiful English language, the language of Shakespeare, the King James Bible, and, er, *South Park*. This idea is also a fiction. In this world, at this point in its history, NO ONE can withstand the overpowering force of the English language. It is everywhere and it is 24/7. TV and American pop culture are the great assimilators — final proof that the world really is flat. I know wealthy people in Lima who complain that they can barely get their children to speak Spanish, so besotted are they with American culture. Americanization is relentless. •

According to a study published last month in the *Population & Development Review*, by the third generation, the grandchildren of the original immigrants, only 17 percent of Mexican Americans speak fluent Spanish. By the fourth generation, the generation represented by my children, only 5 percent do. Regardless of ability to speak Spanish, by the third generation, 96 percent of Mexican Americans

• Using the story of his Uncle Lupe to rebut the claim of disloyalty is an appeal to pathos, or emotion.

• Again, the speaker bases a claim on his personal authority/ credibility—on personal acquaintances. In contemporary terms, this is called an authoritative warrant. In classical terms, it is an appeal to ethos.

prefer to speak English at home. I am not saying this is an unalloyed good thing, only that it is inevitable. ●

My grandparents spoke very little English. My parents are bilingual. I am ashamed to admit my Spanish is pretty poor. And my children speak only the Spanish they've learned in school. It is only a question of time. It is true, and very upsetting, that the educational achievement of Mexican Americans, while improving, continues to lag behind the general population, even into the second and third generations. There are certainly lots of reasons for that. (Personally, having spent some time volunteering in our modern urban schools, it's a minor miracle anyone gets educated in them.) But do these educational shortcomings mean, as Los Tres Amigos imply, that Mexicans are stupid? Of course not. My father is a high school graduate—as are all of his siblings—a considerable achievement for their time. My mother is a high school dropout, but she would be angry with me if I failed to point out that she later received her GED and, indeed, a couple of semesters of credit at a local junior college. They each held a series of tough, dead-end jobs until they were both lucky enough to become federal employees. ●

But money was always tight. They had two sons. Though my parents did not get very far in school, they understood the importance of education and sacrificed to send their children to the best schools they could afford, the local Catholic schools. Their oldest son graduated from Columbia, and then from the Yale Law School; their youngest son earned two bachelor's degrees from the University of Texas.

Gesture beckons daughters to stand and focuses audience's attention on them

My daughters, who are both here tonight, are the real Luceros. Both of my children were identified early on as "gifted" by the Johns Hopkins Center for Talented Youth. My oldest daughter, Elena (named after the family matriarch), is now 15 years old and a sophomore at the Hopkins School in New Haven—a private school founded in 1660 and the favorite school for the children of the Yale faculty.

● Moving away from evidence based on personal experience, the speaker offers facts and statistics—so-called "external evidence," or evidence that is drawn from reliable outside sources.

● The speaker moves back to personal experience as a basis for rebutting the notion that Mexican Americans achieve less than other groups.

Elena took the SAT when she was 12, with no prior preparation, and scored almost as high as I did when I took the test at age 17. This summer, she took an AP Government course at Yale and wrote her term paper on the Commercial Speech Doctrine of the Supreme Court. She got an A+ on it. I know a little bit about legal writing. I thought her paper was at the level of a good first year law student. And, guess what, Professor Huntington? That paper was written in English, not Spanish! •

My 12-year-old, Elizabeth, is also here. She's in

Warm smile connects with audience

the seventh grade at the Middlebrook Public School in Wilton, Connecticut. (She will go to Hopkins, too.) Earlier this year, Elizabeth took a test administered by the Johns Hopkins Center for Talented Youth. Like the SAT, which it resembles, the test measures both verbal and math ability. She did extraordinarily well. Indeed, Johns Hopkins advised us that Elizabeth got the highest verbal score in the State of Connecticut. Most recently, she took the CT State Mastery Tests. Seventh-graders are tested on math, reading and writing skills. The grading scale is 0-400. Elizabeth did extremely well on the math section, but in reading and writing she scored a perfect 400—about 130 points higher than the average score in her school district—which is one of the best in the state. And, guess what Pat Buchanan and Tom Tancredo? Both tests were administered in English!

So take a good look at my girls. According to Los Tres Amigos, they represent the greatest existing

Hand gesture underscores irony

threat to the future of America. They may look like nice kids, but don't let appearances fool you. They are actually busy plotting an insurrection and refusing to learn to speak English. •

And it is on the basis of these absurd fictions that Los Tres Amigos, and others who agree with them, propose to conduct a debate on the need for immigration "reform." I think that Los Tres Amigos should be afraid of my daughters. They, and millions of Latinos just like them, are growing up fast. They are

• One could argue that the speaker's evidence here represents an exceptional case—whether among Mexican Americans or any other group. Again the speaker bases his evidence on personal experience.

• In a sense, the speaker is offering a syllogism: my children are highly accomplished. They are Mexican American. Thus all Mexican Americans at least have the potential to be highly accomplished.

growing up strong, and they are growing up smart, and they will have zero patience for the prejudiced and the ignorant. And THAT, Mis Tres Amigos, that is what you need to be afraid of.

These attacks upon Mexican Americans are, I confess, particularly hard to take from the Buchanans and Tancredos of this world who descend from immigrants who were themselves once derided as stupid, criminally predisposed, uneducable and genetically inferior. In 1891, the "great" Henry Cabot Lodge had this to say about the wave of immigration that brought Representative Tancredo's grandparents to the United States. He warned "that immigration to this country is increasing and is making its greatest relative increase from races most alien to the body of the American people and from the lowest and most illiterate classes among those races." These immigrants, "half of whom have no occupation and most of whom represent the rudest form of labor," are "people whom it is very difficult to assimilate and do not promise well for the standard of civilization in the United States." "They form an element in the population which regards home as a foreign country." "They have no interest or stake in the country, and they never become American citizens." The same sorts of stereotypes greeted the Irish ancestors of Pat Buchanan. Indeed, for a long time the Irish were not even considered "white" by native born Americans. Newspaper cartoonists often depicted them as apelike with a jutting jaw and sloping forehead. The Irish had terrible and well-known problems with alcohol, violence and crime. That is why police vans are still called "Paddy Wagons." •

So, the more things change, the more they stay the same. Not fundamental differences amongst immigrants, but, instead, merely a persistence of prejudice, ignorance and xenophobia — and, oh yes, a total absence of any sense of irony.

About 90 years ago, my Grandfather Francisco crossed the Rio Grande River illegally, settling eventually in San Antonio, where I was born and raised. He came to America because his father, a policeman,

• Here the speaker again uses a warrant by analogy in which he infers that what is [not] true in one case is [not] true in another.

had been assassinated. He worked for many years in a menial job at an Air Force base in Texas. Many times, he was hidden from immigration officers seeking to clear the base of Negroes and Mexicans by a sympathetic German-American. Today, he and my grandmother have almost 200 living descendants. I do sometimes wonder what my grandfather must have been thinking as he crossed the Rio Grande into a strange new land, just as I sometimes wonder what my Uncle Lupe must have been thinking as he felt his landing boat bump against the beaches of France. I am sure they were both afraid. But both of them found the courage and the strength to keep moving forward — as we all must.

I like to think they would have been pleased to see me accept this award. They would have been proud of me and even prouder, I believe, of my astounding daughters. They led hard and unsentimental lives, as did all my grandparents and their children. But, in the end, they found a home here. This country was brave and strong enough to give their descendants a chance to succeed or fail — their own chance to Achieve the Dream. One of my greatest fears is that we are seeing the passing of that Great Country — replaced by one governed by fear — of the future, of the present, and of "the other." •

● The speaker concludes this stirring speech by weaving his personal accomplishments into the larger fabric of the American tapestry. The speech works because of the dramatic interplay of ethos and pathos.

Two paths are open to us. One path would keep us true to our fundamental values as a nation and a people. The other would lead us down a dark trail; one marked by 700-mile-long fences, emergency detention centers and vigilante border patrols. Because I really am an American, heart and soul, and because that means never being without hope, I still believe we will ultimately choose the right path. We have to.

Thank you for listening. And thanks once again to PRLDEF for this great honor.

As he exits, Villarreal raises his award to acknowledge the great honor

Sample Visually Annotated Persuasive Speech

Video

The Importance of Community Service and Civic Engagement

STEPHANIE POPLIN

University of Oklahoma

In this speech, Stephanie Poplin argues that by volunteering we can enrich our lives (a claim of value). Organizationally, the speech incorporates elements of the comparative advantage pattern, in which Stephanie describes the many positive effects of volunteering and then addresses the alternative of inaction. As a final step, she drives home the advantages of engagement.

Stands at attention before the speech

"Great social forces are the mere accumulation of individual actions." Think about that — "Great social forces are the mere accumulation of individual actions." • That was said by noted economist and antipoverty activist Jeffrey Sachs in a *Time* magazine article written about helping the world's poor. And it's true, right? Everything from the Red Cross to the Peace Corps to the civil rights movement was made up of individual actions, yet all those actions were history changing.

• Stephanie uses a quotation from a noted activist both as an attention-getter and to introduce her theme.

I'm Stephanie Poplin, and I would like to speak to you today about why it is imperative that you give yourself the opportunity to live a successful and meaningful life. •

• Stephanie introduces herself with a direct statement of persuasive intent.

Appropriate dress — casual but respectful

One way of achieving this seemingly unattainable lifestyle is by contributing — by putting yourself into the community that surrounds you. I'm referring to community service and civic engagement. Today, I will talk to you about what you can personally gain from your involvement and participation in your community, and I will also address some concerns and reservations you may have about donating your time and your talents. •

• Stephanie clearly states her claim and previews the two main points she will cover.

Now, traditionally, when you hear the word *volunteer*, what do you think of? Someone who wants to do good, someone who wants to improve the lives of those who are less fortunate. And while this remains true, the attitudes of volunteers are beginning to change. Volunteers are beginning to realize that there are some major personal benefits that come along with their involvement in community service. No longer are volunteers getting involved purely for altruistic reasons. Student Volunteering UK conducted large-scale research into the benefits of volunteering. • The study looked at how volunteering can enhance employability, and it emphasized that volunteer participation helps to develop and strengthen new and different skills and to improve job prospects. In our own country, the Corporation for National and Community Service found that volunteering makes us better problem solvers, another key trait employers look for. I think we would all agree that's a necessity for us, especially in the stages we are in in our lives right now. •

Warm smile connects with audience

In today's job market, it is becoming evident that college graduates need more than just paper qualifications. We will need to be able to stand out from the crowd, to be resourceful, to be initiators, to be team players, and to possess a get-up-and-go attitude. • These are now the desired skills of employers, and volunteering can provide all of this. According to both Student Volunteering UK and the Corporation for National and Community Service, virtually every paid job can be mirrored by a volunteering opportunity. Taking part in community service is a new and pioneering form of work experience. Not only is it seen as work experience, but employers look at the act of volunteering as taking great initiative and commitment. •

The evidence from these two major organizations dedicated to unpaid service also lists benefits, other than résumé building, that students felt they had gained through their participation in volunteering. These included building confidence and influencing career choices; they were able to experience making a difference, and volunteering opened up new opportunities and challenges. The Corporation

• Stephanie offers two studies that students are likely to find credible.

• Stephanie shows topic relevance to audience by drawing a link between community service and job prospects.

• Here Stephanie appeals to the audience's social and self-actualization needs.

• Stephanie understands that she must demonstrate a benefit to listeners before they will care about her topic.

for National and Community Service cites community building as a key outcome of volunteering and notes that in the United States, volunteers are absolutely crucial to creating and sustaining healthy communities. Fortunately, since the tragedy of 9/11 seven years ago, there has been a tremendous surge in student volunteers. Volunteering is up so much since this national tragedy that today's student volunteers are sometimes called the "9/11 generation" by leaders of charitable organizations. In 2005, for example, 3.3 million college students gave of their time, or over 30 percent of the college population, up from 27 percent before the tragedy. Tutoring and mentoring were cited as the most popular volunteer activities among student volunteers, with 44 percent of students spending at least 12 hours a week volunteering. • Interestingly, students taking service learning courses and students who work part time volunteer more often than those who don't have jobs. The corporation also recently published a report titled "The Health Benefits of Volunteering." It documents a strong relationship between volunteering and physical health, including lowered rates of depression and even lowered mortality rates.

• One technique for getting listeners to adopt a behavior is to show them that people like themselves have adopted the behavior.

So whether you want to make new friends, improve your job prospects, test a potential career, or build confidence, help build communities, beat depression, and even live longer, volunteering can be the answer. •

Effective hand gesture

Now that we have seen some personal benefits you can gain, I would like to address some concerns you may have. • I realize that some of you may have some reservations about volunteering. Namely, can one person really make a difference? You may be thinking, "If I am giving my time, and my talents, and my effort, to one specific cause, can I even make a dent in the desired outcome?" So next, I would like to elaborate on the idea

• Stephanie directly states the benefits of volunteering.

• Here Stephanie anticipates reservations listeners may have and addresses them.

Quick pause to check notecard

that one person can make a difference. You might be thinking, "What can I possibly do?" But if you have ever spent any time reading or just hanging out with a lonely child, you know that even a small amount of attention and compassion can make a world of difference.

I have experienced this firsthand through my involvement in Habitat for Humanity. • Habitat for Humanity is an international organization fueled by hundreds of thousands of volunteers who join with future homeowners to build simple and affordable houses. It wasn't until my first experience building a home, here in Norman, that I realized the impact this organization has on its volunteers and the families involved. I have always had a bedroom of my own to escape to, and I have always had a kitchen to make breakfast in the morning, but there are two little boys who will have this for the first time, thanks to the OU chapter of Habitat for Humanity. I have always taken my home for granted, but now I can be a part of giving these little boys a home of their own. • We need to prepare ourselves for the possibility that sometimes big changes follow from small events, such as me sheetrocking an empty space that will eventually become a living room that these little boys and their mom and dad can enjoy together.

In summary, we have seen how you can personally benefit from contributing to your community. • Not only do you gain valuable work experience, as well as the opportunity to develop new skills and improve your job prospects, but people who have spent time volunteering report they get back in personal fulfillment and satisfaction more than they ever expend in inconvenience and effort. I've also talked about the theory that one person can make a difference, and I encourage you to explore every possibility and as many organizations as you can to find the volunteer opportunity that fits your personality — one that you will enjoy and love to do.

Someone once told me, "You don't find yourself; you create yourself." As college students, we have every opportunity in the world to create a life that is successful and meaningful. Use your good fortune, and choose to create a life that is service-oriented. Give back to the community that surrounds you. We all have the power to make an impact one way or another. After all, "Great social forces are the mere accumulation of individual actions." •

Brief pause adds emphasis

Thank you.

● Personal testimony builds credibility and demonstrates how one person's volunteer work can have a major impact.

● Stephanie lends power to her words by twice repeating the phrase "I have always had" (the technique of anaphora; see Chapter 16).

● Stephanie uses the transition "In summary" to signal her conclusion and her summary of points.

● Stephanie repeats the quote from the introduction, reinforcing her points and bringing the speech full circle.

Works Cited

Corporation for National and Community Service. *College Students Helping America.* October 2006. www.nationalservice.gov/pdf/06_1016_RPD_college_full.pdf (accessed January 8, 2008).

Sachs, Jeffrey D. "The End of Poverty." *Time.* March 6, 2005.

Student Volunteering UK. *The Art of Crazy Paving: Volunteering for Enhanced Employability.* n.d. www.studentvolunteering.org.uk/ (accessed January 8, 2008).

Special Occasion Speeches 27

Special occasions stand out from the ordinary rhythm of life, marking passages, celebrating life's highlights, and commemorating events. Such occasions often include the observance of important ceremonies and rituals as well as speeches. The ceremonies and rituals symbolically express the event's meaning to the gathered community, while the speaker's words literally give voice to that meaning. When it is delivered well, a special occasion speech forges a bond among audience members and helps them put the significance of the occasion in perspective.

Functions of Special Occasion Speeches Web links

There are many kinds of occasions that call for speeches, some serious and some lighthearted. As is evidenced by its name, a **special occasion speech** is one that is prepared for a specific occasion and for a purpose dictated by that occasion. In the special occasion speech, the rhetorical situation truly gives rise to the speech content. Dedication ceremonies call for speeches that pay tribute. Awards ceremonies call for presentation speeches that acknowledge accomplishments, and acceptance speeches that display gratitude. In each of these instances, audiences have definite expectations of the speaker. More so than in other kinds of speeches, they look to the speaker to fulfill specific functions dictated by the event.

Special occasion speeches can be informative or persuasive or a mix of both. However, neither of these functions is the main goal; the underlying function of a special occasion speech is to entertain, celebrate, commemorate, inspire, or set a social agenda.

ENTERTAINMENT

Many kinds of special occasions call for a speech that entertains. Banquets, awards dinners, and roasts, for example, frequently feature speakers whose main purpose is to entertain those in attendance. In such cases, listeners expect a lighthearted speech that amuses them. Depending on the event, they may also expect the speaker to offer a certain degree of insight into the topic at hand.

CELEBRATION

Often a special occasion speech will celebrate a person, a place, or an event. Weddings, anniversaries, retirement parties, and awards banquets all call for speeches that recognize the person(s) or event being celebrated. The audience expects the speaker to praise the subject of the celebration and to cast him or her in a positive light. The listeners also expect a certain degree of ceremony in accordance with the norms of the occasion.

COMMEMORATION

Certain special occasion speeches, called *commemorative speeches,* focus on remembrance and tribute. Commemorative speeches mark important anniversaries, such as the fiftieth anniversary of the landing of Allied troops in Normandy or the anniversary of the shootings at Virginia Tech. Speakers deliver commemorative speeches about events or people of note at memorials dedicated to them or at gatherings otherwise held in their honor.

INSPIRATION

Inaugural addresses, keynote speeches at conventions, and commencement speeches all have inspiration as their main function. With their examples of achievement and heroism, many commemorative speeches also inspire audiences as well as pay homage to the person or event being commemorated.

SOCIAL AGENDA–SETTING

Yet another function of the special occasion speech is social agenda–setting — establishing or reinforcing the goals and values of the group sponsoring the event. Occasions that call for agenda-setting speeches include gatherings of issues- or cause-oriented organizations, fund-raisers, campaign banquets, conferences, and conventions. Speakers asked to deliver keynote addresses at conferences or conventions are charged with establishing the theme of the meeting and with offering a plan of action related to that theme. Similarly, politically oriented organizations also routinely hold meetings at which invited speakers perform the function of agenda-setting.

TABLE 27.1 • Functions of Special Occasion Speeches

- Entertainment
- Celebration
- Commemoration
- Inspiration
- Social agenda–setting

Types of Special Occasion Speeches

 WEB Video

Special occasion speeches include (but are not limited to) speeches of introduction, speeches of acceptance, award presentations, roasts and toasts, eulogies and other speeches of tribute, after-dinner speeches, and speeches of inspiration.

SPEECHES OF INTRODUCTION

A **speech of introduction** is a short speech with two goals: to prepare or "warm up" the audience for the speaker, and to motivate audience members to listen to what he or she has to say. Many occasions call for speeches of introduction. You might be asked to introduce a guest speaker at a monthly meeting of a social organization to which you belong, to introduce an award presenter at your company's annual banquet, or to introduce an outside expert at a quarterly sales meeting. A good speech of introduction balances four elements: the speaker's background, the subject of the speaker's message, the occasion, and the audience.

Describe the Speaker's Background

A key part of the introducer's task is to tell the audience something about the speaker's background and qualifications for speaking. The object is to heighten audience interest and build the speaker's credibility. If you don't know the speaker personally, be sure to contact him or her days or even weeks before the event. Ask the speaker to describe important achievements, offices held, and other activities that will show audience members what kind of speaker they are about to hear and why they should listen.

Briefly Preview the Speaker's Topic

Part of the introducer's job is to give audience members a sense of why the speaker's subject is of interest to them. Is the subject timely? What significance does it have for the audience? What special connections exist between the subject or the speaker and the occasion? Is he or she an expert on the topic? Why was the speaker invited? Details like these help the audience to understand the speaker's role and build his or her credibility. Keep in mind, however, that it is not the introducer's job to evaluate the speech or otherwise offer critical commentary on it. *The rule is: Get in and cut quickly with a few well-chosen remarks.* Introducers who linger on their own thoughts run the risk of stealing the speaker's thunder.

Ask the Audience to Welcome the Speaker

A final part of the introducer's task is to cue the audience to welcome the speaker. This can be done very simply by saying something like "Please welcome Anthony Svetlana." Hearing this, the audience will provide applause, thereby paving the way for the speaker to take his or her place at the podium.

In the following excerpt from a speech by Frank D. Stella, of F. D. Stella Products Company, Stella introduces Richard A. Grasso, former chairman and chief executive officer of the New York Stock Exchange, to the Economic Club of Detroit. Notice how Stella makes use of the date of the occasion — April 15, or income tax day — to engage the audience. Stella also provides a quick overview of who the speaker is and a reference to why he was a good choice for this occasion.

> Happy April 15! This may be only a quirk of history, but do you realize that not only is today Tax Day, it is also the anniversary of the sinking of the *Titanic*! Talk about double jeopardy!

It's interesting, therefore, that we have scheduled today's speaker for April 15: If your company or individual stock did well and was listed on the New York Stock Exchange, you can, in part, thank Dick Grasso for keeping the Exchange so strong and competitive; but if your taxes went up because your stocks did so well, you can thank Dick for capital gains, the market upsurge, and profitability.

It is a distinct honor for me to introduce Richard A. Grasso, chairman and chief executive officer of the New York Stock Exchange. He has enjoyed a remarkable 28-year-career at the Exchange. [Mr. Stella goes on to provide a more detailed background on Mr. Grasso.][1]

Respond to Introductions

Speakers who have been introduced should respond to the introduction in some way. Acknowledging and thanking the introducer is the most common method. For example:

- I appreciate those kind words.
- Thank you for making me feel welcome today.
- This is a wonderful event, and I appreciate being a part of it.

If you are comfortable ad-libbing, you might decide to respond to the introducer's remarks. Notice how the following speakers use this strategy:

- Thank you so much, Helen. I have to agree with you that this audience must really be committed to the United Way—or hungry!—to be here on a stormy day like this.
- I am honored to be with you tonight. Something that Brad said in his remarks earlier really struck me. If we are to truly make a difference, we have to be able to think out of the box. The box I would like for us to think our way out of tonight is . . .

Most of us are not used to being publicly honored, and accepting praise and accolades from a speaker who introduces us can be awkward. One of the ways to show your humility toward a gracious introduction is through humor:

- That introduction was so gracious; you were more than halfway through it before I realized you were talking about me.[2]
- Thank you, Mr. Secretary, for that incredible introduction. If I had known you were going to eulogize me, I would have done the only decent thing and died.[3]
- I'm really not as good as she said, but neither am I as bad as my mother-in-law thinks. So I guess it averages out.[4]

SPEECHES OF ACCEPTANCE

A **speech of acceptance** is made in response to receiving an award of some sort. Its purpose is to express gratitude for the honor bestowed on the speaker. The speech should reflect that gratitude.

> ✓ **CHECKLIST**
>
> **Guidelines for Introducing Other Speakers**
>
> _____ 1. Clearly demonstrate to the audience why the speaker is relevant to the occasion. Describe his or her achievements, offices held, and other facts that are germane to the occasion.
>
> _____ 2. Identify the speaker correctly. Assign him or her the proper title, such as "vice president for public relations" or "professor emeritus."
>
> _____ 3. Correctly pronounce the speaker's name. Practice difficult-to-pronounce names several times before actually introducing the speaker.
>
> _____ 4. Contact the speaker ahead of time to verify the accuracy of any facts about him or her that you plan to cite.
>
> _____ 5. Mention enough of the speaker's awards and achievements to convince audience members that they should be interested in this person, but not so many that they cause their eyes to glaze over.
>
> _____ 6. Consider devices that will capture the audience's attention, such as quotes, short anecdotes, and startling statements (see Chapter 14). Don't burden the speaker with the added task of having to overcome the audience's boredom brought on by your introduction.
>
> _____ 7. Be brief. The introducer should speak just long enough to accomplish the goals of preparation and motivation. One well-known speaker recommends a two-minute maximum.
>
> _Source:_ Roger E. Axtell, _Do's and Taboos of Public Speaking: How to Get Those Butterflies Flying in Formation_ (New York: Wiley, 1992), 150.

Prepare

If you know that you will be given an award, be sure to prepare an acceptance speech. Because the award is not a surprise, the audience will probably expect a fairly sophisticated acceptance speech. If you think it is at all likely that you will receive an award, prepare in advance so that your acceptance will go smoothly and you can avoid using standard responses such as "I really just don't know what to say."

React Genuinely and with Humility

Genuineness and humility are possibly the most important parts of expressing gratitude. Offering a sincere response shows your audience how much the award means to you. If you are surprised to receive the award, show it. If you are not surprised, don't try to feign excitement. Explain why the award is important to you and describe the value you place on it. Tell your listeners how it will affect your future and how it gives meaning to whatever you did in the past that led to its receipt. Express your gratitude with humility, acknowledging your good fortune in having received it.

✔ **CHECKLIST**

Guidelines for Delivering Speeches of Acceptance

_____ 1. If you know or even suspect that you are to receive an award, prepare an acceptance speech in advance of the event.

_____ 2. In the speech, explain why the award is important to you and describe the value you place on it.

_____ 3. Express your gratitude to the people who are giving you the award. Be specific in citing each of the organizations or individuals involved in the award.

_____ 4. Thank any significant people who helped you attain the achievement for which you are being honored.

_____ 5. Do not belabor your acknowledgments.

_____ 6. Accept the award gracefully by showing that you value it and the people who gave it to you.

_____ 7. End your speech with an explicit expression of gratitude for the award.

Thank Those Giving the Award

Even though the attention is focused on you, don't forget to express your gratitude to the people who are giving you the award. If the award is given by an organization, specifically thank that organization. If it is given by a combination of organizations, remember to mention all of them. If there is a sponsor of the award, such as a donor that makes the award possible, remember to acknowledge the donor as well.

Thank Others Who Helped You

If the reason for your award represents a team effort, be sure to thank all members. If there are people who gave you the inspiration that helped you achieve the award, thank them.

SPEECHES OF PRESENTATION

The job of presenting an award can be an honor in itself. Whether you are presenting a bowling trophy or a Video Music Award, your goal in the **speech of presentation** is twofold: to communicate the meaning of the award and to explain why the recipient is receiving it.

Convey the Meaning of the Award

It is the presenter's task to explain the meaning of the award to the audience. What is the award for? What kind of achievement does it celebrate? Who or what does the award represent? What is the significance of its special name or title? You might offer a brief history of the award, such as when it was founded and the names of some of its previous recipients. If the award has a unique shape or design, explain the significance of that shape or design. If there is an inscription, read it. Because you are a presenter, it is also your job to identify the sponsors or organizations that made the award possible and to describe the link between the sponsor's goals and values and the award. This is information that the audience will be curious about, and mentioning it establishes the award's credibility and increases the honor for the recipient.

The following excerpt is a common way of communicating to the audience the significance of an award:

> It is an honor and a privilege to be the one making this presentation today. This plaque is only a token of our appreciation for Seamus's achievements, but we hope that this symbol will serve as a daily reminder of our admiration for his great work. Let me read the inscription. "Seamus O'Leary, in appreciation for the outstanding work . . ."

Talk about the Recipient of the Award

The second part of the presenter's task is to explain why the recipient is receiving the award. Tell the audience why the recipient has been singled out for special recognition. Describe this person's achievements, the kind of work he or she does, and special attributes that qualify him or her as deserving of the award. Explain how the recipient was selected. What kind of selection process was used? What set this individual apart from other nominees or finalists? The following example illustrates how this can be done:

> And, I might add, these were just some of the accomplishments of Carol Bosno. When the selection committee reviewed all the nominees (some eighty-four of them), it became clear that Carol would be our choice. The committee met four times to narrow the list of nominees, and at each meeting it was clear who our winner would be. The other nominees were outstanding in their own right, but Carol stood apart in many ways.

Consider the Physical Presentation

Plan the actual presentation of the award. Don't set yourself or the recipient up for an awkward presentation. If you are to hand the award to the recipient, make sure that you do so with your left hand so that you can shake hands with your right hand.

ROASTS AND TOASTS

A **roast** is a humorous tribute to a person, one in which a series of speakers jokingly poke fun at him or her. A **toast** is a brief tribute to a person or an event being celebrated. Both roasts and toasts call for short speeches whose goal is to celebrate an individual and his or her achievements. Should you be asked to speak at such events, it will be helpful to follow these guidelines.

Prepare

Remember that the audience is looking to you to set the tone and to express the purpose of the gathering. Being caught off guard and stammering for something to say can really let the air out of your speech and make it less than meaningful.

Also, remember that others who speak before you may use material you had planned to use. Don't be alarmed. Make reference to this fact and put a different spin on it.

Before delivering a roast or a toast, many speakers rehearse in front of a trusted friend or friends. This is especially helpful if you are considering telling a joke that you are unsure about. Practicing with friends also allows them to time your speech. People often speak much longer than they realize. Have someone listen to your presentation and time you. In that way you can see if your speech fits into the time limitations set for your presentation.

Highlight Remarkable Traits of the Person Being Honored

Because these speeches are usually short, try to restrict your remarks to one or two of the most unique or recognizable attributes of the person. Convey what sets this person apart—the qualities that have made him or her worthy of celebrating. In other words, what would you want said about you if you were being honored?

Be Positive

Even if the speech pokes fun at someone, as in a roast, keep the tone good-natured and positive. Remember, the overall purpose of your speech is to pay tribute to the honoree. It's great to have fun, but avoid saying anything that might embarrass the person being honored. Doing so could turn what should be a festive atmosphere into an uncomfortable situation.

Be Brief

Usually several speakers are involved in roasts and toasts. Be considerate of the other speakers by refraining from taking up too much time. This is particularly important for toasts, which are expected to be very short. Violating these expectations can make the toast awkward, especially if everyone is holding a glass in anticipation of the toast ending.

EULOGIES AND OTHER TRIBUTES

The word **eulogy** derives from the Greek word meaning "to praise." Those delivering eulogies, usually close friends or family members of the deceased, are charged with celebrating and commemorating the life of someone while consoling those who have been left behind. Given these goals, the eulogy can be one of the most difficult and challenging special occasion speeches to deliver. At the same time, probably more people with little or no experience in public speaking deliver a eulogy at one time or another than all other types of special occasion speeches.

Should you be called upon to give a eulogy, the following guidelines will help to ensure an effective speech.

Balance Delivery and Emotions

Many speakers fight the tendency to become overly emotional in a eulogy. Despite the sense of grief the speaker may be feeling, his or her job is to help others feel better. The audience looks to the speaker for guidance in dealing with the loss, and for a sense of closure. Therefore, it is essential to stay in control. Showing intense grief will probably make the audience feel worse. If you do feel that you are about to break down, pause, take a breath, and focus on your next thought.

Refer to the Family of the Deceased

Families suffer the greatest loss, and a funeral is primarily for their benefit. Make sure your presentation shows respect for the family; mention each family member by name. Make it clear that the deceased was an important part of a family by humanizing that family.

Commemorate Life — Not Death

Make sure that you focus on the life of the person rather than on the circumstances of his or her death. A eulogy should pay tribute to the deceased as an individual and remind the audience that he or she is still alive, in a sense, in our memories. Talk about the contributions the person made and the achievements that he or she accomplished. Focus on demonstrating the kind of character the person had. You might want to tell a story or an anecdote that illustrates the type of person you are eulogizing. Even humorous stories and anecdotes may be appropriate if they effectively humanize the deceased.

Be Positive but Realistic

Emphasize the deceased's positive qualities. This seems obvious, but care must be taken in selecting stories and anecdotes, as well as in planning descriptions of the person, to ensure that none of the speech is interpreted as casting the deceased in a negative light. It is also important, however, to avoid excessive praise. This may ultimately sound insincere and provide a distorted picture of the person.

✓ CHECKLIST

Tips for Delivering Effective Eulogies

_____ 1. Stay in control of your emotions.

_____ 2. Refer to the family of the deceased, mentioning each family member by name.

_____ 3. Rather than focusing on the circumstances of the death, talk about the contributions the deceased person made during his or her lifetime.

_____ 4. Consider telling a story or an anecdote that illustrates the type of person you are eulogizing. Humor that is respectful may be appropriate.

_____ 5. Emphasize the person's positive qualities, but do not be insincere.

AFTER-DINNER SPEECHES

In the course of his career, Mark Twain, the nineteenth-century humorist and writer, was said to have given more than 150 after-dinner speeches. Extremely popular at the time, lavish dinner affairs were attended by a host of male notables who spent several hours eating and drinking, after which they spent several more hours listening to humorous toasts and speeches.[5] Twain's speeches were so well received that many of them were reprinted in the next day's newspaper.

Today, after-dinner speaking continues to take place around the time of a meal, although not necessarily at a dinner. The contemporary **after-dinner speech** is just as likely to occur before, during, or after a breakfast or lunch seminar or other type of business, professional, or civic meeting as it is to follow a formal dinner. In general, an after-dinner speech is expected to be light-hearted and entertaining (see the following exceptions). At the same time, listeners expect the speaker to provide insight into the topic at hand. Balancing these two goals can make the after-dinner speech one of the most challenging but enjoyable kinds of speeches you deliver.

Recognize the Occasion

Be sure to connect the speech you are giving with the occasion. Delivering a speech that is unrelated to the event that has given rise to it may leave the impression that the speech is canned — that is, one that the speaker uses again and again in different settings. **Canned speeches** can be an immediate turnoff for many audiences. Further, audience members want to be recognized for who they are and for the event they have come to participate in.

Avoid Stand-Up Comedy

Many speakers are tempted to treat the after-dinner speech as an opportunity to engage in stand-up comedy, stringing together a series of jokes only loosely centered on a theme. There are two problems with this approach. First, the after-dinner speech is still a speech. A comedy routine does not have a recognizable introduction, body, or conclusion. This absence of a structure makes it difficult to deliver the serious point that the after-dinner speaker seeks to make because there will be no place where such points naturally fit. Second, most people are not comedians. Keeping an audience laughing for any length of time requires a great deal of practice and skill, as well as a major investment in speechwriting. For noncomedians, this can be a challenge too difficult to overcome.

The most convincing speakers are the ones who are most naturally believable. Trying to become funnier — or more serious — than you normally are will probably set you up to fail because it will make your job harder. The speech becomes an acting challenge. If you are naturally very funny, use that skill. If you have more of a dry sense of humor, plan jokes that reflect that kind of humor. Do not be fooled into thinking that expressing humor means that you have to become a Chris Rock or a Jerry Seinfeld.

The After-Dinner Speech and Social Agenda–Setting

Rather than entertainment, the purpose of certain after-dinner speeches is **social agenda–setting**. For example, each year the members and supporters of the Sierra Club gather to celebrate the date that the organization was founded. At every dinner event, an individual who is prominent in politics or the environmental movement addresses the group. Clearly, when the purpose of the after-dinner speech is agenda-setting, the speaker must focus more closely on the serious side of the equation than on entertainment. Nevertheless, even when charged with this goal, the after-dinner speaker should make an effort to keep his or her remarks low-key enough to accompany the digestion of a meal.

SPEECHES OF INSPIRATION

Many of the types of special occasion speeches discussed so far may well be inspiring. For example, presentation and acceptance speeches might inspire by highlighting the receiver as a model of the values embodied in the award. Certain occasions, however, call for a speech that is meant to inspire as its main goal. Every week, ministers, rabbis, priests, and mullahs deliver inspirational speeches in the form of **sermons**. Commencement addresses, "pep talks" at sales meetings, and nomination speeches at rallies and conventions are all inspirational in nature. In the business world, occasions for inspirational speeches are so frequent that some people earn their living as inspirational speakers. A **speech of inspiration** seeks to uplift the members of the audience and to help them see things in a positive light. Effective speeches of inspiration touch on deep feelings in the audience. Their emotional force is such that our better instincts are aroused. They urge us toward purer motives and harder effort and remind us of a common good.

Thus, as in a persuasive speech, to create an effective inspirational speech you'll need to appeal to the audience's emotions (pathos) and display positive ethos. Two means of evoking emotion, or pathos, are *vivid description* and *emotionally charged words* (see Chapter 24). This and other techniques of language, such as repetition, alliteration, and parallelism, can help transport the audience from the mundane to a loftier level (see Chapter 16).

Use Real-Life Stories

Another way to inspire listeners is through real-life examples and stories. Few things move us as much as the example of the ordinary person who achieves the extraordinary, whose struggles result in triumph over adversity and the realization of a dream. Recognizing this, in their State of the Union addresses several recent U.S. presidents have taken to weaving stories about "ordinary American heroes" into their remarks. Ever cognizant of the power of the televised sound bite, the politicians usually invite these people to attend the speech and then strategically seat them to permit the best camera angles.

✓ **CHECKLIST**

Delivering a Successful Speech of Inspiration

_____ 1. Focus the speech on uplifting the audience.

_____ 2. Seek to arouse the audience's better instincts.

_____ 3. Use emotional appeals.

_____ 4. Concentrate on creating positive speaker ethos (see Chapter 24).

_____ 5. Appeal to the audience's emotions through vivid description and emotionally charged words.

_____ 6. Consider the use of repetition, alliteration, and parallelism (see Chapter 16).

_____ 7. Consider using real-life stories and examples.

_____ 8. Strive for a dynamic style of delivery.

_____ 9. Clearly establish your speech goal.

_____ 10. Consider using an acronym to organize your inspirational message.

_____ 11. Make your conclusion strong.

Be Dynamic

If it fits your personality, use a dynamic speaking style to inspire not only through content but through delivery as well. An energetic style can do a great deal to motivate the audience; when it is combined with a powerful message, this can be one of the most successful strategies for inspirational speaking.

Make Your Goal Clear

Inspirational speeches run the risk of being vague, leaving the audience unsure what the message was. Make sure that the audience cannot mistake your message for something else. Whatever you are trying to motivate your listeners to do, let them know. If you are speaking about a general goal, such as remaining positive in life, let your listeners know that. Make it clear that you are speaking on a general level, and that you are trying to motivate them in a manner that will affect their lives in a broad way. If you are trying to motivate your listeners to perform a specific action, such as donating money to a particular charity, clearly tell them so.

Consider a Distinctive Organizing Device

Many successful inspirational speakers, especially those in the business world, use devices such as _acronyms_ or steps to organize their speeches. This clarifies the organizational pattern of the speech and helps the audience to remember the message. For example, a football coach speaking at a practice session might organize a short inspirational speech around the word _win_. His main points might be Work, Intensity, and No excuses, forming the acronym WIN. This device emphasizes the goal of the constituent elements of the speech. All three are aimed at winning games.

Ethically Speaking
Beware of Violating Audience Expectations

More so than in other kinds of speeches, audience expectation that the speaker will fulfill a specific need is quite high in the special occasion speech. People listening to a eulogy, for example, will be very sensitive to what they perceive to be inappropriate use of humor or a lack of respect shown to the deceased. Those attending a dedication ceremony for a war memorial will expect the speaker to offer words of inspiration and will be disappointed if the speaker's attempts fall flat. Participants in a roast will expect humor but may balk at a speaker who crosses the line by making obscene or racist jokes. When a speaker violates audience expectations in situations like these, the reaction is usually pronounced. When giving a special occasion speech, it is therefore critical to plan your speech with audience expectations firmly in mind.

Here is an example of using steps. Giving an inspirational speech titled "Give Your Life a Dream with Design" to a graduating high school class, David Magill organized his presentation around three steps: "1. Design Your Vision," "2. Just Do It," and "3. Dig Deeper." Magill introduced his main points by saying, "My advice is simple, has three steps, and is easy to remember because the operative word in each step begins with the same letter with which *dream* begins — the letter *D*."[6]

Close with a Dramatic Ending

Using a dramatic ending is one of the best means of inspiring your audience to feel or act in the ways suggested by the theme of your speech. Recall from Chapter 15 the various methods of concluding a speech, including with a quotation, story, rhetorical question, or call to action.

Sample Visually Annotated Special Occasion Speech

Remarks at the Virginia Tech Convocation (after April 16, 2007, Shootings)

GOVERNOR TIM KAINE

The day after the horrific shootings of thirty-two people, mostly students, on the campus of Virginia Tech University in April 2007, Tim Kaine, Governor of the Commonwealth of Virginia, delivered a speech of inspiration. Rather than giving a eulogy of the shooting victims, the governor sought to encourage the shocked and grieving Virginia Tech family. Using the theme of community, he challenged his listeners to both rely on and reach out to each other in overcoming their despair. He effectively included himself as part of the community.

What an amazing community this is! •

Mr. President and Mrs. Bush and to all who are part of this Virginia Tech community in this room, on this campus, worldwide today: It is a very bitter and sad day, and yet my wife Anne and I are very privileged to be here with you, and there is nowhere else in the world we would rather be than with you at this moment. •

Scans the audience to emphasize importance of community

As Charlie [Steger, Virginia Tech University president] mentioned, Anne and I had left on Sunday morning from Richmond to go on a two-week trade mission to Asia. One of the events is actually an event in India to spotlight a wonderful program of Virginia Tech's. We had been in Tokyo in the hotel for about five hours and we were awakened with a call about one in the morning to report the horrible tragedy on this campus, and we were stunned. Our first thought was that we need to get home — we need to be in Blacksburg, with this community that we care so much about. •

We had the experience of being up in the middle of the night and not being able to get home for about 10 hours. So we did what people all across the world had been doing in the last couple of days. We sat there at first in our hotel room and then in a coffee shop and then in an airport waiting lounge with the television on watching to get news about what was happening on the campus and how the campus was handling this. •

It was different being away from home, being halfway across the world, and seeing what was happening on this campus, and what you, you students were showing to the world. And even in the midst of the darkest day in the history of this campus, what you showed to the world yesterday — you students — was an amazing thing. •

Again, and again, and again, and from all these various news outlets, the students were called forth to offer their thoughts and asked what they thought about their campus and how they were dealing with this tragedy. The grief was real and very raw and the

• The governor opens with an emphatic, upbeat attention statement.

• Immediately Governor Kaine focuses positive attention on the audience by highlighting their and his commonality in this place and at this time.

• As many people do when reflecting on such marked tragedies, Governor Kaine recalls where he was and what he was doing when the bad news reached him, and he stresses the desire and effort to get back home to be with the community he is speaking to.

• Governor Kaine combines chronological and spatial/geographical arrangements to account for his time away from and return to Virginia.

• The governor quickly turns attention back to the audience, referring specifically to the university students. The message is mostly for them.

questions were deep and troubling — but again the students came back wearing the Virginia Tech sweat-shirts, wearing the Virginia Tech caps, and the incredible community spirit, and sense of unity here on this campus and how — before it was about who was to blame or what could have been done different — it was about how we take care of each other in this wonderful, wonderful community. How proud we were even in the midst of a sad day, to see how well you represented yourselves and this university to a worldwide community! •

Uses gesture and facial expression to demonstrate sympathy with the audience

There are deep emotions that are called forth by a tragedy as significant as this; grieving and sadness by the boatload. Anne and I have unashamedly shed tears about this and I know virtually all of you have as well. That is the thing we should be doing. You should be grieving. There are resources here on this campus and others who are on this campus to help you if you find need for consolation that is so important. •

A second reaction — that is a natural reaction — is anger. Anger at the gunman, anger at the circumstance, what could have been done different. If something had happened — that's natural as well. One of the most powerful stories in the human history of stories is that great story central to Judaism, Islam and Christianity: the story of Job from the Old Testament, afflicted with all kinds of tragedy in his family and health, and he was angry. He was angry with his circumstances. He was angry at his Creator. He argued with God and he didn't lose his faith. It's OK to argue. It's OK to be angry. Those emotions are natural as well.

And finally the emotions of the family members most affected, beyond grief — losing a son, losing a daughter, a brother, a sister, losing a close friend. You can go beyond grief to isolation and feeling despair. Those haunting words that were uttered on a hill on Calvary: "My God, my God, why hast thou forsaken me?" •

Despair is a natural emotion at a time like this. They're all natural, they're all appropriate — but let

• His comments about students' reactions affirm their common strength and support in the face of tragedy.

• In this and the next two paragraphs, the governor identifies the various emotions elicited by the tragedy and the groups of people who naturally experience them. With these points he shows how emotional response is a common quality among members of the community.

• The governor legitimates the students' and the families' emotions, inviting them to feel what is natural, and expressing his own grief.

me ask one thing of you, this community, as you wrestle with your sadness, as you wrestle with your own feelings of anger, of confusion; as you wrestle with the despair, even you family members who have lost people so close to you: Do not let go of that spirit of community that makes Virginia Tech such a special place. Do not lose hold of that. ●

● He continues the theme of community, suggesting its power to overcome despair.

You need it as a university because you've always had it. You need to maintain it. We do not need that spirit of community to be a victim of yesterday. No, you need that. You, as a community unified together — there is so much you can do for these family members to help bear them up, to help them deal with their grief. If you are unified there is an incalculable amount you can do to help family members and friends deal with the loss. ●

● The governor calls on the students to use their own strength to help sustain and encourage the families who lost loved ones. This draws the students' attention from their own grief to the needs of others.

We need in Virginia that spirit of community that you ● have here. We are bold enough to call ourselves, not a state, but a Commonwealth. A state is a dotted line, a state is a political subdivision — but Commonwealth has a meaning. The meaning is what we have, the god-given and man-made resources that we have, we hold in common for a community. And you at Virginia Tech can be that community and demonstrate that community for us in a way that will benefit the entirety of Virginia.

Effective hand gesture underscores the definition of Commonwealth

● Notice the governor's use of *you* as a transitional element in the series of paragraphs just prior to and following this one. His focus is on the audience, and each of his points is directed to them.

And finally, I would say to you from having that vantage point of hearing about this on the other side of the world: It is not just you that needs to maintain the spirit; the world needs you to. Because the world was watching you yesterday — and in the darkest moment in the history of this university, the world saw you and saw you respond in a way that built community. ●

● Governor Kaine extends the bond of community at the university to the people of Virginia and indeed the entire world. His point is that the loss is not just a local one, but a global one, and that support is found in the global community.

I was reminded in the airport as we got ready to board to come back that I've seen this story before. I've turned on television and seen the bad news of a shooting, or a weather emergency, or a famine. I've seen these stories — and there will be more stories — but there was something in the story yesterday

Upright posture and eye contact reinforces message of hope and optimism

that was different and it was you. Your spirit even in a dark day of optimism and community and hope, and of wanting to be together. You taught something good yesterday, even on a dark day, to people all around the world — and the world needs that example put forward.

And so I pledge to do all I can, President Steger, members of the community and my team • as well, to be with you in the coming days. To be alongside of you in difficult times as we sort through and try to work with your families and friends. You have a remarkable community here; just look around and see this. And see the thousands of students next door. •

This is a remarkable place. Do not let go of that sense of community which is so powerful in this room.

• The Governor's conclusion includes promising action in support of those affected by the tragedy.

• The governor closes by assuring his audience that their community has gained strength to an extent that will endure indefinitely, if they will hold onto it.

Speaking beyond the Speech Classroom

Speaking beyond the Speech Classroom

Speaker's Reference
Speaking beyond the Speech Classroom

28. Communicating in Groups

Keep Your Focus on the Goal(s) of the Group

- Keep in mind that your purpose is to address a specific issue. (p. 463)
- Critically evaluate information in light of the group's goals. (p. 463)
- Create and follow an agenda. (p. 463)

Center Disagreements on Issues Rather than Personalities

- Engage in issues-based conflict, not personal-based conflict. (p. 465)

Don't Accept Information and Ideas Uncritically Merely to Get Along

- Resist groupthink. (p. 465)
- Apply critical thinking skills to solve the problem at hand. (p. 465)
- Engage in devil's advocacy and dialectical inquiry. (p. 466)

As Leader, Set Goals and Identify the Problem

- Set a performance goal. (p. 466)
- Identify the resources necessary to achieving the goal. (p. 466)
- Recognize contingencies that may arise. (p. 467)
- Obtain feedback. (p. 467)

As Leader, Encourage Active Participation among Group Members

- Directly ask members to contribute. (p. 467)
- Redirect the discussion. (p. 467)
- Set a positive tone. (p. 467)

Adopt the Six-Step Framework for Making Decisions and Reaching Goals

- Identify the problem. (p. 468)
- Conduct research and analysis. (p. 468)
- Establish guidelines and criteria. (p. 468)
- Generate solutions. (p. 468)
- Select the best solution. (p. 468)
- Evaluate solutions. (p. 468)

29. Business and Professional Presentations

Prepare a *Sales Presentation* to Persuade Potential Buyers to Purchase a Service or Product

- Consider basing the organization of your sales presentation on Monroe's motivated sequence. (p. 472)
    Draw the potential buyer's attention to the product.
    Isolate and clarify the buyer's need for the product.
    Describe how the product will satisfy the buyer's need.
    Invite the buyer to purchase the product.

Prepare a *Proposal* When Promoting an Idea, Product, or Procedure

- Organize lengthy proposals as follows: (p. 473)
    Introduce and state the problem.
    Describe the method of inquiry.
    Describe the facts learned.
    Offer explanations and interpretations of the findings.
    Offer recommendations.
- Organize brief proposals as follows: (p. 473)
    State the recommendations.
    Offer a brief overview of the problem.
    Review the facts on which the recommendations are based.
    Offer 1–3 recommendations.

Prepare a *Staff Report* When Informing Personnel of Developments Affecting Them and When Reporting on the Completion of a Task

- Organize the staff report as follows: (p. 474)
    State the issue.
    Provide a description of procedures and facts used in addressing the issue.
    Discuss facts that are most pertinent to the issue.
    State the conclusions and the recommendations.

Prepare a *Progress Report* to Offer Updates on Developments in an Ongoing Project

- For long-term projects, prepare reports at designated intervals throughout the duration of the project. (p. 475)
- For short-term projects, prepare reports daily or as requested. (p. 475)
- Provide the following information in the progress report: (p. 475)
    Briefly review progress made up to the time of the previous report.
    Describe new developments since the previous report.
    Describe the personnel involved and their activities.
    Detail time spent on tasks.

Describe supplies used and costs incurred.
Explain any problems and their resolution.
Provide an estimate of tasks to be completed for the next reporting period.

Prepare a *Crisis-Response Presentation* When Seeking to Reassure an Organization's Various Audiences and Restore Its Credibility

30. Speaking in Other College Courses

Expect to Prepare Oral Presentations in a Variety of Formats

- You will be asked to prepare both *individual* and *team presentations.* (p. 480)
- You may engage in *debates.* (p. 481)
- You may prepare *poster sessions.* (p. 487)

Expect to Adjust Your Presentations for Various On-the-Job Audiences

- Expert or insider audience. (p. 484)
- Colleagues within the field. (p. 484)
- Lay audience. (p. 484)
- Mixed audience. (p. 484)

In Science and Mathematics Courses, Expect to Present the Results of Experiments or Solutions to Problems

- The *research (oral scientific) presentation* describes original research you have done, either alone or as part of a team. (p. 485)
- The *methods/procedure presentation* describes and sometimes demonstrates an experimental or mathematical process, including the conditions under which the report can be applied. (p. 486)
- The *research overview presentation* provides context and background for a research question or hypothesis that will form the basis of an impending undertaking. (p. 486)
- The *field study presentation* describes an extended field study or research project. (p. 487)

Ground Scientific and Mathematical Presentations in the Scientific Method

- Provide detailed information about the methods used in gathering and analyzing data. (p. 488)
- Be prepared to use observations, proofs, and experiments as support for the presentation. (p. 488)

Speaker's Reference

- Be selective in your choice of details. (p. 489)
- Use presentation aids. (p. 489)
- Use analogies to build on prior knowledge. (p. 489)

In Technical Courses such as Engineering, Computer Science, and Architecture, Expect to Describe Projects

- *Engineering* and *architecture design reviews* report on the results of a design project. (p. 489)
- The *request for funding* provides evidence that a project is worth funding. (p. 490)
- Incorporate diagrams, prototypes, and other aids into the technical presentation. (p. 490)

In Social Science Courses, Expect to Focus on Qualitative *and* Quantitative Research

- Be prepared to describe experiments, naturalistic observations, case studies, and surveys. (p. 491)
- Expect to explain social or psychological phenomena by answering *what, how,* and *why* questions. (p. 491)

In Social Science Courses, Expect to Review and Evaluate the Research

- The *review of the literature presentation* examines the body of research related to a given topic or issue and offers conclusions about the topic based on this research. (p. 491)
- The *explanatory research presentation* reports on studies that attempt to analyze and explain a phenomenon, such as teen alcohol abuse or infant neglect. (p. 492)
- The *evaluation research presentation* examines the effectiveness of programs developed to address various issues. (p. 492)
- The *policy recommendation report* offers recommendations to solve a problem or address an issue. (p. 493)

In Arts and Humanities Courses, Focus on Interpreting and Analyzing the Topic

- Explain in an informative speech the relevance of a historical or contemporary person or event; a school of philosophical thought; or a piece of literature, music, or art. (p. 494)

- Compare and contrast events, stories, artifacts, or people in order to highlight the similarities or differences between them. (p. 494)
- Engage in debates. (p. 494)
- Research a topic and then lead a classroom discussion on it. (p. 494)

In Education Courses, Expect to Prepare Lectures and to Lead Group Activities and Classroom Discussions

- Pay careful attention to organizing and supporting presentations in education courses. (p. 496)
- Demonstrate how material in the lecture relates to the overall course content. (p. 497)
- Use student-friendly examples as evidence and support. (p. 497)

In Nursing and Allied Health Courses, Expect to Address a Range of Audiences on Health-Care Practices and Techniques

- You may be assigned a *community service learning project,* in which you report on the agency and its client base and your role in the project. (p. 497)
- You may prepare a *case conference,* in which you describe the patient's status, outline steps for treatment, review financial needs, and assess resources. (p. 498)
- You may be assigned a *shift report,* in which you give an oncoming caregiver a concise report of the patient's needs and status. (p. 498)
- You may prepare a *policy recommendation report,* in which you recommend a new or modified health plan or policy. (p. 498)

KEY TERMS

Chapter 28

small group	interpersonal roles	collective mind
virtual group	counterproductive roles	groupthink
presentational speaking	productive conflict	devil's advocacy
agenda	personal-based conflict	dialectical inquiry
task roles	issues-based conflict	participative leader

Chapter 29

presentational speaking	proposal	crisis-response
sales presentation	staff report	presentation
basic sales technique	progress report	

Speaker's Reference

Chapter 30

review of academic article

team presentation

debate

individual debate format

team debate format

claim

reasoning

evidence

expert or insider audience

colleagues within the field audience

lay audience

mixed audience

research presentation (oral scientific presentation)

methods/procedure presentation

research overview presentation

panel discussion

field study presentation

poster session

engineering design review

prototype

architecture design review

request for funding presentation

qualitative research

quantitative research

review of the literature presentation

explanatory research presentation

evaluation research presentation

policy recommendation report

lecture

group activity presentation

classroom discussion presentation

community service learning project

case conference

shift report

evidence-based practice

Communicating in Groups 28

Many of the experiences you'll have as a speaker and an audience member are likely to be related to your job, and most of those occasions will be in the context of a **small group** (usually between three and twenty people) as opposed to a large public audience. In fact, a substantial portion of your professional life will be spent participating in groups and teams.[1] Many of you will also participate in **virtual groups**, in which members who are geographically dispersed interact and exchange ideas through mediated communication such as e-mail, chat rooms, and video conferencing.[2]

Whether they are virtual or face-to-face, groups that form for work-related purposes frequently report orally on the results they've achieved. A manager might ask a committee to devise a new system for promoting employees, for example. As part of their assignment, the committee members must present their findings to senior management. Many professionals are called upon to address a small group of peers, colleagues, or customers on a business or a professional issue. Oral reports such as these are a form of **presentational speaking** — reports delivered by individuals or groups within the business or professional environment. (See Chapter 29 for distinctions and comparisons between public speaking and presentational speaking.)

Becoming an Effective Group Participant WEB Chapter quizzes

Clear communication is vital to working cooperatively in groups and to getting to the point where you have something worthwhile to report. Unfortunately, not all interactions in groups are effective, efficient, or productive. The quality of a group's product is largely determined by how closely the participants keep sight of the group's goals and avoid behaviors that detract from these goals. The more you use the group's goals as a steadying guide, the less likely you are to be diverted from your real responsibilities as a participant. Setting and following an agenda can help you do this. An **agenda** identifies the items to be accomplished during a group meeting; often it will specify time limits for each item of business.[3] Figure 28.1 offers an example of an agenda.

ASSUMING ROLES WITHIN THE GROUP

Group members generally assume two types of roles within the group: a task role and an interpersonal role. **Task roles** directly relate to the group's accomplishment of its objectives and missions — these are roles that directly "make

---

AGENDA

Staff meeting, June 4, 2008
Creative Communication Innovations
9 to 11 A.M.
Third Floor Conference Room

Participants: Lisa Gomez, Jonathan Halberstat, Juliann Chen,
Georgianna Walker, Carol Ludlow, Jerry Freely

1. Welcome and call to order
2. Opening remarks
3. Introduction of guests
4. Approval of minutes from previous meeting
5. Briefing from product line managers
6. Update from auditors
7. Report from consultants on new product line rollouts
8. Report on architecture designs for new assembly plant in Mexico
9. Summary
10. Adjournment

Figure 28.1 Sample Meeting Agenda. *Source:* Adapted from H. Dan O'Hair, James S. O'Rourke, and Mary John O'Hair, *Business Communication: A Framework for Success* (Cincinnati: South-Western, 2001), 492.

things happen." "Recording secretary" and "moderator" are examples of task roles. Other common task roles include "initiator" (helps the group get moving by generating new ideas, offering solutions), "information giver" (offers input), and "information seeker" (seeks clarification and input from the group).[4]

Members also adopt various **interpersonal roles**, or styles of relating in the group. These "relational" roles facilitate group interaction. For example, one person will act to smooth out tension in the group ("the harmonizer"), another will assume the role of keeping the discussion moving and getting everyone's input ("the gatekeeper"), while a third will express group feelings or mood in an effort to clarify the climate.[5]

Both task roles and interpersonal roles help the group maintain cohesion and achieve its mission. Sometimes, however, group members focus on individual versus group needs. These needs are usually irrelevant to the task at hand and are not oriented toward maintenance of the group as a team. Such individuals can be said to display negative interpersonal roles, or **counterproductive roles**. Examples of counterproductive roles include "hogging the floor" (not allowing others to speak), "blocking" (being overly negative about group ideas or raising issues that have been settled), "distracting" (distracting the group from tasks at hand), and "recognition seeking" (acting to call attention to self rather than to group tasks).

USING PRODUCTIVE CONFLICT TO FOCUS ON THE ISSUES

Whenever people come together to consider an important issue, conflict is inevitable. But conflict doesn't have to be destructive. In fact, the best decisions are usually those that emerge from productive conflict.[6] It is through productive conflict that groups grow, mature, and realize a heightened sense of accomplishment. In **productive conflict**, questions are clarified, ideas are challenged, counterexamples are presented, worst-case scenarios are considered, and proposals are reformulated. After a process like this, the group can be confident that its decision has been put to a good test. Because the group members have had a part in analyzing synthesizing, and constructing the decision, it will be one that the entire group can support. Group members will have considerable investment in and therefore ownership of the decision that is reached.

Productive conflict is *issues-based* rather than *personal-based*. In **personal-based conflict**, members argue about one another instead of about the issues, subsequently wasting time and impairing motivation. The group's assigned tasks remain incomplete and issues remain unresolved. Whereas personal-based conflict detracts a group from its mission, **issues-based conflict** allows members to test and debate ideas and potential solutions. It requires each member to ask tough questions, press for clarification, and present alternative views.[7]

PURSUING A COLLECTIVE MIND WHILE AVOIDING GROUPTHINK

For groups to be truly effective, group members eventually need to form a **collective mind**.[8] Groups that manifest a collective mind engage in communication that is critical, careful, consistent, and conscientious.[9] Maintaining a collective mind obviously requires the careful management of issues-based and personal-based conflict, but at the same time group members must avoid the tendency to think too much alike. **Groupthink** is the tendency to accept information and ideas without subjecting them to critical analysis.[10] Groupthink results from strong feelings of loyalty and unity within a group. When these feelings are more motivating than the desire to critically analyze ideas and test solutions, the quality of the group's decisions suffers.

Groups prone to groupthink typically exhibit these behaviors:

- Participants reach a consensus and avoid conflict in order not to hurt others' feelings, but they do so without genuinely agreeing.
- Members who do not agree with the majority of the group are pressured to conform.
- Disagreement, tough questions, and counterproposals are discouraged.
- More effort is spent rationalizing or justifying the decision than testing it.

The best way to maintain a collective mind while avoiding groupthink is to engage in productive conflict, as described above, and to make sure that the discussion includes some level of **devil's advocacy** (arguing for the sake of raising issues or concerns about the idea under discussion) or **dialectical inquiry** (devil's advocacy that goes a step further by proposing a countersolution to the idea).[11] Like productive conflict management, these methods of argument are invaluable for finding a more optimal solution and avoiding groupthink during a group process.

Leading a Group

 Web links

Capable leadership is critical to the success of any group effort. It is the group leader's task to set goals and to encourage active participation among group participants. Four broad styles of leadership are possible within groups: *autocratic* (leaders make decisions and announce them to the group), *consultative* (leaders make decisions after discussing them with the group), *participative* (leaders make decisions with the group), and *delegative* (leaders ask the group to make the decision).[12] Research suggests that of these four types of leaders, the most effective is the **participative leader** — that is, one capable of facilitating a group's activities and interaction in ways that will lead to a desired outcome. Following the steps below will help you become an effective participative leader.

SETTING GOALS

Most negative experiences in groups result from a single underlying problem: lack of a clear goal. Each member of a group should be able to clearly identify the purpose(s) of the group and the goals it is charged with reaching. The group leader should be a catalyst in setting these goals and ensuring that they are reached, either independently or in collaboration with other group members. The latter option is preferable because group members are likely to be more committed and excited about goals that they have helped create. The accompanying checklist contains guidelines for setting group goals.

✓ **CHECKLIST**

Guidelines for Setting Group Goals

_____ 1. Identify the problem.

_____ 2. Set a performance goal.

_____ 3. Identify the resources necessary to achieving the goal.

_____ 4. Recognize contingencies that may arise.

_____ 5. Obtain feedback.

ENCOURAGING ACTIVE PARTICIPATION

Each group member has something unique to contribute, but perhaps not at all times. Sometimes, however, a group member does not participate even if he or she has something valuable to offer. The following are a few reasons for nonparticipation:

- *Apprehension:* Members may experience fear or anxiety about expressing themselves in the group.
- *Lack of self-esteem:* Members may doubt the value of their contributions.
- *Dominance:* Other group members may control the floor.
- *Status differences:* Group members lower in the hierarchy of positions may choose not to comment on stances taken by superiors in the group. Some group members may not participate because they are sensitive to differences in class, race, or gender.
- *Being unprepared:* Group members failing to do outside work ahead of the meeting.

Whatever the root cause, problems arise when participation is unbalanced. A study by Hoffman and Maier,[13] for example, found that groups adopt solutions that receive the largest number of favorable comments, whether these comments emanate from one individual or from many. If only one or two members participate, it is their input that sets the agenda, whether or not their solution is optimal. The following checklist offers guidelines for encouraging group participation.

 CHECKLIST

Techniques to Encourage Group Participation

✓ *Directly ask members to contribute.* The leader can influence involvement by taking note of participants who are quiet and asking them to contribute ("Patrice, we haven't heard from you yet" or "Juan, what do you think about this?").

✓ *Redirect the discussion.* Sometimes one person or a few people can dominate the discussion. To encourage others to contribute, the leader can redirect the discussion in their direction.

✓ *Set a positive tone.* Some people are reluctant to express their views because they fear ridicule or attack. A good leader minimizes such fears by setting a positive tone, stressing fairness, and encouraging a climate of politeness and active listening.

✓ *Ensure that some level of devil's advocacy and dialectical inquiry takes place.*

Making Decisions in Groups

 Web links

Effective groups do not make decisions arbitrarily or haphazardly. Rather, they engage in a deliberate process resulting in decisions that all participants understand and are committed to. Group decision making is best accomplished through a six-step process of reflective thinking based on the work of the educator John Dewey.[14] The steps include: (1) identifying the problem, (2) conducting research and analysis, (3) establishing guidelines and criteria, (4) generating solutions, (5) selecting the best solution, and (6) evaluating solutions. In the words of John Dewey, this sequence of steps encourages group members to "think reflectively" about their task. In this way, all the relevant facts and opinions can be discussed and evaluated, thereby ensuring a better decision. See Figure 28.2 for an explanation of each step.

Step 1   Identify the Problem
- What is being decided upon?
Group leader summarizes problem, ensures that all group members understand problem, and gains agreement from all members.

↓

Step 2   Conduct Research and Analysis
- What information is needed to solve the problem?
Research and gather relevant information.
Ensure that all members have relevant information.

↓

Step 3   Establish Guidelines and Criteria
- Establish criteria by which proposed solutions will be judged.
Reach criteria through agreement and record criteria.

↓

Step 4   Generate Solutions
- Conduct brainstorming session.
Don't debate ideas yet, simply gather and record all ideas.

↓

Step 5   Select the Best Solution
- Weigh the relative merits of each idea against criteria.
Select one alternative that can best fulfill criteria.
If more than one solution survives, select solution that best meets criteria.
Consider merging two solutions if both meet criteria.
If no solution survives, return to problem identification step.

↓

Step 6   Evaluate Solutions
- Does the solution have any weaknesses or disadvantages?
- Does the solution resemble the criteria that were developed?
- What other criteria would have been helpful in arriving at a better solution?

Figure 28.2 Making Decisions in Groups: John Dewey's Six-Step Process of Reflective Thinking

Making Presentations in Groups

Once the group has achieved its goal, members face the task of communicating their results to others in the form of a written report, an oral presentation, or a combination of the two. Group presentations have many of the same characteristics as presentations done individually, but there are differences; while in an individual presentation one person assumes all responsibility for presenting a topic, in a group presentation some or all of the group members share responsibility.

Group presentations (also called *team presentations*) can be an exciting way to present information and to motivate and persuade an audience to accept your communication goals. In order for this to occur, however, all members must be willing to pull their weight. Successful group presentations require cooperation and planning. The first step is to select a leader. See Chapter 30, p. 480, for guidelines on creating effective team presentations.

29 Business and Professional Presentations

In many sectors of the workplace, business and professional presentations serve as a primary medium for disseminating vital company information. These presentations cover a wide range of topics, audiences, and speech purposes. Rather than being formal public speeches, business and professional presentations are forms of **presentational speaking** — reports delivered by individuals or groups within the business or professional environment. Presentational speaking includes individual speakers addressing groups of colleagues, managers, clients, or customers, as well as multiple members of work groups addressing similarly composed audiences. Giving effective business presentations is one of the most important ways that business professionals gain visibility in their organization.[1]

Public versus Presentational Speaking

Business and professional presentations have much in common with formal public speeches. Still, Priscilla Rogers, a professor of business communication, notes that there are some important differences between speeches delivered in public and presentations delivered in a business and professional environment.[2] First, the audience for a presentation can be as small as three people. Second, presentational speaking is less formal than public speaking. Rogers suggests that on a continuum presentational speaking would lie midway between public speaking at one end and conversational speaking at the other.[3] In addition, presentational speaking usually occurs in more limited settings than does public speaking. Public speeches can be delivered just about anywhere an audience can gather — indoors or outdoors, at a large arena or a small park. In contrast, presentations made in a business or a professional context are more likely to be delivered indoors at a business site, notes Frank Dance, a professor of communication and business consultant.[4]

In addition to audience size, level of formality, and setting, Dance suggests several other factors that distinguish presentational from public speaking. These include topic selection, audience composition, audience participation, and speaker expertise.[5]

TOPIC SELECTION

Topics for public speeches can be assigned but are often left to the speaker's discretion. Even when a topic is assigned, public speakers are given some leeway in developing and presenting it. They can even be excused for deviating from a predetermined topic if the topic they prefer to present is relevant to the audience. In contrast, topics for business presentations are either assigned by the presenter's superiors or clients or assumed as part of one's role in a work group or a project. Presentational speakers often follow a prescribed or traditional approach depending on the kind of presentation being made. Presentational topics are more specific, task-oriented, and management- or client-directed.

AUDIENCE COMPOSITION

Public speaking audiences may be more diverse than presentation speaking audiences. They are more likely to be self-selected or voluntary, and they probably expect to be attending a onetime event. In contrast, listeners who attend a business or a professional presentation are more likely to be part of a "captive" audience. As a group they are also more similar, in that there is an ongoing relationship among the participants; that is, they work closely together over a period of time and are sometimes part of a team.

AUDIENCE PARTICIPATION

In general, the public speaker delivers his or her speech uninterrupted. If there is a question-and-answer period, it almost always takes place at the end of the speech. In business and professional presentations, verbal interaction between speaker and audience is generally the rule rather than the exception. Audience members ask questions and make comments during and after the talk, and it isn't unusual for a presentation to be stopped midway when a discussion ensues or time runs out. Presentational speakers learn to be flexible and adaptable in such situations.

SPEAKER EXPERTISE

Listeners generally assume that a public speaker has more expertise or considerably more firsthand knowledge than they do on a topic. The speaker is frequently the reason many audience members attend a speech, regardless of the topic. Presentational speakers, in contrast, are more properly thought of as "first among equals," in that they may be no more expert on the topic than the members of the audience. It just happens that the presenter has been designated to fulfill this particular task for the moment or for a time. A presentation audience attends more to gain information than to hear the presenter.

Common Types of Business and Professional Presentations

Five of the most common types of business and professional presentations are *sales presentations, proposals, staff reports, progress reports,* and *crisis-response presentations.*[6] Any of these oral reports can be delivered by individuals or by multiple presenters. Keep in mind that many industries and professions have their own preferred styles and requirements. The following discussion provides some basic and common features of these presentations.

SALES PRESENTATIONS

Purpose

A **sales presentation** attempts to lead a potential buyer to purchase a service or a product described by the presenter. The general purpose of sales presentations is to persuade.

Audience

A sales presentation can be directed to an audience of one or many. It depends on who has the authority to make the purchase under consideration. Some sales presentations are invited by the potential buyer. Others are "cold sales" in which the presenter/seller approaches a first-time potential buyer with a product or a service. In some cases the audience might be an intermediary—a community agency's office manager, for example, who then recommends to the agency director whether the purchase would be worthwhile. Sales presentations are most successful when they are clearly audience-directed. That is, the product or service must be presented in such a way as to show how it meets the needs of the potential buyer.

Organization

With its focus on audience needs, the motivated sequence pattern developed by Alan Monroe (see Chapter 26) offers an excellent way to organize sales presentations. Sometimes referred to as the **basic sales technique**, Monroe's sequence involves (1) drawing the potential buyer's attention to the product, (2) isolating and clarifying the buyer's need for the product, (3) describing how the product will satisfy the need and provide other long-term benefits, and (4) inviting the buyer to purchase the product. The extent to which the speaker focuses on each segment depends on the nature of the selling situation. In cold-call sales situations, the seller/presenter may have to spend more time discovering the potential buyer's needs. Being a good listener is critical in these situations.[7] (See Chapter 4 on listening.) For invited sales presentations, the buyer's needs will probably be known in advance. In this event, the presenter can spend more time detailing the characteristics of the product and showing how it will satisfy the buyer's needs.

✓ CHECKLIST

Using Monroe's Motivated Sequence to Organize a Sales Presentation*

_____ 1. Draw the potential buyer's attention to the product.
_____ 2. Isolate and clarify the buyer's need for the product.
_____ 3. Describe how the product will satisfy the buyer's need.
_____ 4. Invite the buyer to purchase the product.
_____ 5. Anticipate and prepare for objections.

*See Chapter 26, pp. 412–415.

PROPOSALS

Purpose

Organizations must make decisions constantly on whether to modify or adopt a product, procedure, or policy. Should Armen Construction purchase new drill bits? Should K-mart stores implement a new employee-grievance procedure? Such information is routinely delivered as a **proposal**. For example, the Giant Lollipop Company might be interested in upgrading its telephone system. The facilities manager is given the task of consulting the original system provider to learn about the recommended equipment for making the upgrade. The manager then prepares a presentation that will provide the necessary information to assist the company in making its decision.

Proposals may be strictly informative, as in the example of the facilities manager providing information to his or her superiors. Often, proposals are persuasive in nature, with the presenter arguing in favor of one course of action over another.

Audience

The audience for a proposal can vary from a single individual to a large group; the individual or individuals have primary or sole decision-making responsibility. In the example of the telephone system, the facilities manager will present his or her report to company officers who are authorized to decide, on the basis of the report, whether to upgrade to the newer system. Because many proposals seek to persuade listeners, careful adaptation to the audience is critical to an effective presentation.[8]

✓ CHECKLIST

Preparing a Proposal

Organize lengthy proposals as follows:

_____ 1. Introduce the issue.
_____ 2. State the problem.
_____ 3. Describe the method by which the problem was investigated.
_____ 4. Describe the facts learned.
_____ 5. Offer explanations and an interpretation of the findings.
_____ 6. Offer recommendations.

Organize brief proposals as follows:

_____ 1. State your recommendations.
_____ 2. Offer a brief overview of the problem.
_____ 3. Review the facts on which the recommendations are based.
_____ 4. Offer 1–3 recommendations.

Organization

Depending on its subject, a proposal can be quite lengthy and formally organized or relatively brief and loosely structured. The organization of a lengthier, more formal report includes a full introduction, a statement of the problem, the method of inquiry, a summary of the facts learned, an explanation, a conclusion, and a recommendation. If the facilities manager of the aforementioned telephone system must interview several people and read several sources of information pertaining to the upgrade, the presentation might be suited to the more formal plan. On the other hand, if the information is relatively straightforward and limited in scope, the presenter can begin with a statement of recommendation (or offer a list of 1–3 prioritized recommendations), a brief overview of the problem, and a review of the facts on which the recommendation is based.

STAFF REPORTS

Purpose

A **staff report** informs managers and other employees of new developments that affect them and their work. For example, a company's personnel division might implement a new plan for subscribers to the company's health insurance program. To explain the changes, the personnel director will present the plan at a meeting of the sales division. He or she will review the reasons for the new plan, explain how it works, and describe its ramifications. Another function of staff reports is to provide information on the completion of a project or task. For instance, the district manager of a restaurant chain might assign three local restaurant managers the task of devising a plan for expanding the seating capacity at each location. The managers will present their designs at the next district meeting.

Audience

The audience for a staff report is usually a group, but it can be an individual. The managers of the chain restaurant will make their report in a meeting attended only by the district manager, or in a meeting at which managers from the entire

---

✓ CHECKLIST

Preparing a Staff Report

_____ 1. State the problem or question under consideration.
_____ 2. Provide a description of procedures and facts used to address the issue.
_____ 3. Discuss the facts that are most pertinent to the issue.
_____ 4. Provide a statement of the conclusions.
_____ 5. Offer recommendations.

district are present. The recipients of a staff report then use the information to implement new policy, to coordinate other plans, or to make other reports to other groups.

Organization

Formal staff reports typically include a statement of the problem or question under consideration (sometimes called a "charge" to a committee or a subcommittee), a description of procedures and facts used in addressing the problem, a discussion of the facts that are most pertinent to the problem, and a statement of conclusions followed by recommendations.

PROGRESS REPORTS

Purpose

A progress report is similar to a staff report, with the exception that the audience can include people *outside* the organization as well as within it. A **progress report** updates clients or principals on developments in an ongoing project. On long-term projects, such reports may be given at designated intervals or at the time of specific task completions throughout the duration of the project. For example, subcontractors on a housing-construction project meet weekly with the project developers. On short-term projects, reports can occur daily. For example, medical personnel in the intensive-care unit of a hospital meet each morning to review the treatment protocol and progress of each patient.

Audience

The audiences for progress reports vary greatly. An audience might be a group of clients or customers, developers and investors, next-line supervisors, company officers, media representatives, or same-level co-workers assigned to the same project. For example, a work team consisting of workers from various departments (engineering, marketing, and cost analysis) may be assigned to the

---

✔ CHECKLIST

Preparing a Progress Report

_____ 1. Briefly review progress made up to the time of the previous report.
_____ 2. Describe new developments since the previous report.
_____ 3. Describe the personnel involved and their activities.
_____ 4. Detail time spent on tasks.
_____ 5. Describe supplies used and costs incurred.
_____ 6. Explain any problems and their resolution.
_____ 7. Provide an estimate of tasks to be completed for the next reporting period.

development of a new product. Once a week, members of the team present the rest of the division with a progress report, especially during the early stages. Once the project is well under way and activity is focused on one particular segment, such as marketing, those representatives may be the only personnel to make progress reports, and the audience may extend to potential buyers, corporate officers, and other staff in the various departments. Progress reports are commonplace in staff and committee meetings where subcommittees report on the development of their designated tasks. Audience questions are common at the end of progress reports. (See Appendix A, "Handling Question-and-Answer Sessions" and Chapter 4, "Listeners and Speakers.")

Organization

There is no set pattern of organization for a progress report. In many instances the report begins with a brief statement to review progress made up to the time of the previous report, followed by a more thorough statement of new developments since the previous report was made. This statement may include descriptions of personnel involved and their activities, time spent on tasks, supplies used and costs incurred, problems encountered and how they were handled, and an estimate of tasks to be completed for the next reporting period.

CRISIS-RESPONSE PRESENTATIONS

Purpose

The purpose of the **crisis-response presentation** (also called *crisis communication*) is to reassure an organization's various audiences (its "publics") and restore its credibility in the face of potentially reputation-damaging situations such as contaminated products, layoffs, chemical spills, or bankruptcy. For example, in 1982 Tylenol was faced with a potentially disastrous reputation-damaging crisis when seven people were killed as a result of a lethal contamination of the company's extra-strength painkiller. In addition to recalling the product and improving safety packaging, top management held numerous press conferences and otherwise made themselves available to the press and the public. Today, perhaps as a result of an increase in natural disasters, terrorism, and societal violence, the need for crisis communication arises in both the profit and the nonprofit sectors.[9] In 2005, for example, following Hurricane Katrina, local police and local, state, and federal officials briefed the public on the status of the evacuation and rebuilding efforts.

Audience

Crisis-response presentations may target one, several, or multiple audiences, both inside and outside of an organization. A personnel manager may address a group of disgruntled employees who are unhappy about a new vacation policy. Seeking to allay fears of ruin and shore up stockholder confidence, the CEO of an embattled corporation may target anxious employees and shareholders alike.

ESL Speaker's Notes
Steps to Counteract Problems in Being Understood

With the exception of young children, virtually everyone who learns to speak another language will speak that language with an accent. This issue is especially important in business and professional settings, where being understood can have a direct impact on your career. What steps can you take when your accent will make your oral presentation difficult for the audience to understand?

In the long term, interacting with native speakers in everyday life will help enormously. Engaging in dialogue with cross-cultural partners is an excellent way to adjust to native communication styles.[1] With immersion, non-native speakers can begin to stop translating word for word and start thinking in English. Using a tape recorder and practicing your speech in front of others is also very important.

But what if, although your experience with English is limited, you must nonetheless give an oral presentation? Robert Anholt, a scientist and author, suggests the following:

1. Practice the presentation often, preferably with a friend who is a native English speaker.
2. Learn the presentation almost by heart.
3. Create strong presentation aids that will convey most of the story by themselves, even if your speech is hard to understand.

By practicing often and ensuring that your presentation aids convey the bulk of your meaning, you can be confident that you will get your message across. And with time and effort, be assured that even the most difficult accent can be tamed to the point where speech is clearly understood.

1. Yuxia Z, "Using Authentic Cross-Cultural Dialogues to Encourage International Students' Participation in Tutorial Activities," *Business Communication Quarterly* 70 (2007): 43–47.

Source: Robert Anholt, *Dazzle 'Em with Style: The Art of Oral Scientific Presentation* (New York: W. H. Freeman, 1994), 156.

Organization

Of all the types of business and professional presentations, the crisis-response presentation is perhaps the most complex to plan and deliver. A variety of strategies exist, ranging from simple denial to "mortification," or admitting responsibility for a crisis and asking forgiveness.[10] Familiarity with a range of *image-restoration strategies* will allow the speaker to select the techniques that best apply to the situation at hand.[11] In essence, however, the crisis-response presentation is based on persuasion and argument. Sound reasoning and evidence are essential to its effectiveness. Depending on the issue and the audience(s) involved, one of the four organizational patterns described in Chapter 26 would be appropriate.

Ethically Speaking
Code of Ethics for Professional Communicators

Because hundreds of thousands of business communicators worldwide engage in activities that affect the lives of millions of people and because this power carries with it significant social responsibilities, the International Association of Business Communicators developed the Code of Ethics for Professional Communicators.

Articles

1. Professional communicators uphold the credibility and dignity of their profession by practicing honest, candid, and timely communication and by fostering the free flow of essential information in accord with the public interest.

2. Professional communicators disseminate accurate information and promptly correct any erroneous communication for which they may be responsible.

3. Professional communicators understand and support the principles of free speech, freedom of assembly, and access to an open marketplace of ideas, and act accordingly.

4. Professional communicators are sensitive to cultural values and beliefs and engage in fair and balanced communication practices that foster and encourage mutual understanding.

5. Professional communicators refrain from taking part in any undertaking that the communicator considers to be unethical.

6. Professional communicators obey laws and public policies governing their professional activities and are sensitive to the spirit of all laws and regulations. Should any law or public policy be violated, for whatever reason, they act promptly to correct the situation.

7. Professional communicators give credit for unique expressions borrowed from others and identify the sources and purposes of all information disseminated to the public.

8. Professional communicators protect confidential information and, at the same time, comply with all legal requirements for the disclosure of information that affects the welfare of others.

9. Professional communicators do not use confidential information gained as a result of professional activities for personal benefit and do not represent conflicting or competing interests without the written consent of those involved.

10. Professional communicators do not accept undisclosed gifts or payments for professional services from anyone other than a client or an employer.

11. Professional communicators do not guarantee results that are beyond the power of the practitioner to deliver.

12. Professional communicators are honest not only with others but also, and most important, with themselves as individuals; for a professional communicator seeks the truth and speaks that truth first to the self.

Source: International Association of Business Communicators (IABC) Web site, www.iabc.com/members/joining/code.htm (accessed September 20, 2002).

Speaking in Other College Courses **30**

Your opportunities to speak publicly at college won't end once you complete the introductory public speaking course. Often, you will be called on to prepare oral presentations in your major classes and in other general-education courses. No matter which major you select or what profession you choose, oral presentations will be required. As an engineering major, for example, you might prepare a design review of your major project. A student of history might deliver a presentation linking a historical event with a contemporary issue. Nursing majors might be asked to communicate a treatment plan to a medical team.

Before familiarizing yourself with the various course-specific formats beginning on p. 484, consider the following kinds of presentations that are assigned across the curriculum: academic articles, team presentations, and debates. Whatever your major, you will likely be asked to prepare one or more of these.

Review of Academic Articles

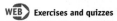 **WEB** Exercises and quizzes

A commonly assigned speaking task across disciplines is the **review of academic articles**. A biology instructor might ask you to review a study on cell regulation published in *Cell Biology*, for example, while a psychology teacher may require that you talk about a study on fetal alcohol syndrome published in the journal *Neuro-Toxicology*. The checklist below details what instructors typically expect from students in a review of an academic article.

 CHECKLIST

Preparing an Oral Review of an Academic Article

Typically, when you are asked to review an academic article, your instructor will expect you to:

✓ Identify the author's thesis.

✓ Explain the methods by which the author arrived at his or her conclusions.

✓ Explain the author's findings.

✓ Identify the author's theoretical perspective, if applicable.

(Continued)

✓ Evaluate the study's validity, if applicable.

✓ Describe the author's sources and evaluate their credibility.

✓ Show how the findings of the study might be applied to other circumstances, and make suggestions for how the study might lead to further research.

Source: With thanks to Michal Dale of Southwest Missouri State University's Department of Communication.

Team Presentations

Team presentations are oral presentations prepared and delivered by a group of three or more individuals. Regularly required in many college courses, successful team presentations require cooperation and planning (see Chapter 28, "Communicating in Groups").

DESIGNATE A TEAM LEADER

First, designate a leader to map out a strategy for presenting the information and to ensure coordination among all members. Once the strategy is in place, the team should assign roles and tasks.

ASSIGN ROLES AND TASKS

In some group presentations, one person may present the introduction, one or several others may deliver the body of the speech, and another may conclude the presentation. Together with the group leader, members must decide who will do what. The Checklist on p. 481 provides guidelines on assigning roles for the group presentation.

ESTABLISH A CONSISTENT FORMAT

The verbal and the audiovisual portions of the presentation should follow a consistent format. Members should use shared terminology, and all visual aids such as slides should be similarly formatted (see Chapter 21). Designate one person to check that these elements are consistent in terms of style, content, and formatting. (See Chapters 21 and 22.)

ESTABLISH TRANSITIONS BETWEEN SPEAKERS

Work out transitions between speakers ahead of time — for example, whether one team member will introduce every speaker or whether each speaker will introduce the next speaker upon the close of his or her presentation.

REHEARSE THE PRESENTATION

Together with the whole group, members should practice their portions of the presentation in the order they will be given in the final form, and they should do so until the presentation proceeds smoothly. This is particularly important to ensure consistency of delivery. Practicing together is key, and rehearsal should include presentation aids. Apply the techniques for rehearsal described in Chapter 19 on delivery.

 CHECKLIST

Assigning Roles for the Group Presentation

✓ Choose the person with the strongest presentation style and credibility level for the opening.
✓ Put the weaker presenters in the middle of the presentation.
✓ Select a strong speaker to conclude the presentation.
✓ Assign someone to handle the presentation aids.
✓ Assign someone with good listening skills to manage the question-and-answer session.

Source: Lin Kroeger, *The Complete Idiot's Guide to Successful Business Presentations* (New York: Alpha Books, 1997), 113.

 CHECKLIST

Team Presentation Tips

✓ Find out who will be attending and what audience members expect to hear.
✓ Write out each member's responsibilities regarding content and presentation aids.
✓ Practice introductions and transitions to create a seamless presentation.
✓ Determine when and how to introduce the speakers — by having one person introduce all at once at the beginning or by having each speaker introduce the next one.
✓ Establish an agreed-upon set of hand signals that will indicate when a speaker is speaking too loud or soft, or too slow or fast.
✓ Rehearse the presentation, with presentation aids, several times from start to finish.

Debates

 Exercises and quizzes

Debates are another popular presentation format in many college courses. Much like a political debate, in an *academic debate* two individuals or groups consider or argue an issue from opposing viewpoints. Generally there will be a winner and a loser, lending this form of speaking a competitive edge.

TAKE A SIDE

Opposing sides in a debate are taken by speakers in one of two formats. In the **individual debate format**, one person takes a side against another person. In the **team debate format**, multiple people (usually two) take sides against another team, with each person on the team assuming a speaking role.

The *pro* side (also called "affirmative") in the debate supports the topic with a *resolution* — a statement asking for change or consideration of a controversial issue. "Resolved, that the United States government should severely punish flag burners" is a resolution that the affirmative side must support and defend. The pro side tries to convince the audience (or judges) that the topic under consideration should be addressed, supported, or agreed with. The *con* side (also called "negative") in the debate attempts to defeat the resolution by dissuading the audience from accepting the pro side's arguments.

ADVANCE STRONG ARGUMENTS

Whether you take the affirmative or negative side, your primary responsibility is to advance strong arguments in support of your position. Arguments usually consist of the following three parts (see also Chapter 25):[1]

- **Claim:** A claim makes an assertion or declaration about an issue. "Females are discriminated against in the workplace." Depending on your debate topic, your claim may be one of fact, value, or policy (see Chapter 25).

- **Reasoning:** Reasoning (also called the *warrant*; see Chapter 25) is a logical explanation of the claim. "Females make less money and get promoted less frequently than males."

- **Evidence:** Evidence is the support offered for the claim. "According to a recent report by the U.S. Department of Labor, women make 28 percent less than men in comparable jobs and are promoted 34 percent less frequently."

Debates are characterized by *refutation,* in which each side attacks the arguments of the other. Refutation can be made against an opponent's claim, reasoning, evidence, or some combination of these elements. In the previous argument, an opponent might refute the evidence by arguing "The report used by my opponent is three years old, and a new study indicates that we are making substantial progress in equalizing the pay among males and females; thus we are reducing discrimination in the workplace."

Refutation also involves rebuilding arguments that have been refuted or attacked by the opponent. This is done by adding new evidence or attacking the opponent's reasoning or evidence.

"FLOW" THE DEBATE

In formal debates (in which judges take notes and keep track of arguments), debaters must attack and defend each argument. "Dropping" or ignoring an argument can seriously compromise the credibility of the debater and her or his side.

Affirmative → Negative		Affirmative → Negative		Affirmative → Negative	
Nonviolent prisoners should be paroled more often.	Nonviolent prisoners can become violent when they are paroled.	Studies show non-violent prisoners commit fewer crimes upon their release.	Those studies are outdated and involve only a few states.	My studies are recent and include big states like New York and California.	The studies from New York and California were flawed owing to poor statistics.

Figure 30.1 Flowchart of the Arguments for the Resolution "Resolved That Nonviolent Prisoners Should Be Paroled More Often"

To ensure that you respond to each of your opponent's arguments, try using a simple technique adopted by formal debaters called "flowing the debate" (see Figure 30.1). Write down each of your opponent's arguments, and then draw a line or arrow to indicate that you (or another team member) have refuted it.

 CHECKLIST

Tips for Winning a Debate

Keep these tactics in mind when participating in debates:

✓   Present the most credible and convincing evidence you can find.

✓   Before you begin, describe your position and tell the audience what they must decide.

✓   If you feel that your side is not popular among the audience, ask them to suspend their own personal opinion and judge the debate on the merits of the argument.

✓   Don't be timid. Ask the audience to specifically decide in your favor, and be explicit about your desire for their approval.

✓   Point out the strong points from your arguments. Remind the audience that the opponent's arguments were weak or irrelevant.

✓   Be prepared to think on your feet (see Chapter 17 on impromptu speaking).

✓   Don't hide your passion for your position. Debate audiences appreciate enthusiasm and zeal.

Prepare to Address Audiences on the Job   Quizzes

When preparing the following course-specific presentations, your professors may require that you tailor your remarks to a mock on-the-job audience, with your classmates representing that audience. Corresponding to the audience types you will likely address once you are employed in your field of training, these audiences include the **expert or insider audience**, the **colleagues within the field audience**, the **lay audience**, and the **mixed audience**. Table 30.1 describes each type of audience. For tips on addressing one of the most common of these types, see the nearby Checklist: Tips on Presenting to a Mixed Audience.

TABLE 30.1 • Types of Audiences in the Working World

Type of Audience	Characteristics
Expert or insider audience	People who have intimate knowledge of the topic, issue, product, or idea being discussed—such as researchers on the same project, design team members, technicians working on similar challenges, and clinicians working with similar clients.
Colleagues within the field audience	People who share the speaker's knowledge of the general field under question (e.g., psychology or computer science) but may not be familiar with the specific topic under discussion (e.g., short-term memory or voice-recognition systems, respectively)—such as academic colleagues, managers, project coordinators, and team leaders.
Lay audience	People who have no specialized knowledge of the general field related to the speaker's topic or of the topic itself.
Mixed audience	An audience composed of a combination of people—some with expert knowledge of the field and topic and others with no specialized knowledge. This is perhaps the most difficult audience to satisfy.

Speaking in Science and Mathematics Courses

Science-related disciplines include the physical sciences (e.g., chemistry and physics), the natural sciences (e.g., biology and medicine), and the earth sciences (e.g., geology, meteorology, and oceanography). Fields related to mathematics include accounting, statistics, and applied math. Oral presentations in science and mathematics often describe the results of original or replicated research. Instructors want to know the processes by which you arrived at your experimental results. For example, your biology instructor might assign an oral report on the extent to which you were able to replicate an experiment on cell mitosis. A mathematics instructor might ask you to apply a mathematical concept to an experiment or issue facing the field. For a geology course, you might be asked to describe the findings of your fieldwork.

 CHECKLIST

Tips on Presenting to a Mixed Audience

✓ Find out as much information as you can about the audience.

✓ Prepare both detailed and general content.

✓ Alert the audience to the order of your coverage: "I will first focus on the big picture and on management (marketing/sales) issues. I will then present design specifications and data analysis." In this way, each audience segment will know what to expect and when.

✓ Consider devoting half to two-thirds of your time to an introduction or overview of your subject and saving the highly technical material for the remaining time.[1]

(Continued)

✓ Be clear about the level at which you are speaking: "I am going to present the primary results of this project with minimal detailed information, but I'll be happy to review the statistics or experimental results in more detail following the presentation."

✓ If you notice that your listeners are experiencing discomfort, consider stopping and asking for feedback about what they want. You might then change course and opt for a more in-depth, high-level approach, depending on what they say.[2]

1. Office of Naval Research, "Tips for Preparing and Delivering Scientific Talks and Using Visual Aids," www.onr.navy.mil/onr/speak (accessed January 1, 2001).
2. Frederick Gilbert Associates, "Power-Speaking Tips," http://www.powerspeaking.com/powerspeaking/pstips.cfm (accessed August 30, 2000).

THE RESEARCH (ORAL SCIENTIFIC) PRESENTATION

In the **research presentation** (also called an **oral scientific presentation**) you describe original research you have done, either alone or as part of a team. The research presentation usually follows the model used in scientific investigations (see Figure 30.2) and includes the following elements:

1. *Introduction* describing the research question and the scope and objective of the study

2. *Description of methods* used to investigate the research question including where it took place and the conditions under which it was carried out

3. *Results* of the study summarizing key findings and highlighting the answers to the questions/hypotheses investigated

4. *Conclusion* (also called "Discussion"), in which you interpret the data or results and discuss their significance

Formulate a Hypothesis

↓

Select a Research Method

↓

Collect the Data

↓

Analyze the Data

↓

Report the Findings

Figure 30.2 Steps in a Scientific Investigation

Evaluating Your Original Research Presentation

✓ Do you state the research question?

✓ Do you clearly state the hypothesis, or hypothetical answer to the research question?

✓ Do you adequately describe and explain the study's research design?

✓ Do you describe the methods used to obtain the results?

✓ Do you explain and evaluate the results of the study?

✓ Do you address the significance of the study?

THE METHODS/PROCEDURE PRESENTATION

Some instructors may require you to describe how an experimental or mathematical process works and under what conditions it can be used. This is generally a ten- to fifteen-minute individual presentation. In a theoretical math class, for example, your assignment might be to describe an approach to solving a problem, such as the Baum Welch algorithm, including examples of how this approach has been used, either inappropriately or appropriately. This type of **methods/procedure presentation** generally does the following:

1. Identifies the conditions under which this particular process should be used

2. Offers a detailed description of the process (at times including an actual demonstration; see Chapter 23)

3. Discusses the benefits and shortcomings of the process

THE RESEARCH OVERVIEW

The **research overview presentation** provides background for a research question that will form the basis of an impending experiment or investigation. Instructors often ask students to organize research overviews into the following sections:

1. Overview of research relevant to the question at hand

2. Discussion of key studies that are central to the question

3. Analysis of the strengths and weaknesses of research in light of the current hypothesis or question

The format for the research overview may be an individual presentation or a **panel discussion**, in which a group of individuals explores specific lines of research that contribute to a general hypothesis or question. (See Appendix C for a review of panel discussions and symposiums.)

FIELD STUDY PRESENTATION

You may sometimes be called on to describe an extended research or field study. A geology student may be asked to report on a dig, for example. The **field study presentation** can be delivered individually, in teams, or in poster session format. A **poster session** presents information about a study or an issue concisely and visually. Presenters display their findings on posters, which are hung on freestanding boards; on hand are copies of the written report, with full details of the study highlighted in the poster session (see the accompanying checklist for more on producing effective poster sessions).

 CHECKLIST

Tips for Producing Effective Poster Sessions

In anticipation of future professional requirements on the job, instructors in scientific, technical, and social scientific disciplines (and, to a lesser extent, the humanities) sometimes direct students to prepare poster sessions.

When you prepare for a poster session, pay particular attention to the following:

✓ Select a concise and informative title for your display.

✓ Include an *abstract* (a brief summary of the study) along with several key points related to a study's research questions/problems, methodologies, results, and conclusions.

✓ Present two to three key points from each section of your paper.

✓ Begin the display by placing, in the upper right-hand corner, a concise introduction that indicates the purpose of the presentation.

✓ Place your conclusions and summary in the lower right-hand corner of the display.

✓ Use standard-size poster board of 1.1 m (3'8") by 1.75 m (5'8").

✓ Select a muted background color such as gray, beige, light blue, or white.

✓ Make sure your type is large enough to be read comfortably from a distance of at least three feet.

✓ Design figures and diagrams to be viewed from a distance.

✓ Label each figure.

✓ Place concise summaries of each figure in legends beneath the figure.

✓ Be prepared to provide brief descriptions of your poster when asked to do so, remembering to keep your explanations short.

✓ Be prepared to answer questions.

Source: Some points derived from Robert Anholt, *Dazzle 'Em with Style: The Art of Oral Scientific Presentation* (New York: W. H. Freeman, 1994); see also "Guides about Speeches and Presentations" Section on Poster Sessions, Colorado State University, http://writing.colostate.edu/references/speaking.htm, August 28, 2000 (accessed September 2, 2000).

Whatever the format, included in the extended research study are the following details:

- Overview of the field research
- Methods used in the research
- Analysis of the results of the research
- Time line indicating how the research results will be used in the future

PREPARING EFFECTIVE PRESENTATIONS IN SCIENCE AND MATHEMATICS

Science and mathematics instructors will expect your presentations to be grounded in the scientific method and to provide detailed information about methods used in gathering and analyzing data. Credible presentations must clearly illustrate the nature of the research question and the means by which results were achieved. Clearly executed presentation aids often are critical to these kinds of reports, and instructors generally require them. Often instructors will expect you to do the following:

- *Use observation, proofs, and experiments as support.* Depending on the nature of the report, instructors may also expect you to recount experiences in the field or to offer observations or experimental findings (e.g., describe what happened to the chemicals in a chemistry experiment or to the physical objects in a physics experiment).

 CHECKLIST

Tips for Preparing Successful Scientific Presentations

- ✓ Create an informative title that describes the research.
- ✓ Place your presentation in the context of a major scientific principle.
- ✓ Focus on a single issue and adjust it to the interests of your audience.
- ✓ Identify the underlying question you will address, divide it into subquestions, and answer each question.
- ✓ Follow a logical line of thought.
- ✓ Explain scientific concepts unambiguously, with a minimum of professional jargon.
- ✓ Use appropriate analogies and metaphors to associate the unknown with familiar knowledge.
- ✓ End with a concise, clearly formulated conclusion in the context of your chosen scientific principle.

Source: Based on Robert Anholt, *Dazzle 'Em with Style: The Art of Oral Scientific Presentation* (New York: W. H. Freeman, 1994), 89–90.

- *Be selective in your choice of details,* highlighting evidence critical to the outcome of the study but not overwhelming listeners with details they can learn about by referring to the written paper and the cited sources.

- *Use presentation aids* (ranging from slides to equations drawn on a chalkboard) to visually illustrate important processes and concepts. Remember that the more simply you can render complex information (without distorting findings), the more likely it is that audience members will grasp your points.

- *Use analogies to build on prior knowledge and demonstrate underlying causes.* See Chapter 23 for detailed guidelines on explaining difficult concepts.

Speaking in Technical Courses

Technical disciplines include the range of engineering fields (mechanical, electrical, chemical, civil, aerospace, industrial, nuclear), computer-science fields (computer and software engineering), and design-oriented fields (industrial design, architecture, graphic design). Oral presentations in technical courses often focus on a project, whether it is a set of plans for an architecture firm, a prototype robot, or an innovative computer-circuit design. Rather than addressing research, as is often the case in scientific and social scientific reports, the focus of technical presentations usually rests on the product or design itself.

Of the various types of presentations assigned in technical courses, the design review is perhaps the most common. Design reviews in engineering-related fields differ somewhat from those delivered in art and architecture courses. Other types of presentations you are likely to deliver in technical courses are requests for funding and progress reports (see Chapter 29, p. 475, for progress reports).

THE ENGINEERING DESIGN REVIEW

The **engineering design review** provides information on the results of a design project. Many capstone-engineering courses require that students prepare design reviews, which are generally informative in nature, although their purpose may include convincing the audience that the design decisions are sound. Design reviews often incorporate a prototype demonstration. A **prototype** is a model of the design. Design reviews often are delivered as team presentations (about twenty-five to thirty minutes in length) or in poster-session format. Design reviews typically include the following:

1. Overview of the design concept
2. Description of the unique specifications
3. Discussion of any experimental testing that has been completed on the design
4. Discussion of future plans and unresolved problems
5. Discussion of schedule, budget, and marketing issues

THE ARCHITECTURE DESIGN REVIEW

The **architecture design review** combines two functions: it enables the audience to visualize the design, and it sells it. A narrative approach, in which you tell the "story" of the design, combined with a *spatial organizational pattern*, in which you arrange main points in order of physical proximity of the design (see Chapter 13), can help you do this. At a minimum, architecture design reviews typically cover:

1. Background on the site
2. Discussion of the design concept
3. Description and interpretation of the design

THE REQUEST FOR FUNDING

In the **request for funding presentation**, a team member or the entire team provides evidence that a project, proposal, or design idea is worth funding. As such, this kind of presentation is persuasive in nature. Requests for funding usually cover the following ground:

1. Overview of customer specifications and needs
2. Analysis of the market and its needs
3. Overview of the design idea or project and how it meets those needs
4. Projected costs for the project
5. Specific reasons why the project or idea should be funded

The request for funding may be delivered as an individual or team presentation. On the job, the audience for the request for funding is made up of people who are concerned with the marketing, economic, and customer aspects of the idea or project (e.g., colleagues within the field; see Table 30.1).

PREPARING EFFECTIVE TECHNICAL PRESENTATIONS

Technical presentations sell ideas, provide hard data, rely on visual aids, and are results oriented.[2] As you prepare your technical presentation, pay particular attention to the following:

- *Lead with the results.* Technical disciplines such as engineering are about results — the end product. When organizing your presentation, consider telling the audience the most important result first. Then fill in the details.[3]
- *Use ample presentation aids.* Use diagrams, prototypes, and drawings, including design specifications, computer simulations, physical models, and spreadsheets. Construct aids early in the process, and use them as you practice the presentation.
- *Use a persuasive design — sell your ideas.* The technical presenter must persuade clients, managers, or classmates that a design, idea, or product is a

good one. As one instructor notes, "You can never assume that your product or design will just sell — you have to do that."[4]

- *Provide hard data.* Good technical presentations are detailed and specific and use numbers as evidence. Instead of general, sweeping statements, provide hard data and clearly stated experimental results.

- *Help listeners visualize* how your design will appear in its intended site (in architecture) by using concrete imagery.

- *Gear the information to the appropriate level.* Because of the complexity of technical information, it is especially important to convey it at a level appropriate to the audience. Typically, people who attend technical presentations possess a range of technical knowledge — from little or none to an expert understanding of the topic at hand (see Table 30.1). See also the checklist on p. 484 for tips on presenting to a mixed audience.

Speaking in Social Science Courses

Students in the social sciences (including psychology, sociology, political science, and communication) learn to evaluate and conduct **qualitative research** (in which the emphasis is on observing, describing, and interpreting behavior) as well as **quantitative research** (in which the emphasis is on statistical measurement).[5]

Research methods and areas of investigation can be far-ranging, from experiments on biological bases of behavior to participant observation studies of homelessness. For students in the social sciences, the focus is often on explaining or predicting human behavior or social forces, answering such questions as "What," "How," and "Why?"[6] Instructors may ask you to evaluate a theory or body of research, debate an issue, review the relevant literature, or make policy recommendations. Additionally, as in science and mathematics courses, you might prepare a research, field study, or methods/procedure presentation.

DEBATE CONTROVERSIAL TOPICS

Students enrolled in social science courses often must prepare for *debates* on controversial issues (see pp. 481–483). Sometimes an assignment involves advocating a position that you do not support. For example, a sociology instructor may require students who oppose euthanasia to defend the practice. Whichever side of an issue you address, you will need to prepare a well-composed argument with strong supporting evidence.

PROVIDE A REVIEW OF THE LITERATURE

The **review of the literature presentation** reviews the body of research related to a given topic or issue and offers conclusions about the topic based on this research. A psychology student, for example, might review the literature on psychological dysfunction in the military family. In addition to describing the available research, the student would offer conclusions uncovered by the research and suggest directions for future research. A review of the literature presentation typically includes the following:

1. Statement of the topic under review
2. Description of the available research, including specific points of agreement and disagreement among sources
3. Evaluation of the usefulness of the research
4. Conclusions that can be drawn from the research
5. Suggested directions for future study

EXPLAIN SOCIAL PHENOMENA

Social scientists often attempt to explain social or psychological phenomena such as "Why do some college students abuse alcohol?" "What leads to child abuse?" This type of **explanatory research presentation** typically addresses the following:

1. Description of the phenomenon under discussion (e.g., *"What* is taking place?")
2. Description of *how* and *why* it occurs as described by research
3. Explanation of the research and suggestions for future research

EVALUATE POLICIES AND PROGRAMS

In addition to explaining phenomena, social scientists often measure the effectiveness of programs developed to address these issues. Rather than asking "How?" or "Why?" evaluation research asks "Does it work?"[7] Typically, the **evaluation research presentation** addresses the following considerations:

1. Explanation of the program's mission
2. Description of the program's accomplishments
3. Discussion of how the accomplishments were measured, including any problems in evaluation
4. Conclusions regarding how well or poorly the program has met its stated objectives

RECOMMEND POLICIES

As well as evaluating programs and policies, you may be asked to recommend a course of action on a current issue or problem. This mirrors what is sometimes required of psychologists, sociologists, communications specialists, and others who investigate an issue and then present their findings to the person or body commissioning the report. A **policy recommendation report** typically includes the following:

1. Definition and brief discussion of the problem
2. Recommendations to solve the problem or address the issue
3. Application of forecasting methods to show likely results of the recommended policy
4. Plan for implementation of the recommendations
5. Discussion of future needs or parameters to monitor and evaluate the recommendations

PREPARING EFFECTIVE PRESENTATIONS IN THE SOCIAL SCIENCES

Good social scientific presentations clearly explain the research question, refer to current research, and use timely data.

- *Illustrate the research question.* Pay attention to clearly illustrating the nature of the research question and the means by which the results were achieved.
- *Refer to current research.* Credible social scientific presentations refer to recent findings in the field. Instructors are more likely to accept experimental evidence if it is replicated over time and supported by current research.
- *Use timely data.* Instructors expect student presentations to include recent data and examples. A report on poverty rates for a sociology course must provide up-to-date data because poverty rates change yearly. A research presentation on treatments for the mentally ill, should accurately reflect current treatments.

Speaking in Arts and Humanities Courses

Speaking assignments in arts and humanities courses (including English, philosophy, foreign languages, art history, theater, music, religion, and history) often require that you interpret the meaning of a particular idea, event, person, story, or artifact. Your art history professor, for example, might ask you to identify the various artistic and historical influences on a sculpture or painting. An instructor of literature may ask you to explain the theme of a novel or a poem. A theater instructor might ask you to offer your interpretation of a new play.

Rather than focusing on quantitative research, presentations in the arts and humanities often rely on your analysis and interpretation of the topic at hand. These interpretations are nonetheless grounded in the conventions of the field and build on the research within it. Oral presentation assignments in arts and humanities courses can range from informative speeches of explanation to individual and team debates. Some presentations may be performative in nature, with students expressing artistic content.

INFORMATIVE SPEECHES OF DESCRIPTION AND ANALYSIS

Often in the arts and humanities, students prepare informative speeches (see Chapter 23) in which they explain the relevance of a historical or contemporary person or event; a genre or school of philosophical thought; or a piece of literature, music, or art. For example, an art history professor may require students to discuss the artist Bernini's contribution to St. Peter's Cathedral in Rome. Visual aids are often a key part of such presentations; in this case, audiences would expect to see relevant reproductions and photographs.

PRESENTATIONS THAT COMPARE AND CONTRAST

Instructors in the arts and humanities often ask students to compare and contrast events, stories, people, or artifacts in order to highlight their similarities or differences. For example, you might compare two works of literature from different time periods, or two historical figures or works of art. These presentations may be informative or persuasive in nature. Presentations that compare and contrast include the following items:

1. *Thesis statement* outlining the connection between the events, stories, people, or artifacts
2. *Discussion of main points* including several examples that highlight the similarities and differences
3. *Concluding evaluative statement* about the comparison (e.g., if the presentation is persuasive, why one piece of literature was more effective than another; if informative, a restatement of similarities and differences)

DEBATES

Often students will engage in debates on opposing ideas, historical figures, or philosophical positions. In a history class, for example, students might argue whether sixteenth-century women in Western Europe experienced a Renaissance. The speaker must present a brief assertion (two to three minutes) about the topic; the opposing speaker then responds with a position. Whatever side of an issue you address, prepare a well-composed argument with strong supporting evidence.

CLASSROOM DISCUSSIONS

Many students taking arts and humanities courses must research a question and then lead a classroom discussion on it. For example, an English student leading a discussion on Anton Chekov's *The Cherry Orchard* would be expected to provide a synopsis of the play's plot, theme, and characters, as well as an analysis of the play's meaning.

PREPARING EFFECTIVE ARTS AND HUMANITIES PRESENTATIONS

Good presentations in the arts and humanities are original in some way. They help the audience think of the topic in a new way by providing a unique interpretation. A presentation on slavery in the United States will be more effective if you offer a new way of viewing slavery, for example, rather than reiterating what other people have said or what is already generally accepted knowledge about slavery. A debate on two philosophical ideas will be most effective when you assert issues and arguments that are different from those that the audience has thought of before. Since many speaking events in the arts and humanities call for interpretation, the more original the interpretation (while remaining logical and grounded in sound evidence), the more persuasive and engaging the audience will perceive the presentation to be. As you prepare your presentation, pay particular attention to the following:

- *Clearly state your thesis.* Tell the audience early on what it is you are trying to explain or prove.
- *Link the discussion to the relevant period in history, school of thought, and/or movement in music, art, or literature.* Provide context for your topic by locating it within its relevant framework.
- *Practice using visual aids.* Often, instructors will expect to see representations of the works under discussion, so spend the necessary time to coordinate slides and other aids with relevant speech points (see Chapter 22).
- *Anticipate questions.* Be prepared to address questions and engage in further discussion after you've delivered the presentation.

Speaking in Education Courses

In education courses (including subfields such as curriculum and instruction, physical education, secondary and elementary education, and educational administration), the most common and practical speaking event is *teaching in a classroom*. Assignments in education courses often focus on some form of instructional task, such as giving a lecture or demonstrating an activity. In a mathematics education course, you might give a mini-lecture on a particular geometric theorem. In a learning-styles course, you may tailor an activity to a variety of different learners. Each of these tasks requires that you deliver an effective informative speech (see Chapter 23). Encouraging participation and using vocabulary and examples appropriate to students' learning level are key, as is enthusiasm in delivery.

DELIVERING A LECTURE

A **lecture** is an informational speech for an audience of student learners. Standard lectures range from fifty minutes to an hour and a half; *a mini-lecture presentation*, designed to give students an opportunity to synthesize information in a shorter form, generally lasts about fifteen to twenty minutes. Effective lectures tend to be interactive, incorporating frequent questions designed to assess student understanding and encourage students to engage in the material.

Typically, lectures include the following:

1. A clear introduction of the topic to be covered (see Chapter 14)
2. Statement of the central idea/thesis
3. Statement of the connection to previous topics covered
4. Discussion of the main points
5. Summary of the lecture and preview of the next assigned topic

FACILITATING A GROUP ACTIVITY

In the **group activity presentation**, the instructor provides an overview of group activity following a lecture with clear directions on how to complete it. Typically, group activity presentations include the following:

1. A succinct review of the lecture thesis
2. A description of the goal of the activity
3. Directions on carrying out the group activity
4. A preview of what students gain from the activity and what the discussion following the activity will cover

FACILITATING A CLASSROOM DISCUSSION

In the **classroom discussion presentation**, the speaker facilitates a discussion following a lecture or class activity, offering preliminary remarks and guiding the discussion as it proceeds.

1. Begin by outlining critical points to be covered.
2. Prepare several general guiding questions to launch the discussion.
3. Prepare relevant questions and examples to use during the discussion.

PREPARING EFFECTIVE PRESENTATIONS IN EDUCATION

Good presentations in education are marked by clear organization, integration of the material into the broader course content, and student-friendly supporting material. Presentations should be interactive in nature.

- *Invite participation.* Effective education presentations engage students in the learning process by posing frequent questions and eliciting answers. Begin a lecture by posing a question about the topic, for example, and allow time for discussion. Avoid monologues in favor of dialogue.
- *Organize material logically.* Presentations in education must be tightly organized so that the audience can easily access information. Thus, pay

careful attention to selecting an organizational pattern (see Chapters 12 and 26). In educational settings, the simpler the organizational structure, the better. Use organizing devices such as preview statements and transitions to help listeners follow ideas in a lecture, for example. Provide clear and logical directions for group activities.

- *Integrate discussion to overall course content.* Effective lectures, activities, or discussions are clearly connected to other parts of the course, topic, or other content. To do this, describe how the lecture for the day relates to the previous days' lectures. In a discussion or group activity, make clear connections between students' comments and other topics that have been raised or will be raised later in the course.

- *Tailor examples and evidence to the audience.* Effective educational presentations use familiar examples and evidence that the audience can grasp easily. The successful instructor will not support an idea with a statistical proof, for example, unless students are trained in statistics. Use familiar examples that will enhance learning (see the section on analogies in Chapter 23); try to choose examples that are close to students' experiences.

Speaking in Nursing and Allied Health Courses

Speaking assignments in nursing and allied health courses — physical therapy, occupational therapy, radiology, and other areas of health care — range from reviews of research articles in professional journals to reports on community service projects in a clinical setting. Students are assigned a mix of individual and team presentations that instruct clients on health-care practices and techniques, describe plans of care to medical teams, communicate patients' status at shift changes, and make policy recommendations to managers. Visual aids such as PowerPoint slides may be required; certain courses also entail preparation of individual or team poster sessions.

The ability to communicate information about patients or clients is important for all health-care providers.

COMMUNITY SERVICE LEARNING PROJECTS

In a **community service learning project**, students learn about and help address a need or problem in a community agency, such as may exist in an adult daycare center, a mental health facility, or a burn center. Typically, presentations about your participation in these projects should include the following:

1. Description of the community agency and its client base
2. Overview of the service project and your role in it
3. Description of your accomplishments

4. Report of any problems encountered

5. Relationship of service learning to course content

6. Summary of what you learned

TREATMENT PLAN REPORTS (CASE CONFERENCES/SHIFT REPORTS)

Either individually or as part of a health-care team, persons in the helping professions report to other health-care providers on the patient's status and discuss plans of treatment. These reports can take the form of a case conference or a shift report. Typically, the **case conference** includes the following:

1. Description of patient status

2. Explanation of the disease process

3. Steps in the treatment regimen

4. Goals for the patient and family

5. Plans for the patient's care at home

6. Review of financial needs

7. Assessment of available resources

A **shift report** is a concise report of the patient's status and needs that is delivered to the oncoming caregiver. It includes the following information:

1. Patient's name, location, and reason for care

2. Current physical status

3. Length of stay in setting

4. Pertinent psychosocial data, including plans for discharge and involvement of family

5. Care needs (physical, hygiene, activity, medication, nutritional)

POLICY RECOMMENDATION REPORTS

In the **policy recommendation report**, the speaker recommends the adoption of a new (or modified) health practice or policy, such as introducing a new treatment regimen at a burn center. This report, sometimes assigned as part of a capstone course, includes the following:

1. Review of the existing policy or practice

2. Description of the proposed policy recommendation

3. Review of the existing scientific literature on the policy recommendation

4. Plan of action for implementing the policy or practice

PREPARING EFFECTIVE PRESENTATIONS IN NURSING AND ALLIED HEALTH COURSES

Good presentations in health-related courses accurately communicate medical information while simultaneously assessing practical conditions. Depending on the audience (e.g., patient or staff), the communication will shift in tone from therapeutic/empathetic to more matter-of-fact, and instructors will expect to see these shifts in tone reflected in your presentations. They will also want you to support any assertions and recommendations with relevant scientific literature and other reports containing evidence of effective clinical practice. Instructors will expect you to do the following:

- Use **evidence-based practice** (EBP) based on current research findings for all assignments. Evidence-based practice is an approach to treatment in which caregivers make decisions based on current research and "best practices."
- Apply concepts in the literature to your work with patients
- Evaluate the results of your interventions

Sample
Speeches

Sample Speeches

SAMPLE SPEECHES
(501–519)

Sample Speeches

Sample Visually Annotated Informative Speech

 WEB Video

Nonmonetary Uses of Gold

CHRISTA KIM

Santa Rosa Junior College

In this speech about an object or phenomenon (gold), Christa Kim reveals a "treasure trove" of new information about the world's most venerated metal. Christa's speech is organized topically, in which the main points describe gold's various properties and applications.

Conveys enthusiasm during the introduction

King Midas was desperately poor but had a good heart. As a reward for his compassion, the gods granted him a single wish, and King Midas, seeking to alleviate his poverty, immediately wished that everything he touched would turn into solid gold. •

The story illustrates the point that, like King Midas, when we think of gold, we too usually focus only on the monetary value of it, whether it is the gold bricks in Fort Knox or expensive jewelry.

What we don't realize is that gold plays a much bigger role in all of our lives. So tonight we are going to explore the nonmonetary uses of gold. To do this, we will first unearth the unique properties of this metal. We will then see how these characteristics have panned out in the medical field to both prevent and alleviate diseases. Finally, we will sift through some applications made by NASA. •

Now, the first unique characteristic of gold is its extreme density. •

When we usually think of dense elements, we think of lead, which is extremely dense. In fact, lead is so dense that whenever we get an X-ray, we wear a lead apron to protect us from radiation. Well, gold, according to the 1996 Macmillan *Encyclopedia*

• Kim captures listeners' attention with an interesting story.

• Kim succinctly states the thesis, previews the main points, and makes skillful use of metaphoric language ("unearth," "pan," and "sift").

• Kim uses a full-sentence transition to move into her first main point.

of Earth Sciences, is one and a half times more dense than lead. •

Engineers have already taken advantage of this characteristic by using extremely thin films of gold to coat electronic switches and relays. In telephones,

for example, there are over thirty-three of these gold-plated contacts, which work within the main component of the phone, the diaphragm, to transform electric signals into sound.

Reveals visual aid no. 1

• Kim uses a series of blown-up illustrations to help the audience visualize her points. Placing them face down on an easel, she turns them over to show listeners only when she makes her point. In this way, the images do not distract audience members.

Now, besides being one of the most dense of all metals, gold is also one of the most ductile, which means that it can

be easily stretched while maintaining its shape. • The Gold Institute states that gold is so ductile that a single ounce can be drawn out into a thin wire over five miles long. *The Minerals Yearbook,* published by the U.S. Department of the Interior, claims

Puts visual aid away when finished discussing it

• Kim defines difficult terms such as *ductile.*

that these thin gold wires are essential to the manufacture of every single computer and that other electronics, such as televisions and VCRs, also depend on these thin gold wires to process messages and sounds.

Not only is gold one of the most dense and ductile of all metals, it's also the least corrosive. According to the Joint Research Center for Atom Technology, as reported in the June 5, 1994, issue of *Nature,* • gold's surface structure provides little or no room for bonding. Now, what this means is that

Gestures to highlight visual aid no. 2

• Here and elsewhere, Kim establishes the credibility of her sources by citing author, date, and publication title.

molecules tend to slip away, without chemically affecting, or latching onto, gold's surface. • This is why we can never find any gold with any rust or mold.

• Rather than merely stating facts, Kim offers clear explanations.

Now, combined, these characteristics set the stage for many applications within the health and

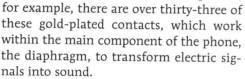

medical field. For example, gold is being used to treat lagophthalmos. Lagophthalmos is a condition caused by disease or injury that leads to the inability to close the eye because the eyelid muscle is too weak. In the past, doctors would have had to use a needle and thread to physically sew the eyelids shut in order to keep the eyes from

Strides across stage, adding dynamism

drying out. But now, according to Dr. Donald J. Bergen at the Southeastern Eye Center for North Carolina, doctors are able to utilize the dense and noncorrosive qualities of gold in the form of a gold implant.

These implants, weighing between 0.6 and 1.6 grams, ● are surgically inserted into the upper lid of the eye and work with gravity to give the eye the extra weight it needs in order to close properly. And what's more, because gold is so noncorrosive, it will not react with the human tear — the reason why, in the United States alone, more than 15,000 patients are able to benefit from the use of this procedure.

● Kim uses statistics in the form of frequencies ("between 0.6 and 1.6 grams" and "more than 15,000 patients") as evidence for the medical function and benefits of gold.

But gold isn't used only to treat conditions like lagophthalmos. It's also being used to treat diseases such as rheumatoid arthritis. Gold has been used in the treatment of this painful disease since 1927, when European physicians first discovered that injecting gold compounds into the body alleviated pain. The Arthritis Foundation states that when gold is injected into the human body, it affects the process of the disease that causes joint pain and swelling and in so doing lessens the chance of joint deformity and disability. This procedure has been so effective that the January 22, 1997, issue of *The Lancet* calls gold vital to the treatment of rheumatoid arthritis. ●

Maintains good eye contact and posture from a new position onstage

● Kim clearly credits her sources throughout the speech.

The medical industry isn't the only one that is able to take advantage of gold's unique characteristics. ● NASA is also using gold in several different ways in space. One is in the area of communication. According to Ned Rozell from the Geophysical Institute at the University of Alaska, satellites in space depend on gold to process static-free signals when broadcasting messages back from Earth. In fact, the *Pathfinder,* the robotic geologist developed by NASA, which recently took photographs of rocks and soil on Mars, wouldn't have been able to relay its findings back to Earth without the use of gold circuitry.

● Kim makes ample use of examples to ensure that her points are understood.

Besides enabling communication in space, gold also aids in the exploration of space in two unique ways. The first way takes advantage of gold's noncorrosiveness. The Geophysical Institute at the University of Alaska states that fine powder gold makes the world's best lubricant for rocket engines. It makes the best lubricant because unlike oil, gold does not inevitably break down from solar radiation or evaporation. •

The second way that gold aids in the exploration of space takes advantage of gold's extreme density. According to a 1997 exhibit at the California State Mining and Mineral Museum, a gold coating of only six millionths of an inch thick can reflect away all heat, all light, and all radiation. As seen here, this astronaut's helmet, suit, and visor are completely coated with gold to shield and protect the astronaut from harmful radiation. • Gold, therefore, has become a critical element in space travel.

Shows visual aid no. 3

In addition to enabling communication and exploration in space, gold, believe it or not, is also working to preserve a bit of our own culture. Once formed, gold maintains its shape whatever the environmental conditions. It is for this reason that gold was the material selected to press the record *Sounds of Earth,* which, according to Carl Sagan in his book *Cosmos,* was sent aboard the *Voyager* spacecraft in 1977 and is only now exiting our solar system. The record jacket gives instructions in scientific notation for how to play the record, while the record itself contains information about Earth's cultures and civilizations.

Included on this record is information about our genes, our anatomy, and our DNA. The record includes greetings from over sixty different cultures as well as music. We placed the record on *Voyager* with the hope that a bit of our culture would be preserved and perhaps even found by distant beings. And because gold is so durable, this golden record, which tells so much about the planet's journey through space and time, will long outlive all life on Earth.

Visual aid no. 4 includes two complementary images

While gold will continue to play an important role monetarily, it should now be clear that the nonmonetary uses of gold have a huge impact on our

• To encourage understanding, Kim tells audience members *why* gold is a good lubricant.

• A photograph helps the audience visualize Kim's verbal description.

daily lives. • On Earth, doctors are able to utilize the characteristics of density, ductility, and noncorrosiveness to treat conditions such as lagophthalmos, rheumatoid arthritis, and potentially even the HIV virus. In space, NASA is able to utilize these very same characteristics to enable satellite communication and exploration and to preserve a bit of our own culture. It should now be apparent that these doctors, researchers, and engineers who are using gold in nonmonetary ways to enrich our everyday lives truly do possess the real Midas touch. •

Offers a warm smile after closing the speech

• Kim concludes her speech by summarizing her main points.

• She brings the speech full circle with her reference to the "Midas touch."

Sample Visually Annotated Persuasive Speech

Tales of the Grandmothers: Women and Work

ANITA TAYLOR

George Mason University, Fairfax, Virginia

Anita Taylor is a professor of communication and women's studies. She delivered the following speech to the Woman of the Year Celebration at the Aerospace Corporation in Chantilly, Virginia, on September 13, 2004. The central argument in this persuasive speech, shortened from the original, is that the U.S. economy would not be where it is today without the range of "home work" that women have traditionally performed. The speaker supports this claim of fact with various kinds of evidence, from personal experience to facts and statistics. The entire speech is offered as a series of stories, illustrating beautifully the narrative pattern of organization described in Chapter 12 (see p. 209). Using internal previews, summaries, and other kinds of transitions, Taylor frequently leaves off and picks up the thread of the story in order to orient her listeners and drive home her theme.

I begin with the story of a girl baby, born 1826 in Massachusetts, Luna Puffer Squire (Squier). As a seven-year-old, Luna came with her family to Illinois, where she married at 19. The family farmed; their place was about 100 miles up the Illinois River north of St. Louis. • That gave them easy access for harvesting timber and shipping wood to build the growing city during the U.S. years of westward expansion. One piece of family lore holds that they owned barges and tugs that moved the logs to the city, until these were lost during the Civil War.

Luna, by then several months pregnant, with 5 other children . . . in late summer 1863 saw husband John off to the South as a soldier in the Union Army. Fix this picture in your mind. • This now 37-year-old woman in a farming/lumber family has 5 children ranging in age from 19 to 2, and a baby due before the year ends. Her husband is hundreds of miles away fighting a war to preserve the union. No census taker would record her as employed. But, for sure, this woman is working. There, in part, is my point. But, let's go on with Luna Puffer Squire Nairn's story. •

"Captain" John as the family always thereafter referred to him was later wounded in the war. . . .

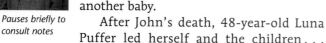

Family stories related that when Luna Puffer learned of his injury, . . . she boarded a river vessel, headed down the Mississippi and retrieved him. . . . And in 1866 birthed another baby.

Pauses briefly to consult notes

After John's death, 48-year-old Luna Puffer led herself and the children . . . west to homestead in Kansas . . . Luna received a land patent in 1887 in Pawnee Rock, KS, a town where she is considered a founder of the local Methodist Church. The new Kansans encountered years of drought and subsequent crop failures; some moved at least temporarily to Raton, NM (perhaps drawn by prospect of railroad jobs); one moved South drawn by the prospect of more "free" land when the Oklahoma Indian territory was opened for white settlement; others returned to Illinois where Squire and Nairn families live today.

I start with the tale of Luna Puffer Squire Nairn for several reasons. • First, I am in her family a century later . . . and I never heard of her as a child. My family "dropped" her story and told us about later immigrants, male of course. Second, she and

> • Taylor alerts listeners that her speech will be a narrative with the simple phrase, "I begin with the story . . ."

> • Taylor invites listeners to enter the story by telling listeners to "Fix this in your mind."

> • Here Taylor alerts listeners that the story continues.

> • Taylor "exits" the story to establish her credibility and state her thesis.

her daughters and granddaughters (my grandmothers) illustrate the points I want to make. They explode the myth that has pervaded my adult life: that women in the U.S. first entered the workforce in large numbers during the 20th century women's revolution. That myth lives on for two reasons, both illustrated by Luna Puffer and her granddaughters: We have buried the stories of women's lives, and we have discounted their labor as "not-work." •

• Taylor states her thesis and previews her two main points: women's work has been ignored, and women's work has been discounted.

The two reasons weave together to support that myth that women first entered the workforce in large numbers during and as a result of the "women's liberation" movement of the 1960s and 70s. The myth usually credits the many "Rosie the Riveter's" of World War II with showing women they could hold nontraditional employment, but it does not credit the long history of other income-earning labor by women prior to WW II. The myth does recognize that women often worked outside the home for pay prior to marriage, especially as garment industry factory workers. But it ignores the many other kinds of income production in which women engaged prior to the "second wave feminism" of the 20th century. And it ignores the role of women's work in what Anne Ferguson has described as "reproductive labor," a category that refers to far more than birthing babies. It includes all work, paid or otherwise, required to reproduce the culture (not just the species).

Good posture, professional dress, and sustained eye contact support credibility

The myth of the nonworking woman deep sixes the history of urban homes as craft shops. Only when the economy industrialized did production for sale move outside homes where everyone had been involved, although often children were apprenticed to someone else's home. When factories took the laborers "out" to work, childcare became an issue, so an ideology was needed to provide for it without the factory owner being responsible. Voila! Childcare becomes women's work. Only, no surprise, turns out that it's not "really" work because it doesn't earn any wages. With the full development of Victorian era beliefs, the cult of true womanhood reached fruition.

Never mind that the cult was built on the experiences of the generally well-to-do families. The culture developed the idea that such a role was ideal, so not only do these elite groups largely populate the opinion making classes; they constitute a class and way of life toward which even working class and poor families aspired. . . . Since the "nonworking" life was the ideal, failing to achieve it was not much talked about. That would have been a mark of failure. . . .

Along with the concept of the "nonworking" woman came a view of motherhood as the primary role for women, a role for which they are uniquely suited by biology and god. To accomplish the widespread acceptance of these twin myths, our culture elevated certain stories about our past and it rendered other narratives invisible. And there I want to focus on the story of invisible working women. •

Stories usually told are illustrated by these data from the Population Resource Center: In 1900, census reports identify just 19 percent of women being paid for their work. Today, nearly 60 percent of U.S. women participate in the cash economy. Does that mean that in 1900 81% of women did not work? Or that today 40% do not? Far from it. So what's wrong with the picture? •

To fill in the many missing spaces let me trace my maternal ancestors after Luna Puffer Squire Nairn. I'll quickly look at five generations, ending with mine. • These stories are relevant because there is no reason to believe the women in my family are particularly unusual. Indeed, in that our family represents women of moral background and little wealth, we are probably more representative of families in general than the typical well-to-do Victorian model of "true womanhood." Most women who traced their maternal descent line would find a similar kind of story. •

Over half the population relied on agriculture for livelihood in the middle 1800s. . . . So let me give you a short description of the typical farm family's life in the years before our current era of industrialized farming. Economists and historians often describe the "farmer" as the male parent in such families. That is an abomination. It leaves unmeasured

• Taylor previews her next main point.

• The speaker offers factual evidence to support her argument that women always worked.

• Taylor offers an internal preview of the next part of the speech. This helps listeners follow along.

• Taylor establishes the relevance of her topic to the audience by pointing out that her ancestors were typical for their time.

and usually unnoticed labors of other members of those families, labors required in pre-industrial farming for survival, and increasingly, to produce income. Farm and ranch families' income often came from a "cash crop" of wheat, corn, sheep, cattle, etc., but their farms also supplied most of their food and much of their clothing. One of my earliest memories is going with my mother to the feed store, where she spent a bit extra to buy chicken feed in sacks instead of bulk. I would be taken along at these times to pick out the pattern of the sacks so that when they were emptied, we could wash them and mother could make my school clothes for the year. ● . . . There was food preparation and preservation, quilt and blanket making, wood chopping and (sometimes) coal carrying, retrieving and disposing of water, AND production of meager cash crops, whether that was hay, milk, cream, cotton, corn, cattle, pigs, chickens, eggs, or lumber. Farm women did all these activities. And farm children, girls and boys, also engaged in this work as soon as they were old enough to tote a feed pail, pull a weed or pick a strawberry. Income as well as subsistence of farm families depended on the labor of ALL the adults and most of the children.

Scans the audience; a smile shows goodwill

● Here Taylor offers as evidence her own knowledge and opinions.

So, regardless of how economists might measure the labor, in families that remained the typical nuclear one, women were farmers, not just helpmates for the man of the farm. And that was work. In short, farm women have worked just as long as there have been farm families. And while at the end of the 20th century, farmers constituted only a tiny percentage of the population in the U.S., the comparable figure at the century's beginning was 40%. That's 40% of the women in the country in 1900 engaging in both subsistence and income producing labor — none of it counted in the reported statistics.

Beyond this part of the story, however, is the fact that virtually all nonfarm women did much of the same work I've just described. For the vast numbers of small shopkeepers, those who were part of the urban merchant class, women worked in the shops right along with the men and the children. Other urban women worked in other ways to earn income. Some were laborers outside the home before being married. They were mill workers, school teachers, domestic help in homes of the well-to-do; they were dressmakers, milliners, midwives, cooks, laundry workers, etc. When married and with children, many women did piece work, and they took in sewing — or boarders. Both kinds of working women are among my grandmothers. My great grandmother outlived her husband by 39 years. And this was pre social security. Family stories have it that "aunt Mary" as her obituaries said she was known, was fiercely independent. She supported herself for 35 + years by taking in roomers. . . . My mother was a farmer; one of her sisters farmed, then later moved to the state's largest city and became a real "Rosie Riveter," building B-29 bombers during World War II. After the war she was among the women entering the clerical staff of the growing economy. . . . The five women of this family in the next generation (mine) have all worked for pay, outside the home, for most of our lives. . . .

As I noted before, these stories are not unique. What I want to do, finally, is pull both threads of this argument together. . . . The economic system as we have built it with paid labor largely done outside the home would not survive without the whole range of "home" work. After "employment" moved out of the home into factories and institutions, fathers had to leave home on a daily basis for long hours. We don't even need to think about the need for women to birth babies (the literal reproductive labor) required to replace the workforce as existing workers age and die; there was a whole other range of things that had to be done just so that "father" could "go to work" in the developing industrial economy. Think of all the support systems the paid employee had to have, especially in the days when "he" worked from dawn to dusk. Early industrial institutions weren't known as benevolent organizations — they didn't have child care, health

Taylor turns to connect with the far corners of the room

services, on site laundry facilities, cafeterias or lunchrooms, etc. ALL those services had to be provided for the worker. All those services are labor. . . .

. . . So here we are today. • Some things have not changed. Some women in families who can afford it don't do paid work outside the home. Many other women work two jobs, one paid and one unpaid — or sometimes two paid and one unpaid. But much has changed. Large numbers of women are now working at professional and other relatively high paid jobs, including all of us here in this room I suspect. That, surely we will all agree, is great progress related to women and work. And that is why it is wonderful to be here today as part of this celebration honoring your Woman of the Year. Virtually all of us here today have found our way into roles not traditional for women. And I suspect all of us here have been blessed in doing so. . . . Those of us now with relatively well paid employment have a remaining responsibility. We need always to remember that those unheralded unpaid women workers are, in fact, working; and we need to begin talking in ways that reflects such recognition. We need to reflect our awareness that all labor is work whether compensated or not. We need to talk in ways that distinguish paid from unpaid labor. • Ironically, recent technological changes will help in this process. As "working at home" grows, we'll have to find new ways to describe which workers get paid by salary or wage and which are compensated only by the love and affection of those they serve. We all should consider, for instance, banishing the term "working mothers" from our vocabulary. All mothers work, whether for pay or not. . . . •

And finally, we must attend to our own lives so that we do not entrench this new situation I describe. We do not want to repeat the old model where the wealth of some depended on the relative poverty of others. We surely do not want to build our success and that of the women who follow us on the backs of low paid women. Achieving that goal will require our constant vigilance. I invite you to join me in such awareness as we celebrate working women everywhere.

• This signal phrase indicates the conclusion.

• Taylor emphasizes her points by repeating the phrase "We need."

• The speaker's call to action asks listeners to actively focus on recognizing the range of women's work.

Sample Visually Annotated Special Occasion Speech

2004 University of Pennsylvania Commencement Address

BONO

In this commencement address delivered to the graduating class of the University of Pennsylvania on May 17, 2004, Bono, activist and lead singer of the rock group U2, nicely incorporates several qualities of an effective special occasion speech. He combines a serious message about the abolition of poverty and AIDS in Africa with a more relaxed, laid-back attitude typically associated with rock stars. This juxtaposition makes it more likely that Bono's student audience will be receptive to his call to action.

My name is Bono and I am a rock star. •

Bono addresses the crowd at graduation

. . . Doctor of Laws, wow! I know it's an honor, and it really is an honor, but are you sure? . . . I never went to college, I've slept in some strange places, but the library wasn't one of them. I studied rock and roll and I grew up in Dublin in the '70s; music was an alarm bell for me, it woke me up to the world.

I was 17 when I first saw the Clash, and it just sounded like revolution. The Clash were like, "This is a public service announcement—with guitars." •

I was the kid in the crowd who took it at face value. Later I learned that a lot of the rebels were in it for the t-shirt. They'd wear the boots but they wouldn't march. They'd smash bottles on their heads but they wouldn't go to something more painful, like a town hall meeting. By the way, I felt like that myself until recently. I didn't expect change to come so slow. So agonizingly slow. I didn't realize that the biggest obstacle to political and social progress wasn't the Free Masons, or the Establishment, or the boot heel of whatever you consider the man to be, it was something much more subtle.

Bono acknowledges the occasion. His appearance mixes formal robes with casual sunglasses and open collar

. . . So for better or worse that was my education. I came away with a clear sense of the difference music could make in my own life, in other people's lives if I did my job right, which if you're a singer in a rock

• Of course he is. Bono's opening remark is a guaranteed crowd-pleaser. His audience knows who he is, but stating it is unexpected and humorous.

• Bono uses personal history to argue that rock music can be revolutionary. He will revisit the theme when he addresses poverty in Africa.

band means avoiding the obvious pitfalls, like say a mullet hairdo. If anyone here doesn't know what a mullet is, by the way, your education's certainly not complete. I'd ask for your money back. For a lead singer like me, a mullet is, I would suggest, arguably more dangerous than a drug problem. Yes, I had a mullet in the '80s. •

Now this is the point where the faculty start smiling uncomfortably and thinking maybe they should have offered me the honorary bachelor's degree instead of the full blown ("He should have  been the bachelor's one; he's talking about mullets and stuff . . ."); and if they're asking what on earth I'm doing here, I think it's a fair question: what am I doing here? More to the point: what are you doing here? Because if you don't mind me saying so, this is a strange ending to an Ivy League education. Four years in these historic halls thinking great thoughts and now you're sitting in a stadium better suited for football listening to an Irish rock star give a speech that is so far mostly about himself. What are you doing here?

Smile underscores humor

. . . For four years you've been buying, trading, and selling, everything you've got in this marketplace of ideas. The intellectual hustle. Your pockets are full, even if your parents are empty, and now you've got to figure out what to spend it on. Well, the going rate for change is not cheap. Big ideas are expensive. The University has had its share of big ideas. Benjamin Franklin had a few, so did Justice Brennan and in my opinion so does Judith Rodin. What a gorgeous girl. • They all knew that if you're gonna be good at your word, if you're gonna live up to your ideals and your education, it's gonna cost you. So my question, I suppose, is: What's the big idea? What's your big idea? What are you willing to spend your moral capital, your intellectual capital, your cash, your sweat equity in pursuing outside of the walls of the University of Pennsylvania? •

There's a truly great Irish poet; his name is Brendan Kennelly, and he has this epic poem called the *Book of Judas,* and there's a line in that poem that never leaves my mind: "If you want to serve the age,

• Self-effacing humor establishes rapport with the listeners and shows Bono to be more personable than they might expect of a celebrity.

• References to U Penn history build credibility. Franklin was the founder of the college, Brennan a famous alumnus, and Rodin the president.

• Appropriate for a commencement speech, Bono challenges the graduates to question what they plan to do with their education.

betray it." • What does that mean to betray the age? Well to me betraying the age means exposing its conceits, its foibles, its phony moral certitudes. It means telling the secrets of the age and facing harsher truths. Every age has its massive moral blind spots. We might not see them, but our children will. Slavery was one of them and the people who best served that age were the ones who called it as it was, which was ungodly and inhuman. Ben Franklin called it when he became president of the Pennsylvania

Pauses for emphasis

Abolition Society. Segregation. There was another one. America sees this now but it took a civil rights movement to betray their age. And 50 years ago the U.S. Supreme Court betrayed the age [when on] May 17, 1954, *Brown vs. Board of Education* came down and put the lie to the idea that separate can ever really be equal. Amen to that.

Fast forward 50 years [to] May 17, 2004: What are the ideas right now worth betraying? What are the lies we tell ourselves now? What are the blind spots of our age? What's worth spending your post-Penn lives trying to do or undo? It might be something simple. It might be something as simple as our deep down refusal to believe that every human life has equal worth. Could that be it? Could that be it?

Each of you will probably have your own answer, but for me that is it. And for me the proving ground has been Africa. Africa makes a mockery of what we say, at least what I say, about equality. It questions our pieties and our commitments because there's no way to look at what's happening over there and its effect on all of us and conclude that we actually consider Africans as our equal before God. There is no chance.

An amazing event happened here in Philadelphia in 1985, Live Aid, that whole "We Are the World"

Looks down at notes

phenomenon, the concert that happened here. Well after that concert I went to Ethiopia with my wife, Ali; we were there for a month and an extraordinary thing happened to me. We used to wake up in the morning and the mist would be lifting; we'd see thousands and thousands of people

• Bono effectively quotes a poem to support and extend his message.

who'd been walking all night to our food station where we were working. One man — I was standing outside talking to the translator — had this beautiful boy and he was saying to me in Amharic, I think it was, I said I can't understand what he's saying; and this nurse who spoke English and Amharic said to me, he's saying will you take his son. He's saying please take his son; he would be a great son for you. I was looking puzzled and he said, "You must take my son because if you don't take my son, my son will surely die. If you take him he will go back to where he is and get an education." (Probably like the ones we're talking about today.) I had to say no; that was the rules there and I walked away from that man. •

In this sequence, Bono effectively uses hand gestures

I've never really walked away from it. But I think about that boy and that man and that's when I started this journey that's brought me here into this stadium. Because at that moment I became the worst scourge on God's green earth, a rock star with a cause. Except it isn't the cause. Seven thousand Africans dying every day of preventable, treatable disease like AIDS? That's not a cause. That's an emergency. And when the disease gets out of control because most of the population lives on less than one dollar a day? That's not a cause. That's an emergency. •

. . . But the scale of the suffering and the scope of the commitment, they often numb us into a kind of indifference. Wishing for the end to AIDS and extreme poverty in Africa is like wishing that gravity didn't make things so damn heavy. We can wish it, but what the hell can we do about it? Well, more than we think. We can't fix every problem — corruption, natural calamities are part of the picture here — but the ones we can, we must. The debt burden, as I say, unfair trade, as I say, sharing our knowledge, the intellectual copyright for lifesaving drugs in a crisis; we can do that. And because we can, we must. Because we can, we must. • Amen.

. . . The fact is that this generation — yours, my generation — we're the first generation that can look

• A story humanizes Bono's cause and puts a face on suffering in Africa.

• Bono uses repetition for emphasis.

• Again, Bono uses repetition for emphasis.

at poverty and disease, look across the ocean to Africa and say with a straight face, we can be the first to end this stupid extreme poverty, where, in a world of plenty, a child can die for lack of food in its belly. . . . We can be that generation that says no to stupid poverty. It's a fact, the economists confirm it. It's an expensive fact but cheaper than say the Marshall Plan that saved Europe from communism and fascism. And cheaper I would argue than

Bono becomes more animated as the speech becomes more passionate

fighting wave after wave of terrorism's new recruits. . . . So why aren't we pumping our fists in the air and cheering about it? Probably because when we admit we can do something about it, we've got to do something about it. For the first time in history we have the know-how, we have the cash, we have the lifesaving drugs, but do we have the will? •

. . . I know idealism is not playing on the radio right now; you don't see it on TV; irony is on heavy

• Multiple examples support Bono's claim that his humanitarian goals are reachable.

rotation, the knowingness, the smirk, the tired joke. I've tried them all out but I'll tell you this, outside this campus, and even inside it, idealism is under siege beset by materialism, narcissism and all the other isms of indifference.

Bono scans the crowd during his call to action

. . . But I don't want to make you cop to idealism, not in front of your parents, or your younger siblings. But what about Americanism? Will you cop to that at least? It's not everywhere in fashion these days. . . . But it all depends on your definition of Americanism. Me, I'm in love with this country called America. I'm a huge fan of America, I'm one of those annoying fans, you know the ones that read the CD notes and follow you into bathrooms and ask you all kinds of annoying questions about why you didn't live up to that. I'm that kind of fan. •

. . . I love America because America is not just a country; it's an idea. You see my country, Ireland, is a great country, but it's not an idea. America is an idea, but it's an idea that brings with it some

• Good use of humor and a nice ironic touch — Bono is used to being on the other side of that kind of fandom.

baggage, like power brings responsibility. It's an idea that brings with it equality, but equality, even though it's the highest calling, is the hardest to reach. The idea that anything is possible, that's one of the reasons why I'm a fan of America. It's like hey, look there's the moon up there, let's take a walk on it, bring back a piece of it. That's the kind of America that I'm a fan of.

. . . So what's the problem that we want to apply all this energy and intellect to? Every era has its defining struggle and the fate of Africa is one of ours. It's not the only one, but in the history books it's easily going to make the top five, what we did or what we did not do. It's a proving ground, as I said earlier, for the idea of equality. But whether it's this or something else, I hope you'll pick a fight and get in it. • Get your boots dirty; get rough; steel your courage with a final drink there at Smoky Joe's, • one last primal scream and go. Sing the melody line you hear in your own head; remember, you don't owe anybody any explanations; you don't owe your parents any explanations; you don't owe your professors any explanations.

• Bono makes his call to action, challenging his listeners to pick their fight.

• Mentioning a local bar builds credibility.

. . . The world is more malleable than you think and it's waiting for you to hammer it into shape. Now if I were a folksinger I'd immediately launch

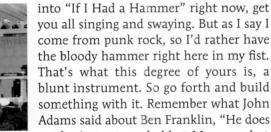

into "If I Had a Hammer" right now, get you all singing and swaying. But as I say I come from punk rock, so I'd rather have the bloody hammer right here in my fist. That's what this degree of yours is, a blunt instrument. So go forth and build something with it. Remember what John Adams said about Ben Franklin, "He does not hesitate at our boldest Measures but rather seems to think us too irresolute." Well this is the time for bold measures and this is the country and you are the generation. •

Bono concludes with emphasis

Thank you.

• Bono's final call to action revisits his opening themes of music and revolution.

Reference and Research Appendices

Reference and Research Appendices

Handling Question-and-Answer Sessions

Deftly fielding questions is a final critical component of making a speech or a presentation. As the last step in preparing your speech, anticipate and prepare for questions the audience is likely to pose to you. Write these questions down, and practice answering them. Spend time preparing an answer to the most difficult question that you are likely to face. The confidence you will gain from smoothly handling a difficult question should spill over to other questions.[1]

Protocol during the Session

As a matter of courtesy, call upon audience members in the order in which they raise their hands. Consider these guidelines:

- *Repeat or paraphrase the question* ("The question is, 'Did the student council really vote against . . '"). This will ensure that you've heard it correctly, that others in the audience know what you are responding to, and that you have time to reflect upon and formulate an answer. Note that there are a few exceptions to repeating the question, especially when the question is hostile. One expert suggests that you should always repeat the question when speaking to a large group; when you're in a small group or a training seminar, however, doing so isn't necessary.[2]

- *Initially make eye contact with the questioner, then move your gaze to other audience members.* This makes all audience members feel as though you are responding not only to the questioner but to them as well.

- *Remember your listening skills.* Give questioners your full attention and don't interrupt them.

- *Don't be afraid to pause while formulating an answer.* Many speakers feel they must feed the audience instantaneous responses; this belief sometimes causes them to say things they later regret. This is especially the case in media interviews (see Appendix B). Pauses that seem long to you may not appear lengthy to listeners.

- *Keep answers concise.* The question-and-answer session is not the time to launch into a lengthy treatise on your favorite aspect of a topic.

Handling Hostile and Otherwise Troubling Questions

When handling hostile questions, do not get defensive. Doing so will damage your credibility and only encourage the other person. Maintain an attitude of respect, and stay cool and in control. Attempt to defuse the hostile questioner with respect and goodwill. Similarly, never give the impression that you think a question is stupid or irrelevant, even if it clearly is.

- *Do not repeat or paraphrase a hostile question.* This only lends the question more credibility than it is worth. Instead, try to rephrase it more positively[3] (e.g., in response to the question "Didn't your department botch the handling of product X," you might respond, "The question was, 'Why did product X experience a difficult market entry?' To that I would say that . . .").

- *If someone asks you a seemingly stupid question, do not to point that out.* Instead, respond graciously.[4]

Ending the Session

Never end a question-and-answer session abruptly. As time runs out, alert the audience that you will take one or two more questions and then must end. The session represents one final opportunity to reinforce your message, so take the opportunity to do so. As you summarize your message, thank your listeners for their time. Leave an air of goodwill behind you.

Preparing for Mediated Communication

B

Public speaking today often involves communicating through an electronic medium such as television, radio, or videoconference. The underlying principles described throughout this guide will stand you in good stead as you prepare for these circumstances. These speaking situations do present some unique challenges, however.

Speaking on Television

On television, you are at the mercy of reporters and producers who will edit your remarks to fit their time frame. Therefore, before your televised appearance, find out as much as you can about the speech situation — for example, how long you will be on camera and whether the show will be aired live or taped. You may need to convey your message in **sound bite** form — succinct statements that summarize your key points in twenty seconds or less.

EYE CONTACT, BODY MOVEMENTS, AND VOICE

The question of where to direct your gaze is critical on televised appearances, as is controlling body movement and voice. The following are some guidelines:

- Don't play to the camera. In a one-on-one interview, focus on the interviewer. Do not look up or down or tilt your head sideways; these movements will make you look uncertain or evasive.[1]

- If there is an audience, treat the camera as just another audience member, glancing at it only as often as you would at any other individual during your remarks.

- If there is only you and the camera, direct your gaze at it as you speak.

- Keep your posture erect.

- Exaggerate your gestures slightly.

- Project your voice, and avoid speaking in a monotone.

DRESS AND MAKEUP

To compensate for the glare of studio lights and distortions caused by the camera, give careful consideration to dress and grooming:

- Choose dark rather than light-colored clothing. Dark colors such as blue, gray, green, and brown photograph better than lighter shades.

525

- Avoid stark white, because it produces glare.
- Avoid plaids, dots, and other busy patterns, as they tend to jump around on the screen.
- Avoid glittering jewelry, including tie bars.
- Wear a little more makeup than usual because bright studio lights tend to make you look washed out.

Speaking on Radio: The Media Interview

The following are guidelines for preparing for media interviews on the radio. These same guidelines can also be applied to the television interview.

- Know the audience and the focus of the program. What subjects does the broadcast cover? How long will the interview be? Will it be taped or live?
- Brush up on background information, and have your facts ready. Assume that the audience knows little or nothing about the subject matter.
- Use the interviewer's name during the interview.
- Prepare a speaking outline for the interview. Remember that the microphone will pick up the sound of papers being shuffled.
- Remember that taped interviews may be edited. Make key points in short sentences, and repeat them using different words.[2] Think in terms of sound bites.
- Anticipate questions that might arise, and decide how you will answer them.
- Use transition points to acknowledge the interviewer's questions and to bridge your key message points, such as "I am not familiar with that, but what I can tell you is . . ."; "You raise an interesting question, but I think the more important matter is. . . ."[3]
- Avoid the phrase "No comment." It will only exaggerate a point you are trying to minimize. Instead, say "I am not at liberty to comment/ discuss. . . ."

Speaking in the Videoconference

The **videoconference** integrates video and voice to connect students and instructors, or businesspeople, in remote sites with each other in real time. To deliver an online presentation, prepare as you would for one on-site, but pay particular attention to good diction, delivery, and dynamic body language.[4]

- Look into the camera to create eye contact; speak directly to the long-distance audience.

- To prevent video "ghosting" (pixelation), avoid sudden, abrupt, or sweeping movements.
- To compensate for audio delays, speak and move a little more slowly and deliberately than normal.
- Wear pale, solid colors and avoid flashy jewelry (see additional tips on dress in the section "Speaking on Television").
- Prepare visual aids following the principles described in Chapter 21.[5]

C Public Discussions: Panels, Symposiums, and Forums

Panels, symposiums, and forums are common formats in which multiple speakers share their expertise with an audience. Topics run the gamut from *A* to *Z*, and in virtually every field.

The Panel Discussion

In a **panel discussion**, a group of people (at least three, and generally not more than nine) discusses a topic in the presence of an audience. Panel discussions do not feature formally prepared speeches. Usually the participants are arranged in a semicircle or behind a table placed in front of the audience; participants address their remarks to each other. The purpose of a panel discussion can be either to inform or to persuade audience members on the issue being addressed.

Panels require the presence of a skilled chairperson or moderator to direct the discussion. During the presentation phase, the moderator describes the purpose and topic, or agenda, of the presentation and introduces the panel members. He or she begins the discussion by directing a question to one or more of the participants. At the conclusion of the panel, the moderator summarizes the discussion and directs questions from the audience.

When preparing remarks for a panel discussion, consider the following:

- What is the agenda for the discussion? (Generally, the moderator will deliver one to you.)
- Who is your audience? What do audience members know about the topic? What do they need to know about it?
- What are the ground rules? (Generally, the moderator will prepare a list and distribute it to each participant.)
- What aspects of the topic are the other participants likely to address? What are their areas of expertise?
- Will questions from the audience be permitted during the discussion or deferred until the panel has ended?
- How much time is allotted for the question-and-answer session? You will need to plan accordingly.

The Symposium

A **symposium** is a formal meeting at which several speakers (usually three to five) deliver short speeches on the same topic. Symposiums are organized to inform audiences about different aspects of a topic. Participants either address different aspects of a topic or offer contrasting viewpoints. Sometimes the symposium concludes with a question-and-answer period; at other times, it is followed by a panel discussion among members of the symposium.

When preparing a presentation for a symposium, consider the following:

- What aspects of the topic will the other participants address?
- In what order will the speakers address the audience?
- What are your time constraints?
- Who is your audience?
- Will you engage in questions and answers with the other speakers, or just with the audience?
- How much time is allotted for the question-and-answer session? You will need to plan accordingly.

The Forum

A **forum** is an assembly for the discussion of issues of public interest. Forums are often convened to help policymakers and voters alike deliberate about key policy issues. Forums can take place in a physical space, such as a town hall, or online, in moderated Web chats and other forms of virtual forums.

Forums may feature a panel or a symposium, followed by an extensive question-and-answer period by the audience. One well-known forum is the *town hall meeting*, in which citizens deliberate on issues of importance to the community. Often, city and state governments will sponsor town halls in order to gather citizen input about issues that affect them, using this input to formulate policy. Sometimes the media will gather citizens together for a town hall meeting and will televise the event.

When participating in public forums (not as a featured speaker, but as a member of the audience), consider the following:

- Organize your thoughts as much as possible in advance by jotting down your question or comment on a piece of paper. Use the guidelines for impromptu speaking described in Chapter 17, page 275.
- Do not duplicate someone else's questions or comments unless it adds to the discussion.
- Be conscious of not wasting the audience's time. Use no more time than necessary to make your points.
- If appropriate, include a call to action at the conclusion of your comments.

D Commonly Mispronounced Words

The following lists of errors in pronunciation are from *Basic Public Speaking*, Third Edition, by Paul L. Soper (Oxford University Press, 1968), with gratitude. The correct pronunciation or proper spelling is given in parentheses.

Misplacing the Accent

admir'able (ad'mirable)

applic'able (ap'plicable)

ce'ment (cement')

compar'able (com'parable)

exemplar'y (exemp'lary)

exig'ency (ex'igency)

finan'cier (financier')

formid'able (for'midable)

hor'izon (hori'zon)

i'dea (ide'a)

impi'ous (im'pious)

impot'ent (im'potent)

incompar'able (incom'parable)

incongru'ous (incon'gruous)

infam'ous (in'famous)

in'terest'ed (in'terested)

irrepar'able (irrep'arable)

municip'al (munic'ipal)

prefer'able (pref'erable)

proj'ectile (projec'tile)

reg'ime (regime')

respite' (res'pite)

superflu'ous (super'fluous)

u'nited (unit'ed)

vehe'ment (ve'hement)

vehi'cle (ve'hicle)

Addition of Sounds

attack-ted (attacked)

athaletics (athletics)

barbarious (barbarous)

colyum (column)

corpse (corps)

drawr (draw)

drownded (drowned)

elum (elm)

enterance (entrance)

ekscape (escape)

filum (film)

grievious (grievous)

height-th (height)

hinderance (hindrance)

idear (idea)

lightening (lightning)

mischievious (mischievous)

of-ten (of[t]en)

rememberance (remembrance)

sing-ger (singer)

stastistics (statistics)

sub-tle (su[b]tle)

sufferage (suffrage)

umberella (umbrella)

warsh (wash)

Omission of Sounds

accerate (accurate)

actully (actually)

assessory (accessory)

blong (belong)

canidate (candidate)

defnite (definite)

guarntee (guarantee)

jography (geography)

ineffecshal (ineffectual)

nuclus (nucleus)

particlar (particular)

pome (poem)

plice (police)

quite (quiet)

reconize (recognize)

resume (résumé)

sedimentry (sedimentary)

simlar (similar)

superntenent (superintendent)

sussinct (succinct)

temperture (temperature)

vilent (violent)

uzhal (usual)

Sound Substitutions

agin (again)

blaytant (blatant)

boquet (bouquet)

brochr (brochure)

calvary (cavalry)

capsl (capsule)

tshasm (chasm)

click (clique)

conscious (conscience)

crooks (crux)

cullinary (culinary)

dictionury (dictionary)

diptheria (diphtheria)

dipthong (diphthong)

dis-hevel (dishevel)

fewtyle (futile)

gesture (*g* is soft)

genuwine (genuine)

gigantic (first *g* is soft)

hiccough (hiccup)

homidge (homage)

ullusion (illusion)

interduce (introduce)

irrevelent (irrelevant)

jist (just)

larnyx (larynx)

lenth (length)

loose (lose)

longgevity (longevity)

memor (memoir)

miradge (mirage)

preelude (prelude)

preform (perform)

prespiration (perspiration)

prestidge (prestige)

rench (rinse)

saloon (salon)

strenth (strength)

statue (stature)

substantuate (substantiate)

theayter (theater)

tedjius (tedious)

E Chicago Documentation

Two widely used systems of documentation are outlined in *The Chicago Manual of Style,* Fifteenth Edition (2003). The first, typically used by public speakers, provides for bibliographic citations in endnotes or footnotes. This method, which is also frequently used by journalists and scholars in the humanities, is illustrated in this appendix. The second system, often used by writers in the physical and natural sciences, employs an author-date system: sources are cited in the text with full bibliographic information given in a concluding list of references. For information about the author-date system — and more information generally about Chicago-style documentation — consult the *Chicago Manual,* 15th ed., Chapters 16 and 17.

1. Book by a Single Author   Give the author's full name followed by a comma. Then italicize the book's title. In parentheses, give the city of publication followed by a colon, the publisher's name followed by a comma, and the publication date. Place a comma after the parentheses, and then give the page numbers from which your paraphrase or quotation is taken.

   1. Eric Alterman, *What Liberal Media? The Truth about Bias and the News* (New York: Basic Books, 2003), 180–85.

2. Book by Multiple Authors   Give all the authors' full names, the book's title in italics, the publication information in parentheses, and the pages from which your paraphrase or quotation is taken.

   2. Bill Kovach and Tom Rosenstiel, *The Elements of Journalism: What Newspeople Should Know and the Public Should Expect* (New York: Three Rivers Press, 2001), 57–58.

   2. Bill Kovach and Tom Rosenstiel, *The Elements of Journalism: What Newspeople Should Know and the Public Should Expect,* rev. ed. (New York: Three Rivers Press, 2007), 57–58.

   2. Leonard Downie Jr. and Robert G. Kaiser, *The News about the News: American Journalism in Peril* (New York: Knopf, 2002), 72–75.

3. Edited Work without an Author   Give the editor's full name followed by a comma, "ed." for *editor,* and another comma. Then give the title in italics, publication information in parentheses, and the pages you're citing.

3. Joseph B. Atkins, ed., *The Mission: Journalism, Ethics, and the World* (Ames: Iowa State University Press, 2002), 150–57.

4. Encyclopedia or Dictionary   Give the title of the work in italics followed by a comma, the edition (if any), the letters "s.v." (from the Latin *sub verbo,*"under the word"), and then the term you looked up, in quotation marks, and a period. If the citation is from an online reference work, add the URL (Internet address) and the access date.

4. *Routledge Encyclopedia of Philosophy,* s.v. "Ethics of journalism."

4. *Encyclopedia Britannica,* s.v. "Yellow Journalism," http://www.britannica .com/eb/article-9077903/yellow-journalism (accessed October 17, 2007).

5. Article in a Magazine   Include the author's full name, the title of the article in quotation marks, the title of the magazine in italics, and the publication date. If you use a quotation, give the page number of the quotation. Otherwise, there is no need to cite the page numbers of the article.

5. John Leo, "With Bias toward All," *U.S. News & World Report,* March 18, 2002, 8.

6. Article in a Journal   Give the author's full name, the title of the article in quotation marks, the title of the journal in italics, the volume number, the issue number (if available), the year of publication in parentheses followed by a colon, and the pages used. If the journal article was found online, give the URL and, if timeliness is an issue, the date of access.

6. Tom Goldstein, "Wanted: More Outspoken Views; Coverage of the Press Is Up, but Criticism Is Down," *Columbia Journalism Review* 40 (2001): 144–45.

6. Tom Goldstein, "Wanted: More Outspoken Views; Coverage of the Press Is Up, but Criticism Is Down." *Columbia Journalism Review* 40 (2001), http://backissues.cjrarchives.org/year/01/6/goldsteinpresscrit.asp (accessed October 29, 2007).

7. Article in a Newspaper   Include the author's full name, the title of the article in quotation marks, the title of the newspaper in italics, the date of publication, the edition (such as "national edition") if relevant, and the section of the paper in which the article appeared. Omit page numbers, even for a citation to a quotation. If the article was found online, give the URL to the article itself (or to the newspaper's home page, if the article is archived) and the access date.

7. Felicity Barringer, "Sports Reporting: Rules on Rumors," *New York Times,* February 18, 2002, sec. C.

7. Arthur Schlesinger Jr., "Fixing the Electoral College," *Washington Post*, December 19, 2000, final edition, http://www.washingtonpost.com (accessed October 23, 2007).

8. Web Site Give the name of the author (if available), the title of the page in quotation marks followed by a comma, the title (italicized) or owner of the Web site if relevant, and the site's URL. If there is no author, give the owner of the site as the author. The date you accessed the site is optional; if you include it, add it in parentheses at the end.

8. FAIR (Fairness & Accuracy in Reporting), "Challenging Hate Radio: A Guide for Activists," http://www.fair.org/index.php?page=112 (accessed September 21, 2007).

9. E-mail Message Treat e-mail messages like personal communications. Give the sender's full name, the phrase "e-mail message to author," and the date of the message.

9. Grace Talusan, e-mail message to author, March 20, 2005.

10. E-mail Discussion List Message Give the author's full name, the phrase "e-mail to" followed by the name of the discussion list, the date of the posting, and the URL of the list. Your date of access is optional.

10. Ola Seifert, e-mail to Society of Professional Journalists mailing list, August 23, 2002, http://f05n16.cac.psu.edu (accessed September 14, 2005).

11. Newsgroup Message Include the author's full name, the phrase "message to" followed by the name of the newsgroup, the date of the posting, and the URL of the newsgroup. Your date of access is optional.

11. Jai Maharaj, message to alt.journalism.newspapers.newsgroup, November 11, 2002, http://groups.google.com (accessed December 19, 2005).

12. Article in an Electronic Database Give the author's full name, the title of the article (in quotation marks), the title of the periodical (in italics), publication information for the periodical, the pages you are citing, and the URL of the database. Your date of access is optional.

12. Mark J. Miller, "Tough Calls: Deciding When a Suicide Is Newsworthy and What Details to Include Are among Journalism's More Sensitive Decisions," *American Journalism Review* 24, no. 10 (2002): 43, http://infotrac.galegroup.com (accessed March 1, 2005).

13. Government Document Use the governmental body or office as the author. Give the governmental body's name ("U.S. Congress," "U.S. House,"

"Senate Committee on Foreign Relations"), the title of the article (in quotation marks) or publication (italicized), the usual publication information, and the page numbers you are citing.

13. U.S. Congress, *The Electronic Freedom of Information Improvement Act: Hearing before the Subcommittee on Technology and the Law of the Committee on the Judiciary, 1992* (Washington, D.C.: GPO, 1993), 201.

14. Personal Communication   Give the author's name, the type of communication (e.g., "letter to author," "conversation with author," "telephone conversation with author"), and the date.

14. Soo Jin Oh, letter to author, August 13, 2000.

15. Interview   Give the name of the interviewee, the interviewer, the name of the program or forum, the publication or network, and the date. Interviews that have not been published or broadcast should be cited with a description of the type of interview (e.g., "tape recording") and the place the interview was conducted.

15. Walter Cronkite, interview by Daniel Schorr, *Frontline*, PBS, April 2, 1996.

16. Video Recording   Give the title of the film or other work, the medium (VHS, DVD), the director, the place and name of the film distribution company, and the date of release.

16. *All the President's Men*, VHS, directed by Alan J. Pakula (Burbank, Calif.: Warner Brothers, 1976).

17. Sound Recording   List the composer or writer, the title of the work, the performer or conductor, the recording company or publisher, and the recording number or date of release.

17. Noam Chomsky, *Case Studies in Hypocrisy: U.S. Human Rights Policy*, read by the author (AK Press, 2000).

17. Antonio Vivaldi, *The Four Seasons*, conducted by Seiji Ozawa, Telarc CD-80070.

F APA Documentation

Most disciplines in the social sciences — psychology, anthropology, sociology, political science, education, and economics — use the author-date system of documentation established by the American Psychological Association (APA). This citation style highlights dates of publication because the currency of published material is of primary importance in these fields. For more information about APA format, see the *Publication Manual of the American Psychological Association, Sixth Edition* (2010).

The *Publication Manual* advises users to omit retrieval dates for content that is in permanent form, such as published journal articles, and to provide the DOI (digital object identifier) for that content. If no DOI is available, list the home page URL of the sponsor or publisher of the site. Including the database from which the content was sourced is not recommended, as this can be subject to change.

The numbered entries that follow introduce and explain some conventions of this citation style using examples relating to the topic of stress management. Note that in the titles of books and articles only the first word of the title and subtitle and proper nouns are capitalized.

1. Book by a Single Author   Begin with the author's last name and initials followed by the date of publication in parentheses. Next, italicize the book's title and end with the place of publication, including city and state or country, and the publisher.

Rabin, B. S. (1999). *Stress, immune function, and health: The connection.*

New York, NY: Wiley-Liss.

2. Book by Multiple Authors or Editors   Begin with the authors' last names and initials followed by the date of publication in parentheses. Next, italicize the book's title and end with the place of publication and the publisher. Invert all authors' names and use an ampersand before the last name.

Williams, S., & Cooper, L. (2002). *Managing workplace stress: A best practice*

blueprint. New York, NY: Wiley.

3. Article in a Reference Work   List the author of the article, the publication date, and the article title. This information is followed by the word *In* and the italicized title of the reference work. Include the volume number and inclusive page numbers of the article in parentheses, followed by the place of publication and the publisher. If an online edition of the reference work is cited, give the retrieval date and the URL. Omit end punctuation after the URL.

Kazdin, A. E. (2000). Stress. In *Encyclopedia of psychology* (Vol. 7,

pp. 479–489). New York, NY: Oxford University Press.

Biofeedback. (2007). In *Encyclopaedia Britannica online.* Retrieved from

http://www.britannica.com/eb/article-9079253

4. Government Document Use the office or governmental department as the author followed by the publication date. Italicize the title of the document and end with the place of publication and the publisher (usually "Washington, DC," and "U.S. Government Printing Office"). This example refers to a book; for other formats, refer to Appendix D in the APA *Publication Manual.*

U.S. Department of Health and Human Services. (1997). *Violence in the*

workplace: Guidelines for understanding and response. Washington, DC:

Government Printing Office.

5. Journal Article Begin with the author's last name and initials followed by the date of publication in parentheses. Next, list the title of the article and italicize the title of the journal in which it is printed. Then give the volume number, italicized, and the issue number in parentheses if the journal is paginated by issue. End with the inclusive page numbers of the article.

Dollard, M. F., & Metzer, J. C. (1999). Psychological research, practice, and

production: The occupational stress problem. *International Journal of*

Stress Management, 6(4), 241–253.

6. Journal Article Online For an article found online, include the issue number regardless of how the journal is paginated. If a DOI number is given, add "doi:" and the number after the end period of the citation. Otherwise, add "Retrieved from" and the URL for an open-content article or the URL for the journal home page for subscription-only content. It is no longer necessary to include the database from which an article is retrieved or the date of retrieval for a published article. Omit the end period after a DOI or URL.

Hardie, E. A., Critchley, C., & Swann, K. (2007, June 12). Self-coping

complexity: The role of relational, individual, and collective self-

aspects and corresponding coping styles in stress and health. *Current*

Research in Social Psychology, 12(10), 134–150. Retrieved from

http://www.uiowa.edu/~grpproc/crisp/crisp12_10.pdf

7. Magazine Article Begin with the author's last name and initials followed by the date of publication, including the month or the month and day, in parentheses. Next, list the title of the article and the title of the magazine, italicized. Give the volume number, italicized, followed by the inclusive page numbers of the article.

Cobb, K. (2002, July 20). Sleepy heads: Low fuel may drive brain's need to

sleep. *Science News, 162,* 38.

8. Newspaper Article   Begin with the author's last name and initials followed by the date of publication, including the month and day, in parentheses. Next, list the title of the article and, in italics, the newspaper in which it is printed. End with the section and page or pages on which the article appears. Note that the abbreviation *p.* or *pp.* is used for newspaper page numbers. If the article was found online, omit page numbers, give the URL for the retrieval site, and do not add end punctuation.

Goode, E. (2002, December 17). The heavy cost of chronic stress.

The New York Times, p. D1.

Goode, E. (2002, December 17). The heavy cost of chronic stress.

The New York Times. Retrieved from http://www.nytimes.com

9. Unsigned Newspaper Article   If a newspaper article does not list an author, give the title, the publication date in parentheses, the name of the newspaper in italics, and the page on which the article appears.

Stress less: It's time to wrap it up. (2002, December 18). *Houston Chronicle,*

p. A1.

10. Document from a Web Site   List the author, or, if no author is given, the title of the document and the publication date. List the date of access only if no publication date is given. List the URL without end punctuation.

Stress management: Measuring stress. (2009, April 22). Retrieved from

http://www.webmd.com/balance/stress-management-evaluating-stress

11. Personal Web Site   To cite a personal Web site, it's usually sufficient to simply note the site in your speech. For example,

Dr. Wesley Sime's stress management page is an excellent resource

(http://www.unl.edu/stress/mgmt/).

The APA manual states that personal Web sites should not be included in a bibliography; check with your instructor to see what his or her expectations are for your APA bibliography.

12. Electronic Mailing List Message   Cite the author's name, the posting date in parentheses, the subject line, and the name of the list, followed by "archived at" and the address for the archive or for the specific message.

> Greenberg, G. (2002, May 26). Re: Job Stress & Mortality: Psychosomatic
> Med, U-T Houston [Electronic mailing list message]. Retrieved from
> http://list.mc.duke.edu/cgi-bin/wa?A2=ind0205&L=oem-announce&
> P=R13114&I=-3&O=A&T=0

13. Newsgroup, Online Forum, or Discussion Group Message   Cite the author's name, the posting date, the subject line, and the URL of the group or the archived item.

> Dimitrakov, J. (2001, February 21). Immune effects of psychological stress
> [Online discussion group message]. Retrieved from http://groups.google
> .com/groups?q=stress&start=40&hl=en&lr=&ie=UTF-8&selm=3A9ABDE
> 4%40MailAndNews.com&rnum=44

14. E-mail Message   To cite personal e-mail correspondence, it's sufficient to simply note the message in your speech. For example,

> An e-mail message from the staff of AltaVista clarifies this point
> (D. Emanuel, personal communication, May 12, 2005).

The APA manual states that e-mail correspondence, like other personal communications, should not be included in a bibliography; check with your instructor to see what his or her expectations are for your APA bibliography.

15. Abstract from an Information Service or Online Database   Begin with the author's last name and initials, followed by the date of publication in parentheses. Next, list the title of the document and the name of the journal, the volume number, the issue number, and the page numbers. Indicate "Abstract retrieved," followed by your access date and the name of the database.

> Viswesvaran, C., Sanchez, J., & Fisher, J. (1999). The role of social support in
> the process of work stress: A meta-analysis. *Journal of Vocational Behavior,*
> *54,* 314–334. Abstract retrieved from http://www.elsevier.com

16. Personal Interview   To cite a personal, unpublished interview, it's usually sufficient to note the interview in your speech. For example,

> During her interview, Senator Cole revealed her enthusiasm for the new
> state-funded stress management center (M. Cole, personal communi-
> cation, October 7, 2005).

The APA manual states that personal interviews, like other personal communications, should not be included in a bibliography; check with your instructor to see what his or her expectations are for your APA bibliography.

G MLA Documentation

Created by the Modern Language Association, MLA documentation style is fully outlined in the *MLA Handbook for Writers of Research Papers* (Seventh Edition, 2009). Disciplines that use MLA style include English literature, the humanities, and various foreign languages. The sample citations below all relate to a single topic: film appreciation and criticism.

1. Book by a Single Author   Citations for most books are arranged as follows: (1) author's name, last name first; (2) title and subtitle, italicized; and (3) city of publication, an abbreviated form of the publisher's name, and the date. Each of these three pieces of information is followed by a period and one space. End the citation with the medium of publication (*Print*) and a period.

> Berg, Charles Ramírez. *Latino Images in Film: Stereotypes, Subversion, and Resistance.* Austin: U of Texas P, 2002. Print.

2. Book by Multiple Authors or Editors   Give the first author's name, last name first; then list the name(s) of the other author(s) in regular order with a comma between authors and the word *and* before the last one. The final name in a list of editors is followed by a comma and "ed." or "eds."

> Hill, John, and Pamela Church Gibson, eds. *The Oxford Guide to Film Studies.* New York: Oxford UP, 1998. Print.

3. Article in a Reference Work   Begin with the author of the article; if none is provided, begin with title of the article in quotation marks. Cite the name of the reference work, followed by edition (if provided) and date of publication. If the work is arranged alphabetically, no volume or page numbers are required.

If the citation is to an online version of the work, give the author, article title, and Web site. Then add the publisher or sponsor of the site, the date of publication or last update, the medium (*Web*), and the date you accessed the work (day, month, year). End with a period.

> Katz, Ephraim. "Film Noir." *The Film Encyclopedia.* 4th ed. 2001. Print.

> "Auteur Theory." *Encyclopaedia Britannica Online.* Encyclopaedia Britannica, 2007. Web. 22 Oct. 2007.

4. Government Document   Give the name of the governmental body or office followed by the agency and any subdivision as the author, using standard abbreviations. Italicize the title of the document. Congressional documents should include congressional number and session, house, and type of document (report, resolution, etc.) in abbreviated form, and number of the material. Add the publication information (the publisher is often the Government

Printing Office [GPO]). Then end with the medium (*Print*). For an online government document, after the title of the document, give any additional print information, database you accessed, medium (*Web*), and your date of access.

> United States. Cong. House. Committee on the Judiciary. *National Film Preservation Act of 1996*. 104th Cong., 2nd sess. H. Rept. 104-558. Washington: GPO, 1996. Print.

> United States. Cong. House. Committee on House Administration. *Library of Congress Sound Recording and Film Preservation Programs Reauthorization Act of 2008*. 110th Cong., 2nd sess. H. Rept. 110-683. *GPOAccess, Congressional Reports*. Web. 15 Jan. 2009.

5. Magazine Article Along with the author's name, title of the article in quotation marks, and title of the magazine in italics, include the full date of publication and inclusive page numbers of the article. The date of publication should be listed as day, month, year, with no commas between them. For monthly magazines, list the month and year only. Use three-letter abbreviations for all months except May, June, and July. End with the medium (*Print*).

If citing the article from an online edition of the magazine, after the article title, add name of the Web site in italics, followed by a period. Add the publisher or sponsor of the site, date of publication, medium (*Web*), and your access date.

> Ansen, David. "Lights! Action! Cannes!" *Newsweek* 19 May 1997: 76-79. Print.

> Ansen, David. "Boomer Files: 7,714 Movies, and Counting." *Newsweek. Newsweek*, 29 Oct. 2007. Web. 3 Nov. 2007.

6. Journal Article Follow the format for magazine articles, but include the journal's volume number and the issue number (if any), with a period between them. Give the year in parentheses followed by a colon and the page numbers. End with the medium (*Print*).

If an article is accessed online through a database service, after the publication information, add the name of the database in italics, followed by a period. Then give the medium (*Web*) and your date of access. End with a period.

> Kingsley-Smith, Jane E. "Shakespearean Authorship in Popular British Cinema." *Literature-Film Quarterly* 30.3 (2002): 159-61. Print.

> Holcomb, Mark. "A Classic Revisited: *To Kill a Mockingbird*." *Film Quarterly* 55.4 (2002): 34-40. *JSTOR*. Web. 22 Oct. 2007.

7. Newspaper Article Documenting a newspaper article is similar to documenting a magazine article. In citing the name of the newspaper, do not include any initial *A, An,* or *The*. Add the city in brackets after the name if the newspaper is not well known and the city's name is not part of the newspaper's title. Give the date, edition (if any), a colon, a space, section number or letter (if any), and page number(s). If the article appears on discontinuous pages,

give the first page followed by a plus sign (+) to indicate that the article continues on other pages. End with the medium (*Print*).

When citing a newspaper article found online, after the article title, give the
name of the newspaper's Web site followed by a period. Specify the publisher or
sponsor of the site, publication date, medium consulted (*Web*), and your access date.

> Sebastian, Pamela. "Film Reviews Have a Delayed Effect on Box-Office Re-
> ceipts, Researchers Say." *Wall Street Journal* 13 Nov. 1997: A1+. Print.

> Dargis, Manohla. "Unblinking Eye, Visual Diary: Warhol's Films." *New York
> Times.* New York Times, 21 Oct. 2007. Web. 30 Oct. 2007.

8. Newspaper Editorial Document an editorial as a standard newspaper article, but add the label "Editorial" after the title. If the editorial is signed, list
the author's name first; otherwise, begin with the title.

> "The Edgy Legacy of Stanley Kubrick." Editorial. *New York Times* 10 Mar.
> 1999: A18. Print.

9. Single-Issue CD-ROM, Diskette, or Magnetic Tape Cite these electronic
sources as you would books, with title of the source in italics. Add number of the
electronic edition, release, or version (if applicable), city and publisher of the
source, and year of publication. End with the medium (*CD-ROM, Diskette*, etc.).

> "Pulp Fiction." *Blockbuster Movie Trivia.* 3rd ed. New York: Random, 1998.
> CD-ROM.

10. Online Scholarly Project or Reference Database Begin with the author
if one is listed. Then give the title of the work you are citing, in quotation
marks, followed by title of the site, in italics. If the site has an editor, give the
abbreviation "Ed." followed by the editor's name. Then cite the name of the
sponsoring organization, date of electronic publication or of the latest update,
medium (*Web*), and your date of access.

> "Origins of American Animation." *American Memory.* Lib. of Cong. 31 Mar.
> 1999. Web. 26 June 2003.

11. Commercial Web Site Include the creator of the Web site (if known); title of the work you are citing, in quotation marks; the site's title, in italics; and
name of any sponsoring organization or publisher (if none is found, use *N.p.*).
Then give the date the site was last updated (if none is listed, use *n.d.*), medium
(*Web*), and your date of access.

> "American Beauty." *Crazy for Cinema.* N.p., n.d. Web. 24 Oct. 2003.

12. Personal Web Site Guidelines for citing a personal Web site are similar to
those for a commercial site. Include creator of the site and title of the site in italics.
If there is no title, include a description such as "Home page." Give the publisher
or sponsor of the site, date of the last update, medium (*Web*), and your access date.

> Last, Kimberly. *007.* Kimberly Last, n.d. Web. 18 Oct. 2007.

13. Article in an Online Periodical Begin with the author, title of the article in quotation marks, and name of the Web site in italics, followed by a period. Then add the publisher or sponsor of the site, date of publication, the medium (*Web*), and your date of access.

> Taylor, Charles. "The Pianist." *Salon.com.* Salon Media Group, 27 Dec.
> 2002. Web. 1 Jan. 2005.

14. Posting to a Discussion Group Begin with the author's name; title of the posting in quotation marks (if there is no title, use the label "Online posting," not in quotation marks). Then give the name of the Web site, e-mail discussion list, or newsgroup, in italics; sponsor or publisher of the site (if none, use *N.p.*); and date of the posting. Add the medium (*Web*) and your date of access.

> Granger, Susan. "Review of *The Cider House Rules.*" *Rotten Tomatoes.* IGN
> Entertainment, 30 Mar. 2000. Web. 2 Oct. 2000.

15. E-mail Message Give the writer's name, subject of the message in quotation marks, and the phrase "Message to" and the name of the recipient (if the message was addressed to the author of the work in which the message is being cited, write "Message to the author"). Include the date of the message. End with the medium (*E-mail*).

> Boothe, Jeanna. "Re: Top 100 Movies." Message to the author. 16 Feb.
> 2005. E-mail.

16. Work of Art or Photograph Include the name of the artist, the work's title, date of composition (if unknown, use *n.d.*), medium of composition (*Oil on Canvas, Bronze, Photograph*), museum or other location, and city. For artwork cited in a book, use the basic citation followed by publication information for the book, and end with the medium consulted (*Print*). For artwork cited online, omit the medium of composition, and then after the city, add the Web site or database, medium consulted (*Web*), and your date of access.

> Christenberry, William. *Coleman's Café.* 1971. Ektacolor Brownie Print.
> Hunter Museum of Art, Chattanooga.

> Christenberry, William. *Signs Near Greensboro, Alabama.* 1973. Smithsonian
> American Art Museum, Washington. *Smithsonian American Art Museum.*
> Web. 14 Jan. 2003.

> Vermeer, Jan. *A Woman Weighing Gold.* 1664? Oil on Canvas. Natl. Gallery
> of Art, Washington. Ed. Gerald F. Brommer. *Discovering Art History.* 2nd
> ed. Worcester: Davis, 1988. 308. Print.

17. Personal Interview Begin with the name of the person interviewed. Then specify the type of interview (Personal, Telephone, or Internet interview) and the date on which it was conducted.

> Sanderson, Andrew. Telephone interview. 12 June 2002.

H CBE/CSE Documentation

The CSE (Council of Science Editors, formerly the Council of Biology Editors) style is most frequently used in the fields of biology and environmental science. The current CBE/CSE style guide is *Scientific Style and Format: The CSE Manual for Authors, Editors, and Publishers,* Seventh Edition (2006). Publishers and instructors who require the CBE/CSE style do so in three possible formats: a citation-sequence superscript format, a name-year format, or a citation-name format, which combines aspects of the other two systems.

- Citation-sequence superscript format: Use superscript numbers for in-text references. In the references list, number and arrange the references in the sequence in which they are first cited in the speech.

- Name-year format: Use the name and year, in parentheses, for the in-text reference. In the references list, give the references, unnumbered, in alphabetical order.

- Citation-name format: Use superscript numbers for in-text references. In the references list, arrange the references in alphabetical order and number the list sequentially.

In the following examples, all of which refer to environmental issues, you will see that the citation-sequence format calls for listing the date after the publisher's name in references for books and after the name of the periodical in references for articles. The name-year format calls for listing the date immediately after the author's name in any kind of reference. Notice also the absence of a comma after the author's last name, the absence of a period after an initial, and the absence of underlining in titles of books or journals.

1. Book by One Author   Be sure to list the total number of pages in the book.

CITATION-SEQUENCE AND CITATION-NAME

1. Leggett JK. The carbon war: global warming and the end of the oil era. New York: Routledge; 2001. 341 p.

NAME-YEAR

Leggett JK. 2001. The carbon war: global warming and the end of the oil era. New York: Routledge. 341 p.

2. Book by Two or More Authors

CITATION-SEQUENCE AND CITATION-NAME

2. Goldstein IF, Goldstein M. How much risk? a guide to understanding environmental health hazards. New York: Oxford University Press; 2002. 304 p.

NAME-YEAR

Goldstein IF, Goldstein M. 2002. How much risk? a guide to understanding environmental health hazards. New York: Oxford University Press. 304 p.

3. Journal Article CBE/CSE style uses standard scientific abbreviations for titles of journals (*Am Sci* for *American Scientist* and *J Am Med Assoc* for *Journal of the American Medical Association,* for instance). One-word titles are never abbreviated. To cite a journal article on the Internet, add the medium ([Internet]), date cited, and the URL (Internet address). Also give the DOI (digital object identifier) code, if available. Omit end punctuation after a URL or DOI.

CITATION-SEQUENCE AND CITATION-NAME

3. Brussard PF, Tull JC. Conservation biology and four types of advocacy. Conserv Biol. 2007; 21(1):21–24.

3. Brussard PF, Tull JC. Conservation biology and four types of advocacy. Conserv Biol [Internet]. 2007 [cited 2007 Oct 22]; 21(1):21–24. Available from http://www.blackwell-synergy.com/toc/cbi/21/1 doi:10.1111/j.1523–1739.2006.00640.x

NAME-YEAR

Brussard PF, Tull JC. 2007. Conservation biology and four types of advocacy. Conserv Biol. 21(1):21–24.

Brussard PF, Tull JC. 2007. Conservation biology and four types of advocacy. Conserv Biol. [Internet]. [cited 2007 Oct 22]; 21(1):21–24. Available from http://www.blackwell-synergy.com/toc/cbi/21/1 doi:10.1111/j.1523-1739.2006.00640.x

4. Magazine Article

CITATION-SEQUENCE AND CITATION-NAME

4. Wilcott B. Art for Earth's sake. Mother Jones 2000 Jun:16.

NAME-YEAR

Wilcott B. 2000 Jun. Art for Earth's sake. Mother Jones: 16.

5. Newspaper Article

CITATION-SEQUENCE AND CITATION-NAME

5. Parson EA. Moving beyond the Kyoto impasse. New York Times 2001 Jul 1; Sect. A:23 (col. 1).

NAME-YEAR

Parson EA. 2001 Jul 1. Moving beyond the Kyoto impasse. New York Times. Sect. A:23 (col. 1).

6. Web Site For material found on a Web site, give the author's name (if any) and the title of the material, followed by "Internet" in brackets. Add the place of publication, the publisher, and the date of publication, followed by the date of citation, in brackets. Add "Available from:" and the URL.

CITATION-SEQUENCE AND CITATION-NAME

6. Water Pollution Control: Watershed Management Cycle [Internet]. Nashville: Tennessee Department of Environment and Conservation; 2007 [cited 2007 Oct 23]. Available from: http://www.tennessee.gov/environment/wpc/watershed/cycle.shtml

NAME-YEAR

Water Pollution Control: Watershed Management Cycle [Internet] 2007. Nashville: Tennessee Department of Environment and Conservation. [cited 2007 Oct 23]. Available from: http://www.tennessee.gov/environment/wpc/watershed/cycle.shtml

7. E-Mail Message CBE/CSE style recommends mentioning personal communications, such as letters and e-mails, in text but not listing them in the list of references. An explanation of the material should go in a separate "Notes" section.

. . . (2003 e-mail from Maura O'Brien to me; unreferenced, see "Notes") . . .

8. E-Mail Discussion List Message or Newsgroup Message

8. Affleck-Asch W. Three hundred pesticides to be withdrawn in Europe [discussion list on the Internet]. 2002 Dec 2, 6:37 pm [cited 2003 Jan 2]. [about 8 paragraphs]. Available from: http://www.mail-archive.com/ecofem%40csf.colorado.edu

IEEE Documentation

The Institute of Electrical and Electronics Engineers (IEEE) style requires that references appear at the end of the text, not in alphabetical order but in the order in which the sources are cited in the text. A bracketed reference number beginning with *B* precedes each entry. For speakers, this means creating a bibliography of sources listed in the order in which they are cited in the speech. For more information on IEEE documentation, check the *IEEE Standards Style Manual* online at http://standards.ieee.org/guides/style/index.html.

1. Book List the author by last name and first initial followed by a comma. Then list the book's title in italics and the edition (if applicable). Finally, list the place of publication, the publisher, the date of publication, and the pages cited.

[B1] Vorpérian, V., *Fast Analytical Techniques for Electrical and Electronic Circuits.* New York: Cambridge University Press, 2002, p. 462.

2. Periodical List the author, the title of the article in quotation marks, the title of the periodical in italics, the volume number, the issue number, the pages cited, and the date. Only the first word of the article title and subtitle and proper nouns are capitalized.

[B2] Brittain, J. C., "Charles F. Scott: A pioneer in electrical power engineering," *IEEE Industry Applications Magazine*, vol. 287, no. 6, pp. 6–8, Nov./Dec. 2000.

3. Web Page List the author, the title of the Web page, the medium (enclosed in brackets), volume and issue number (for an online journal), page number (if relevant or given), and the year and the month of publication in parentheses. Then add "Available at:" and provide the full URL (Internet address) or the name of the online service provider.

[B3] Harnack, A., and Kleppinger, E., "Beyond the MLA Handbook: Documenting Electronic Sources on the Internet" [On-line style sheet] (June 1996), Available at: http://english.ttu.edu.kairos/1.2/

J Glossary

abstract language   Language that is general or nonspecific. See also *concrete language.*

active listening   A multistep, focused, and purposeful process of gathering and evaluating information.

active voice   The feature of a verb indicating that the subject performs the action. Effective speeches make ample use of the active voice. See also *passive voice.*

ad hominem argument   A form of fallacious argument that targets people instead of issues and attempts to incite an audience's dislike for an opponent.

after-dinner speech   A speech that is likely to occur before, after, or during a formal dinner, a breakfast or lunch seminar, or other type of business, professional, or civic meeting.

agenda   A document identifying the items to be accomplished during a meeting.

agora   In ancient Greece, a public square or marketplace. See also *forum.*

alliteration   The repetition of the same sounds, usually initial consonants, in two or more neighboring words or syllables.

allusion   A figure of speech in which the speaker makes vague or indirect reference to people, historical events, or concepts to give deeper meaning to the message.

almanac   A reference work that contains facts and statistics in many categories, including those that are related to historical, social, political, and religious subjects.

analogy   An extended metaphor or simile that compares an unfamiliar concept or process with a more familiar one in order to help the listener understand the one that is unfamiliar.

anaphora   A rhetorical device in which the speaker repeats a word or phrase at the beginning of successive phrases, clauses, or sentences.

anecdote   A brief story of an interesting, humorous, or real-life incident that links back to the speaker's theme.

antithesis   Setting off two ideas in balanced (parallel) opposition to each other to create a powerful effect.

appeal to tradition   A fallacy of reasoning in which the speaker argues for the truth of a claim based solely on common practices in the past.

architecture design review   Oral presentation with the dual goal of helping listeners visualize the design concept while also selling it.

argument   A stated position, with support, for or against an idea or issue; contains the core elements of claim, evidence, and warrants.

arrangement   The strategic process of deciding how to order speech points into a coherent and convincing pattern for your topic and audience; also refers to one of the five parts of the classical canons of rhetoric.

articulation   The clarity or forcefulness with which sounds are made, regardless of whether they are pronounced correctly.

atlas   A collection of maps, text, and accompanying charts and tables.

attitudes   A predisposition to respond to people, ideas, objects, or events in evaluative ways.

audience analysis   The process of gathering and analyzing demographic and psychological information about audience members with the explicit aim of adapting your message to the information you uncover.

audience-centered approach   An approach to speech preparation in which in each phase of the speech preparation process — from selection and treatment of the speech topic to making decisions about organization, language, and method of delivery — is geared toward communicating a meaningful message to the audience.

audience perspective   A stance taken by the speaker in which he or she adapts the speech to the needs, attitudes, and values of an audience.

audio clip   A short recording of sounds, music, or speech. Introducing sound into a speech can add interest, illustrate ideas, and even bring humor to the mix.

aural channel   A nonverbal channel of communication made up of the vocalizations that form and accompany spoken words. These vocalizations, also called *paralanguage,* include the qualities of volume, pitch, rate, variety, and articulation and pronunciation.

authoritative warrant   A warrant that appeals to the credibility the audience assigns to the source of the evidence; also called an *ethos-based appeal.*

average   A summary of a set of data according to its typical or average characteristics; may refer to the *mean, median,* or *mode.*

balance   A principle that suggests that appropriate emphasis or weight be given to each part of the speech relative to the other parts and to the theme.

bandwagoning   A fallacious argument that presents itself as true because "general opinion" supports it.

bar graph   A type of graph used to compare quantities or magnitudes with the use of bars of varying lengths.

basic sales technique   A synonym for *Monroe's motivated sequence,* a five-part process of persuasion. See also *motivated sequence pattern of arrangement.*

begging the question   A fallacious argument presented in such a way that it is necessarily true, even though no evidence has been presented.

beliefs   The ways in which people perceive reality or determine the very existence or validity of something.

biased language   Any language that relies on unfounded assumptions, negative descriptions, or stereotypes of a given group's age, class, gender, abilities, and geographic, ethnic, racial, or religious characteristics.

body   The part of the speech in which the speaker develops the main points intended to fulfill the speech purpose.

brainstorming   A problem-solving technique, useful for developing speech topics, that involves the spontaneous generation of ideas. You can brainstorm by making lists, using word association, and mapping a topic, among other techniques.

brief example   A single illustration of a point.

call to action   A challenge to audience members to act in response to a speech, see the problem in a new way, change their beliefs about the problem, or change both their actions and their beliefs with respect to the problem; placed at the conclusion of a speech.

canned speech   A speech used repeatedly and without sufficient adaptation to the rhetorical speech situation.

canons of rhetoric   A classical approach to speechmaking in which the speaker divides a speech into five parts: invention, arrangement, style, memory, and delivery.

captive audience   An audience in attendance not because they necessarily freely choose to listen to a speech but because they must.

case conference   An oral report prepared by health-care professionals evaluating a patient's condition and outlining a treatment plan.

causal (cause-effect) pattern of arrangement   A pattern of organizing speech points in order, first of causes and then of effects or vice versa; it is used when the cause-effect relationship is well established.

central processing   A mode of processing a persuasive message that involves thinking critically about the contents of the message and the strength and quality of the speaker's arguments. People who seriously consider what the speaker's message means to them are most likely to experience a relatively enduring change in thinking.

channel   The medium through which the speaker sends a message (e.g., sound waves, air waves, electronic transmission, and so forth).

chart   A method of visually organizing complex information into compact form. Several different types of charts are helpful for speakers: flowcharts, organization charts, and tabular charts or tables.

cherry-picking   To selectively present only those facts and statistics that buttress your point of view while ignoring competing data.

chronological pattern of arrangement   (also called *temporal pattern*) A pattern of organizing speech points in a natural sequential order; it is used when describing a series of events in time or when the topic develops in line with a set pattern of actions or tasks.

circular pattern of arrangement   A pattern of organizing speech points so that one idea leads to another, which leads to a third, and so forth until the speaker arrives back at the speech thesis.

claim   The declaration of a state of affairs, often stated as a thesis statement, in which a speaker attempts to prove something.

claim of fact   An argument that focuses on whether something is or is not true or whether something will or will not happen.

claim of policy   A claim that recommends that a specific course of action be taken, or approved, by an audience.

claim of value   A claim that addresses issues of judgment.

classroom discussion presentation   A type of oral presentation in which the speaker presents a brief overview of the topic under discussion and introduces a series of questions to guide students through the topic.

cliché   An expression that is predictable and stale.

closed-ended question   A question designed to elicit a small range of specific answers supplied by the interviewer. See also *scale question* and *open-ended question*.

co-culture   A community of people whose perceptions and beliefs differ significantly from those of other groups within the larger culture.

coherence   Clarity and logical consistency within a speech or an argument.

colleagues within the field audience   An audience of individuals who share a speaker's knowledge of the general field under question but who may not be familiar with the specific topic under discussion.

collective mind   A state of mind adopted by group members in which they determine that the group communication will be careful, consistent, and conscientious.

collectivist culture   A culture that tends to emphasize the needs and desires of the larger group rather than those of the individual.

colloquial expression   An informal expression, often with regional variations of speech.

common knowledge   Information that is likely to be known by many people and is therefore in the public domain; the source of such information need not be cited in a speech.

community service learning project   Oral report in which the speaker describes a community agency and its client base, his or her role and accomplishments in working with the agency, any problems encountered, and what was learned.

comparative advantage pattern of arrangement   A pattern of organizing speech points so that the speaker's viewpoint or proposal is shown to be superior to one or more alternative viewpoints or proposals.

conclusion   The part of the speech in which the speaker reiterates the speech purpose, summarizes main points, and leaves the audience with something to think about or act upon.

concrete language   Specific, tangible, and definite language (nouns or verbs). See also *abstract language.*

connotative meaning   The individual associations that different people bring to bear on a word.

contractions   Shortened forms of the verb *to be* and other auxiliary verbs in conjunction with pronouns; the use of contractions makes the speaker's language more concise.

conversation stopper   Speech designed to discredit, demean, and belittle those with whom one disagrees.

coordinate points   The alignment of points in a speech outline according to their equal importance to the topic and purpose.

coordination and subordination   The logical placement of ideas relative to their importance to one another. Ideas that are coordinate are given equal weight. An idea that is subordinate to another is given relatively less weight.

copyright   A legal protection afforded original creators of literary or artistic works, including works classified as literary, musical, dramatic, choreographic, pictorial, graphic, sculptural, audiovisual, sound recording, or architectural.

counterproductive roles   Negative interpersonal roles of group members who focus on individual versus group needs. These needs are usually irrelevant to the task at hand and are not oriented toward maintenance of the group as a team.

crisis-response presentation   Oral presentation in which the speaker seeks to reassure an organization's various audiences ("publics") and restore its credibility in the face of potentially reputation-damaging situations.

critical and conflicted audience   Audience members whose attitudes are critical or conflicted with respect to the speaker's topic.

critical thinking   The ability to evaluate claims on the basis of well-supported reasons.

cultural intelligence   The willingness to learn about other cultures and gradually reshape your thinking and behavior in response to what you've learned.

cultural norms   A group's rules for behavior; attempts to persuade people to do things contrary to their cultural norms will usually fail.

cultural premises   A group's shared beliefs and values about personal identity and relationships; persuasive attempts that challenge cultural premises will usually fail.

culture   The language, beliefs, values, norms, behaviors, and even material objects that are passed from one generation to the next.

database   A searchable place, or "base," in which information is stored and from which it can be retrieved.

debate   An oral presentation in which two individuals or groups consider or argue an issue from opposing viewpoints.

decoding   The process of interpreting a message.

deductive reasoning   Reasoning from a general condition to a specific instance. See also *inductive reasoning; syllogism.*

defensive listening   A poor listening behavior in which the listener reacts defensively to a speaker's message.

definition by etymology (word origin)   Defining something by providing an account of a word's history.

definition by example   Defining something by providing an example of it.

definition by negation   Defining something by explaining what it is not.

definition by synonym   Defining something by comparing it with another term that has an equivalent meaning. For example: A friend is a comrade or a buddy.

deliberative oratory   In ancient Greece, speech addressing legislative or political policy issues.

delivery   The vocal and nonverbal behavior that a speaker uses in a public speech; one of the five canons of rhetoric.

delivery cues   Brief reminder notes or prompts placed in the speaking outline; can refer to transitions, timing, speaking rate and volume, presentation aids, quotations, statistics, and difficult-to-pronounce or-remember names or words.

demagogue   An unethical speaker who relies heavily on irrelevant emotional appeals to short-circuit listeners' rational decision-making process.

demographics   Statistical characteristics of a given population. Characteristics typically considered in the analysis of audience members include age, gender, ethnic or cultural background, socioeconomic status (including income, occupation, and education), and religious and political affiliation.

denotative meaning   The literal or dictionary definition of a word.

devil's advocacy   Arguing for the sake of raising issues or concerns about the idea under discussion.

Dewey decimal number   An identifying number that allows the user to retrieve library books and other works that have been classified according to the Dewey decimal system.

diagram   A schematic drawing that explains how something works or how it is constructed or operated; used to simplify and clarify complicated procedures, explanations, and operations.

dialects   Subcultural variations of the mainstream pronunciation and articulation of a language.

dialectical inquiry   Devil's advocacy (see above) that goes a step further by proposing a countersolution to an idea.

dialogic communication   The sharing of ideas and open discussion through words.

dialogue   "through words" (from the Greek *dia,* "through" and *logos,* word)

dignity   The feeling that one is worthy, honored, or respected as a person.

direct quotation   A statement quoted verbatim, or word for word, from a source. Direct quotations should always be acknowledged in a speech. See also *paraphrase.*

disinformation   The deliberate falsification of information.

domain   The suffix at the end of a Web address that tells you the nature of the Web site: educational (.edu), government (.gov), military (.mil), nonprofit organization (.org), business/commercial (.com), or network (.net). A tilde (~) in the address usually indicates that it is a personal page rather than part of an institutional Web site. Understanding the domain can help you assess the credibility of a site.

dyadic communication   Communication between two people, as in a conversation.

effective delivery   The skillful application of natural conversational behavior to a speech in a way that is relaxed, enthusiastic, and direct.

eight-by-eight rule   Rule of design according to which the speaker does not include more than eight words on a line or eight lines on one PowerPoint slide or other kind of visual aid.

either-or fallacy   A fallacious argument that is stated in terms of two alternatives only, even though there may be multiple ways of viewing the issue.

elaboration likelihood model of persuasion (ELM)   A model of persuasion that states that people process persuasive messages by one of two routes — either central processing or peripheral processing — depending on their degree of involvement in the message.

elocutionary movement   An approach to public speaking in which speechmaking is regarded as a type of performance, much like acting.

encoding   The process of organizing a message, choosing words and sentence structure, and verbalizing the message.

encyclopedia   A reference work that summarizes knowledge found in original form elsewhere and provides an overview of subjects.

engineering design review   An oral presentation providing information on the results of a design project.

enthymeme   A syllogism stated as a probability rather than as an absolute. Because the enthymeme states either a major or a minor premise, but not both, the premise not stated remains implied.

epideictic oratory   In ancient Greece, speech addressing special occasions, such as celebrations and funerals.

ethical appeal   An attempt to persuade audience members by appealing to speaker credibility.

ethics   The rules or standards of moral conduct, or how people should act toward one another. In terms of public speaking, *ethics* refers to the responsibilities speakers have toward both their audience and themselves. It also encompasses the responsibilities that listeners have toward speakers.

ethnocentrism   The belief that the ways of one's own culture are superior to those of other cultures. Ethnocentric speakers act as though everyone shares their point of view and points of reference, whether or not this is in fact the case.

ethos   The Greek word for "character." According to the ancient Greek rhetorician Aristotle, audiences listen to and trust speakers if they exhibit competence (as demonstrated by the speaker's grasp of the subject matter) and good moral character.

eulogy   A speech whose purpose is to celebrate and commemorate the life of someone while consoling those who are left behind; typically delivered by close friends and family members.

evaluation research presentation   An oral presentation reporting on the effectiveness of programs developed to address various issues; frequently delivered in social scientific fields.

evidence   Supporting material that provides grounds for belief.

evidence-based practice   An approach to medical treatment in which caregivers make decisions based on current research and "best practices."

example   An illustration whose purpose is to aid understanding by making ideas, items, or events more concrete and by clarifying and amplifying meaning.

expectancy-outcome values theory   A theory of persuasion developed by Icek Aizen and Martin Fishbein positing that audience members act according to the perceived costs and benefits ("value") associated with a particular action; useful when developing a persuasive speech targeting behavior.

expert (or insider) audience   An audience composed of individuals who have an intimate knowledge of the topic, issue, product, or idea being discussed.

expert testimony   Any findings, eyewitness accounts, or opinions by professionals who are trained to evaluate or report on a given topic; a form of supporting material.

explanatory research presentation   An oral presentation focusing on studies that attempt to analyze and explain a phenomenon; frequently delivered in social scientific fields.

extended example   Multifaceted illustrations of the idea, item, or event being described, thereby getting the point across and reiterating it effectively.

external listening distraction   Anything in the environment that distracts listeners from receiving the speaker's message.

fabrication   The making up of information, such as falsifying data or experiments or claiming a source where none exists.

fact book   A reference work that includes key information on a given topic (e.g., facts about the geography, government, economy, and transportation of a given country).

facts   Documented occurrences, including actual events, dates, times, places, and people involved.

fairness   One of four "ground rules" of ethical speaking, fairness is the act of making a genuine effort to see all sides of an issue and to be open-minded.

fair use   Legal guidelines permitting the limited use of copyrighted works without permission for the purposes of scholarship, criticism, comment, news reporting, teaching, and research.

fear appeal   A persuasive appeal to audience members that deliberately arouses their fear and anxiety.

feedback   Audience response to a message, which can be conveyed both verbally and nonverbally through gestures. Feedback from the audience often indicates whether a speaker's message has been understood.

feedback loop   The continual flow of feedback between speaker and listener. A situation in which successful speakers adjust their message based on their listeners' reactions, and vice versa (also known as *circular response*).

field searching   (often called **advanced search**) A search tool in most Internet search engines that targets specific search parameters to narrow search results.

field study presentation   An oral presentation, typically delivered in the context of science-related disciplines, in which the speaker provides (1) an overview of field research, (2) the methods used in the research, (3) an analysis of research results, and (4) a time line indicating how the research results will be used to go forward.

fighting words   A speech that uses language that provokes people to violence.

figures of speech   Expressions, such as metaphors, similes, analogies, and hyperbole, in which words are used in a nonliteral fashion.

First Amendment   The amendment to the U.S. Constitution that guarantees freedom of speech ("Congress shall make no law . . . abridging the freedom of speech . . .").

fixed alternative question   A closed-ended question that contains a limited choice of answers, such as "Yes," "No," or "Sometimes."

flip chart   A large (27–34 inches) pad of paper on which a speaker can illustrate speech points.

flowchart   A diagram that shows step-by-step progression through a procedure, relationship, or process. Usually the flow of a procedure or process is drawn horizontally or vertically and describes how key components fit into a whole.

font   A set of type of one size and face.

forensic oratory   In ancient Greece, speech addressing legal matters, such as the settlement of disputes.

forum   In ancient Rome, a public space in which people gathered to deliberate about the issues of the day; see also *agora, public forum.*

free speech   The right to be free from unreasonable constraints on expression.

frequency   A count of the number of times something occurs or appears.

full-sentence transitions   Signals to listeners, in the form of declarative sentences, that the speaker is turning to another topic.

full-text database   A database in which at least some of the records contain the full text of articles.

gender   Our social and psychological sense of ourselves as males or females.

gender stereotypes   Oversimplified and often severely distorted ideas about the innate nature of men or women.

general case   See *major premise.*

general encyclopedia   A reference work that attempts to cover all important subject areas of knowledge.

general speech purpose   A declarative statement that answers the question "Why am I speaking on this topic for this particular audience and occasion?" Usually the general speech goal is to inform, to persuade, or to mark a special occasion. See also *specific speech purpose.*

generational identity   The collective cultural identity of a generation or a cohort.

graph   A graphical representation of numerical data. Graphs neatly illustrate relationships among components or units and demonstrate trends. Four major types of graphs are line graphs, bar graphs, pie graphs, and pictograms.

group activity presentation   An oral presentation that introduces students to an activity and provides them with clear directions for its completion.

groupthink   The tendency of a group to accept information and ideas without subjecting them to critical analysis. Groupthink results from strong feelings of loyalty and unity within a group and can lead to a decline in the quality of the group's decisions.

hackneyed language   Language that is poorly crafted and lacking in freshness.

handheld (or fixed) microphone   A microphone that is attached by a cord to an electrical power source.

handout   Page-size items that convey information that is either impractical to give to the audience in another manner or is intended to be kept by audience members after a presentation.

hasty generalization   A fallacy of reasoning in which the speaker attempts to support a claim by asserting that a particular piece of evidence (an isolated case) is true for all individuals or conditions concerned.

hate speech   Any offensive communication—verbal or nonverbal—directed against people's racial, ethnic, religious, gender, or other characteristics. Racist, sexist, or ageist slurs, gay bashing, and cross burnings are all forms of hate speech.

heckler's veto   Speech meant to drown out a speaker's message; such speech silences freedom of expression.

hedges   Unnecessary words and phrases that qualify or introduce doubt into statements that should be straightforward.

high-uncertainty avoidance culture   One of five "value dimensions," or major cultural patterns, that are significant across all cultures to varying degrees; identified by Geert Hofstede.

hostile audience or **one that strongly disagrees**   One of four potential types of audiences the persuasive speaker may encounter.

hyperbole   A figure of speech in which the speaker uses obvious exaggeration to drive home a point.

hypothetical example   An illustration of something that could happen in the future if certain things occurred.

identification   A feeling of commonality with another; when appropriate, effective speakers attempt to foster a sense of identification between themselves and audience members.

indentation   In an outline, the plotting of speech points to indicate their weight relative to one another; subordinate points are placed underneath and to the right of higher-order points.

individual debate format   A debate in which one person takes a side against another person.

individualistic culture   A culture that tends to emphasize personal identity and the needs of the individual rather than those of the group, upholding such values as individual achievement and decision making.

individual search engine   A search engine that compiles its own database of Web pages, such as Google or AltaVista. See also *meta-search engine*.

inductive reasoning   Reasoning from specific instances to a general condition; see also *deductive reasoning*.

information   Data set in a context for relevance.

informative speech   Public speaking that is intended to increase an audience's understanding and awareness by imparting knowledge. Informative speeches provide an audience with new information, new insights, or new ways of thinking about a topic.

inoculation effect   A theory of persuasive speaking in which a speaker anticipates and addresses counterarguments. The theory is modeled on the biological principle of inducing resistance through exposure to small quantities of a harmful substance.

integrity   The quality of being incorruptible, or able to avoid compromise for the sake of personal expediency.

intellectual property   The ownership of an individual's creative expression.

internal listening distraction   Thoughts and feelings, both positive and negative, that intrude on our attention as we attempt to listen to a speaker.

internal preview   An extended transition used within the body of a speech that alerts audience members to ensuing speech content.

internal summary   An extended transition that draws together important ideas before proceeding to another speech point.

interpersonal roles   Types of roles or styles of interacting in a group that facilitate group interaction.

interview   A type of communication conducted for the purpose of gathering information. Interviews can be conducted one-on-one or in a group.

intonation   The rising and falling of voice pitch across phrases and sentences. Intonation is what distinguishes a question from a statement.

introduction   The first part of a speech, in which the speaker establishes the speech purpose and its relevance to the audience and previews the topic and the main points.

invective   Abusive speech; accusatory and attacking speech.

invention   The classical rhetorical term for the process of selecting information to illustrate or prove speech points.

invisible Web   The portion of the Web that includes pass-protected sites, documents behind firewalls, and the contents of proprietary databases.

irony   A figure of speech in which the speaker uses humor, satire, or sarcasm to suggest a meaning other than the one that is actually being expressed.

issues-based conflict   Conflict that allows group members to test and debate ideas and potential solutions. It requires each member to ask tough questions, press for clarification, and present alternative views.

jargon   Specialized terminology developed within a given endeavor or field of study.

key-word outline   The briefest of the three forms of outlines, the key-word outline uses the smallest possible units of understanding associated with a specific point to outline the main and supporting points. See also *phrase outline* and *sentence outline*.

lavalier microphone   A microphone that attaches to a lapel or a collar.

lay audience   An audience of individuals who have no specialized knowledge of the general field related to a speaker's topic or of the topic itself.

lay testimony   Testimony by a nonexpert; a form of supporting material.

lazy speech   A poor speech habit in which the speaker fails to properly articulate words.

LCD display technology   Liquid crystal diode display technology.

learning styles   Preferred ways of processing information; one learning theory model suggests visual, aural, read/write, and kinesthetic modes of learning.

lecture   An informative speech prepared for an audience of student learners.

Library of Congress call number   An identifying number that allows the user to retrieve books and other works that have been classified according to the Library of Congress classification system.

library portal   An entry point into a large collection of research and reference information that has been selected and reviewed by librarians.

linear-active culture   A culture in which members approach tasks systematically, preferring to do things one at a time and in an orderly fashion; one of three cultural types identified by Richard D. Lewis. See also *multi-active culture* and *reactive culture*.

line graph   A type of graph used to represent trends and other information that changes over time. A line graph displays one measurement on the horizontal axis and other units of measurement or values on the vertical axis. The values or points are connected with a line.

listening   The conscious act of recognizing, understanding, and accurately interpreting the messages communicated by others.

listening distraction   Anything that competes for a listener's attention; the source of the distraction may be internal or external.

logical fallacy   A statement that is based on an invalid or deceptive line of reasoning.

logos   An appeal to the audience's reason and logic.

low-uncertainty avoidance culture   One of five "value dimensions" or major cultural patterns that are significant across all cultures to varying degrees; identified by Geert Hofstede.

main points   The key ideas or primary points intended to fulfill the speech purpose. Their function is to make claims in support of the thesis. See also *subordinate points*.

major premise   A general case; used in syllogisms and enthymemes. See also *minor premise*.

malapropism   The inadvertent use of a word or phrase in place of one that sounds like it.

Maslow's hierarchy of needs   A model of human action based on the principle that people are motivated to act on the basis of their needs.

mass communication   Communication that occurs between a speaker and a large audience of unknown people. In mass communication the receivers of the message are not present with the speaker, or they are part of such an immense crowd that there can be little or no interaction between speaker and listeners. Communication that occurs via a television or radio news broadcast or a mass rally is an example of mass communication.

mean   The sum of the scores divided by the number of scores; the arithmetic (or computed) average.

median   A type of average that represents the center-most score in a distribution; the point above and below which 50 percent of the scores fall.

memory   One of five parts of the classical canons of rhetoric; refers to the practice of the speech until it can be artfully delivered.

message   The content of the communication process — thoughts and ideas put into meaningful expressions. A message can be expressed both verbally (through the sentences and points of a speech) and nonverbally (through eye contact and gestures).

metaphor   A figure of speech used to make an implicit comparison without the use of *like* or *as* (e.g., "Love is a rose"). See also *simile*.

meta-search engine   A search engine that searches several search engines simultaneously. Examples include MetaCrawler and Dogpile. See also *individual search engine*.

methods/procedure presentation   An oral presentation describing and sometimes demonstrating an experimental or mathematical process, including the conditions under which that process can be applied; frequently delivered in scientific and mathematical fields.

minor premise   A specific case; used in syllogisms and enthymemes. See also *major premise*.

misinformation   Information that is false.

mixed audience   An audience composed of a combination of individuals, some of whom have expert knowledge of the field and topic while others have no specialized knowledge.

mixed metaphor   A metaphor that juxtaposes or compares unlike images or expressions ("Before plunging into the pool, let's walk through these steps").

mode   A type of average that represents the most frequently occurring score(s) in a distribution.

model   A three-dimensional, scale-size representation of an object such as a building.

Monroe's motivated sequence   See *motivated sequence pattern of arrangement*.

motivated sequence pattern of arrangement   A five-step process of persuasion developed by Alan Monroe.

motivational warrant   A warrant that uses the needs, desires, emotions, and values of audience members as the basis for accepting evidence in support of a claim.

multi-active culture   A culture in which members do many things at once, are people oriented, and extroverted; one of three cultural types identified by Richard D. Lewis. See also *linear-active culture* and *reactive culture*.

multimedia   A single production that combines several types of media (stills, sound, video, text, and data).

mumbling   Slurring words together at a very low level of volume and pitch so that they are barely audible.

narrative   A story; it can be based on personal experiences or imaginary incidents.

narrative pattern of arrangement   A pattern of organizing speech points so that the speech unfolds as a story, with characters, plot, setting, and vivid imagery. In practice, this pattern often is combined with other organizational patterns.

noise   Anything that interferes with the communication process between a speaker and an audience, so that the message cannot be understood; noise can derive from external sources in the environment or from internal psychological factors.

non sequitur   An argument in which the conclusion is not connected to the reasoning.

onomatopoeia   A figure of speech in which the speaker imitates natural sounds in word form in order to add vividness to a speech (e.g., "The rain dripped a steady plop, plop, plop").

open-ended question   A question designed to allow respondents to elaborate as much as possible. Open-ended questions are particularly useful for probing beliefs and opinions. They elicit more individual or personal information about audience members' thoughts and feelings. See also *closed-ended question*.

operational definition   Defining something by describing what it does (e.g., "A computer is something that processes information").

oratory   In classical terms, the art of public speaking.

organizational chart   A chart that illustrates the structure or chain of command in an organization, plotting the interrelationships among different positions, divisions, departments, and personnel.

organizational pattern   The arrangement of speech content into a specific organizational model, such as the chronological or cause-effect pattern. Different patterns produce different outcomes, depending upon the type of information contained in the speech, as well as the speaker's goals.

outlining   The physical process of plotting speech points on the page in hierarchical order of importance.

overgeneralization   An attempt to support a claim by asserting that a particular piece of evidence is true for everyone concerned.

overhead transparency   An image on a transparent background that can be viewed by transmitted light, either directly or through projection onto a screen or wall. The images may be written or printed directly onto the transparency or handwritten during the presentation.

paid inclusion   The practice of paying a fee to a search engine company for inclusion in its index of possible results, without a guarantee of ranking.

paid placement   The practice of paying a fee to a search engine company for inclusion in its search results and a guaranteed higher ranking within those results.

pandering   To identify with values that are not your own in order to win approval from an audience.

panel discussion   An oral presentation in which a group of three to nine people discuss a topic in the presence of an audience and under the direction of a moderator.

paralanguage   See *aural channel*.

parallel form   The statement of equivalent speech points in similar grammatical form and style.

parallelism   The arrangement of words, phrases, or sentences in similar grammatical and stylistic form. Parallel structure can help speakers emphasize important ideas in a speech.

paraphrase   A restatement of someone else's statements or written work that alters the form or phrasing but not the substance of that person's ideas. See also *direct quotation*.

participative leader   A leader who facilitates a group's activities and interactions in ways that will lead to a desired outcome.

patchwrite plagiarism   A form of plagiarism in which you copy material from a source and then change and rearrange occasional words and sentence structures to make it appear as if the material were your own. See also *plagiarism*.

pathos   The appeal to an audience's emotions.

pauses   Strategic elements of a speech used to enhance meaning by providing a type of punctuation emphasizing a point, drawing attention to a key thought, or allowing listeners a moment to contemplate.

percentage   The quantified portion of a whole, or 100 percent.

performance anxiety   A form of *public speaking anxiety (PSA)* that occurs the moment a speaker begins to deliver a speech. See also *preparation anxiety*.

periodical   A regularly published magazine, journal, or newspaper.

peripheral processing   A mode of processing a persuasive message that does not consider the quality of the speaker's message but is influenced by such noncontent issues as the speaker's appearance or reputation, certain slogans or one-liners, or obvious attempts to manipulate emotions. Peripheral processing of messages occurs when people lack the motivation or the ability to pay close attention to the issues.

personal-based conflict   Conflict in which group members personalize disagreements over issues, thereby wasting time, distracting the group from its mission, and impairing motivation.

personification   A figure of speech in which the speaker endows an abstract idea or inanimate object with human qualities (e.g., "Computers have become important members of our family").

persons with disabilities (PWD)   A person whose physical or mental impairment substantially limits his or her major life activities.

perspective-taking   The identification of audience members' attitudes, values, beliefs, needs, and wants and the integration of this information into the speech context.

persuasion   The process of influencing others' attitudes, beliefs, values, and behavior.

persuasive speaking   Speech whose general purpose is to effect some degree of change in the audience's beliefs, attitudes, values, or behavior.

phrase outline   A delivery outline that uses a partial construction of the sentence form of each point instead of using complete sentences that present precise wording for each point. See also *key-word outline* and *sentence outline*.

pictogram   A type of graph that illustrates comparisons in picture form. The pictures represent numerical units and are drawn to relate to the items being compared.

picture   A two-dimensional representation of people, places, ideas, or objects produced on an opaque backing; types of pictures commonly used by speakers include photographs, line drawings, diagrams, maps, and posters.

pie graph   A type of graph used to depict the division of a whole. The pie, which represents 100 percent, is divided into portions or segments called "slices." Each slice constitutes a percentage of the whole.

pitch   The range of sounds from high to low (or vice versa). Pitch is determined by the number of vibrations per unit of time; the more vibrations per unit (also called frequency), the higher the pitch, and vice versa.

plagiarism   The act of using other people's ideas or words without acknowledging the source. See also *patchwrite plagiarism* and *wholesale plagiarism*.

policy recommendation report   An oral presentation that offers recommendations for solving a problem or addressing an issue.

poster session   A format for the visual presentation of posters, arranged on freestanding boards, that contains the concise display of a study or an issue for viewing by participants at professional conferences. The speaker prepares brief remarks and remains on hand to answer questions as needed.

power distance   As developed by Geert Hofstede, a measure of the extent to which a culture values social equality versus tradition and authority.

preparation anxiety   A form of *public speaking anxiety* (PSA) that arises when the speaker begins to prepare for a speech, at which point he or she might feel overwhelmed at the amount of time and planning required. See also *performance anxiety*.

pre-performance anxiety   A form of *public speaking anxiety* (PSA) that occurs when the speaker begins to rehearse a speech.

pre-preparation anxiety   A form of *public speaking anxiety* (PSA) that occurs the moment speakers learn they must give a speech.

presentation aids   Objects, models, pictures, graphs, charts, video, audio, and multimedia, used alone or in combination within the context of a speech; such aids help listeners see relationships among concepts and elements, store and remember material, and critically examine key ideas.

presentational speaking   Reports delivered by individuals or groups within a business or professional environment.

preview statement   A statement included in the introduction of a speech in which the speaker identifies the main speech points that will be covered in the body of the speech.

primary research   Original or firsthand research, such as interviews and surveys conducted by the speaker. See also *secondary research*.

problem-cause-solution pattern of arrangement   A pattern of organizing speech points so that they demonstrate (1) the nature of the problem, (2) reasons for the problem, (3) unsatisfactory solutions, and (4) proposed solutions.

problem-solution pattern of arrangement   A pattern of organizing speech points so that they demonstrate the nature and significance of a problem first, and then provide justification for a proposed solution.

productive conflict   A form of group conflict in which questions are clarified, ideas are challenged, counterexamples are presented, worst-case scenarios are considered, and proposals are reformulated.

progress report   A report that updates clients or principals on developments in an ongoing project.

pronunciation   The formation of word sounds.

prop   Any live or inanimate object used by a speaker as a presentation aid.

propaganda   Information represented in such a way as to provoke a desired response.

proposal   A type of business or professional presentation in which the speaker provides information needed for decisions related to modifying or adopting a product, procedure, or policy.

prototype   A physical model of a design.

public domain   Bodies of work, including publications and processes, available for public use without permission; not protected by copyright or patent.

public forum   Any physical or virtual space in which people gather to voice their ideas about public issues.

public speaking   A type of communication in which the speaker delivers a message with a specific purpose to an audience of people who are physically present during the delivery of the speech. Public speaking always includes a speaker who has a reason for speaking, an audience that gives the speaker its attention, and a message that is meant to accomplish a purpose.

public speaking anxiety (PSA)   Fear or anxiety associated with a speaker's actual or anticipated communication to an audience.

qualitative research   Research with an emphasis on statistical measurement.

quantitative research   Research with an emphasis on observing, describing, and interpreting behavior.

questionnaire   A written survey designed to gather information from a large pool of respondents. Questionnaires consist of a mix of *open-* and *closed-ended questions* designed to elicit information.

reactive culture   A culture in which members rarely initiate discussions or actions, preferring to listen to what others have to say first; one of three cultural types identified by Richard D. Lewis. See also *linear-active culture* and *multi-active culture*.

reasoning   Drawing inferences or conclusions from the evidence the speaker presents.

receiver   The recipient (an individual or a group) of a source's message.

reckless disregard for the truth   A quality of defamatory speech that is legally liable. See also *defamatory statement*.

red herring fallacy   A fallacy of reasoning in which the speaker relies on irrelevant information to support an argument.

reference librarian   A librarian trained to help library users locate information resources.

refutation pattern of arrangement   A pattern of organizing speech points in which each main point addresses and then refutes (disproves) an opposing claim to the speaker's position.

request for funding presentation   An oral presentation that provides evidence that a project, proposal, or design idea is worth funding; it is frequently delivered in such technical fields as engineering, computer science, and architecture.

research overview presentation   A type of oral presentation in which the speaker provides the context and the background for a research question or hypothesis that will form the basis of an impending undertaking; it is typically delivered within the context of scientific and mathematical disciplines.

research presentation (oral scientific presentation)   An oral presentation describing original research undertaken by the speaker, either alone or as part of a team; it is frequently delivered in scientific and social scientific fields.

respect   To feel or show deferential regard. For the ethical speaker, respect ranges from addressing audience members as unique human beings to refraining from rudeness and other forms of personal attack.

responsibility   A charge, trust, or duty for which one is accountable.

restate-forecast form   A type of transition in which the speaker restates the point just covered and previews the point to be covered next.

review of academic article   Oral presentation in which the speaker reports on an article or study published in a scholarly journal.

review of the literature presentation   An oral presentation in which the speaker reviews the body of research related to a given topic or issue and offers conclusions about the topic based on this research; it is frequently delivered in social scientific fields.

rhetoric   The practice of oratory, or public speaking.

rhetorical device   A technique of language to achieve a desired effect.

rhetorical proof   In classical terms, a means of persuasion (*ethos, pathos, logos*).

rhetorical question   A question that does not invite an actual response but is used to make the audience think.

rhetorical situation   The circumstances that call for a public response; in broadest terms, consideration of the audience, occasion, and overall speech situation when planning a speech.

roast   A humorous tribute to a person, one in which a series of speakers jokingly poke fun at the individual being honored.

roman numeral outline   An outline format in which main points are enumerated with roman numerals (I, II, III), supporting points with capital letters (A, B, C), third-level points with arabic numerals (1, 2, 3), and fourth-level points with lowercase letters (a, b, c).

rules of engagement   Standard of conduct for communicating with others in the public arena, including speaking the truth, listening, and responding coherently.

sales presentation   A presentation that attempts to persuade a potential buyer to purchase a service or product described by the presenter.

sans serif typeface   Typefaces that are blocklike and linear and are designed without tiny strokes or flourishes at the top or bottom of each letter. See also *serif typeface*.

scale question   Also called an "attitude scale," a closed-ended question that measures the respondent's level of agreement or disagreement with specific issues.

scanning   A technique for creating eye contact with large audiences; speakers move their gaze across the audience from one listener to another and from one section to another, pausing as they do so to gaze briefly at individual listeners.

search engine   Using powerful software programs, a search engine scans millions of Web documents that contain the keywords and phrases you command it to search. A program then creates a huge index from the Web pages that have been read, compares it with your search request, and returns matching results to you, usually in order of relevance.

secondary research   The vast world of information gathered by others; can include published facts and statistics, texts, documents, and any other information not originally collected and generated by the researcher. See also *primary research*.

selective perception   A psychological principle that posits that listeners pay attention selectively to certain messages and ignore others.

sentence outline   An outline in which each main and supporting point is stated in sentence form and in precisely the way the speaker wants to express the idea. Generally, sentence outlines are used for working outlines. See also *key-word outline* and *phrase outline*.

serif typeface   Typefaces that include small flourishes, or strokes, at the top and bottom of each letter. See also *sans serif typeface*.

sermon   A speech of inspiration given in a religious context.

sexist language   Language that oversimplifies or distorts ideas about the innate nature of what it means to be male or female. For example the generic use of the pronoun *he* or *she*.

sexist pronoun   A pronoun that is used restrictively to refer to one or the other gender when the antecedent may in fact be either male or female.

shared meaning   The mutual understanding of a message between speaker and audience. Shared meaning occurs in varying degrees. The lowest level of shared meaning exists when the speaker has merely caught the audience's attention. As the message develops, depending on the encoding choices made by the source, a higher degree of shared meaning is possible.

shift report   An oral report prepared by health-care workers that concisely relays patient status and needs to incoming caregivers.

signposts   Conjunctions or phrases (such as "Next," "First," "Second," and so forth) that indicate *transitions* between supporting points.

simile   A figure of speech used to compare one thing with another by using the word *like* or *as* (e.g., "He works *like* a dog"). See also *metaphor*.

slander   Defamatory speech.

slippery slope   An argument based on a faulty assumption that one case will necessarily lead to a series of events or actions.

small group   A group that consists of between three and twenty people as opposed to a large public audience.

small group communication   Communication involving a small number of people who can see and speak directly with one another, as in a business meeting.

social agenda–setting   In a special occasion speech, a type of speech purpose whose goal is to focus on a social/political issue and reinforce a message that relates to it.

socioeconomic status (SES)   A cluster of demographic characteristics of audience members, including income, occupation, and education.

sound bite   A succinct statement that summarizes key points in twenty seconds or less.

source   The source, or sender, is the person who creates a message. The speaker transforms ideas and thoughts into messages and sends them to a receiver, or an audience.

spatial pattern of arrangement   A pattern of organizing main points in order of their physical proximity or direction relative to each other; it is used when the purpose of a speech is to describe or explain the physical arrangement of a place, a scene, or an object.

speaking extemporaneously   A type of delivery that falls somewhere between impromptu and written or memorized deliveries. Speakers delivering an extemporaneous speech prepare well and practice in advance, giving full attention to all facets of the speech — content, arrangement, and delivery. Instead of memorizing or writing the speech word for word, they speak from a *key-word outline* or *phrase outline*.

speaking from manuscript   A style of delivery in which the speaker reads the speech verbatim — that is, from a prepared written text (either on paper or on a TelePrompTer) containing the entire speech.

speaking from memory   A type of delivery in which the speaker puts the entire speech, word for word, into writing and then commits it to memory.

speaking impromptu   A type of delivery that is unpracticed, spontaneous, or improvised.

speaking outline   A delivery outline to be used when practicing and actually presenting a speech.

speaking rate   The pace at which a speech is delivered. The typical public speech occurs at a rate slightly below 120 words per minute.

specialized encyclopedia   A reference work that delves deeply into one subject area, such as religion, science, art, sports, or engineering.

specialized search engine   A search engine that searches for information only on specific topics.

special occasion speech   A speech whose general purpose is to entertain, celebrate, commemorate, inspire, or set a social agenda.

specific case   See *minor premise*.

specific speech purpose   A refined statement of purpose that zeroes in more closely than the general purpose on the goal of the speech. See also *general speech purpose*.

speculative claim   A type of *claim of fact* that addresses questions for which answers are not yet available.

speech of acceptance   A speech made in response to receiving an award. Its purpose is to express gratitude for the honor bestowed on the speaker.

speech of inspiration   A speech whose purpose is to inspire or motivate the audience to positively consider, reflect on, and sometimes even act on the speaker's words.

speech of introduction   A short speech defined by two goals: to prepare or "warm up" audience members for the main speaker and to motivate them to listen to what that speaker has to say.

speech of presentation   A speech whose purpose is twofold: to communicate the meaning of an award and to explain why the recipient is receiving it.

staff report   A report that informs managers and other employees of new developments relating to personnel that affect them and their work.

statistic   Quantified evidence; data that measures the size or magnitude of something, demonstrates trends, or shows relationships with the purpose of summarizing information, demonstrating proof, and making points memorable.

stereotype   A generalization about an apparent characteristic of a group, culture, or ethnicity that falsely claims to define all of its members.

story   See *narrative*.

style   The speaker's choice of words and sentence structure.

subject (Web) directory   A searchable database of Web sites organized by categories (e.g., Yahoo! Directory).

subordinate points   The alignment of points within a speech outline that have somewhat lesser weight than main points; they provide support for or extend the more central ideas or *main points*.

substantive warrant   A warrant that relies on factual evidence to link a claim to evidence. See also *warrant by analogy, warrant by cause,* and *warrant by sign*.

supporting points   Information (examples, narratives, testimony, and facts and statistics) that clarifies, elaborates, and verifies the speaker's assertions.

syllogism   A form of rational appeal defined as a three-part argument consisting of a major premise or general case, a minor premise or specific case, and a conclusion. See also *deductive reasoning*.

sympathetic audience   An audience that already shares much agreement with the speaker; one of four types of potential audiences that persuasive speakers may encounter.

symposium   A formal meeting at which several speakers deliver short speeches on the same topic.

table   A systematic grouping of data or numerical information in column format.

tag questions   Unnecessary questions appended to statements or commands; the use of such weak language undermines a speaker's authority.

talking head   A speaker who remains static, standing stiffly behind a podium, and so resembles a televised shot of a speaker's head and shoulders.

target audience   Those individuals within the broader audience who are most likely to be influenced in the direction the speaker seeks.

task roles   Types of roles that directly relate to the accomplishment of the objectives and missions of a group. Recording secretary and moderator are examples of task roles.

team debate format   A debate in which multiple people take sides against another team, with each person on the team assuming a speaking role.

team presentation   An oral presentation prepared and delivered by a group of three or more people.

TelePrompter   A device that contains a magnified script of a speech; it is commonly used when a speaker's remarks are televised.

testimony   Firsthand findings, eyewitness accounts, and opinions by people, both lay (nonexpert) and expert.

thesis statement   The theme, or central idea, of a speech that serves to connect all the parts of the speech. The main points, the supporting material, and the conclusion all relate to the thesis.

tilde (~)   A symbol that appears in the domain of a Web address; it usually indicates a personal page rather than an institutional Web site.

toast   A brief tribute to a person or an event being celebrated.

topic   What the speech is about; a topic may be assigned to the speaker, or the speaker may have to choose one based on personal interests, experience, and knowledge.

topical pattern of arrangement (also called *categorical pattern*)   A pattern of organizing main points as subtopics or categories of the speech topic; of all organizational patterns, this one offers the most freedom to structure speech points as desired.

topic map   A brainstorming technique in which you lay out the words in diagram form to show categorical relationships among them; it is useful for selecting and narrowing a speech topic.

transitions   Words, phrases, or sentences that tie speech ideas together and enable a speaker to move smoothly from one point to the next.

triad   A rhetorical device that makes use of three parallel elements.

trustworthiness   The quality of displaying both honesty and dependability.

typeface   An assortment or set of type or characters(fonts) all of one style and sometimes one size (called the "point size"). Typefaces come in a variety of lettering styles, such as Arial, Times Roman, or Courier.

uncertainty avoidance   The extent to which people feel threatened by ambiguity.

understatement   A figure of speech in which a speaker draws attention to an idea by minimizing its importance (e.g., "Flunking out of college might be a problem").

uninformed, less educated, or **apathetic audience**   An audience that knows or cares little about a specific topic.

unity   The quality of a speech in which only those points that are implied by the purpose and thesis statements are included. Nothing is extraneous or tangential. Each main point supports the thesis, and each supporting point provides evidence for the main points.

U.S. Government Printing Office (GPO)   Responsible for publishing and distributing all information collected and produced by federal agencies, from the Census Bureau to the Department of Education and the Environmental Protection Agency. GPO publications also include all congressional reports and hearings.

valid generalization   A generalization that is supported by different types of evidence from different sources and that does not make claims beyond a reasonable point.

values   Our most enduring judgments or standards of what's important to us (e.g., equal opportunity, democracy, change and progress, or perseverance).

video   Presentation aids (including movies, television programs, and other recording segments) that combine sight, sound, and movement to illustrate key speech concepts.

videoconference   Synchronized visual and audio communication between two or more remote locations.

virtual group   A group in which members who are physically dispersed interact and exchange ideas through mediated communication such as e-mail and *videoconferencing*.

virtual library   A collection of library holdings available online.

visual channel   A nonverbal channel of communication that includes the speaker's physical actions and appearance—facial expressions, gestures, general body movement, physical appearance, dress, and objects held.

visualization   An exercise for building confidence in which the speaker closes his or her eyes and envisions a series of positive feelings and reactions that will occur on the day of the speech.

vocal fillers   Unnecessary and undesirable phrases or utterances that are used to cover pauses, such as "uh," "hmm," "you know," "I mean," and "it's like."

vocal variety   The variation of volume, pitch, rate, and pauses to create an effective delivery.

volume   The relative loudness of a speaker's voice while giving a speech.

warrant   A core component of an argument that serves to justify the link made between the claim and the evidence.

warrant by analogy   A statement, based on the comparison of two similar cases, that infers that what is true in one case is true in the other. The assumption is that the characteristics of case *A* and case *B* are so similar, if not the same, that what is true for *B* must also be true for *A*.

warrant by cause   The provision of a cause-effect relationship as proof of a claim.

warrant by sign   A statement based on an inference that such a close relationship exists between two variables that the presence or absence of one may be taken as an indication of the presence or absence of the other (e.g., smoke is a sign of fire).

wholesale plagiarism   A form of plagiarism in which you "cut and paste" material from print or online sources into your speech and represent that material as your own. See also *plagiarism*.

word association   A *brainstorming* technique in which you write down ideas as they occur to you, beginning with a single word, in order to generate and narrow speech topics.

working bibliography   An in-process list of source materials used to support the claims made in a speech.

working outline   A preparation or rough outline that refines and finalizes the *specific speech purpose*, firms up and organizes *main points*, and develops *supporting material*.

World Wide Web   The most frequently used portion of the Internet, the Web is a graphics-rich environment of electronic pages or documents that contain text, graphics, sound, video, and—its most distinguishing feature—hyperlinks.

Notes

Chapter 1

1. Peter D. Hart Research Associates, "How Should Colleges Prepare Students to Succeed in Today's Global Economy?" (survey conducted on behalf of the Association of American Colleges and Universities, 2006). D. Uchida, M. J. Cetron, and F. McKenzie, "What Students Must Know to Succeed in the Twenty-first Century" (special report by the World Future Society based on "Preparing Students for the Twenty-first Century," a report on a project by the American Association of School Administrators, 1996).
2. W. Barnett Pearce, "Toward a National Conversation about Public Issues," in *The Changing Conversation in America: Lectures from the Smithsonian*, ed. William F. Eadie and Paul E. Nelson (Thousand Oaks, Calif.: Sage, 2002), 16.
3. Daniel Yankelovich, *Coming to Public Judgment: Making Democracy Work in a Complex World* (Syracuse, N.Y.: Syracuse University Press, 1991).
4. "Who Votes, Who Doesn't, and Why," Pew Research Center for the People and the Press Web site, October 18, 2006, http://people-press.org/reports/display.php3?ReportID=292 (accessed June 29, 2007).
5. Rebecca Rimel, "Policy and the Partisan Divide: The Price of Gridlock" (speech given at the Commonwealth Club in San Francisco, November 2004), Pew Charitable Trusts Web site www.pewtrusts.com/ideas/ideas_item.cfm?content_item_id=2763&content_type_id=19&issue_name=Global%20warming&issue=19&page=19&name=Speeches (accessed May 10, 2007).
6. For a discussion of Daniel Yankelovich's 3-step process by which public judgments occur, see Yankelovich, *Coming to Public Judgment.*
7. For a discussion of conversation stoppers and rules of engagement, see Pearce, "Toward a National Conversation."
8. James L. Golden, Goodwin F. Berquist, William E. Coleman, and J. Michael Sproule, *The Rhetoric of Western Thought: From the Mediterranean World to the Global Setting,* 8th ed. (Dubuque, Iowa: Kendall/Hunt, 2003), 37–43.
9. *Compton's Online Encyclopedia,* s.v. "public speaking," http://www.comptons.com/encyclopedia (accessed June 10, 2000).
10. The scholarly basis for this model is an integration of rhetorical theory (Aristotle), information theory (Shannon and Weaver), semantics (Ogden and Richards), and systems theory (Bertalonffy). Taken together, these important concepts allow us to view communication as a highly interactive yet holistic process.
11. Lloyd F. Bitzer, "The Rhetorical Situation," *Philosophy and Rhetoric* 1 (Winter 1968): 1–14.
12. Robert Perrin, "The Speaking-Writing Connection: Enhancing the Symbiotic Relationship," *Contemporary Education* 65 (1994): 62–64.
13. James Henslin, *Sociology: A Down-to-Earth Approach,* 8th ed. (Boston: Pearson, 2007), 36–37.
14. David C. Thomas and Kerr Inkson, *Cultural Intelligence: People Skills for a Global Business* (San Francisco: Berrett-Koehler Publishers, 2004), 14.
15. Ibid., 14.

Chapter 3

1. James C. McCroskey, "Classroom Consequences of Communication Anxiety," *Communication Education* 26 (1977): 27–33; James C. McCroskey, "Oral Communication Apprehension: A Reconceptualization," in *Communication Yearbook 6,* ed. M. Burgoon (Beverly Hills: Sage, 1982), 136–170; Virginia P. Richmond and James C. McCroskey, *Communication Apprehension, Avoidance, and Effectiveness,* 5th ed. (Boston: Allyn & Bacon, 1998).

2. See, for example, M. J. Beatty "Situational and Predispositional Correlates of Public Speaking Anxiety," *Communication Education* 37 (1988): 28–39.

3. Adapted from James C. McCroskey, "Oral Communication Apprehension: A Summary of Recent Theory and Research," *Human Communication Research* 4 (1977): 79–96.

4. K. Weisul, "Does Giving a Speech Spook Women More?" *Business Week,* April 8, 2002.

5. R. Behnke and C. R. Sawyer, "Anticipatory Anxiety Patterns for Male and Female Public Speakers," *Communication Education* 49 (2000): 187–95.

6. Adapted from S. Tobia, "Anxiety and Cognitive Processes of Instruction," in *Self-Related Cognitions in Anxiety and Motivation,* ed. Ralf Schwarzer (Hillsdale, N.J.: Lawrence Erlbaum, 1986): 35–54.

7. R. Behnke, C. R. Sawyer, and R. Chris, "Milestones of Anticipatory Public Speaking Anxiety," *Communication Education* 48 (April 1999): 165–72.

8. Ibid.

9. David-Paul Pertaub, Mel Slater, and Chris Barker, "An Experiment on Public Speaking Anxiety in Response to Three Different Types of Virtual Audience," *Presence: Teleoperators and Virtual Environments* 11 (2002): 670–78.

10. Lenny Laskowski, "Overcoming Speaking Anxiety in Meetings and Presentations," Speakers Platform Web site, http://www.speaking.com/articles_html/ LennyLaskowski_532.html (accessed July 26, 2007).

11. John Robert Colombo, "Speech Anxiety: Overcoming the Fear of Public Speaking," SpeechCoachforExecutives.com, http://www.speechcoachforexecutives.com/ speech_anxiety.html (accessed July 25, 2007).

12. Ibid.

13. Joe Ayres, "Coping with Speech Anxiety: The Power of Positive Thinking," *Communication Education* 37 (1988): 289–96; Joe Ayres, "An Examination of the Impact of Anticipated Communication and Communication Apprehension on Negative Thinking, Task-Relevant Thinking, and Recall," *Communication Research Reports* 9 (1992): 3–11.

14. Pamela J. Feldman, Sheldon Cohen, Natalie Hamrick, and Stephen J. Lepore, "Psychological Stress Appraisal, Emotion, and Cardiovascular Response in a Public Speaking Task," *Psychology and Health* 19 (2004): 353–68; S. Hus, S. Romans-Kroll, and Joung-Min, "Effects of Positive Attitude toward Giving a Speech on Cardiovascular and Subjective Fear Responses during Speech on Anxious Subjects," *Perceptual and Motor Skills* 81 (1995): 609–10.

15. M. T. Motley, "Public Speaking Anxiety qua Performance Anxiety: A Revised Model and Alternative Therapy," *Journal of Social Behavior and Personality* 5 (1990): 85–104.

16. Elizabeth Quinn, "Visualization in Sport: Imagery Can Improve Performance," About.com: Sports Medicine, http://sportsmedicine.about.com/cs/sport_psych/a/ aa091700a.htm (accessed August 29, 2007).

17. Joe Ayres, C. S. Hsu, and Tim Hopf, "Does Exposure to Visualization Alter Speech Preparation Processes?" *Communication Research Reports* 17 (2000): 366–74.

18. Quinn, "Visualization in Sport."

19. Joe Ayres and Tim Hopf, "Visualization: Is It More Than Extra Attention?" *Communication Education* 38 (1989): 1–5; Joe Ayers and Tim Hopf, *Coping with Speech Anxiety* (Norwood, N.J.: Ablex, 1993).

20. Ayres and Hopf, "Visualization," 2–3.

21. Laurie Schloff and Marcia Yudkin, *Smart Speaking* (New York: Plume, 1991).

22. Mayo Clinic Staff, "Relaxation Techniques: Learn Ways to Calm Your Stress," MayoClinic.com, http://www.mayoclinic.com/health/relaxation-technique/SR00007 (accessed August 29, 2007).

23. Lars-Gunnar Lundh, Britta Berg, Helena Johansson, Linda Kjellén Nilsson, Jenny Sandberg, and Anna Segerstedt, "Social Anxiety Is Associated with a Negatively Distorted Perception of One's Own Voice," *Cognitive Behavior Therapy* 31 (2002): 25–30.

Chapter 4

1. M. Burley-Allen, *Listening: The Forgotten Skill: A Self-Teaching Guide* (New York: Wiley, 1995); M. G. Eskaros, "Fine-Tune Your Listening Skills," *Hydrocarbon Processing* 83 (2004).

2. H. E. Chambers, *Effective Communication Skills for Scientific and Technical Professionals* (Cambridge: Perseus Publishing, 2001).

3. Andrew Wolvin and C. Coakley, *Listening,* 4th ed. (Dubuque, Iowa: Brown, 1992).

4. Philip Vassallo, "Dialogue: Speaking to Listen: Listening to Speak," *ETC* (Fall 2000): 306–13.

5. Ronald D. Gordon, "Communication, Dialogue, and Transformation," *Human Communication* 9, no. 1 (2006): 17–30.

6. Ibid.

7. S. Golen, "A Factor Analysis of Barriers to Effective Listening," *Journal of Business Communication* 27 (1990): 25–36.

8. Thomas E. Anastasi Jr., *Listen! Techniques for Improving Communication Skills* (Boston: CBI Publishing, 1982).

9. Ibid.

10. Carole Wade and Carol Tavris, *Psychology,* 4th ed. (New York: HarperCollins, 1996), 31–35.

11. Ron Hoff, *I Can See You Naked,* rev. ed. (Kansas City, Mo.: Andrews McMeel, 1992), 300–301.

Chapter 5

1. Michael Josephson, interview by author, May 10, 1996.

2. *The Compact Edition of the Oxford English Dictionary,* 1971 ed., 2514.

3. Cited in Edward P. J. Corbett, *Classical Rhetoric for the Modern Student* (New York: Oxford University Press, 1990).

4. Dominic A. Infante, Andrew S. Rancer, and Deanna F. Womack, *Building Communication Theory,* 3rd ed. (Prospect Heights, Ill.: Waveland Press, 1997).

5. Rebecca Rimel, "Policy and the Partisan Divide: The Price of Gridlock" (speech delivered at the Commonwealth Club in San Francisco, November 2004), Pew Charitable Trusts Web site (accessed May 10, 2007).

6. For an excellent discussion of the tension between these two rights, see Douglas M. Fraleigh and Joseph S. Tuman, *Freedom of Speech in the Marketplace of Ideas* (New York: Bedford/St. Martins, 1997).

7. David L. Hudson, "Fighting Words," First Amendment Center Web site, firstamendmentcenter .org/Speech/arts/topic.aspc?topic=fighting_words (accessed May 20, 2007).

8. Steven E. Gillen, "Rights Clearance and Permissions Guidelines" (paper prepared by the law firm Greenebaum, Doll, and McDonald, Cincinnati, 2002).

9. Ann Coulter, *Godless: The Church of Liberalism* (New York: Crown Forum, 2006.)

10. W. Barnett Pearce, "Toward a National Conversation about Public Issues," in *The Changing Conversation in America: Lectures from the Smithsonian,* ed. William F. Eadie and Paul E. Nelson (Thousand Oaks, Calif.: Sage, 2002), 16.

11. W. Gudykunst, S. Ting-Toomey, S. Suweeks, and L. Stewart, *Building Bridges: Interpersonal Skills for a Changing World* (Boston: Houghton Mifflin, 1995), 92.

12. Ibid.

13. Josephson, interview.

14. Louis A. Day, *Ethics in Media Communications: Cases and Controversies,* 2nd ed. (Belmont, Calif.: Wadsworth, 1997).

15. Josephson, interview.
16. "President Tobin to Step Down," Hamilton College Web site, October 2, 2002, http://www.hamilton.edu/news (accessed February 10, 2005).
17. Rebecca Moore Howard, "A Plagiarism Pentimento," *Journal of Teaching Writing* 11 (1993): 233.
18. With thanks to Keith Perry, Department of Humanities, Abraham Baldwin Agricultural College.
19. "How to Recognize Plagiarism." Indiana University Bloomington School of Education Web site, http://www.indiana.edu (accessed June 16, 2002).
20. Skyscraper Museum Web site, http://www.skyscraper.org (accessed June 26, 2002).
21. U.S. Copyright Office Web site, www.copyright.gov (accessed January 11, 2006).
22. Gillen, "Rights Clearance."
23. U.S. Copyright Office Web site, section on fair use, http://www.copyright.gov/fls/fl102.html (accessed February 19, 2005).
24. Gillen, "Rights Clearance."

Chapter 6

1. James C. McCroskey, Virginia P. Richmond, and Robert A. Stewart, *One-on-One: The Foundations of Interpersonal Communication* (Englewood Cliffs, N.J.: Prentice-Hall, 1986).
2. Daniel O'Keefe notes that while attitudes and behavior are "generally consistent," there are "a large number of possible moderating variables," including the relative demands of the behavior, whether there is a vested position, and others. Daniel J. O'Keefe, *Persuasion: Theory and Research,* 2nd ed. (Thousand Oaks, Calif.: Sage, 2002), 17.
3. McCroskey, Richmond, and Stewart, *One-on-One.*
4. E. D. Steele and W. C. Redding, "The American Value System: Premises for Persuasion," *Western Speech* 26 (1962): 83–91; Robin M. Williams Jr., *American Society: A Sociological Interpretation,* 3rd ed. (New York: Alfred A. Knopf, 1970).
5. Inter-University Consortium for Political and Social Research, *World Values Survey, 1981–1984 and 1990–1993* (Irvine: Social Science Data Archives, University Libraries, University of California, 1997).
6. "Crafting a Communications Project," Biodiversity Project, March 2003, www.biodiversityproject.org/EF%20Kit/EFCraftingcommunication (accessed July 10, 2007).
7. Ibid.
8. Kenneth Burke, *A Rhetoric of Motives* (Berkeley: University of California Press, 1969).
9. Hillary Rodham Clinton, "Abortion Is a Tragedy," *Vital Speeches of the Day* 71, no. 9 (2005): 266–70.
10. Ann Neville Miller, "An Exploration of Kenyan Public Speaking Patterns with Implications for the American Introductory Public Speaking Course," *Communication Education* 51, no. 2 (2002): 168–82.
11. "Community College Statistics," American Association of Community Colleges Web site, http://www2.aacc.nche.edu/research/index.htm (accessed May 20, 2007).
12. J. G. Melton, *Encyclopedia of American Religions,* 7th ed. (Detroit: Gale Research, 2002).
13. Daniel Canary and K. Dindia, eds., *Sex Differences and Similarities in Communication* (Mahwah, N.J.: Lawrence Erlbaum, 1998).
14. "Facts for Features," *Newsroom,* U.S. Census Bureau Web site, May 29, 2007, http://www.census.gov/Press-Release/www/releases/archives/facts_for_features_special_editions/010102.html (accessed June 5, 2007).
15. "Foreign-Born Population by Sex, Age, and World Region of Birth 2003," *Foreign-Born Population of the United States American Community Survey — 2003 Special Tabulation (ACS-T-2),* Table 3.1a, U.S. Census Bureau Web site, http://www.census.gov/population/www/socdemo/foreign/acst2.html (accessed June 5 2007).
16. Richard D. Lewis, *When Cultures Collide: Leading across Cultures,* 3rd ed. (Boston: Intercultural Press-Nicholas Brealey International, 2005), p 27.

17. Geert Hofstede, *Culture's Consequences: International Differences in Work-Related Values* (Beverly Hills: Sage, 1980). Adapted from a discussion in Larry A. Samovar, Richard E. Porter, and Lisa A. Stefani, *Communication between Cultures* (Belmont, Calif.: Wadsworth, 1998).
18. Lewis, *When Cultures Collide*, 27.
19. Samovar, Porter, and Stefani, *Communication between Cultures*.
20. Rushworth M. Kidder, *Shared Values for a Troubled World: Conversations with Men and Women of Conscience* (San Francisco: Jossey-Bass Publishers, 1994).

Chapter 8

1. Rodney Reynolds and Michael Burgoon, "Evidence," in *The Persuasion Handbook: Developments in Theory and Practice,* ed. J. P. Dillard and M. Pfau (Thousand Oaks, Calif.: Sage, 2002), 427–44.
2. Ibid.
3. Barrington D. Parker, "International Exodus: Visa Delays and Denials," *Vital Speeches of the Day* 70, no. 19 (2004): 583–87.
4. Risa Lavizzo-Mourey, "Childhood Obesity: The Killer Threat Within," *Vital Speeches of the Day* 70, no. 13 (2004): 396–400.
5. Quoted in K. Q. Seelye, "Congressman Offers Bill to Ban Cloning of Humans," *New York Times,* March 6, 1997, sec. A.
6. Mark Turner, *The Literary Mind* (New York: Oxford University Press, 1996).
7. Ibid.
8. Helen Zia (speech delivered to the annual convention of the Asian American Journalists Association), reprinted in *Voices of Multicultural America: Notable Speeches Delivered by African, Asian, Hispanic, and Native Americans, 1790-1995,* ed. Deborah Straub (New York: Gale Research, 1996).
9. Brock Evans, "A Gift for All of America" (address delivered to the biennial session of the Wyoming Conservation Congress, Casper, Wyo., July 10, 1999), http://www.votd.com/evans.htm (accessed May 1, 2000).
10. Testimony of Derek P. Ellerman to Subcommittee on Human Rights and Wellness, Committee on Government Reform, U.S. House of Representatives, July 8, 2004, Polaris Project, http://www.polarisproject.org/polarisproject/news_p3/DPETestimony_p3.htm (accessed March 15, 2005).
11. J. C. Reinard, *Foundations of Argument* (Dubuque, Iowa: William C. Brown, 1991).
12. Steve Jobs (keynote address delivered at Worldwide Developers Conference, San Francisco's Moscone West, June 11, 2007).
13. U.S. Census Bureau American Factfinder, *Profile of General Demographic Characteristics 2000, Geographic Area Colorado,* http://factfinder.census.gov/servlet/QTTable?_bm=n&_lang=en&qr_name=DEC_2000_SF1_U_DP1&ds_name=DEC_2000_SF1_U&geo_id=04000US08.
14. Sara Kehaulani Goo, "Airbus Hopes Big Plane Will Take Off, Beat Boeing," *Washington Post,* December 19, 2004, http://www.washingtonpost.com/wp-dyn/articles/A9900-2004Dec18.html (accessed May 13, 2005).
15. Centers for Disease Control and Prevention, "Births to Youngest Teens at Lowest Levels in Almost 60 Years," http://www.cdc.gov/od/oc/media/pressrel/r041115.htm (accessed May 13, 2005).
16. Bureau of Transportation Statistics, "Airlines On-Time Performance in April Better Than March but Slips from Previous Year," June 4, 2007, www.bts.gov/press_releases/2007/dot055_07/html/dot055_07.html (accessed June 4, 2007).
17. Center on Budget and Policy Priorities, "Behind the Numbers: An Examination of the Tax Foundation's Tax Day Report," April 14, 1997, http://www.cbpp.org/taxday.htm (accessed June 7, 2005).
18. Data from Centers for Disease Control and Prevention, "Youth Risk Behavior Surveillance—United States, 2003," *Morbidity and Mortality Weekly Report,* May 21, 2004, 1–96, http://www.cdc.gov/mmwr/preview/mmwrhtml/ss5302a1.htm (accessed February 3, 2005).

19. Roger Pielke Jr., "The Cherry Pick," *Ogmius: Newsletter for the Center for Science and Technology Research* 8 (May 2004), http://sciencepolicy.colorado.edu/ogmius/archives/issue_8/index.html (accessed May 24, 2005).
20. Ibid.
21. Ralph Underwager and Hollida Wakefield, "The Taint Hearing," *IPT*, 10 (1998). Originally presented at the 13th Annual Symposium in Forensic Psychology, Vancouver, British Columbia, April 17, 1997, www.ipt-forensics.com/journal/volume10/j10_7.htm#en0 (accessed September 1, 2007).

Chapter 9

1. James C. McCroskey, *An Introduction to Rhetorical Communication*, 8th ed. (Boston: Allyn and Bacon, 2001), makes this point throughout his text, and particularly on pages 188–89.
2. Jennifer Keohane, reference librarian, Simsbury Public Library, conversation with author, Simsbury, Conn., June 23, 2002.
3. Robert G. Torricelli, *Quotations for Public Speakers: A Historical, Literary, and Political Anthology* (New Brunswick, N.J.: Rutgers University Press, 2002).
4. Robert J. Morgan, *Nelson's Complete Book of Stories, Illustrations, and Quotes: The Ultimate Contemporary Resource for Speakers* (Nashville, Tenn.: Thomas Nelson, 2000).
5. "The Art of Asking Questions," Poynteronline, http://www.poynter.org/content (accessed January 11, 2006).

Chapter 10

1. Barbara Burg et al., "Writing with Internet Sources," Lamont Library of the Harvard College Library Web site, http://hcl.harvard.edu/lamont/resources/guides (accessed July 17, 2007); Susan Gilroy, "The Web in Context: Virtual Library or Virtual Chaos?" Lamont Library of the Harvard College Library Web site, http://hcl.harvard.edu/lamont/resources/guides (accessed May 5, 2005).
2. Harvard College Library, "Evaluating Web Sites," October 5, 2005, hcl.harvard.edu/research/guides/evaluatingweb/index.html (accessed July 12, 2007); Sandra Kerka, "Myths and Realities: Information Management," 1997, ERIC, http://www.eric.ed.gov:80/ERICWebPortal/Home.portal?_nfpb=true&_pageLabel=Home_page (accessed May 16, 2005).
3. Jorgen J. Wouters, "Searching for Disclosure: How Search Engines Alert Consumers to the Presence of Advertising in Search Results," *Consumer Reports WebWatch*, November 8, 2004, http://www.consumerwebwatch.org/dynamic/search-report-disclosureabstract.cfm (accessed May 7, 2005).
4. See, for instance, recommendations made by librarians at University of California Berkeley Teaching Library Internet Workshops, http://www.lib.berkeley.edu/TeachingLib/Guides/Internet/MetaSearch.html (accessed May 10, 2005).
5. Wouters, "Searching for Disclosure."
6. Ibid.

Chapter 11

1. E. Thompson, "An Experimental Investigation of the Relative Effectiveness of Organization Structure in Oral Communication," *Southern Speech Journal* 26 (1960): 59–69.
2. R. G. Smith, "Effects of Speech Organization upon Attitudes of College Students," *Speech Monographs* 18 (1951): 292–301.
3. H. Sharp Jr. and T. McClung, "Effects of Organization on the Speaker's Ethos," *Speech Monographs* 33 (1966): 182ff.
4. "Communication Skills, Honesty/Integrity Top Employers' Wish List for Job Candidates," *Job Outlook 2005 Survey*, January 20, 2005, National Association of Colleges and Employers, http://www.naceweb.org/products/jo2005report.htm (accessed June 12, 2005).

5. G. H. Bower, "Organizational Factors in Memory," *Cognitive Psychology* 1 (1970): 18–46.
6. Rodney Reynolds and Michael Burgoon, "Evidence," in *The Persuasion Handbook: Developments in Theory and Practice,* ed. J. P. Dillard and M. Pfau (Thousand Oaks, Calif.: Sage, 2002), 427–44.
7. Leonard J. Rosen and Laurence Behren, *The Allyn & Bacon Handbook* (Needham, Mass.: Allyn & Bacon, 1992), 103.

Chapter 12

1. PBS, "Life on the Internet Timeline," http://www.pbs.org/internet/timeline/index.html (accessed April 3, 2000).
2. Anita Taylor, "Tales of the Grandmothers: Women and Work," *Vital Speeches of the Day* 71, no. 7 (2005): 209–12.
3. Sonja K. Foss and Karen A. Foss, *Inviting Transformation: Presentational Speaking for a Changing World* (Prospect Heights, Ill.: Waveland Press, 1994).

Chapter 13

1. For an enlightening review of the history of outlining from Cicero to electronic software, see Jonathan Price, "STOP: Light on the History of Outlining," *Journal of Computer Documentation* 23.3 (August 1999): 69–78.
2. Mark B. McClellan (speech presented at the fifth annual David A. Winston lecture, Washington, D.C., October 20, 2003), http://www.fda.gov/oc/speeches/2003/winston1020.html (accessed August 14, 2005).
3. Gratitude goes to Carolyn Clark, Ph.D., of Salt Lake Community College, for sharing this assignment with us.

Chapter 14

1. Ron Hoff, *I Can See You Naked,* rev. ed. (Kansas City, Mo.: Andrews McMeel, 1992), 41.
2. "Openings," *Executive Speaker* 26, no. 5 (2005): 1.
3. William Safire, *Lend Me Your Ears: Great Speeches in History* (New York: Norton, 1992), 676.
4. For a rich discussion of the role of stories and narratives in communication, see Walter Fisher, "Narration as a Human Communication Paradigm: The Case of Public Moral Argument," *Communication Monographs* 51, no. 1 (1984): 1–22.
5. Edward P. J. Corbett, *Classical Rhetoric for the Modern Student,* 3rd ed. (New York: Oxford University Press, 1990).
6. Bas Andeweg and Jap de Jong, "May I Have Your Attention? Exordial Techniques in Informative Oral Presentations," *Technical Communication Quarterly* 7, no. 3 (1998): 271–84.
7. Antoinette M. Bailey, "Thoughts on Building a House for Diversity," *Vital Speeches of the Day* 66, no. 13 (2000): 400–402.
8. Quoted at http://www.executive-speaker.com/spkopxxx.html (accessed July 3, 2005).
9. Vance Coffman, "Help Wanted: 'Busineers,'" *Vital Speeches of the Day* 66, no. 16 (2000): 488–92.
10. Nelson Mandela, "Our March to Freedom Is Irreversible," in *The Penguin Book of Twentieth-Century Speeches,* ed. B. MacArthur (New York: Penguin, 1992).
11. C. A. Kiesler and S. B. Kiesler, "Role of Forewarning in Persuasive Communication," *Journal of Abnormal and Social Psychology* 68 (1964): 547–69, cited in James C. McCroskey, *An Introduction to Rhetorical Communication,* 8th ed. (Boston: Allyn & Bacon, 2001), 253.
12. Marvin Runyon, "No One Moves the Mail Like the U.S. Postal Service," *Vital Speeches of the Day* 61, no. 2 (1994): 52–55.
13. Robert L. Darbelnet, "U.S. Roads and Bridges: Highway Funding at a Crossroads," *Vital Speeches of the Day* 63, no. 12 (1997): 379.
14. Andeweg and de Jong, "May I Have Your Attention?"

Chapter 15

1. R. O. Skovgard, interview by author, June 10, 1995.
2. Holger Kluge, "Reflections on Diversity," *Vital Speeches of the Day* 63, no. 6 (1997): 171–72.
3. William E. Kirwan (speech delivered to the SUNY Stony Brook Student–Community Wellness Leadership Symposium, Stony Brook, N.Y., February 15, 2000).
4. Hillary Rodham Clinton, "Women's Rights Are Human Rights" (speech delivered to the United Nations Fourth World Conference on Women, Beijing, China, September 5, 1995).
5. Sue Suter, "Adapting to Change, while Holding on to Values: *Star Trek*'s Lessons for the Disability Community" (speech delivered to the Annual Conference of the Association for the Severely Handicapped, Springfield, Ill., September 22, 1999).
6. Oprah Winfrey (speech delivered at Wellesley College commencement, Wellesley, Mass., May 30, 1997), http://www.wellesley.edu/PublicAffairs/Commencement/1997/winfrey.html (accessed April 2, 2000).

Chapter 16

1. Robert Harris, "A Handbook of Rhetorical Devices," July 26, 2002, *Virtual Salt,* http://www.virtualsalt.com/rhetoric.htm (accessed August 5, 2002).
2. Michael J. Lewis, "When Presidents Speak," *Commentary* 111, no. 6 (2001): 48–51.
3. Peggy Noonan, *Simply Speaking: How to Communicate Your Ideas with Style, Substance, and Clarity* (New York: Regan Books, 1998), 51.
4. William Safire, *Lend Me Your Ears: Great Speeches in History* (New York: Norton, 1992), 26.
5. Dan Hooley, "The Lessons of the Ring," *Vital Speeches of the Day* 70, no. 20 (2004): 660–63.
6. Katherine E. Rowan, "A New Pedagogy for Explanatory Public Speaking: Why Arrangement Should Not Substitute for Invention," *Communication Research* 44 (1995): 245.
7. James E. Lukaszewski, "You Can Become a Verbal Visionary" (speech delivered to the Public Relations Society of America, Cleveland, Ohio, April 8, 1997), Executive Speaker Library, http://www.executive-speaker.com/lib_moti.html.
8. "Information for Decision Makers. Population Estimates of Disability and Long-Term Care. February 1995," *ASPE Research Notes,* DisabilityInfo.gov, http://www.disabilityinfo.gov (accessed April 24, 2005).
9. David C. Thomas and Kerr Inkson, *Cultural Intelligence: People Skills for a Global Business* (San Francisco, Calif.: Berrett-Koehler Publishers, 2004), 14.
10. Ibid.
11. Catherine H. Zizik, "Powerspeak: Avoiding Ambiguous Language," *Speech Communication Teacher* (Summer 1995): 8–9.
12. Andrea Lunsford and Robert Connors, *The St. Martin's Handbook,* 3rd ed. (New York: St. Martin's Press, 1995), 101.
13. Safire, *Lend Me Your Ears,* 496–97.
14. L. Clemetson and J. Gordon-Thomas, "Our House Is on Fire," *Newsweek,* June 11, 2001, 50.
15. Gloria Anzaldúa, "Entering into the Serpent," in *The St. Martin's Handbook,* ed. Andrea Lunsford and Robert Connors, 3rd ed. (New York: St. Martin's Press, 1995), 25.
16. P. H. Matthews, *The Concise Oxford Dictionary of Linguistics* (New York: Oxford University Press, 1997).
17. Howard K. Battles and Charles Packard, *Words and Sentences,* bk. 6 (Lexington, Mass.: Ginn & Company, 1984), 110.
18. Robin Lakoff, *Language and Woman's Place* (New York: Harper & Row, 1975); Deborah Tannen, *You Just Don't Understand: Women and Men in Conversation* (New York: William Morrow, 1990); Deborah Tannen, *Talking from 9 to 5* (New York: William Morrow, 1994); Anthony Mulac, "The Gender-Linked Language Effect: Do Language Differences Really Make a Difference?" in D. Canary and K. Dindia (eds.), *Sex Differences and Similarities in Communication* (Mahwah, N.J.: Lawrence Erlbaum, 1998); Phyllis Mindell, *A Woman's Guide to the Language of Success: Communicating with Confidence and Power* (Englewood Cliffs, N.J.: Prentice Hall, 1995).
19. Remarks of Senator Barack Obama, New Hampshire Primary, Nashua, New Hampshire, January 8, 2008, www.barackobama.com.

20. Cited in Safire, *Lend Me Your Ears,* 22.
21. Remarks of Senator Barack Obama, New Hampshire Primary.
22. Jesse Jackson, in *Voices of Multicultural America: Notable Speeches Delivered by African, Asian, Hispanic, and Native Americans, 1790-1995,* ed. Deborah Straub (New York: Gale Research, 1996), 594-99.
23. Ibid.
24. Lunsford and Connors, *The St. Martin's Handbook,* 345.

Chapter 17

1. James A. Winans, *Public Speaking* (New York: Century, 1925). Professor Winans was among the first Americans to contribute significantly to the study of rhetoric. His explanation of delivery is considered by many to be the best coverage of the topic in the English language. His perspective infuses this chapter.
2. James C. McCroskey, *An Introduction to Rhetorical Communication,* 8th ed. (Englewood Cliffs, N.J.: Prentice Hall, 2001), 273.
3. Winans, *Public Speaking,* 17.
4. Thomas M. Conley, *Rhetoric in the European Tradition* (New York: Longman, 1990).
5. William Safire, PBS *NewsHour,* August 15, 1996, http://www.pbs.org/newshour/gergen/july-dec96/safire_8-15.html (accessed July 15, 2005).
6. Robbin Crabtree and Robert Weissberg, *ESL Students in the Public Speaking Classroom: A Guide for Teachers* (Boston: Bedford/St. Martin's, 2000), 24.

Chapter 18

1. Kyle James Tusing and James Price Dillard, "The Sounds of Dominance: Vocal Precursors of Perceived Dominance during Interpersonal Influence," *Human Communication Research* 26 (2000): 148-71.
2. Caryl Raye Krannich, *101 Secrets of Highly Effective Speakers* (Manassas Park, Va.: Impact Publications, 1998), 121-22.
3. Kenneth C. Crannell, *Voice and Articulation,* 4th ed. (Belmont, Calif.: Wadsworth, 2000), 41.
4. MaryAnn Cunningham Florez, *Improving Adult ESL Learners' Pronunciation Skills,* National Clearinghouse for ESL Literacy Education, 1998, http://www.cal.org/caela/digests/Pronun.htm (accessed July 16, 2005).
5. Tusing and Dillard, "Sounds of Dominance."
6. The digitized audio of King's "I Have a Dream" speech can be accessed at http://www.americanrhetoric.com/speeches/Ihaveadream.htm.

Chapter 19

1. Robert Rivlin and Karen Gravelle, *Deciphering the Senses: The Expanding World of Human Perception* (New York: Simon & Schuster, 1998), 98; see also A. Warfield, "Do You Speak Body Language?" *Training & Development* 55, no. 4 (2001): 60.
2. Judee K. Burgoon, David B. Buller, and W. Gill Woddall, *Nonverbal Communication,* 2nd ed. (New York: McGraw-Hill, 1996).
3. Ibid.
4. Ibid.
5. Reid Buckley, *Strictly Speaking: Reid Buckley's Indispensable Handbook on Public Speaking* (New York: McGraw-Hill, 1999), 204.
6. Laurie Schloff and Marcia Yudkin, *Smart Speaking* (New York: Plume, 1991), 108.
7. Buckley, *Strictly Speaking,* 209.
8. J. P. Davidson, "Shaping an Image That Boosts Your Career," *Marketing Communications* 13 (1988): 55-56.
9. See speaking consultant Rick Segel's witty comments on the problems of dressing down in the workplace at http://www.ricksegel.com/reprints8.html (accessed July 18, 2005).
10. Along with speeches at the White House, economic conferences, and elsewhere, Bono delivered the 2001 commencement address at Harvard University,

http://www.commencement.harvard.edu/2001/bono_address.html (accessed August 1, 2005), and the 2004 commencement address at the University of Pennsylvania, http://www.dailypennsylvanian.com/vnews/display.v/ART/4057faca6b12a (accessed August 1, 2005).

11. David Wolfe, *Women's Wear Daily,* as quoted by image consultant Lisa Duncan at http://www.lisaduncan.com/tipstrends.html (accessed July 18, 2005).

Chapter 20

1. Robert Heinich, Michael Molenda, and James D. Russell, *Instructional Media and the New Technologies of Instruction,* 4th ed. (New York: Macmillan, 1993), 66.
2. Cheryl Currid, *Make Your Point: The Complete Guide to Successful Business Presentations Using Today's Technology* (Rocklin, Calif.: Prima Publishing, 1995), 117.
3. *Merriam-Webster's Collegiate Dictionary,* 10th ed. (Springfield, Mass.: Merriam-Webster, 1993).

Chapter 21

1. David M. Orchard, Barry D. Perow, Kenneth Frankes, and Torin Reed, *Figuratively Speaking in the Computer Age: Techniques for Preparing and Delivering Presentations* (n.p.: American Association of Petroleum Geologists, 2000), 83–86.
2. Cheryl Currid, *Make Your Point: The Complete Guide to Successful Business Presentations Using Today's Technology* (Rocklin, Calif.: Prima Publishing, 1995).

Chapter 22

1. Ron Hoff, *I Can See You Naked,* rev. ed. (Kansas City, Mo.: Andrews McMeel, 1992), 143.

Chapter 23

1. Tina Blythe et al., *The Teaching for Understanding Guide* (Hoboken, N.J.: Jossey-Bass, 1997); Kenneth D. Frandsen and Donald A. Clement, "The Functions of Human Communication in Informing: Communicating and Processing Information," in *Handbook of Rhetorical and Communication Theory,* ed. Carroll C. Arnold and John Waite Bowers (Needham, Mass.: Allyn & Bacon, 1984), 334.
2. E. Thompson, "An Experimental Investigation of the Relative Effectiveness of Organization Structure in Oral Communication," *Southern Speech Journal* 26 (1966): 59–69.
3. Katherine E. Rowan, "A New Pedagogy for Explanatory Public Speaking: Why Arrangement Should Not Substitute for Invention," *Communication Education* 44 (1995): 236–50.
4. Vickie K. Sullivan, "Public Speaking: The Secret Weapon in Career Development," *USA Today,* May 2005, 24.
5. Howard K. Battles and Charles Packard, *Words and Sentences,* bk. 6 (Lexington, Mass.: Ginn & Company, 1984), 459.
6. Rowan, "A New Pedagogy."
7. S. Kujawa and L. Huske, *The Strategic Teaching and Reading Project Guidebook,* rev. ed. (Oak Brook, Ill.: North Central Regional Educational Laboratory, 1995).
8. Shawn M. Glynn et al., "Teaching Science with Analogies: A Resource for Teachers and Textbook Authors," National Reading Research Center, Instructional Resource No. 7, Fall 1994.
9. Altoona List of Medical Analogies, "How to Use Analogies," Altoona Family Physicians Residency Web site, http://www.altoonafp.org/analogies.htm (accessed June 13, 2005).
10. Glynn et al., "Teaching Science," 19.
11. Altoona List of Medical Analogies, "How to Use Analogies."
12. Wolfgang Porod, "Nanotechnology," *Vital Speeches of the Day* 71, no. 4 (2004): 125–28.
13. Tina A. Grotzer, "How Conceptual Leaps in Understanding the Nature of Causality Can Limit Learning: An Example from Electrical Circuits" (paper presented at the annual conference of the American Educational Research Association, New Orleans, April 2000), http://pzweb.harvard.edu/Research/UnderCon.htm (accessed June 17, 2005).
14. Neil D. Fleming and C. Mills, "Helping Students Understand How They Learn," *Teaching Professor* 7, no. 4 (1992).

Chapter 24

1. Edward P. J. Corbett, *Classical Rhetoric for the Modern Student,* 3rd ed. (New York: Oxford University Press, 1990).
2. Communications scholars Winston Brembeck and William Howell define the goal in this way: "Persuasion is communication intended to influence choice." See Winston L. Brembeck and William S. Howell, *Persuasion: A Means of Social Influence,* 2nd ed. (Englewood Cliffs, N.J.: Prentice Hall, 1976).
3. Kathleen K. Reardon, *Persuasion in Practice* (Newbury Park, Calif.: Sage, 1991), 210.
4. Richard E. Petty and John T. Cacioppo, *Communication and Persuasion: Central and Peripheral Routes to Attitude Change* (New York: Springer-Verlag, 1986).
5. Reardon, *Persuasion in Practice,* 210.
6. Russel H. Fazio, "How Do Attitudes Guide Behavior?" in *The Handbook of Motivation and Cognition: Foundations of Social Behavior,* ed. Richard M. Sorrentino and E. Tory Higgins (New York: Guilford, 1986).
7. Sarah Trenholm, *Persuasion and Social Influence* (Englewood Cliffs, N.J.: Prentice Hall, 1989).
8. Joseph R. Priester and Richard E. Petty, "Source Attributions and Persuasion: Perceived Honesty as a Determinant of Message Scrutiny," *Personality and Social Psychology Bulletin* 21 (1995): 637–54. See also Kenneth G. DeBono and Richard J. Harnish, "Source Expertise, Source Attractiveness, and the Processing of Persuasive Information: A Functional Approach," *Journal of Personality and Social Psychology* 55 (1987): 541.
9. Priester and Petty, *Personality,* 11.
10. Eveline Feteris, "A Pragma-Dialectical Approach of the Analysis and Evaluation of Pragmatic Argumentation in a Legal Context," *Argumentation* 16 (2002): 349–67.
11. Nathan Crick, "Conquering Our Imagination: Thought Experiments and Enthymemes in Scientific Argument," *Philosophy and Rhetoric* 37 (2004): 21–41.
12. Edward Corbett, *Classical Rhetoric for the Modern Student,* 1356a, 1377b.
13. Ibid.
14. Elpidio Villarreal, "Choosing the Right Path," Speech Delivered to the Puerto Rican Legal Defense and Education Fund Gala in New York City, October 26, 2006, *Vital Speeches of the Day* 72, no. 26 (2007), 784–86.
15. Kim Witte and Mike Allen, "A Meta-Analysis of Fear Appeals: Implications for Effective Public Health Campaigns," *Health Education and Behavior* 27 (2000): 591–615.
16. Robert A. Stewart, "Perceptions of a Speaker's Initial Credibility as a Function of Religious Involvement and Religious Disclosiveness," *Communication Research Reports* 11 (1994): 169–76.
17. For an extensive review of the history of the field of communication from the classical period to the present era, see Dominic A. Infante, Andrew S. Rancer, and Deanna F. Womack, *Building Communication Theory,* 4th ed. (Prospect Heights, Ill.: Waveland Press, 2003).
18. Abraham Maslow, *Motivation and Personality* (New York: Harper & Row, 1954).
19. B. Soper, G. E. Milford, and G. T. Rosenthal, "Belief When Evidence Does Not Support the Theory," *Psychology and Marketing* 12 (1995): 415–22, cited in Stephen M. Kosslyn and Robin S. Rosenberg, *Psychology: The Brain, the Person, the World* (Boston: Allyn & Bacon, 2004), 330.
20. Icek Ajzen and Martin Fishbein, *Understanding Attitudes and Predicting Social Behavior* (Englewood Cliffs, N.J.: Prentice Hall, 1980).
21. Richard Petty and John T. Cacioppo, "The Elaboration Likelihood Model of Persuasion," in *Advances in Experimental Social Psychology* 19, ed. L. Berkowitz (San Diego, Calif.: Academic Press, 1986), 123–205; Richard Petty and Duane T. Wegener, "Matching versus Mismatching Attitude Functions: Implications for Scrutiny of Persuasive Messages," *Personality and Social Psychology Bulletin* 24 (1998): 227–40.
22. For good reviews of the literature on source credibility in general, see Richard M. Perloff, *The Dynamics of Persuasion* (Hillsdale, N.J.: Lawrence Erlbaum, 1993), and Infante, Rancer, and Womack, *Building Communication Theory.*

23. K. K. Sereno and G. I. Hawkins, "The Effects of Variations in Speakers' Nonfluency upon Audience Ratings of Attitude toward the Speech Topic and Speakers' Credibility," *Speech Monographs* 34 (1967): 58–64.
24. Priester and Petty, "Source Attributions and Persuasion."

Chapter 25

1. *Merriam-Webster's Collegiate Dictionary*, 10th ed. (Springfield, Mass.: Merriam-Webster, 1993).
2. Austin J. Freeley, *Argumentation and Debate*, 8th ed. (Belmont, Calif.: Wadsworth, 1993), 158.
3. Thomas A. Hollihan and Kevin T. Baaske, *Arguments and Arguing* (New York: St. Martin's Press, 1994), 27.
4. The model of argument presented here follows Steven Toulmin, *The Uses of Argument* (New York: Cambridge University Press, 1958), as described in James C. McCroskey, *An Introduction to Rhetorical Communication*, 6th ed. (Englewood Cliffs, N.J.: Prentice-Hall, 1993).
5. Annette Rottenberg, *Elements of Argument*, 4th ed. (Boston: Bedford/St. Martin's, 1994), 10.
6. American Council on Science and Health, "What's the Story? Drug-Supplement Interaction," November 2000, http://www.acsh.org/publications/story/index.html (accessed August 27, 2002).
7. Transcript of President George W. Bush's address to the United Nations, September 13, 2002, *New York Times*, September 13, 2002, A10.
8. Based on McCroskey, *An Introduction to Rhetorical Communication*.
9. See the discussion of the relationship between attitudes and behavior in Daniel J. O'Keefe, *Persuasion: Theory and Research*, 2nd ed. (Thousand Oaks, Calif.: Sage, 2002), 16–17.
10. Dennis S. Gouran, "Attitude Change and Listeners' Understanding of a Persuasive Communication," *Speech Teacher* 15 (1966): 289–94; J. P. Dillard, "Persuasion Past and Present: Attitudes Aren't What They Used to Be," *Communication Monographs* 60 (1966): 94.
11. Freeley, *Argumentation and Debate*, 175.
12. Edward P. J. Corbett, *Classical Rhetoric for the Modern Student*, 3rd ed. (New York: Oxford University Press, 1990).
13. Herbert Simon, *Persuasion in Society* (Thousand Oaks, Calif.: Sage, 2001), 385–87.

Chapter 26

1. *Motor Vehicle Facts and Figures* (American Automobile Manufacturers Association, 1997), 84.
2. Herbert Simon, *Persuasion in Society* (Thousand Oaks, Calif.: Sage, 2001), 385–87.
3. A. H. Monroe, *Principles and Types of Speeches* (Chicago: Scott, Foresman, 1935).
4. James R. DiSanza and Nancy J. Legge, *Business and Professional Communication: Plans, Processes, and Performance*, 2nd ed. (Boston: Allyn & Bacon, 2002), 236.

Chapter 27

1. Frank D. Stella, "Introductory Remarks Delivered to the Economic Club of Detroit, Detroit, Michigan," *Executive Speaker* 17 (April 15, 1996): 3.
2. G. Parret, *I Love My Boss and 969 Other Business Jokes* (New York: Sterling Publishing, 1993).
3. H. H. Shelton, "Victory, Honor, Sacrifice," *Vital Speeches of the Day* 66, no. 20 (2000): 627.
4. Ibid.
5. Paul Fatout, ed., *Mark Twain Speaks for Himself* (West Lafayette, Ind.: Purdue University Press, 1978).
6. David Magill, "Give Your Life a Dream with Design," *Vital Speeches of the Day* 62, no. 21 (1996): 671–72.

Chapter 28

1. H. Dan O'Hair, James S. O'Rourke, and Mary John O'Hair, *Business Communication: A Framework for Success* (Cincinnati: South-Western, 2001).
2. W. L. Tullar and P. R. Kaiser, "The Effect of Process Training on Process and Outcomes in Virtual Groups," *Journal of Business Communication* 37 (2000): 408–27.
3. H. Dan O'Hair, Gustav Friedrich, and Linda Dixon, *Strategic Communication in Business and the Professions,* 4th ed. (Boston: Houghton Mifflin, 2002).
4. K. D. Benne and P. Sheats, "Functional Roles of Group Members," *Journal of Social Issues* 4 (1948): 41–49.
5. Ibid.
6. M. S. Poole and J. T. Garner, "Perspectives on Workgroup Conflict and Communication," in *The SAGE Handbook of Conflict Communication,* J. Oetzel and S. Ting-Toomey, ed. (Thousand Oaks, Calif.: Sage, 2002), 267–92.
7. H. Dan O'Hair, Gustave Friedrich, John Wiemann, and Mary Wiemann, *Competent Communication,* 2nd ed. (New York: Bedford/St. Martin's, 1997).
8. Karl E. Weick and K. Roberts, "Collective Minds in Organizations: Heedful Interrelating on Flight Decks," *Administrative Science Quarterly* 38 (1993): 357–81.
9. Geoffrey A. Cross, "Collective Form: An Exploration of Large-Group Writing," *Journal of Business Communication* 37 (2000): 77–100.
10. Irving Lester Janis, *Groupthink: Psychological Studies of Policy Decisions and Fiascoes* (Berkeley: University of California Press, 1982).
11. O'Hair, Friedrich, and Dixon, *Strategic Communication.*
12. J. K. Winter, J. C. Neal, and K. K. Waner, "How Male, Female, and Mixed Gender Groups Regard Interaction and Leadership Differences in the Business Communication Course," *Business Communication Quarterly* 64 (2001): 43–58.

Chapter 29

1. R. Weinholdt, "Taking the Trauma out of the Talk," *Information Management Journal* (November/December 2006): 62.
2. For a review, see Priscilla S. Rogers, "Distinguishing Public and Presentational Speaking," *Management Communication Quarterly* 2 (1988): 102–15.
3. Ibid.
4. Frank E. X. Dance, "What Do You Mean: Presentational Speaking?" *Management Communication Quarterly* 1 (1987): 260–71.
5. Ibid.
6. Part of this classification of business presentations is adapted from Raymond V. Lesikar, John D. Pettit Jr., and Marie E. Flatley, *Basic Business Communication,* 8th ed. (New York: McGraw Hill, 1999).
7. M. Hunter, "Shut Up, Listen and Sell," *B to B* 92 (2007): 11.
8. H. Dan O'Hair, James S. O'Rourke, and Mary John O'Hair, *Business Communication: A Framework for Success* (Cincinnati: South-Western, 2001).
9. H. D. O'Hair, and R. L. Heath, eds., *Handbook of Risk and Crisis Communication* (Mahwah, N.J.: Erlbaum, in press).
10. William L. Benoit, *Accounts, Excuses, and Apologies: A Theory of Image Restoration Strategies* (Albany: State University of New York Press, 1995).
11. Ibid.

Chapter 30

1. Edward S. Inch and Barbara Warnick, *Critical Thinking and Communication: The Use of Reason in Argument,* 3rd ed. (Boston: Allyn & Bacon, 1998).
2. Deanna P. Daniels, "Communicating across the Curriculum and in the Disciplines: Speaking in Engineering," *Communication Education* 51 (July 2002): 3.
3. Ibid.
4. Ibid.

5. James M. Henslin, *Sociology: A Down-to-Earth Approach,* 8th ed. (Boston: Allyn & Bacon, 2007), 138.

6. William E. Thompson and James V. Hickey, *Society in Focus: An Introduction to Sociology,* 2nd ed. (New York: HarperCollins, 1996), 39.

7. Ibid.

Appendix A

1. Patricia Nelson, "Handling Questions and Answers." Toastmasters International, Edmonton and Area, revised November 3, 1999, http://www.ecn.ab.ca/toast/qa.html (accessed September 1, 2000).

2. Diane DiResta, *Knockout Presentations: How to Deliver Your Message with Power, Punch, and Pizzazz* (Worcester, Mass.: Chandler House Press, 1998), 236.

3. Ibid., 237.

4. Lilyan Wilder, *Talk Your Way to Success* (New York: Eastside Publishing, 1986), 279.

Appendix B

1. Patricia Nelson, "Handling Questions and Answers." Toastmasters International, Edmonton and Area, revised November 3, 1999, http://www.ecn.ab.ca/toast/qa.html (accessed September 1, 2000).

2. Daria Price Bowman, *Presentations: Proven Techniques for Creating Presentations That Get Results* (Holbrook, Mass.: Adams Media, 1998), 177.

3. Oklahoma Society of CPAs (OSCPA), "Tips for Successful Media Interviewing," http://www.oscpa.com/?757 (accessed June 10, 2006).

4. Diane Howard, "Guidelines for Videoconference Presentations, Performances, and Teaching," dianehoward.com (accessed June 10, 2006).

5. Some tips adapted from "Videoconferencing," AT&T Education Web site, http://www.kn.pacbell.com/wired/vidconf/compressedVid.html (accessed June 13, 2006).

Acknowledgments

About.com. "About.com:Welcome" logo. Copyright © 2002 About Inc. Used with permission of About, Inc. which can be found online at www.about.com. All rights reserved.

Maya Angelou. "Phenomenal Woman." Copyright © 1978 by Maya Angelou. From *And Still I Rise* by Maya Angelou. Used by permission of Random House, Inc.

Roger E. Axtell. "Guidelines for Introducing Other Speakers." From *Do's and Taboos of Public Speaking: How to Get Those Butterflies Flying in Formation.* Copyright © 1992 John Wiley & Sons, Inc. Reprinted with permission of John Wiley & Sons, Inc.

Joe Ayres and Tim Hopf. "Visualization: Is It More than Extra Attention?" From *Communication Education* 38(1989):1–5. Reprinted by permission of the publisher (Taylor & Francis, http://www.informaworld.com).

Kenneth Beare. "Using Contractions." Copyright © 2007 by Kenneth Beare (esl.about.com/library/grammar/blgr_contractions.htm). Used with permission of About, Inc. which can be found online at www.about.com. All rights reserved.

Bono. Commencement Speech at the University of Pennsylvania, 2004 (with 13 images). Copyright © Creative Video Souvenir Productions, Inc. Reprinted with permission.

Brooklyn Public Library. Screenshot of "Brooklyn Info Bridge: Basic Search by Subject" page. Copyright © Brooklyn Public Library. Reprinted by permission.

Cheryl Currid. Two tables, 21.1, 21.2. Adapted from *Make Your Point: The Complete Guide to Successful Business Presentations Using Today's Technology* by Cheryl Currid, p. 74. Copyright © 1995 by Cheryl Currid. Reprinted with permission.

Michal Dale. "Preparing an Oral Review of an Academic Article." With thanks to Michal Dale of Southwest Missouri State University's Department of Communication.

Edward J. Epstein. Title Page from *The Big Picture.* Copyright © 2005 by Random House, Inc. Used by permission of Random House, Inc.

Lauren Fleishman. "Vegetable Platter" photo from *Newsweek* article "How to Fix School Lunch," August 8, 2005, p. 50. Copyright © Lauren Fleishman, 2005. Reprinted with permission of the photographer.

Isabella Golmier. Abstract of article, "Can Cigarette Warnings Counterbalance Effects of Smoking Scenes in Movies." From *Psychological Reports*, February 2007. Copyright © 2007 by Ammons Scientific, Ltd. Reproduced with permission of Ammons Scientific, Ltd. in the format Textbook via Copyright Clearance Center.

Google. Google Trademark and Google Scholar Beta Trademark. Copyright © 2008 Google, Inc. Used with permission.

International Association of Business Communicators. "Code of Ethics for Professional Business Communicators." www.iabc.com/members/joining/code.htm. Accessed September 20, 2002. Copyright © 2002 IABC. Reprinted by permission.

Tim Kaine. "Remarks at the Virginia Tech Convocation (After 4/16 Shootings)" (with photos). www.governor.virginia.gov/MediaRelations/Speeches/2007/VT-convo.cfm. Copyright © 2007 by Governor Tim Kaine. © Michaele White, Governor Kaine's photographer. Reprinted by permission.

Martin Luther King, Jr. Excerpts from "I Have a Dream." Reprinted by arrangement with The Heirs to the Estate of Martin Luther King Jr., c/o Writers House as agent for the proprietor New York, NY. Copyright 1963 Dr. Martin Luther King Jr.; copyright renewed 1991 Coretta Scott King.

Lin Kroeger. "Checklist on Assigning Roles for the Group Presentations." From *The Complete Idiot's Guide to Successful Business Presentations* by Lin Kroeger. Copyright © 1997 by Lin Kroeger. Used by permission of Alpha Books, an imprint of Penguin Group (USA) Inc.

Julian Makey. Photo of Jamie Oliver from *Newsweek*, August 8, 2005, p. 50. Reprinted by permission from Rex USA.

National Academy of Sciences. Screenshot of Institute of Medicine Web site (www.iom.edu). Copyright © 2008 National Academy of Sciences. All rights reserved.

New York Public Library. NYPL.ORG logo. Reprinted by permission of the New York Public Library.

New York Times. Screenshot of Op-Ed article "Emergency in the Emergency Rooms." From *The New York Times*, June 21, 2006. Copyright © 2006 The New York Times. Reprinted by permission.

The Nobel Foundation. Screenshot of Anders Culhed homepage, http://nobelprize.org/nobel_prizes/literature/articles/cullhed/index.html. © Nobel Web AB. Reprinted by permission.

Open Directory. Search page. Copyright © 2008 Netscape. All Rights Reserved. Used with permission.

Milton Rokeach. "Values Survey." Reprinted with the permission of The Free Press, a Division of Simon & Schuster Adult Publishing Group. From *The Nature of Human Values* by Milton Rokeach, p. 28. Copyright © 1973 by The Free Press. All rights reserved.

Peter L. Soper. "Commonly Mispronounced Words." From *Basic Public Speaking* (1968) by Soper, P.L. Reprinted by permission of Oxford University Press, Inc.

Anita Taylor. "Tales of the Grandmothers: Women and Work" (with photos). Speech to the *Woman of the Year Celebration*, Aerospace Corporation, Chintilly, Virginia, September 13, 2004. Originally published in *Vital Speeches*, January 2005, and *Educational Video Group* for video version. Reprinted by permission of the author.

Peg Tyre and Sarah Staveley-O'Carroll. "How To Fix School Lunch: Celebrity Chefs, Politicians and Concerned Parents Are Joining Forces to Improve the Meals Kids Eat Every Day." From *Newsweek*, August 8, 2005. Copyright © 2005 Newsweek. Reprinted by permission.

Elpidio Villarreal. "Speech to Puerto Rican Legal Defense and Education Fund Gala, October 26, 2006." Reprinted by permission of the author. Photos reprinted by permission of the Puerto Rican Legal Defense and Education Fund.

Lilyan Wilder. "Thirteen Commonly Mispronounced Words." From *Seven Steps to Fearless Speaking*. Copyright © 1999 by Lilyan Wilder. Reprinted with permission of John Wiley & Sons, Inc.

Audrey Hepburn Images: © John Springer Collection/CORBIS; © Sunset Boulevard/Corbis; © Sunset Boulevard/Corbis; © Sunset Boulevard/Corbis; © Sarah Chalmers, Artist; © CinemaPhoto/CORBIS; © Bettmann/CORBIS; © Bettmann/CORBIS.

Source to Speech Images: Trips for Kids Web site logo: Courtesy of Trips for Kids; Southern Off-Road Bicycle Association Logo and Photographs (2): Courtesy of SORBA, Southern Off-Road Bicycle Association; Mountain biking photograph: Stockbyte. Getty Images; Child in plastic waste photograph: China Photos. Getty Images; Garbage Dump Photograph: Sami Sarkis. Getty Images; Whole Foods bag: David McNew. Getty Images.

Part Opener Photos
p. 1 (Dr. Jane Goodall), Getty; p. 33 (King Abdullah of Jordan Addresses Joint Session of Congress), Getty; p. 81 (Jon Stewart), Getty; p. 125 (two students studying), Getty; p. 183 (girl in library), Getty; p. 229 (Bono), Getty; p. 265 (the Dalai Lama), Getty; p. 295 (businessman), Getty; p. 339 (Kielburger), AP; p. 455 (doctor), Corbis; p. 501 (General Petraeus), Getty.

Index

ESL SPEAKER'S NOTES

ETHICALLY SPEAKING

PUBLIC SPEAKING IN CULTURAL PERSPECTIVE

CITING SOURCES

✓ CHECKLISTS

SAMPLE SPEECHES